Penguin Education

Problems of Modern Society
A Sociological Perspective

Edited by Peter Worsley

Contributing Editors

M. R. Chatterton
Isabel Emmett
J. R. E. Lee
J. Clyde Mitchell
D. H. J. Morgan
C. G. Pickvance
Bryan Roberts
W. W. Sharrock
Robin Ward
D. T. H. Weir
Peter Worsley

Problems of Modern Society
A Sociological Perspective

Edited by Peter Worsley

Contributing Editors: M. R. Chatterton, Isabel Emmett,
J. R. E. Lee, J. Clyde Mitchell, D. H. J. Morgan,
C. G. Pickvance, Bryan Roberts, W. W. Sharrock,
Robin Ward, D. T. H. Weir, Peter Worsley

Penguin Books

Penguin Books Ltd, Harmondsworth,
Middlesex, England
Penguin Books Inc, 7110 Ambassador Road,
Baltimore, Md 21207, USA
Penguin Books Australia Ltd, Ringwood,
Victoria, Australia

First published 1972
This selection copyright © Peter Worsley and contributing editors, 1972
Introduction and notes copyright © Peter Worsley and contributing
editors, 1972

Made and printed in Great Britain by
Cox & Wyman Ltd, London, Reading and Fakenham
Set in Intertype Times

Contents

Introduction

This book of Readings is designed to complement two earlier books from Penguin Education, the textbook *Introducing Sociology*, and the accompanying *Modern Sociology: Introductory Readings*. The Readings selected in the latter volume were closely tied to the layout of the textbook, chapter by chapter, so as to provide the reader with further material in the form of extracts from some of the original sources we had drawn upon in writing the textbook, and to enable him to read them at first hand, rather than mediated by our own reworking of the ideas they contain.

The present volume has a quite different focus: that of 'social problems'. In Part One of the textbook, we distinguished between a sociological problem and a social problem by suggesting that a sociological problem occurs when we have to explain some piece of social behaviour in terms of sociological theory; a social problem is 'some piece of social behaviour that causes public friction and/or private misery and calls for collective action to solve it'. We went on to insist that sociology was concerned with the normal as well as the abnormal; with happy families as much as 'problem families'; with the everyday as well as the exotic; and with respectability as much as with vice. Hence, as sociologists, we were not only concerned with 'social problems', with things that go wrong, or with 'social pathology'. What is normal, untroublesome, or acceptable, equally constitute sociological problems, for we have to explain theoretically how it is that societies persist, or why (in Britain) nine couples out of ten preserve their marriages despite the well-known tribulations of married life.

Yet people do have problems, and they seek to understand what has caused them and work out what they can do to solve them. Few sociologists are unconcerned about these things either, because they have values, like anyone else, which lead them to like some things and hate others. They may be able to direct their researches, therefore, to those things people find troublesome. By 'people' we do not necessarily mean governments or social workers, for they are only special sets of people, and may be defined by the citizen as 'part of the trouble'. Nor are we ourselves administrators, policy-makers, planners, or therapists. We wish to help in the only relevant way we can in our capacities as social scientists. By looking at social problems as sociological problems, we may, we hope, in whatever small degree, help others to arrive at a better understanding of why and how unpleasant things happen to them and to their fellows. As C. Wright Mills put it, we may then be better able to see that apparently purely personal 'private troubles', local to the places where we live our lives: poverty, sickness, loneliness are part of general social processes that afflict thousands in similar life-situations.

Such an understanding may require us to identify who the people are who take the crucial decisions which affect the lives of millions, so that we may be able to influence them or perhaps have them replaced. But in modern society, many of the key decisions do not seem to be the special responsibility of any clearly identifiable persons at all: bureaucratization has made the decision-taking process opaque, and hidden the 'controllers' from view. In other vital areas – such as the control of the world's population and natural resources, the poverty of the great majority of mankind, or the spiralling nuclear arms race – there appear to be no controllers at all, and human intervention and social control seem all the more urgent.

In trying to identify the social factors which generate personal problems, in showing that they are not purely personal, we do not mean to imply that misfortunes do not happen to persons. Of course it is the individual who experiences the breakup of his marriage, who goes to prison or is robbed, or who is fired from his job. Yet these are *social* problems in the sense that the marriage may have broken down because the partners had absorbed absurdly romantic notions of what marriage would be like; the criminal may have started on his career because he was brought up in a milieu where crime was common or even admired; and the worker usually shares the misfortune of losing his job with many others who are laid off and is not just an isolate.

These misfortunes, then, are things that happen to particular people, but they are often not unique experiences: they are personal in their impact, but patterned both in their causation and distribution.

We begin to see, then, that what constitutes a 'social problem' is itself quite problematic. When we use those words, such things as poverty, sickness, delinquency and crime, or family troubles, normally spring to mind. Yet war, evil governments, religious conflict, swindles practised on the consumer, oversized school classes, corrupt trade unions, or third-rate television programmes, are just as much social problems. The conventional conception of what are social problems not only misses all these things out; it also focuses primarily on the end-product: the individual affected: and not the agencies doing the affecting, as if poverty and sickness had nothing to do with governments, corporations or professional bodies. Such a conception of social problems, that is, *de-politicizes* our thinking, for we can only fully understand 'private troubles' by tracing the larger malfunctioning which causes the individual suffering, or, to put it in the positive mode, how social problems are *produced* by society and *distributed* to victims. We pointed out in the textbook that our ideas as to what constitutes a social problem are strongly influenced by traditional cultural notions which go back to the nineteenth century: then *the* 'Social Problem' was a euphemistic label used to describe prostitution. The Victorians similarly used the euphemistic phrase 'the condition of England question' to refer to the widespread misery of the working classes and the possibility that they might rise in revolution. And 'social problems' were those misfortunes which were commonly held to be the result of individual weakness or moral obliquity: thus the poor were poor because they were lazy or improvident; the sick because they had dirty habits and were foolhardy; and so on. Even today, then, when we begin to discuss social problems, these archaic definitions and their implicit moral undertones can affect our thinking if we do not watch out. Terms like 'problem families' are likely to be one of the first things mentioned in any discussion of social problems, and the social worker is likely to be invoked as the crucial relevant person to solve people's problems for them, rather than the citizen himself, or, perhaps, the politician. There are thus moral assumptions of blame and responsibility historically embedded in the very phrase 'problem families', whereas for the poor person, the rich may be his problem, or the Government, or inhuman laws and administrators of laws. To the Black revolutionary, then, the 'pigs' are a social problem; to the policeman, it may be the other way round.

Each person and each group will thus define social problems differently. But, it may be objected, surely there are some things we could all agree which were undesirable and therefore universally acceptable as constituting a 'problem'. Yet we are not always of one mind as to whether, say, even poverty is an evil to be absolutely condemned. There are many groups of men and women who have chosen poverty – in monasteries and nunneries – because, to them, the renunciation of material things was the highest use to which a person could put his life.

The very same behaviour, then, can be quite differently evaluated. The virtues that we apply will vary according to the groups (tribe, nation, class, gang, family, etc.) that we have belonged to, or identify with. Since there are many such groups, providing us with reference-points we may use in evaluating behaviour, we are likely to evaluate the same behaviour differently in different company or at different points in our moral careers. For a girl to expose her legs in a beauty parade, on the beach, to her lover, or in a mini-skirt, are all socially acceptable contexts; if a lady's legs are suddenly exposed in a Marx Brothers film because somebody has stepped on the train of her evening gown, it raises a horse-laugh: it is a 'social disaster'. More seriously, what is 'suicide' in one context may be 'heroic self-sacrifice for the mother-country' in another; murder may earn you your country's highest honours if you commit it in the 'right' place in the 'right' ways: in battle with the enemy. We are sadly all too inured to 'justifications' of the use of torture by torturers, but it is less often known that even torture may be endured, if not enjoyed, by those who undergo it, for North American Indian cultures regarded dying 'well' under torture as the ultimate in nobility, a death devoutly to be desired and even spun out.

What is acceptable behaviour or not varies not only between groups and within different situational contexts, but also over time. Abortion was a crime in Britain until recently, when, under a new law, it became both legal and redefined primarily as a decisional problem of medical treatment rather than the prerogative of the police and the courts.

Obviously, this relativity of what constitutes 'normal' and 'deviant', 'good' and 'bad' behaviour raises profound ethical and philosophical issues, and, in our daily lives, we often have to take positions on these matters when we come across them. This does not mean that we are necessarily led to systematize our thinking, for we may practise avoidance of difficult situations, or may be inconsistent, or operate *ad hoc*, or justify differential treatment of the same behaviour by different people by invoking some underlying general principle, as when we honour our nation's spies and hang those from other countries. For the most part, our daily life does not require us to abstractly formulate a coherent philosophy; we tend to leave that to specialists in that kind of operation: to philosophers or theologians. Yet people do reflect about life, and try to systematize their thinking, if only because intellectual inconsistencies come home to roost when we practise inconsistent *behaviour*, as that gets us into trouble. And in any case, anthropologists have shown that ordinary men in all societies show a concern with trying to make sense of the world that goes beyond understanding merely those kinds of things that are of practical use to them.

We cannot say, then, that certain acts are *intrinsically* 'good' or 'normal', and others 'bad' or 'deviant'. 'Deviancy', it is pointed out below, 'is not a quality inherent in certain acts'. It is, firstly, a construction put upon certain acts by certain kinds of people. Thus we may treat people we know personally differently from strangers; we react to them as *persons*. We may treat others, not as persons, but as members of *categories*: 'black' or 'artist', 'old man' or 'professional', or as members of organized and distinctive *groups*: as a 'Russian', as the 'night porter at the X factory', the 'lead guitar of the Beatles', or as 'sergeant of No. 1

platoon, B Company, 705 Battalion, No. 4 Brigade, 5th Infantry Division, People's Liberation Army'.

They, too, will treat us differentially. Each of us has had a distinctive individual life-experience in terms of the groups we have grown up in, moved into, belonged to, moved through and out of: a unique set of contexts and memberships, involving contacts with a distinctive set of 'significant others'. It is this which generates our individual personality. Yet we also share common life-situations and identities: we may work in the same plant as forty thousand other employees, or in the same shop as two hundred others; may be called to serve in the Army along with all other eligible young men, or we may find ourselves in a seminar group of five in the first year of the teacher training course in X College. Hence our experiences are by no means purely individual, even if the particular set is never quite the same for any two people. Thus, the particular set of beliefs one holds is peculiar to oneself, in one sense, insofar as nobody shares quite the same beliefs, but in another sense, millions do 'think alike', and consequently act in similar ways. Yet we must be careful not to assume that what might look like the 'same' overt acts have identical meanings, for many acts, such as that of voting the same party ticket, are not so much common as parallel behaviour – the motivations and meanings informing the behaviour are very different. The ideologist may see trade unionism as an expression of the solidarity of all workers, whatever the colour of their skin; the racialist may build up the union as a way of keeping Blacks out.

Values, then, are neither purely individual nor randomly distributed. They are produced, carried, propagated and absorbed by virtue of one's memberships of social groups. In our reactions to other people's behaviour, then, we employ these values in a variety of situations. We often do so inconsistently, using conflicting values in different situations to deal with different kinds of people.

We are always hard at work, then, *constructing* reality: analysing other people's behaviour in the light of our general ideas and our experience, deciding how we will treat them, and so forth. It might seem that people with rigid ideologies, say, political or religious ones, would find life easier insofar as they only have to apply absolute rules to all situations and treat people according to pre-ordained categories. But even for the pacifist, the revolutionary or the religious 'enthusiast', general rules still have to be applied to particular cases. Hence they have to interpret the rules, and this leaves considerable latitude for individual manoeuvre and for uncertainty. The history of vicious sectarian quarrels between revolutionary 'comrades' totally devoted to the 'same' cause is eloquent testimony of this.

When we talk about 'constructing' reality, we do not mean to imply that we observe some non-social 'acts' which we then proceed to stick labels on; for we never perceive *any* behaviour as socially neutral. All behaviour has 'instant' social meanings for us (though we may alter our interpretations as time goes on): we approve or disapprove; we understand it or we don't. This is why the concept of 'secondary deviation', discussed below, is so important, for in condemning or approving the behaviour of others, we are going to affect the way they will respond to us. We are part of their social environment, to which they must react. Thus we find that the drug addict is not only physically affected by the physical action of the drug on his bodily metabolism – taking the drug and being physically affected by it are the 'primary' behaviours which get him labelled as a deviant. He is also socially affected by the reactions of those who condemn him, as well as the more supportive responses of those who share his habit. He then reacts to these reactions, a development which is *also* likely to be deviant since he joins the company of others in the same boat in order to protect himself: they become his friends and allies as against the hostile agents of orthodoxy, repression and persecution. He thus finds himself part of a new social group: a second stage of deviation.

We tend to think of those who are different from us as not being 'normal', and treat them as both irrational and immoral, as inferior, or as unimportant or unrepresentative minorities, or as unnecessary or untypical nuisances. University authorities often talk of revolutionary students as being 'unbalancd' or 'sick'; managers regard shop stewards as witch-like malevolent agitators who dominate but do not represent the mass of sane healthy workers. Or we may define the behaviour of those we dislike as being quite devoid of any guiding notions of 'good' and 'bad': thus classical musicians declare jazz or pop music not to *be* music at all: white racists commonly believe that black people are animals, and have 'no morals'. Yet once we penetrate into other people's cultural worlds, once we get under the skin of the persons we condemn as deviant, we find, all too commonly, that they behave according to very rigid and principled moral codes. There is 'honour among thieves' and *esprit de corps* in SS battalions; and the slum sex code described below by Whyte is puritanical in its rigour. Some unrespectable sub-cultures may have such rigid moral and behavioural codes of behaviour that they are codified in ritual. Thus the Mafia in Sicily, before killing one who deviated from their code, gave him the ritualized 'kiss of death'. Revolutions became such normal a part of nineteenth century French culture that symbolic expressions of the revolutionary spirit became institutionalized: when you saw the troops with their muskets upside-down on their shoulders, they were telling you symbolically that they had defected to the revolutionary cause.

Revolutions have their own logic and norms of behaviour; they are not blind destruction. At the level of personal deviance, too, individual deviants are also usually perfectly normal. Shaw, in his description of a youthful delinquent who eventually becomes a criminal of a rather unpleasant kind, says that Stanley, the 'Jack-Roller' (who practised 'queer-bashing') was no psychopath, but psychologically quite normal. Strikes, Lane and Roberts insist, 'can be perfectly normal events, conducted by perfectly normal people, in perfectly normal circumstances'. Children who perform badly at school may have more than their share of ability rather than being incapable: they may simply be pouring more of their psychic energy into organizing street gangs than into passing exams. In extreme, people may torture others, as some Frenchmn did during the Algerian Revolution, not because they are sadists, but in a quite clinical and instrumental fashion (they were out to produce information fast), and they could even, as 'professionals,' admire someone who could stand up to it.

Because moral values vary in these ways, it is impossible – or arbitrary – to define only certain kinds of behaviour as 'problems', as 'wrong', or 'nutty', in ways that will command assent from everybody. One man's 'deviance' is, indeed, another man's 'custom'. Even to use the word 'deviance' is to accept someone's standards as constituting the norm which is 'deviated' *from*: for what orthodox society terms the criminal's *deviation* from their moral code can be phrased differently in terms of *his* moral code: as *loyalty* to the gang or as the exhibition of technical *competence* as a thief. We might be better off, scientifically speaking, in talking simply of 'variance' of moral codes, rather than 'deviance', though we seem stuck with this established term now. Similarly, to speak of, say, a criminal gang as constituting a '*sub*-culture' implies that the dominant culture is our norm, from which this particular sub-culture deviates. To say that one code is dominant is not to accept that it is *better,* but simply that it is held by those who have the power to get others to conform to their values.

If by 'sub-culture' we merely wish to indicate that the cultural behaviour in question is that of a minority group, the term may be more permissible. But right and wrong are not functions of numbers, and minorities can be right, as Hitler's Germany showed, and majorities, silent or vocal, can be wrong. Our yardsticks of what constitute 'good' and 'bad' behaviour, then, in the end, are rooted in values we acquire from society, whether we get them from religion or from quite 'secular' sources.

The resolution of conflicts between groups of men who hold different sets of values is acted out in a variety of exchanges and contests, ranging from war to debate. It would be naïve to think that differences involving deeply-held ideologies or material interests can necessarily be resolved by the mutual accommodation of men of goodwill, For not all men profess goodwill to others, or are willing to be accommodating. There are those who would consider themselves to be 'better dead than Red'. In the final analysis the conflict may not be resolved and just persists, or may be resolved by one party imposing its will upon the other, for power emanates from the barrels of guns. But the great bulk of social disputes, even international ones, are not resolved by recourse to the gun. Guns may be there as the ultimate resort, but the ultimate is not necessarily resorted to. Hence even major international disagreements, let alone interpersonal quarrels, remain matters of continuing dispute, permanent 'contests' which erupt periodically in the form of 'incidents' and 'social dramas'. Under such conditions, both sides will develop formal or informal rules regulating the conflict, as Sudnow's description below of 'negotiated pleas' in the courts show. Even armies in war will (sometimes) respect Geneva conventions; at other times, the code will be quite unofficial, as when German and English troops 'fraternized' at Christmas-time in the First World War, defying their High Commands in deference to an even higher commandment: that of a shared cultural value placed on a time traditionally set aside for friendship, peace and love.

We are not, however, able to freely choose how we will act, just like that. There are whole sets of more or less powerful 'others' limiting our range of action or forcing our hand. Life is not a cafeteria, or to the extent that it is, the goods available and the amount of money we have to spend limit what we can buy. What we want to buy – or to sacrifice our lives for – depends on our values. These are both positive and negative: we have different wants, and abhor different things. The latter are the source of our 'social problems', insofar as things happen to us that we do not want to happen; the former insofar as we cannot get everything we want.

In the end, then, there can be no absolute definition of what constitutes a social problem. We may all agree that some issues are troublesome, but they trouble us in different ways, so that we cannot agree on a common solution. But our own lists of those issues we deem to be social problems will include many things excluded from other people's.

This may seem a very 'agnostic' position. It means that the selection of issues to treat as social problems is itself problematic, for whose definitions are we to use? Those of criminals, governments, policemen, lawyers, housewives, or criminologists? Our answer is the resultant of the intersection of several different sets of definitions: in part, those issues which have conventionally been defined in our culture as 'social problems' – disease, poverty, crime, bad housing, etc. – which, we agree, are largely 'Establishment' ways of defining 'social problems'. In part, we are guided by asking people what issues they would expect to see treated in a book on social problems, and in part, again, we have introduced a whole range of issues which *we* see as social problems but which are not necessarily defined in those terms by most people. Many of these latter are the large-scale, societal problems – of war and peace, pollution and nuclear war – rather than purely interpersonal troubles. If this is a compromise, it has to be, for at its widest, one could say that *everything* is a 'social problem', in that all social action involves making choices between competing values in guiding the way we allocate our scarce resources: that all actions have their 'opportunity cost' in terms of the other things we might have done, or in terms of the effort involved. We hope, in treating even the conventional 'social problems', however, that we have done so in a way that challenges conventional perspectives, and even the very assumption that these are necessarily problems, or that the answers usually sought are sound, or that the blame normally allocated has been laid at the right door. In the nature of things, then, it is the reader who must decide on his own interpretations after he has thought through the various kinds of analysis he will encounter in this volume.

Finally, we make no apology for introducing two sections, the first and the last, on 'Population, Resources and Pollution' and on 'The Future' respectively, which are not usually found in books on social problems, for these, in the end, are perhaps the greatest of all, and Ehrlich's gloomy scenario of 'eco-catastrophe' may increasingly come to look less like the science-fiction it is if we do not begin to give more urgent thought to finding solutions than we do at present.

Editor's note

The introductory essays and the selections for each respective Part of this volume were the work of: Part One, J. Clyde Mitchell; Part Two, Isabel Emmett, David Morgan and John Lee; Part Three, Chris Pickvance; Part Four, John Lee and Peter Worsley; Part Five, David Morgan; Part Six, Isabel Emmett and Bryan Roberts; Parts Seven and Eight, Michael Chatterton and David Weir; Part Nine, Robin Ward; Part Ten, David Morgan, Wes Sharrock and Robin Ward; and Part Eleven, Wes Sharrock and Peter Worsley.

Part One
Population, Resources and Pollution

Whatever other problems beset mankind, the simple numerical one of how many people there are to be fed, housed, clothed and provided with the services that make life as satisfying as possible, is basic. Whether we are concerned with highly industrialized communities such as in Western Europe or the United States of America or with societies living barely at subsistence levels, the consequences of the rate at which the population is consuming the resources available are equally serious for the people concerned. How the 'population problem' actually presents itself, however, will vary from one society to another, but here we are interested in examining some of the general implications of the relationships of population growth on the one hand to the consumption of services and resources on the other.

The size of a particular population, indeed of its rate of growth, is related to several different factors: the resources that the population has available, the standard of living that that population considers to be desirable, and the capacity of that population to make use of those resources in order to achieve that standard of living. Sociologists therefore consider the size and growth of any population in relation to an 'eco-system', of which the population is only a part. The eco-system may be thought of as the set of interconnection among four analytically separate elements. The first is, of course, the *number of people* involved and the rate at which they are increasing. The second is the *environment* in which they are placed and upon which they rely immediately or indirectly for their living. But the environment itself must be manipulated and exploited by people if they are to live in it successfully, and to do this they must have at their command the necessary skills and knowledge. They must have available therefore a *technology*, whether it is of the highly complex industrial kind found in a country, say, like the United Kingdom, or of a relatively simple kind like, say, that of hunting and gathering peoples like the Bushmen of the Kalahari Desert, or – as with the majority of the peoples of the world throughout history – of a fairly simple kind of 'subsistence' agriculture. Finally, the technology itself cannot be effective unless there is some *organization* by means of which the people are able to coordinate their activities and so make use of their skills and knowledge for what they deem to be their own benefit. Organization, then, includes not only the social structure of the community but also the scheme of values which determine what the community deems to be desirable. These four elements: population, environment, technology and organization, constitute the eco-system, and provide a set of intellectual tools with which the sociologist is able to approach what is known generally as 'the population problem'.

When we say that these four analytically separable elements constitute a system – an ecological system in fact – we mean that looking at the interrelationships of these somewhat different aspects of human life, helps us understand the significance of each in 'the population problem' in general. To take a very simple example, if we consider a band of Bushmen living in the Kalahari Desert, the supply of food, animals, insects, roots and fruits is so limited that too large an increase of population would simply mean that there was not enough food to go round. Normally, hunting is men's business and the gathering of food that of women and children. This organized division of labour enables the band to use their resources to the full, given the capabilities and limitations of the different members of the band. The men use poisoned arrows and sharpened stakes in their hunting, and the women and children use stakes to dig up roots. A good deal of field-lore has been handed down from their forebears, and new knowledge is constantly being developed which enables them to determine where the most fruitful places are in which they can find food, and to track and to predict the movements of animals. These tools and skills are what we have called technology. Clearly the use of more powerful tools and weapons, or more extensive knowledge, would increase their access to foodstuffs, as would perhaps a greater division of labour and specialization within the band. A greater and more regular supply of food would enable more babies to survive and older people to live longer. The result would be that foodstuffs would begin to be consumed more quickly than they could be replaced, leading eventually to starvation amongst some at least of the band.

Modern industrial societies are infinitely more complex than societies of hunting and gathering peoples. But the general relationships between population, technology, organizations and resources are, in principle, the same. Too rapid consumption of resources, arising either from an increased population or a higher level of living, ultimately destroys basic resources and demands one or more new technological developments through which additional resources can be tapped, a general lowering of the standard of living, or a reduction of the population which depends on these resources.

The most striking difference between modern industrial societies and subsistence or hunting and gathering societies lies primarily in the degree of sophistication of modern technology. Modern industrial societies have been able to achieve their present exalted level of living in the first instance through the extensive understanding and control of natural phenomena. Among these, the production of inanimate energy has probably been of crucial importance, but an understanding of biological processes, such as plant and animal growth as applied in agriculture, or of nutrition and disease as applied in medicine, is of similar significance. Modern technology could hardly be effective, of course, without the complex social organization with which it is usually associated. But while modern technology may not be a sufficient condition for a complex industrial society it is at least a necessary condition.

Man's knowledge of natural and material phenomena, however, may be used in several different ways, and sometimes the long-range consequences of how he uses his knowledge may not be apparent. The most direct and immediate way in which knowledge can be used, of course, is in making available more, and different sorts of goods and services. The extent to which food, clothing, housing, transportation, light, warmth and comfort in modern industrial societies surpasses that in simpler subsistence societies, is immediate evidence of this. Environments hostile to people with crude technologies can be exploited by others who are able to call upon extensive engineering and other technical resources. Cities of considerable populations now flourish within the Arctic Circle in the USSR, and in the desert in Libya, where, as recently as fifty years ago, these environments were too harsh to support any but the scantiest of human populations. Extensive agronomic research has led to the development of wheat strains which, on the one hand, are able to produce grain in the semi-arctic climates of Northern Russia as well as in the semi-tropical climate of Australia. Careful selection of animals has led to the breed of cattle which provide more meat for the smallest amount of foodstuffs, or chickens that produce more eggs per unit weight of grain they consume, than ever before in history. Perhaps even more striking are artificial fibres – from which clothing, carpets and drapery can be manufactured without having to use valuable agricultural land for their production – or plastic materials which replace increasingly scarce metals.

But while scientific and technical knowledge can be applied to make more and more goods available for consumption, it is also used to enable more and more people to be born and to survive to consume those goods.

One of the most dramatic developments in human history has been the application of biological knowledge to the control of diseases, especially those which have their sharpest incidence in childhood. Antibiotics have made it possible virtually to eliminate diseases which formerly killed an appreciable proportion of young people. Medical skills have also made it possible for people to have babies who formerly would have been sterile all their lives. Insulin allows diabetics to survive where only fifty years ago they were doomed to early deaths; modern surgeons are increasingly able to repair injuries from accidents which would have formerly proved fatal, or to repair gross congenital abnormalities and thus allow children to survive who previously would have died.

But equally, the same skills may be used to prevent children from being conceived, and so allow people voluntarily to control the number of children they have. Surgical practices such as vasectomy or the tying-off of the Fallopian tubes, and physiological procedures such as the use of oral contraceptives, are examples of the application of such technology.

Technology, however, may have undesirable as well as desirable consequences. Misgivings, for example, have been expressed in some countries in which modern technology is highly developed about the consequences of enabling children severely malformed at birth to survive, or using highly complex medical devices such as kidney and heart machines to keep old people alive.

More dramatic, however, are the effects on the environment of the widespread use of technology, particularly by industrial concerns in towns. The refinement and processing of raw products, and the manufacture of new material upon which so much modern living depends frequently not only destroys and disrupts much of the countryside, but also uses vast quantities of water, generates heat and produces noxious waste products. The pollution of the environment consequent upon modern technological processes has only recently become a matter of popular concern. Yet all use of resources must lead to some production of waste material and hence some pollution of the environment. What is significant about the present state of affairs is the speed at which water is being used, heat generated and discharged, land covered by sterile dump-heaps and non-biodegradable garbage, noxious gases and solids discharged into the air and poisonous waste materials poured into the rivers, lakes and sea (see Reading 1). Relatively small amounts of pollutant, particularly if they are mostly the residues of natural products, can usually be reabsorbed by the natural recycling of waste products. But now that the total volume of pollutants is so large, and because many of the products are chemicals not found extensively in nature and not easily reabsorbed by natural biological and chemical process (for example the extreme radio-active isotopes), normal recycling is impaired, and we stand in grave danger of permanently destroying the natural environment which for so long has provided a congenial setting for human life.

Technology then is a good servant but a bad master. It is used to create the goods and services people demand for their comfort and well-being. The use of technology gets out of hand when its noxious products are discharged into the environment without sufficient attention to the long-term, possibly inevitable, effects of those products on the environment. The sheer volume of effluent produced by industrial processes or by motor vehicles or by domestic grates, however, becomes a problem only because people in the past have not been prepared to bear the costs of ensuring that the effluents are rendered benign before they are discharged. The ingenuity that has led to the invention of procedures for producing the substances needed so extensively in modern societies is surely capable of devising means of detoxicating the waste products of these processes. But such devices would no doubt increase the cost of production of the original substances, so that in the end the population at large must choose between the alternatives of living in an increasingly polluted environment, paying more for the products they require to maintain their present level of living, or of consciously electing to forego the use of these substances and thereby accepting a lower standard of living.

Population increases

Even if the standard of living remains constant, however, the environment is at risk of destruction notwithstanding pollution, if the population increases unrestrictedly. At present (1970), the size of the world population is approximately 3500 million. This population appears to be increasing geometrically at approximately 2 per cent per year, so that if present birth and death rates maintain themselves, the population of the world in AD 2000, barring holocausts, will be 6500 million.

This is, of course, a broad average. To gauge more accurately what the trends are we must determine what the main factors in the increase are and how these are likely to change (see Reading 2). The trend in population of any country is determined by the difference between births and immigration on the one hand and deaths and emigration on the other. If we are considering world population then we need take only births and deaths into account. Insofar as deaths are concerned, the long-term trend appears clearly to be towards a steady diminution. Crude death-rates which take no account of the differences in ages between populations, are likely to be deceptive, but if differences in age-structure are taken into account, it is clear that death-rates are falling everywhere. This is, as previously mentioned, because of the raising of the standard of living and the spread of medical skills. The biggest fall in death-rates has been among young children. The younger the child, the more likely it is to die, and health improvements show themselves particularly in the lowering of the death-rate in early childhood. Equally, if a child survives to the age of, say, five, then it is very likely to survive to maturity, so that improvements in the rate of the survival in childhood have a cumulative effect on population increases because this means that more people survive to have children themselves. But general improvements in levels of living and in health reduce the death-rate throughout life, although from the point of view of population increase the decrease of the death-rate among the people who are still capable of producing children, is most significant.

The trend in the birth-rate, however, is more variable. While in highly industrialized countries the birth-rate has fallen, or is falling dramatically, the same trend has not yet manifested itself very significantly in the underdeveloped countries. Why this should be so is not very clear. Basically it seems to be related to the extent to which people living at a fairly high standard use the technological resources available to them to control the size of their families and so enable them to maintain that standard of living. In underdeveloped countries it appears that people maintain the large family-sizes which were consistent with formerly high death-rates, long after the death-rate has in fact fallen substantially. The consequence is that while industrial countries have high levels of living, low death-rates and low birth-rates, underdeveloped countries have, in general, low levels of living, falling death-rates and high birth-rates. Under these circumstances, the very countries which are least able to support increasing populations are exactly those in which the rates of population increase are highest.

Rates of population increase, and the differential effects of the birth- and death-rates upon which they are based, have several different consequences for the welfare of the societies to which they relate. The most obvious of these is, of course, competition for basic resources such as food and housing. But the resource requirements for the subsistence of the population can be imported, so that agricultural land, given international trade, need not necessarily be the constraining factor. In the most extreme form, the competition is simply for space, for, given a finite area, the population that can live in that area will be limited by the actual physical space available in which people can live. In many industrialized countries this state is beginning to be approximated by the constant increase in proportions living in towns. England and Wales provides an example of this, where in 1970, 70 per cent of its population lives in settlements of 100,000 or more. All over the world the proportion of the population living in cities is increasing (see Reading 3). In some parts of the world, dense settlement is so extensive that literally hundreds of miles of territory, as for example, from Boston to Washington in the United States, is one large urban agglomeration. Some biologists, basing their conclusions on experiments and observations on animals, have attempted to analyse the consequences for human life of extreme densities of settlement, as for example in slum areas of large towns. They point out that when the number of animals exceed some optimum density various forms of bizarre behaviour begin to manifest themselves. Mothers begin to eat their litters, some show extreme aggression, while others show extreme withdrawal. They conclude that this derives from the frustration of deep biological attachment to 'territory', and argue that human populations in analogous situations are likely to manifest equivalent forms of behaviour. There is no doubt that living in large towns presents peculiar personal and social problems, but in general the form of behaviour associated with them can be explained in terms of the *quality* of social relationships in towns rather than basic biological dispositions. Large agglomerations of population do indeed present considerable difficulties of organization and planning, of living accommodation, transportation, and the provision of services such as water, light and the disposal of refuse. But these problems are amenable to solution, given sufficient time and money. The problems that arise out of the *quality* of social relationships in large cities, similarly, while less completely understood, may nevertheless be ameliorated by appropriate actions consciously taken by those involved in them.

The consequences of differing birth- and death-rates for populations may not be quite so apparent. As a broad generalization, we may say that the production of goods for consumption, including the construction of buildings, roads and similar amenities in a community, as well as the provision of services upon which the community relies, falls particularly upon the active adult population. Which particular age-groups may be included in the 'active adults' population obviously will vary from one society to another, depending for example upon the extent to which the population depends upon muscular strength for its well-being or the extent to which the young must be trained before they are able to contribute directly to the national income. As a rough measure, demographers take the ages of twenty to sixty-five (of both sexes) to represent the 'active' population, and those under twenty and those over sixty-five to represent the 'inactive' (see Reading 4). The assumption here is that young people under twenty, and older people over the age of sixty-five, will on the whole be consuming more than they are producing and using more services than they are providing. They thus depend upon the active population. The proportions of population in these three categories arise out of the combined operation of changes in the birth-rate and the death-rate. A country which has a rising birth-rate and a falling death-rate is thus likely to have a small proportion of 'active' as against young and old dependants. Such a country is Pakistan, where for every 100 people aged twenty to sixty-five there are 167 aged less than twenty and ten aged sixty-five or more. In contrast, England and Wales has a young dependency rate of fifty-four and an old dependency rate of twenty-five, so that the burden of dependancy here arises distinctly from the high proportion of older people. Sweden, also economically affluent, has seventy-three persons aged twenty or less and twenty-six persons aged sixty-five and over per 100 'active' persons, showing a somewhat higher dependancy rate than that in England and Wales. The United States has seventy-four persons aged twenty or less and only eighteen persons aged sixty-five and over per 100 'active' persons, Japan has fifty-nine and twelve respectively, reflecting the considerably lower dependancy rate in its present industrial and demographic phase. The cost of dependancy of the under-twenties, however, is likely to differ from those of the over-sixty-fives. Without more information about the contribution that children and old people make to the national product therefore we cannot draw simple conclusions about the social implications of national differences in young and old dependancy rates. It is likely, however, that children, as against old people, on the average consume proportionately more than they produce. The 'burden of dependancy' is thus more likely to be heavier in those populations such as in present-day developing countries, in which birth-rates and death-rates are both high.

An even more subtle change in population structure which is likely to have very real consequences for people arises out of the different proportions of boy babies born as against girl babies. On the average, in industrial countries there are 106 boys born for every 100 girls born. Possibly because of the improving health of mothers where the levels of living are increasing this ratio has been tending to increase over the years. Boy babies, however, appear to be less robust than girl babies, so that mortality rates amongst boys are higher, with the result that by about age of five the ratios have approximately equated. With steady improvements in pediatric care, however, more boy babies are surviving than formerly, so that proportionately more boys are surviving into adulthood than girls. This means of course that, excluding the possibility of wars, in which the mortality among males is likely to be higher than among females (by no means certain in future wars), some adjustments will need to be made in marriage institutions if some young men in the future are going to have the opportunity of marrying. In the United Kingdom in 1901, for example, there were ninety men aged twenty to twenty-four to every 100 group in which most people first marry. By 1931, the proportion had risen to ninety-five, by 1971 to 102, and it is estimated it will be 103 in the year 2001. At older ages, however, the greater risk of mortality among men will presumably continue to operate so that, as at present, older women will heavily outnumber older men.

Levels of living and population growth

The consequences of population growth, combined with expected standards of living, are likely to be as significant for international affairs as they are internally, within nations. At present, the consumption of resources in industrialized countries is out of all proportion to that in underdeveloped countries. Figure 1 sets out the consumption of foodstuffs for various countries in comparison with a standard diet set up by the United Nations Food and Agricultural Organization. The extent to which the countries of Asia and Africa fall far short of this standard is immediately apparent. What is true for foodstuffs is equally true for practically every other resource needed to sustain human life. Figure 1 of Reading 1 'Sources of Power and Damage' shows that the energy consumption in North America is about four times that of Asia. This is equally true for other resources. Modern industrialized countries are using far greater quantities *per capita* of metals, water, petroleum, coal and wood-products (particularly for paper-production) than under-developed countries, much of it being imported from 'underdeveloped' countries. This is the natural consequence of the higher general standard of living in present-day industrialized countries. Assuming that the population of present-day underdeveloped countries remains fixed at present levels, it follows that if the standards of living in these countries are to reach those of present-day developed countries, a considerable increase in production and hence considerably higher consumption of resources – of energy, of water, and so on – will be unavoidable. From this will follow even higher levels of pollution and the production of even more refuse. If the populations of present-day underdeveloped countries are going to keep expanding, and at the same time approximate the standard of living in industrial countries, the world consumption of basic resources and production of pollutants will be increased even more. A technological breakthrough is possible, of course, by means of which

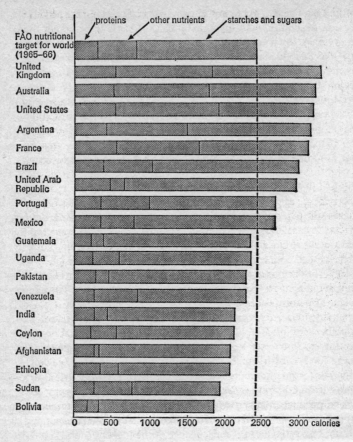

Figure 1 Quality of diet in selected countries.
The United Nations Food and Agricultural Organization (FAO) set a
world target of 2400 calories per person in 1965-66; for a diet of
reasonably good quality. 12·5 per cent of these calories were to be
provided by proteins, 20·8 per cent by other nutrients, and 66·7 per cent by
sugars and starches. Few developing countries met the total caloric target
in 1965–66 and fewer still consumed nutrients in the proper proportion.
Source: Fisher, 'The many-faceted food problem', *Population
Bulletin*, vol. 24, December 1968.

the requirements of the world population at a fairly high level of living may be met without such prodigal destruction of basic resources and without necessarily polluting the environment. But at present limitations in available basic resources and the deleterious consequences of their use for the environment put an inexorable constraint on both population growth and the overall improvement in the levels of living.

The implications for the future are disturbing. The marked disparity of levels of living between the industrialized nations of the world and the rest – in terms of sheer struggle for resources – could easily become a bone of international contention. If the people of the underdeveloped world of today set themselves a target of a higher level of consumption, given present-day methods of agricultural and industrial production, conflict with present-day developed countries for the limited available resources of the world, with all the danger of international relationships that this implies, seems inescapable. An alternative would be that present-day levels of living in industrial countries be reduced and the savings in consumption so produced be redistributed among the less privileged people of the world. A third alternative – which in fact is being actually prosecuted in many developing nations – is that of reducing the present rate of population growth, which at least will offset further falls in the levels of living, but this is, obviously, only part of the solution, since the ultimate objective surely is a better life for all, not merely a common low standard of life for all.

The 'population – resources – standards of living' problem is peculiarly insidious, since it usually takes concrete, if dramatic and obvious form, only when famine stalks a country. The essentially private decision of a pair of individuals to have another child inevitably has social and economic consequences which for the individual pair may be almost negligible, but when multiplied up by millions of times for a large population assumes Gargantuan proportions. Furthermore, the consequences of actions taken now may take decades to manifest themselves as problems, so that a child born now will consume most heavily not immediately, but only twenty years hence; a factory which starts polluting a water-course now may upset the ecological balance irreversibly only in twenty years' time. The current popular interest in both pollution and population among middle-class people in affluent countries is a hopeful augury for the future, but they are only a tiny handful, who, by reason of their affluence, can afford to sit back and take thought. Paradoxically, the hungry and deprived of the word have little incentive to be so objective about these problems, though they are likely to be the first to suffer from the effects of undue population pressure and the depradations of environmental pollution. And their reaction is not likely to be merely a cerebral one.

1 Charles Ogburn, Jr

The Sources of Power and Damage

Excerpts from Charles Ogburn, Jr, 'The sources of power and damage',
Population Bulletin, vol. 26, June 1970, pp. 17–33.

Sources of power and damage

Energy consumption is a reliable gauge of a society's economic status. It is therefore no surprise that the US produces and consumes nearly three times as much electrical energy per person as any other continental region.

Last year the US consumed 1451 billion kilowatt hours (KWH) of electrical energy. If the whole world were to reach our current *per capita* KWH level at a time when the human population was 5 billion, it would necessitate almost a ninefold increase in the generation of electricity. Nuclear or conventional power plants would have to be built on most of the world's large and accessible rivers, lakes and bays. The metals industry would be enormously challenged to support the generation, transmission and use of such an imposing increase in electrical energy. Pollution hazards – thermal, air and radioactive – would grow much more intense.

Europe and the Soviet Union do not have far to go to reach the present US level of *per capita* electrical energy consumption – over 6600 KWH per year. But for Africa, Asia and Latin America, the power increases would have to exceed an order of magnitude. How might such increases be provided? What might the environmental consequences be?

Solar Energy

Power available to man has in the main four derivations:

1. Muscle power, which counts for little in a highly industrialized society.

2. The energy of water flowing downhill, which in a simpler age turned our millwheels and today spins huge electric generators in the penstocks of giant dams.

3. The burning of carbonaceous fuels – wood, coal, petroleum and natural gas.

4. Atomic fission and atomic fusion, the latter heretofore uncontrollable and unusable except as a super-explosive.

There is another source of energy theoretically capable of supplying all the power the human race could ever use, and that is the sun. But as Daniels of the University of Wisconsin points out: 'Even the unrealistic enthusiasts have come to realize that there are no quick and easy sol-

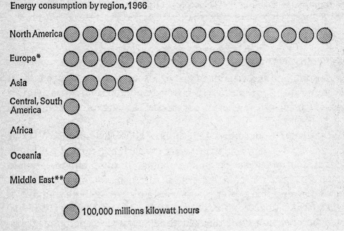

Energy consumption by region, 1966

North America
Europe*
Asia
Central, South America
Africa
Oceania
Middle East**

100,000 millions kilowatt hours

*excludes USSR   USSR total – 516,480 MKW
**includes Southern Yemen   Yemen figures not available
Cyprus (381 MKW) is included in Europe

Figure 1 Energy consumption by region, 1966.
Energy consumption, a good gauge of both pollution and development, is more than an order of magnitude greater in the West than other regions. Closing the gap while the West's energy use continues to rise would vastly increase the threats to the global environment.
Source: US Federal Power Commission, *World Power Data*, 1966.

utions to the intermittency of the sun and the high cost of collecting its energy' [. . .]

Hydroelectric power

Hydroelectric power is clean [. . .] Nevertheless, the tangible and intangible costs can be high. Where large impoundments are necessary to produce a profitable head of water, vast areas of land are lost to inundation. The sacrificed acres are likely to be fertile and important to man, in terms of both agriculture and fisheries. Commercially valuable fish are often blocked from their spawning grounds by dams [. . .]

Electric power from falling streams may be supplemented by power from tides. The tides [can be harnessed] by damming indentures of the coast, and utilizing the flow of water in and out of the basins thus formed as the sea rises and falls. [. . .] Tidal generation of power has the advantage of causing far less damage to the environment than conventional hydro-electric impoundments, but the world's potential tidal power is less than 1 per cent of its potential water power.

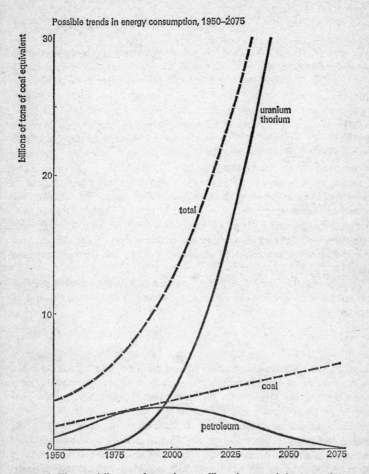

Possible trends in energy consumption, 1950–2075

Figure 2 The world's use of petroleum will peak around the turn of the century, while coal consumption continues to rise slowly. After about 1975, most of the increase in energy use will be provided by nuclear fuels.
Source: Brown, *et al, The Next Hundred Years,* Viking Press.

Carbonaceous fuels

In many parts of the world even today, life would be all but impossible without wood for fuel. Of the world total of wood cut, over 40 per cent is burned – not only to cook food and heat homes but to produce steam for small ships and locomotives. The continued widespread use of wood for such purposes will probably be unthinkable, for tomorrow's billions will be hard pressed to satisfy their growing needs for lumber and paper. Wood as a source of power will have to be replaced by more efficient fuels in greater supply.

The other carbonaceous fuels, on which industry has largely depended since its beginnings and on which it will largely depend for some time to come, are the so-called 'fossil fuels': coal, oil, gas and derivative compounds. The consumption of all these fuels continues to rise rapidly, though coal has been accounting for a diminishing proportion of the total.

The fossil-fuel story is one of the remarkable episodes in man's history – and the word 'episode' is deliberately chosen. Writing in 1968, Hubbert observed that 'half of the world's cumulative production of petroleum has occurred during the twelve-year period since 1956. . . . In brief, most of the world's consumption of energy from fossil fuels during its entire history has occurred during the last twenty-five years.' The reasons for this pell-mell consumption can be found largely in Europe and the US, which are using fossil fuels at a record, steadily rising rate. The example of petroleum illustrates how abnormal is the period of rapid industrial growth which has prevailed, at least in the West, for the last few centuries. [. . .]

While destined to a relatively short remaining life, the massive burning of fossil fuels for energy can be expected to continue beyond the end of this century. [. . .]

Air pollution

No city dweller today needs to be reminded of the atmospheric pollution caused by the combustion of coal, oil and gasoline. Our urban areas are overhung most of the time by a pall of smog whose more toxic compounds irritate the membranes of the eyes and respiratory system, produce cancer and otherwise shorten lives [. . .]

Carbon dioxide is produced by the oxidation of carbon, as in the burning or decay of organic matter and in animal metabolism. It is essential to plant life. Nevertheless, this tasteless, odorless, colorless gas is today under scrutiny for its potentially ominous role as an environmental heat trap. Carbon dioxide permits most solar energy to pass through, but it is relatively impervious to heat radiated from the earth. Thus, it acts like a global greenhouse. [. . .]

The rapid depletion of the known reserves of coal and oil could raise the concentration of carbon dioxide in the atmosphere by as much as seventeen times – an enormous increase indeed.

What causes deep concern among informed persons as the level of atmospheric carbon dioxide mounts is that the increased retention of heat in the atmosphere through the 'greenhouse effect' may melt a good deal of the Greenland and Antarctic ice caps. This would raise the level of the ocean by as much as 250 feet, drowning every port city in the world and inundating every coastal plain. The oceans are gradually encroaching on the world's coasts as it is, presumably in part as a result of the release of water tied up in ice. [. . .]

That the continued use of fossil fuels will increasingly warm the earth is by no means certain, however. It might even have the opposite effect. Some scientists, impressed by evidence that the earth has recently been experiencing a cooling trend, believe that this is the consequence of dust and other particulates disgorged into the air from the burning of fossil fuels. [. . .]

There is, moreover, a third possible consequence of rising fossil-fuel combustion. We may be faced with a very dangerous degree of oxygen depletion, for this vital element is bound up in carbon dioxide. [. . .]

We have seen that for a further damming of rivers for electric power, we must pay a high price in land. Likewise, our still-mounting use of fossil fuels may be placing the global environment of our species in jeopardy. Under these circumstances, we now look to the third of the great power sources after falling water and fossil fuels.

Nuclear power

Circumstances are highly propitious for exploiting atomic fission as a source of energy. Much of the basic technology has been mastered. If 'breeder' reactors come strongly into the field by the end of the century, as is now expected, we shall have an almost limitless supply of fuel for the fission process. [. . .]

Meanwhile, as our use of fossil fuels fast approaches its peak, our demands for electric power are growing faster than the population. They are, indeed, doubling in under ten years. More than 100 nuclear power plants are already planned for the US. The Atomic Energy Commission (AEC) predicts that the proportion of electricity in the United States which is nuclear generated will increase from 3 per cent today to 50 per cent by the year 2000. With considerable enthusiasm, the Commission portrays nuclear power plants as instruments of a greatly expanded economic development both at home and overseas:

A typical industrial complex . . . could include interrelated industrial processes for the production of fertilizers, aluminium, phosphorus, caustic-chlorine and ammonia. The agro-industrial complex would be located on the sea coast and include large-scale desalting of sea water for highly intensified irrigated agriculture. Nuclear reactors producing low-cost power would serve as the energy source for the electrical and other energy requirements of the complexes. . . . The energy-center concept might have application in Australia, India, Mexico, the Middle East, Peru and the United States.

Recent studies by the United Nations Economic and Social Council also envisage nuclear reactors of one or two million kilowatts' capacity serving as power generators for large-scale industrial and agricultural developments in arid regions. With the rapid depletion of fossil fuels and the prospects of a nearly limitless supply of nuclear fuels, we can expect other nations to leap on the nuclear bandwagon as fast as their competence and resources allow. A large share of the world's power generation will be nuclear by the year 2000 – perhaps 35 per cent [. . .]

In the last two or three years, misgivings about the effects of nuclear power plants have become more widespread and articulate [. . .]

Little is known with certainty about the costs to the environment of nuclear power generation. Its adoption on a wide scale would vastly reduce the levels of sulfur oxides, hydrocarbons and particulate matter which are now spewn into the air by conventional coal-fired plants. This lessening of air pollution has been put forward as one of the major contributions we can expect from nuclear power. But other imposing environmental problems would emerge. Nuclear power plants (like conventional coal plants) produce about three times as much heat as they can use to generate electricity.

Thermal pollution

Nuclear plants must therefore be located near a plentiful water supply – normally a lake or stream. To get rid of the surplus two-thirds of the heat from the reactor, the cooling water is returned downstream of its source a good deal warmer than at the intake point [. . .] For the amount of electricity generated, the newer atomic plants will release about the same amount of heat into the cooling water as the newer coal-fired plants. The difference, however, is that forthcoming nuclear plants will generate much more electricity and discharge much more heat at a given site than their fossil-fueled predecessors.

Thermal pollution above a certain level can undoubtedly play havoc with the life of a stream: 'It can kill, it can affect the movement of some species, and it can regulate rates of biochemical and physiological processes, especially those associated with reproduction.' It can increase the

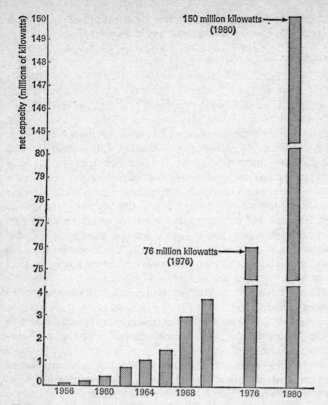

Figure 3 Estimated growth of nuclear power with United States 1956–80.
Sources: J. McHale, *The Future of the Futures*, Braziller, 1969.
Projections for 1976 and 1980 given by Scaborg. Remarks at
the Financial Forum on Nuclear Energy, Waldorf Astoria Hotel, New
York, 30 October 1968.

susceptibility of aquatic life to toxic chemicals and disease, stimulate
the growth of bottom-rooted plants and thus retard flow and increase
siltation, and encourage the excessive growth of algae.

Heat pollution of estuaries is also particularly menacing, for [. . .] these
areas are vital to marine fisheries [. . .] Biologists argue that the effects of
heating even a small area may spread, because the chain of life in an
entire estuary is threatened when a major link is damaged or destroyed.

What gives the problem its disquieting dimensions is the prospect that
nuclear plants will explosively proliferate – in the United States and

around the world. Indeed, any significant narrowing of the global income gap must be based at least in part on this likelihood [. . .]

Radioactive pollution

In addition to the enormous quantities of heat that a million-kilowatt nuclear plant must get rid of, there are several billion Curies of radioactive materials that accumulate in the course of a year and must also be removed.[1] Of these radioactive materials, small amounts take care of themselves by quickly decaying. The remainder contain large quantities of the long-lived isotopes of strontium-90, iodine-131, cesium-137 and the form of hydrogen known as tritium. Some of these pass into the local environment in gaseous or liquid form. Most of them accumulate in the reactor fuel. These wastes – materials of moderate to high-level radiation – are periodically drawn off, packaged and shipped to waste-storage facilities where various measures are taken to withhold them permanently from circulation. Some wastes are converted into granular form and stored in underground concrete vaults. Others are buried deep in salt beds. Still others – the liquid slurries – are held in stainless steel tanks or pumped into the earth.

The problem of radioactive waste accumulation is directly related to the amount of electricity generated [. . .] Thus, as increasingly affluent and large human populations require more and more nuclear plants to power their industries, the risks of radioactive pollution will correspondingly increase. [. . .]

While most high-level wastes are removed from the reactor and buried in natural salt beds or underground concrete and metal bins, intermediate wastes have proved harder to dispose of – especially the aqueous varieties. Pumped deep into the earth or stored in earth ponds, they have been known to escape into circulating ground water. Some have even been dumped into the sea in the hope that it would disperse and dilute them to 'harmless' levels [. . .]

How significant a threat to human and other life are the 'radio isotopes' released into the environment?

Assessing the danger from the discharge of these radioactive materials into the air and waters is impossible at this stage of our knowledge. We do know that radiation can cause cancers, the fatality rate being about twenty in one million from exposure to a level of radiation ten times higher than that occurring naturally. We have it on the authority of the International Commission for Radiological Protection that the genetic

1. A Curie equals the activity of one gram of radium. The explosion of the atomic bomb at Hiroshima released only a few hundred thousand Curies of long-lived radiation.

risks from exposure to radiation are greater than the bodily effects; this fact entails the possibility of the genetic contamination of the human race.

While the AEC would allow the public to be exposed to five times the natural background dose of radiation per year, most biologists believe there is no minimum level of exposure below which damage does not occur, and they generally recommend that the public be exposed to no more than 2·7 times the natural background radiation.

So far we have been speaking of the radioactive by-products which are released to the environment by design – wise or otherwise. What about the high-level wastes that are removed from the reactor for safe-keeping? Some of these longer-lasting isotopes have been described as a million to a billion times more lethal than any other known industrial chemical.

Unfortunately, there is no known way for man to neutralize them. Only time will do so, and a great deal of time at that – between 600 and 1000 years. [. . .]

These ingredients will have to be monitored for hundreds of years. To visualize governments equal to such a trust, one must indeed be optimistic. Nine cases of tank-failure out of 183 tanks stored in Washington, North Carolina, have already been reported by the AEC.

Radioactive accidents

A final danger in the multiplication of nuclear plants is the possibility, however remote, of an accident. Rather than having the form of a monstrous blast, such an accident would amount to the forceful discharge of radioactive material of up to several million Curies. Needless to say, every effort is made in the design of nuclear plants to guard against an accident. But no one who has had much experience with human fallibility or is acquainted with the instances of negligence and equipment failure in nuclear plants will be fully reassured. [. . .]

The current type of nuclear reactor does not, of course, necessarily represent the last word. There is the prospect that the dangers to which present plants subject the environment will be significantly mitigated with the advance of reactor technology; some of these dangers may be completely eliminated.

'Breeder' reactors

Today's reactors, called 'burners', are dependent for fuel upon the naturally occurring fissionable isotope of uranium, uranium-235. This is a serious drawback in view of the fact that less than 1 per cent of natural uranium consists of uranium-235. And uranium ores are limited [. . .] For this and other reasons, the pressure is on for the development of the 'breeder' reactor, in which more fissile material is produced than is consumed and in which virtually the whole available supply of low-grade uranium and thorium can be converted at high temperatures into fissionable isotopes of plutonium and uranium [. . .]

For these gains a price in new risks will evidently have to be paid. The heat-transfer medium in present experimental breeders is molten sodium raised to 1000°F.; it becomes highly radioactive and ignites if exposed to air. For these reasons an alternative circulant is being sought [. . .]

Components, however, have failed. It was such a failure that caused a melting of a portion of the reactor fuel in the Lagoona, Michigan breeder plant – the only commercial breeder – in January 1966 [. . .]

The danger seems to be that the nuclear chain reaction could go too far in part of the reactor, causing the fuel to melt and assume a 'critical configuration' leading to a nuclear explosion. [. . .]

One scientific commentator states that 'a tremendous number of experimental and test facilities must be built and operated both by the government and by industry', and that 'the operation of large, safe, reliable commercial breeders [is] still another ten, and perhaps fifteen to twenty years away'.

Nuclear fusion

Difficulties vastly more formidable, it would appear, still lie in the way of physicists seeking to go beyond nuclear fission altogether to exploit the energy of nuclear fusion, the source of the sun's heat. The fuel – an isotope of hydrogen – must be heated to between 100 million and five billion degrees Kelvin, and the ions produced, called the plasma, must be held for tenths of a second in a configuration of correct density.

Despite the difficulties, scientists involved in the nuclear fusion field appear to be hopeful of eventually overcoming them. Success would put at man's disposal an amount of energy equivalent to 500 Pacific oceans of high-grade fuel oil. Furthermore, since fusion power plants would operate at very high efficiency, they would create much less thermal pollution than conventional plants. They also would not emit radioactive by-products.

Writing on the still-remote harnessing of nuclear fusion, Walter Sullivan of the *New York Times* states: 'Success would provide ample energy for the remaining lifetime of the earth and should enable man, under wise leadership and assuming some method of population control, to work out ways to live in equilibrium with his environment and its resources.'

That could be so, but an effective and politically viable method of population control is not even in sight, while 'wise leadership' would be a novelty indeed in man's treatment of his environment. The record of the new damage to the environment which has accompanied every increase in power production warrants little confidence that man will wisely handle the quantum jump in power we could expect from the control of atomic fusion.

In any case, as long as the world's population continues to grow and mankind seeks ever-rising levels of consumption, the demand for increased power will be difficult to deny if the means of supplying it are at hand, regardless of what those means entail. [. . .]

Therefore, in looking ahead, we had better prepare ourselves for a global landscape liberally sprinkled with giant reactors. If a world population of 5 billion is to achieve the present US level of industrialization, it must be able to increase power output many times above the present levels, not only for individual consumption and for producing the mountains of metals and fertilizer that will be needed, but also for extracting the fuel to feed the reactors themselves.

Clearly, then [to close the gap in levels of living in different countries today] – that is a world population of five billion enjoying present US material standards of living – would, if realized, pose an enormous threat to our environment. This would be true whether our energy source was largely fossil fuels or nuclear power. Furthermore, the demand for power involves an immense drain on metals, for energy consumption and metals consumption are closely related. Only a sophisticated metals technology can support an advanced power-generating, power-distributing network. To provide power for five billion people at current US kilowatt-hour standards would therefore vastly speed up the depletion of many irreplaceable metals. This dilemma is but one of many that will confront us if our population and consumption continue to grow while we and other nations seek to narrow the global income gap [. . .]

Facing up to the future

It may of course be argued that the attainment or approximation of a present-day American style of living by the entire human species is nothing we need anticipate. But the possibility of such a future – and its appeal to our equalitarian instincts – should give us food for thought.

1. It might move us to a less leisurely approach to the problem of runaway population growth. This would include a hard look at the 'right' of every family to have as many offspring as it pleases. If the human race meets with the disaster toward which its accelerating rate of increase seems to be rushing it, that 'right' will be among the least of our pos-

sessions to be lost. The message indeed, is that an industrializing world simply cannot afford to have five billion people. We must lower our sights even lower than this conservative projection if we are to preserve a livable environment.

2. It might lead us to a deliberate policy of working more with than in disregard of nature, even if this means – for the wealthier nations that can well afford it – foregoing certain increases in consumption in order to undertake greater conservation. Resources could be allocated from frills to the restoration and protection of the environment. Efforts could be made to produce food increasingly within the natural scheme, in ways that do not require heavy power inputs or drastic disruptions of the natural economy. It has been found, for example, that Africa's savannas yield more proteins if left in possession of the native antelope than if transformed into cattle ranches. Inland waters of all kinds, estuaries, bays of the sea and artificial impoundments could be protected and cultivated for the high-grade proteins they can produce. The development of methods for 'farming' organic wastes of every type through the agency of yeasts and algae could be given a high priority.

3. It might dispose the industrialized nations, and above all the United States, to be less prodigal in their consumption of resources and to salvage more of their wastes. (Some municipalities on both sides of the Atlantic are already engaged in the latter effort as a means of dealing with rising mountains of trash.) We are befouling our waterways with organic wastes that might replace the nutrients which we extract from our farmlands. Nearly all the wastes of our industrial civilization, the effluents of factories, the bottles, papers, cans and car bodies, are resources we strew across the landscape at the same time that we mine the earth to obtain their constituents. This is currently an economical practice, but it is madness none the less.

4. It might prompt us to examine other 'economies' we seek at the expense of the environment. Radioactive products seep from nuclear reactors because trapping them would 'prohibitively' raise the cost of the electricity generated. Mountains and the forests they support are devastated by strip-mining to keep costs of extraction low. Urban sprawl consumes acreage wholesale because land is valued in terms not of its role in the environment but of its market price.

It might bring us to recognize that the lands and their vegetative cover, their resources of minerals and waters, and the seas themselves, are the indispensable commons of the human species as a whole, and that any individual or organizational proprietary rights to any part of them are subordinate to the environmental rights of all people, including at least our immediate heirs. The destruction of forests and the pollution of the oceans for individual or corporate gain may impair our grandchildren's ability to breathe. We may even come to hold that the manufacturer or government bureaucrat responsible for the discharge of poisons into the environment should be as accountable as if he had dumped the crankcase drainings of his motorcar down his neighbor's well or his garbage on his neighbor's porch.

A choice

The hardest choices are those between alternatives which both seem right and good. Today we face such a dilemma. Do we wish to see an ever-rising human population? Do we wish to go on getting and spending at ever-higher levels?

Or, as we prefer to believe about ourselves, do we truly seek a more equitable world in which all people can claim their due share of the earth's bounty? The burden of [the argument] is that we cannot have it both ways. We and our descendants are fated to make a painful choice.

2 Annabelle Desmond and Michael Amrine

The Population Problem

Excerpts from Annabelle Desmond and Michael Amrine, 'A distinguished Frenchman views the population problem', *Population Bulletin*, vol. 18, May 1962, pp. 43–62.

For many centuries, there has been overcrowding in some areas of the globe. Many – perhaps most – human societies have always lived close to hunger. [. . .]

In his book *Fertility and Survival: Population Problems from Malthus to Mao Tse-Tung*, Alfred Sauvy (1961) speculates whether the public attention given to population growth today may be due simply to better record-keeping because 'our statistical magnifying-glass' has been perfected? Or is it because we are becoming 'more sensitive and more humane'? He thinks not and he believes neither point is relevant. He says that during the past twenty years important changes have quietly been taking place upon our planet:

The new factor in our world, let us repeat, is neither over-population – an imprecise term – nor misery – a partly subjective notion – nor hunger, or rather, under-nourishment, which is part of the data that can be measured scientifically.

The struggle for existence and the poverty of the greatest number have been part of the fate of mankind for a very long time. Of course, we might consider that the moment has come to stop this age-old tragedy, now that we have achieved so much in the way of dominating nature, and to say therefore that the new factor is our ability to conquer a scourge of nature. But there is another new factor, very new and very important: mankind has quite suddenly entered into a period of rapid growth in numbers.

In the twentieth century, Sauvy observes, there are not only great increases in absolute terms in population, in comparison with previous centuries, *there is also an increase in the rate of increase*. In his introductory pages, Sauvy shows how in a few centuries the world has gone from an annual population increase rate of 0·5 per cent to 1·7 per cent. That is more than a 200 per cent increase in the rate of increase.

At older, slower rates, the world doubled in population, from 545 million in 1650, to 1175 million in 1850. That doubling took 200 years – but human population doubled again in less than a century.

In absolute numbers, the annual world population increment now is tremendous because the base is so large. Today's population of three billion, growing at 1·7 per cent, means an additional 51 million people a year. If that growth rate continues unchanged, world population will double to six billion in only 40 years.

The problem of population is further complicated by the fact that the rate of increase is even higher than the world average in precisely those crowded areas where intense population pressure stifles economic growth. In some of these regions, population is increasing at rates between 2 and 3·5 per cent a year.

To indicate what these rates mean in time and numbers, if a population were growing at 2 per cent a year, it would double in thirty-five years and grow sevenfold in a century. If a population were growing at 3·5 per cent, it would double in only twenty years and grow thirty-two fold in a century!

This speed-up in the rate of growth is the new thing. This is the reason, in Sauvy's phrase, for 'an unprecedented anxiety'.

Growth rates differ in regions

Medical progress continually is lowering the death rate nearly everywhere. But birth rates remain traditionally high in the less-developed countries. [. . .]

Generally speaking, Europe is an area of stable population growth with low birth and death rates combining to keep growth down.

Western Europe had an average growth rate of about 0·7 per cent a year in 1958. The uniformity of the rate among the countries is striking [. . .]

In southern Europe, notably in southern Italy, Spain, Portugal and Greece, Sauvy found more rapid growth, greater poverty, and less industrial development.

Sauvy also notes the high rate of growth, 1·7 per cent, in the USSR. This is equal to the world average and very close to the growth rates found in North America.

North America v. South America

Canada and the United States have higher annual rates of population growth (1·7 per cent) than most European countries. This is because the birth rates of Canada and the United States are much higher and their death rates are comparable to the low rates of Europe. Although the birth rates of Canada and the United States today are exceptionally high for industrial countries, they are less than half of what they were a century ago; and they are considerably lower than the birth rates of the less-developed countries today [. . .]

Annabelle Desmond and Michael Amrine 47

A striking difference in the pattern of population growth is found in North and South America. Here are two continents in the same hemisphere, both possessed of great natural resources and both colonized from Europe in the last few hundred years at about the same time. Their historical traditions have been different, and today their cultures and political and economic systems are different.

Population is growing faster in Latin America than in any other major region of the world, 2·5 to 3 per cent per year. There, sharply declining death rates combine with traditionally high birth rates to increase the growth rate.

Sauvy divides Latin America into two zones: the tropical zone, including Mexico, Central America and tropical South America, and the temperate zone of South America. The tropical zone has traditionally high birth rates, falling death rates and growth rates of 3 per cent a year. In the temperate zone, lower birth rates combine with falling death rates to give slower rates of growth. In all of Latin America, only Argentina and Uruguay have birth rates similar to those found in Canada and the United States [. . .]

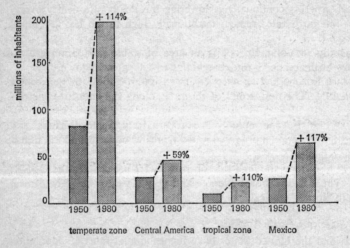

Figure 1 Population increase in Latin America.
The populations of various regions of Latin America are shown in comparison with the population projected to 1980 (United Nations high projection). Tropical Latin America has the highest rate of increase of any major region of the world.
Source: Sauvy.

Asia

Sauvy notes that 'the great migrations came out of Asia, and the greatest human masses are now in Asia, as well as the greatest expansions in numbers' [. . .]

Since Sauvy's book was written, the Indian census of 1961 reported 438 million people, about seven million more than the official estimates which were based on the 1951 census. The Pakistani census for 1961 reported ninety-four million, a total which was four million above the country's official estimates. In 1953, the Chinese census reported almost 583 million people, a total which exceeded the official estimates by about 100 million.

Japan, whose pre-war population growth was the most rapid in Asia, is the only Asian country today whose birth rate has declined to within a reasonable balance of its low death rate. As a result, Japan's population is growing at about 1 per cent a year [. . .]

Sauvy summarizes the Asian situation in these broad terms:

In Asia as a whole, the growth of population is fairly rapid; but there are great regional variations in the relationship between the population and the natural resources, at least as these are at present exploited. Whereas Iran, Iraq, Burma, Vietnam and even Turkey and Syria apparently still have, like Soviet Asia, vast resources at their disposal, India, China and Formosa, Japan, Israel, Korea, Pakistan even and Malaya, are finding it difficult to cope with their demographic growth.

We are very badly documented on Soviet Asia but there is good reason to believe that its rate of increase is higher than that of the Soviet Union as a whole, 1·7 per cent per annum. It is very probably over 2 per cent per annum, including immigration. [. . .]

Africa

Africa was a very dark continent, demographically speaking, before the Second World War, and up to that time posed 'no problem of over-population'. [. . .]

Sauvy speculates that under-population rather than over-population may have been the issue in what is sometimes called 'Black Africa', including Madagascar. He writes that the loss of people to sleeping sickness, malaria and other diseases has caused concern.

In South Africa, 'the white population is vastly outnumbered by the increasing Indian, half-caste and Bantu populations. In thirty years, the European population is expected to increase by 50 per cent, whereas the coloured increase will be 75 per cent for the Bantus, 100 per cent for the half-caste, and 150 per cent for the Asiatics. In pure figures, the increase would be of 1,200,000 for the Europeans and of 7,800,000 for the non-Europeans. . . .'

Like many others, Sauvy notes that the situation there 'is all the more explosive because segregation aggravates the social pressure'.

Death takes a holiday

Deaths from epidemics and famines – Sauvy calls this 'excess mortality' – which used to decimate populations in earlier times, have practically disappeared in time of peace. Furthermore, what he calls 'normal mortality' is also much lower than it was because medical progress is now carried to virtually every corner of the earth. Sauvy says that medical advances, especially in hygiene and preventive medicine, 'have everywhere lowered that dismal figure of 30 per 1,000 [this he postulates as 'normal mortality'] which seemed like a heavy stone laid on the head of mankind, and much lower rates have been reached, varying from 15 to 25 per 1000, even among very poor people'.

This lower death rate has not been matched by a lower birth rate; so population is growing rapidly throughout the vast reaches of Africa, Asia (except in Japan) and Latin America (except in Argentina and Uruguay). While agreeing with other demographers that the falling death rate is the key factor in today's rapid population growth in those areas, Sauvy seeks to emphasize another very important fact: *'the death rate is and will be lowering without the help of economic progress'*. (Italics ours.)

During Europe's great population expansion, economic progress from the Industrial Revolution moved along with medical progress. The two were thought to be inextricably linked to each other. But in most less-developed areas today, there is a serious lag between population growth and economic growth.

Declining mortality increases life expectancy

In primitive societies, high death rates, particularly high infant mortality rates, held life expectancy down. Life expectancy at birth in the early eighteenth century was very little, if any, higher than in prehistoric times.

Today, a longer life is the prospect of people nearly everwhere, even in underdeveloped countries. Humane health measures are keeping people alive *even when they are close to starvation* (see Figure 2) [. . .]

Sauvy makes a distinction between chronic undernourishment and actual hunger to the point of death from starvation in a famine. Millions of people in the world today are not starving in the literal sense of the word, but it is remarkable that, with a diet so far below minimal requirements accepted by nutritionists, they still live on without succumbing to one of the many diseases – infectious, parasitic or others – that affect the human race.

More people now live to reproduce

Sauvy points out that 'to say that the average life has risen from thirty to sixty years does not mean that death used to strike men at thirty and now allows them a respite of the same duration. The rise is in fact chiefly caused by the decrease in infant mortality.'

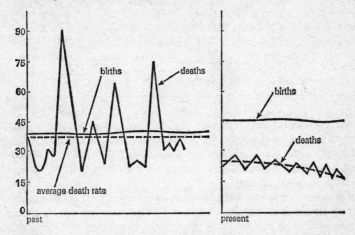

Figure 2 Changing patterns of births and deaths in underdeveloped countries.
Until very recently death rates throughout the world showed sharp variations often from year to year. Over the long pull, births exceeded deaths slightly, and population grew slowly. Beginning in the West about 1800, increasingly effective mortality control eliminated wide swings in death rates, and they have fallen steadily since then. Birth rates also followed a downward course. In the underdeveloped countries today, the birth rate has not declined. Thus, the rate of population growth has increased.
Source: Sauvy.

Fewer infants die now. Most of them live to have children of their own. In former times, there might be six children born in a family but only two or three would live to be adults. Now virtually all children born reach their reproductive years [. . .]

Sauvy illustrates his point by showing the number of persons surviving at different age groups in three quite different societies: a country before the demographic revolution, a less developed and a developed country today (see Table 1).

Table 1

	France 18th century	India 1941–50	Norway 1946–50
	(*number of survivors*)		
Birth	1000	1000	1000
1 year	767	818	970
20 years	502	574	950
40 years	369	422	916
60 years	214	216	818
80 years	35	27	388
85 years	12	2	214

From this table, Sauvy observes that in Europe the number of survivors to the age of twenty years per 1000 babies born has doubled in two centuries, and the number of persons reaching sixty has quadrupled. More important, the proportion of babies born who live to adult age has risen from 50 to 95 per cent.

Sauvy notes that lower death rates, an increased life expectancy and a larger proportion of surviving adults are demographic realities which are common to all countries; and that 'some under-developed countries, with a younger age group composition, already have a lower death rate than that of France and England, lower, even, than that of the United States.'

However, the birth rate is quite a different matter. In the less-developed countries, the birth rate has remained at traditional levels, around forty to forty-five per 1000. It may have risen slightly in some countries as health and sanitation improved. With well over half of the population under twenty years of age, the potential for continued rapid growth is obviously great.

In contrast, the birth rate in the countries of Europe is between fifteen and twenty per 1000. Sauvy says that 'this lowering is voluntary and the result of contraceptives and abortive practices'. He notes that in France the use of contraceptives and the lengthening of life began about the same time, in the eighteenth century; and that in the other countries of Europe, the lowering of the birth rate came later: 'it was the time-lag between the two lowering rates, the birth rate and the death rate, which caused the great demographic impetus in the nineteenth century' [. . .]

Can science and technology match the increase?

Under a favorable social organization, modern methods in agriculture, production and technology make it *possible* for human beings to produce much more than they have in the past. Many persons believe that through science and technology man will always be able to produce more than enough food and goods to keep up with an expanding population. However, the facts of *per capita* income *as they exist today* show tremendous disparities, and these indicate that the benefits of science and technology still remain more theoretical than real for a great part of the earth.

Conceding that 'the standard of living' really cannot be measured too precisely, although many have tried, Sauvy makes some estimates of the quantity of goods consumed per individual in different nations at different times. Emphasizing that his estimates are rough, he observes that the differences are so large and the conclusions so obvious that one need not make a 'search of decimal-points'.

Sauvy takes as a standard of comparison the amount of goods and services consumed per human being in Western Europe in 1938, just before the outbreak of the Second World War, and considers that amount equal to 100. He estimates that in 1870 Western Europe had a standard of living of about 40, and that production, and therefore consumption, per person more than doubled by 1938. He compares the standards of living of various regions and times [. . .]

Table 2

	Standard of living	Duration of life	
		in years	in indices
France 1788	25	30	50
Western Europe in 1870	40	40	66
Western Europe in 1938	100	60	100
Present-day Asia	10	40 to 45	66 to 75
Present-day Africa	12	40	66
Present-day Latin America	35	50 to 55	84 to 92

Wealth and poverty

If a family has a steady income while it is growing, it has less and less income per person with each addition. If the income grows, but not in proportion to the family growth, there still is less income *per capita* than when the family was small.

The basic arithmetic of population growth and income growth in a nation is similar. But a comparison between nations and families cannot be carried too far without becoming meaningless in terms of human needs, and complicated in terms of the definition of income and questions of productivity *per capita*.

If a nation has in its total population a greater proportion of old persons or children – or both – than it had before, then it has a smaller proportion of fully productive workers. Thus, the dependency load is greater. There may not be enough producers to keep up with consumer demands [. . .]

Observing that the *per capita* income of a nation measures the wealth or poverty of a people, Sauvy shows the great disparities of wealth from one country to another. The estimates he used were those available at the time he was writing. They are calculated in American dollars.

From nearly 2000 dollars per inhabitant in the United States, the income per head scales down to 600–1100 in Western Europe (850 in France), in Australia and New Zealand, and falls to below 150 in the poverty-stricken underdeveloped countries.

	dollars
Rhodesia and Nyasaland	100
Thailand	80
South Korea, Pakistan, Belgian Congo	75
Kenya, India, Uganda, Burma, etc.	60

Sauvy states that these figures should be considered 'extremely rough, with a margin of error of as much as 25 to 30 per cent'. The figures are *averages per inhabitant*, and 'since the national income is often very unequally distributed in under-developed countries (India, especially), the income of workers is in fact below these figures'.

The estimates serve to emphasize how far many of the less-developed countries must go in terms of economic growth before the development necessary to meet the 'rising expectations' of the people begins to get off the ground.

The different possibilities

If the death rate continues to fall in the less-developed world and if the birth rate does not decline, population would grow even faster in the years ahead. Only very special circumstances, such as a thermo-nuclear war, could quickly alter the trends now in motion. Barring such a catastrophe, there is little reason to doubt that human population growth will continue to set new records, for a short time at least.

Can this revolutionary rate of growth continue for long? No, Sauvy answers. 'A new factor will emerge, which will modify present conditions and the present [rate] of growth.' He does not explicitly define that new factor, but he outlines different broad possibilities which alone – or in differing combinations – are likely to change the present course. These are:

Return to an increased death-rate, either voluntarily . . . or involuntarily, as a result of shortages or of cataclysms, such as war.
Emigration to other lands. The population decreases by exits from the territory. This would be a geographical solution.
Progress in production of subsistence-means, sufficient to feed everyone and even to improve welfare . . . The [rate] of growth remains, but without harmful results.
Reduction of the birth, rate, sufficient to slow down or stop the growth of the population [. . .]

The only two possibilities worthy of consideration, Sauvy believes, are the economic (production in means of sustenance) and the demographic (reduction in the birth rate) [. . .]

The economic solution

In Sauvy's words, 'the "economic" solution consists in increasing the means of subsistence at least as fast as the number of human beings'. He gives three main reasons for stressing why this solution is central to all others:

An improvement in the standard of living is, as we shall see, an essential condition for the limitation of births, or at least a very favourable factor. The 'economic solution' can therefore facilitate the 'demographic solution'.
. . . we must expect an important increase of population in under-developed countries for at least a generation. . . .
. . . an improvement in the standard of living is of the utmost importance; it would be inhuman and dangerous to allow human beings to multiply in wretchedness.

Sauvy contrasts in some detail the truly *economic investments* – those which increase the production of consumer goods or create new methods of production for the future – and demographic investments – those which provide the necessary facilities to maintain a given level of living. As its population grows, a nation must invest more in schools, hospitals, highways, etc., merely to accommodate the increased number of persons. [. . .]

A country whose population is growing at a rate of 2 to 3 per cent a year must spend up to 10 per cent of its national income merely to keep living levels from declining. 'People must contribute one out of ten working days, that is, pay a tithe.' Sauvy states that the standard of living cannot be raised except by an investment over and above this 10 per cent [. . .]

Can these countries raise living levels?

Facing such conditions, how can these countries hope to save and build up capital in order to achieve a brighter future? Sauvy is aware that human beings may not have the strength to perform extra work in such circumstances, and he concludes that nations cannot rely upon the savings of their poor to achieve development dreams:

In all these countries, income is very low, often lower than ninety-five dollars a year per person; this income (or rather this produce) is seldom enough even for purely physiological needs. How then, or by what magic, can this under-nourished and debilitated man renounce part of his vital food and that of his children? Can a voluntary saving equivalent to 300 calories a day really be expected from a man who hardly has 2000?

And yet the 15 per cent saving on the national income which was quoted above represents a minimum; two-thirds of it, i.e. 10 per cent, will meet demographic needs and maintain the same standard of living, and the remaining third will enable the country to raise its standard of living by an average of 1·25 per cent per annum – a very modest result which means a whole half-century to double the standard of living and bring the annual income to a still abysmal level of 190 dollars per person!

In spite of such a depressing outlook for 'the economic solution', Sauvy repeatedly emphasizes the necessity of increasing economic measures to a scope which may really help.

However, Sauvy insists that even the development of all the arable land available to man, the spread of new methods throughout the world, and foreseeable scientific advances – all of these together cannot guarantee a solution to population pressures. Economic and technical advances are of basic importance to human survival, he contends, but in themselves they will not be enough to assure a decent world for the children of tomorrow. At best, he appears to believe that the 'economic solution' might buy the time needed for implementation of the 'demographic solution'.

The demographic solution: prevention of births

Examining the demographic solution, Sauvy discusses various aspects of birth prevention including methods used and the attitudes of the individual and of couples, and of different governments. He surveys the policies of Japan and India, and reviews Communist doctrine and attitudes.

Sauvy believes that many governments are beginning to get over their former tendency to be 'populationistic', i.e., to favour more population as an obvious way to increase their strength. A nation that seeks to improve the living levels of its people is less 'natalistic' than one which seeks to increase its power. In general, Sauvy's survey of attitudes and policies remains valid today, even though the book was written in 1958.

3 Robert C. Cook

The World's Great Cities

Excerpts from Robert C. Cook, 'The world's great cities: evolution or Devolution?', *Population Bulletin*, vol. 16, September 1960, pp. 109–30.

A major side-effect of the unprecedented speed-up in world population growth today is the ever-increasing concentration of people in cities the world over.

The rate of city growth will continue to vary in different areas of the world, decelerating in the older, industrial countries and accelerating in the agrarian, underdeveloped countries which hold two thirds of the world's people.

Urbanization is a vastly different process in those countries than it was in the West where the Industrial Revolution generated the capital needed to build the economies which could provide for the growing populations. Jobs were plentiful in the industrial cities of the West, and this provided the 'pull' for the countless millions who migrated, and still do, from country to city.

The situation is often the reverse in the underdeveloped countries today. There, the 'push' is the gross overcrowding of the rural population living at or near the bare subsistence level. More often than not, the migrant goes to an even more precarious urban situation where he cannot find work readily and must spend his limited savings. From the socio-economic and humanitarian points of view, the trek to the cities in the underdeveloped countries will continue to be more of a curse than a blessing as it absorbs limited capital and generates tension.

Today [1960] there are sixty-one cities with a million people or more in the world, compared with only ten in 1900.

Now, two people out of every ten live in cities of 20,000 or more population. If the present trend continues – and there is every indication that it will for some time – almost half the world's population will live in cities that size by 2000; and by 2050, nine people out of every ten.

The giant of all time, the New York–northeastern New Jersey metropolitan agglomeration, has a population of over 14·5 million, according to preliminary tabulations from the 1960 census. That is more than the combined population of Australia and New Zealand; and it is almost half the entire population of Mexico.

New York's borough of Manhattan shows a 15 per cent decline in population since the 1950 census. But with 1·7 million people Manhattan's population density is 75–900 per square mile.

On the other side of the world, Calcutta's population of 5·7 million is small in comparison. But projections based on current trends would give Calcutta a population of between thirty-five and sixty-six million by the year 2000! [...]

Obviously, such a projection is merely a *reductio ad absurdum*. The problems of food distribution and sanitation in the absence of very rapid economic development, are only two of many factors which would cause death rates to rise and check such multiplication of people long before standing-room-only develops.

Few people seem to understand that the pattern of tomorrow's city is being formed by today's rapid population growth. Will the city remain the traditional center of culture or will it degenerate into a socio-economic sinkhole for mankind?

Can the sprawling shantytowns which make up the cities of Asia, Africa and Latin America evolve into habitable places which provide adequate services so necessary to urban life?

Will the shabby, decaying, smog-ridden cities of the industrial West be cleansed of the blight which has been accumulating since the Industrial Revolution began? Or, will the deteriorating central cities continue to sprawl out at an even faster rate, consuming untold acres of prime farm land with their insatiable appetite for space? Will these cities be able to win back the fleeing, more prosperous residents and the industries whose tax revenue is essential to their financial stability?

As man increasingly becomes a city-born and city-bred creature, the problems of city living and city organization will intensify in complexity and embrace the planet. Drift and improvisation cannot solve them. Dynamic global action is essential now if the cities of tomorrow are to have a true, not imagined, relationship to the needs and enduring values of the people who will live in them [...]

England, the world's most highly urbanized country today, is the classical example of the processes of industrialization and urbanization because she led the world in both. By 1801, 26 per cent of the population of England and Wales lived in cities of 5000 or more; and 21 per cent in cities of 10,000 or more. The United States did not reach this degree of urbanization until 1880 when 25 per cent of the population lived in cities of 5000 or more. In contrast, only about 20 per cent of India's population live in cities of that size today.

By 1861, 55 per cent of the total population of England lived in urban areas; and by 1891, 72 per cent, with only 1·3 per cent of the population living in urban districts smaller than 3000 population. Until 1861, the rural population suffered a relative decline in numbers as cities grew more rapidly. The numerical peak of the rural population, 9·1 million, was reached in 1861. It declined 11 per cent, to 8·1 million by 1891.

London, a mud-flat on the banks of the Thames when Caesar arrived, grew from 864,800 to 4,232,000 between 1801 and 1891 – an increase of almost 400 per cent. In 1891, Greater London with 5·6 million people, three-fourths of whom lived in the city proper and the remainder in the 'outer ring', had the distinction of being the world's largest city. It covered an area of 690 square miles and included every parish of which any part was within twelve miles of Charing Cross. Today, it has an area of 722 square miles, and includes the Administrative County of London (London AC), also Middlesex County, and parts of Surrey, Hertfordshire, Essex and Kent counties. The population of Greater London is slightly over 8·2 million. London AC which includes the City of London and twenty-eight metropolitan boroughs is identical with the 1891 area. It comprises 117 square miles and has a population of 3·2 million that represents a 28 per cent decline from its 1901 peak.

Between 1811 and 1891, England's large cities with 100,000 population increased from 1·2 million to more than 9·2 million. Although London absorbed a lesser share of this growth, 14·6 per cent of Britain's population lived in the capital city of 1891 and 17·3 per cent lived in the other large cities. In terms of the aggregate urban population, 44 per cent resided in London and the twenty-three large cities [. . .]

World-wide urbanization 1900–1960

World population is growing at an unprecedented rate today. The world still is far from a city world, even though it has been moving in that direction at an ever-accelerating rate since 1800. However, urbanization will continue to spread for some time to come as the underdeveloped areas strive for economic development.

Today, over 20 per cent of the world's people, or more than 500 million, live in urban areas of 20,000 or more, compared with only about 2 per cent in 1800. Over three fifths of today's urbanites live in large cities of 100,000 or more, and they represent 13 per cent of total world population.

In 1900, there were ten cities with one million or more population in the world: five in Europe, three in North America and only one in Asia and one in Russia. In 1955, there were sixty-one cities of that size. Of the twenty-eight in Asia, nine were in China and six in India. Europe had sixteen cities of a million or more and the United States had five.

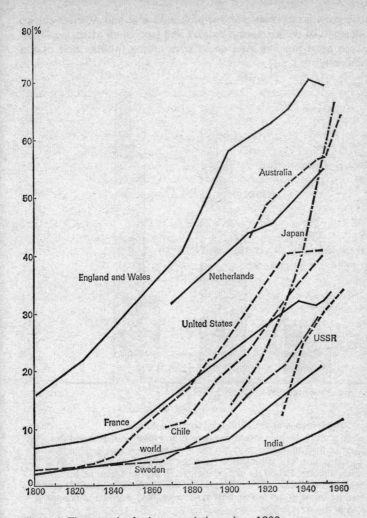

Figure 1 The growth of urban populations since 1800.
This shows the percentage of the total population of various countries living in localities of 20,000 or more. (The unit is 25,000 or more for the United States and Sweden.) For the world as a whole the proportion of dwellers in medium sized and large cities has quadrupled, from under 5 per cent to over 20 per cent. In the United States the proportion has increased tenfold as the nation has shifted from predominantly rural to one of the most highly urbanized countries.
Source: United Nations, *Report on the World Social Situation* (1957).

Urban growth rates reached their peak in Europe and America during the latter part of the nineteenth century and tapered off after that. They have been most rapid in Asia and Africa during the first half of the twentieth century [. . .]

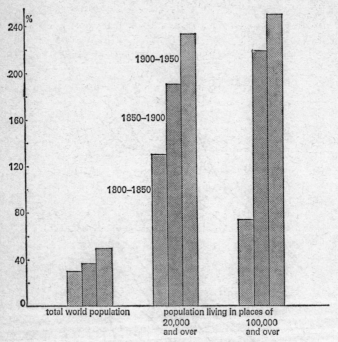

Figure 2 The increase in world and urban population.
This graph shows the percentage increase in the total population of the world and of the population living in the medium-sized and large cities since the early part of the Industrial Revolution. During this time, world population increased at a rate unprecedented in previous history, but the movement into cities was far more rapid. In these explosive growing urban areas will be found some of the most serious political, social and economic problems in the next fifty years.

The speed-up in population growth in the economically under-developed areas of the world is accompanied by the traditional acceleration in the growth of cities in those areas. Discussing present and future trends, the United Nations, *Report on the World Social Situation* (1957) states:

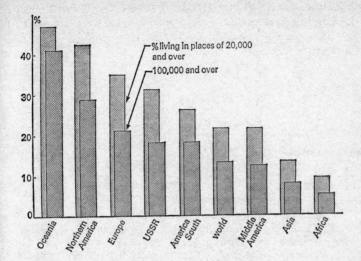

Figure 3 Percentage of population living in big cities.
The trek to the cities has gone on for centuries. Yet today, even with the
enormous increase in urban population in recent decades, man remains
predominantly a country dweller. If present trends continue for a century,
he will become predominantly a city dweller.

The large-city population of Asia and Africa has increased much more
rapidly during the twentieth century than it did during the nineteenth century
while in Europe and America, urban growth reached its peak in the latter
part of the nineteenth century and slowed down thereafter. These shifting
rates of growth have meant that Asia, which contained nearly two-thirds of
the world's population in large cities in 1800, had less than a fourth by 1900;
but then the trend started to reverse, and by 1950 Asia had one-third of the
world's large-city population.

Noting that there are important differences in the levels and trends of
urbanization among the industrially more advanced countries and
among the less developed countries, the Report states:

Several of the economically less-developed countries, particularly in Latin
America, have higher levels of urbanization – as measured by this particular
criterion – than certain European countries.
  . . . Some of the more urbanized and industrialized countries experienced a
marked slowing-down of their urbanization rate during the period between
1930 and 1950 . . . France, the United States and (between 1940 and 1950)
Japan; England and Wales actually experienced a slight drop between 1941

Table 1 Population in large Cities (100,000 and over) by Major Continental Regions

Area	Population (in millions) in large cities				As % of total population			
	1800	1850	1900	1950	1800	1850	1900	1950
World	15·6	27·5	88·6	313·7	1·7	2·3	5·5	13·1
Asia	9·8	12·2	19·4	105·6	1·6	1·7	2·1	7·5
Europe*	5·4	13·2	48·0	118·2	2·9	4·9	11·9	19·9
Africa	0·30	0·25	1·4	10·2	0·3	0·2	1·1	5·2
America	0·13	1·8	18·6	74·6	0·4	3·0	12·8	22·6
Oceania	—	—	1·3	5·1	—	—	21·7	39·2

* Including USSR.

Source: United Nations, *Report on the World Social Situation*, New York, 1957, p. 114 (based on data from Kingsley Davis and Hilda Hertz).

and 1951. Such a slowing-down or regression may be due to several possible factors: the reaching or approaching of a natural limit of urbanization, depending upon the economy of the country; the effects of the depression of the 1930s and of the Second World War; a shift from city growth to suburban growth – with the improvement of transportation and the overcrowding of cities, suburban localities are growing much more rapidly than cities proper in a number of countries (the United States is an outstanding example). The relative weight of these different factors is not known.

Other countries have shown a remarkable increase in degree of urbanization since 1930. This includes Puerto Rico and the USSR. In the latter country, between 1926 and 1955, while the total population increased only 34 per cent, the population in cities of 100,000 or more increased more than four times.

... Ceylon on the other hand, is remaining relatively stable at a low level of urbanization.

Differences in the pattern of urbanization

In 1950, the world's major regions of industrial urban settlement were Australasia, Northwestern Europe, Northern America, Northeast Asia and Southern South America. These areas included about 25 per cent of total world population, but 52 per cent living in cities of 100,000 or more. By major world areas, Africa was the least urbanized, with only 9 per cent of the population in cities of 20,000 or more. Australasia was the most heavily urbanized, with 47 per cent in cities of that size.

During the past 25 years, the two largest countries of the communist world, USSR and China, have experienced very rapid urbanization. In the USSR in 1959, 48 per cent of the total population was living in cities, compared with only 32 per cent in 1939. In twenty years, the urban population grew by almost forty million, an increase of two thirds. In 1959, 23 per cent of the total population and almost 50 per cent of the urban population lived in cities of 100,000 or more [. . .]

It has been estimated that twenty million Chinese migrated from rural to urban areas between 1949 and 1956. This almost equals the total population of the three Benelux countries and 'undoubtedly constitutes one of history's largest population shifts in so short a time . . .'. China's inland cities have experienced fantastic growth. Estimates indicate that in the western provinces alone, Lanchow grew from 200,000 in 1950 to 680,000 in 1956; Paotow from 90,000 in 1949 to 430,000 in 1957; Kalgan from 270,000 in 1949 to over 630,000 in 1958; Sian from less than one-half million in 1949 to 1,050,000 in 1957.

Furthermore there is a heavy concentration of China's urban population in her large cities. In 1953, 13 cities of 100,000 or more accounted for forty-nine million people, or 63 per cent of the total urban population. However, only 13 per cent of the total population lived in cities. In contrast, about 46 per cent of the United States urban population lived in cities of 100,000 or more in 1950, and 64 per cent of our total population lived in urban localities.

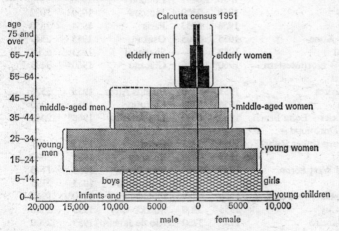

Figure 4 Age-sex distribution of the population of Calcutta.
This graph shows the enormous preponderance of males between twenty and forty in a great Asian city. The excess of males is found in all ages except among those under five and seventy-five and over. Multitudes of men in the prime of life, separated from their families and living under primitive conditions, pose a most serious problem of urban adjustment in the underdeveloped countries.

The growth rate of the urban population of the USSR between 1950 and 1959 was 4 per cent per annum. In China between 1949 and 1956 the urban growth rate appears to have been at the rate of 6·5 per cent per annum. [. . .]

In some regions of the world, a single large city – usually the capital city – contains a high proportion of a nation's total population and its urban population. In many countries, well over 50 per cent of all the urban population is concentrated in the capital cty. This is especially true of several Latin American countries [. . .]

Table 2 Estimated Population of World's Twenty Greatest Metropolitan Agglomerations

Metropolitan area	Year	Population (in thousands)	Principal City	Year	Population (in thousands)
New York – Northeastern New Jersey	1960*	1,4577	New York City	1960*	7710
Tokyo – Yokohama	1955	1,1349	Tokyo	1955	6969
London	1956	1,0491	London	1956	3273
Moscow	1956	7300	Moscow	1959	5032
Paris	1954	6737	Paris	1954	2850
Osaka – Kobe	1955	6405	Osaka	1955	2547
Shanghai	1953	——	Shanghai	1953	6204
Chicago – Northwestern Indiana	1960*	6726	Chicago	1960*	3493
Buenos Aires	1955	5750	Buenos Aires	1955	3575
Calcutta	1955	5700	Calcutta	1955	2750
Los Angeles – Long Beach	1960*	6690	Los Angeles	1960*	2448
Essen – Dortmund – Duisburg (Inner Ruhr)	1955	5353	Essen	1955	691
Bombay	1955	4400	Bombay	1955	3600
East and West Berlin	1955	4245	East Berlin	1955	1140
			West Berlin	1955	2195
Philadelphia – New Jersey	1960*	4289	Philadelphia	1960*	1960
Mexico City	1955	3900	Mexico City	1955	2800
Rio de Janeiro	1955	3750	Rio de Janeiro	1955	2900
Detroit	1960*	3761	Detroit	1960*	1672
Leningrad	1955	3500	Leningrad	1959†	2888
São Paulo	1955	3300	São Paulo	1955	2600

Source: International Urban Research, *The World's Metropolitan Areas*, Berkeley, University of California Press, 1959, unless otherwise indicated.

* US Bureau of the Census; 1960 data are preliminary.

† USSR All-Union Population Census of 1959.

In 1955, the world had 1107 metropolitan areas of 100,000 or more. Asia contained almost one third of these or 341 and Europe over one fourth or 279. North America had 202, Latin America seventy-eight and Oceania only eleven. The nations with the largest number were the United States, 189; USSR, 148; and China, 103. Of the world's 108 metropolitan areas with one million or more, thirty-four were in Europe, excluding USSR, thirty two were in Asia, and twenty-six were in North America [...]

Contrasts in city life

Despite the ever-accelerating rate of urbanization since 1800, modern man continues to be tied to the land. Four out of every five people in the world still live in the country. However, the trek to cities will accelerate during the decades ahead as the economically underdeveloped countries strive to become industrial societies.

But the speed-up in the rate of social change makes the urbanization process a very different one today in those countries than it was in the Western world. Since the Industrial Revolution began, the continuous migration in the West from country to city has been a flight from low-paid rural jobs to more lucrative jobs and greater opportunities in urban areas. But in underdeveloped countries today the movement to cities is more of a shift from unproductive rural situations to even less productive urban situations with no income gain and with grievous drain on limited savings due to higher living costs.

Because there is such a vast gulf between life in the traditional village and life in a large city, the rural–urban transition can be a painful experience. More often than not, the migrant ends up in a dingy shanty-town shelter, with no means of transportation and no job. Thus, in this pattern of urbanization, rural poverty is transferred to the cities where it becomes more concentrated and conspicuous. Observing that 'the overflow of rural distress into urban districts is an outstanding characteristic of economically underdeveloped countries today', the United Nations Report states:

The rapidly growing cities of the less developed regions of the world generally have several districts or zones which are imperfectly integrated:

1. A modern commercial, administrative, and upper-class residential centre.
2. An 'old city' of narrow streets and densely occupied buildings.
3. A zone of huts or shacks, within or without the city limits proper, lacking most urban features except density of settlement and urban types of employment among the residents.

Table 3 Levels of Urbanization

Country	Year	% of population in localities of 20,000 and over
Europe, Northern America and Oceania		
England and Wales	1951	69
Australia	1958	64
Netherlands	1950	56
Germany (West)	1950	45
United States	1950	43
Belgium	1950	42
Denmark	1955	42
Italy	1951	41
Austria	1951	40
Hungary	1954	36
USSR	1959	36
Sweden	1950	35
Canada	1951	35
France	1954	33
Switzerland	1950	31
Finland	1950	24
Czechoslovakia	1947	21
Poland	1946	18
Yugoslavia	1948	13
Africa, Asia and Latin America		
Japan	1955	66
Argentina	1947	48
Israel	1950	46
Chile	1952	41
Uruguay	1950	36
Cuba	1953	36
Venezuela	1950	31
Egypt	1947	29
Mexico	1950	24
Iran	1950	21
Brazil	1950	20
Ecuador	1950	18
Turkey	1950	15
India	1951	12
Guatemala	1950	11
Ceylon	1953	10
Pakistan	1951	8
Haiti	1950	5
Afghanistan	1951	4

Compiled from United Nations and US Bureau of the Census sources.

This pattern has many variations. In some cases, particularly in Asia and North Africa, the modern city is completely separate from the old, and the latter has retained its traditional artisan industries, commercial activities (e.g., bazaars) and social organization, often being divided into sharply defined quarters along ethnic or religious lines. A few of the old cities (e.g., Damascus) have grown to considerable size with only a minor admixture of modern elements. In other cases, particularly in Latin America, the modern city and the old are intermingled, with the recent expansion of the former sometimes almost obliterating the latter, or reducing it to a zone of deteriorating tenement houses. In most of Africa south of the Sahara, and in various industrial mining and oil-producing centres in other regions, the old city has never existed.

The zone of huts or shacks is usually on the periphery of the city. In some cases it is made up of coherent villages maintaining traditional values and social controls similar to those of the rural villages; more frequently, however, this zone consists largely of amorphous mushrooming shantytowns, lacking any formal administration or any apparent informal social organization. Such shanty-towns may be outside the administrative boundary of the city, so that no authority is responsible for providing urban services and enforcing housing regulations; even when the shanty-town is within the city limits, however, the municipal authorities may pay little attention to its needs, particularly if, as is often true, the residents are 'squatters' with no legal right to the land on which they build their shacks.

The pattern of urban growth is also complicated by the location of factories, usually around the periphery of the cities; their workers may come from neighbouring shanty-towns or from more substantial workers' housing built by the employers or the state.

The Report states that the limited evidence available indicates that the housing situation in many cities, particularly in Asia, has deteriorated in recent years 'since new building has not kept up with the natural increase in urban population, let alone the flood of migrants'. The shanty-town sprawl creates miserable living conditions:

Under present conditions, the great majority of the urban poor are housed either in the older parts of the cities or in the peripheral villages and shanty-towns. Except for housing built by employers for their own workers, there has been very little private construction with rents or purchase prices within the means of even the better-paid workers. Public low-cost housing and 'aided self-help' housing, while increasingly important have in most cities thus far reached only a limited part of the low-income groups.

Whether migrants to the cities move into the older tenement slums or into peripheral shantytowns depends on various factors. ... Peripheral shantytowns spring up on land that is not being used for one reason or another. The occupant may simply set up a hut as a squatter, may pay a small rent to the owner of the land or, in the case of some better organized groups of workers, may obtain recognition from the Government of his right of occupancy. The land is often unused because it is undesirable or unsuitable for permanent buildings. It may consist of swamps (as in certain districts of Bangkok), steep hillsides (as in the *favelas* of Rio de Janeiro), low ground subject to flooding (as in the outskirts of Baghdad), or refuse dumps. Waste areas of these types may be found near the center of the city as well as on the outskirts. In other cases, the land is too arid for cultivation and outside the scope of the city water system. Many shantytowns also occupy land that is held vacant by urban investors in anticipation of future city growth, so that the occupants face eventual eviction; these include shacks on scattered vacant lots in the inner parts of the cities.

The quality of the dwellings in the peripheral areas varies with the occupants' incomes, security of tenure, and standards of housing (the last usually derived from rural village housing). There may be a progressive change in the character of the improvised housing as the migrant stays longer in the urban area. The best of the peripheral settlements can sometimes be raised to acceptable standards by methods of aided self-help – provision of some building materials, tools and advice – plus enforcement of minimum sanitary and occupancy regulations, provision of safe water supplies, sewerage, electricity and paved streets. The lack of any community identification, however, in dwelling areas which the occupants themselves may regard as temporary and makeshift, as well as the lack of any formal or informal types of social organization, may render difficult group action for local improvement.

The occupant-built peripheral zones are able to develop more freely in the cities of sparsely peopled countries in Africa and Latin America, where desert or other uninhabited land is often found at the city limits. In densely populated parts of Asia, the sudden massive movement of population to the cities, particularly the waves of refugees, has often forced the creation of shantytowns, but as a rule, the growth of peripheral shantytowns is limited in such places by the fact that land is intensively cultivated up to the edge of the city and thus too valuable for occupation by migrants. This difficulty has not prevented rapid city growth, but it has resulted in the most extreme overcrowding, both in the older parts of the cities and in the improvised slums that have sprung up on the few available pieces of vacant land – river banks, swamps, even the city streets; many also live on boats in rivers, canals and ports. It is well known that thousands of working class individuals and families in Indian cities have no shelter at all, sleeping in the streets. In the tenements of some Asian cities, families that occupy a single room may subdivide it by horizontal and vertical partitions and sublet the resulting windowless cubicles to other families. Under these conditions of extreme competition for housing, rents naturally become exhorbitant in relation to incomes.

Such overcrowding also contributes to the unstable character of urban labour in Asia. The man who migrates to the city looking for wage labour is not tempted to bring his family from his home village if they will have to sleep in the street, although he might be contented with an improvised shack. The single worker may crowd in with a family of relatives or fellow-villagers, sleep in an alley, or even sleep in the premises of a sweat shop, until he has earned enough to return home.

Life in megalopolis – USA

Problems of urbanization are not confined to the economically under-developed regions of the world. As people continue to pile up in cities in the already heavily urbanized Western countries, pressures and tensions will cause unsolved social problems to grow worse and will create many new problems.

Today, population is growing very rapidly in the United States. The greatest part of this growth is, and will continue to be for some time to come, in the metropolitan agglomerations. Furthermore, multitudes will continue to leave the farm for city and suburb each year.

Will our cities rise to the challenge of rebuilding and revitalizing which faces them? How will they cope with the even higher rates of juvenile delinquency, mental illness, alcoholism and other social ills which ever-increasing congestion in living inevitably will bring? How will they meet the numerous other problems which grow in size as cities grow: traffic congestion, air pollution, city blight, congested slums, inadequate housing and dwindling water supplies? [. . .]

Fortunately, many people are becoming aware of the dire implications in this trend toward the monstrous-sized city. Regional, state and city planning groups, and in some cities citizen groups, are being formed in an effort to correct disastrous trends and to alert public opinion to their implications.

The city of tomorrow

When the city of antiquity first began to emerge, transportation was by foot, communication by word of mouth, and space – that playground of twentieth-century man – was thought to be an inverted bowl with holes punched in it. In the field of transportation and communication, invention and technology have moved farther in one century than in the pre-ceeding two thousand centuries.

Generations of scientific research and highly sophisticated planning have brought man to the stage where he can bounce messages off a balloon orbiting in space. By jet plane he can reach any spot on the planet in less than a day. But in the area of social invention man's approach to many urgent problems, among them population control and city planning, still smacks of the Dark Ages rather than the technological age of invention and creative improvisation. A do-nothing, know-nothing approach or a Micawberish hope that 'something will turn up' does not resolve crises.

Robert C. Cook 71

It is very likely that in the city man first will have to face the fact that space is the finite factor in the multiplication of people. In all probability, projections which indicate that a century hence Calcutta's population could increase by thirty-five to sixty-six million, or that New York City could be half or two-thirds that size, will never materialize. However, they serve to warn of nightmares to come unless man begins to apply his foresight and his great inventive skills to check his unprecedented population growth and to solve the problems which that growth has created.

4 W. Petersen

The Three Main Age-Groups

Excerpts from W. Petersen, *Population*, Macmillan Co., 1961, pp. 76–84.

In order to summarize the effect of [age] structure on society, we can divide the population into three main age-groups: dependent children, under fifteen years, the active population, fifteen to sixty-four years; and dependent aged sixty-five years and over. This distribution is shown in Table 1 for the period since 1880, the date at which America's transformation from an agrarian to an industrial society passed its preliminary stage.

Table 1 Distribution by Per Cent among Three Main Age-Groups, United States, 1880–1955

Year	Total	Dependent children (under 15 years)	The active population 15–64 years)	Dependent aged (65 years and over)	Index of aging (5)/(3) ×100
(1)	(2)	(3)	(4)	(5)	(6)
1800	100	38·1	58·5	3·4	8·9
1890	100	35·5	60·4	3·9	11·0
1900	100	34·4	61·3	4·1	11·9
1910	100	32·1	63·4	4·3	13·4
1920	100	31·7	63·4	4·7	14·8
1930	100	29·3	65·1	5·4	18·4
1940	100	25·0	68·1	6·8	27·2
1950	100	26·8	65·3	8·2	30·6
1955	100	29·6	61·8	8·6	28·7

Sources: Conrad Taeuber and Irene B. Taeuber, *The Changing Population of the United States*, (Wiley, 1958, p. 31); US Bureau of the Census, *Current Population Reports*, series P-25, no. 121 (27 September 1955).

Dependent children

From the censuses of 1790 and 1800, when half of the white population was under sixteen years, until 1940, there was a steady decline in the proportion of children, at first slow and then more rapid. In 1850 two fifths of the population was under fifteen years, and in 1910 almost one third. After the depression of the 1930s, the proportion fell to one fourth. Then the trend was reversed.

The most obvious reason for these changes in the proportion of children, of course, was the long-term decline in fertility and its revival after 1945. The decline in the death rate, since it was concentrated in infant and child mortality, was in demographic terms equivalent to a rise in the birth rate. That is to say, the fall in the proportion of children up to 1940 was less, and the rise since 1940 was greater, because of declining mortality. The effect of immigration was complex. Since most immigrants were young adults, the immediate consequence of their entry was to decrease the proportion of children in the population; but in the somewhat longer run this effect was countered by their higher than average fertility.

The gradual reduction in the proportion of children, a concomitant of the country's urbanization, varied according to regional differences in fertility, mortality, and immigration. In 1880, when 38 per cent of the whole population was under fifteen, among the various states this percentage ranged from twenty-four in Montana to forty-six in Mississippi. 'In general, proportions of youth in the southern States in 1880 were as high as those in the national population in the colonial period, while the proportions in the northeastern industrial States were as low as those in many modern industrial nations' (Taeuber and Taeuber, 1958). Today these regional differences are much smaller.

The proportion aged five to fourteen years, which more or less defines the school population through junior high school, also decreased steadily, from 24·3 per cent in 1880 to 20·1 per cent in 1930 and, more sharply, to 16·2 per cent in 1950. Although the proportion in school ages fell off, the allocations for education increased greatly, partly because of the larger percentage of these cohorts that attended schools and even more because of the spectacular rise in the *per capita* cost.[1] Even so, during the depression of the 1930s and the war of the 1940s minimum amounts of money and attention were allocated to keeping the school plant and personnel up to par, so that in any case a determined postwar effort was necessary to make up deficiencies. The problem was considerably aggravated by the baby boom. During the first postwar decade more than thirty six million infants were born to American parents, and as these children move up into adult life, they disrupt one after another institutions built to accommodate more modest numbers. By 1955, when the

1. The expenditure per pupil in elementary and secondary schools jumped from $20 in 1900 (or $62 in 1949–1950 dollars) to $259 in 1950, and even this increase has not kept pace with the rising costs.

percentage of the population aged five to fourteen years had increased to 18·6, greatly swollen student bodies had burst the grammar schools, and administrators of high schools and colleges were well aware that their turn was coming. Under these conditions, it will be particularly difficult to improve, or even to maintain, the quality of instruction over the next decades. In the public debate over the low standards in American education, the very statement of the issue, to be complete, must refer to the reversal of the secular trend in population structure: the percentage of dependent children increased from twenty-five in 1940 to almost thirty in 1955.

The active population

The definition of adulthood, while it has a biological base, varies greatly from one culture to another, and in the United States from one period or region to another. Children on a farm are assigned their chores; in today's cities child labor is prohibited. And delimitation of active adulthood in terms of chronological ages rather than functions, therefore, must be approximate and to some degree arbitrary. The definition used here, the group aged fifteen to sixty-four, has the advantage of conforming with statistical and legal conventions, but in several respects it overstates the actual size of the active population. Few outside this age-group perform adult roles, and many in it do not.

If we define the active population in economic terms, then the principal deviations result from education beyond the high school and from early retirement. Among white males only 38·8 per cent of the fourteen to nineteen age-group were in the labor force in 1950 and, at the other end, less than 80 per cent of the sixty–sixty-four age group. In 1950 more than nine-tenths of fifteen-year-old boys were in school, and more than one-fifth of those aged twenty. And if we define the active population also by noneconomic roles, the same deviations can be noted. The median age at marriage, though it has been going down, is still nearer twenty than fifteen; and women's childbearing period ends between forty-five and fifty. The age at which young men are conscripted has usually been around eighteen; and meaningful military service ends long before sixty-five. In most states legal maturity is set at eighteen or twenty-one. Voting usually begins at twenty-one and gradually sloughs off in the advanced ages.

As the proportion of the active population becomes larger, 'the burden of dependency' declines. From 1880 to 1940, as can be seen from Table 1, the proportion of children decreased faster than that of the aged increased, so that the percentage in the active sector rose from 58·5 to

68·1. After 1940, however, this adult sector fell off sharply, so that by 1955 it constituted almost the same proportion as in 1900. Why should the burden of dependency, which had been getting less for the whole of the nation's history, have become heavier in the last decades? No single answer can be given to this question. It is decidedly relevant, for example, that the massive pre-1914 immigration, which used to supplement the native-born adults, has been very much smaller since that date. The youngest cohorts in the active population in 1955, those aged fifteen to twenty-five, had been born during the 1930s, when the nation's birth rate was at the lowest point in its history; and these very small cohorts will remain as part of the active population for almost half a century. In the postwar years, as we have seen, the baby boom increased the proportion of dependent children, and the percentage of dependent aged continued to rise, though more slowly.

The burden of dependency will continue to get heavier, at least for a period. If we were to take age twenty rather than fifteen to define the beginning of adulthood (and, as we have seen, in many respects this would be a realistic choice), then the full effect of the low fertility during the depression would appear only in 1960. Meanwhile, the proportionately much larger cohorts born in the early years of the century will successively reach sixty-five and add to the number of dependents at that end of the scale. This trend will be partly balanced by the larger cohorts born from 1945 on, who will begin to enter the active sector in the early 1960s. Whether the burden of dependency will continue to rise once the boom babies have all assumed adult roles will depend on two unknown factors – the size of future families and the future control of death at advanced ages.

Dependent aged

The proportion of the population aged sixty-five and over increased from 3·4 per cent in 1880 to 8·6 per cent in 1955. In absolute numbers the growth was from 3·1 million in 1900 to about sixteen million in 1960; the population as a whole increased by 2·4 times and the aged by 5·3 times. Few demographic developments have received wider public attention than this 'problem'. Newspaper readers have had to learn the meaning of *gerontology* (from the Greek *gerōn*, old man), the study of the aged, and *geriatrics* (from the Greek *gēras*, old age), the healing of the aged. Much that has been written on the subject, however, is distinguished more by the authors' noble sentiments, not to say sentimentality, than by their knowledge and acuity. 'Viewed as a whole the "problem of aging" is no problem at all. It is only the pessimistic way of looking at a great triumph of civilization.'

What caused the increase in the proportion of the aged in the population of the United States and of all other Western countries? The common-sense answer to this question might be that it was the combined effect of falling mortality and falling fertility, but such an answer would be misleading. The increase in the *number* of old people was indeed the consequence of improvements in death control. However, declines in mortality have been greater among infants and children, and the larger proportion who remained alive retarded the aging of the population. 'In most Western countries the fraction over sixty-five would be *larger* than it is if mortality rates had remained at their 1900 level. The average age of the population would be *greater* if [control over] mortality had *not* improved.'

The increase in the *proportion* of old people, thus, was due to the fall in fertility, and this means that prognoses must take into account the postwar revival in the birth rate. As we can see from column 5 of Table 1, the growth in the proportion of dependent aged has been slowed down by the baby boom. The two influences can be combined into a single figure, as follows:

$$\text{index of aging} = \frac{\text{persons 65 years and over}}{\text{children under 15 years}} \times 100.$$

According to this index, shown in column 6, the increase has not only slowed down but actually been reversed from 1950 to 1955. Most writers are still discussing the aging of Western populations when actually – unless the death rates at older ages are reduced considerably – a new 'younging' may be in prospect.

The problem of aging may well have been overstated also in other senses. In a preindustrial familistic culture, like America of *circa* 1850 or traditional China, the old were no 'problem'.

The social status given them was of the best. They did not fear to grow old; for the old were not pitied or shoved aside, and were not treated as objects of charity and special worry. This situation (ideal from the standpoint of the aged) was made possible by the social and economic structure of the society in two ways. First, the structure was of the static, agricultural, and familistic type in which the old could perform useful functions. Second, it produced such high mortality that there were few relatively old people in the population.

In a dynamic industrial society, the aged can play fewer useful roles. The family ties of young Americans are to their children more than to their parents; and the more extended kin, who have an important place in traditional rural cultures, in an urban society are often less meaningful than friends. Even if the proportion of aged had remained constant, it would have been more difficult to accommodate them in the city apartments, say, of their married children; and the actual much larger proportion could be given the same deference and care as once had been standard only by sacrificing some other significant values.

If we correct the sentimentality and other false perspectives that have often been used to define the problem of aging, this does not, of course, dispose of it. While the proportion of elderly persons is increasing more slowly, their absolute number is great and is going up together with that of the growing population. Sociologists and social psychologists have barely begun to analyse the characteristics of aging possibly susceptible to amelioration by changes in the social environment beyond the secure provision for basic physical needs. In 1960, though persons sixty-five and over earned only $1576 on the average, they laid out more than twice as much in medical expenditures, and spent almost three times as many days in hospitals, as those under sixty-five.

In the United States the percentage of aged varies among subgroups by a complex interrelation of several factors. The aged group carries in itself, as it were, the history of the past and changes over time are reflected in present differences between it and the rest of the population. When today's very old were children, for example, about a quarter of the population were given no more than four years of schooling, an amount now considered so inadequate that it is used to define the upper limit of the 'functionally illiterate'. In 1950, thus, the proportion functionally illiterate among whites ranged from 18 per cent of the sixty-five to sixty-nine age-group down to only 3 per cent of those aged twenty-five through twenty-nine. Similarly, since immigration was sharply curtailed after 1914, the proportion of aged among foreign-born is much higher than in the native population. The out-migration of young adults left disproportionate numbers of older persons on the farms, and in eastern cities the earlier decline in fertility also resulted in a more rapid aging. These differential patterns have been altered also by a substantial postretirement migration to states with a pleasant climate, particularly Florida and California.

Perhaps the most significant difference among subgroups of the aged is that between males and females. In the United States today females live on the average more than five years longer than males. Thus, unless her husband is five years younger than she, the probability is that the wife will survive him. Since, on the contrary, men generally marry women younger than themselves, widows outnumber widowers by a considerable proportion. Moreover, whenever a marriage is dissolved by either death or divorce, the man is more likely to remarry than the woman. For all these reasons, the sex ratio of widowed and divorced persons is very low; for the United States in 1950 it was only 420 [...][2]

The proportion of children and aged combined thus measures the burden of dependency that has to be carried by the active population. In the United States this burden decreased over the whole of the national history up to 1940, and since that date it has been increasing. The percentage aged sixty-five and over went up from 3·4 in 1880 to 8·6 in 1955; and when in the last decade of this rise it was combined with the baby boom, the joint proportion of all dependents began to increase. It is very easy, however, to overstate the problem of the aging, for the rise in fertility has brought about, at least potentially, a 'younging' of the population. By one index, the aging of the American population was reversed in 1950.

2. Sex ratio is defined as $\dfrac{\text{number of males}}{\text{number of females}} \times 1000.$

Part Two Industrialization: People at Work

The 1970s have brought large-scale unemployment to Britain again, but for many of those who do have jobs, the fear of losing them is less immediate than boredom inherent in their work. New forms of class conflict have appeared: shipyard workers on the Clyde have occupied their factories in order to keep them working. But older forms of class conflict are still with us. Strikes, as Lane and Roberts show (Reading 7), are indeed 'normal', and can appear even in apparently quite placid industrial situations. It is still a principal interest of management to make profit through the labour of workers and a principal interest of the work-force to maximize wages. Thus conflict is endemic in industrial society. But the conflict takes many forms and varies in intensity and incidence. Management and workers do not face each other in conflict across the work bench: very often, indeed, they are not looking in each other's direction. For managers in industry, the world is not mainly filled by workers but by other kinds of people to whom they must respond: by business competitors, impatient customers and tardy suppliers; and they are affected, too, by 'impersonal' forces: market trends and government regulations. To managers, when they are acting in their role as managers, workers are seen simply as one of several 'costs', rather than as a set of persons, and in any case, at workshop level, conflict between management and workers is mediated by supervisors who handle conflict on behalf of management. But the conflict, and the daily running outcome of the conflict, are there, and contribute to many of the private problems and public issues we are concerned with. The raw material of the conflict does not consist solely of strikes and lock-outs, wage-demands and turn-downs. It also concerns such issues as radios being off or on, absenteeism, lateness, turnover, the degree of capitalization and supervision. And it takes place at a national level, as Blumer argues here (Reading 9), but also at other levels.

Work has been the locus of many of the most severe and chronic conflicts in industrial society, so it is appropriate that the first passage below should start us off in the middle of the Industrial Revolution.

In this extract, a spinner spells out what exploitation meant to those workers and the hardships they suffered during that phase of capitalist development. Academic discussion of these hardships in terms of 'necessary wars', 'terms of trade', and the economic difficulties facing Britain as a nation at that time, is exposed by Thompson (Reading 5), who translates such abstractions into relationships between people.

The tale of the human cost of economic changes is brought right up to date in Cottrell's article (Reading 6) which shows how people in a modern American town wrestled to achieve some sociological understanding of what was happening to their own community, and some political maturity, when technological change, in an economy geared to profit, led to the closing of their major industry.

Historically, to protect themselves from some of the hardships and injustices that come in the wake of industrialization, workers developed trade unions. However, Allen (Reading 8) suggests that trade unions, in Britain at least, constitute no revolutionary challenge to the social order since they are deeply embedded in capitalism and dependent upon the working of free market mechanisms. They are supportive of the system of government and fail even in their limited objective of protecting their members. This extract implicitly raises the question of how the very different characteristics which he suggests are typical of modern British unions are able to coexist side by side, for he suggests they display democratic, authoritarian, bureaucratic, traditional and competitive characteristics.

Blumer's article argues that the activities of unions and employers at national level are a more appropriate field of study for sociologists than intensive studies of single factories. Current industrial sociology, he suggests, neither takes into account adequately the degree to which the antagonistic relations between workers and management are constantly in flux, nor adequately recognizes that such relationships are in large measure not conducted at local level at all, but at national level – not between individuals in a factory but between large organizations of unions and federations of employers.

But the broad national movements Blumer would have us bear in mind have their effects in each particular workplace in particular struggles and confrontations.

In his essay 'Fun in Games', from the book *Encounters*, Erving Goffman argues that we are always encountering people in situations which have boundaries in time and space: that is, we interact with particular people at particular times in particular places. Goffman likens these boundaries to the membrane of a cell in a living organism. Each party to the encounter within such a boundary has social characteristics which he brings in from the outside world, and these find expression in the encounter, but in ways determined by the structure of the encounter itself. Some characteristics are ruled to be irrelevant: in most workplaces a man's religion is held to be his own affair; in other cases, hostilities between skilled and unskilled workers may find expression in terms of existing religious differences. Thus differences of religion, or of social class, age and sex may permeate the 'membrane' of the workshop wall, becoming changed as they do so; or may be ruled irrelevant, according to the technical, market and social factors that are combined in a particular workshop. In some industrial situations, whether you are Black or White, man or woman, is irrelevant; in other situations these factors may be used to reinforce workers' solidarity or to divide them.

In a similar fashion, because of local variations in markets for labour and commodities, national wage agreements are most commonly amended and elaborated in each workplace to fit in with the particular 'effort-bargain' which is hammered out from day to day on each particular shop floor.

Blumer is correct to stress the dynamic character of worker–management relationships, and the degree to which a struggle affecting both sides is taking place at a level higher than any particular factory between huge national organizations. There has not been a great deal of research into this national struggle, nor into the 'huge armies' to which Blumer refers: the employers' federations and unions, the arbitration bodies before which they appear; nor into the meetings and negotiations which make up the struggle. But the sociological investigation of the single factory is still needed, and study at the national level will not explain what happens at the local level.

Intensive studies of a single factory are of interest to sociologists not only because work is important in society, but also because the study of work-situations helps us extend our understanding of social relationships more generally. For people are divided and united in all kinds of social settings and industrial sociologists are simply sociologists looking at the relationships between human groups in an industrial setting.

The sociologist finds equal interest and importance in the study of committee rooms and offices, for these too are workplaces. Conflict in the 'power game' at the top is as dramatic as conflict on the shop floor, and certainly as important. Yet it is all too little studied sociologically.

Conflict on the shop floor, too, is always taking on new forms in ever-changing industrial settings. Thompson and Cottrell paint hardship and injustice as normal in early industrial capitalism. They and others who draw attention to the hardships brought by capitalism, do not argue that preindustrial society was 'better' than capitalism in terms of human happiness. None the less, a myth of a golden, craftsman past in the pre-industrial era, when work was 'meaningful', has crept into the literature and into our thinking from a variety of sources. Yet even the early period of the Industrial Revolution itself gets romanticized as a result of dissatisfaction with the present, as Blauner points out; and because wants are constantly changing, it is difficult to know how workers feel about industrial work today in a society which has brought affluence for many, as compared with previous periods. It would be naïve to believe that this kind of affluence has brought contentment. Blauner (Reading 10) argues that when you ask workers if they are satisfied, they frequently say they are, and he gives excellent reasons for not taking these replies at face value or thinking that satisfaction is measurable at all.

Blauner's and other contributions are concerned primarily with factory work. But manufacture is of shrinking importance in British and American economies today: it has been said that today more people work on the manipulation of people and bits of paper than on the manipulation of things. This fact has been reflected only slowly in the work of industrial sociologists, but our extracts from Hughes (Reading 11) shows a welcome move towards the study of organizations and occupations whose primary function is service to others. And where Blauner stresses the importance of work in the life of the man who does it, Hughes stresses the importance of work in the lives of those for whom a man does it.

5 E. P. Thompson

The Making of the English Working Class

Excerpts from E. P. Thompson, *The Making of the English Working Class*, Gollancz, 1963, Penguin 1968, pp. 218–26.

For most working people the crucial experience of the Industrial Revolution was felt in terms of changes in the nature and intensity of exploitation. Nor is this some anachronistic notion, imposed upon the evidence. We may describe some parts of the exploitive process as they appeared to one remarkable cotton operative in 1818 – the year in which Marx was born. The account – an Address to the public of strike-bound Manchester by 'A Journeyman Cotton Spinner' – commences by describing the employers and the workers as 'two distinct classes of persons':

First, then, as to the employers: with very few exceptions, they are a set of men who have sprung from the cotton-shop without education or address, except so much as they have acquired by their intercourse with the little world of merchants on the exchange at Manchester; but to counterbalance that deficiency, they give you enough of appearances by an ostentatious display of elegant mansions, equipages, liveries, parks, hunters, hounds, etc., which they take care to shew off to the merchant stranger in the most pompous manner. Indeed their houses are gorgeous palaces, far surpassing in bulk and extent the neat charming retreats you see round London ... but the chaste observer of the beauties of nature and art combined will observe a woeful deficiency of taste. They bring up their families at the most costly schools, determined to give their offspring a double portion of what they were so deficient in themselves. Thus with scarcely a second idea in their heads, they are literally petty monarchs, absolute and despotic, in their own particular districts; and to support all this, their whole time is occupied in contriving how to get the greatest quantity of work turned off with the least expence. ... In short, I will venture to say, without fear of contradiction, that there is a greater distance observed between the master there and the spinner, than there is between the first merchant in London and his lowest servant or the lowest artisan. Indeed there is no comparison. I know it to be a fact, that the greater part of the master spinners are anxious to keep wages low for the purpose of keeping the spinners indigent and spiritless ... as for the purpose of taking the surplus to their own pockets.

The master spinners are a class of men unlike all other master tradesmen in the kingdom. They are ignorant, proud, and tyrannical. What then must be the men or rather beings who are the instruments of such masters? Why, they have been for a series of years, with their wives and their families, patience itself – bondmen and bondwomen to their cruel taskmasters. It is in vain to insult our common understandings with the observation that such men are free; that the law protects the rich and poor alike, and that a spinner can leave his master if he does not like the wages. True; so he can: but where must he go? why, to another, to be sure. Well: he goes; he is asked where did you work last: 'did he discharge you?' No; we could not agree about wages. Well I shall not employ you nor anyone who leaves his master in that manner. Why is this? Because there is an abominable *combination existing among the masters*, first established at Stockport in 1802, and it has since become so general, as to embrace all the great masters for a circuit of many miles round Manchester, though not the little masters: they are excluded. They are the most obnoxious beings to the great ones that can be imagined. ... When the combination first took place, one of their first articles was, that no master should take on a man until he had first ascertained whether his last master had discharged him. What then is the man to do? If he goes to the parish, that grave of all independence, he is there told – We shall not relieve you; if you dispute with your master, and don't support your family, we will send you to prison; so that the man is bound, by a combination of circumstances, to submit to his master. He cannot travel and get work in any town like a shoemaker, joiner, or taylor; he is confined to the district.

The workmen in general are an inoffensive, unassuming, set of well-informed men, though how they acquire their information is almost a mystery to me. They are docile and tractable, if not goaded too much; but this is not to be wondered at, when we consider that they are trained to work from six years old, from five in a morning to eight and nine at night. Let one of the advocates for obedience to his master take his stand in an avenue leading to a factory a little before five o'clock in the morning, and observe the squalid appearance of the little infants and their parents taken from their beds at so early an hour in all kinds of weather; let him examine the miserable pittance of food, chiefly composed of water gruel and oatcake broken into it, a little salt, and sometimes coloured with a little milk, together with a few potatoes, and a bit of bacon or fat for dinner; would a London mechanic eat this? There they are (and if late a few minutes, a quarter of a day is stopped in wages) locked up until night in rooms heated above the hottest days we have had this summer, and allowed no time, except three-quarters of an hour at dinner in the whole day: whatever they eat at any other time must be as they are at work. The negro slave in the West Indies, if he works under a scorching sun, has probably a little breeze of air sometimes to fan him: he has a space of ground, and time allowed to cultivate it. The English spinner slave has no enjoyment of the open atmosphere and breezes of heaven. Locked up in factories eight stories high, he has no relaxation till the ponderous engine stops, and then he goes home to get refreshed for the next day; no time for sweet association with his family; they are all alike fatigued and exhausted.

This is no over-drawn picture: it is literally true. I ask again, would the mechanics in the south of England submit to this?

When the spinning of cotton was in its infancy, and before those terrible machines for superseding the necessity of human labour, called steam engines, came into use, there were a great number of what were then called *little masters*; men who with a small capital, could procure a few machines, and employ a few hands, men and boys (say to twenty or thirty), the produce of whose labour was all taken to Manchester central mart, and put into the hands of brokers. ... The brokers sold it to the merchants, by which means the master spinner was enabled to stay at home and work and attend to his workmen. The cotton was then always given out in its raw state from the bale to the wives of the spinners at home, when they heat and cleansed it ready for the spinners in the factory. By this they could earn eight, ten, or twelve shillings a week, and cook and attend to their families. But none are thus employed now; for all the cotton is broke up by a machine, turned by the steam engine, called a devil: so that the spinners' wives have no employment, except they go to work in the factory all day at what can be done by children for a few shillings, four or five per week. If a man then could not agree with his master, he left him, and could get employed elsewhere. A few years, however, changed the face of things. Steam engines came into use, to purchase which, and to erect buildings sufficient to contain them and six or seven hundred hands, required a great capital. The engine power produced a more marketable (though not a better) article than the little master could at the same price. The consequence was their ruin in a short time; and the overgrown capitalists triumphed in their fall; for they were the only obstacle that stood between them and the complete controul of the workmen.

Various disputes then originated between the workmen and masters as to the fineness of the work, the workmen being paid according to the number of hanks or yards of thread he produced from a given quantity of cotton, which was always to be proved by the overlooker, whose interest made it imperative on him to lean to his master, and call the material coarser than it was. If the workman would not submit *he must summon his employer before a magistrate*; the whole of the acting magistrates in that district, with the exception of two worthy clergymen, being gentlemen who have sprung from the same source with the master cotton spinners. The employer generally contented himself with sending his overlooker to answer any such summons, thinking it beneath him to meet his servant. The magistrate's decision was generally in favour of the master, though on the statement of the overlooker only. The workman dared not appeal to the sessions on account of the expense . . .

These evils to the men have arisen from that dreadful monopoly which exists in those districts where wealth and power are got into the hands of the few, who, in the pride of their hearts, think themselves the lords of the universe.

This reading of the facts, in its remarkable cogency, is as much an *ex parte* statement as is the 'political economy' of Lord Brougham. But the

'Journeyman Cotton Spinner' was describing facts of a different order. We need not concern ourselves with the soundness of all his judgements. What his address does is to itemize one after another the grievances felt by working people as to changes in the character of capitalist exploitation: the rise of a master-class without traditional authority or obligations; the growing distance between master and man; the transparency of the exploitation at the source of their new wealth and power; the loss of status and above all of independence for the worker, his reduction to total dependence on the master's instruments of production; the partiality of the law; the disruption of the traditional family economy; the discipline, monotony, hours and conditions of work; loss of leisure and amenities; the reduction of the man to the status of an 'instrument'.

That working people felt these grievances at all – and felt them passionately – is itself a sufficient fact to merit our attention. And it reminds us forcibly that some of the most bitter conflicts of these years turned on issues which are not encompassed by cost-of-living series. The issues which provoked the most intensity of feeling were very often ones in which such values as traditional customs, 'justice', 'independence', security, or family-economy were at stake, rather than straightforward 'bread-and-butter' issues. The early years of the 1830s are aflame with agitations which turned on issues in which wages were of secondary importance; by the potters, against the Truck System; by the textile workers, for the Ten-Hour Bill; by the building workers, for cooperative direct action; by all groups of workers, for the right to join trade unions. The great strike in the north-east coalfield in 1831 turned on security of employment, 'tommy shops', child labour.

The exploitive relationship is more than the sum of grievances and mutual antagonisms. It is a relationship which can be seen to take distinct forms in different historical contexts, forms which are related to corresponding forms of ownership and State power. The classic exploitive relationship of the Industrial Revolution is depersonalized, in the sense that no lingering obligations of mutuality – of paternalism or deference, or of the interests of 'the Trade' – are admitted. There is no whisper of the 'just' price, or of a wage justified in relation to social or moral sanctions, as opposed to the operation of free market forces. Antagonism is accepted as intrinsic to the relations of production. Managerial or supervisory functions demand the repression of all attributes except those which further the expropriation of the maximum surplus value from labour. This is the political economy which Marx anatomized in *Das Kapital*. The worker has become an 'instrument', or an entry among other items of cost.

In fact, no complex industrial enterprise could be conducted according to such a philosophy. The need for industrial peace, for a stable labour-force, and for a body of skilled and experienced workers, necessitated the modification of managerial techniques – and, indeed, the growth of new forms of paternalism – in the cotton-mills by the 1830s. But in the overstocked outwork industries, where there was always a sufficiency of unorganized 'hands' competing for employment, these considerations did not operate. Here, as old customs were eroded, and the old paternalism was set aside, the exploitive relationship emerged supreme.

This does not mean that we can lay all the 'blame' for each hardship of the Industrial Revolution upon 'the masters' or upon *laissez faire*. The process of industrialization must, in any conceivable social context, entail suffering and the destruction of older and valued ways of life. Much recent research has thrown light upon the particular difficulties of the British experience; the hazards of markets; the manifold commercial and financial consequences of the Wars; the post-war deflation; movements in the terms of trade; and the exceptional stresses resulting from the population 'explosion'. Moreover, twentieth-century preoccupations have made us aware of the overarching problems of economic growth. It can be argued that Britain in the Industrial Revolution was encountering the problems of 'take-off'; heavy long-term investment – canals, mills, railways, foundries, mines, utilities – was at the expense of current consumption; the generations of workers between 1790 and 1840 sacrificed some, or all, of their prospects of increased consumption to the future.

These arguments all deserve close attention. For example, studies of the fluctuations in the demand of the South American market, or of the crisis in country banking, may tell us much about the reasons for the growth or retardation of particular industries. The objection to the reigning academic orthodoxy is not to empirical studies *per se,* but to the fragmentation of our comprehension of the full historical process. First, the empiricist segregates certain events from this process and examines them in isolation. Since the conditions which gave rise to these events are assumed, they appear not only as explicable in their own terms but as inevitable. The Wars had to be paid for out of heavy taxation; they accelerated growth in this way and retarded it in that. Since this can be shown, it is also implied that this was *necessarily* so. But thousands of Englishmen at the time agreed with Thomas Bewick's condemnation of 'this superlatively wicked war'. The unequal burden of taxation, fund-holders who profited from the National Debt, paper-money – these were not accepted as given data by many contemporaries, but were the staple of intensive Radical agitation.

But there is a second stage, where the empiricist may put these fragmentary studies back together again, constructing a model of the historical process made up from a multiplicity of interlocking inevitabilities, a piecemeal processional. In the scrutiny of credit facilities or of the terms of trade, where each event is explicable and appears also as a self-sufficient cause of other events, we arrive at a *post facto* determinism. The dimension of human agency is lost, and the context of class relations is forgotten.

It is perfectly true that what the empiricist (historian) points to was there. The Orders in Council had in 1811 brought certain trades almost to a standstill; rising timber prices after the Wars inflated the costs of building; a passing change of fashion (lace for ribbon) might silence the looms of Coventry; the power-loom competed with the hand-loom. But even these open-faced facts, with their frank credentials, deserve to be questioned. Whose Council, why the Orders? Who profited most from corners in scarce timber? Why should looms remain idle when tens of thousands of country girls fancied ribbons but could not afford to buy. By what social alchemy did inventions for saving labour become engines of immiseration? The raw fact – a bad harvest – may seem to be beyond human election. But the way that fact worked its way out was in terms of a particular complex of human relationship: law, ownership, power. When we encounter some sonorous phrase such as 'the strong ebb and flow of the trade cycle' we must be put on our guard. For behind this trade cycle there is a structure of social relations, fostering some sorts of expropriation (rent, interest, and profit) and outlawing others (theft, feudal dues), legitimizing some types of conflict (competition, armed warfare) and inhibiting others (trade unionism, bread riots, popular political organization) – a structure which may appear, in the eyes of the future, to be both barbarous and ephemeral [. . .]

It is scarcely possible to write the history of popular agitations in these years unless we make at least the imaginative effort to understand how such a man as the 'Journeyman Cotton Spinner' read the evidence. He spoke of the 'masters', not as an aggregate of individuals, but as a class. As such, 'they' denied him political rights. If there was a trade recession, 'they' cut his wages. If trade improved, he had to fight 'them' and their state to obtain any share in the improvement. If food was plentiful, 'they' profited from it. If it was scarce, some of 'them' profited more. 'They' conspired, not in this or that fact alone, but in the essential exploitive relationship within which all the facts were validated. Certainly there were market fluctuations, bad harvests, and the rest; but the experience of intensified exploitation was constant, whereas these other causes of hardship were variable. The latter bore upon working people, not directly, but through the refraction of a particular system of ownership and power which distributed the gains and losses with gross partiality.

6 W. F. Cottrell

Death by Dieselization

Excerpts from W. F. Cottrell, 'Death by dieselization: a case study in the reaction to technological change', *American Sociological Review*, vol. 16, 1951, pp. 358–65.

In the following instance it is proposed that we examine a community confronted with radical change in its basic economic institution and trace the effects of this change throughout the social structure. From these facts it may be possible in some degree to anticipate the resultant changing attitudes and values of the people in the community, particularly as they reveal whether or not there is a demand for modification of the social structure or a shift in function from one institution to another. Some of the implications of the facts discovered may be valuable in anticipating future social change.

The community chosen for examination has been disrupted by the dieselization of the railroads. Since the railroad is among the oldest of those industries organized around steam, and since therefore the social structure of railroad communities is a product of long-continued processes of adaptation to the technology of steam, the sharp contrast between the technological requirements of the steam engine and those of the diesel should clearly reveal the changes in social structure required [. . .]

The town 'Caliente' was built in a break in an eighty-mile canyon traversing the desert. Its reason for existence was to service the steam locomotive. There are few resources in the area to support it on any other basis, and such as they are they would contribute more to the growth and maintenance of other little settlements in the vicinity than to that of Caliente. So long as the steam locomotive was in use, Caliente was a necessity. With the adoption of the diesel it became obsolescent.

This stark fact was not, however, part of the expectations of the residents of Caliente. Based upon the 'certainty' of the railroad's need for Caliente, men built their homes there, frequently of concrete and brick, at the cost, in many cases, of their life savings. The water system was laid in cast iron, which will last for centuries. Businessmen erected substantial buildings, which could be paid for only by profits gained through many years of business. Four churches evidence the faith of Caliente people in the future of their community. A twenty-seven-bed hospital serves the town. Those who built it thought that their investment was as well warranted as the fact of birth, sickness, accident, and death. They believed in education. Their school buildings represent the investment of savings guaranteed by bonds and future taxes. There is a combined park and play field which, together with a recently modernized theatre, has been serving recreational needs. All these physical structures are material evidence of the expectations, morally and legally sanctioned and financially funded, of the people of Caliente. This is a normal and rational aspect of the culture of all 'solid' and 'sound' communities [. . .]

There are the usual unions, churches, the myriad little clubs to which the women belong. In short, here is the average American community with normal social life, subscribing to normal American codes. Nothing its members had been taught would indicate that the whole pattern of this normal existence depended completely upon a few elements of technology which were themselves in flux. For them the continued use of the steam engine was as 'natural' a phenomenon as any other element in their physical environment. Yet suddenly their life pattern was destroyed by the announcement that the railroad was moving its division point, and with it destroying the economic basis of Caliente's existence.

Turning from this specific community for a moment, let us examine the technical changes which took place and the reasons for the change. Division points on a railroad are established by the frequency with which the rolling stock must be serviced and the operating crews changed [. . .]

In its demands for service, the diesel engine differs almost completely from a steam locomotive. It requires infrequent, highly skilled service, carried on within very close limits, in contrast to the frequent, crude adjustments required by the steam locomotive. Diesels operate at about 35 per cent efficiency, in contrast to the approximately 4 per cent efficiency of the steam locomotives in use after the Second World War in the United States. Hence diesels require much less frequent stops for fuel and water. These facts reduce their operating costs sufficiently to compensate for their much higher initial cost [. . .]

The shift to diesels was greatly facilitated by the war. In consequence, every third and sometimes every second division point suddenly became technologically obsolescent.

Caliente, like all other towns in similar plight, is supposed to accept its fate in the name of 'progress'. The general public, as shippers and consumers of shipped goods, reaps the harvest in better, faster service and eventually perhaps in lower charges. A few of the workers in Caliente will also share the gains, as they move to other division points, through higher wages. They will share in the higher pay, though whether this will be adequate to compensate for the costs of moving no one can say. Certain it is that their pay will not be adjusted to compensate for their specific losses. They will gain only as their seniority gives them the opportunity to work. These are those who gain. What are the losses, and who bears them?

The railroad company can figure its losses at Caliente fairly accurately. It owns thirty-nine private dwellings, a modern clubhouse with 116 single rooms, and a twelve-room hotel with dining-room and lunch counter facilities. These now become useless, as does much of the fixed physical equipment used for servicing trains. Some of the machinery can be used elsewhere. Some part of the roundhouse can be used to store unused locomotives and standby equipment. The rest will be torn down to save taxes. All of these costs can be entered as capital losses on the statement which the company draws up for its stockholders and for the government. Presumably they will be recovered by the use of the more efficient engines [. . .]

Probably the greatest losses are suffered by the older, 'nonoperating' employees. Seniority among these men extends only within the local shop and craft. A man with twenty-five years' seniority at Caliente has no claim on the job of a similar craftsman at another point who has only twenty-five days' seniority. Moreover, some of the skills formerly valuable are no longer needed. The boilermaker, for example, knows that jobs for his kind are disappearing and he must enter the ranks of the unskilled. The protection and status offered by the union while he was employed have become meaningless now that he is no longer needed. The cost of this is high both in loss of income and in personal demoralization.

Operating employees also pay. Their seniority extends over a division, which in this case includes three division points. The older members can move from Caliente and claim another job at another point, but in many cases they move leaving a good portion of their life savings behind. The younger men must abandon their stake in railroad employment. The loss may mean a new apprenticeship in another occupation, at a time in life when apprenticeship wages are not adequate to meet the obligations of mature men with families. A steam engine hauled 2000 tons up the hill out of Caliente with the aid of two helpers. The four-unit diesel in command of one crew handles a train of 5000 tons alone. Thus to handle the same amount of tonnage required only about a fourth of the manpower it formerly took. Three out of four men must start out anew at something else.

The local merchants pay. The boarded windows, half-empty shelves, and abandoned store buildings bear mute evidence of these costs. The older merchants stay, and pay; the younger ones, and those with no stake in the community, will move; but the value of their property will in both cases largely be gone.

The bondholders will pay. They can't foreclose on a dead town. If the town were wiped out altogether, that which would remain for salvage would be too little to satisfy their claims. Should the town continue, there is little hope that taxes adequate to carry the overhead of bonds and day-to-day expenses could be secured by taxing the diminished number of property owners or employed persons.

The church will pay. The smaller congregations cannot support services as in the past. As the churchmen leave, the buildings will be abandoned.

Home owners will pay. A hundred and thirty-five men owned homes in Caliente. They must accept the available means of support or rent to those who do. In either case, the income available will be far less than that on which the houses were built. The least desirable homes will stand unoccupied, their value completely lost. The others must be revalued at a figure far below that at which they were formerly held.

In a word, those pay who are, by traditional American standards, *most moral*. Those who have raised children see friendships broken and neighborhoods disintegrated. The childless more freely shake the dust of Caliente from their feet. Those who built their personalities into the structure of the community watch their work destroyed. Those too wise or too selfish to have entangled themselves in community affairs suffer no such qualms. The chain store can pull down its sign, move its equipment, and charge the costs off against more profitable and better located units, and against taxes. The local owner has no such alternatives. In short, 'good citizens' who assumed family and community responsibility are the greatest losers. Nomads suffer least.

The people of Caliente are asked to accept as 'normal' this strange inversion of their expectations. It is assumed that they will, without protest or change in sentiment, accept the dictum of the 'law of supply and demand'. Certainly they must comply in part with this dictum. While their behavior in part reflects this compliance, there are also other changes perhaps equally important in their attitudes and values.

The first reaction took the form of an effort at community self-preservation. Caliente became visible to its inhabitants as a real entity, as meaningful as the individual personalities which they had hitherto been taught to see as atomistic or nomadic elements. Community survival was seen as prerequisite to many of the individual values that had been given precedence in the past. The organized community made a search for new industry, citing elements of community organization themselves as reasons why industry should move to Caliente. But the conditions that led the railroad to abandon the point made the place even less attractive to new industry than it had hitherto been. Yet the effort to keep the community a going concern persisted.

There was also a change in sentiment. In the past the glib assertion that progress spelled sacrifice could be offered when some distant group was a victim of technological change. There was no such reaction when the event struck home. The change can probably be as well revealed as in any other way by quoting from the Caliente *Herald*:

[. . .] Smart big corporations the country over encourage their employees to own their own homes – and loud are their boasts when the percentage of such employees is favorable! But in contrast, a high [company] official is reported to have said only recently that 'a railroad man has no business owning a home!' Quite a departure from what has appeared to be [company] tradition.

It is difficult for the *Herald* to believe that this official, however 'big' he is, speaks for the . . . [company] . . . when he enunciates a policy that, carried to the letter, would make tramps of [company] employees and their families!

No thinking person wants to stand in the way of progress, but true progress is not made when it is overshadowed by cold-blooded disregard for the loyalty of employees, their families, and the communities which have developed in the good American way through the decades of loyal service and good citizenship.

This editorial, written by a member of all the service clubs, approved by Caliente businessmen, and quoted with approbation by the most conservative members of the community, is significant of changing sentiment.

The people of Caliente continually profess their belief in 'the American way', but like the editor of the *Herald* they criticize decisions made solely in pursuit of profit, even though these decisions grow out of a clear-cut case of technological 'progress'. They feel that the company should have based its decision upon consideration for loyalty, citizenship, and community morale. Caught between the support of a 'rational' system of 'economic' forces and laws, and sentiments which they accept as significant values, they seek a solution to their dilemma which will at once permit them to retain their expected rewards for continued adherence to past norms and to defend the social system which they have been taught to revere, but which now offers them a stone instead of bread.

Implications

We have shown that those in Caliente whose behavior most nearly approached the ideal taught are hardest hit by change. On the other hand, those seemingly farthest removed in conduct from that ideal are either rewarded or pay less of the costs of change than do those who follow the ideal more closely. Absentee owners, completely anonymous, and consumers who are not expected to cooperate to make the gains possible are rewarded most highly, while the local people, who must cooperate to raise productivity, pay dearly for having contributed [. . .]

It rapidly became apparent to the people of Caliente that they could not gain their objectives by organized community action or individual endeavor but there was hope that by adding their voices to those of others similarly injured there might be hope of solution. They began to look to the activities of the whole labor movement for succor. Union strategy, which forced the transfer of control from the market to government mediation or to legislation and operation, was widely approved on all sides. This was not confined to those only who were currently seeking rule changes, but was equally approved by the great bulk of those in the community who had been hit by the change. Cries of public outrage at their demands for makework rules were looked upon as coming from those at best ignorant, ill-informed, or stupid, and at worst as being the hypocritical efforts of others to gain at the workers' expense. When the union threat of a national strike for rule changes was met by government seizure, Caliente workers, like most of their compatriots across the country, welcomed this shift in control, secure in their belief that if 'justice' were done, they could only be gainers by government intervention. These attitudes are not 'class' phenomena purely, nor are they merely occupational sentiments. They result from the fact that modern life, with the interdependence that it creates, particularly in one-industry communities, imposes penalties far beyond the membership of the groups presumably involved in industry. When makework rules contributed to the livelihood of the community, the support of the churches, and the taxes which maintain the schools; when featherbed practices determine the standard of living, the profits of the businessman, and the circulation of the press; when they contribute to the salary of the teacher and the preacher, they can no longer be treated as accidental, immoral, deviant, or temporary. Rather they are elevated into the position of emergent morality and law. Such practices generate a morality which serves them just as the practices in turn nourish those who participate in and preserve them. They are as firmly a part of what one 'has a right to expect' from industry as are parity payments to the farmer, bonuses and pensions to the veterans, assistance to the aged, tariffs to the industrialist, or the sanctity of property to those who inherit. On the other hand, all these practices conceivably help create a structure that is particularly vulnerable to changes such as that described here.

Practices which force the company to spend in Caliente part of what has been saved through technological change, or failing that, to reward those who are forced to move by increased income for the same service, are not, by the people of Caliente, considered to be unjustifiable. Confronted by a choice between the old means and resultant 'injustice' which their use entails, and the acceptance of new means which they believe will secure them the 'justice' they hold to be their right, they are willing to abandon (insofar as this particular area is concerned) the liberal state and the omnicompetent market in favor of something that works to provide 'justice'.

The study of the politics of pressure groups will show how widely the reactions of Caliente people are paralleled by those of other groups. Amongst them it is in politics that the decisions as to who will pay and who will profit are made. Through organized political force, railroaders maintain the continuance of rules which operate to their benefit rather than for 'the public good' or 'the general welfare'. Their defense of these practices is found in the argument that only so can their rights be protected against the power of other groups who hope to gain at their expense by functioning through the corporation and the market. [. . .]

The case cited is not unique. Not only is it duplicated in hundreds of railroad division points, but also in other towns abandoned by management for similar reasons. Changes in the location of markets or in the method of calculating transportation costs, changes in technology making necessary the use of new materials, changes due to the exhaustion of old sources of materials, changes to avoid labor costs such as the shift of the textile industry from New England to the South, changes to expedite decentralization to avoid the consequences of bombing, or those of congested living, all give rise to the question, 'who benefits, and at whose expense?'

The accounting practices of the corporation permit the entry only of those costs which have become 'legitimate' claims upon the company. But the tremendous risks borne by the workers and frequently all the members of the community in an era of technological change are real phenomena. Rapid shifts in technology which destroy the 'legitimate' expectations derived from past experience force the recognition of new obligations. Such recognition may be made voluntarily as management foresees the necessity, or it may be thrust upon it by political or other action. Rigidity of property concepts, the legal structure controlling directors in what they may admit to be costs, and the stereotyped nature of the 'economics' used by management make rapid change within the corporation itself difficult even in a 'free democratic society'. Hence while management is likely to be permitted or required to initiate technological change in the interest of profits, it may and probably will be barred from compensating for the social consequences certain to arise from those changes. Management thus shuts out the rising flood of demands in its cost accounting only to have them reappear in its tax accounts, in legal regulations or in new insistent union demands. If economics fails to provide an answer to social demands, then politics will be tried.

It is clear that while traditional morality provides a means of protecting some groups from the consequences of technological change, or some method of meliorating the effects of change upon them, other large segments of the population are left unprotected. It should be equally clear that rather than a quiet acquiescence in the finality and justice of such arrangements, there is an active effort to force new devices into being which will extend protection to those hitherto expected to bear the brunt of these costs. A good proportion of these inventions increasingly call for the intervention of the state. To call such arrangements immoral, unpatriotic, socialistic, or to hurl other epithets at them is not to deal effectively with them. They are as 'natural' as are the 'normal' reactions for which we have 'rational' explanations based upon some prescientific generalization about human nature, such as 'the law of supply and demand' or 'the inevitability of progress'. To be dealt with effectively, they will have to be understood and treated as such.

7 Tony Lane and Kenneth Roberts

Strikes are Normal

Excerpt from Tony Lane and Kenneth Roberts, *Strike at Pilkingtons*, Fontana, 1971, pp. 223-7.

No two strikes are identical. The strike we have described in St Helens at the Pilkington glass works in the spring of 1970 will never happen again, either there or anywhere else. But there are elements common to many strikes. The Pilkington strike was a wildcat – it was spontaneous and completely unpremeditated – and developed into a protracted struggle. These features, either taken separately or together, are far from unusual.

We will attempt to generalize from our own study of this particular strike to other strikes having similar characteristics. While we cannot be certain that the conclusions we draw from the Pilkington strike will stand up to the sort of generalizations about to be emptied on to the reader, we nevertheless feel bound to suggest that our bucket has dredged up something of more than local importance. Just how important is for our readers to judge, and for other social scientists to confirm or dispute by further research.

Very few people at Pilkingtons had been expecting a strike. How and why the strike spread from a small beginning remained a mystery to most of the participants. Shop stewards, rank and file workers, and managers all confessed to an inability to understand the events of the first weekend. The dispute over the clerical error which sparked it all off surprised nobody, for small localized conflicts were not unknown in the Flat Drawn department, where the strike began, or in other departments in other plants. What *was* so amazing was the way it became converted into a demand for a large increase on the basic pay and the way it snowballed right around St Helens.

In what was an otherwise extremely complex series of events only one thing stands out with clarity: there was no organized plot. The strike had not been engineered by a group of subversives who had deliberately infiltrated Pilkingtons in order to undermine the economy. Cloaks, daggers, Kremlin agents, the Church of Rome, and small groups of 'politically motivated men' – all those mythical progenitors of natural and political 'calamities' belong firmly in the pages of Ian Fleming and Dennis Wheatley. Drama there was in St Helens – but it was unscripted. Such script as there was, was made up by people as they went along: the strike in its beginnings was a genuine spontaneous movement. In the early stages many workers did not know why they were striking – it was during the process of spreading through the factories that the strike acquired definite objectives.

Previous explanations of this type of wildcat have treated it as an emotional explosion following upon pent-up grievances that have not been resolved. Yet while this theory fits approximately the department in which the strike started, the same could not be said for all of the departments in all of the works. Morale in the Pilkington factories did not appear to be unusually low in the period immediately preceding the strike. If top management had been warned that they were sitting on a 'powder keg' and had noticed that they were 'getting rather less cooperation in change than (they) had in the past', they certainly weren't prepared for what they woke up to on the morning of Saturday, 4 April. There had been no sudden acceleration in labour turnover, and the incidence of localized disputes had shown no sharp upswing.

Most of the workers had not anticipated the strike either: they had seen no build-up of tensions or problems that had led them to want to strike or to believe that one was imminent. Problems and grievances certainly existed. Dissatisfaction with wage levels was widespread. In some departments there had been almost continuous friction between labour and management. Some employees (including most of those who became members of the Strike Committee) had felt that quite a lot of things were badly wrong at Pilkingtons. But, if it could not be claimed that the firm was purring along in a state of glorious harmony, there was certainly nothing to indicate that on the day the strike started, grievances had been more numerous or more deeply felt than they had been in the preceding months.

This means of course that workers can be drawn into a strike without being conscious of an exceptionally wide range of grievances, and without being subject to unusual stress on the shop-floor. A strike, in other words, can gather momentum under 'normal' working conditions. The prospect of a sizeable pay increase, apparent support from workmates, and advice from shop stewards, can together encourage people to join a strike and thereby add to its momentum – all without any change in the feelings and attitudes characteristic of previous months. Those people who actually set a strike in motion undergo rather different experiences from those who subsequently join it, and a large-scale strike can be triggered off by the decisive action of only a small number of men. This however will not always be the case. It has to be remembered that the great majority of the Pilkington workers had never before been involved in a strike-prone work situation. In firms where workers are more strike-experienced it is much less likely that a departmental-based dispute would have a bush-fire effect – even if it were to be converted into an issue of wider application.

In contemporary Britain strikes have been defined as a 'problem', and the attachment of this label has created the allied impression that strikes are aberrations and atypical events which must therefore occur only amongst aberrant workers or under atypical conditions. It has accordingly been assumed that if certain features of the industrial landscape were remodelled the 'problem' could be buried.

This conception of strikes may well be false. The implication of our observation – that the Pilkington strike occurred in normal conditions – is that strikes generally should be regarded as *normal* features of industrial life in those sectors of the economy where large numbers of workers are gathered together under one roof.

The Pilkington workers' complaints about their jobs were mainly centred around money: 'We have to work a lot of overtime to get a decent living wage', and of course during the strike a return to work was made conditional upon the payment of cash. This suggests that work was primarily regarded as a matter of exchanging time and labour for cash – not as a source of interest or stimulation, or a moral obligation to the employer. This attitude to work is far from uncommon amongst semi-skilled and unskilled manual workers in large firms. Employers treat labour as a commodity and workers regard their labour-power in a similar way.

This is not to suggest that people look only for financial rewards from their work; there is in fact more than enough evidence to show that ideally workers would like to derive a much wider range of satisfactions. The suggestion is simply that as a matter of fact the nature of work is such that money is about the only reward that can be obtained.

This instrumental approach towards work may have several repercussions for industrial relations. Workers with such a disposition may well use whatever tactics appear to be most effective to maximize their earning power. They may bargain through their union officials or shop stewards, they may work-to-rule, go slow, ban overtime, or strike.

From the point of view of explaining the way in which the Pilkington strike gained momentum over the first week-end, the implications of this instrumental approach to work are obvious. If there is no sense of moral obligation towards work, no feeling of personal involvement, then the possibility of a quick financial return will be sufficient to get people outside the factory gates. This certainly seemed to be one of the features in the first crucial forty-eight hours of the Pilkington strike, for, to repeat, there did not seem to have been any accumulation of tensions throughout all the plants in St Helens.

Some sections of industry are more strike-prone than others. The breadth and depth of bonds that tie individuals to their jobs and their employers will vary, and so the extent to which apparent trivia such as the miscalculation of bonuses are likely to spark off something larger will also vary. There can be no doubt that some industrial conditions are more conducive to strikes than others, but to claim that strikes can be normal is not to deny this. The fact remains that in much of large-scale industry, millions of workers are employed under conditions in which periodic upsets are bound to occur, and when they do there is the continuous possibility of a wildcat strike.

Pilkington's management admitted that problems did exist: clerical errors in the calculation of wages were far from unusual; anomalies did exist in the wages structure; some jobs were not particularly pleasant, and others were either distinctly unpleasant or dangerous. But management was also quick to point out that most other large firms had identical problems, and anyway what could be done about them? The answer is: very little. And this is precisely why strikes can be perfectly normal events, conducted by perfectly normal people, in perfectly normal circumstances.

8 V. L. Allen

The Paradox of Trade Unionism

Excerpts from V. L. Allen, 'The paradox of trade unionism', in R. Miliband and
J. Saville (eds.), *The Socialist Register, 1964*, Merlin Press, pp. 158–65.

The paradox of trade unionism

Trade unionism is a universal phenomenon and is the collective act of
protecting and improving living standards by people who sell their
labour power against people who buy it. Clearly this protective, improving function can be performed in various ways, depending upon the
precise nature of the environment in which unions find themselves, but
before it can start certain necessary and sufficient conditions have to be
present. The necessary conditions are the existence of a free market for
labour in which it is possible for buyers to discriminate against, and
therefore exercise power over, sellers, and enough political tolerance to
permit potential opposition groups to arise. The sufficient conditions can
be almost any factor which injects realism into the lives of people who
sell their labour. In Britain in the eighteenth century the most significant
sufficient condition was the excessive use of apprentices by employers;
later the introduction of machinery. In the mid-twentieth century the
main factor which impelled white-collar workers to organize was a fall
in real incomes, and therefore status, through inflation. But in every case
workers were responding to obvious, well-formed forces. Trade unions
from the very beginning were devised to protect their members from the
exigencies of capitalism. They belonged essentially to capitalism because
they grew out of the conditions it created.

This fact throws some light, but not all, on the present role of unions.
Trade unions are patently not initiators. What they do is always in response to well-established forces such as rising prices, falling prices, unemployment, government action which influences living standards, and
over which they have little or no control. They are not, and never have
been, revolutionary bodies. They have never been in the vanguard of
revolutionary change though they have been vehicles for change. In a
number of revolutionary situations unions have formed the organized
basis for mass industrial support once the movements for change have
commenced. Where revolutions have started without the existence of

unions then the unions have had to be created. In Russia before the October Revolution, unions were largely the creation of a revolutionary political party. In the struggle for political independence in Ghana and Tanganyika the nationalist parties had to ally themselves with unions to make political action apparently and decisively effective.

The fact alone, however, that unions originated as protective societies does not invalidate them as revolutionary, or even initiatory, bodies, unless there is something in their nature which inhibits quick movement. Two factors in concert inhibit quick movement. The first is that trade unionism is a mass act in that it depends for its effectiveness upon the widest possible basis of support. A union must include at least a substantial minority but more often a majority of its potential membership before it can command respect from an employer. Secondly, because a union is operating in a conflict situation in which serious adverse consequences might flow from a decision, every major act of policy must be based on the consent, tacit or overt, of a majority of its members. In other words, trade unions are relatively large-scale democratic organizations. Decisions which are acceptable to the majority of the members must necessarily resemble compromises of extreme possibilities and before the need to take a decision is obvious to the majority, the impact of the forces creating the need for a decision must be experienced by most of the people involved. Trade union decisions then are relatively slowly reached compromises. The speed at which a decision is reached is finally determined by the democratic processes within the union. The more serious a matter is, the wider and lengthier must the consultation with the members be. When a decision is reached the situation will most probably have so changed, because to create the need for collective action at all it must be dynamic, that the decision becomes a response to forces. Every organization, of course acts in response to forces external to it. But some can anticipate the nature, intensity and direction of the forces and by the speed of their responses appear to initiate change. It is not fortuitous that revolutionary bodies practise what is called democratic centralism.

Trade unions have always been sluggish in their assessment of circumstances, even when their democratic processes were simple and direct. Their responses, however, have been considerably slowed down because as their organizations have grown democracy has become institutionalized. In 1962, nine per cent of the 176 unions affiliated to the Trades Union Congress organized 71 per cent of the 8,315,332 members. More than 47 per cent of the total membership was in five unions. In these large unions there are rigid, formal bureaucratic structures because only with these can numerous geographically scattered members with diverse interests be serviced. Communications in these structures, however, are slow because every part of them has to be functionally related to and synchronized with every other part. It may take months for communications to pass from one end of the hierarchy to the other. There are also informal obstacles to quick movement. The ability to respond is in part a function of age. The longer the unions exist the more deeply they become tied by vested interests and tradition. In trade unions tradition is a significant determinant of motivation. Unfortunately traditions carry over from one set of circumstances to another. Attitudes evolved, say, during a long period of unemployment become traditional during a phase of full employment and inhibit responses which full employment makes necessary.

These disabilities would not matter if trade unions could satisfy their moderate aims of protection satisfactorily without revolutionary change. As it is, they cannot. It is not possible to state the precise part unions have played in determining the living standards of their members because so many variables are involved. Changes in the demand for labour have a swift impact on workers' living standards while improvements in technology have a longer-term, and perhaps more substantial, effect. These and other variables cannot be isolated and controlled and assessed but it is possible to examine the general effectiveness of unions.

The protective function of unions means more than simply holding what is already possessed. It involves insulating workers from the uncertainty, the insecurity and the differentials which characterize capitalism, and this can only be done effectively by making positive demands for security against contingencies such as sickness and unemployment; by providing for that level of income which would act as a buffer against fluctuations in living costs; by narrowing differentials, including the differential between wages and profits, to remove any sense of injustice; and by providing physical amenities in work and out which would protect against excessive fatigue, discomfort and the like. The protective function is based on certain ethical considerations which have their origin in the exigencies of capitalism. The plight of individual employees *vis-à-vis* employers has given rise to a deep sense of solidarity. Protection must involve all in the group, or, depending on the circumstances, the class. Secondly, the injustices of differentials, particularly within a group, have created a desire for equality so that everyone in a group should not only be protected but treated equally. There is a direct relationship between protection and the belief in equality because equality means removing friction-creating differences, not levelling everyone irrespective of function, to the same standard. All of these basic trade union demands are made initially within the context of the existing distribution of income because trade unionists at large have been socialized to accept their economic and social ratings and to couch their demands, therefore, in 'reasonable' terms. But the logic of the implementation of the protection function is that there should be changes in the distribution of the national income in favour of trade unionists. The extent to which there have been changes is one measure of trade union effectiveness.

The full cost of protecting workers under capitalism is the price of labour. This price, to employers, is a production cost which can be manipulated. If it is regarded as excessive it can either be minimized by using more capital-intensive methods or passed on to consumers through higher commodity prices. In each case the distributive process so works as to maintain the *status quo*. The switch to more capital-intensive methods will displace labour so that if the workers who remain in employment obtain gains they will be at the expense of those who have lost their jobs. But even if no labour is displaced there will be an argument about the distribution of the gains and the likelihood is that at the best from the workers' point of view it will follow the traditional pattern. This is because if a union is strong enough to obtain what an employer regards as a disproportionate share he will attempt, and in general succeed, in passing the cost to the consumer. A problem for unions is that they rarely know the gains from improved technology so that they are not able to make definite claims about their distribution anyway. If the commodity market is rising then it will be possible for employers to pass on the cost of all trade union demands to consumers simply by increasing prices. As trade unionists are consumers their real incomes remain as they were before the demands were made. Only if unions can increase the price of labour on a falling commodity market, thus making it impossible for employers to pass the cost on, can they increase their share of the national income and even then the increase is temporary because as soon as the market conditions improve employers can recoup their losses. It rarely happens that unions are able to increase the price of labour when employers are finding it difficult to sell their commodities because a deteriorating state of trade normally produces unemployment and this weakens unions by making it difficult for workers to pay their union subscriptions and to be militant because they fear unemployment. It is an anomaly that unions are weakest when the possibility of gains is greatest; and are strongest when the possibility of gains is least. There are exceptions in occupations, firms or industries but in general, so long as unions work within the free price mechanism, their basic aims are frustrated. The share of wages in the national income has remained remarkably stable since the last quarter of the nineteenth century. One estimate showed that the share was 41·4 per cent in 1880 and 41·8 per cent in 1935.

There were variations between these dates but not sharp ones. In 1913 the share of wages was 39·4 per cent and in 1931 it was 43·7 per cent. Another estimate showed that between 1870 and 1950 wages were never less than 36·6 per cent of the national income and never more than 42·6 per cent. In the period 1946–50 when the money earnings of industrial workers rose by about one-third, the ratio of wages to profits remained roughly at the level of the inter-war years. The main determinant of the share of wages was the market environment and unions had no control over this.

The point emerges then that although unions are incapable of initiating revolutionary change it is only through such change that they will achieve their basic aims. That is, if an effective means of protection cannot be applied under the present system then it is necessary to alter the systems fundamentally. A step, however, which altered the process of distribution would involve other changes. Unions would not achieve their ends directly but through the agency of a central government with planning authority. The relative shares in the national income could only be disturbed by interfering with the free price mechanism and thus by taking from unions their right to bargain over wages. In order, then, to escape from the restrictions and frustrations imposed by a capitalist society, unions would have to undergo a radical character transformation. There are important sociological reasons why this transformation is resisted.

Union leadership

Trade union officials provide leadership at all levels. Because of the inevitable oligarchic control in unions, leadership involves directing the organizations in all of their major activities and is, therefore, a role which must be analysed if the obstacles to the radical character transformation of unions are to be understood. The role of a union official is set so that the behaviour of any person who becomes an official is almost entirely predictable. The only significant variations which occur are those which exist within the hierarchy of roles in a union. If a person moves from being a local to a national official then different behaviour will be expected of him. The dominance of the role over the individual explains why the union behaviour of communist and anti-communist officials varies so little; why, in other words, there is continuity of activities despite marked changes in personnel. A new union leader might give greater meaning to his role because of his intellectual ability but if this results in a significant difference in the direction of union activities it will be because the environment of the union has changed.

The behaviour of a union official is confined by various kinds of sanctions which have been created by social and administrative factors. The first set comprise the process of socialization whereby the role of union officials has been conditioned to be consistent with the norms and values of a capitalist society. The second set can be described by the bureaucratization of union organizations.

The process of socialization was an inevitable one, for unions could not perpetually stand out against the system, fail to change it and yet continue to exist without taking on some of the values of the system itself. The consequence has been to make unions work with and to some extent for the system. This is what the non-legalistic integration of trade unions into society is all about. The results of the process can be seen in many ways. A dominant trade union ethic is a belief in solidarity. This was forced on unions by their need for cohesion in a hostile environment yet their practice of solidarity is disrupted by the way in which each individual union stoutly protects its own vested interests. The trade union movement reflects the competitive nature of British society through the competition of unions with each other over wages policies, members, and, in the case of craft unions, jobs. Trade unions have imbibed capitalist values to the extent of becoming involved in the competitive process. The unions have welded themselves to the price mechanism through uncritical belief in collective bargaining so that it would be difficult for any government, no matter how sympathetic towards trade union aspirations, to interfere with the wage bargaining process without evoking strong union protests and arousing their antipathy. The unions advocate limited forms of planning for other sections of the economy but insist that wage determination, the vital variable in the planning process, should remain free. Unions support the principle of equity and through the introduction of uniform rates for jobs attempt to apply it. Yet in collective bargaining they practise the most iniquitous form of wage determination. Free collective bargaining is an institutionalized way of operating the play of market forces and their interaction with the subsidiary forces which make up the balance of industrial power. Workers, irrespective of their needs, are in a strong or weak bargaining position because of market forces. In the inter-war years the coal miners, for instance, suffered privations because the export demand for coal declined; in the immediate post-Second World War period they obtained relatively high wages because the demand for coal increased; now that alternative sources of power are established the demand for coal is again decreasing, with the obvious depressing effect upon miners' living standards. The treatment of the miners in the past has been iniquitous, as is that of the railway workers at the present compared with motor production workers. The justification for allocating reward according to market forces is crudely economic; it has no basis in equity.

The acceptance of free collective bargaining has led, too, to what can be called the myth of achievement. This is simply a situation where union officials are so preoccupied with the means of achievement that they create an illusion about the ends. Instead of being directly concerned about the redistribution of income and devising a means to achieve this, they show satisfaction with fractional changes in money wage rates. In doing this they accept the expectations which employers have deemed suitable for them. These expectations are buttressed by disarming notions of compromise and fairmindedness. Any departure from what is equitable can be justified if the result can be construed as being fair, the meaning of which is set by the limits of voluntary concessions from employers [. . .] Union leaders lose sight of the reality that they are in a conflict situation. But then this, too, is a consequence of socialization. There is an illusion about a harmony of industrial interests which also influences the role of union officials.

The sanctions on union leaders are of a prohibitive, prescriptive or permissive character and can be seen in attitudes to making 'unreasonable' demands, breaking negotiated agreements, refusals to compromise and 'irresponsibility' to society at large. There are also sanctions which are derived from the integration of unions into the political parliamentary democratic system. There have always been occasions when the objectives of unions demanded political action. At first the need was for legislation to protect women and children in industry, then to protect union funds, enforce industrial safety standards and establish minimum wage rates for workers in sweated industries. Now the need arises from the growth of the government as an employer and its frequent and decisive interventions in industry. Unions are forced into an intensive relationship with the government but are confronted by limitations on the political action they can take which are set by a belief in political democracy in general and party politics in particular. The sanctions from this situation concern acts which challenge the authority of an elected government or usurp the party system. There is, in consequence, a general prohibition on industrial action for political ends; indeed on anything which savours of coercion of the government; and union leaders respect it. When union leaders during the General Strike realized they were challenging the authority of the government they backed down as quickly as they could. The unwillingness of the Trades Union Congress to support the London busmen in their 1958 strike indicated that most union leaders did not want even to appear to challenge the government. These restrictions can be extensive for there can be so many points of conflict between unions and the government and when they are expressed, the government invariably adopts a constitutional position which gives it automatic protection.

Bureaucracy does not belong to any particular economic system but it is authoritarian and is consistent, therefore, with the private ownership and control of the means of production. It has been associated with achievement and is a dominant feature of contemporary capitalism. It is understandable, though not necessarily justifiable, that unions should copy bureaucratic practices as far as their allegiances to democratic control permit. Whereas the socialization process has set limits to the uses to which the role of union leadership may be put, bureaucratization has prescribed limits to the role itself. It has combined all the roles involved in trade unions in a hierarchical structure with fixed layers of command and lines of communication and has prescribed their duties. Formally, union officials must act towards each other and committees they serve according to regulations. Their informal relationships may differ from the formal ones but only in so far as this accords either with tradition or greater efficiency. The informal power of a general secretary is generally much greater than that provided for by his union constitution because he commands power as a specialist in addition to his formal authority. This is not usually disputed so long as the specialist power produces greater efficiency. But all the time he has to be guided by the formal limits to his activities.

Bureaucracy inevitably slows down movement but it does not necessarily result in faulty movement. Faultiness is the product of an inability to respond to changing circumstances. There are two elements in bureaucratic organizations which make accurate and immediate responses to changes difficult. The first is the constitutional provision for action. Rules and regulations are difficult to change unless the need for change is intense and imperative. Unions, moreover, deliberately make constitution-changing difficult because alterations not associated with variations in circumstances can be a handicap to action. Secondly it is possible for bureaucratic attitudes to develop which make a ritual of adherence to regulations. If circumstances alter but not the regulations then people with these attitudes cannot cope with the situation.

Trade unions, then, have acquired aims which are legitimate within the context of a capitalist society. They are limited aims, concerning wages, hours of work and working conditions, which can be achieved without unduly disturbing the fabric of capitalism; without, indeed, unduly disturbing capitalists because it is possible to conceive of them being obtained through labour market pressures. These legitimate aims are pursued through institutionalized practices. So long as the environment of unions remains stable there need be no inconsistency between the aims and the practices; that is, the ordinary members may feel they are getting satisfaction. But if there are sharp environmental changes, equally sharp inconsistencies develop because institutionalized practices are relatively unresponsive to change. This is what has happened in Britain. Trade unions now are not capable by themselves of achieving satisfactorily even their limited aims.

9 Herbert Blumer

Sociological Theory in Industrial Relations

Excerpts from Herbert Blumer, 'Sociological theory in industrial relations',
American Sociological Review, vol. 12, 1947, pp. 272–8.

The evaluation of current theory and research in industrial relations
requires as a background a brief sketch of the nature of industrial relations in our present-day American society. The primary parties to these
relations are workers and management. The extent and variety of the
relations between workers and management cannot be dealt with in this
paper. I wish merely to note the obvious point that these relations in
American industry are not in the nature of a simple contract between a
worker selling his labor and an employer purchasing that labor. That
bare fundamental relation has been elaborated in our society into an
extensive, diversified, complex and indirect network of relations in which
the individual worker becomes an insignificant and inconspicuous figure.
With unionization, especially with industrial unionization, workers have
become incorporated in organizations, usually of vast dimensions. The
relations of workers to management become increasingly led by, directed by, mediated by and expressed through such organizations. The
organization as such functions through a heirarchy of officers and central committees who formulate policies, establish objectives, decide on
strategy and tactics, and execute decisions. On the side of management
one finds similar organization which takes out of the hand of the individual manager the determination of the major outlines of his relation to
the worker. Relations between workers and management become primarily a matter of relations between organized groups. The formation of
huge national unions had especially given a new dimension and character
to these relations.

To my mind the most noteworthy feature of the relations between
workers and management in American industry is that the relations are
dynamic, uncrystallized and changing. They may be regarded as in a
state of continuous tension, even though the degree of this tension will
vary significantly from time to time. The tension is, itself, an inevitable
consequence of a variety of factors which lead workers and management
to exercise pressure against each other at shifting points and in new ways.
Each of these two parties is forced to meet such pressure – to resist it if it

can, to adjust to it in some way if it must. The result is that the relations are either moving, or if not moving, in tenuous accommodation poised to move.

That this is true should be apparent on an analysis of the basic and accessory conditions which impart impetus to the relations between workers and management. Fundamentally, workers and management in our economy are necessarily in conflict with each other. I don't say this in a Marxian sense. I refer merely to the fact that workers, especially in their organized groups, are seeking to secure benefits and to preserve benefits and that management is seeking managerial freedom and opportunities for business profit. As our economy is organized, these respective interests enter normally in opposition. As either of the two parties moves in the direction of what it is seeking, it encroaches on the interest of the other party. Thus, an advance is in the nature of pressure and as such encounters resistance. Whenever such advances are initiated the pattern of relations changes. This bare statement merely sketches the fundamental fact that industrial relations between workers and management under our economy are intrinsically instable and inherently disposed toward rearrangement.

All that is needed to set such relations in movement is the initiation of seeking efforts by workers or by management. The conditions which initiate such seeking efforts are rife in our society and are likely to remain so. I call attention to only a few of the more conspicuous ones: competition in business with the inevitable effort to achieve efficient, low-cost production and managerial freedom; the effort of management to coup the gains of improved efficiency through technological improvements; the shifting and changing of management personnel with divergent philosophies; the development of new wishes and conceptions of rights on the part of workers; the exercise of pressure by the rank and file, particularly in large democratic unions; the formation of national unions, leading to uniform demands on diversified industrial concerns; the pressure on union leaders to produce increased benefits; the struggle for position on the part of union leaders or those seeking to be leaders; the development of a militant, aggressive psychology on the part of unions; the rivalry between unions for prestige, membership and the efforts to weaken rival unions; the change in price-wage relationships and the movement of the business cycle; shifts in political power offering to either organized workers or to management the opportunity to actively advance its particular interest; shifts in public opinion which yield the same encouragement; and the appearance of new legislation or new judicial interpretation which open new vistas of what is permissible. Such conditions – and the list is by no means complete – lead and coerce workers and management into new relations as each party seeks to pursue and to protect its respective interests. In response to such forces, industrial relations in our society become tense, changeable and ever moving.

The mobile character of industrial relations has taken on a new dimension and nature with the organization of workers in vast national unions. The focal point of relationship has been shifted away from the contact between workers and local management to the contact between big union organization and management organization. Although there are exceptions, the usual consequence of the organization of workers on a national basis has been a centralized guidance of labor activities over an industry-wide area. Bargaining is done for the industry as a whole or for large segments of the industry represented by huge corporations. Thus labor relations become increasingly a matter of relationship between gigantic organizations of workers and management, each of which functions through central policy and executive groups. Relations between workers and management in the local plants in the industry tend to lose separate and autonomous character and instead are determined in their basic outlines by the policies, objectives, plans and strategy of the central organizations. Thus to suggest an analogy, workers and management become related and aligned like vast opposing armies, with many outposts and points of contact but with the vast relationship operating along lines set up by the central organizations [. . .]

A proper orientation to the study of industrial relations in our society must be based, in my judgment, on the recognition that such relations are a moving pattern of accommodative adjustments largely between organized parties. In a valid sense industrial relations may be likened to a vast, confused game evolving without the benefit of fixed rules and frequently without the benefit of any rules. The setting of this game is itself not stable, but instead is shifting and presenting itself in new forms. This occasions strains on the pattern of the game. In addition, each of the parties is subject to the play of pressures and forces inside its own ranks which impart further tension and shifts in the game situation. Still further, the participants are far from satisfying their respective wishes and objectives in the temporal accommodations which they make to each other, with a consequence of constant pressure on their relations and an opportunistic readiness to change them. I think that we deceive ourselves and perhaps engage in wishful thinking when we regard this shifting flow of relations in industry as temporary and transitory, to be followed by a shaking down of relationships into a permanent orderly system. This, to my mind, is not at all likely as long as we live in a dynamic, democratic, competitive society. The degree of tension, the rapidity of accommodations and the extent of shifts in relations may vary from time to time, but the mobile character of the relations remains.

In my judgment the fruitful study of present day industrial relations requires a new perspective – one that is compatible with the mobile, indirect and large-dimensional character of such relations. I sense the blurred outlines of such a perspective. It must visualize human beings as acting, striving, calculating, sentimental and experiencing persons and not as the automatons and neutral agents implied by the more dominant of our current scientific ideologies and methodologies. It must further visualize such human beings in their collective character – as arranged in diverse ways and incorporated in intricate and indirect network of relations. It must embrace the complicated behavior of these collectivities, particularly as they act and prepare to act toward one another.

The observation necessary to sharpen and fill in this vague perspective must meet the two requirements of intimate familiarity and broad imaginative grasp [. . .] In addition to being based on intimate acquaintance with what is being observed, observation must be suited to the imaginative grasping of intricate complexes of data. It is unfortunate that observation in the field of industrial relations has to be made in the form of large intricate patterns – but it has to be, in order to be realistic. In a way, the necessities of observation in industrial relations are quite similar to those required in modern warfare. The individual soldier in his single observation post, regardless of how competent he may be as an observer, can understand little of what is taking place over the broad area of a campaign. A sociological investigator making observations in a single factory suffers, I believe, from a corresponding limitation. Effective observation requires the observer to sense the movement in the field, to take many varied roles, to size up a variety of different situations and in doing so to perform the difficult task of fitting such things into somewhat of an integrated pattern. This type of observation, whether we like it or not, requires a high degree of imaginative judgment in order to be accurate. It may be noted, in passing, that this type of observation is not nurtured in our training programs for sociologists; indeed, our current conventions of research discourage this type of observation.

Assuming that observation based on intimate familiarity and using broad imaginative judgment is made of industrial relations, its findings, I suspect, will not lend themselves to treatment by our present kind or current stock of sociological theories. Our sociological thinking has been fashioned in the main from the consideration of matters which are quite apart from the central character of modern dynamic life. Our thinking has been derived from images of stable societies and of nicely ordered association; or from highly abstracted and emasculated data such as census and demotic items; or from a miscellany of imported theories which were formed with reference to matters different from those in our field; or from a variety of social philosophies which have appeared from time to time in our western civilization. Our sociological thinking has not been shaped from empirical consideration of the dynamic character of modern life. We need a scheme of treatment suited to the analysis of collective and mass interaction – the interaction between active and relatively free collectivities with different degrees and kinds of organization. To formulate such a scheme is the theoretical task which confronts sociologists in the field of industrial relations. I do not believe that sociologists have begun this task.

10 Robert Blauner

Work Satisfaction and Industrial Trends in Modern Society

Excerpt from Robert Blauner, 'Work satisfaction and industrial trends in modern society', in W. Galenson and S. M. Lipset (eds.), *Labor and Trades Unionism*, Wiley, 1960, pp. 352-6.

When we read modern accounts of what work and workers were like before the Industrial Revolution, we continually find that the dominant image of the worker of that period is the craftsman. Viewed as an independent producer in his home or small shop with complete control over the pace and scheduling of his work, making the whole product rather than a part of it, and taking pride in the creativity of his skilled tasks, his traits are typically contrasted with those of the alienated factory worker – the allegedly characteristic producer of modern society.

It is remarkable what an enormous impact this *contrast* of the craftsman with the factory hand has had on intellectual discussions of work and workers in modern society, *notwithstanding its lack of correspondence to present and historical realities*. For, indeed, craftsmen, far from being typical workers of the past era, accounted for less than 10 per cent of the medieval labor force, and the peasant, who was actually the representative laborer, was, in the words of the Belgian socialist Henri De-Man, 'practically nothing more than a working beast'. Furthermore, the real character of the craftsman's work has been romanticized by the prevalent tendency to idealize the past, whereas much evidence suggests that modern work does not fit the black portrait of meaningless alienation. In fact, it has been asserted 'that in modern society there is far greater scope for skill and craftsmanship than in any previous society, and that far more people are in a position to use such skills'.

For intellectuals, it seems to be particularly difficult to grasp both the subjective and relative character of monotony and the capacity of workers to inject meaning into 'objectively meaningless' work. Their strong tendency to view workers as dissatisfied suggests the idea that the alienation thesis, though a direct descendant of Marxist theory and related to a particular political posture, also reflects an intellectual perspective (in the sociology of knowledge sense) on manual work.

Surprisingly enough, business executives also tend to view manual workers as alienated. Perhaps this attitude reflects, in part, the growing influence of intellectual ideas, including neo-Marxist ones, on the more progressive business circles; perhaps, more importantly, this stems again, as in the case of the intellectual, from the middle-class businessman's separation and distance from the workaday world of his industrial employees. At any rate, such industrial spokesmen as Drucker and Heron are likely to generalize much as does Worthy of Sears Roebuck, who, in discussing 'overfunctionalization', has written:

The worker cannot see that total process, he sees only the small and uninteresting part to which he and his fellows are assigned. In a real sense, the job loses its meaning for the worker – the meaning, that is, in all terms except the pay envelope. Thus a very large number of employees in American industry today have been deprived of the sense of performing interesting, significant work. In consequence, they have little feeling of responsibility for the tasks to which they are assigned.

But, work *has* significant positive meanings to persons who do not find overall satisfaction in their immediate job. A still viable consequence of the Protestant ethic in our society is that its work ethic (the notion of work as a calling, an obligation to one's family, society, and self-respect, if no longer to God), retains a powerful hold. This is most dramatically seen in the reactions of the retired and unemployed. The idea is quite common to American workers at all occupational levels that soon after a worker retires, he is likely to either 'drop dead' or 'go crazy' from sheer inactivity. An English industrial psychiatrist states that this is actually a common calamity in British industry. Similarly, the studies made in the 1930s of unemployed people show that the disruption of the work relationship often leads to the disruption of normal family relations, to political apathy, and to a lack of interest in social organizations and leisure-time activities.

Studies of job satisfaction further question the prevailing thesis that most workers in modern society are alienated and estranged. There is a remarkable consistency in the findings that the vast majority of workers, in virtually all occupations and industries, are moderately or highly satisfied, rather than dissatisfied, with their jobs.

However, the marked occupational differences in work attitudes and the great significance which workers impute to being, at least to some extent, masters of their destiny in the work process, along with the fact that surrender of such control seems to be the most important condition of strong dissatisfaction are findings at least as important as the overall one of general satisfaction. Perhaps the need for autonomy and independence may be a more deep-seated human motive than is recognized by those who characterize our society in terms of crowdlike conformity and the decline of individualism.

These findings also have clear implications for industrial engineering. If industry and society have an interest in workers' experiencing satisfaction and pride in their work, a major effort must be made to increase the areas of control which employees have over the work process, especially in those industries and occupations where control is at a minimum. Charles Walker, who has written perceptively of the automobile worker's lack of control, has advocated two major solutions for humanizing repetitive assembly line work: job rotation and job enlargement. Where job rotation was introduced in one section of the automobile plant he studied, job satisfaction increased without loss of efficiency or production. The idea of recombining a number of jobs into one enlarged job seems especially to appeal to the line workers: as one man said, 'I'd like to do a whole fender myself from the raw material to the finished product.' But such radical job enlargement would be a negation of the assembly line method of production. Therefore, we must anticipate the day when the Utopian solution of eliminating assembly line production entirely will be the practical alternative for a society which is affluent and concerned at the same time that its members work with pride and human dignity.

Finally, the findings of this paper indicate a need for considerable further research on industrial statistics and industrial trends. If the evidence shows that extreme dissatisfaction is concentrated among assembly line workers, it becomes terribly important, for a total assessment of the conditions of work in modern America, to know what proportion of the labor force works on assembly lines or in other job contexts involving little control over their work activities. It is startling, considering the importance of such data, that such figures do not exist. This situation helps maintain the conventional belief that the mechanized assembly line worker is today's typical industrial worker in contrast to the craftsman of the past.

An indication that the actual proportion of assembly line workers is quite small is suggested by figures of the automobile industry, the conveyor belt industry par excellence. If we consider total employment in the industrial groupings involved in the manufacture, sales, repair, and servicing of automobiles, we find that assembly line workers make up less than 5 per cent of all workers in this complex. There are approximately 120,000 automobile workers who are line assemblers, yet the number of skilled repair mechanics in all branches of the industry, a job which in many ways resembles the craft ideal, exceeds 500,000. In addition, the 120,000 assemblers are outnumbered by 400,000 managers who own or operate gas stations, garages, new and used car lots, and wrecking yards, and by 200,000 *skilled* workers in automobile plants.

Recent developments, especially automation, have served further to decrease the proportion of assembly line operatives in the industry.

If the situation in the automobile industry is at all typical, research might well show that those kinds of job contexts which are associated with high work satisfaction and control over one's time and destiny, such as skilled repair work and self-employment, are more representative than is commonly believed, and are even increasing over the long run. Such a prospect should bring considerable satisfaction to all those in the diverse intellectual traditions who have been concerned with what happens to human beings in the course of their major life activity, their work. And yet, this would not necessarily mean that the problem of the lack of fulfillment in work had become less serious. For as one industrial sociologist has suggested, this problem *may become more acute,* not because work itself has become more tedious, fractionated, and meaningless, but because the ideal of pride in creative effort is shared by an increasingly large proportion of the labor force as a result of the rise of democratic education and its emphasis on individualism and occupational mobility.

Note on methodological problems in job satisfaction research

By far the most common technique employed in job satisfaction studies is the poll-type questionnaire in which workers are asked directly, 'How satisfied are you with your occupation?' or, 'Do you like your job?' These questions have a number of advantages. They are quite straightforward and, in general, are easily understood in a common-sense fashion. Research costs are relatively economical, and what may be the guiding consideration is that the data are quantifiable and easily expressed in a form which can both indicate the total distribution of work satisfaction and dissatisfaction in a given population, and can readily locate differences among workers according to occupation, industry, educational level, sex, etc.

However, such a direct questionnaire runs certain risks which are common to all opinion polls. The respondent may not want, or may not be able, to answer honestly. In this case we suggest a cultural bias toward indicating contentment; the meaning of the question may not always be the same to the worker as it is to the interviewer; and simply the manner in which the question is phrased or asked may favor one response rather than another. For example, it has been suggested that dichotomizing responses into only 'satisfied' and 'dissatisfied' categories has the effect of overestimating the actual degree of satisfaction by pushing those who are in a middle category toward the satisfied alternative.

There are further problems which stem from the special character of work attitudes. There is a certain naïveté in expecting frank and simple answers to job satisfaction questions in a society where one's work is so important a part of one's self that to demean one's job is to question one's very competence as a person. In addition, even if a person could be as honest in reporting about his job satisfaction as in reporting the number of children in his family, this problem is as inherently vague and nebulous as the latter question is precise. While most empirical investigators in this field operate with a common-sense notion of satisfaction, a few writers have been aware of the problem of conceptualization. In the first full-length book on job satisfaction, Hoppock wrote in 1935:

The problem is complicated by the ephemeral and variable nature of satisfaction. Indeed, there may be no such thing as *job* satisfaction independent of the other satisfactions in one's life. Family relationships, health, relative social status in the community, and a multitude of other factors may be just as important as the job itself in determining what we tentatively choose to call job satisfaction. A person may be satisfied with one aspect of his job and dissatisfied with another. Satisfactions may be rationalized, and the degree of satisfaction may vary from day to day. A person may never be wholly satisfied.

Assuming that we are able to arrive at some kind of definition or delimitation of the concept, the problem then arises as to who is to judge a person's satisfaction in work. Are people really satisfied because they say they are satisfied: since Freud this question has become standard currency. If they are honest with the interviewer, can they be honest with themselves? And if people who say they are satisfied are actually so, is this not on a superficial level, a kind of normal adjustment to reality? What about the depth of satisfaction? How many people derive profound, creative fulfillment in work? And does not the existence of general satisfaction reflect a generally low level of aspiration; an adaptation to what Marx called an *animal*, rather than a *human*, level of living?

The above considerations suggest the extent to which the study and analysis of work satisfaction is fraught with problems not only of conceptualization, but of differences in ideals and value premises. At the heart of the question is the philosophic controversy between those who uphold an objective, and those who advocate a subjective theory of values. For the latter, people are satisfied in work if they truly feel themselves satisfied. The former approach, however, organizes a set of objective standards of behaviour which individuals must meet. True fulfillment involves meeting the standards of the observer (an intellectual), rather than the standards of the individuals themselves. This is the characteristic approach of the critics of mass culture who do not find reassurance in the fact that most viewers today actually like the movies and television fare.

Although the above discussion indicates the enormous difficulties involved in getting a fair estimate of the absolute level of job satisfaction, we can speak with far greater assurance about relative levels of satisfaction experienced by members of different occupational groups. It is difficult to interpret a finding that 70 per cent of factory workers report satisfaction with their jobs because we do not know how valid and reliable our measuring instrument is. But when 90 per cent of printers compared to only 40 per cent of automobile workers report satisfaction, the relative difference remains meaningful.

11 Everett C. Hughes

Mistakes at Work

Excerpt from Everett C. Hughes, 'Mistakes at work', *Canadian Journal of Economics and Political Science*, vol. 17, 1951, pp. 220–27.

Some mistakes are more fateful than others, either for the person who makes them, for his colleagues, or for the persons upon whom the mistakes are made. Those who train students for research which requires receiving the confidence of living people and getting and keeping entrée to groups and institutions of various sorts are aware of this problem. (We are at present working on a project to discover how to train students to a high level of skill in social observation with the least risk of damage to all concerned.) In occupations in which mistakes are fateful and in which repetition on living or valuable material is necessary to learn the skills, it is obvious that there is a special set of problems of apprenticeship and of access to the situations in which the learning may be done. Later on, when the neophyte is at his work, there arises the problem of his seeming always to have known how, since the very appearance of being a learner is frightening. At any rate, there are psychological, physical, social, and economic risks in learning and doing one's work. And since the theoretical probability of making an error some day is increased by the very frequency of the operations by which one makes one's living, it becomes natural to build up some rationale to carry one through. It is also to be expected that those who are subject to the same work risks will compose a collective rationale which they whistle to one another to keep up their courage, and that they will build up collective defenses against the lay world. These rationales and defenses contain a logic that is somewhat like that of insurance, in that they tend to spread the risk psychologically (by saying that it might happen to anyone), morally, and financially. A study of these risk-spreading devices is an essential part of comparative study of occupations. They have a counterpart in the devices which the individual finds for shifting some of the sense of guilt from his own shoulders to those of the larger company of his colleagues. Perhaps this is the basis of the strong identification with colleagues in work in which mistakes are fateful, and in which even long training and a sense of high calling do not prevent errors.

Now let us approach the subject from the side of the person who, since he receives the services, will suffer from the mistakes when they are made. In a certain sense, we actually hire people to make our mistakes for us. The division of labor in society is not merely, as is often suggested, technical. It is also psychological and moral. We delegate certain things to other people, not merely because we cannot do them, but because we do not wish to run the risk of error. The guilt of failure would be too great. Perhaps one reason why physicians do work gratis for each other's families is to keep completely free from the economic necessity of treating people with whom they are so closely involved that mistakes would be hard to face.

Sometimes a person requires an assurance that can be had only by being in a strictly lay frame of mind. Belief in the charism of skill is a lay, rather than a professional, attitude. The professional attitude is essentially statistical; it deals in probabilities. But there are matters about which we prefer to think in absolutes. In dealing with such matters we delegate the relative way of thinking to another, who becomes our agent. He runs our risks for us. We like to believe him endowed with charism. Gold, who studied some of the building trades, found that the housewife likes to believe that the plumber she calls in is perfect, not merely *relatively* good. He keeps the mysterious entrails of her precious house in order. How much more does one want to believe absolutely in one's dentist, lawyer, physician, and priest? (There are of course other nontechnical factors involved in delegation of tasks. Some work is *infra dignitate*. Some is necessary, but shady, or forbidden by one's particular taboos and aversions.)

Now this does not mean that the person who delegates work, and hence, risk, will calmly accept the mistakes which are made upon him, his family, or his property. He is quick to accuse; and if people are in this respect as psychiatrists say they are in others, the more determined they are to escape responsibility, the quicker they may be to accuse others for real or supposed mistakes.

In fact, I suppose that we all suspect just a little the objectivity of those to whom we delegate the more fateful of our problems. We suspect them for that very experimental spirit which we know is, in some degree, necessary to hardy and progressive skill in meeting our crises. Thus there is probably always some ambivalence in our feelings towards the people whom we hire to make our mistakes, or at least to run the risk of making them. The whole problem or set of problems involved in delegating work – and risks – to others is one on which there is not much to be found in the anthropological, sociological, or psychological literature. For each occupation that one studies one should, I believe, seek to determine just what it is that is delegated to the persons in the occupation and what are the attitudes and feelings involved on both sides.

We now have before us the problem and the characters. The characters are the people who, because they do something often and for others, run the risk of making mistakes and of causing injury; and those other people who, for technical, economic, psychological, moral, or status reasons, delegate some of their tasks and problems to others and who therefore may have mistakes made upon them and at their expense. These are not really two kinds of people, but are the same people in different roles. The relation of these two roles is part of the personal adjustment of everyone who works. The problem is the reduction and absorption of the risk of failure on both sides, and of the kinds of conflicts within and between persons, which arise from the risk of error, mistakes and failures.

As soon as we go into these problems we are faced with another: that of defining what a failure or mistake is in any given line of work or in a given work operation. This leads to still another, which turns out to be the significant one for the social drama of work: who has the right to say what a mistake or a failure is? The findings on this point are fairly clear; a colleague-group (the people who consider themselves subject to the same work risks) will stubbornly defend its own right to define mistakes, and to say in the given case whether one has been made. Becker has found that professional jazz musicians will do considerable injury to themselves rather than let any layman, even the one who is paying their wages, say that a musician is playing badly or even that he has struck the wrong note. An orchestra leader who would even relay a layman's complaint to a member of his band would be thought already on the road to becoming a 'square', one of those outsiders who do not understand jazz music. Now you may say that jazz music is so lacking in any canons of correctness that there is no such thing as a single false note within the larger noise. It is all a matter of individual opinion. There is no clear and objective standard by which a judgement can be made.

But how clear is it in other lines of work? When one starts comparing occupations in this regard one finds that in most of them it is very difficult to establish criteria of success or failure, and of mistakes as against proper execution of work. The cases where all parties to the work drama would agree are few indeed. In factories which make precision parts the criteria are finely measured tolerances, but usually there is an informally agreed upon set of tolerances which are slightly looser than those in the book. Workmen and inspectors are continually at odds over the difference, even when the workmen want the parts they make to be workable. This is a case of the clearest kind of criterion. In medicine the criteria of success and failure are often far from clear. Bettelheim recently stated that psychotherapists do not discuss together their successes and failures because there are no standards to go by; that is why, he said, they spend so much time discussing whether their historical reconstructions of the troubles of their patients are correct or not. Health is, after all, a relative matter. Most people are interested in making the old body do as long as possible; this makes medicine quite a different matter from the automobile industry (where the garage man makes his work easier by persuading you the old car isn't worth mending).

Even where the standards may be a little clearer than in medicine and education, the people who work and those who receive the product as goods or services will have quite different degrees and kinds of knowledge of the probabilities and contingencies involved. The colleague-group will consider that it alone fully understands the technical contingencies, and that it should therefore be given the sole right to say when a mistake has been made. The layman, they may contend, cannot even at best fully understand the contingencies. This attitude may be extended to complete silence concerning mistakes of a member of the colleague-group, because the very discussion before a larger audience may imply the right of the layman to make a judgment; and it is the *right* to make the judgment that is most jealously guarded.

In some occupations it is assumed that anyone on the inside will know by subtle gestures when his colleagues believe a mistake has been made. Full membership in the colleague-group is not attained until these gestures and their meaning are known. When they are known, there need not be conscious and overt discussion of certain errors even within the colleague-group. And when some incident makes an alleged failure or mistake a matter of public discussion, it is perhaps the feeling that outsiders will never understand the full context of risk and contingency that makes colleagues so tight-lipped. And if matters have gone to such a point that mistakes and failures are not freely discussed even within the trusted in-group, public discussion may be doubly feared; for in addition to questioning the prerogative of in-group judgment, the outside inquisitor lifts the veil from the group's own hidden anxieties, the things colleagues do not talk about even among themselves. This may be the source of the rather nervous behavior of school teachers when my colleagues and I report to them – at their own request – some of the things we are finding out about them.

One of the differences between lay and professional thinking concerning mistakes is that to the layman the technique of the occupation should be pure instrument, pure means to an end, while to the people who practice it, every occupation tends to become an art. David Riesman, who was once a clerk to Justice Brandeis, and an assistant in the office of the District Attorney of New York, tells of the wonderful briefs which young lawyers draw up for presentation to lower court judges who can scarcely read them, much less judge the law that is in them. The ritual of looking up all the past cases, and the art of arguing out all possibilities are gone through, even when the lawyer knows that the decision will be made upon a much simpler – perhaps also a much sounder – basis. What is more: the ritual and the art are respected, and the men who perform them with brilliance and finesse are admired. The simple client may be dazzled, but at some point he is also likely to think that he is being done by the whole guild of lawyers, including his own, the opposing counsel, and the court. In a sense, the art and cult of the law are being maintained at his expense. The legal profession believes, in some measure, in the cult of the law. The individual case is thought of not merely as something to be decided, but as part of the stream of observance of the cult of the law.

And here we come to the deeper point of Bettelheim's remarks concerning his own colleagues, the psychotherapists. A part of their art is the reconstruction of the history of the patient's illness. This may have some instrumental value, but the value put upon it by the practitioners is of another order. The psychotherapists, perhaps just because the standards of cure are so uncertain, apparently find reassurance in being adept at their art of reconstruction (no doubt accompanied by faith that skill in the art will bring good to patients in the long run).

Another example of these ways of thinking is to be found in social work. This profession is said to make a distinction between successful and professional handling of a case. The layman thinks of success as getting the person back on his feet, or out of his trouble. The social worker has to think of correct procedure, of law, of precedent, of the case as something which leaves a record. She also appreciates skilful interviewing, and perhaps can chuckle over some case which was handled with subtlety and finish, although the person never got 'well' (whatever that would be in social work).

In teaching, where ends are very ill-defined – and consequently mistakes are equally so – where the lay world is quick to criticize and blame, correct handling becomes ritual as much as or even more than an art. If a teacher can prove that he has followed the ritual, the blame is shifted from himself to the miserable child or student; the failure can be and is put upon them.

Ritual is also strongly developed in occupations where there are great unavoidable risks, as in medicine. In such occupations the ritual may, however, be stronger in the second and third ranks of the institutions in which the work is done. Thus, in medicine, the physician, who stands at the top of the hierarchy, takes the great and final risks of decision and action. These risks are delegated to him, and he is given moral and legal protection in taking them. But the pharmacist, who measures out the prescribed doses, and the nurse, who carries out the ordered treatment, are the great observers of ritual in medicine. Pharmacists are said often to become ritualistic wipers and polishers, flecking infinitely small grains of dust from scales on which they are only going to weigh out two pounds of Paris green. The ritualistic punctiliousness of nurses and pharmacists is a kind of built-in shock-absorber against the possible mistakes of the physician. Indeed, in dramatizing their work, these second-rank professions explicitly emphasize their role as saviors of both patient and physician from the errors of the latter. And here again we get a hint of what may be the deeper function of the art, cult, and ritual of various occupations. They may provide a set of emotional and even organizational checks and balances against both the subjective and the objective risks of the trade.

I suspect that it is a rare occupation whose practitioners develop no criteria of good work, and no concept of mistake or failure other than simply defined successful conclusion of the given case or task. Usually the professional judgment will contain explicit or implicit references to an art, a cult, and a ritual. The function of the art, cult, and ritual is not so much to bring the individual case to an early successful conclusion as to relate it to the on-going occupation itself, and to the social system in which the work is done. In most occupations, a man can be judged as quite wrong by his colleagues for an action which the lay client might consider very successful indeed. The quack, defined functionally and not in evaluative terms, is the man who continues through time to please his customers but not his colleagues. On the contrary, a man may be considered by his colleagues to have done a piece of work properly and without error, even when the client may accuse him of error, mistake, or failure.

Part Three Urbanization: Living in Towns and Cities

What the sociologist means by 'urban problems' is usually something quite different from what the man in the street understands by that phrase. For the ordinary citizen, urban problems are troubles that occur to him because he lives in a town or city rather than in a village, for example, traffic jams, having to live in a slum, having freedom of action limited by by-laws and planning regulations, or inadequate local shopping facilities. For the sociologist, urban problems are those patterns of social behaviour among city dwellers which raise questions for sociological theory.

This definition itself is problematic and many sociologists would question it. Since the majority of the population of industrialized countries like Britain and the United States lives in cities and towns, one might argue that anything and everything that goes on in urban life is part of the subject-matter of urban sociology; in other words, that almost all sociology is urban sociology. But city life itself is characterized by the specialization of activities. Organizations and groups emerge concerned with the different areas of social life, religious, political, educational, etc., and sociology in its turn reflects this specialization in its own sub-divisions: the sociology of religion, political sociology, etc. Yet, if we adopt this approach, nothing seems to be left as a substantive field for a specifically 'urban' sociology.

One solution to this dilemma is to say that urban sociology is only concerned with the way space affects life in dense urban agglomerations. Thus studies of the 'journey to work', or housing densities, or neighbour relations in suburban housing estates, are all studies of the way social life is conditioned by spatial factors. Yet space has more than a physical or geographical dimension. Individuals, groups or organizations pursue their goals both within a physical environment and within an environment of other individuals, groups and organizations. This latter environment we may call 'social space'. It is the social relations between individuals, groups and organizations, arising out of their position in physical and social space that is the subject-matter of urban sociology.

Thus while, for example, industrial sociologists study factories, and educational sociologists study schools, the urban sociologist focuses on the inter-relations between the two; on the multiplex personal relationships and inter-organizational relations which develop as a result of the existence of factories and schools. It is this field of overlapping relations and interdependence which escapes the 'institutional' sociologies. This geographical and social interdependence can be seen in a variety of contexts. Organizations are represented on each other's committees and ruling bodies (for example, city councillors on the city police authority, church leaders on local neighbourhood-improvement committees); individuals and organizations are each other's clients (local newspaper, local businesses, and local customers; industrial firms and employment exchanges). Organizations and groups also have overlapping memberships (angling club and sports club, church congregation and political party). These relations of interdependence, and overlapping membership among organizations create multiplex relationships, that is, relationships in which two persons associate in more than one social context.

The individual's experience of the city, however, depends very much on his social position: it is never the same for any two men. With the increasing division of labour and specialization of occupations, most city dwellers work as employees in organizations – factories, shops or offices – where they have little influence. They are also clients and customers of specialized organizations such as shops, schools, cinemas, or hospitals, in which their power is again limited. The fact that most of these organizations are part of national chains, corporations, Ministries, or other organizational systems, reduces still further the influence of local participants, since major decisions are taken at the organizational headquarters.

City dwellers do have a wider sphere of choice, however, as to whether they will join 'voluntary associations', that is, churches, political parties, sports clubs and other leisure-time groupings, which display a minimum degree of formal organization. Yet 40 to 50 per cent of the population of Britain do not belong to any such association, and this large minority is largely working-class in occupation, has lower incomes, and is less well-educated. Conversely, those who do belong to one or more voluntary association tend to be middle-class, better-paid, and better-educated. Leaders within these associations are even more heavily concentrated within the ranks of the middle classes, and many of them occupy leadership positions in several organizations at once. But for the large majority of the population, the typical pattern of organizational involvement is a negative one of exclusion from voluntary associations (and from interlocking memberships in other associations), or of participation only at the lowest levels of authority, whether as workers in work-organizations, or as customers or clients in others.

It is the ranks of the 'excluded' that most migrants to the city go to swell. Urbanization is one of the main processes going on in modern society across the globe. The main source of the constant increase in urban populations is migration from the rural areas and from foreign countries.

As Hauser shows in Reading 12, urbanization in poor countries produces special problems different in kind from those generated by urbanization in rich countries. In underdeveloped countries, though cities and towns have flourished for centuries, even millennia, urban development took on new forms with the advent of colonialism. Coastal cities sprang up in response to new market-patterns, and became entrepôts through which raw materials were exported to the metropolitan territory of the colonial Power. New job-opportunities were largely created in the capital. But this was – and is – urbanization without industrialization, or 'over-urbanization'. One consequence is the growth of shanty-towns of unemployed or casually-employed persons who have emigrated to town from the poorer regions of the country. In rich countries, urbanization usually started at the same time as industrialization, and the problems of the unemployed, though severe, were not of the same order. Migration and urbanization remain important features of the growth of even the richer countries. The contemporary European economy involves the migration of millions of Turks, Spaniards, Algerians and Italians to richer countries such as West Germany and Switzerland. The heterogeneous ethnic and national composition of American cities is a further result of massive international migration over decades.

Rapid urbanization poses additional problems of social order, since it produces new and very diversified populations living in these cities. Many of them have only recently arrived there, and for these immigrants, the city represents only a part of their total life-experience. They may continue to adhere to the values and institutions of their former place of residence, and only interact with other migrants. The extent to which anonymity and isolation are inevitable features of 'urbanism as a way of life' varies considerably for migrants as between ethnic groups and between individuals. All of them, however, must experience the characteristic features of urban living to some extent, simply because they live there. They will be unable to entirely avoid entering situations in which the norms of behaviour are unknown to them, and which involve their interacting with individuals with whom they are unfamiliar. But there are ways in which migrants may endeavour, often with a high degree of success, to shield themselves against the full effects of urbanism. They may choose or even be forced to live in relatively segregated communities, in the extreme in 'ghettoes', where they work in establishments owned by their countrymen; they may choose their leisure-time associates exclusively from among their own group; and they may rely on each other for finding jobs. In these ways, a migrant may largely restrict his associates to those with whom he has common understandings. Conversely, a migrant who has no friends or relatives, and who is forced to rely on his own initiative in finding a job and a place to live, is more likely to experience the full variety of city life.

Migrants go to the city hoping for a better life; yet they find themselves part of the urban poor. Poverty is thus a relative concept. Men measure themselves against others; such groups are said to constitute their 'reference groups'. They may aspire to become members of such groups themselves. And once they succeed – if they ever do at all – they will develop new wants, and new conceptions of what constitutes 'wealth' and 'poverty'. Because of this variability and change in the meaning and measure of 'poverty' amongst different groups and over time, sociologists talk of 'relative deprivation'. The people who feel most deprived are not necessarily those with the lowest living-standards (for they may be resigned to their lot in one way or another), but those who do not accept its inevitability and who aim at something higher.

Poverty means more than low individual consumption: it becomes a 'way of life' for whole communities and classes. The poor have different values of the more affluent, and may even constitute a threat to the society's ruling groups. The existence of poverty in society thus has a different significance for the poor themselves and for the affluent. Nor is poverty a uniquely urban phenomenon. The peasantry throughout history have rarely had an enviable lot. But there are sizeable poor populations in most cities, too. In many cases, problems of poverty and problems of ethnic relations go hand in hand, because the poor population usually belongs to underprivileged ethnic groups. In the selection from *Poverty and Culture*, Valentine (Reading 13) examines existing conceptions of poverty, and shows how there is no single 'culture of poverty', but a variety of responses to the condition of being poor. Valentine argues further that the concept of 'culture' has principally been used to label patterns of human behaviour which diverge from those found in the milieux inhabited by the middle-class sociologist. Too often, the social life of the poor has been described as 'disorganized' – a label unsupported by the evidence. What we do find is not so much lack of organization as simply ways of organizing life different from our own.

'Difference', however, is by no means synonymous with 'disorganization', and although there is an abundance of literature on the tendency of middle-class people to join and dominate voluntary associational life, there is an equally rich literature on the tightly-integrated cultures of the poor. Misconceptions of the life of the poor as being 'disorganized' have had serious and negative consequences, for example, in the United States where it has often been assumed in 'poverty programmes' that what was needed was a 'stiffening' of a 'disorganized' lower-class culture (by the strengthening of family life for example). This has diverted attention from the structural causes of urban poverty, such as unequal occupational and educational opportunities. Moreover, even studies of 'shanty-town' life show people actively responding to their situation – creating informal local government, improving their dwellings, organizing themselves politically – as well as being organized and manipulated. They are not cut off from the rest of the world, nor are they inert.

Their activity may, however, take forms unacceptable to those who control such unequal societies, for whom the preservation of 'law and order' and the protection of property are major problems. The less fortunately placed often challenge the social rules which regulate the established order: they attempt to acquire the goods of society in ways that are illegal or at least illegitimate, or, more widely, adopt styles of life considered 'deviant' by those who set the dominant codes of society. In discussing the social context of crime, in an extract from her book *The Death and Life of Great American Cities,* Jacobs (Reading 14) argues that the crime-rate depends on street safety. But the social life of the city varies from one zone to another: the city's streets are used in very different ways by different users. The central and inner areas attract many strangers because of the varied and specialized services they offer. In such areas, the problem of street safety is, at base, a problem of ensuring order in situations where there are many strangers who do not share common norms of conduct. In suburbs and small towns, services available are less specialized and thus less likely to attract non-residents. Hence the problem of public order is a different one, since there will be greater mutual acquaintance among co-users of streets and other facilities, and hence more likelihood of a common code of behaviour in public places widely shared as part of common understandings about what is right and proper and what is not.

Jacobs thus argues that the control of crime and the security of urban life cannot be ensured primarily by the presence of police officers, but depends on informal surveillance by the citizenry itself. Planners can influence the amount of surveillance through their control of land-use. If the street is planned to attract a variety of users, with different time-schedules, for example, residents, shoppers, pub-goers, cinema-goers, their coming and going will provide 'eyes' to watch the street, and this activity will itself be a reason for watching the streets. Public control is thus something which emerges simply as a by-product of the use of the street for everyday purposes. But if each citizen's pair of eyes is an unofficial agency of social control, it can only be so insofar as it be backed up by public opinion.

The absence of a sense of community identity and responsibility, and of shared codes of behaviour, even where attempts have been made to 'engineer' it, has been particularly widely reported in a variety of studies which have examined dissatisfaction with new housing estates. In the extract from *Societies in the Making* (Reading 15), Jennings discusses what aspects of life in new housing estates, and what aspects of the transition from old to new areas provoke these feelings: whether it is because many residents did not choose to live there; because there are great social differences among them; because contacts with members of the extended family are more difficult; because the 'corner shop' is replaced by a single, impersonal shopping centre, and so forth.

The nature of the informal relationships that grow up among co-residents is obviously very important for their feelings of satisfaction. There has been a long tradition in urban sociological studies which stresses the absence of strong, diffuse, intimate relationships among city-dwellers, and which has led to an under-emphasis and an under-valuing of the role of weak, segmental, restricted relationships. Yet the number of people with whom the former kind of relationship can be maintained is limited, because of the time and energy they call for and because they involve a high degree of commitment and of mutual obligation. Weak relationships, however, involve only light obligations and are therefore less burdensome permitting greater choice in whether to deepen the relationship or not; they can be maintained by quick conversations on a limited number of subjects of general interest. Yet they are important, because they help people order their relationships with others by providing a minimum basis of knowledge about them, thus facilitating the emergence of local leaders, since knowledge is a basis of trust and hence of the acceptance of leaders. Such relationships also allow vital, and not so vital, information to be passed around among the residents of an area about local events, customs and personalities, in the form of 'gossip' for instance. Such talk embodies local codes of values about how people should behave. Lastly, weak relationships create links between people who do not have enough in common to sustain more complex relationships of friendship, and indirect links between people scattered over a geographical area, who lack any direct ties. Weak relationships are probably more important than strong ones in urban situations of this kind.

Jennings (Reading 15) argues that the development of sets of weak ties of this kind was hindered by some of the physical characteristics of the housing estate she studied. Shops and public facilities were centrally located, so that using them meant longer journeys, and hence less frequent use. The wider catchment area of the shops meant that many users were strangers to each other, the reverse of the situation in the corner shop in older urban areas. The chance of meeting neighbours was thus much reduced, and with it the chance of developing networks of informal ties of acquaintanceship among neighbours. The absence of voluntary associations on the estate was a further reason for the failure of weak ties to proliferate as such associations are an important source of weak ties. Jenning's comments on the efforts to develop a Community Association, and to find acceptable leaders for it, is another indication of the importance of weak ties.

Housing estates are one expression of the demand for space generated by the expansion of the city into surrounding areas as the urbanization process takes place. But pressure on land within the city has increased too, and high buildings, whether office-blocks or flats, have become a common part of the urban landscape. In recent years high flats have come to be seen, not as the ideal communities planners imagined, but as the cause of various social problems for their residents: loneliness, restricted play-space for children, delinquency, vandalism, etc. Statements to this effect are often made by magistrates, councillors, police officers, church leaders, social workers and others whose position in urban organizations lends authority to their claims.

The extract from 'Living off the ground' (Reading 16) is from a study generated by the recognition that there is a considerable social distance, both in terms of ideas and values, and of housing experience and preferences, between planners and architects and the people they plan and design for. The study aimed at providing a knowledge of popular preferences and values about housing, and shows that, contrary to public opinion, only a minority of residents of high flats are unhappy with them. The most important correlate of preference for high flats was the respondent's stage in the life-cycle: there were large differences in attitude between old people, and families with young children.

Studies of this type ('user' studies) have many limitations. Apart from problems concerning the representativeness of the sample, or of the value of interview data in general (for example, the interviewer may be perceived as someone who can change the respondent's situation), measures of satisfaction are inherently problematic. A person may hold very high aspirations, or he may adjust his aspirations downwards 'realistically', lessening his relative deprivation. It is difficult, if not impossible, to know what level of aspirations a respondent has in mind when he answers questions about his satisfaction. Secondly, people have very different intentions for the future and these colour their answers. Some may intend to move shortly to somewhere better, and thus see their present accommodation as transitional; others may intend to spend the rest of their lives there. Thirdly, questions concerning satisfaction often assume a degree of 'crystallization' of attitudes on the part of respondents which they may not possess. For example, dissatisfied replies to specific questions about the flat, lifts or play facilities may reflect a general dissatisfaction which has its origin outside the immediate physical environment. (The article below mentions a case of this kind.) Life in high flats, then, is a difficult subject about which to obtain standardized and comparable measures of satisfaction.

The basic reason for this is that living anywhere involves a whole complex of experiences. The social experience of high flat dwellers is thus the resultant of a number of factors operating at once, only one of which is the height of the flat itself. Other factors affecting satisfaction might be the husband's occupation; whether the wife works or not; the age of their children; the proximity of kin; whether the flat was chosen or not; previous housing experience, etc. If we were able to separate out the effects of the various factors involved and assign weights to them it would become possible to test the hypothesis that it is the physical environment of the high flat as such which is responsible for the various social phenomena attributed to it, but the problems involved in the design of the research of this sort are considerable. (For an attempt to draw together and assess the literature on this subject, see J. and R. Darke's *Health and Environment: High Flats*.)

An alternative approach would be to identify a set of characteristics which occur together fairly frequently, and which include living in high flats. For example, low socio-economic position and restricted choice of housing situation, previous residence in slum-clearance areas and rehousing due to redevelopment, higher rent, kin living at a distance, and reserved attitude towards immediate neighbours, etc. This approach would draw attention to the overall situation of the high flat dweller, rather than to his type of housing alone. These variables which are regularly linked to living in high flats would be taken together, and their joint action examined rather than simply regarding the high flat as the cause of problems.

The role of the planner is one final and important theme which emerges from several of the extracts. The planner sees his contribution to the shaping of the city as that of a specialist possessing certain technical skills. Yet there is a wide variety of ideologies held by different planners. For some, planning means improving the balance of land-use, with the concomitant belief that a free market in land and property would produce an inferior pattern of land-use: the degeneration and commercialization of the environment. For others, control of land-use is seen as a means of shaping social behaviour, for example, building 'communities'.

The planner has some control over physical and social space. Individuals, groups and organizations will be affected by his actions. Whether they in turn will make known their views depends on the organizational and individual links they can activate with planning bodies and with individual planners. In the planning of new housing estates, local churches, social welfare agencies, and breweries may be consulted. In city-centre development, existing large businesses, credit institutions, and property developers are likely to make known their interests. Within the local authority itself, there will be pressures from other departments, such as the City Treasury, with its interest in the rating revenue, as well as national directives. In these circumstances, planning decisions may reflect and encourage market forces rather than countering them.

The residents of slum-clearance areas, on the other hand, are unlikely to have many personal ties with planners, and the organizations which are consulted on their behalf are often outside groups of professionals with a common definition of the slum as a 'problem area', rather than groups of local residents. Thus the influence of individuals and organizations on planning decisions is highly unequal. The result is that planning comes to resemble a tug-of-war between competing interest-groups rather than a cool, dispassionate scientific exercise.

And now that large-scale developments are increasingly taking place on regional or even national levels, with the development of motorways, airports and rapid transit systems, new interest groups are threatened. The suburban middle classes and rural landowners are now involved and threatened by planning decisions. It is likely that their integration with local government bodies and officials, through personal ties and organizational links, will create new pressures on planning decisions, and possibly lead to the emergence of new structures, embodying more public participation, for the overall management of the environment.

12 Philip Hauser

Problems of Rapid Urbanization

Excerpt from Philip Hauser, 'The social, economic and technological problems of rapid urbanization', in B. F. Hoselitz and W. E. Moore (eds.), *Industrialization and Society*, UNESCO-Mouton, 1963, pp. 207–15.

The most visible consequence of over-urbanization and rapid rates of urban growth is the decadence of the urban environment in under-developed areas. The physical city is characterized by a large proportion of shanty-towns and tenement slums; inadequate urban services, including housing, water supply, sewerage, utilities, and transport; uncontrolled land use; excessive population densities; deficient educational and recreational facilities and inefficient commercial and marketing services. Rapid urbanization in the underdeveloped areas is accompanied by not only a defective but, also, by a deteriorating urban environment. It is estimated that, in Latin America alone, some four or five million families live in urban shanty-towns and slums. The miserable physical conditions of cities create great pressure for 'social' instead of 'productive' investments. However, many of the public housing and physical improvement programs which have been undertaken in such areas have necessarily tended to benefit families with moderate incomes rather than to meet the needs of the lowest-income families – the residents of the shanty-towns and slums.

Of course the underdeveloped nations are very aware of the need for city and regional, as well as national planning. But the city planner in the underdeveloped country is confronted with insuperable difficulties. These stem largely from low income levels; from rapid population growth, including hordes of immigrants from rural areas who are ill-adapted to urban living; from inadequate urban infrastructure development – all in all, from a bewildering array of needs, each of which seems to have first priority.

Although urban agglomerations of the size of Western cities are to be found, the physical amenities associated with such in the West have not yet developed – at least, not for the mass population. The amenities of urban existence are available only to very small fractions of the total urban population. It is in the impact on the already inadequate urban physical plant that the rapid rate of urbanization produces some of its more serious consequences.

Economically developed areas

Economically advanced urban centers also have acute physical problems. Although these vary from nation to nation, we may focus here on those most apparent in the United States. The urban plant of the United States – residential, commercial, industrial, and governmental – has been constructed rapidly in response to rapid urbanization. Land-use patterns have been largely the product of market forces which have caused remarkable physical development but have also permitted swift obsolescence and decay. Much of the contemporary urban plant in the United States today is blighted or threatened with blight. Although the physical plant of cities in the West in general, and in the United States in particular, is incomparably superior to that in the underdeveloped areas, Western *cities* include, by Western standards, relatively large proportions of substandard housing and are pockmarked by slums. The urban United States has only recently begun to try to cope with these physical problems on a major scale, through programs of 'urban renewal', public housing, and extended efforts at city planning. The worst slums in many of the cities in the United States have now been razed; but the larger portion of the task of urban renewal still lies ahead. Moreover, it is doubtful that urban renewal is, at the present time, advancing as rapidly as the process of decay. In the United States, as in some other Western countries, it has yet to be demonstrated that the urban plant can be maintained – i.e., that blight and slum can be prevented. There can be little doubt that problems of urban renewal and urban maintenance are made much more difficult by continued rapid growth.

Rapid growth is also aggravating acute difficulties of circulation in cities in the United States. Although the automobile has been a leading factor in the growth of the urban center, it is beginning to strangle the city with congestion, and is causing large portions of it to be converted into highways and parking space. Rapid growth is augmenting the 'commuter crisis' and is forcing metropolitan areas to re-examine the role of mass transportation in the circulation of persons and goods. This paper cannot elaborate on the physical problems of economically advanced cities; but there *are* such problems, and these problems are aggravated by rapid urbanization.

The city represents not only a new form of economic organization and a changed physical environment. It also is a profoundly modified social order affecting man's conduct and thought. Urbanization produces the city as a physical and economic artifact, and also produces 'urbanism as a way of life'. The size, density, and heterogeneity of population – aspects of 'social morphology' – affect the nature, intensity, and frequency of contact, and, therefore, influence the nature of the process of socialization and human nature itself. The city is a type of mutation in culture that has far-reaching effects on social structure and process and on social institutions, including the structure and function of government. The transition from pre-urban to urban living necessarily involves frictions, which are manifested in social and personal problems. Rapid urbanization exacerbates these frictions.

The effects of living in large urban agglomerations have frequently been treated in the sociological literature. A number of frameworks for the analysis of the impact of urbanization on the social order and on the person have emerged. Among these are the distinction between 'organic' and 'mechanical' solidarity; between 'community' and 'society'; and between 'folk' and 'urban' ways of life. The chief effects of urban living on the personal level are, probably, discernible in the changed nature of interpersonal relations and in the relative flexibility of personal patterns of behavior. On the cultural and social level, they are to be found in the changed nature of the forces making for cohesion, in the changed genesis and function of social institutions, and in the changed structure and role of government.

On the personal level, contacts in the urban setting become secondary, segmental, and utilitarian, rather than primary, integral, and sentimental as in the traditional social order. Personality tends to change from a relatively rigid structure molded by the traditional social heritage to more fluid flexible patterns, arising from the necessity to exercise choice and from rationalism in behavior, as the hold of tradition loosens and new urban problems emerge. On the social level, cohesion in the urban social order becomes a function of interdependence engendered by increased specialization and division of labor; it is no longer the product of the constraint of convention in a relatively homogeneous and closed traditional order. Social institutions in the urban setting become 'enacted' rather than 'crescive' as older functions become attenuated or disappear and new instrumentalities arise to cope with unprecedented situations and problems. Even the basic social institutions – the family and the church – are subjected to forces which modify their structure, their role, and their hold on the behavior of the person.

In the urban setting, the role of government is one of increasing interventionism as organizational complexity and interdependence increase. In the West, the transition from a feudal to an industrialized and urbanized order has been characterized by the emergence of complex formal organization – bureaucracy – not only in government, but also in business, labor, voluntary associations, and virtually all organized aspects of the mass society.

In this macrocosmic consideration of the impact of urbanization, we must emphasize that the transition from the traditional to the urban society does not proceed in an orderly and synchronized manner. The process of urbanization and its impact proceed with different tempos in different sectors of the society and among the several nations. In fact, one of the basic social problems of urbanization is to be found in the coexistence, at any one time, of different stages and of differential impacts of urbanization on the social order. Moreover, the more rapid the rate of urbanization, the greater becomes the probability that divers sectors of the social order will be characterized by anachronistic relationships.

Underdeveloped areas

These general elements provide a framework for more specific manifestations of the social problems associated with rapid urbanization. The acute as well as chronic aspects of social problems that result from rapid urbanization are, perhaps, most discernible in the adjustment of in-migrants to urban living. The rural in-migrant to the city is typically from a relatively homogeneous origin. In the city, he is confronted with a bewildering and almost incomprehensible vastness and heterogeneity. He usually lives for some time with his fellow villagers or relatives and only gradually becomes accommodated to city life. He must adapt to new and unfamiliar ways of making a living; a money economy; regular working hours; the absence of warm family living; large numbers of impersonal contacts with other human beings; new forms of recreation; and a quite different physical setting, often involving new kinds of housing, sanitation, traffic congestion, and noise. One of the greatest adjustment problems centers around the transition from a subsistence to a monetary economy, and dependence on a job for subsistence.

Furthermore, the in-migrant often finds his area of first settlement is the shanty town, in which the decadence of the underdeveloped urban environment is manifest in its most extreme form. Consequently, superimposed on problems of adjustment there may be severe problems of health and nutrition, and of extreme poverty and squalor in living conditions. In such a setting, the in-migrant frequently displays personal disorganization as the subjective aspect of social disorganization. It is in the in-migrant family that the greatest incidences of personal and social pathology are found – delinquency, crime, prostitution, mental illness, alcoholism, drug addiction, etc.

Another element contributes to the social problems and is source of severe problems for the economy as well. This is the fact that rural in-migrant workers often lack rudimentary skills for industrial work, possess high rates of illiteracy, and are otherwise ill-prepared for city living. Throughout the underdeveloped countries, the need to increase literacy and to provide minimum vocational training for urban employment is acute. In fact, the provision of adequate educational and vocational training, both to the in-migrant and to the more permanent inhabitant of urban places, is among the most critical social problems which confront the underdeveloped areas.

Rapid urbanization is accompanied by increasing tempos of cultural, social, and personal change. A number of scholars have maintained that underdeveloped areas with non-Western cultures possess ideologies and value systems that tend to resist change in general and, therefore, changes of the type induced by urbanization. A rapid rate of urbanization, as contrasted with a slow one, conceivably increases the frictions of transition from non-Western to urban (and presumably Western) value systems. It is, of course, disputable whether Western values identified with urbanism as a way of life are an antecedent or a consequence of industrialization and urbanization; and whether they are the only values consonant with urban living. Conceivably, the difference between non-Western outlooks produces different kinds of 'urban mentality' and interpersonal and social relations in the urban setting. Whatever the answer to this question may be, it *is* true that rapid urbanization increases the tensions and frictions of adjustment in value systems from pre-urban ways of life.

Also among the more pressing social problems in the urban setting are the series constituting 'the population problem'. As dramatically demonstrated in Ceylon, contemporary public health methods permit startlingly rapid decreases in mortality to be effected in short periods of time, while fertility rates and aggregate product remain relatively unchanged. In consequence, the underdeveloped areas of the world are just beginning the type of 'population explosion' which the economically advanced nations have undergone over the past three centuries. Since the capacity to decrease mortality rates is growing more rapidly, the population-explosion potential of the underdeveloped areas is of considerably greater magnitude. Urban growth rates are fed by immigration from rural areas, as well as by the natural increase resulting from lower death rates; but the large streams of migration from rural to urban areas are a function of the national explosions in the underdeveloped nations. Rapid rates of urbanization could, in the longer run, contribute to the solution of the population problem in so far as urbanization can accelerate literacy, change value systems, and prepare the populace for limiting fertility.

Another group of serious problems created or augmented by rapid rates of urbanization are those of internal disorder, political unrest, and governmental instability fed by mass misery and frustration in the urban setting. The facts that the differences between the 'have' and 'have not' nations, and between the 'have' and 'have not' peoples within nations, have become 'felt differences', and that we are experiencing a 'revolution in expectations', have given huge urban population agglomerations an especially incendiary and explosive character. In the domestic and international settings in which many underdeveloped areas find themselves, huge and rapidly swelling urban populations constitute supersensitive tinderboxes with explosive potential. Newspaper headlines of the last few months provide adequate documentation of this observation.

Another major social problem that is precipitated by rapidly increasing urbanization is the task of planning and devising programs designed to deal with urban social problems. Planning agencies, health and welfare services, educational, vocational training, and recreational facilities, etc., are either inadequate or non-existent in many of the underdeveloped nations. In particular, agencies for receiving and dealing with the problems of the in-migrant are inadequate or non-existent. Planning and programming the solution of social problems entail difficult decisions involving national planning, in general. They involve, among other things, the complex task of maximizing the participation of the urban dwellers themselves by motivating them to play a major role in helping to solve their own problems.

Economically advanced areas

Rapid urban growth is not without its accompaniment of social problems in the economically advanced nations. Although hardly assuming a magnitude comparable with the social problems of the underdeveloped areas, rapid urbanization in the United States, for example, is aggravating or creating a number of social problems. Among these are the problem of inter-group relations arising from the changing composition of newcomers to American cities; the problem of providing urban services; the problems of local governmental structure; the problem of the role of government in general. This listing is not by any means exhaustive; but it may suffice to illustrate such problems in the more advanced nations.

In the United States, rapid urbanization has historically meant both larger and more heterogeneous urban population. During the nineteenth and twentieth centuries, the United States was the foremost recipient of emigrants, mainly from Europe. Immigration contributed materially to urban, as well as to total national, growth. Rapid rates of urbanization were accompanied by increased diversity of ethnic groups in American cities and, therefore, by difficult problems of adjustment incident to the acculturation and assimilation of foreign stock. This process, by no means finished yet, has created many melting-pot problems in urban areas. The difficulties of these intergroup relations have, in recent years, been in part augmented, and in part replaced, by the adjustment problems of great streams of internal migrants who, since the passage of restrictive immigration legislation, have replaced the immigrants who formerly fed urban growth in the United States. The in-migrants include white and Negro rural populations and, in some cases, appreciable numbers of Puerto Ricans as well. The adjustment problems of these in-migrants, largely unprepared for urban living, are compounded, in the cases of the Negro and Puerto Rican, by the racial differences which make them more conspicuous than was the white immigrant.

At present rapid urbanization in the United States involves the absorption of new streams of in-migrants with difficult problems of adjustment to urban life. The in-migrant to the American city, like the immigrants before him and like the in-migrant to the city in underdeveloped areas, also experiences the highest incidence of personal and social disorganization. Although the social problems engendered by streams of newcomers to American cities are not so intransigent as those in underdeveloped areas, they are by no means insignificant. The difficulties of intergroup relations – especially that of white–Negro relations – are particularly troublesome; and they are being greatly aggravated by the high rate of in-migration and by rapid urban growth.

As American metropolitan populations continue to grow explosively, it has become increasingly difficult to provide adequate urban services. Although the problems are of an entirely different order from those in the underdeveloped nations, urban services – including water, sanitation, drainage, police and fire protection, courts, education, and recreation – have not kept pace with growing population in many areas.

Explosive urban growth has created many problems in local government structure and relationships. The structure of local government inherited from the eighteenth and nineteenth centuries is evincing increasing strain under the pressure of metropolitan area problems. This is manifested by the growing number of elections about consolidated, or metropolitan, forms of government; and by the emergence of special agencies for dealing with specific metropolitan planning or administrative functions. Rapid urbanization in the United States is tending to add to pressure for 'home rule', and to aggravate 'upstate-downstate' conflict. It is also accelerating the trend toward direct relationship between the federal and the city governments, wherein state governments are by-passed.

Finally, this metropolitan growth in the United States is unquestionably a major factor in the proliferation and expansion of government functions – on the federal and the state, as well as the local, levels. For metropolitanism, as a way of life, is synonymous with increased complexity and interdependence of living, and necessarily engenders greater interventionism.

Concluding observations

Forces now in motion point to the future increased industrialization and increased urbanization of the world as a whole, and particularly of the economically underdeveloped nations. In their urban centers, the social, economic, and technological problems that accompany urban living are already acute; and they are becoming even more inflamed by the accelerated pace of urbanization. Important among the forces contributing to this acceleration are explosive total population growth, forcing the migration of population from the impoverished rural countryside to urban centers; and the efforts of underdeveloped nations themselves to induce economic development by means of increased industrialization.

The patterns of urbanization in the underdeveloped nations have not followed the Western lines, and are not likely to do so in the future. The differences in the patterns of urbanization and the nature of the problems which emerge are, in large measure, attributable to the differences between present domestic and world situations and those which obtained when Western nations were first experiencing industrial and urban transformation. Some of these differences arise from the fact that in many underdeveloped areas, urban development is largely an outgrowth of colonialism and thus to a great extent reflects the troubled conditions of postwar adjustments and newly won independence, or chronic political unrest and governmental instability. Others derive from the extent to which central planning and government interventionism, as contrasted with the play of free market forces, are necessary in the underdeveloped areas. There are contrasts between the state of industrial and agricultural technology in the twentieth century and that in the eighteenth and nineteenth centuries. There are differences in the ratio of population to resources, and in the availability of open land for surplus population emigration. The basic outlooks and value systems in the underdeveloped nations differ from those of the West. Finally, there are extremely important differences between the total world situation – economic, social, and political – at the present time and that during the eighteenth and nineteenth centuries.

Despite these differences, however, it may be anticipated that the urban environment in the underdeveloped nations, as in the West, will produce economic, social, physical, and personal changes. They will not necessarily take the same forms as they did in the economically advanced countries; but changes there will be – and, accompanying them, will be the frictions of change.

It must be emphasized, in closing, that the total impact of the city is far from a negative one. Urbanization, and particularly rapid rates of urbanization, precipitate many economic, social, and technological problems. However, it is also true that the city, and urbanism as a way of life, have paved the way for the great achievements of civilization. They have done more than to advance technology, increase productivity, and raise levels of living. In addition, they have stimulated intellectual and cultural developments of the type represented by the universities, the development of science, the creation of new art forms, and, in general, the increased mastery of man over nature. Hence, although rapid urbanization is producing acute problems, it is undoubtedly challenging the ingenuity of man to find solutions for these problems.

13 C. A. Valentine

Poverty and Culture

Excerpts from C. A. Valentine, *Culture and Poverty*, University of Chicago Press, 1968, pp. 1–24 and 48–82.

The concept of culture, as used in the parlance of the human sciences, arose from a great human confrontation. The idea of culture was one of the principal intellectual outgrowths of the worldwide meeting between the expansionist West and exotic non-Western peoples. The confrontation began with the contacts of exploration and matured into the relationships of empire. From this experience the West derived a growing need to find order in its increasing knowledge of immensely varied human lifeways. As the emerging science of anthropology developed the culture concept, it thereby provided an important means to this end of discovering order in variation [. . .]

Culture in the anthropological sense has come to mean, most simply, the entire way of life followed by a people. The bearers of a culture are understood to be a collectivity of individuals such as a society or a community. One important implication of this formulation is that culture and society are not the same, though of course they are closely related. The cultural patterns that shape the behavior of people in groups should not be confused with the structure of institutions or social systems, even though each is obviously dependent on the other. A classical anthropological definition of culture is 'that complex whole which includes knowledge, belief, art, morals, laws, customs, and any other capabilities and habits acquired by man as a member of society'. A more modern definition refers to the 'organization of experience' shared by members of a community, including 'their standards for perceiving, predicting, judging, and acting'. This means that culture includes all socially standardized ways of seeing and thinking about the world; of understanding relationships among people, things, and events; of establishing preferences and purposes; of carrying out actions and pursuing goals. In a general sense, then, culture consists of the rules which generate and guide behavior. More specifically, the culture of a particular people or other social body is everything that one must learn to behave in ways that are recognizable, predictable, and understandable to those people [. . .]

Today we are witnessing another great human confrontation, comparable in some ways to that which produced the modern idea of culture. In the mid-twentieth century, the more privileged and comfortable strata of Western society are finding themselves confronted as never before by the poor at the bottom of their social order. While present interest tends to focus on this confrontation as it occurs within the developed societies of the West, particularly the United States, this is becoming a universal phenomenon as the modern, urban, industrial social order becomes worldwide.

As a result of this new situation, there is again a demand for systematic knowledge about groups or categories of humanity to which relatively little attention was previously given. Again, there is also a need for concepts to render this knowledge coherent and to help shape both public attitudes and public policy. The principal result so far is the well-known idea of a 'culture of poverty'. Though less well known popularly, similar and closely related conceptions abound in the technical literature: 'lower-class culture'; 'low-income life styles'; 'lower-class Negro culture'; 'culture of unemployment'; 'culture of the uninvolved'; 'culture of violence'; 'slum culture'; and even 'dregs culture'. Indeed, these labels are part of what amounts to an intellectual fad of attributing a 'culture' or 'subculture' to almost any social category [. . .]

In the work of E. Franklin Frazier there are many contributions to the developing idea of class culture. Chief among these is the theme of disorganization in the life of the urban black poor. This image is developed virtually to the point of denying that the Negro masses in American cities live by any coherent cultural system at all [. . .]

Frazier creates an image of the black poor as so abysmally disorganized and so hopelessly infected with social pathologies that they even lack public opinion, social control, or community institutions. This appears to be a major source of one of the most prominent and logically confused themes in the later conceptions of 'lower-class culture' and the 'culture of poverty'. While these constructs are labeled and treated as 'cultures', they are nevertheless presented as so lacking in basic elements of organization universal among human lifeways that they stand quite outside any usual definition of the term culture. Thus life in the culture of the poor takes on the paradoxical meaning of life without culture, or at least without major elements previously understood as necessary aspects of culture [. . .]

An essential element in Frazier's reasoning is one that is perpetuated by later thinkers. This is a direct logical leap from social statistics, which are deviant in terms of middle-class norms, to a model of disorder and instability. Such reasoning effectively eliminates consideration of possible cultural forms that, in spite of differing from Frazier's assumed standard, might have their own order and functions. For example, an implicit assumption is continually evident that female family heads receive no significant support from any social network. Yet there is no indication of the careful study that would be required to determine whether or not female-headed households maintain functional relationships with nonresident male consorts, maternal or paternal kinsmen, other relatives by blood or marriage, or indeed any other sources of support except welfare agencies.

Frazier, like his successors, fails to follow up leads in his data that might help to clarify issues otherwise glossed over. The reader searches in vain for any investigation into the role of the temporarily absent males who upset social workers by returning to their families. Have these men been in communication with the households to which they return? Are they links in a wider network? Or what? Frazier does not attend to such empirical questions, preferring instead to cover everything with the blanket concept of disorganization. It is difficult to avoid the impression that this conceptualization admits only two possibilities: order on a conventional middle-class model, or disorder [...]

For an anthropologist or anyone who appreciates the anthropological approach, turning to Lewis' writings on the 'culture of poverty' after reviewing many sociological works on 'lower-class culture' is likely to be a refreshing experience. Lewis is an anthropologist who knows what the theoretical concept of culture has meant in the works of his professional colleagues. He has employed ethnographic methods in much of his own research. It is clear that he shares many of the positive values associated with the idea of culture. Reading the published results of his field work with Mexicans and Puerto Ricans, where his notion of the 'culture of poverty' is presented, one often feels that he came to know some of these people very well and achieved an empathetic rapport with them [...]

We have seen that in the social science literature there is a considerable emphasis on a heavily negative approach to the behaviors and values that are thought to be distinctive of the lower class or the poor. Scarcely a description can be found that does not dwell on the noxiousness, pathology, distortion, disorganization, instability, or incompleteness of poverty culture as compared with life of the middle classes. Lewis has taken some pains to dissociate himself from this orientation, in its more simplistic forms at least. Discussing his view of the 'culture of poverty', he writes as follows:

This view directs attention to the fact that the culture of poverty in modern nations is not only a matter of economic deprivation, of disorganization or of the absence of something. It is also something positive and provides some rewards without which the poor could hardly carry on [. . .] That is, the core of culture is its positive adaptive function. I, too, have called attention to some of the adaptive mechanisms in the culture of poverty. . . .

In spite of all this, however, Lewis' description of poverty culture runs very heavily to such negative traits as 'lack of effective participation', 'minimum of organization', 'absence of childhood', 'high incidence of the abandonment of wives and children', and 'a high incidence of maternal deprivation, of orality, of weak ego structure, confusion of sexual identification, a lack of impulse control . . . little ability to defer gratification and to plan for the future . . . and a high tolerance for psychological pathology of all sorts'. This is, of course, much the same list of disabilities found in standard sociological descriptions of 'lower-class culture' [. . .]

None of the various works focused on poverty culture show, either in manifest method or in reported data, the fully rounded ethnographic approach employed by Lewis in earlier research, such as his descriptions of the Mexican village Tepozotlan. In these earlier studies, as in most ethnographic accounts, family life is only one among many equally important aspects of social existence: the economic system, the wider social structure, the political order from village to nation, the individual life cycle, and ritual and ideology [. . .]

In the poverty-culture studies, on the contrary, the focus is so restricted to the family that the social system as a whole and its culture patterns become little more than a shadowy backdrop for personal and household intimacies. There is no doubt that this orientation is perfectly legitimate for some kinds of research. What this approach cannot adequately support, however, is the portrayal of a culture, a whole way of life. If Lewis presented these works as studies of family life among the poor, there would be no quarrel of this sort with his method or his selection of evidence. He could then quite properly leave the broader problem of the whole culture of the poor to other research workers, or perhaps to later works of his own. The serious weakness of these studies as they stand is that, in them, Lewis has insisted on returning to the cultural level of portrayal and analysis without presenting evidence adequately supporting his abstract model at this level. The wider importance of this weakness stems from the fact that this very notion of a *culture* of poverty has so greatly influenced public knowledge, attitudes, and policies [. . .]

The twin concepts, 'culture of poverty' and 'lower-class culture', have essentially identical implications in relation to major issues of public attitudes and policies. The salient common element is the insistence on absolute priority for doing away with the perceived behavioral, or 'cultural', distinctions of the lower class. When one asks what could be the source of this insistence, a likely possibility seems to be a conviction that the behavior of the unworthy poor is dangerous and threatening. Is this anything other than a defensive projection of the values and interests of the middle class? [. . .]

A minority of scholars have been expressing doubts for some time about the prevailing formulations of class cultures and poverty culture. Several books appearing in the middle 1960s may herald a general reassessment of these formulations. None of the works so far available deals with the whole problem. None has yet presented a full-scale alternative intellectual framework. Nevertheless, several have raised searching questions about the supposed cultural distinctiveness of disadvantaged communities and collectivities as presently understood by social scientists and others.

One important source of such queries is the recent research by Kenneth Clark and his associates in Harlem. This work was conceived as a study of disorganization and powerlessness. One finds in it some of the same problems of inappropriate methods and inadequate data repeatedly identified as other studies were discussed in earlier chapters. At the same time, however, certain key elements found in earlier research and writings are absent here. The classbound moralistic derogation of the Frazier tradition is one missing element. Another is the device of wrapping up the whole problem of lower-class life in the neat conceptual package of a self-contained cultural system which distracts attention from the impingements and impositions of the wider society. Being relatively free of these conceptual blinders enables Clark to raise some challenging issues [. . .]

Yet something important is still lacking. A major deficiency is that the Harlem community is still not presented in terms of its *own* social order, cultural idiom, or life style [. . .]

The question whether this community might have its own distinct forms of social organization has hardly been posed and could not be answered from the kinds of data presented. The comparative structuring of the evidence insures that the distinctiveness of social statistics from Harlem will be interpreted only as departures from general American norms. Thus the possibility of sociocultural coherence specific to Central Harlem is automatically ruled out by the frame of reference within which data are gathered and analyzed. It is as if a scholar set about describing and interpreting the distinctiveness of American society simply by comparing social statistics from the United States with norms for England or for the English-speaking world in general, using the known forms of British social structure as the standard of social order. Such a scholar would be bound to find many indications of 'disorganization' in his American data. If he were a sensitive and humane individual, he might visit the United States to interview some of its citizens and discuss the 'problems' and 'conditions' of their social existence with them. This would probably give him further insights into the 'instability' of American society, and some of these insights might be valid. Yet if our imagined scholar did no more than this, he might well leave the United States without ever grasping the fact that America has some forms of social order that do not exist in England or elsewhere in the English-speaking world.

While one hopes they do not exist in the world of serious scholarship, such commentators and visitors to the United States are of course not totally figments of fantasy. There are at least two major reasons why they are a vanishing type. First, America is obviously much too wealthy, powerful, and successful to be dismissed simply as an unstable deviant off-shoot of British society. Second, the unique patterns of American society have long been extensively portrayed and interpreted in a huge body of art and scholarship that itself is both a creation of American culture and part of a developing international culture. By contrast, of course, the Harlems within America are neither wealthy nor powerful in the American context, and they are only beginning to portray themselves or communicate their own patterns through media that are understandable to the outside world of white, middle-class America. Perhaps this helps to explain how commentators and visitors from the larger America, including some who are both sophisticated intellectually and genuinely sympathetic toward the denizens of the 'Dark Ghetto', persist in viewing this ghetto in terms of external criteria alone. In a different but not irrelevant context, ethnography has proved the key to understanding the internal coherence of other 'deviant' social systems. Hence the thesis of this essay – that America needs an ethnography of its poor and its minorities.

Further reading

CLARK, K. B. (1965), *Dark Ghetto, Dilemmas of Social Power*, Gollancz.
FRAZIER, E. FRANKLIN (1939), *The Negro Family in the United States*, University of Chicago Press.
FRAZIER, E. FRANKLIN (1957), *Black Bourgeoisie*, Free Press.
LEWIS, O. (1966), *La Vida*, Random House.

14 Jane Jacobs

Eyes on the Street

Excerpts from Jane Jacobs, *The Death and Life of Great American Cities*, Cape, 1962, pp. 29–39.

Streets in cities serve many purposes besides carrying vehicles, and city sidewalks – the pedestrian parts of the streets – serve many purposes besides carrying pedestrians. These uses are bound up with circulation but are not identical with it and in their own right they are at least as basic as circulation to the proper workings of cities.

A city sidewalk by itself is nothing. It is an abstraction. It means something only in conjunction with the buildings and other uses that border it, or border other sidewalks very near it. The same might be said of streets, in the sense that they serve other purposes besides carrying wheeled traffic in their middles. Streets and their sidewalks, the main public places of a city, are its most vital organs. Think of a city and what comes to mind? Its streets. If a city's streets look interesting, the city looks interesting; if they look dull, the city looks dull.

More than that, and here we get down to the first problem, if a city's streets are safe from barbarism and fear, the city is thereby tolerably safe from barbarism and fear. When people say that a city, or a part of it, is dangerous or is a jungle what they mean primarily is that they do not feel safe on the sidewalks.

But sidewalks and those who use them are not passive beneficiaries of safety or helpless victims of danger. Sidewalks, their bordering uses, and their users, are active participants in the drama of civilization versus barbarism in cities. To keep the city safe is a fundamental task of a city's streets and its sidewalks.

This task is totally unlike any service that sidewalks and streets in little towns or true suburbs are called upon to do. Great cities are not like towns, only larger. They are not like suburbs, only denser. They differ from towns and suburbs in basic ways, and one of these is that cities are, by definition, full of strangers. To any one person, strangers are far more common in big cities than acquaintances. More common not just in places of public assembly, but more common at a man's own doorstep. Even residents who live near each other are strangers, and must be, because of the sheer number of people in small geographical compass.

The bedrock attitude of a successful city district is that a person must feel personally safe and secure on the street among all these strangers. He must not feel automatically menaced by them. A city district that fails in this respect also does badly in other ways and lays up for itself, and for its city at large, mountain on mountain of trouble.

Today barbarism has taken over many city streets, or people fear it has, which comes to much the same thing in the end. 'I live in a lovely, quiet residential area', says a friend of mine who is hunting another place to live. 'The only disturbing sound at night is the occasional scream of someone being mugged.' It does not take many incidents of violence on a city street, or in a city district, to make people fear the streets. And as they fear them, they use them less, which makes the streets still more unsafe.

To be sure, there are people with hobgoblins in their heads, and such people will never feel safe no matter what the objective circumstances are. But this is a different matter from the fear that besets normally prudent, tolerant and cheerful people who show nothing more than common sense in refusing to venture after dark – or in a few places, by day – into streets where they may well be assaulted, unseen or unrescued until too late.

The barbarism and the real, not imagined, insecurity that gives rise to such fears cannot be tagged a problem of the slums. The problem is most serious, in fact, in genteel-looking 'quiet residential areas' like that my friend was leaving.

It cannot be tagged as a problem of older parts of cities. The problem reaches its most baffling dimensions in some examples of rebuilt parts of cities, including supposedly the best examples of rebuilding, such as middle-income projects. The police precinct captain of a nationally admired project of this kind (admired by planners and lenders) has recently admonished residents not only about hanging around outdoors after dark but has urged them never to answer their doors without knowing the caller. Life here has much in common with life for the three little pigs or the seven little kids of the nursery thrillers. The problem of sidewalk and doorstep insecurity is as serious in cities which have made conscientious efforts at rebuilding as it is in those cities that have lagged. Nor is it illuminating to tag minority groups, or the poor, or the outcast with responsibility for city danger. There are immense variations in the degree of civilization and safety found among such groups and among the city areas where they live. Some of the safest sidewalks in New York City, for example, at any time of day or night, are those along which poor people or minority groups live. And some of the most dangerous are in streets occupied by the same kinds of people. All this can also be said of other cities.

Deep and complicated social ills must lie behind delinquency and crime, in suburbs and towns as well as in great cities. This book will not go into speculation on the deeper reasons. It is sufficient, at this point, to say that if we are to maintain a city society that can diagnose and keep abreast of deeper social problems, the starting point must be, in any case, to strengthen whatever workable forces for maintaining safety and civilization do exist – in the cities we do have. To build city districts that are custom made for easy crime is idiotic. Yet that is what we do.

The first thing to understand is that the public peace – the sidewalk and street peace – of cities is not kept primarily by the police, necessary as police are. It is kept primarily by an intricate, almost unconscious, network of voluntary controls and standards among the people themselves, and enforced by the people themselves. In some city areas – older public housing projects and streets with very high population turnover are often conspicuous examples – the keeping of public sidewalk law and order is left almost entirely to the police and special guards. Such places are jungles. No amount of police can enforce civilization where the normal, casual enforcement of it has broken down.

The second thing to understand is that the problem of insecurity cannot be solved by spreading people out more thinly, trading the characteristics of cities for the characteristics of suburbs. If this could solve danger on the city streets, then Los Angeles should be a safe city because superficially Los Angeles is almost all suburban. It has virtually no districts compact enough to qualify as dense city areas. Yet Los Angeles cannot, any more than any other great city, evade the truth that, being a city, it *is* composed of strangers not all of whom are nice. Los Angeles' crime figures are flabbergasting. Among the seventeen standard metropolitan areas with populations over a million, Los Angeles stands so pre-eminent in crime that it is in a category by itself. And this is markedly true of crimes associated with personal attack, the crimes that make people fear the streets [. . .]

The reasons for Los Angeles' high crime rates are undoubtedly complex, and at least in part obscure. But of this we can be sure: thinning out a city does not insure safety from crime and fear of crime. This is one of the conclusions that can be drawn within individual cities, too, where pseudo-suburbs or superannuated suburbs are ideally suited to rape, muggings, beatings, holdups and the like.

Here we come up against an all-important question about any city street: How much easy opportunity does it offer to crime? It may be that there is some absolute amount of crime in a given city, which will find an outlet somehow (I do not believe this). Whether this is so or not, different kinds of city streets garner radically different shares of barbarism and fear of barbarism.

Some city streets afford no opportunity to street barbarism. The streets of the North End of Boston are outstanding examples. They are probably as safe as any place on earth in this respect. Although most of the North End's residents are Italian or of Italian descent, the district's streets are also heavily and constantly used by people of every race and background. Some of the strangers from outside work in or close to the district; some come to shop and stroll; many, including members of minority groups who have inherited dangerous districts previously abandoned by others, make a point of cashing their paychecks in North End stores and immediately making their big weekly purchases in streets where they know they will not be parted from their money between the getting and the spending [. . .]

Meantime, in the Elm Hill Avenue section of Roxbury, a part of inner Boston that is suburban in superficial character, street assaults and the ever present possibility of more street assaults with no kibitzers to protect the victims, induce prudent people to stay off the sidewalks at night. Not surprisingly, for this and other reasons that are related (dispiritedness and dullness), most of Roxbury has run down. It has become a place to leave.

I do not wish to single out Roxbury or its once fine Elm Hill Avenue section especially as a vulnerable area; its disabilities, and especially its 'great blight of dullness', are all too common in other cities too. But differences like these in public safety within the same city are worth noting. The Elm Hill Avenue section's basic troubles are not owing to a criminal or a discriminated against or a poverty-stricken population. Its troubles stem from the fact that it is physically quite unable to function safely and with related vitality as a city district [. . .]

This is something everyone already knows: a well-used city street is apt to be a safe street. A deserted city street is apt to be unsafe. But how does this work, really? And what makes a city street well used or shunned? [. . .]

A city street equipped to handle strangers, and to make a safety asset, in itself, out of the presence of strangers, as the streets of successful city neighborhoods always do, must have three main qualities.

1. There must be a clear demarcation between what is public space and what is private space. Public and private spaces cannot ooze into each other as they do typically in suburban settings or in projects.

2. There must be eyes upon the street, eyes belonging to those we might call the natural proprietors of the street. The buildings on a street equipped to handle strangers and to insure the safety of both residents and strangers, must be oriented to the street. They cannot turn their backs or blank sides on it and leave it blind.

3. The sidewalk must have users on it fairly continuously, both to add to the number of effective eyes on the street and to induce the people in buildings along the street to watch the sidewalks in sufficient numbers.

Nobody enjoys sitting on a stoop or looking out a window at an empty street. Almost nobody does such a thing. Large numbers of people entertain themselves, off and on, by watching street activity.

In settlements that are smaller and simpler than big cities, controls on acceptable public behavior, if not on crime, seem to operate with greater or lesser success through a web of reputation, gossip, approval, disapproval and sanctions, all of which are powerful if people know each other and word travels. But a city's streets, which must control not only the behavior of the people of the city but also of visitors from suburbs and towns who want to have a big time away from the gossip and sanctions at home, have to operate by more direct, straightforward methods. It is a wonder cities have solved such an inherently difficult problem at all. And yet in many streets they do it magnificently.

It is futile to try to evade the issue of unsafe city streets by attempting to make some other features of a locality, say interior courtyards, or sheltered play spaces, safe instead. By definition again, the streets of a city must do most of the job of handling strangers for this is where strangers come and go. The streets must not only defend the city against predatory strangers, they must protect the many, many peaceable and well-meaning strangers who use them, insuring their safety too as they pass through. Moreover, no normal person can spend his life in some artificial haven, and this includes children. Everyone must use the streets.

On the surface, we seem to have here some simple aims: to try to secure streets where the public space is unequivocally public, physically unmixed with private or with nothing-at-all space, so that the area needing surveillance has clear and practicable limits; and to see that these public street spaces have eyes on them as continuously as possible.

But it is not so simple to achieve these objects, especially the latter. You can't make people use streets they have no reason to use. You can't make people watch streets they do not want to watch. Safety on the streets by surveillance and mutual policing of one another sounds grim, but in real life it is not grim. The safety of the street works best, most casually, and with least frequent taint of hostility or suspicion precisely where people are using and most enjoying the city streets voluntarily and are least conscious, normally, that they are policing.

The basic requisite for such surveillance is a substantial quantity of stores and other public places sprinkled along the sidewalks of a district; enterprises and public places that are used by evening and night must be among them especially. Stores, bars and restaurants, as the chief examples, work in several different and complex ways to abet sidewalk safety.

First, they give people – both residents and strangers – concrete reasons for using the sidewalks on which these enterprises face.

Second, they draw people along the sidewalks past places which have no attractions to public use in themselves but which become traveled and peopled as routes to somewhere else; this influence does not carry very far geographically, so enterprises must be frequent in a city district if they are to populate with walkers those other stretches of street that lack public places along the sidewalk. Moreover, there should be many different kinds of enterprises, to give people reasons for criss-crossing paths.

Third, storekeepers and other small businessmen are typically strong proponents of peace and order themselves; they hate broken windows and holdups; they hate having customers made nervous about safety. They are great street watchers and sidewalk guardians if present in sufficient numbers.

Fourth, the activity generated by people on errands, or people aiming for food or drink, is itself an attraction to still other people.

This last point, that the sight of people attracts still other people, is something that city planners and city architectural designers seem to find incomprehensible. They operate on the premise that city people seek the sight of emptiness, obvious order and quiet. Nothing could be less true. People's love of watching activity and other people is constantly evident in cities everywhere [. . .]

A lively street always has both its users and pure watchers. Last year I was on such a street in the Lower East Side of Manhattan, waiting for a bus. I had not been there longer than a minute, barely long enough to begin taking in the street's activity of errand goers, children playing, and loiterers on the stoops, when my attention was attracted by a woman who opened a window on the third floor of a tenement across the street and vigorously yoo-hooed at me. When I caught on that she wanted my attention and responded, she shouted down, 'The bus doesn't run here on Saturdays!' Then by a combination of shouts and pantomime she directed me around the corner. This woman was one of thousands upon thousands of people in New York who casually take care of the streets. They notice strangers. They observe everything going on. If they need to take action, whether to direct a stranger waiting in the wrong place or to call the police, they do so. (Action usually requires a certain self-assurance about the actor's proprietorship of the street and the support he will get if necessary.) But even more fundamental than the action and necessary to the action, is the watching itself.

Not everyone in cities helps to take care of the streets, and many a city resident or city worker is unaware of why his neighborhood is safe. The other day an incident occurred on the street where I live, and it interested me because of this point.

My block of the street, I must explain, is a small one, but it contains a remarkable range of buildings, varying from several vintages of tenements to three-and four-story houses that have been converted into low-rent flats with stores on the ground floor, or returned to single-family use like ours. Across the street there used to be mostly four-story brick tenements with stores below. But twelve years ago several buildings, from the corner to the middle of the block, were converted into one building with elevator apartments of small size and high rents.

The incident that attracted my attention was a suppressed struggle going on between a man and a little girl of eight or nine years old. The man seemed to be trying to get the girl to go with him. By turns he was directing a cajoling attention to her, and then assuming an air of nonchalance. The girl was making herself rigid, as children do when they resist, against the wall of one of the tenements across the street.

As I watched from our second-floor window, making up my mind how to intervene if it seemed advisable, I saw it was not going to be necessary. From the butcher shop beneath the tenement had emerged the woman who, with her husband, runs the shop; she was standing within earshot of the man, her arms folded and a look of determination on her face. Joe Cornacchia, who with his sons-in-law keeps the delicatessen, emerged about the same moment and stood solidly to the other side. Several heads poked out of the tenement windows above, one was withdrawn quickly and its owner reappeared a moment later in the doorway behind the man. Two men from the bar next to the butcher shop came to the doorway and waited. On my side of the street, I saw that the locksmith, the fruit man and the laundry proprietor had all come out of their shops and that the scene was also being surveyed from a number of windows besides ours. That man did not know it, but he was surrounded. Nobody was going to allow a little girl to be dragged off, even if nobody knew who she was.

I am sorry – sorry purely for dramatic purposes – to have to report that the little girl turned out to be the man's daughter.

Throughout the duration of the little drama, perhaps five minutes in all, no eyes appeared in the windows of the high-rent, small-apartment building. It was the only building of which this was true. When we first moved to our block, I used to anticipate happily that perhaps soon all the buildings would be rehabilitated like that one. I know better now, and can only anticipate with gloom and foreboding the recent news that exactly this transformation is scheduled for the rest of the block frontage adjoining the high-rent building. The high-rent tenants, most of whom are so transient we cannot even keep track of their faces, have not the remotest idea of who takes care of their street, or how. A city neighborhood can absorb and protect a substantial number of these birds of passage, as our neighborhood does. But if and when the neighborhood finally *becomes* them, they will gradually find the streets less secure, they will be vaguely mystified about it, and if things get bad enough they will drift away to another neighborhood which is mysteriously safer.

15 Hilda Jennings

Suburban Housing Estates

Excerpt from Hilda Jennings, *Societies in the Making*, Routledge & Kegan Paul, 1962, pp. 216–25.

Perhaps the most significant point which emerges from recent comparative studies of old near-central areas and twentieth century housing estates is the general agreement that the inhabitants of the latter have less feeling of belonging to a local society and are less friendly to their neighbours in general.

This suggests that a different type of society is emerging in areas which are still largely, though not now exclusively, designed as the homes of wage-earners. In some ways they would appear to be conforming to the way of life already established in a number of middle-class districts, in which privacy is thought of as either a good in itself, or as a necessary adjunct to social status.

Before attempting to consider this change in relation to place and class, the major change from private development to municipal provision and ownership must be recognized as a new factor.

In the old ninteenth-century areas, the local society came into being largely as the result of a multiplicity of individual choices, opportunities and compulsions, operating primarily in the economic field.

In the new areas both the nature and incidence of compulsions and choices are different. Choice has largely passed from the individual to the municipal owner, designer and administrator. For the Corporation tenant or would-be tenant, the pressures are thus social rather than economic.

Yet both place and economic factors still exercise compulsions, and these are in some respects as binding on the local authority as they would have been on the private developer.

The growing shortage of land within big cities compels development outwards. Either by the creation of new towns or overspill areas or by the extension of boundaries, the pressing need for additional dwellings has to be met. Thus we see the extension of residential areas through the inner-ring, inter-war estates and suburbs to post-war estates whose location has been dictated solely by the availability of land. In the city with which we are concerned in this study this was almost entirely situated on the side opposite to the main concentrations of industry, in what had previously been rural areas outside the County Borough boundaries.

The new estates were therefore inevitably in the nature of dormitories. Travel from them to places of employment often entailed long cross-city journeys. Place was thus robbed, at least for the time being, of what had so far been its main function, and no longer bound its inhabitants to it by providing the means of livelihood.

Such development of outlying areas was of course only made possible by the growth of transport facilities. Greater accessibility, the second attribute of place which we discussed in an earlier chapter, did not, however, mean that the individual tenant had a greater choice of the area of his voluntary association. For many families, the enforced journey to work, especially when taken in conjunction with the higher rents incidental on the move from rent-restricted property to a Corporation house imposed a severe strain on the budget. Leisure-time journeys by workers and journeys by non-earning members of the household often had to be limited to what were felt to be pressing necessities. Even so, some families found that in order to meet their enforced higher commitments they had to retrench in other ways, such as forgoing an annual holiday or other non-essential expenditure.

The journey to work also largely nullified the effects of shorter working hours. After an hour's travel each way, even without taking into account the effects of increased overtime in order to make ends meet, many workers felt little disposed to undertake more travel outside the home area.

The choice between associations and leisure-time interests in the city and locally based interests and relationships was in fact largely illusory. 'City' was not in practice an effective alternative to 'neighbourhood'.

The alternative idea more recently put forward by some sociologists is that the city-based community which they desire to see come into being should consist of a series of inter-penetrating neighbourhoods converging on the centre.

Apart, however, from the social dissimilarities of the districts to be penetrated, the enforced use of public transport which would be involved in much of such penetration would appear severely to limit the practical application of this idea. To our informants, intervening areas between the home and work places were to a great extent only a vacuum, devoid of human content, and to be crossed as quickly and with as little effort and expenditure as possible. In contrast to this, the former ties between adjoining districts of similar type had resulted from common near-local work easily accessible from both home areas and from the gradual growth of personal relationships by intermarriage and the spread of acquaintanceship.

The neighbourhood remained an important element in the lives of workers outside it and even more so in those of housewives tied to it by the needs of dependent children, as well as by the exigencies of finance. It is necessary therefore to look more closely at what it had to offer in respect of human relationships and associational ties.

In default of accepted machinery for consultation between the local authority as sole owner, designer and landlord and the body of the inhabitants, the latter proved to have little opportunity of voicing their preferences and needs effectively. They were, and resentfully recognized themselves to be, relegated to the role of consumers and users of the accommodation and services provided by corporate society. The fact that they acknowledged the provision made to be good as far as their actual dwellings were concerned did not remove their sense of non-participation and lack of partnership with the authority.

Here again, however, ownership did not mean that the authority itself was free from compulsions from outside sources. These exterior compulsions and pressures were partly economic, reflecting prevalent new patterns of demand and supply, and partly derived from the realm of ideas. In both cases they were increasingly expressed through corporative bodies of a functional and specialized nature.

The local Planning Authority, which finally determined the disposal of land and the design and services, found it necessary to consult with and to take into account, the desires and needs of other bodies which were influential in their own fields. Such bodies and interests included those representing the major religious denominations and the brewers, both of which were faced with a diminished demand and a consequent need to make the most efficient and economical use of their resources. The traders whom it was hoped to attract to the estates also required facilities in line with modern commercial trends.

In addition to such private interests, the component bodies within the local authority itself demanded recognition of the needs of education, public health and housing in particular. To a considerable extent these specialized branches of local government were influenced by the growing expertise of professional and technical officers. These were themselves members of professional associations which exerted influence both in local government and central government spheres. There grew up in fact, professional dogmas and assumptions which were largely accepted as the criteria of satisfactory planning and its ancillary services both by local officers and to varying but substantial degrees by the elected councillors who served on the respective committees.

The families who moved to the outlying and still developing estates which we studied in most detail found that the cumulative effect of the current economic and professional factors was bringing into being a physical environment very different from that to which many of them were accustomed.

Its most marked physical differences were in greater size, less compact lay-out, due to lower densities of population and houses and the provision of private gardens and public open spaces and school playing fields. Services, such as shops and public houses, were fewer and served wider areas; there was no provision for the corner or general shop, or for the small shop which was a subsidiary source of income and catered for little intimate groups of neighbours from a particular sub-district.

The coordination of plans by the religious bodies also led to a decrease in the number and types of places of worship, and these, like the shops, were planned with a view to drawing in people from wider areas. The old type of mission and gospel hall was lacking.

The effect of this changed form of provision, much of which did not come into being in the early years of estate development, was twofold.

Occasions of informal and involuntary contacts were markedly fewer, since neighbours no longer met each other in the course of their daily shopping and the more centralized shops did not, because of their specialized character and greater range of customers, serve in the same way as centres of public opinion. Similarly, it was no longer so easy to indulge in frequent chats on the doorsteps, or to 'pop in and out' without formality. 'You almost feel that you ought to take your overall off before you go down your path and up your neighbour's.'

Secondly, lack of services or of the familiar type of service took people off the estate to shop by bus where the goods were cheaper and more varied. Many such shoppers went back to their old area where they could combine visits to relatives and friends with shopping, and where the shopkeeper also was often an old friend.

Frequent journeys 'home' were indeed felt by most of the former residents in the old areas to be inevitable, since the move to the estate had involved separation from their parents, whose society and help had so far formed a main part of their lives and who often themselves needed regular help from their children.

In the field of institutional membership also, the decrease in participation after leaving the old area was marked. Far fewer of the adults claimed membership of or association with any type of organization, whether secular or religious, and the great majority of those who did so returned to their former organizations which were almost entirely centred in the old home area.

The decrease was most pronounced in the sphere of religion, and affected not only the adults, but the children also.

Thus, at least in the first few years after removal, except in a few cases, the social bond with the new estate was not strengthened significantly by the formation of new relationships either through formal or informal associations.

There were other reasons why intercourse tended to be restricted. The first of these was connected with the initial lack of choice of district. Many of the residents had not wished to be housed there and from the start hoped to move away as soon as opportunity offered. The rate of mobility was therefore high, and the number of unsettled families awaiting transfer was higher still. On the group of outlying estates which we are describing, some three-and-a-half years after they moved there exactly half of the ninety families from the old area had moved again or were awaiting removal. This state of affairs did not conduce to a sense of belonging or to a desire to become involved in estate activities.

To some extent delay in bringing facilities into being was a primary cause of unsettlement. On the other hand, more permanent features of the estate led to settled desire to leave it and inhibited the growth of attachments to neighbourhood.

A second factor which was influential in forming social attitudes was the heterogeneity of the population and the lack of any discernible basis of unity such as had been operative in the residents in the old area.

Both the change from multiple private ownership to comprehensive public ownership and changes which were taking place in the class structure conduced to a diversity of tenants.

In order not only to be just, but to be demonstrably just, to all claimants for accommodation, the 'points' system of allocation was based on defined categories of housing needs. Comparatively little regard could be paid to individual preferences for area or type of dwelling which arose from more personal considerations. Effective choice was between acceptance and refusal of a dwelling which became available rather than between alternative dwellings. Varying degrees of prestige or good or bad reputation soon began to be attached to the developing post-war estates, and by no means always conformed to the social aspirations or desires of the tenants who were housed there.

On the estates described there soon came into being three divergent social groups; the 'social climbers' who applied for a council house in default of privately owned accommodation, but had a strong desire to live among people with similar aspirations to status; the respectable 'working class' who wished only to live among their own kind and to be free to continue in their customary modes of living; and a minority of markedly anti-social or socially sub-standard families whose conduct was a source of annoyance to both the other groups. This last section of the tenants came to the estates as a result of the avowed policy of the municipal landlord, which sought to disperse, rather than congregate, their less satisfactory tenants.

More general and far-reaching changes than municipal policy in the allocation of dwellings were, however, affecting the basis of working-class unity. Scientific and technical advances, the development of new industries and the growth of ever-larger units of production, distribution and administration, called for a new kind of worker with new technical and administrative skills. The 'working class' became less easily definable and recognizable; on its fringes there was growing up an increasing number of 'lower middle class' or 'doubtfully middle class' wage-earners and small-salaried workers, some of whom were black-coated and inclined to disassociate themselves from the old-established artisan class. Their rewards in earnings were not always greater but they tended to claim superior status.

Since such claims were often not accepted and indeed were usually resented by their neighbours of 'respectable' status their dispersal among these was likely to inhibit the growth of general good will and neighbourliness.

In the absence of the humanizing and personalizing influence of place operating through services and established kinship and neighbour groups, the isolated one-generation family on the estate tended either to remain aloof, with one or two 'special friends' with similar claims to superiority as their only effective local contacts, or to seek a 'better-class' neighbourhood. Where, as often happened, they openly acknowledged this latter ambition, their 'swank' and 'snobbishness' aroused general resentment.

Moreover, since they were not known as persons, they could only assert their status through their material possessions, their curtains, furnishings, television sets and cars, or their up-to-date hair styles and dress. There was a great temptation for their less stable neighbours to follow their example, regardless of their income and other commitments. Thus debt, sometimes linked with increasing marital disharmony, became more common. The urge to make a similar showing in the eyes of their neighbours was accentuated because many of them were young and for the first time in their lives were removed from the restraining influence of parents and neighbour codes. 'They think they're very grand,' said some of the respectable who maintained their old customs and criteria of judgement, 'but I ask you, do they pay their bills?'

It was for such reasons that material and snobbish values began to be widely attributed to the inhabitants of the estates.

On the other hand, the great majority of the families whose histories on the estates we studied continued to judge their neighbours by their friendliness and 'dependability', their practice of the virtues of thrift and solvency and by their upbringing of their children. This, however, they felt to be threatened on all sides.

The example of the anti-social families, who were given to quarrelling, brawls, bad language, and offences against the law, and whose children were unruly and 'dragged up', made them fearful of the inevitable contacts between neighbours' children.

Exclusive and often antagonistic groups, therefore, were common even in one street, and the daily kindnesses which were often shown were confined within these exclusive groups.

The one common desire of all three sections was to live among 'their own kind', and for the attainment of this they were largely dependent on the local authority. 'Why must they mix the good and the bad on these estates?' said a young wife from the old area. Many others asserted that caution in making or pursuing acquaintances had proved necessary, because of the uncertainty of response and the too frequent abuse of confidences or approaches to friendliness by 'people of a different sort'.

On the other hand, loneliness in a strange and distant area was keenly felt, particularly by housewives. Although the idea of a Community Association and centre embracing people drawn from a wide area and previously unknown to each other, was strange to many of them, considerable numbers joined the Mossdene Association in its early days. They wanted to make friends without committing themselves to undue intimacy with neighbours.

Unfortunately, but probably inevitably, the rivalries and tensions in the streets were carried into the association; as a result membership fell off, and the general attitude on the estate became that of apathy or antagonism towards the movement.

A number of causes conduced to this state of affairs. The obvious need for a means of expression of grievances and needs of the tenants as a whole in such matters as rents and lack of amenities was not met by the association to any great extent. The centre was not built, although considerable contributions were made by the members to the building fund.

Moreover, the divisions among the tenants made it difficult to find acceptable and accepted leadership. There were none of the overlapping *élites* of the old area. Abilities and personal characteristics were unknown and had to be taken on trust. People whose roles and functions were familiar were almost non-existent.

The very fact that a number of those who claimed superior status came forward to act as leaders was seen as another sign of 'swank' and 'bossiness'. Despite the obvious abilities of some of these, and their willingness to undertake hard work, they too often proved to be 'touchy', resentful of criticism, and prone 'to go off in a huff'. Nor were they practised in the kind of diffused and interlocking functional authority which had grown up in the old area. The association experienced recurrent crises and was soon in imminent danger of collapse.

There was, however, another possible source from which it appeared that responsible leaders might be drawn. As time went on a growing number of functional workers whose professional status was accepted by the inhabitants came into the estate. At first some of these threw in their lot with the association and in some instances helped to avert disputes and to soften acrimony.

Soon, however, they grew tired of its apparent ineffectiveness and in their concern for the welfare of the estate formed a separate body. A number of them, including almost all the teachers and many of the specialized social workers sent in by Bristol agencies, did not live in the locality and were little known outside their particular fields of work. Others were thought to 'throw their weight about' and the very success of the new body in calling attention to local needs disposed the key members of the association to look on it as a rival which wanted to usurp its functions and prestige.

Although there was provision for cross-representation between the two bodies, the new organization was largely professional in composition and outlook. By some people it was thought of as a reversion to the paternalistic and authoritarian type of leadership existing in the old area at the time when the factory owners and managers with their class associates in the church and medicine, were largely responsible for the welfare of the wage-earners.

It was only when as a result of a common sense of frustration both bodies disbanded and a new organization which included professional and functional workers and key tenants was formed that a new and more promising start was made. With the end of divided leadership developments came rapidly. A paid warden was appointed and a centre built. Although the estate was still in a state of flux and lacked the older unity of class and place, the desire for social intercourse was not lacking and membership grew steadily during the first eighteen months of the new venture.

The picture which we have painted of an old local society in the course of disintegration and of new ones without any accepted basis of unity has many parallels elsewhere. At first sight it seems to be a gloomy one. Yet it is not new, but an old story retold.

If we turn back to the history of the old area, we find that it went through similar phases of change. In its early days there was the same severance from familiar places and kinship ties, the same preponderance of the young; in it too, there emerged a new and ambitious class, the skilled artisans, who tended to 'ape' the way of life of those above them in status, and were only gradually integrated into a larger class of kinship and place. For long periods also there was an obsession with material and physical needs, though this was the result of pressing economic distress rather than of full employment and rising standards of living.

The old society also knew changing conceptions of the functions of the corporate society, ranging from the *laissez faire* assumptions of an expanding economic system to the welfare state of the first half of the twentieth century, when the social evils accompanying the growth of towns and the fluctuations of trade could no longer be ignored.

Out of all this emerged a society in which individuals counted and the social bond was strong and found expression in the wider society.

Such a comparison offers hope for the future. Yet some new factors seem to demand explicit recognition and purposive action if the old ideals of individual significance, social unity and effective democracy are to be given new and appropriate forms of expression.

Firstly, the traditional ties with defined localities may be increasingly threatened by the conquest of space and by the fragmentation of interests and bonds resulting partly from new types of economic organization. Secondly, there is a danger that the individual may come to count for less if the tendency to large-scale organization and administration continues. Thirdly, the growth of powerful and specialized and professionalized corporate bodies within the state may tend to make the man-in-the-street less able to play an effective part in the shaping of society. It may be that another age of discovery demands a rethinking of the aims, machinery and functions of corporate society in relation to the individual and to organized groups.

16 Ingrid Reynolds and Charles Nicholson

Living in High Flats

Excerpts from Ingrid Reynolds and Charles Nicholson, 'Living off the ground', *Architects' Journal*, 20 August 1969, pp. 459–70.

This paper describes attitudes to living off the ground on six local authority estates [in London and Sheffield]. It relies almost entirely on the responses of housewives, but as these were so like their husbands' the data can be considered to reflect the views of both.

Because of the few examples of each block type surveyed conclusions cannot be drawn with much certainty. Further, residents living off the ground were partly self selected since housing departments do not generally force people to live off the ground where alternatives are available – and also because some unhappy residents had probably moved out already. The sample therefore does not give a representative cross section of tenants even in Sheffield or Greater London. These limitations should be kept in mind and generalizations from the data should be made cautiously.

The method

The survey. The survey was designed as a comparative study to find out, among other matters, how different types of households reacted to different kinds of buildings, e.g., houses, point blocks, balcony-access blocks. Thus estates were chosen to give various block types and the sample was arranged in pre-defined household types.

A range of topics was covered generally rather than a few subjects studied in depth. Questions were asked about layout, socio-economic and background subjects, and on social and personal matters.

The sample. 1334 housewives and 369 husbands were interviewed. Of the former, 984 lived off the ground. The four household categories analysed were:

1. Families comprising parents and children under sixteen. This category was split up into those households where all children were under five years; those with some under and some over, and those with all children five or over.

2. Adults (only) under pensionable age.
3. Mixed households of parents with children under sixteen and other adults under pensionable age.
4. Husbands and wives over pensionable age.

Other households, e.g., three-generation households, husbands and wives where only one partner was pensionable, were excluded.

Estates and block types. Five types of block were studied – houses, point blocks, internal corridor slab blocks, balcony-access blocks and deck-access blocks. Usually two examples of each were surveyed; they were typical and had been occupied at least a year.

Ideally a large random sample of each block type should have been studied but this would have prolonged the work. It is hoped, however, to survey further examples [. . .]

Housewives' judgements. Housewives' judgements whether they were 'satisfied' or 'happy' have been taken as meaningful. These terms are related to people's experience and aspirations – a limitation of all user reaction studies. Architects' personal judgements are also limited in the same way and the advantage of user surveys is that they obtain the opinion of many users and can help overcome some of the limitations in the designer's personal experience and knowledge.

Analysis of data has shown that housewives answered the questionnaire consistently and could explain reasons for their attitudes [. . .]

The findings
Attitudes to living off the ground

All housewives living off the ground (definition: access doors not at ground level) were asked 'How do you feel now about living off the ground . . . happy? No feelings either way? Unhappy?' Sixteen per cent said 'unhappy' and 68 per cent 'happy', leaving 16 per cent with 'no feelings either way'.

Percentages of housewives from different household types who were *unhappy* living off the ground are shown in Figure 1. A much higher proportion of housewives with children under five felt unhappy living off the ground than any others. Housewives with all children over five differed little from those with no children [. . .]

Although the sample cannot be considered a representative cross-section it is reasonable to conclude from this and other survey data that there are many, particularly without young children, who feel happy living off the ground.

Housewives were also asked how they felt about living off the ground when they first moved in. Feelings 'at first' and 'now' correlated significantly, indicating little change in views. There was a slight tendency for more family households to become unhappy, and more of the

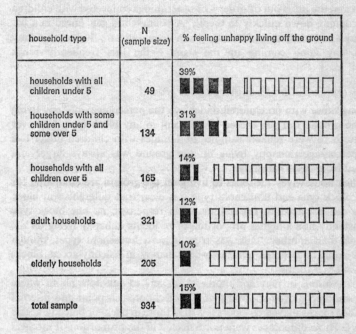

Figure 1 Percentage of various household types unhappy living off the ground. (The discrepancy between the number in the total sample and the cumulative total of subgroups is due to exclusion of mixed households from the analysis.)

others, particularly the adult and elderly, to become happy. Those who had previously lived off the ground were not happy more frequently than those who had not.

Advantages and disadvantages of living off the ground

Residents felt the advantages were: they were away from noise, the view was good, they had more privacy, air was fresher and cleaner, and they were away from the nuisance of children. This last was mentioned by housewives whether childless or not. Typical comments were 'I took to it right away – very fresh air and we don't get as much dirt as we used to when we lived on the ground'; 'There is more privacy and I feel free and away from it all'; 'Don't get so much noise – outlook is nice'.

Disadvantages were: lifts were often broken down and dirty, the stairs were difficult to climb, and children's play was a problem. Comments included 'It's more difficult with the baby – if you want to get out with a pram and the lift is out of order – or other things connected with children like running down quickly to them'; 'A young child gets bored in a flat all day and I can't always be taking him up and down'; 'It doesn't do my heart any good coming up the stairs – the lifts frequently break down' [. . .]

Block type and attitudes to living off the ground

Among those with no children under five the percentage unhappy living off the ground did not exceed 19 per cent in any block type. However where there were reliable samples of families with children under five the percentage unhappy living off the ground was always larger and ranged from twenty to sixty.

When housewives' attitudes to living off the ground are compared for each block type and household type it is clear that differences in block types did not account for differences in responses; no one block type consistently had a higher proportion of residents unhappy living off the ground than another. This was true of most household types, though more adult households tended to be unhappy in balcony-access blocks than in other forms.

Observations of play and mothers' answers to questions about where their children played showed that young children in point and internal corridor blocks played outdoors less than those in deck- or balcony-access blocks. These differences were not reflected in the proportion of mothers unhappy living off the ground; housewives in point or internal corridor blocks were not more unhappy living off the ground than those in deck- or balcony-access blocks.

Height of blocks and attitudes to living off the ground

Very high buildings were regarded less favourably than lower counterparts. In very high blocks disadvantages of lifts breaking down, waiting for lifts and problems of children's play and supervision of children playing outdoors often outweighed advantages of quietness, cleanness, view, privacy and being away from the nuisance of children. In slightly lower blocks advantages nearly always outweighed disadvantages which were seemingly less severe. However, with so few examples of each type of block, generalization is hazardous, though analysis of open-ended responses adds some support to these findings.

In medium-rise balcony-access blocks the disadvantages of too few lifts or of having to walk up stairs and the nuisance of children often outweighed advantages of view, privacy and protection from children which the blocks might have afforded.

That there was no significant correlation between actual height of housewives' dwellings and their attitudes to living off the ground indicates that replies were not related to height of dwelling at all or else that the proportion of those living very high who were unhappy there was no greater than that living near the ground, and that those in between were more happy. Whatever the reason, it seems that three- or four-storey buildings are not necessarily more satisfactory to residents than high-rise solutions.

When people live only a few floors up they seem to benefit less from better views and air and less noise than those higher up. Yet they also have their access problems – dirty or unreliable lifts or none at all. In very high blocks on the other hand lift and play problems become severe. Perhaps blocks between these extremes maximize advantages and minimize disadvantages of living off the ground. However, high blocks may be satisfactory if occupied only by households without children. This needs further testing.

Factors related to attitude to living off the ground

To find out what factors were associated with attitudes to living off the ground, housewives' responses to all rating questions – covering most aspects of housing layout as well as socio-economic, social-emotional and background variables – were correlated with their feelings about living off the ground.

Correlations indicate that unhappiness off the ground was mainly associated with variables denoting general dissatisfaction, i.e., dissatisfaction with dwelling and estate indicating a desire to move, with some social-psychological variables, i.e., loneliness, 'nervousness', and wanting to be away from people; and with variables indicating difficulties in bringing up children, e.g., safety from traffic, wanting under-fives to play out more, play a problem.

Socio-economic group, rent, income, length of residence and previous housing experience did not correlate with attitudes to living off the ground, and nor did satisfaction with lifts and access arrangements [. . .]

Comparison of the responses of housewives living in houses with those of housewives living in flats and maisonettes on and off the ground

[. . .] *Children's play.* Sixty-eight per cent of all housewives with children under sixteen found children's play a problem. Mothers in houses and balcony-access blocks thought play as great a problem as those in point blocks, internal corridor blocks and deck-access blocks. Further, there was no significant correlation between height above ground and mothers' feelings about play problems. Systematic observation, however, has shown that children under five living off the ground played outside less than those on the ground. Despite this, it was found that mothers of these children did not find play more of a problem than those with older children.

Loneliness. Sixteen per cent of all housewives said they 'often' felt lonely but there was no difference between housewives living on and off the ground or between those living in houses and multi-storey blocks. There was also no significant correlation between height above ground and loneliness.

'Nervousness'. There was no evidence that more tenants in high rise buildings were 'nervous' than in medium rise balcony-access blocks or houses. 48 per cent of housewives suffered at least one of four symptoms (nerves, depression, irritability, sleeplessness), but those in houses seemed somewhat worse than those in other buildings. There was no relationship between 'nervousness' and height above ground. Housewives with children were more 'nervous' than others.

Housewives' choice of estates

Half the housewives said they had particularly wanted to live on their present estate. There were fairly low but statistically significant correlations between wanting to come to the estate and the general satisfaction variables, so that those who had chosen their estate were somewhat more satisfied than those who had not.

Choice of dwelling type

When tenants were asked if they would rather live in a house farther out of London (or on the outskirts of Sheffield) or in blocks of flats or maisonettes near the centre, 42 per cent chose the house. When this was analysed by household type the house was chosen by 53 per cent of the family households, 42 per cent of the adult households, 63 per cent of the mixed, and 19 per cent of the elderly households. Housewives tended, particularly in Sheffield, to choose what they already had. Results must therefore be interpreted cautiously.

Interviews with housing managers

Housing managers of the six estates said that tenants were generally more reluctant to move into high blocks than into low blocks or houses.

At Sheffield, with an easier housing situation, residents could say what type of dwelling and estates they preferred although they could not always get them. In London on the other hand even this limited choice was mostly impossible because of the housing shortage. Letting dwellings on the six estates presented no difficulty except in point blocks at Canada Estate, and it was here – and only here – that requests for transfers were above average. Most tenants came from cleared slums near the estate they now lived on, except at Canada Estate, where most came from the waiting list, drawn from all over London, because people were reluctant to live on the estate.

Findings of other research

Very little hard evidence supports often passionately held views for or against housing people in multi-storey dwellings. Results of other surveys supported some of these findings as they show a large proportion of people tended to be satisfied living off the ground and no great difference in levels of satisfaction was found between people in high buildings, low buildings and houses. Findings, that, for families with young children living off the ground, play problems were worse, and that the children tended to play outside less, is also supported by earlier research. A health study found more illness in those families in three- and four-storey blocks of flats than in houses. This was most marked in respiratory infections in young women and children and of psychoneurotic disorders in women.

Conclusions

Taking all housewives together play problems, 'nervousness' and loneliness appeared as serious for those on the ground as off, but young children play outdoors more when living on the ground.

Findings, however, clearly support the view that living off the ground is least satisfactory for families with children, particularly when these are under five. They suggest that there are many households, particularly those without children and the elderly, who feel happy living off the ground and that many may choose to do so if this gave them a central location. However, some of them will not be happy off the ground. Where possible therefore offering a choice of block type is important.

The major factor influencing a housewife's attitude to living off the ground was whether she had children, particularly young children. Block type or height at which housewives lived were less important. Some evidence suggests that blocks up to seven storeys and very high blocks may be less satisfactory than those between, i.e., those about eight to sixteen floors – though this will partly depend on the type of household occupying them.

Ingrid Reynolds and Charles Nicholson 177

'Nervousness', loneliness and desire to be more separated from others were related to feelings about living off the ground. This suggests that personality characteristics may influence attitudes [. . .]

As one would expect, those on the estate of their choice seemed rather more satisfied than those who were not.

It seems therefore that attitudes to living off the ground are important in feelings of satisfaction and that the needs of families with young children are the most pressing. There are also some of the other household types who strongly dislike living off the ground. These should be given priority for living on the ground.

Part Four **The Politics of Inequality**

In ordinary everyday life we are constantly competing and jockeying with each other to obtain a greater share of society's scarce goods and resources. As members of society, we attempt to use power and influence, argument and persuasion in an effort to improve our lot in life and sometimes even to improve the lot of others. In this way we all play politics in an attempt to resolve our problems, though we may never read, let alone write, a political manifesto, never storm a barricade, nor even vote for a local councillor. The argument with the neighbour as to who shall cut the hedge, the would-be lover's attempts to seduce a reluctant partner, and the scheming of the careerist attempting to curry favour with his employers, are all 'political' in this sense.

In this widest sense politics refers to the ways in which individuals and groups attempt to set and fulfil goals and ambitions. In some cases an individual may realize his goal on his own, as with the would-be seducer referred to above. But his skills are carefully employed to take account of social rules, norms and conventions. Even in this case then, politics is a social enterprise. Sometimes, however, an individual's aims and goals may only be realized with the cooperation of an army of allies who need convincing of the righteousness of the case and of the advantages of following it, and who need organizing into an effective political army to defeat powerful opposition. Both Christ and Lenin, for example, set about such tasks, both having ambitions to change the world, to alter men's social relations and attitudes both to each other and to society's limited stock of scarce goods and resources. Hence for them and for their disciples it was necessary to provide a dream or an ideology that could win and maintain support by demonstrating the immorality and injustice of existing society, by exposing society's problems and by providing a programme to end them.

The dividing line between the politics of interpersonal life and involvement in organized mass politics is not as clear-cut as might first appear. The personalities and programmes of political leaders are formed by their reflections upon the successes and failures of their own direct experience and the successes and failures of others that they have knowledge of. Equally, grounded in their own everyday interpersonal experience, potential followers develop views of their needs and problems, and on the basis of these may become or be made receptive to the programmes of politicians. They may see such programmes as answers to their needs and may then be persuaded to participate. Alternatively, they may never encounter such programmes at all, or may turn away in anger or apathy.

From this brief discussion it should be clear that the basis of an individual's involvement in any form of mass politics is highly complex. Many needs cannot be made into bases for mass action, and even when mass action does occur, this does not usually happen spontaneously but requires the development and maintenance of an organized and energetic mass movement. The precise course of the Russian Revolution was unpredictable but the Revolution itself was not unexpected as years of preparatory organization went into the making of it. In an article on the nature of mass movements, Blumer, in Lee's *Principles of Sociology* (Barnes & Noble, 1946) has shown that it is a major task for such organizations to constantly relate the movement's programme and ideals to the feelings of frustration and the sense of needless suffering of the movemen's membership and the following outside its ranks. By so doing, it links the movement to its social roots: the problems experienced by the disprivileged.

At its most abstract level, therefore, political sociology is concerned with the analysis of the relationships which men forge in their attempts to solve social problems and with the analysis of the problems that these relationships themselves can create.

In the Readings to follow we shall primarily be concerned with problems of political organization as these apply to mass movements and not directly with the details of interpersonal politics. It will be necessary for us to select from the infinite variety of social problems which could be labelled political and which have stimulated political organization. In the passages below we have decided to concentrate upon one theme: the seemingly endemic conflict in modern industrial society between the 'haves' and 'have-nots' and the way in which inequality generates revolutionary and reformist challenges to the *status quo*. The most dominant revolutionary challenge of our time is Communism.

Let the ruling class tremble at a Communistic revolution.
The proletarians have nothing to lose but their chains.
They have a world to win.
Working men of all countries, unite!

With this concluding statement of the Communist Manifesto, Marx and Engels, having analysed the conflicts and miseries engendered by the capitalist mode of production and appropriation, announce their programme of revolutionary action.

They both believed that the emancipation of the underprivileged could only occur as a consequence of the mass organization of the working class, who, dwelling upon their common life-experiences of exploitation, poverty and political and economic tyranny, would join together as part of a Communist movement to overthrow inequality and property ownership. To Marx, the institutions of justice, politics and administration in capitalist society were little more than devices employed by the propertied ruling class to consolidate their rule. They gave the appearance of democracy, but in effect were instruments of ruling-class control. A workers' revolution would overthrow the bourgeois State and abolish property ownership for the first time in history, because the class which constituted the majority of society would hold the reins of power.

In Reading 17, Michels (1876–1936) argues that the Marxist view, and indeed the programmes of all socialist reformists and revolutionaries, are utopias and doomed to failure. In his classical analysis of political parties, he follows Weber in the contention that bureaucratic organization is the most efficient means of performing large-scale administrative tasks. Also like Weber, he views organizational structures as power-hierarchies which are essentially undemocratic, since administrative expertise and power centres in the leadership. Even socialist movements which aim at equality and democracy are no exception; they too require bureaucratic machinery and skilled leaders. These leaders then become distanced from the needs and outlook of the party's grass-roots members; they become bureaucrats. They participate in the activities of the ruling class, become part of that class and are sooner or later corrupted. Because of their organizational power and expertise, they are able to resist political challenges, and come to form a semi-permanent élite. Michels summed this up in his famous 'Iron Law of Oligarchy' which pre-dates Orwell's *Animal Farm,* but which is just as pessimistic.

Michels' analysis of the Social Democratic movements of the day appears to explain the seemingly unending procession of Labour leaders who accept positions of power, prestige and wealth in capitalist societies. The thesis finds common expression in popular opinion. That Labour leaders sell out, and that 'they're all in it for themselves', are arguments often used by the cynical or apathetic to justify their detachment from reformist or revolutionary politics. Many conservatives also use a lay version of Michels' ideas to justify their position when they suggest that

'Socialism is all right in theory' or that 'some are more equal than others'.

This general acceptance of Michels' position helps to explain the degree of conservatism found amongst the working classes and their lack of participation in Socialist politics. What cannot be explained so easily is the degree of continued support which Socialist movements do achieve. Nor could we explain the processes of revival and democratization that frequently occur in such movements. In his definitive study of *British Political Parties*, though R. T. McKenzie generally accepts Michels' theory as applicable to the British Labour Party, he pointedly remarks that there is certainly no iron law of oligarchy and that 'evidence has also been provided of revolts against the party leaders'. As Gouldner argues in the Reading 18, Michels' Iron Law is not a scientifically established law at all, but an 'ethos of pessimism' which ignores the evidence of men's constant strivings to participate in and control the governing of their lives. The so-called Iron Law ignores all this; it ignores contradictory evidence and is not, therefore, subject to the possibility of refutation.

Michels' views are best treated as a logical model of possible developments within political organizations in which no countervailing forces exist. The conditions under which such developments can occur were never made explicit. Marx himself opposed parliamentary reformism because he believed that if Socialists attempted to reform capitalism from within they would either be corrupted or defeated by the powerful institutions of the capitalist State. Massive working-class activity and involvement in establishing Communism was the only insurance of a successful social revolution; only this would prevent the corruption of leaders.

The years since Marx's death have seen a considerable degree of incorporation of the working class into contemporary capitalist industrial society, and though wide disparities of income and wealth remain, significant political, economic and welfare rights have been extended to the working class. Some people have argued that this was an automatic result of industrial development; others that it was a result of the activities of the Labour Party.

Young (Reading 19) opposes both of these views, suggesting that the working class has had to struggle for any reforms that have been obtained, and has continually produced collective institutions and values which defend the workers against exploitation and which, therefore, challenge the premises upon which capitalist society is based. He suggests that the most important organizational embodiment of this challenge grew out of the trade union movement, and was revealed in industrial struggles, rather than in the emergence of the Labour Party, which quickly became adapted to the political institutions of capitalism, particularly Parliament. Young concludes by suggesting that working-class culture, based on collective industrial and educational experience, continues to present a political challenge to the organization of the state. He does not tell us precisely how contemporary organizations embody this challenge but it is clear that the modern industrial scene remains conflict-ridden. The 1964–70 Labour Government in Britain often found itself unable to contain this strife though the need to do so was declared to be its most fundamental problem.

Unlike Young, McKenzie and Silver (Reading 20) concentrate their analysis upon voting in contemporary society. Thus their concern is with a very limited aspect of participation in institutional politics. They rightly assert that a considerable proportion of workers, and particularly their wives, have always voted Conservative and that Conservative voters today are not as deviant culturally as is often assumed. Their findings suggest that, in terms of national political culture, the deviant might be the consistent anti-Tory who displays firmly-grounded class attitudes. This is not really surprising, as McKenzie and Silver consider that the non-deviant views Britain as essentially undivided by class and as imbued with patriotism. A major difficulty with their analysis revolves around their use of the terms 'dominant' and 'deviant', which suggest that there is a widely-accepted fixed set of British political attitudes that may be characterized as 'non-deviant'. They are thus implying that to be a Conservative is to be normal.

There are further problems attached to studies based upon such ephemeral and intermittent activity as voting. It is difficult to gauge the significance which voting has for a large population, and opinion polls suggest that the basis of the voters' attachments may be very much more flexible than is commonly thought. This is demonstrated by Blondel who shows the importance of the 'floating voter' in recent British elections. In the second extract from *Voters, Parties and Leaders* (Reading 21) he goes on to examine the basis of party preference, and suggests that strictly rational choice on the basis of party programmes is in many ways impossible.

Of course, the nationalistic, conservative political culture which McKenzie and Silver find so pervasive is of long standing, but it has been sharpened and stimulated in opposition to the 'totalitarianism' of Soviet Russia. The British Labour Party has denounced this totalitarianism and has thereby played its part in spreading the view that revolutionary Socialism results in Communistic dictatorship. To many people the existence of world Communism has become the major social problem of our time.

Trotsky's analysis of the course of events in Russia after the Revolution (Reading 22) has many points in common with Michels' analysis of political bureaucracies. However, unlike Michels, Trotsky attempts to stipulate the conditions which made for setbacks for the original spirit of the Revolution and in particular its drives towards equality and cooperation. He observes that the Russian Revolution occurred in a backward country, in which the industrial working class were a minority, forced to compete with backward peasants for scarce objects of consumption. Whilst the Revolution brought equality it was an equality of nothing.

This fact, together with subsequent famine, civil strife and war, and the consequent possibility of counter-revolution, were the conditions which made the rise of the bureaucracy possible, not some inevitable 'iron tendency' which operates under any conditions, and he thus develops the view advanced by Marx that egalitarian revolutions can only be maintained in advanced developed societies.

A common view of Soviet Russia suggests that despite the Revolution, it has a class structure and that this is not all that different from the class structure of capitalist societies. This view is rejected by Goldthorpe (Reading 23), who suggests that the Soviet economy is in principle a planned economy, so that market forces do not govern life-chances and the distribution of wealth, power and prestige. Instead, the situation is subject to political control and to the conscious choice of the state planners. Even if such political control does exist, it is clear that it has not been used to abolish inequalities of wealth, power and prestige.

In the last twenty-five years, the most significant revolutions that have attempted to destroy these inequalities have occurred in backward countries. Perhaps revolution is more easily achieved in countries which have not been able to build the organizations of the underprivileged into the machinery of politics. Certainly, revolutionary parties have succeeded in organizing the masses where the capitalist State has failed. In his detailed analysis of Chinese Communist success between 1923 and 1945, Hofheinz (Reading 24) is unable to point to any one decisive social factor that made for receptivity to Communism. What was crucial instead was the activity of the Communists themselves. We end, therefore, with the reminder that politics is not something that 'happens', but something that is achieved by coordinated social action.

17 Robert Michels

Power in the Party

Excerpt from Robert Michels, *Political Parties*, translated by Eden and Cedar
Paul, Free Press, 1949, pp. 367–76. First published in German in 1911.

Generated to overthrow the centralized power of the state, starting from
the idea that the working class need merely secure a sufficiently vast and
solid organization in order to triumph over the organization of the state,
the party of the workers has ended by acquiring a vigorous centralization
of its own, based upon the same cardinal principles of authority and
discipline which characterize the organization of the state. It thus
becomes a governmental party, that is to say, a party which, organized
itself like a government on the small scale, hopes some day to assume the
reins of government upon the large scale. The revolutionary political
party is a state within the state, pursuing the avowed aim of destroying
the existing state in order to substitute for it a social order of a fundamentally different character. To attain this essentially political end, the
party avails itself of the socialist organization, whose sole justification is
found precisely in its patient but systematic preparation for the destruction of the organization of the state in its existing form. The sub-
versive party organizes the *framework* of the social revolution. For this
reason it continually endeavours to strengthen its positions, to extend its
bureaucratic mechanism, to store up its energies and its funds.

Every new official, every new secretary engaged by the party, is in
theory a new agent of the revolution; in the same way every new section
is a new battalion; and every additional thousand francs furnished by the
members' subscriptions, by the profits of the socialist press, or by the
generous donations of sympathetic benefactors, constitute fresh ad-
ditions to the war-chest for the struggle against the enemy. In the long
run, however, the directors of this revolutionary body existing within the
authoritarian state, sustained by the same means as that state and inspired by the like spirit of discipline, cannot fail to perceive that the
party organization, whatever advances it may make in the future, will
never succeed in becoming more than an ineffective and miniature copy
of the state organization. For this reason, in all ordinary circumstances,
and as far as prevision is humanly possible, every attempt of the party to
measure its forces with those of its antagonists is foredoomed to

disastrous failure. The logical consequence of these considerations is in direct conflict with the hopes entertained by the founders of the party. Instead of gaining revolutionary energy as the force and solidity of its structure has increased, the precise opposite has occurred; there has resulted, *pari passu* with its growth, a continued increase in the prudence, the timidity even, which inspires its policy. The party, continually threatened by the state upon which its existence depends, carefully avoids (once it has attained to maturity) everything which might irritate the state to excess. The party doctrines are, whenever requisite, attenuated and deformed in accordance with the external needs of the organization. Organization becomes the vital essence of the party. During the first years of its existence, the party did not fail to make a parade of its revolutionary character, not only in respect of its ultimate ends, but also in respect of the means employed for their attainment – although not always in love with these means. But as soon as it attained to political maturity, the party did not hesitate to modify its original profession of faith and to affirm itself revolutionary only 'in the best sense of the word,' that is to say, no longer on lines which interest the police, but only in theory and on paper. This same party, which at one time did not hesitate, when the triumphant guns of the bourgeois governors of Paris were still smoking, to proclaim with enthusiasm its solidarity with the communards, now announces to the whole world that it repudiates antimilitarist propaganda in any form which may bring its adherents into conflict with the penal code, and that it will not assume any responsibility for the consequences that may result from such a conflict. A sense of responsibility is suddenly becoming active in the Socialist party. Consequently it reacts with all the authority at its disposal against the revolutionary currents which exist within its own organization, and which it has hitherto regarded with an indulgent eye. In the name of the grave responsibilities attaching to its position it now disavows anti-militarism, repudiates the general strike, and denies all the logical audacities of its past.

The history of the international labor movement furnishes innumerable examples of the manner in which the party becomes increasingly inert as the strength of its organization grows; it loses its revolutionary impetus, becomes sluggish, not in respect of action alone, but also in the sphere of thought. More and more tenaciously does the party cling to what it calls the 'ancient and glorious tactics', the tactics which have led to a continued increase in membership. More and more invincible becomes its aversion to all aggressive action.

The dread of the reaction by which the socialist party is haunted paralyses all its activities, renders impossible all manifestation of force, and deprives it of all energy for the daily struggle. It attempts to justify its misoneism by the false pretence that it must reserve its strength for the final struggle. Thus we find that the conservative tendencies inherent in all forms of possession manifest themselves also in the Socialist party. For half a century the Socialists have been working in the sweat of their brow to create a model organization. Now, when three million workers have been organized – a greater number than was supposed necessary to secure complete victory over the enemy – the party is endowed with a bureaucracy which, in respect of its consciousness of its duties, its zeal, and its submission to the hierarchy, rivals that of the state itself; the treasuries are full; a complex ramification of financial and moral interests extends all over the country. A bold and enterprising tactic would endanger all this: the work of many decades, the social existence of thousands of leaders and sub-leaders, the entire party, would be compromised. For these reasons the idea of such a tactic becomes more and more distasteful. It conflicts equally with an unjustified sentimentalism and a justified egoism. It is opposed by the artist's love of the work he has created with so much labour, and also by the personal interest of thousands of honest bread-winners whose economic life is so intimately associated with the life of the party and who tremble at the thought of losing their employment and the consequences they would have to endure if the government should proceed to dissolve the party, as might readily happen in case of war.

Thus, from a means, organization becomes an end. To the institutions and qualities which at the outset were destined simply to ensure the good working of the party machine (subordination, the harmonious cooperation of individual members, hierarchical relationships, discretion, propriety of conduct), a greater importance comes ultimately to be attached than to the productivity of the machine. Henceforward the sole preoccupation is to avoid anything which may clog the machinery. Should the party be attacked, it will abandon valuable positions previously conquered, and will renounce ancient rights rather than reply to the enemy's offensive by methods which might 'compromise' its position. Naumann writes sarcastically:

The war-cry 'Proletarians of all countries unite!' has had its due effect. The forces of the organized proletariat have gained a strength which no one believed possible when that war-cry was first sounded. There is money in the treasuries. Is the signal for the final assault never to be given? ... Is the work of preliminary organization to go on for ever?

As the party's need for tranquillity increases, its revolutionary talons atrophy. We have now a finely conservative party which (since the effect survives the cause) continues to employ revolutionary terminology, but which in actual practice fulfils no other function than that of a constitutional opposition.

All this has deviated far from the ideas of Marx, who, were he still alive, ought to be the first to revolt against such a degeneration of Marxism. Yet it is quite possible that, carried away by the spectacle of an army of three million men acting in his name, swearing on solemn occasions *in verba magistri*, he also would find nothing to say in reprobation of so grave a betrayal of his own principles. There were incidents in Marx's life which render such a view possible. He certainly knew how to close his eyes, in public at any rate, to the serious faults committed by the German social democracy in 1876.

In our own day, which may be termed the age of the epigones of Marx, the character of the party as an organization ever greedy for new members, ever seeking to obtain an absolute majority, cooperates with the condition of weakness in which it finds itself *vis-à-vis* the state, to effect a gradual replacement of the old aim, to demolish the existing state by the new aim, to permeate the state with the men and the ideas of the party. The struggle carried on by the socialists against the parties of the dominant classes is no longer one of principle, but simply one of competition. The revolutionary party has become a rival of the bourgeois parties for the conquest of power. It therefore opens its doors to all those persons who may assist in the attainment of this end, or who may simply swell its battalions for the struggle in which it is engaged [. . .]

Thus the hatred of the party is directed, not in the first place against the opponents of its own view of the world order, but against the dreaded rivals in the political field, against those who are competing for the same end – power. It is above all in the electoral agitation carried on by the Socialist parties when they have attained what is termed 'political maturity' that this characteristic is most plainly manifest. The party no longer seeks to fight its opponents, but simply to outbid them. For this reason we observe a continual recurrence in Socialist speeches of a claim which harmonizes ill with Socialist principles, and which is often untrue in fact. Not the nationalists, they say, but we, are the best patriots; not the men of the government, but we, are the best friends of the minor civil servants (in Italy) or of the peasants (in Germany); and so on. Evidently among the trade unions of diverse political coloring, whose primary aim is to gain the greatest possible number of new members, the note of competition will be emphasized yet more. This applies especially to the so-called 'free unions' of Germany, neutrally tinted bodies which on principle hold in horror all definiteness in respect of political views or conceptions of the world order, and which are therefore distinguishable in name only (a few trifling terminological differences apart) from the Christian unions. If we study the speeches and polemic writings directed by the leaders of the free unions against the leaders of the Christian unions, we find that these speeches and writings contain no declarations of principle and no theoretical expositions, but merely personal criticisms and accusations, and above all accusations of treachery to the cause of labor. Now it is obvious that these are no more than the means vulgarly employed by competitors who wish to steal one another's customers.

By such methods, not merely does the party sacrifice its political virginity, by entering into promiscuous relationships with the most heterogeneous political elements, relationships which in many cases have disastrous and enduring consequences, but it exposes itself in addition to the risk of losing its essential character as a party. The term 'party' presupposes that among the individual components of the party there should exist a harmonious direction of wills towards identical objectives and practical aims. Where this is lacking, the party becomes a mere 'organization'.

18 Alvin W. Gouldner

Bureaucracy is Not Inevitable

Excerpts from Alvin W. Gouldner, 'Metaphysical pathos and the theory of bureaucracy', *American Political Science Review*, vol. 49, 1955, pp. 469–507.

That gifted historian of ideas, A. O. Lovejoy, astutely observed that every theory is associated with, or generates, a set of sentiments which those subscribing to the theory could only dimly sense. Lovejoy called this the 'metaphysical pathos' of ideas, a pathos which is 'exemplified in any description of the nature of things, any characterization of the world to which one belongs, in terms which, like the words of a poem, evoke through their associations and through a sort of empathy which they engender, a congenial mood or tone of feeling.'

As a result, a commitment to a theory often occurs by a process other than the one which its proponents believe and it is usually more consequential than they realize. A commitment to a theory may be made because the theory is congruent with the mood or deep-lying sentiments of its adherents, rather than merely because it has been cerebrally inspected and found valid. This is as true for the rigorous prose of social science as it is for the more lucid metaphor of creative literature, for each has its own silent appeal and its own metaphysical pathos.

Furthermore, those who have committed themselves to a theory always get more than they have bargained for. We do not make a commercial contract with a theory in which we agree to accept only the consignment of intellectual goods which has been expressly ordered; usually we take also the metaphysical pathos in which the theory comes packaged. In the end, the theory reinforces or induces in the adherent a subtle alteration in the structure of sentiments through which he views the world.

So too is it with the theory of organization. Paradoxically enough, some of the very theories which promise to make man's own work more intelligible to himself and more amenable to his intelligence are infused with an intangible metaphysical pathos which insinuates, in the very midst of new discoveries, that all is lost. For the metaphysical pathos of much of the modern theory of group organization is that of pessimism and fatalism [. . .]

It is the pathos of pessimism, rather than the compulsions of rigorous analysis, that lead to the assumption that organizational constraints have stacked the deck against democracy. For on the face of it there is every reason to assume that 'the underlying tendencies which are likely to inhibit the democratic process' are just as likely to impair authoritarian rule. It is only in the light of such a pessimistic pathos that the defeat of democratic values can be assumed to be probable, while their victory is seen as a slender thing, delicately constituted and precariously balanced.

When, for example, Michels spoke of the 'iron law of oligarchy', he attended solely to the ways in which organizational needs inhibit democratic possibilities. But the very same evidence to which he called attention could enable us to formulate the very opposite theorem – the 'iron law of democracy'. Even as Michels himself saw, if oligarchical waves repeatedly wash away the bridges of democracy, this eternal recurrence can happen only because men doggedly rebuild them after each inundation. Michels chose to dwell on only one aspect of this process, neglecting to consider this other side. There cannot be an iron law of oligarchy, however, unless there is an iron law of democracy.

Much the same may be said for Selznick's study of the Tennessee Valley Authority.[1] He posits certain organizational needs: a need for the *security* of the organization, for *stable lines of authority* and communication, for *stable* informal relationships. But for each of the organizational needs which Selznick postulates, a set of contrary needs can also be posited, and the satisfaction of these would seem to be just as necessary for the survival of an organization. If, as Selznick says, an organization must have security in its environment, then certainly Toynbee's observations that too much security can be stultifying and corrosive is at least as well taken. To Selznick's security need, a Toynbee might counterpose a need for a moderate challenge or threat.

A similar analysis might also be made of Selznick's postulated need for *homogeneity* of outlook concerning the means and role of the organization. For unless there is some heterogeneity of outlook, then where is an organization to find the tools and flexibility to cope with changes in its environment? Underlying Selznick's need for homogeneity in outlook, is there not another *need*, a need that consent of the governed be given – at least in some measure – to their governors? Indeed, this would seem to be at the very core of Selznick's empirical analysis, though it is obscured in his high-level theoretical statement of the needs of organizations. And if all organizations must adjust to such a need for consent, is there not built into the very marrow of organization a large element of what we

1. Philip Selznick, *TVA and the Grass Roots: a Study in the Sociology of Formal Organization*, University of California Press, 1949.

mean by democracy? This would appear to be an organizational constraint that makes oligarchies, and all separation of leaders from those led, no less inherently unstable than democratic organization.

These contrary needs are just as real and just as consequential for organizational behavior as those proposed by Selznick. But they point in a different direction. They are oriented to problems of change, of growth, of challenging contingencies, of provoking and unsettling encounters. Selznick's analysis seems almost to imply that survival is possible only in an icy stasis, in which 'security', 'continuity', and 'stability' are the key terms. If anything, the opposite seems more likely to be true, and organizational survival is impossible in such a state.

Wrapping themselves in the shrouds of nineteenth-century political economy, some social scientists appear to be bent on resurrecting a dismal science [. . .]

Perhaps the situation can be illuminated with an analogy. For many years now infantile paralysis has killed and maimed scores of people. For many years also doctors, biologists, and chemists have been searching for the causes and cure of this disease. Consider the public reaction if, instead of reporting on their newest vaccines, these scientists had issued the following announcement: 'We have not reached any conclusions concerning the causes of the disease, nor has our research investigated defenses against it. The public seems to have perfectionist aspirations of flawless health, they have 'utopian' illusions concerning the possibilities of immortality and it is this – not the disease – that is the danger against which the public needs to be armed. We must remember that the human animal is not immortal and that for definite reasons his lifespan is finite.' It is likely, of course, that such scientists would be castigated for having usurped the prerogatives and functions of clergymen.

This, however, seems to parallel the way in which some social scientists have approached the study of organizational pathology. Instead of telling men how bureaucracy might be mitigated, they insist that it is inevitable. Instead of explaining how democratic patterns may, to some extent, be fortified and extended, they warn us that democracy cannot be perfect. Instead of controlling the disease, they suggest that we are deluded, or more politely, incurably romantic, for hoping to control it. Instead of assuming responsibilities as realistic clinicians, striving to further democratic potentialities wherever they can, many social scientists have become morticians, all too eager to bury men's hopes.

19 Nigel Young

The English Working Class in Capitalist Society

Excerpts from Nigel Young, 'Prometheans or troglodytes? the English working class and the dialectics of incorporation', *Berkeley Journal of Sociology*, vol. 12, 1967, pp. 1–4 and 24–7.[1]

It would be superfluous to emphasize here the importance of the English societal model in the growth of the social sciences. Recent work has challenged the generalizability of the English 'forerunner' model of modernization and industrialization. This model has prevailed since Marx derived his initial schema of class in the process of industrialization from Engels' empirical study of England and in conjunction with the work of the English political economists. But theoretical inquiry into stratification and change, industrialism and national political citizenship, still returns repeatedly to the 'classic ground' of this first industrial nation. Hardly less important than this model of modernization and industrialization have been the paradigms of English legal and constitutional development, for example, the 'evolution' of its parliamentary democracy, first elaborated by such writers as J. S. Mill and Bagehot, Dicey, Maitland and Stubbs. To the degree to which these models remain theoretically relevant, and to the degree to which sociologists depend on the secondary analysis of historians, any major historiographical shift will have important ramifications for the social sciences. This review-essay is in one sense to be seen as an overdue attempt at a sociological response to just such a shift, to what in fact amounts to a new and significant historiography developed in England over the last decade. This historiography has been distinguished by its re-evaluations of the nature of English society since the Industrial Revolution, by its researches into popular traditions and ruling power, and in its emphasis on the cultural and political role of the working class. Springing in part from Marxian revisionism, this new historiography has been characterized as both a 'democratic' and a 'revolutionary' history. Its dominant tone has been a humane if populistic anti-determinism. It has stressed its concern with men as conscious, creative, *acting* beings, both singly and collectively; with those who failed as well as those who succeeded. The recent widespread analytical return to forgotten or neglected social groups and movements – to peasants, anarchists, religious sects, crowds

1. The editors wish to point out that, due to reasons of space, this article has been severely cut and its important footnotes omitted.

and mobs, and revolutionary folk traditions – is symptomatic of this same tendency. It combines anti-economistic and anti-deterministic currents with an emphasis on continuity and epochal change, rather than climactic discontinuities. The position has been expressed in a particularly eloquent passage by E. P. Thompson in the introduction to his analysis of *The Making of the English Working Class*. He criticizes approaches that see the working class as 'determined' by industrialization, composed of passive victims of *laissez-faire*, statistical data, or 'forerunners' and 'progenitors'. Thompson states that he seeks to rescue men whose 'anti-industrialism may have been backward-looking' whose 'communitarian ideals may have been fantasies' and whose 'insurrectionary conspiracies may have been foolhardy', from the 'enormous condescension of posterity' for 'they lived through these times of acute social disturbance and we did not [. . .] Their aspirations were valid in terms of their own experience.' 'Our only criterion of judgement should not be whether or not a man's actions are justified in the light of subsequent evolution [. . .] we are not at the end of social evolution ourselves.' Such statements express a revolt not merely against the tyranny of certain 'Marxist' categories, but against those of sociologism as well: Thompson's position may be seen as a polar one to that taken by Smelser who describes some of the same ideas, movements, and events as mere 'symptoms of disturbance', 'unjustified' negative, emotional reactions, and 'unrealistic aspirations'. Thompson's approach to the working class differs from earlier British historiography not because it argues (or assumes) the 'pessimistic' interpretation of the impact of Industrialism; nor because it emphasises the role of the 'lower orders'; not even because it takes the 'two-nations' approach to nineteenth- and twentieth-century British society – all this has been done before. Where it varies centrally is in its assumption of the usually latent, but continuing, revolutionary and transforming potential of the working class [. . .]

The incorporation of the English working class into the polity and institutional framework of the nation state, was not achieved by the evolving teleology of some mythic, overarching 'citizenship'. Nor did it emerge through a suffusing and monolithic national consciousness. Rather, I have tried to elucidate those specific institutional nexi, in which ideological enlistment, material inducements, social cooptation and political accommodation could be maximized. I argue that the systems of rights and duties invoked by various groups from the eighteenth century onwards, were in fact fraught with contradictions, concealing deep social polarities. I conclude that the civic incorporation of the English working class did not take place during early industrialism. On the contrary, it seems clear that a strong sense of separate identity and intense working-class consciousness developed. This was reinforced by social ostracization and curtailment of rights, symbolized by such acts of state as the 1832 Reform Bill and the Poor Law Act of 1834. The culture of this class is then examined in terms of a continuing popular egalitarian-collectivism. This collectivism is seen to be in part traditional, in part articulated in opposition to the other major normative deviation from paternalist-traditionalism – bourgeois individualism, utilitarianism, and political economy. But it is also stressed that this collectivism is no spontaneous or reactive generation of the factory system. Its major expression is seen as clearly the creation of a set of, what became eventually largely defensive, institutional bulwarks which protected and insulated normative alternatives. Although it does not seem that free-market and individualist values had a profound impact on working men, leading to the 'social capillarity' that many expected, certain working-class institutions were drawn corporatively into the market frame. Moreover, many members of the class became increasingly 'respectable', introspective and for long periods, passive. But the class clearly also became increasingly powerful and well organized. I try to show that if it had abandoned its revolutionary ambitions, the working class had not wholly lost its revolutionary potentialities. In some sense 'hegemonic' consciousness and aspiration began to reappear mechanically at the end of the nineteenth century as the class engaged in successful economistic conflicts and increased its corporative strength. Yet it is clear that this reappearance of consciousness and action was not joined by any intellectual force, assisting the class to set and impose goals for the society. Thus it is concluded that the hermetic culture, whilst preserving class-identity, has by way of introverting consciousness, kept the class, and its ideals, subordinate.

Proletarian collectivism has to be seen not merely as a creative response to the facts of capitalism, but as *the* popular response to the egalitarian rationalism of the Enlightenment. In its democratic institutional forms, this response was concretized. Having been defined as deviant, these institutions were at first repressed, then accommodated, and finally incorporated into the structure of the nation state. For, in conclusion, I have followed the historians in identifying the crucial nexus of civic and national incorporation as the Labour Party in Parliament. Despite the importance of nationalism, and Imperialist distractions, it seems to be here that the mystification of the state, law and constitution, and the cooptive mechanisms prove decisive, drawing even the unions into the national frame.

At the outset of this analysis two major structural orientations to British society since industrialization may be distinguished: one, stressing civic integration and national polity, may be called the 'citizenship' approach. The other, (towards which this present analysis tends) stresses class-culture and polarization; this I shall label the 'two-nations' approach. These two perspectives almost exactly parallel the fundamental bifurcation in social theory between theory which emphasizes normative and functional unity – societal integration – (the approach which, at least since Durkheim's 'moral society', has dominated sociology) and theory which alternatively emphasizes the ubiquity of authority or coercion, 'dysfunctional' conflict, and social change. The former's stress on general value orientations leads to a parallel dichotomy in institutional-normative approaches. At the risk of oversimplification, there is a tendency for the normative-integration approach to stress common culture and overarching or general value orientations (and their essential continuity) at the *societal* and – usually, in application – at the *national* (state) level. As one incisive critique put it: 'Each culture is made to appear as a whole which possesses different parts (sub-cultures) as well as an overall unity (way of life) but in which the actions of individuals and groups are limited to pre-established patterns and tend to reinforce the culture of which they are a part.' Moreover, the normative-integration approach tends to de-emphasize the analysis of institutional levels at which normative alternatives (and thus normative-institutional conflict, dissensus) may be generated and sustained. 'Within the arena of contending groups,' Bendix observes, 'separate and competing subcultures may be distinguished, which may be systematically united only by a minimum of shared values, and largely by coercive conjunctions, law and social control.' As Bendix has also stressed it is necessary to conceptualize the conflicting tendencies inherent in the development of social structures in order to avoid the 'fallacy of retrospective determinism'. Despite the disclaimers of its proponents it is exactly this fallacy – as well as some of the other flaws in the normative-structural functional approach, cited above – that I think is involved in many of the applications of the concept of 'citizenship'. For example, the citizenship approach tends to stress a *national* normative unity, over against the conflicting tendencies inherent in sub-cultural (or counter-cultural) and institutional formations. This approach is individuating: it stresses civic status and hierarchy, over against social class. In emphasizing recognition and reciprocity (of rights, duties, claims and obligations) there is a tendency, as in normative functionalism, to exaggerate the 'dependent adjustment' aspects of human activity, rather than the 'deliberate' and 'innovative' elements.

Recent historical research points to an alternative perspective. Rejecting implicitly this reified national, societal and 'civic' framework, its prime concentration is on firstly the sub-societal group, the counter-institutional formation and the counter-normative developments of the English proletariat, and secondly on the active and innovative roles, in particular the *institutional* creativity, of working people. I shall argue that, drawing on the cultural alternatives embodied in the historical developments of popular institutional forms (political, industrial groups, friendly societies, village life, etc.), there was created an implicit *rival* societal frame, an alternative model of social relations and a separate culture. On the other hand, to a limited degree certain of the 'givens' or assumptions of nineteenth-century bourgeois society *were* partly accepted, more by segmental, situational, and institutional compulsion, than by actual ideological persuasion. Through this acceptance, the notion of a common citizenship was able to grow slowly more influential, after the great working-class defeats of the 1830s and 1840s. But this specific growth (of the notion of a common citizenship) has to be differentiated from other types of parallel ideological developments – including the slow increase in national consciousness. The development of a 'civic-sense' has also to be seen in the context of a variety of institutional changes, not merely at the level of the nation state or the 'polity', but in the local community [. . .]

With the Labour Party, the working class – and, less directly, their unions – became genuine, if subordinate, partners in running the machine, and naturally aspirants for controlling it. It was a machine in which the bourgeoisie daily 'disposed of more ample means of corruption, both material and spiritual'. Whereas for several decades after 1867 parliamentary activity has remained the epiphenomena of the labor movement [. . .] after 1906 it drew increasing popular attention. Parliamentarism was able to physically and culturally sever working-class leadership from its constituency in a way that had not occurred previously; oligarchic control advanced rapidly within the new party. At the same time the grip on this leadership of constitutionalism and the parliamentary 'rules of the game' strengthened. As Miliband shows, the party leaders were from the outset pitted fundamentally against strikes and direct action, especially of the uncompromising Syndicalist sort; class war was permissible, as long as it was not expressed in industrial terms. As MacDonald said, berating the Syndicalists in 1912, 'Socialism must start from the facts of social unity.' Accepting all the characteristic mystagogy and conventions of 'the greatest social club in the world', the Labour Party endorsed in quick succession, ministers in liberal governments, compromising coalitions, cabinet government, royal honors, and the principle of parliamentary autonomy. They were indeed eager victims of the mystique of the 'dignified part of the constitution'.

It must be emphasized that the English working class entered the English state machinery at a moment of its growing power and self-consciousness. The industrial challenges of the pre-war years were to shake it to its foundations, but in 1900, it still deployed all 'those innumerable defenses against any ultimate class confrontation' that characterize its structures. Again, the World-War coalition, into which the Labour Party entered in 1915, proved to be a confirmation of a renewed growth of statism. The Party was recruited to act as an agent of war-mobilization (though with an important dissenting minority, even at the Party's top levels). The spread of the Party as a national electoral organization at this time was perhaps the single most decisive factor in spreading a sense of national identity and obligation, and enhancing 'civic incorporation' through its emphasis on electoral equality and national status. After 1915, it was at last possible for politicians to appeal to a common-community to curtail class conflict (though with the resurgence of union militancy in 1916 these were decreasingly effective). Each successive Labour government has done the same.

The national organization of the Labour Party did not in any sense reflect the collective culture which it purported to represent. It was, in fact, completely imitative of the bourgeois electoral machines developed over the previous fifty years with personalist, vote-catching campaigns, the manipulative use of communications and increasingly bureaucratic central direction. It proved essentially adaptive to the integumental institutional modes; its campaigns were 'respectable' and 'responsible'. Moreover, despite the formal subordination of the party to the unions, the party became first independent, then dominant in the partnership. Neither union nor constituency delegates were able to control their representatives in parliament; rather, they were played off against one another.

The Labour Party, in turn had profound effects on the unions. It drew union leadership into the parliamentary arena and was influential in furthering the bureaucratization of the unions which had hitherto advanced remarkably slowly. The continuous diplomatic contact with the metropolitan bourgeoisie and its august institutions, elicited an almost feudal, deferential response from many union leaders, now separated by parliamentary activity from their union constituents. Much of Michels' analysis of the conditions of social democratic betrayal apply quite perfectly to the English case; but this was the structural entailment of parliamentarism *per se*, not of corporative unionism in itself. Increasingly conscious of media dominance, and the developing internal oligarchy of the party, meant that parliament, where the politics of pressure and various kinds of 'influence' were disguised in argument, became a facile arena for the ideological cooptation of industrial leaders. Only those, like miners' leaders, who stayed outside parliament, retained their militancy.

Parliament, in other words, imposed its own conditions. It ritualized political deference and civility in a traditional institution; it realized a formal corporate assimilation of labor; it then proceeded to coopt the leadership and began to accelerate the individuation of the rank and file. Corporativism, economism and pragmatism could not alone have achieved all this; the evolutionist, reformist and statist perspective of the Fabians, aided by the available forms of Marxism, were initially responsible. From that moment parliamentarism, and the centralizing bipartisanship it produced, increasingly dominated the Labour movement. It directly conflicted with the federalist, localist, and spontaneous elements in unionism. Moreover, it directly undermined the hegemonic logic of unionism's corporative institutional development. When national industrial crises came, and they did, the emollient and obfuscating qualities of the Labour movement's nexi with parliament proved decisive. Parliament itself was, of course, never 'an arena of a genuine class confrontation'.

As Thompson writes, most governing institutions 'operate with a good deal of autonomy ... within a general context of class power ... those moments in which [they] appear as the direct, emphatic, and unmediated organs of a "ruling class" are extremely rare, as well as transient.' In the first three decades of the nineteenth century, and again in the first three decades of the twentieth there were a number of moments when the ruling class deployed its claim of legality and constitutionality against the working class, and in particular against its combinations. When it did so the ruling class revealed its claims as based on too narrow a class interest, thereby decisively undermining its legitimacy. For brief moments the opacity of this link between generalized values and specific interests stood revealed. In these periods, parliament, law, the constitution, rapidly lost credibility; the social structures appeared fragile and malleable, or as Lloyd George put it, 'molten'. In such crises efforts to maintain the system often tended to exacerbate tension and resistance.

In the earlier period, the Labour movement had lacked experience and firmly-rooted organizations; in the latter, it lacked volatility and hegemonic aspirations. In 1926, perhaps the last moment when a climactic syndical transformation was possible, and after deep inroads had been made by parliamentarism, the militancy of sections of the working class overtook a conservative leadership. With immense popular support union militants enforced a national confrontation. In the communities the collective institutions took over; the cooperatives distributed food and printed a news-sheet, the trades-councils became sources of local authority, in some areas even taking over policing duties from the constabulary. As the strike progressed, it was clear that as J. H. Thomas had warned, 'passions that might be difficult to control' had been let loose, and the militants became more influential each day the impasse was prolonged. After nine days, a majority of the trade union leadership, in collaboration with the Labour Party in London, and conferring with the Government, capitulated, in part fearing its own rank-and-file. The following day the strike was a quarter-of-a-million stronger, as if to exemplify the resistance to the new controllers. But in the wake of the repressions that followed, and with union and Labour Party membership declining, class collaboration became the order of the day. Both through the unions and in parliament, the process of centralization, bureaucratization and a-politicization was resumed.

Despite the *civic* incorporation of the English working class, largely by way of the Labour Party, its *culture* has not, as the recurring prophets of embourgeoisement predicted, 'dwindled to a minimum'. There has perhaps been some transition from a traditional 'solidary' type of collectivism to a more 'instrumental' variety. But the educational system remains an instrument of class-differentiation not unification; the incomes-gap has not noticeably narrowed; and consequently the social composition of the élite remains much the same. In material terms a common, national mass-culture has developed, based on mass-production. It was already spreading in the later nineteenth century, to the horror of men like Ruskin and Morris. Thus it is partly true that 'instead of inheriting a simple but distinctive culture', working people have been 'provided with a cheap and shoddy imitation of a civilization that has become national'. Yet as has been argued, that which is distinctive about English working-class culture is not its material artifacts, but its ideas about social relationships, given institutional expression. It is this continuity of ideas and institutions which has led me to interpret 150 years of working-class conflict, not as Smelser puts it, as 'disturbed reactions to specific structural pressures', but as much nearer to a permanent, if often undeclared, state of war. Moreover, sixty years after the parliamentary incorporation of labor was initiated, most of the culture, especially certain of the institutional forms, remain not only intact, but vital to the working-class community. Insofar as they embody an alternative idea of social relationships their continued vitality, and the survival of the ideas they express, represent for British society an unresolved contradiction.

20 Robert McKenzie and Alan Silver

The Working-Class Tory in England

Robert McKenzie and Alan Silver, 'Conservation and the working-class Tory in England', *Transactions of the Fifth World Congress of Sociology*, International Sociological Association, 1962, pp. 191-202.

The most general impression one gets from a comparison of Labour and Conservative working-class voters in this sample is of a prevailing homogeneity between the two groups. There is little difference between them in terms of sex, income, or occupational skill level, and only a moderate difference in terms of age. No comparable studies exist to provide a base line, but previous research does suggest that an earlier tendency for working-class Conservatives to be older and have lower incomes than Labour voters is disappearing, though the Conservatives are still somewhat older.

These aggregate results conceal some diverging trends: among the lower-income group, older voters more frequently vote Conservative than younger (Table 1); and, while age and sex separately are either moderately related or unrelated to voting Conservative, older working-class women vote Conservative with considerably more frequency than do other groups. We shall return to these findings later, in another context.

Table 1 Among Working-Class Voters with Below-Average Incomes, the Older are more often Conservative than the Younger

	Below average incomes		Above average incomes	
	Below age 44	Above age 44	Below age 44	Above age 44
	%		%	
Labour	83	63	71	70
Conservative	17	37	29	30
N (= 100%)	72	162	150	102

The political and social perspectives of Labour and Conservative working-class voters differ where one would expect them to – with respect to objects of partisan concern like the issue of nationalization, key power sources such as the trade unions, big business and the upper classes, and the parties themselves. Yet the differences are not such as to override an impression that Conservative values pervade much of the urban working class, including many Labour voters. There is, for example, a widespread dislike or distrust of trade unions: more than half of the entire sample agrees that unions have too much power. The unions are often perceived – even by working-class Labour voters – as unduly disruptive or officious; and there is a good deal of feeling that strikes are called too frequently, despite the far lower strike rate of Britain compared to that of the United States. The organic view of society, promulgated by the great Conservative spokesmen, Burke and Disraeli, finds a responsive echo in the contemporary urban working class. For such reasons, it is hard to think of working-class Conservatives in Britain as normatively deviant from working-class political culture; on the contrary, they seem to express aspects of a wide national consensus.

It is also difficult to think of working-class Conservatives as apathetic, ignorant, or alienated people – a kind of psychological *lumpenproletariat*. Working-class Conservatism cannot, apparently, be ascribed to political pathology in ways analogous to the alleged link between the 'authoritarian personality' and clinical pathology. In fact, the working-class Conservatives in our sample tend to be better informed than the Labour voters in terms of political knowledge; somewhat more of them (to take but one example) knew the name of the leader of the Labour Party. Furthermore, Conservative voters show no signs of a greater sense of political futility. In short, the Conservatives appear to be as well integrated as Labour voters into the political process in contemporary Britain.

Conservative working-class voters proved to be much more committed to their party in terms of range of criteria than Labour voters. While Labour is widely perceived as more concerned with the interests of the common man, it is often seen as more solicitous than efficacious, while the Conservatives are widely seen as more efficacious than solicitous. In short, many working-class voters believe that the Conservatives have a capacity to get things done – a superior executive ability – which appears to offset their lesser concern with the class interests of manual workers.

'Concern for the interests of the common man' is almost the only criterion on which Labour is consistently ranked higher than the Conservatives. With respect to foreign policy, Commonwealth relations, national prosperity, and the sense of patriotism, the Conservatives are evaluated as far superior by Tory voters, and as almost the equal of (or superior to) Labour by Labour voters. In fact, Conservative voters in the working class appear to enjoy greater congruence between voting behavior and broad perceptions of the parties than do Labour voters, who seem to be linked to Labour almost entirely in terms of class interest. In a political culture which values so highly the Burkean themes of consensus and national community, this suggests that working-class Conservatives may be under less ideological cross-pressure than Labour voters.

Let us turn, for the moment, from the analysis of working-class Conservative and Labour voters, to focus on the population of working-class Conservatives. Here, we can no longer rely upon the dichotomous choice situation imposed by a two-party system to provide the categories of analysis. Rather, it is necessary to develop analytic categories derived from the historical origins of working-class Conservatism in Britain.

Both Marx and Disraeli conceived working-class Conservatism to be based on what Walter Bagehot, in *The English Constitution,* called 'deference': the voluntary abnegation of power by the working class in favour of an hereditary, or quasi-hereditary elite. A reading both of Bagehot and of Conservative propaganda directed at the working class suggests the following set of definitions of 'deferential' Conservatism. Deferentials:

1. Prefer ascribed, socially superior political leadership.
2. Prefer power to originate from the elite, rather than from the mass franchise.
3. Form and express political judgements in terms of the intrinsic characteristics of leader, not pragmatically in terms of issues or the outcome of policy.
4. View political outcomes benefiting the working class as indulgent or paternalistic acts by the elite, not as flowing from the machinery of government or the economy.
5. Prefer continuity to abrupt change.
6. View the Conservative Party as more patriotic than the opposition.

We have also used a typological opposite to deference – perspectives which run counter to these traditional values; we called working-class voters with such outlooks 'seculars'. The question then becomes: are all, or almost all, working-class Conservatives 'deferentials' – as envisioned by observers so diversely committed as Marx, Bagehot, and Disraeli? If not, what are the conditions and consequences of these two kinds of working-class Conservatism?

It is necessary to illustrate at least the single most important criterion used to define deference and secularism. We asked respondents to explain their choice for Prime Minister as between two men – one of them the son of a banker and MP, a graduate of Eton and Oxford, and an officer in the Guards; the other, the son of a lorry (truck) driver who went to a grammar school, won a scholarship to a provincial university, entered the Army as a private and was promoted to officer rank. We have, then, caricatured but not unrealistic pictures of ascribed, elitist leadership and of achieved leadership of working-class origin. A few quotations will give the flavour of the distinctions made possible by this procedure.

Deferential responses: [respondent prefers son of MP.] 'Because he should have the brains or instincts of parents. The qualities to make a Prime Minister are in the breeding. When it comes to critical questions like whether the country should go to war you want someone with a good headpiece who knows what he's doing. It's born in you.'

'The MP's son. Breeding counts every time. I like to be set an example and have someone I can look up to. I know the other man has got a long way on his own merits, and I do admire that, but breeding shows and is most important in that position.'

Secular responses: [respondent prefers lorry (truck) driver's son.] 'He has struggled in life. He knows more about the working troubles of the ordinary person. Those who inherit money rarely know anything about real life. This man has proved he is clever and can achieve something without any help from others.'

'Either of them because it depends upon their individual ruling ability.'

Using this criterion alone, it was possible to compare working-class voters for the two parties. Deference is considerably more common among Conservative than Labour voters. Half of the Conservatives, but only one-fifth of the Labour voters, preferred the Prime Minister of elite social origin. It seems that deferential perspectives continue to sustain the Conservatism of very many working-class voters in contemporary urban England.

Among working-class Conservatives it was possible to classify individuals on the basis of more of the six criteria defining deference and secularism. When we look for social differences between these two ideological kinds of working-class Conservatives, the factors of age, sex, and income that failed to discriminate (or do so decreasingly) between Labour and Conservative voters, come to life; deferentials tend strongly to be older than seculars and to have lower incomes; and there is a marked, but lesser tendency for fewer women than men to be seculars.

Insofar as youth and higher incomes are linked to post-war social change – to which women can be thought of as socially less exposed than men – secularism may be displacing deference as an ideological basis of working-class Conservatism in Britain. It is not possible, however, definitively to establish this conclusion by means of observations at one point in time. Moreover, the themes and motifs of traditional hierarchical Conservatism – so richly available in British culture – may well be available for resuscitation under the impact of future events.

Some political attitudes of deferentials and seculars diverge. Seculars, for example, are less often unconditionally committed to the Conservative Party: almost all the deferentials, but only half the seculars, said that they would definitely vote Conservative in an imminent hypothetical election – a result obtained long before the pressures of the campaign, and of the necessity for choice, precipitated long-standing loyalties. There is a moderate, but consistent tendency for seculars to be more frequently 'leftist' on a variety of issues and judgements. There is considerable evidence to suggest that seculars are more concerned with social mobility: many more of them than deferentials endorse a complaint that it is 'too hard for a man with ambition to get ahead in Britain'. Finally, seculars seem to be more sensitized to economic deprivation: among low-income working-class Conservatives (but not those with high incomes), seculars are much more likely to identify with the working class than are deferentials (Table 2).

Table 2 Among Working-Class Conservatives with Below-Average Incomes, Seculars are more likely than Deferentials to Identify with the Working Class[1]

Class Identification	Below average incomes			Above average incomes		
	Deferential	% Mixed	Secular	Deferential	% Mixed	Secular
Working class	58	70	89	77	73	73
Middle class	34	21	11	23	13	21
Other, don't know	8	9	—	—	14	6
N (= 100%)	26	24	18	13	15	34

1. The income of the chief wage earners of forty-eight respondents could not be ascertained.

Keeping in mind that deferentials are considerably older than seculars, we can now suggest why, as we have reported, low income has a conservatizing effect among older working-class voters, but seems to move younger ones in the direction of Labour. Low income may be tolerated by deferential Conservatives and, indeed, experienced as calling for increased reliance upon the traditional elite. But for seculars, low income may represent a severe strain upon their commitment to the Conservative Party – a commitment based upon pragmatic rather than traditional grounds. The political impact of low income, then, depends on the values and perspectives upon which party loyalty is based. Analogous reasoning may account for the uniquely high level of Conservative voting among older, working-class women: both their age and sex combine to leave them relatively unexposed to 'secularization' among Conservative voters; hence, they are less able to withdraw support from the traditional elite.

We can also suggest why the typical correlates of working-class rightist voting – age, sex, and income – do not obtain, or are decreasing, in contemporary Britain. We are, perhaps, witnessing a shift from the politicized ethos of earlier working-class protest to what has been called the 'post-political' age. In the earlier context, traditionalist ideologies like deference were linked, in the working class, to low income (among unskilled rural migrants from traditional backgrounds), to women (relatively insulated from change), and to the older (who had been socialized into traditional values); hence, these characteristics in turn were often linked to rightist voting. But as working-class Conservatism is stabilized in Britain on the basis of ideologies more appropriate to industrial culture, like secular Conservatism, the earliest empirical correlations between working-class rightist voting and these attributes begin to diminish.

Does this mean that something like Jacksonian, or more generally egalitarian, perspectives are emerging in the working-class electorate? Not necessarily. Even in the United States, as Lane has suggested, inegalitarian values have important functions for the industrial working class. And, as Almond has argued, traditional elements in modern political culture can be seen not as deviant, anachronistic, or atavistic, but as serving critically important expressive and symbolic purposes. Where would these things be more likely to persist than in the peculiarly and triumphantly mixed political culture of Britain, in which traditional themes bear so close a relationship to the very sense of nationality?

The data contain other suggestions as to the future of working-class deference. For example, as younger working-class Conservative voters appear to move away from deference – at least for the present – younger Labour voters are not; indeed, they may be moving toward it. Thus, proportionately more younger than older Conservatives prefer the lorry driver's son as Prime Minister, but somewhat more younger than older Labour voters prefer the candidate of elite social origin (Table 3). It is possible that, while secularism is 'modern' for working-class Conservatives it is less so for Labour voters. It is as if deferential predispositions among working-class voters for both major parties are converging toward a common level.

Table 3 Older Working-Class Voters are more Likely than Younger to Prefer a Prime Minister of Elite Social Origin among Conservative Voters, but not among Labour Voters

	Labour voters		Conservative voters	
	Below age 44	Above age 44	Below age 44	Above age 44
	%		%	
Prefers Prime Minister of:				
Working class origin	70	80	54	39
Elite origin	27	17	40	53
Neither, don't know	3	3	6	8
N (= 100%)	207	218	65	113

It may be, then, that as recent social change in Britain – expanded working-class horizons, improved access to education, higher incomes, the slow erosion of class boundaries – is diluting deference among Conservatives, the resulting greater integration of the working class into British society is confronting Labour voters with traditional themes to which they had previously been unexposed or hostile. Such themes, deference among them, may, in the Britain to come, begin to lose their intimate connection with the Conservative Party and become more than ever norms for the good citizen, regardless of party loyalty. Indeed, the data show that the connection between deference and Conservative voting is far stronger among older than among younger workers (Table 4). Thus, deference may be declining among Conservative working-class voters, increasing or maintaining itself among Labour voters, and thus becoming less factional and more consensual among the working-class electorate.

At least until 1964, however, it appeared that post-war social change in urban Britain had acted less dramatically to change the frequency with which working-class electors voted Conservative than to shift the social and ideological basis of working-class Conservative allegiance from the older and poorer to the younger and better paid, from deferentials to seculars. The Conservative Party is well prepared by its history to cope with this change. But one hundred years after the Reform of 1867,

Table 4 Deference is more Closely linked to Conservative Voting among Older than Younger Working-Class Voters, Regardless of Income

| Prefers Prime Minister of: | Below-average income | | | | Above-average income | | | |
| | Below age 44 | | Above age 44 | | Below age 44 | | Above age 44 | |
	Elite origin (deferential) %	Working-class origin (secular) %	Elite origin (deferential) %	Working-class origin (secular) %	Elite origin (deferential) %	Working-class origin (secular) %	Elite origin (deferential) %	Working-class origin (secular) %
Labour	70	86	36	76	64	75	48	81
Conservative	30	14	64	24	36	25	52	19
N (= 100%)	19	51	47	105	44	95	33	63

the decline of deference among working-class Conservatives sharpens the party's need to attract the increasingly prosperous descendants of the Victorian working men whom Disraeli and his followers enfranchised.

Five years after that reform, Bagehot, fearing the domination of the 'poor ignorant people', saw deference as crucial to 'the happy working of a delicate experiment'. As working-class Conservatives come to include fewer of the poor and the deferential, the shape of the party's relationship to its working-class voters remains to be clarified by time, research, and the course of events.

21 J. Blondel

Voters, Parties and Leaders

Excerpts from J. Blondel, *Voters, Parties and Leaders*,
Penguin Books, 1963, pp. 71–2 and 83–4.

If one tries to analyse the floating vote, one must analyse all the possible movements. If one analyses all the possible movements, one finds that the floating vote is a very complex reality. In a straight fight, in two successive elections, there are three possibilities open to each elector: he can vote Conservative, vote Labour, or abstain. Since he can have voted Conservative, have voted Labour, or abstained at the previous election, there are nine possible courses open to the electors of the constituency. All these courses are in fact taken. Only three of them constitute a form of 'fixed' voting behaviour; each of the other six is a form of floating vote. If the constituency has a three-cornered fight in one of the instances, there are twelve possibilities, nine of which constitute a form of floating vote. With a three-cornered fight in both instances, twelve courses out of sixteen are forms of floating vote. It may be, as Gallup polls showed, that 80 per cent of the population always voted for the same *party*; this does not mean that only 20 per cent are floating voters, because this would amount to discarding the occasional abstainers. We saw that in Bristol in 1955 their role was crucial. It is perhaps nearer the truth to argue, from the evidence of detailed constituency surveys, that as many as a quarter of the electors are in some sense floating voters, *from one election to the next*.

One finds, in each constituency, movements of floating voters in all possible directions. One should not be surprised to find also, as voting studies showed, that the floating voters are not the most rational of electors. Floating voters may play a crucial part in the British system of government. But they do not seem to be aware of their responsibilities. They do not seem to be drawn from the most politically conscious section of the community. The reasons for their change of allegiance are often trivial. They seem to be less committed, not because of a genuine independence of mind, but more out of apathy. They resemble abstainers more than they resemble the image of the perfect voter. Indeed, since many floaters are, or have been, abstainers, there is a natural similarity between the two groups. As the authors of the Bristol surveys said, they are likely to 'resemble, not Hamlet, paralysed by the pale cast of doubt, but Lancelot Gobbo' [. . .]

Party images

Voting cannot be explained by entirely rational criteria. At the beginning of the century, Wallas showed the fairly narrow limits of the rational element in voting behaviour. Even though the two-party system enables electors to choose between two sets of programmes and only between two sets of programmes, it is not true that electors choose between programmes. It is not even true that electors, having only one vote, establish an order of priority and select one 'most important issue' on the basis of which they cast their vote. Studies which have taken place since Wallas have shown that the support which electors give to a party is linked, not with 'issues', but with much broader and vaguer general 'images' with which the party is associated. These images often coincide with a certain view of the class system in the country, particularly among Labour electors, a large majority of whom claim that their party is 'for the working-class' and an even larger majority of whom claim that the Conservative party is 'for the rich or big business'. These images are also associated with some general economic and social notions, such as the 'Welfare State', 'full employment' in the past, 'free enterprise' and, now, quite often, 'nationalization'. The internal unity and the character of the leadership of the parties play a part in the formation of these images. In recent years at any rate, foreign affairs do not: respondents of whatever political views recognize that both parties are 'for peace' in a general sense. Images do not spring up either, in the minds of electors, on humanitarian and libertarian questions. To that extent, the partisanship which one finds on economic and social 'images' corresponds to the partisanship which we found earlier on economic and social issues.

Images differ from issues, but they are connected to them. Images do live. As the authors of the Bristol surveys said, some issues cross the gateway and become images, as, in recent years, nationalization; others, such as full employment, disappear in the wilderness. Images are influenced by issues in a general fashion: they are influenced by what is going on. They are also influenced by leadership and party dynamism. But they are more persistent than issues and some of them, for instance the image of class, are so persistent that they seem to be permanent. They are much vaguer than issues; they indicate that the electors have a general view of society and of the way in which the parties fit in the framework of society. One of the difficulties of the Liberal party seems to be that it does not, as yet, evoke any images in the minds of the electors.

There is nothing inherently wrong in the fact that electors associate the parties with images and not with policies. We have just said that, in the long run, these images are modified and influenced; they are modified by the policies and record of the parties. Moreover, if party support was entirely rational and solely based on policies, representative government would become unworkable. The parties would never be able to count on some loyal support in cases of blunders and difficulties; nor would they ever be able to rally their supporters and thereby educate public opinion. But the decisions at election time would not become any easier, since the parties have comprehensive programmes and since a vote has to be a vote for a package deal. Voting is clearly partly an emotional affair. It is based on prejudices as well as on a rational assessment of the structure of society in general. It is based on the view which the electors have of the future society which the parties are trying to build. It is up to the parties to modify, slowly but profoundly, these prejudices and these views. Party images are the medium through which the party conflict is resolved, every four or five years, at the general election. General elections involve the whole life of the nation. It is natural that they should be decided, not only by views on one or a few fairly specialized questions, but on the whole of the impressions which, rightly or wrongly, electors have of society and of its political forces.

22 Leon Trotsky

What Happened to the Revolution?

Excerpts from Leon Trotsky, *The Revolution Betrayed*,
Pioneer Publishers, 1937, pp. 89–90, 112–14 and 254–6.

The axiom-like assertions of the Soviet literature, to the effect that the laws of bourgeois revolutions are 'inapplicable' to a proletarian revolution, have no scientific content whatever. The proletarian character of the October Revolution was determined by the world situation and by a special correlation of internal forces. But the classes themselves were formed in the barbarous circumstances of Tsarism and backward capitalism, and were anything but made to order for the demands of a socialist revolution. The exact opposite is true. It is for the very reason that a proletariat still backward in many respects achieved in the space of a few months the unprecedented leap from a semi-feudal monarchy to a socialist dictatorship, that the reaction in its ranks was inevitable. This reaction has developed in a series of consecutive waves. External conditions and events have vied with each other in nourishing it. Intervention followed intervention. The Revolution got no direct help from the West. Instead of the expected prosperity of the country an ominous destitution reigned for long. Moreover, the outstanding representatives of the working class either died in the civil war, or rose a few steps higher and broke away from the masses. And thus after an unexampled tension of forces, hopes and illusions, there came a long period of weariness, decline, and sheer disappointment in the results of the Revolution. The ebb of the 'plebeian pride' made room for a flood of pusillanimity and careerism. The new commanding caste rose to its place upon this wave.

The demobilization of the Red Army of five million played no small role in the formation of the bureaucracy. The victorious commanders assumed leading posts in the local Soviets, in economy, in education, and they persistently introduced everywhere that regime which had ensured success in the civil war. Thus on all sides the masses were pushed away gradually from actual participation in the leadership of the country.

The reaction within the proletariat caused an extraordinary flush of hope and confidence in the petty-bourgeois strata of town and country, aroused as they were to new life by the NEP [New Economic Policy], and growing bolder and bolder. The young bureaucracy, which had arisen at first as an agent of the proletariat, began now to feel itself a court of arbitration between the classes. Its independence increased from month to month.

The international situation was pushing with mighty forces in the same direction. The Soviet bureaucracy became more self-confident, the heavier the blows dealt to the world working class. Between these two facts there was not only a chronological, but a causal connection, and one which worked in two directions. The leaders of the bureaucracy promoted the proletarian defeats; the defeats promoted the rise of the bureaucracy. The crushing of the Bulgarian insurrection and the inglorious retreat of the German workers' party in 1923, the collapse of the Estonian attempt at insurrection in 1924, the treacherous liquidation of the General Strike in England and the unworthy conduct of the Polish workers' party at the installation of [Jozef] Pilsudski [as premier] in 1926, the terrible massacre of the Chinese revolution in 1927, and, finally, the still more ominous recent defeats in Germany and Austria – these are the historic catastrophes which killed the faith of the Soviet masses in world revolution and permitted the bureaucracy to rise higher and higher as the sole light of salvation [. . .]

The basis of bureaucratic rule is the poverty of society in objects of consumption, with the resulting struggle of each against all. When there are enough goods in a store, the purchasers can come whenever they want to. When there are few goods, the purchasers are compelled to stand in line. When the lines are very long, it is necessary to appoint a policeman to keep order. Such is the starting point of the power of the Soviet bureaucracy. It 'knows' who is to get something and who has to wait.

A raising of the material and cultural level ought, at first glance, to lessen the necessity of privileges, narrow the sphere of application of 'bourgeois law', and thereby undermine the standing ground of its defenders, the bureaucracy. In reality the opposite thing has happened: the growth of the productive forces has been so far accompanied by an extreme development of all forms of inequality, privilege, and advantage, and therewith of bureaucratism. That too is not accidental.

In its first period, the Soviet regime was undoubtedly far more equalitarian and less bureaucratic than now. But that was an equality of general poverty. The resources of the country were so scant that there was no opportunity to separate out from the masses of the population any broad privileged strata. At the same time the 'equalizing' character of wages, destroying personal interestedness, became a brake upon the development of the productive forces. Soviet economy had to lift itself from its poverty to a somewhat higher level before fat deposits of privilege became possible. The present state of production is still far from guaranteeing all necessities to everybody. But it is already adequate to give significant privileges to a minority, and convert inequality into a whip for the spurring on of the majority. That is the first reason why the growth of production has so far strengthened not the socialist, but the bourgeois features of the state.

But that is not the sole reason. Alongside the economic factor dictating capitalistic methods of payment at the present stage, there operates a parallel political factor in the person of the bureaucracy itself. In its very essence it is the planter and protector of inequality. It arose in the beginning as the bourgeois organ of a workers' state. In establishing and defending the advantages of a minority, it of course draws off the cream for its own use. Nobody who has wealth to distribute ever omits himself. Thus out of a social necessity there has developed an organ which has far outgrown its socially necessary function and become an independent factor and therewith the source of great danger for the whole social organism.

The social meaning of the Soviet Thermidor now begins to take form before us. The poverty and cultural backwardness of the masses has again become incarnate in the malignant figure of the ruler with a great club in his hand. The deposed and abused bureaucracy, from being a servant of society, has again become its lord. On this road it has attained such a degree of social and moral alienation from the popular masses that it cannot now permit any control over either its activities or its income.

The bureaucracy's seemingly mystic fear of 'petty speculators, grafters, and gossips' thus finds a wholly natural explanation. Not yet able to satisfy the elementary needs of the population, the Soviet economy creates and resurrects at every step tendencies to graft and speculation. On the other side, the privileges of the new aristocracy awaken in the masses of the population a tendency to listen to anti-Soviet 'gossips' – that is, to anyone who, albeit in a whisper, criticizes the greedy and capricious bosses. It is a question, therefore, not of specters of the past, not of the remnants of what no longer exists, not, in short, of the snows of yesteryear, but of new, mighty, and continually reborn tendencies to personal accumulation. The first still very meager wave of prosperity in the country, just because of its meagerness, has not weakened, but strengthened, these centrifugal tendencies. On the other hand, there has developed simultaneously a desire of the unprivileged to slap the grasping hands of the new gentry. The social struggle again grows sharp. Such are the sources of the power of the bureaucracy. But from those same sources comes also a threat to its power . . .

To define the Soviet regime as transitional, or intermediate, means to abandon such finished social categories as *capitalism* (and therewith 'state capitalism') and also *Socialism*. But besides being completely inadequate in itself, such a definition is capable of producing the mistaken idea that from the present Soviet regime a transition *only* to Socialism is possible. In reality a backslide to capitalism is wholly possible. A more complete definition will of necessity be complicated and ponderous.

The Soviet Union is a contradictory society, halfway between capitalism and socialism, in which:

1. The productive forces are still far from adequate to give the state property a socialist character.
2. The tendency toward primitive accumulation created by want breaks out through innumerable pores of the planned economy.
3. Norms of distribution preserving a bourgeois character lie at the basis of a new differentiation of society.
4. The economic growth, while slowly bettering the situation of the toilers, promotes a swift formation of privileged strata.
5. Exploiting the social antagonisms, a bureaucracy has converted itself into an uncontrolled caste alien to Socialism.
6. The social revolution, betrayed by the ruling party, still exists in property relations and in the consciousness of the toiling masses.
7. A further development of the accumulating contradictions can as well lead to Socialism as back to capitalism.
8. On the road to capitalism the counter-revolution would have to break the resistance of the workers.
9. On the road to Socialism the workers would have to overthrow the bureaucracy. In the last analysis, the question will be decided by a struggle of living social forces, in both the national and the world arenas.

Doctrinaires will doubtless not be satisfied with this hypothetical definition. They would like categorical formulae: yes – yes and no – no. Sociological problems would certainly be simpler if social phenomena had always a finished character. There is nothing more dangerous, however, than to throw out of reality, for the sake of logical completeness, elements which today violate your scheme and tomorrow may wholly overturn it. In our analysis, we have above all avoided doing violence to dynamic social formations which have had no precedent and have no analogies. The scientific task, as well as the political, is not to give a finished definition to an unfinished process, but to follow all its stages, separate its progressive from its reactionary tendencies, expose their mutual relations, foresee possible variants of development, and find in this foresight a basis for action.

23 John H. Goldthorpe

Have Classes been Abolished in the USSR?

Excerpt from John H. Goldthorpe, 'Social stratification in industrial society', monograph no. 8, *Sociological Review*, 1964, pp. 110–14.

I would like to question the idea that the stratification systems of all industrial societies are *ipso facto* of the same generic type, and thus that they may in principle be expected to follow convergent or parallel lines of development. Against this view, I would like to suggest that social stratification in the advanced societies of the Communist world – or at any rate in the USSR and its closer satellites – is *not* of the same generic type as in the West.

Soviet society is, of course, stratified; and, furthermore, it is true that in spite of the absence of private property in production, it appears to be stratified on an often similar pattern to the capitalist or post-capitalist societies of the West. For example, to a large degree there is apparent similarity in the connections between occupational role, economic rewards and social prestige, in the part played by education in determining occupational level, in the operation of an informal status system, and so on. But, I would argue, this similarity is only of a phenotypical kind: genotypically, stratification in Soviet society is significantly different from stratification in the West.

Primarily, it may be said, this difference derives from the simple fact that in Soviet society the economy operates within a 'monistic', or totalitarian, political order and is, in principle at least, totally planned, whereas in advanced Western societies political power is significantly less concentrated and the economy is planned in a far less centralized and detailed way. From this it results that in the West economic, and specifically market forces act as the crucial stratifying agency within society. They are, one could say, the major source of social inequality. And consequently, the *class* situation of individuals and groups, understood in terms of their economic power and resources tends to be the most important single determinant of their general life-chances. This is why we can usefully speak of Western industrial society as being 'class' stratified. However, in the case of Soviet society, market forces cannot be held to play a comparable role in the stratification process. These forces operate, of course, and differences in economic power and resources between individuals and groups have, as in the West, far-reaching social and human consequences. But, one would argue, to a significantly greater extent than in the West, stratification in Soviet society is subjected to *political* regulation; market forces are not permitted to have the primacy or the degree of autonomy in this respect that they have even in a 'managed' capitalist society. Undoubtedly, the functional requirements of the economy exert pressures upon the system of stratification, and these pressures may in some cases prove to be imperative. But the nature of the political order means that far more than with Western democracy, the pattern of social inequality can be shaped through the purposive action of the ruling party, and still more so, of course, the 'life-fates' of particular persons.

For example, during the years of Stalin's rule, economic inequality in the USSR generally increased. Numerous writers have in fact commented upon the progressive abandonment over this period of the egalitarian aspects of Marxist-Leninist ideology and of post-revolutionary attempts to operate egalitarian economic and social policies. From the early 1930s differential rewards in relation to skill, effort and responsibility were introduced into industry and administration, and thus from this point the range of wages and salaries tended to widen. Further, changes in the 1940s in the income tax and inheritance laws were conducive to greater inequalities in incomes and personal wealth alike. Then again, high ranking officials and other favoured persons appear to have received increasingly important non-monetary rewards in the form of cars, apartments, villas, free holidays and so on. By the end of the war decade, these developments had led to a degree of inequality in Soviet society which, in the view of many commentators, was greater than that which was generally to be found in the industrial societies of the West. However, in more recent years it has become clear that contrary to most expectations, this inegalitarian trend in the USSR has been checked and, moreover, that in certain respects at least it has even been reversed. Minimum wages in industry have been increased several times since the late 1950s and the incomes of the *kolkhozy* have for the most part risen quite considerably. This latter development has had the effect of closing somewhat the income gap between industrial and agricultural workers and has also been associated with a reduction in differentials in the earnings of the *kolkhoz* peasants themselves. At the same time, there is evidence of limitations being placed on the more excessive salaries of higher officials and of more stringent measures being taken against the abuse of privileges. Finally, tax changes in the past few years have tended to favour the poorer against the richer groups, and various kinds of welfare provision have been substantially improved. In these ways, then, economic differences between the manual and nonmanual categories overall have almost certainly been reduced to some extent, as well as differences within these categories.

Now these changes can, of course, be rightly regarded as being in some degree economically conditioned. Clearly, for instance, the increased differentiation in wages and salaries in the Stalin era must in part be understood in terms of the exigencies and consequences of rapid industrialization. But, I would argue, there can be little question that at the same time these changes were the outcome of political decisions – of choices made between realistic alternatives – and, furthermore, that frequently they were brought about with political as well as with specifically economic ends in view. Stalin, it is true, wanted rapid industrialization: but he had the further political objective that this process should be carried through under his own absolute control. Thus, this entailed not only depriving a large section of the population of material returns from their labour in order to achieve maximum expansion of industrial capacity, but also the building-up of a group of exceptionally favoured administrators and managers who would be highly motivated to retain their enviable positions through loyalty to Stalin and through high-level performance. To this latter end, in fact, appropriate status as well as economic inequalities were also developed. For example, during and after the war years, formal titles, uniforms and insignia of rank were introduced into various branches of industry and the governmental bureaucracy. Moreover, the wide social distance which was in this way created between the top and bottom of the stratification hierarchy had the manifest function of insulating the 'elite' from the masses and from their needs and wishes. And thus, as Feldmesser has pointed out, those in high positions were helped to learn 'that success was to be had by winning the favour not of those below them but of those above them, which was exactly what Stalin wanted them to learn'.

Similarly, the more recent moves towards reducing inequalities have again fairly evident political aims, even though, in some cases, they may also have been economically required. On the one hand, it seems clear that the present Soviet leadership is working towards a future Communist society which will be characterized by a high level of social welfare, and indeed eventually by private affluence, while still remaining under the undisputed dominance of the Party. In other words, the creation of the 'good life' for all appears destined to become one of the regime's most important sources of legitimacy. In fact, as Shapiro has noted, the 1961 Programme of the CPSU makes this more or less explicit. The Programme, he writes, 'enunciates squarely the concrete fact that party rule has come to stay. It calls upon the Soviet citizen to recognize and accept this fact, and to abandon the illusion that in this respect, things are going to change. In return, it promises him great material benefits and prosperity.'

On the other hand, the security of the regime also requires that the bureaucratic and managerial 'elite' does not become so well established as to gain some measure of independence from the Party chiefs. Thus, Krushchev has been concerned to show the members of this group that they remain the creatures of the Party and that their privileges are not permanent but still rest upon their obedience and service to the Party. Those whom Djilas has referred to as the 'new class' in Communist society cannot in fact be allowed by the Party leadership to become a class – in the sense of a collectivity which is capable of maintaining its position in society (and that of its children) through its own social power, and which possesses some degree of group consciousness and cohesion. For the emergence of such a class would constitute a serious threat to the Party's totalitarian rule, different only in degree from the threat that would be posed by the emergence of an independent trade union, professional body or political organization. It is awareness of this danger, one would suggest, which chiefly lies behind the recent attacks – verbal as well as material – which have been made upon higher officialdom and the top industrial personnel. For apart from the curtailment of economic rewards in some cases, it is interesting to note that the quasi-military status distinctions of the war decade have now been largely abolished and that the Party has actually encouraged rank and file employees in industry and agriculture to expose inadequacy and inefficiency on the part of their superiors. Furthermore, there has been some weeding out of superfluous posts and demotions appear to have become much more common. Finally, though, it is probably Krushchev's educational reforms which have been of greatest significance. These were carried through at a time when pressure on the institutions of secondary and higher education was reaching a peak; yet they were designed to make access to these institutions less dependent than previously upon economic resources and the new rules for competitive entry which were introduced seem, if anything, to shift the balance of 'social' advantage away from the children of the 'elite' and towards candidates from worker or peasant families. As Feldmesser notes, if a 'new class' – a 'state bourgeoisie' – were in fact in existence in the USSR, then exactly the reverse of this might have been expected; that is, a move to make access to these scarce facilities *more,* rather than less, dependent upon the ability to pay.

It is then not too much to say that in Soviet society hierarchical differentiation is an instrument of the regime. To a significant degree stratification is *organized* in order to suit the political needs of the regime; and, as these needs change, so too may the particular structure of inequality. In other words, the Soviet system of stratification is characterized by an important element of 'deliberateness', and it is this which basically distinguishes it from the Western system, in spite of the many apparent similarities. In the industrial societies of the West, one could say, the action of the state sets limits to the extent of social inequalities which derive basically from the operation of a market economy: in Soviet society the pattern of inequality also results in part from 'market' forces, but in this case these are subordinated to political control up to the limits set by the requirements of the industrial system. For this reason, one may conclude, Soviet society is not, in the same way as Western society, *class* stratified. As Aron has observed, class stratification and a monistic political system are to be regarded as incompatibles.

24 Roy Hofheinz, Jr

Why Did the Chinese Communists Succeed?

Excerpts from Roy Hofheinz, Jr, 'The ecology of Chinese communist success: rural influence patterns, 1923–45', in A. Doak Barnett (ed.), *Chinese Communist Politics in Action*, University of Washington Press, 1969, pp. 1–22, 33, 55–77.

Chinese communism began, at least in its present form, in the villages of China. Despite its pretensions to represent the 'proletariat' of China, it was a predominantly rural phenomenon, and its history, psychology, and etiology are inextricably enmeshed in Chinese country life. Chinese communism as a social movement and a political force must be seen first as a part of a complex rural political process before its wider implications and later evolution can be examined [. . .]

The rise of the Communist movement in China can be, I suggest, put in perspective by examining the background of the regions in which the movement was most successful. I propose to begin a treatment of Chinese Communist success by an examination of the environment or 'ecology' of that success [. . .]

The analysis of political radicalism in the Western world has profited greatly from an accident. The spread of universal voting in this century, while not necessarily favorable to radical causes, has made the measure of their influence considerably easier. Analysts have been able to assume comfortably that either votes for or membership in a political party are sufficiently clear indications of strength or influence that there is no need to probe further. Given that the vote or membership figures are available, the well-developed techniques of opinion sampling, or of ecological correlation could be applied directly to the analysis of 'causes'.

But in China we are several steps removed from such work. Not only do we have little of the background statistical data (not to mention access to interview subjects for the pre-1949 period), we are hard pressed to establish a measure of Communist strength [. . .]

How are we to begin to measure the extent of Chinese Communist success? In the absence of detailed election data we are forced to rely on the gross indicators of growth. There are basically two main approaches to the gross measures: either we can compile what is available in the way of quantified information about the number of individuals involved in the Communist movement – the total membership of the Party, of the

Red Armies, the front organizations, and so forth; or we can describe and analyse the geographic spread of the movement. On the one hand we deal with a numerical constituency, and on the other with a spatial one [. . .]

It should be evident from inspection of Figures 1 to 4 that, first, there is almost no geographical correspondence between the three periods of Chinese Communist success. It is almost as though once a Communist movement had been successfully developed in a particular area and then that movement was suppressed, the area became in some sense immune to further easy inroads by Communist organizers [. . .]

If and when we establish an adequate measure of 'Communist

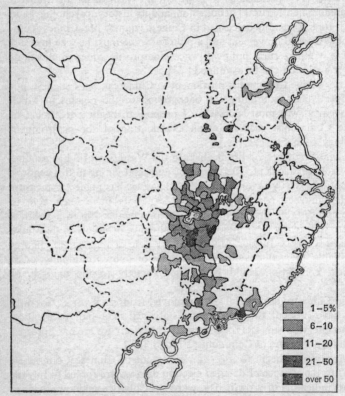

1–5%
6–10
11–20
21–50
over 50

Figure 1 Communist influence in China 1926–7; percentage of rural population in peasant associations.
Source: Kuomintang Peasant Bureau of membership figures of Communist-led peasant movements at *hsien* (county) level.

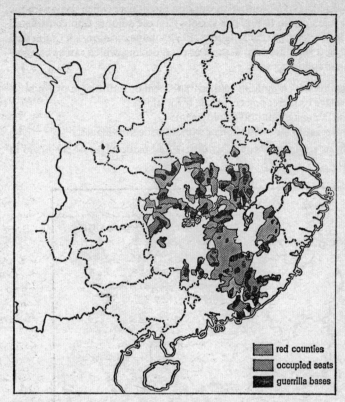

red counties
occupied seats
guerrilla bases

Figure 2 Communist influence in China, 1932.
Source: Intelligence report presented to Japanese Diet, 1932.

influence' in the hundred-score counties of China, what then? Are adequate data available for Republican China, or for any other period for that matter, which might reveal underlying patterns? Did all *hsien* which at one time or another became Communist strongholds exhibit certain common characteristics independent of their connection with the movement? Given the nature of information on Chinese local areas, despair is perhaps the safest reaction [. . .]

On the basis of the limited data that I have so far been able to collect, what can be said about the way various social factors relate to our county level index of Communist success?

Some idea of the complexity of the notion of rural injustice and peasant dissatisfaction in China can be gained by examining the complaints listed in an authoritative work on the subject which deals with the critical years of the 1930s. The various Chinese authors who contributed to the Institute of Pacific Relations' 1939 volume on *Agrarian China* deal with at least six different measures of rural decline, which can be categorized in the following way:

1. Inequality of landholding, either traditional or resulting in or from:
(*a*) extensive or increasing corporate ownership;
(*b*) a rise in nonagricultural employment;
(*c*) an increase in out-migration or work outside the villages.
2. High, or rising, or inequitably distributed percentages of crop paid in rent.

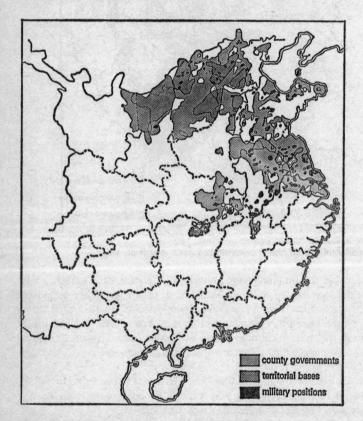

Figure 3 Communist influence in China 1938–41.
Source: Composite map based on three Japanese Intelligence reports.

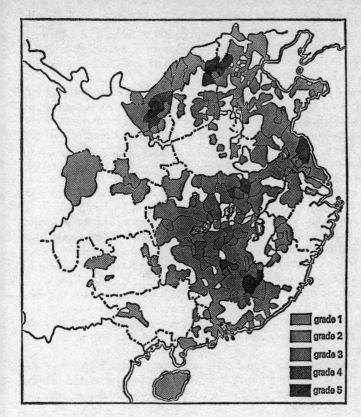

Figure 4 Communist influence, a composite map, 1923–45.

3. Declining *or* rising land prices.

4. High, rising, or overly complicated taxes, surtaxes, or military assessments.

5. High, rising, or unduly complicated interest rates.

6. The use of unfair weights and measures, 'exploitative' subleasing, excessive rent deposits, the loss of *kan-ch'ing* (empathy between owner and tenant), and other noneconomic injustices (including various 'feudal' obligations).

With such a bewildering array of potential causes for dissatisfaction, there is little wonder that no adequate conception of 'grievance potential' has yet been developed. I have some hope, however, that additional data relevant to at least some of these indicators can be assembled. For example, the national government did collect statistics during the early thirties on interest rates, land prices, and taxes at the county level, and some of Buck's work deals precisely with certain of the indicators listed above, including tenancy and rent rates.

Inequality of landholding is one measure of grievance which is very popular with present-day Chinese Communist historians. It has become, in fact, a matter of ritual in Peking accounts to invoke injustices of land distribution in introducing the story of any particular guerrilla movement. Yet by all accounts China in the pre-1949 era did not suffer, by world standards, from an unusual degree of land concentration, even in the worst of areas. Using the figures for land concentration introduced by the Soviet mission to China in the twenties, Russett has estimated that China ranked in the highest third of all nations on a scale of equality of land ownership. Furthermore, the geography of land maldistribution within China itself casts further doubt on a thesis which stresses landholding. The Communists achieved some of their most notable successes in the North China plain, an area of remarkably equitable distribution of the ownership of land.

Kuomintang Ministry of Internal Affairs data illustrate this fact clearly for the provincial level. From its estimates of the percentage of total land owned by rich, middle, and poor peasants, we can rank the provinces along a scale running from low to high concentration of inequality.

A calculation of the 'equal share percentage' – that is to say, of the percentage of all farmers in each province who together owned half the total land owned – reveals the following ranking for the provinces in 1934:

Table 1 Inequality of Land Distribution 1933

Province	Equal Share %	Province	Equal Share %
Shansi	67	Hunan	76
Honan	68	Chahar	78
Kansu	68	Anhwei	79
Shensi	69	Yunnan	79
Shantung	70	Chekiang	80
Kiangsu	72	Hupeh	81
Hopei	73	Chinghai	83
Suiyuan	73	Kwangsi	84
Kwangtung	76		

What is notable about this ranking is that there appears to be a negative relationship between areas of unequal land distribution and areas where the Communist movement blossomed. The south coastal and remote southwestern provinces (Chekiang, Kwangsi, Yunnan, Chinghai), the least fertile for Communist growth, suffered from the highest inequality percentages. The northern provinces of Hopei, Honan, Shansi, and Shantung, into which the Communist movement expanded so rapidly after 1938, reveal rates of land concentration from 5 to 15 per cent lower than in the southern areas where the Communists were less successful [. . .]

A further measure of political development we might introduce is that of rural cooperatives. The cooperatives built by the Nationalist government in the 1930s were widely regarded as a vehicle for the rural reforms necessary to combat Communist influence. We might assume that the measure of cooperative membership would indicate the degree of success of rural 'rehabilitation' as well as of the impact of the national government on village life.

Significantly, the data on the 1930s show that only an extremely small number of these cooperatives were established: the membership of all KMT cooperatives as a proportion of the total rural population remained around one-quarter of 1 per cent, only slightly higher than KMT membership *per capita*. The contrast with the mobilization rates of the Communists is thus overwhelming.

Nonetheless, some interesting patterns emerge from the data on cooperatives. First, the distribution of cooperatives by province suggests that it was not the strongholds of the Kuomintang which enjoyed the highest degree of mobilization in cooperatives [. . .]

The second pattern of interest to emerge from the data on cooperatives is that they do not appear to demonstrate a positive correlation with our distribution of Communist influence. In fact, with the exception of the counties in central Hopei which contributed considerable support both to the CCP in 1937–40 and to the KMT cooperatives in 1937, areas of maximum Communist influence appear to have been only very sparsely organized by the rural cooperative movement [. . .]

Cultural measures

Impressionistic accounts of village life recorded by early twentieth-century travelers in China usually begin with estimates of the extent of 'cultural' progress in the area. Opium smoking, footbinding, and even the wearing of the old Manchu-style queues were still to be seen in the mid-thirties in some villages. Provincial authorities of the Republican period who were interested in bringing such villages into the modern age sometimes recorded their own information of such practices. Can this information be used to shed light on the distribution of Communist influence? We might consider two hypotheses: that the Communists were able to take advantage of the oppressive quality of traditional practices, and that measures of such practices should therefore correlate positively with CCP influence. Or that such practices were signs of the strength of 'backwardness', of traditional customs, social patterns, and political organizations, and that there should therefore be a negative correlation.

One index of 'backwardness' we have used is the proportion of the population with bound feet for Hunan and Shansi (actually the figures for Shansi give a ratio of footbinding to the total number of households, and thus slightly understates the *per capita* incidence). It should be noted that areas of extreme 'backwardness', according to this measure, were not the areas of prime CCP strength. Nor do these maps support any simple hypothesis that there was a direct correlation between Christianity and Communism [. . .]

If the backlands of Hunan were the most susceptible to Christianity, they were the least susceptible to Communism, at least during the peasant movement period. Those relatively remote counties which after 1927 did become Soviet bases (that is, those on the eastern edge of the province bordering Kiangsi) tended to fall in the middle range of Christian susceptibility. Although in Hunan both Communism and Christianity, as we have measured them, seem to be related to the backward-modern variable, the shape of the relationship is quite different: for Christianity it is a U-shaped curve, for communism (in Hunan) a rising straight line [. . .]

Conclusion

There was no single pattern of Communist success or influence in China. Theories of the 'political geography' of the Communist movement which claim that the location of a point of maximum influence might have been predicted from a generalized model of background factors have yet to explain the great variety in the relationships between Communist forces and the villages [. . .]

But what of the broader explanations of the rise of Communism in China with which we began this essay? Has our examination of the 'ecology' of the successful Communist base counties brought us any closer to a general theory of the rise of the movement? I think the answer is a qualified yes. Insofar as the first step in theory building is the questioning of established notions or paradigms of thought, we have made some progress.

By examining the variance in certain background factors which some theories have held to be important, we have been able to cast considerable doubt on a number of the larger explanations of Chinese Communist success. For example, peasant nationalistic hatred could hardly have been the main factor in the remarkable spread of Communist power in the peasant movement period or in the Soviet era. 'Modern revolutionary potential' is not a satisfactory explanation for the high Communist success in the rear areas or even in the North China plain.

This is not to say that all the theories have been put to the test [. . .]

But to go beyond the destructive to the constructive phases of theory building is a more difficult step. It is clear that no single-factor explanation is satisfactory for a phenomenon as complicated as the Chinese Communist revolution. But what is the proper mixture of contextual and motivational factors that seems most satisfactory when the Communist movement in China is seen as a whole? I would suggest that the contextual and motivational theories lie at the two poles of a continuum of explanations which centers on what is perhaps the most important and least examined of all the possible explanations of Chinese Communist success: the behavior of the Chinese Communists themselves. It seems almost impossible to develop quantifiable indicators of such imponderables as the viability and vitality of the movement itself, its organizational dynamism, the quality of its personnel, the vigor of its recruitment. But as we reconstruct it, the sense of forward movement, or at least of an alternative way out of present dilemmas, must have seemed as important an 'appeal' to recruits as personal interest or patriotism. An important part of the motivation to join the movement depended on the very presence within the local context of a Communist political structure. Thus, motivation depended on context and context on motivation, and at the center of the interaction was the vital core of committed individuals that made the movement into a political force in the villages.

To say that the Chinese revolution was a 'rural revolution' is a half truth: at least half of Chinese rural society did not participate in it, and at least half of the credit for the revolution belongs to the Communists themselves. The expansion of Communist forces in any area during any period was likely to be better correlated with Communist presence in the vicinity than with any other social phenomenon. Part band-wagon, part demonstration, part mobility opportunity, part the path of least frustration, the Chinese Communist movement tended to appeal to nonmembers by its very presence and to grow by its known capacity to expand. Once a foothold in a county was gained, within primary communication distance of the county's population, these forces began to work, and combined with the proper mix of symbol manipulation, skills, threats, appeals, cajoleries, and acts of independent bravery, unquestionable honesty, and unusual competence, produced the potential for recruitment and for the establishment of legitimacy that placed the county effectively under Communist control. In the final analysis, any general theory of the rise of Chinese Communism that omits the importance of organizational presence and vitality will remain only a partial explanation.

Part Five The Family

In discussing social problems relating to the family we may make a
distinction between two kinds of problem. In the first place we have
those problems which stem from family relationships themselves, for
conflict and competition within the family are both inevitable to some
degree. We are dealing here with such problems as the relationships
between spouses, between parents and children, or between siblings.
There are also the problems which arise out of the fact that each family
tends to draw a boundary around itself, to define itself as a unique entity
as against other families and social institutions and often to demand
much from its members in terms of loyalty, commitment of material and
non-material resources and identification. As Laing has insisted
in several of his works, an extract from one of which is given below
(Reading 25), the family not merely creates these kinds of problems but
is also able in effect to deny that these *are* problems; because an
individual feels that there is something unique or special about family
relationships – and particularly about *his* family relationships – he will
go to great lengths to deny that there is anything 'wrong' in his particular
family situation. These denials will tend to reinforce the original
problem, say a growing estrangement between husband and wife or
between father and daughter. We are looking at conflict within the
family, conflict which stems from family living itself. Such conflicts are
indeed a central part of family life and have, of course, been recognized
as such in literature and folk-tales. When the story-teller begins with the
words 'a certain man had two sons', we can be sure that a tale of conflict
is to follow.

These then are the kinds of problems that stem from family life itself,
from the fact that a relatively small number of people are living for a
relatively long period of time within each other's social field. Conflict
and competition – for land or for love – almost inevitably enter into such
relationships. At the same time there are those problems which arise
outside the family but which are amplified or modified within the family
situation. Thus, for example, unemployment affects single people as well

as married workers but the effect of prolonged unemployment has a whole series of repercussions on family relationships, on the position of the 'bread-winner', the relationship between the spouses, between father and children, and so on. The fact is that, in most cases, modern society does not impinge directly upon an individual but is, rather, mediated through the family and family relationships. Thus the association between education and social class may be amplified within the family (through the process of socialization, linguistic development and so on), or, alternatively, may be modified so that some working-class families can and do give encouragement to their children.

In any situation, of course, it is difficult to distinguish between these 'internal' and 'external' aspects of family living. As the extract from Goode's important work on divorce points out (Reading 26), the estrangement between a couple which leads to a divorce is not just a function of their relationship alone but also of other ties in which the spouses are involved and other factors outside the conjugal family.

He shows how divorce rates vary between different societies and at different times and suggests that we can analyse these variations in terms of different social structures. Goode also usefully demonstrates why divorce is considered to be a problem in the first place; here again it is necessary to look outside the particular estranged relationship between a husband and wife. Elsewhere in the book (from which this extract is taken) he outlines the societal pressures on the divorced woman to remarry, and suggests that the high rate of remarriage is one way in which the impact of high divorce rates on society is minimized. Goode's study provides an excellent example of the way in which the sociologist can examine such an intimate issue as divorce and demonstrates that we must look beyond the alleged incompatibilities or infidelities of the spouses themselves to wider social pressures and influences.

The difficulties involved in drawing boundaries between the 'internal' and the 'external' in relation to family problems is not merely an academic problem. In the United States the debate about the Negro family – stemming from the controversial Moynihan report – was essentially around this issue. Is it the case that the instability of the Negro family is a major factor contributing to the disadvantaged position of the black population in the United States? Or is it the case that this family, far from being peculiarly pathological, is in fact an institution which has developed and adjusted to meet the particular disadvantages of discrimination and unemployment? Indeed, is the Negro family in fact all that unstable? Gans summarizes some of the themes in this controversy and demonstrates very clearly the way in which social research has important political consequences (Reading 28). Komarovsky (Reading 27) also touches on this theme of the relation between the family and the other institutions in society. She shows the contradiction – in the case among white, working-class families – between the ideal of the companionate marriage and the actuality, which is more often than not shaped by economic uncertainty and social isolation. Her conclusion that the value of companionship, so often stressed in writings about the family, is 'more prescriptive than descriptive' is one that sociologists and others may well take to heart.

We see, therefore, that the family does not stand alone and that it is affected by its relations with other institutions. The major roles within the family are also often the major sources of identity outside the family. Thus, included in the role of 'father' is the role of 'bread-winner' or worker; the 'good father' is expected to provide for his family. The 'generation gap' implies a complex set of inter-relationships between parents and children on the one hand and the development of a specific 'youth culture' in the wider society on the other. If, at its simplest, we see the family as a group structured around the two basic principles of sex and generational differentiation we can see that it is impossible to look at roles within the family without also examining the meaning that these roles have outside the family.

This becomes particularly important when considering the theme of the family in a changing society. Some of the major considerations involved in examining the connections between the family and industrialization and urbanization have been considered elsewhere (see Worsley's *Introducing Sociology*, Penguin, 1970). At this point it should be enough to stress the following very broad conclusions:

1. There is a tendency throughout the world for the conjugal family to become the major family unit. Goode's study *World Revolution and Family Patterns* (Free Press, 1963) summarizes many of these trends and also reminds us of the complexities of this process.

2. This is not to say that kin outside the relationship of spouse, parent and child are unimportant. Indeed, considerable research has shown the continued importance of grandparents at all social levels after a couple has married and set up home together. However, we must also stress that most of the research has shown that it is the *grandparents* who are the main focus of these wider relationships. Other kin, such as siblings, appear to be much less important on the whole. Further, it is probably no longer possible to talk of a kinship 'system' in the sense of a bounded and clearly defined unit. Rather we have a network of relationships (and

one which changes over time) which may include both kin and non-kin, and one where personal preferences appear to play an important part.

The understanding of these changes again takes us back to the complex interplay between the changing nature of work, the changes in the class structure and social and occupational mobility and the changes within the family. Of particular importance here (and of great contemporary relevance) are the changing roles of men and women. The statement that 'a woman's place is in the home' is both a statement about the ideal expectations of the roles of a mother and a wife within the family and the overall position of women in society as a whole. Again we see the intersection between roles within the family and identities in the wider society. What we have seen in the past fifty or one hundred years is change in both these spheres; on the one hand through birth control and earlier marriage the role of the mother within the family has been reduced and, on the other, there have been increasing opportunities as a result of economic and educational change for women to occupy roles outside the homes. Many other factors such as legal and political changes are, of course, also relevant. It is obvious that these changes in roles of women also involve and necessitate changes in the roles of men. The brief extract from the preliminary PEP Report *Women and Top Jobs* (Reading 29) looks to the future, and reminds us of the complex inter-relationships between definitions as to what is 'masculine' and 'feminine' and the roles of men and women in home and at work. The authors look towards a society which is less structured around the factor of sex. While their discussion deals explicitly with women in professional and managerial positions it is likely that these themes have a much wider applicability.

Within this section, therefore, we have discussed the relationships between the 'internal' and 'external' aspects of the family in a changing society and the kinds of problems – marital breakdown, economic uncertainty, etc. – which arise here. Laing looks at the problems that develop within family relationships. Goode reminds us that marital breakdown must be seen in a wider and social and cultural context, and Komarowsky and Gans (Reading 28) point to the problems of 'ordinary' black or white families in modern urban, industrial society. Finally, the extract from the PEP Report focuses directly on change and gives us one glance into possible future patterns of family relationships.

It will be noted that many problems conventionally associated with the family are not dealt with here. Thus there is little directly on changing sexual patterns and standards (pre-marital sex, for example), or on the generation gap. It is to be regretted that many of the studies in this field tend to be either highly impressionistic or, at the other extreme, methodologically sophisticated studies of fairly small populations. The extracts here have been chosen in an attempt to combine immediacy and sociological imagination. It is to be hoped that these pieces illustrate the sociological ideal of linking personal troubles with public issues.

25 R. D. Laing

Series and Nexus in the Family

Excerpt from R. D. Laing, 'Series and nexus in the family', *New Left Review*, no. 15, 1962, pp. 9–14.

Series

At one theoretical extremity is the group that can be termed a *series*.

The series is a type of human multiplicity in which no person is essential, where everyone is quantitatively interchangeable. Yet the members of the series are united in a negative unity, by their reciprocal qualitative indifference to each other, and, simultaneously, by their quantitative concern (what will 'people' think – gossip, scandal, etc.).

The minimal form of unification in a multiplicity in which each member is quantitatively interchangeable and reciprocally indifferent to the others, is achieved through a common object. The anti-Semites are united by a common object, to which they are all *anti*. The members of a bus queue have only the bus as their common object of unification.

A very interesting situation occurs when the members of a series, lacking any direct collateral involvement or concern with each other, achieve a curious form of unification through taking the Other as the common object of each.

Thus, in scandal, gossip groups, the group is always and everywhere *other* people: it is everywhere, but everywhere it is elsewhere. Each person in the series is united by being the serial other to others in the series. The members of such a series are unified, for instance, by serial ideas which are never held by anyone in his own person. Each person is thinking of what he thinks the other thinks. The other, in turn, thinks what yet another thinks. Each person does not mind a coloured lodger, but each person's neighbour does. This serial collection is united by the fact that each person is a neighbour of his neighbour. What the serial 'they' think is held with conviction. It is indubitable and it is incontestable. The scandal group is a series of others which each serial member repudiates in himself.

Since such a series is always the others, and always elsewhere, each member of the series feels unable to make any difference to the series. I have no objection to my daughter marrying a gentile *really*, but we live in a Jewish neighbourhood after all. The series has a collective power in proportion to each person's creation of this power and his own impotence. Thus one finds serialized prejudice and morality. Scandal (of one type) is serialized morality in operation *par excellence*.

This is seen very clearly in the following inverted Romeo and Juliet situation.[1]

John and Mary had a love affair, and just as they were ending it, Mary found she was pregnant. Both families were informed. Mary did not want to marry John. John did not want to marry Mary. But John thought Mary would want him to marry her, and Mary did not want to hurt John's feelings by telling him that she did not want to marry him – as she thought he wanted to marry her, and that he thought she wanted to marry him.

The two families, however, compounded the confusion considerably. Mary's mother took to bed screaming and in tears because of the disgrace – what people are saying about the way she brought her daughter up. She did not mind the situation 'in itself', especially as the girl was going to be married, but she took to heart what everyone would be saying. No one in their own person in either family ('if it only affected me . . .') was in the least concerned for their own sake, but everyone was very concerned about the effect of 'gossip' and 'scandal' on everyone else. The concern focused itself mainly on the boy's father and the girl's mother – both of whom required to be consoled at great length for the terrible blow. The boy's father was worried about what the girl's mother would think of him. The girl's mother was worried about what 'everyone' would think of her. The boy was concerned at what the family thought he had done to his father, and so on.

The serial tension spiralled up within a few days to the complete engrossment of all members of both families in various forms of tears, wringing of hands, recriminations, apologies.

Typical utterances were:

Mother to girl: 'Even if he does want to marry you how can he ever respect you after what people will have been saying about you recently?'
Girl: (some time later) 'I had finally got fed up with him just before I found I was pregnant, but I didn't want to hurt his feelings because he was so in love with me.'
Boy: 'If it had not been that I owed it to my father for all he had done for me, I would have arranged that she got rid of it. But then everyone knew by then.'

1. Because we are describing a concrete situation, many other features are entailed besides those of serial alterity, but this is one element in the situation. The example is fictitious.

Everyone knew because the son told his father who told his wife who told her mother who told her eldest son who told his wife . . . etc.

Serial processes, like other group processes, appear to have a dynamism divorced from the praxis of individuals in the series. But in this and every other case this process (whether serial, organizational, institutional . . .) is alienated praxis – intelligible when, and only when, the steps in the vicissitudes of its alienation from the praxis of each and every person can be retraced back to what at each and every moment is their only origin – the actions of each and every single person.

Now, the peculiar thing about the members of a series of others is that each one repudiates his identity as a member of the group, and by doing so creates a 'group' united by negative reciprocities. The series is a plurality of solitudes in which what each person has in common is his allocation to the other of the necessity for his own actions. Each person, however, as other to the other, is the other's necessity. Each denies any internal bond with the others; each person claims his own inessentiality: 'I just carried out my orders. If I had not done so, someone else would have.' 'Why don't you sign? Everyone else has', etc. Yet although I can make no difference, I cannot act differently. No single other person is any more necessary to me than I claim to be to 'them'. But just as he is 'one of them' to me, so I am 'one of them' to him. In this collection of reciprocal indifference, of reciprocal inessentiality and solitude, there appears to exist no freedom. There is conformity to a *presence* that is everywhere *elsewhere*.

Nexus

A series is hardly yet a group, but it is a human multiplicity which has the rudimentary beginnings of group formation about it.

In order to regard any number of separate people as one group, it is necessary to posit them as together constituting a measure of unity. This act of unifying a multiplicity of persons I shall call an act of group synthesis. If I think of certain others as together with me, and certain others as not together with me, I have already undertaken two acts of synthesis, resulting in *we* and *them*. However, in order that *we* have a group identity, it is not enough that I regard, let us say, you and him as constituting a *we* with myself. You and he have to perform similar acts of synthesis, each on his own behalf. In this *we* (me, and you, and him), each of *us* recognizes not only our own private syntheses, but also the syntheses that each of the others makes. That is, I 'interiorize' your and his syntheses, you interiorize his and mine, he interiorizes mine and yours. Thus in a completely achieved group, the group is not simply a social object, shared by people who have nothing in common except this 'object'. The group to each member of the group (not as a social 'object' observed by an outsider) is the synthesis of the multiplicity of its members and the synthesis of the multiplicity of syntheses that each and everyone here and everywhere, invents and maintains. It is not, and cannot be, an object, a totality. The group can never be finally and conclusively grasped as a whole; any group is in continual *totalization*, a perpetual series of actions that maintain its existence, but can never complete it once and for all.

The group looked at from the outside comes into view as a social object, lending by its appearance and by the apparent processes that go on inside it, credence to the organismic illusion.

This is a mirage; as one approaches closer there is no organism anywhere.

A group, whose unification is achieved through the reciprocal interiorization by each of each other, in which neither a 'common object', nor organizational or institutional structures, etc., have a primary function as a kind of group 'cement', I shall call a *nexus*.

The unity of the nexus is in the interior of each synthesis. Each such act of synthesis is bound by reciprocal interiority with every other synthesis of the same nexus, in so far as it is also the interiority of every other synthesis. The unity of the nexus is the unification of every other synthesis. The unity of the nexus is the unification made by each person of the plurality of syntheses.

This social structure of the completely achieved nexus is its *unity as ubiquity*. It is a ubiquity of *heres*, whereas the series of others is always elsewhere, always *there*.

The series is a circular flight. It is elusive. It is never here and now; never in *my* thinking, always in what I think the others think.

The nexus exists only in so far as each person incarnates the nexus. The nexus is everywhere, in each person, and is nowhere else than in each. The nexus is at the opposite pole from the series, in that each person acknowledges affiliation to it, regards the other as coessential to him, and assumes that the other regards him as coessential to the other.

We are all in the same boat in a stormy sea,
and we owe each other a terrible loyalty.
G. K. Chesterton

In this group of reciprocal loyalty, of brotherhood unto death, each freedom is reciprocally pledged, one to the other.

In the nexal family the unity of the group is achieved through the interiorization by each of the group, and the danger to each person (since the person is essential to the nexus, and the nexus is essential to the person) is the dissolution or dispersion of 'the family'. This can come about only by one person after another dissolving it in themselves. A united 'family' exists only as long as each person acts in terms of its existence. Each person may then act on the other person to coerce him (by sympathy, blackmail, indebtedness, guilt, gratitude, or naked violence) into maintaining his interiorization of the group unchanged.

The nexal family is then the 'entity' that has to be preserved in each person, and served by each person, whom one lives and dies for: and which in turn offers life for loyalty, and death for desertion. Any deflection from the nexus (betrayal, treason, heresy, etc.), is deservedly, by nexus ethics, punishable: and the worst punishment devisable by the 'group men' is exile or excommunication.

The condition of permanence of such a nexus, whose sole existence is each person's interiorization of it, is the successful re-invention of whatever gives such interiorization its *raison d'être*. If there is no external danger, then danger and terror have to be invented and maintained. Each person has to act on the others to maintain the nexus *in them*.

Some families we have studied live in perpetual anxiety of what, to them, is an external persecuting world. The members of the family live in a family ghetto, as it were. This is one basis for so-called maternal over-protection. It is not 'over'-protection from the mother's point of view, nor, indeed, often from the point of view of other members of the family.

The 'protection' that the family offers its members seems to be based on several preconditions: a phantasy of the external world as extra-ordinarily dangerous; the generation of terror inside the nexus at this external danger. The 'work' of the nexus is the generation of this terror. This work I shall call *violence*.

The stability of the nexus is the product of terror generated in its members by the work (violence) done by the members of the group on each other. Such family 'homeostasis' is the product of reciprocities mediated under the statutes of violence and terror.

One way that such rigidity is often 'explained' by social scientists, is by positing the group as a kind of organism, or hyper-organism, and by inventing a physiology and pathology for it. The changelessness of the family is then regarded as a form of group pathology, arising from an undue operation of a homeostatic principle. This is only one instance of the frequent importation of concepts derived from biology into the realm of multiplicities of human beings.

Phenomenologically, a group can feel to its members to be an organism; to those outside it, it can appear to act like one. But to go beyond this, and to maintain that, *ontologically*, it *is* an organism, is to become completely mystified.

Family pathology is an even more corrupt concept than individual *psycho-pathology*. It simply extends the unintelligibility of individual behaviour to the unintelligibility of the group. Why cannot a family change? Because it is a hyper-static system. This is simply a sophisticated tautology mystified by metaphor. It is the *organic analogy* applied now not just to one person, but to a multiplicity of persons. Its initial impact can be seductive and exciting, but it is in fact an even worse mystification than the organic analogy as applied to one person.

The group is *not* to the individual as whole to a part, as a hyper-organism, as hyper-individual. It is not a mechanism except in the sense that the mechanical action of the group may be constituted as such in and through the praxes of each and all of its members.

The highest ethic of the nexus, then, is reciprocal concern. Each person is concerned about what the other thinks, feels, does. He regards it as his right to expect the others to be concerned about him, and an obligation to feel concern toward them. I make no move without feeling it as my right that you should be happy or sad, proud or ashamed, of what I do. Every action of mine is a 'group' action, it is for or against, always the concern of, the other members of the group. And I regard you as callous if you do not concern yourself about my concern for you when you do anything.

A family can act as gangsters, offering each other mutual protection against each other's violence. It is a reciprocal terrorism, with the offer of protection-security against the violence that each threatens the other with, and is threatened by, if anyone steps out of line.

My concern, my concern for your concern, your concern, and your concern for my concern, etc. is an infinite spiral, upon which rests my pride or shame in my father, sister, brother, my mother, my son, my daughter.

My security rests on his or her need for me. My need is for the *other's* need of me. His or her need is that I need him or her. My need is not simply 'need' to satisfy biological drives. It is my need to be needed by the other. My love is a thirst, not to satisfy my love, but a thirst to be loved. My solicitude is not for another, but for another to want me. My want is a want to be wanted: my longing, a longing to be longed for. And in the same way, my emptiness is that the other does not require me to fulfil him or her. And, similarly, the other wants to be wanted by me, longs to be longed for by me. Two alienated loves, two self-perpetuating solitudes, an inextricable and timeless misunderstanding – tragic – and comic – the soil of endless recrimination.

The essential characteristic of the family nexus is that every action of one person is expected to have reference to and to influence everyone else. The nature of this influence is expected to be reciprocal.

Each person is expected to be controlled, and to control the others, by the reciprocal effect that each has on the other.

In such families, it is assumed that to be affected by the others' actions or feelings is 'natural'. It is not 'natural' if father is neither proud nor ashamed of son, daughter, mother, etc. According to this ethic, action done to please, to make happy, to show one's gratitude to the other, is the highest kind of action. This modality of sociality, this reciprocal trans-personal cause-effect, is a self-actualizing presumption. In this 'game', it is a foul to use this inter-dependence to hurt the other, except in the service of the nexus, but the worst crime of all is to refuse to act in terms of this presumption.

Examples of this in action are:

Peter gives Paul something. If Paul is not pleased, or refuses the gift, he is ungrateful for what is being done for him. Or: Peter is made unhappy if Paul does something. Therefore if Paul does it he is making Peter unhappy. If Peter is made unhappy Paul is inconsiderate, callous, selfish, ungrateful: or, if Peter is prepared to make sacrifices for Paul, so Paul should be prepared to make sacrifices for Peter, or else he is selfish, ungrateful, callous, ruthless, etc.

'Sacrifice' under these circumstances consists in Peter impoverishing himself to do something for Paul. It is the tactic of *enforced debt*.

One way of putting this is that each person *invests in the other*.

26 William J. Goode

Women in Divorce

Excerpt from William J. Goode, *Women in Divorce*, Free Press, 1956, pp. 8–15. (First published as *After Divorce*.)

Cultures vary in the *degree* of marital conflict. Undoubtedly, for example, in periods of great change in the role definitions of the sexes there is firstly far *more* disagreement and conflict between spouses, and secondly certainly more expression of this conflict in *overt behavior*. We are merely asserting the inevitability of family conflict and personal unhappiness in all cultures, and the impossibility of there being meaningful, *direct* moral proscriptions against them.

Moreover, what the culture defines as a *bearable* level or degree of conflict will also doubtless vary from one epoch or society to another; and what is more what the society or culture defines as an *appropriate solution* for conflict also varies. The first of these three propositions is borne out by general observations and some theory, although intensity of marital conflict has not been measured in any culture. With reference to the second, there are beginnings of systematic theory in the structural-functional hypotheses of the past decade, specifically those dealing with mechanisms for alleviating and preventing conflict. Here, let us simply note, once more, the possibility of analysing various elements in any kinship system by reference to their effect upon the *stability* of marriage. The universal nuclear family is to be viewed as one type of boundary-maintaining social unit, under various internal and external pressures toward boundary dissolution and maintenance. Marital unhappiness is only a resultant of various factors that predispose toward marital instability.

Among these factors, there are also various mechanisms which:

1. *Prevent* the building of tensions or external forces.
2. Alleviate or deflect such forces.
3. Define various difficulties as bearable.
4. Offer various solutions for changing the structure or direction of these forces, or even for removing them.

Within such a view, divorce is to be seen as one kind of mechanism for dealing with the pressures and problems inevitably *caused by* marriage. Divorce is in a basic sense 'caused' by marriage.

A typical set of preventive mechanisms was found in pre-revolutionary China. According to traditional descriptions of this 'classical' family, the roles of husband and wife were *clearly* defined. Respect and not romantic love was demanded between husband and wife. There was an extended family system, so that intimate emotional interaction between husband and wife was less continuous or intense than in our own system. Extended deviations from proper marital patterns were prevented in part by the continuous supervision by other, older relatives. If the wife built up any large reservoir of hatred and fear, it was more likely to be aimed at the mother-in-law, rather than at the husband, who was only rarely the most powerful member of the family in the first decade of a marriage.

When conflict *does* reach high limits, there are different solutions in different cultures. One rare solution is that of Dobu, where overt conflict is viewed as standard. There are, however, many outlets for aggression. There is an alternation of family residence each year, from the village of wife's family to that of husband's family. Thus, each of the two spouses may look forward to a period in which great freedom of unchecked, mostly unilinear aggression is permitted.

Perhaps the most common solution is that of divorce, the extended families of each spouse offering at times the necessary help. Divorce is, then, an *institutionalized element of certain kinship systems*. It is not always a kind of excrescence, a sort of pathology or unpredictable deviation. This does not ignore or minimize the difficulties that individuals experience in divorce, or the devastation that may occur in their private lives when a divorce conflict occurs. Rather, we are noting that *all* family systems have *some* kinds of escape mechanisms built into them, to permit individuals to survive the pressures of the system, and one of these is divorce.

Nor is this solution confined to industrial societies. As Murdock has shown, and as Hobhouse began to show earlier, divorce is very common in many pre-literate societies. Even without a complete set of data, it is clear that the rate of divorce is often higher than in our own, or than in the other few nations that have at various times had still higher rates than the US.

It is then an error to think that, because primitive societies are mostly 'rural', they are therefore to be identified with the classical family of Western nostalgia, an idealized picture of the rural family in America at some unspecified period prior to the 1900s.

Theoretical importance of divorce

We do not have, unfortunately, any adequate analysis of the values relating to divorce in these societies. We know that in our own, divorce has been a possible, but disapproved, solution for marital conflict. That is, it seems that divorce is not as yet fully *institutionalized* in our own cultural structure. Certainly among some groups of our society it is still disapproved of strongly. It is equally certain that this attitude is *changing*. Thus, although a rise in our divorce rate can not be viewed as a simple index of social pathology or even of personal disorganization, it is without question an index of social change.

In the light of these hypotheses, divorce as a phenomenon and as an experience is theoretically very interesting. It is closely tied to several sets of strong value patterns relating to the family and to marital conflict. It is an index of interpersonal strain, and within our own society it is also an index of strain in the social structure, in that firstly, there are many strong, if gradually weaker, moral proscriptions against it; but secondly, in spite of these proscriptions, the divorces continue to occur and the rate of divorce continues to rise as a mass phenomenon. Moreover, since marital stability in our society is morally approved, since the roots of this attitude are to be found in the three major sects of the Judeo-Christian religious tradition, and since divorce is also judged to be an act of self-seeking or of moral failure, it is likely that few couples divorce in our culture without a guilt component on both sides with specific reference to the divorce (aside from guilts with other sources). Thus, on both the psychodynamic and the socio-structural levels there are interesting ramifications.

Furthermore, divorce as a large-scale solution for marital conflict is a relatively recent reappearance in the cultural history of Western society (for Rome in its 'decline', as for Athens, the rate must have been high), yet it has been an always *potentially* institutionalized element in the social structure because of its many Semitic religious antecedents (both Arab and Hebrew, of course). Since these potentialities did not become actual, divorce as a social deviation is in certain respects not like crime or juvenile delinquency, treason or sacrilege.

These latter and other violations are like divorce in that they can be predicted to some extent on the basis of individual characteristics, and to a very great extent on a mass basis. However, they are very different in that prescribed modes of official and unofficial behavior exist for dealing with such deviations. We are socialized to react against these deviations with a fairly specific behavioral and emotional set, and we are even told to some extent how they ought to be punished.

This is not the case for divorce. Neither the participants nor their close friends and relatives have been taught to react in a culturally approved fashion with respect to divorce. We are all taught how to grieve at the death of a relative. We are not taught how we should behave as a divorcee. We are given many culturally approved rationalizations for failing to achieve high status in our occupation, but we are not taught how to solve or to adjust to the failure of our marriage. The general preferences in our culture for rationalistic approaches to problems fail us in this area of great emotionality. Consequently, we should expect to find a set of social phenomena of considerable interest for understanding the family patterns in our culture. Finally, since divorce is a personal and often familial crisis, study of it should add to our knowledge about how individuals adjust to crises.

Numerical importance of divorce

A rather substantial segment of the population has, at one time or another, been involved in the divorce process. We do not have an exact figure for the segment composing all who have ever divorced. However, even allowing a substantial amount of cohort mortality, this group must number nearly ten million. Davis has estimated that 150,000 to 200,000 children are affected by divorce each year in this country, and calculates further that for the year 1940 the total number of children, then under the age of eighteen years, whose parents had ever been divorced, numbered 1,533,000. The figure has certainly not declined. In addition, although the divorce rate fluctuates somewhat from one year to the next, it is clear that the secular trend of divorce is still upward. It seems a conservative estimate to assert that the experience of divorce is likely to occur to one-fifth to one-sixth of the men and women in this country who live out an average life span.

On the other hand, as we have noted before, several countries have exhibited a *higher* rate of divorce than even the US. Burgess and Locke have assembled these rates for several countries, and show that under the old family system in Japan, there were approximately 367 divorces per 1000 marriages for the years 1884–8. Russia, Palestine, and Egypt had higher rates than the US for the period in or about 1938. As we also noted previously, many primitive societies have relatively high divorce rates. At any given time, approximately 2 per cent of the adult population of the US is in the marital status 'still divorced'. Finally, we must remember that death still dissolves more marriages than does divorce.

The structural importance of divorce

Whether or not we judge this segment of the population or this rate to be large, it seems at least likely that in our society the group impact of divorce is much greater than in most others. We have elsewhere noted some of the behavioral indices of this concern. They may be summarized as follows:

1. A widespread condemnation of the extent of divorce and of its increase.
2. The emotional difficulties suffered by the individuals in the divorce.
3. The number of panaceas offered as general solutions for the problem.
4. Its frequency as an object of clinical research.
5. The development of organizations and experts whose aim is to ameliorate this distress.

The kinship structure fails to define clearly an acceptable behavior pattern for this experience in the life history of a substantial segment of the population. The kinship system fails to furnish unambiguous arrangements for the following kinds of problems.

1. There are no ethical imperatives for relatives or friends that would make them feel constrained to furnish material support during the crisis and afterwards to the divorcees *as* divorcees. This is a period of dissolution of certain household arrangements. Most often, the two spouses separate from one another, and at least one of them must set up a new abode. There are new problems of purchasing food and housing, and, of course, there are various legal fees. These costs cannot usually come out of existing income. There is no room for such added expenses. In addition, of course, one or both spouses may lose their jobs, and there is only rarely enough money for both to continue their usual activities without need for added funds.

2. Similarly, there are no ethical imperatives for friends and relatives to furnish *emotional* support during this period. There is a general ethical imperative to furnish support to close friends during any kind of crisis, and to some extent this is applicable to the divorce situation. It is not comparable, however, to the kind of crisis created by an emergency operation or sudden illness, death, loss of job, etc. In the event of divorce, the friend must make an adjustment among several other imperatives, such as whether he *should* support the break-up of a family, whether he approves his friend's conduct, or how friendly he is to the other spouse. What we are distinguishing here is the difference between a crisis situation in which the imperatives are clear and one in which they are not clear. As we shall show later, friends and relatives actually do help in this situation, but this is not the crucial point at issue. Whether a given individual gives such support is the resultant of many factors, but

he cannot, in our society, base his action upon a simple rule of the kinship or friendship structure. The most striking contrast, of course, is with death of the spouse, for in this case the relative or friend who is unwilling to provide economic or emotional support is viewed with disapproval by all within the group.

3. A further point of ambiguity centers around the *readmission* of participants into their former kinship structure or into a new one. The importance of this ambiguity is not to be underestimated, and it is indeed the base on which other ambiguities rest. By contrast, among the Zuñi, for example, the kinship is matrilineal, divorce is relatively common, and it is accompanied by little public concern and attention. This is the case generally, as it happens, for merely private matters of marital conflict and even marriage. In this society the property in land is owned by the woman's side of the family and descends through her line. In one sense, divorce means that the man is 'dismissed'. We are not, however, concerned with the personal impact of this situation, but with the fact that in the case of a divorce, all the parties concerned know what they are supposed to do. The man returns to his mother's household, where there is a known place for him. He is part of her family line, and marriage has not changed that fact. He does not carry away the corn he has raised, and there is no argument about the ownership of real property, for that remains in the possession of his wife's lineage. There can be no argument about the children, since the children belong to his wife's line. Whether she herself rears the children or they are given to one of her male relatives to rear, the children are nevertheless part of her family, and it is the right of her family to make decisions about the children's welfare. There is no alimony and no child support, since both sides are simply reabsorbed into an existing and usually extended familial network. These provisions exist whether or not either family approves the behavior of either spouse. There may, of course, be some deviations from these rough rules laid down here, for in no society does everyone live up to the ideal. Nevertheless, these are the general moral imperatives, and the individual or family who failed to live by them would be criticized.

In our own society, by contrast, we are not at all clear as to where the members of the divorcing family ought to go. Indeed, in our society the emphasis is so much on the single family unit, the nuclear family, with only rather tenuous and increasingly vague connections with the older generation or with collateral relatives, that often there is almost no other family cell to which the members of the divorced family *can* go. This is a somewhat exaggerated statement, but it does describe the *norms*. The husband's original family has no moral imperative to take him back. He has made a claim to adulthood and independence, having founded his new family. He has left the family nest. There is no room for him, not alone spatially as is so often the situation in our time, but in kinship terms. It is assumed that if he divorces he will continue to work and support himself, together with perhaps his divorced spouse and children, but this is not a necessary concern of the family from which he originally came. Again, we must emphasize that, concretely, his original family may help him and be friendly to him, but there is no moral injunction that *as divorcee* he has such rights.

The wife is in an even more ambiguous position. Our own society is patrilineal, and patriarchal to a degree. By the Judeo-Christian traditions of the Western world, the wife leaves her original family and becomes a member of the husband's family. Actually, because of the pattern of small nuclear families in our generation, husband and wife simply form a new family unit. In any event, she is considered to be part of that new unit, and no longer part of her family of orientation. This is emphasized by the fact that she takes her husband's name and, if she has children, usually keeps her husband's name even after the divorce. The children also have her husband's name, so that even if she returns with her children to her own family's home, her name and kinship designation lie with the family of her husband. To this degree, then, the divorce asserts a legal cleavage which is only partially carried out in institutional fact.

In any event, for all the family members involved in the divorce, there is some ambiguity about the family status and role to which each must *return* when a divorce is made final. Neither of the two families of orientation is given clear definitions of the approved kinship status to be reassumed by the two married children.

4. As an almost necessary consequence of these ambiguities, the kinship structure does not point out avenues for the *formation of new families*. In some strata, after what is considered an appropriate period of emotional recovery, the divorced wife gradually forms new male friendships. In others, this behavior is considered vaguely or definitely improper. What is certain, however, is that the family's obligation to help her form a new family is not clear. This is in contrast with the moral imperatives families feel for helping the younger generation find a first husband or wife. Daughters are admonished by both parents that they must look for the right kind of husband, and parents usually make at least token gestures toward helping in this process. Even the most protective mother gives at least lip service to the notion that she must help her son find a wife. The push toward marriage is strong in our culture, and it affects both generations. The family has, however, discharged its obligations when the child is married. The unhappiness and disorganization of the divorced spouse may lead in time to the parent

family offering help in moving toward a second marriage. However, this is a result of the personal affection of family members for one another and the distress caused by the other's suffering, and is not so much due to a socially recognized obligation to offer this type of aid to a divorced child.

5. Correlative with these gaps is a further ambiguity concerning the proper behavior and emotional attitudes of the spouses most directly concerned. We have just noted the failure to specify the proper behavior for various activities which might be carried out by relatives or even friends. However, the other side of all such sets of definitions is a specification of the appropriate role behavior of the two spouses. There is no clear definition as to whether they should be grieved or relieved. They are in some sense now 'single', but the role behavior of the never married is much more definitely specified. Having *once* been defined as adult and married, a status which is in turn defined as being chronologically *later* than the status of 'never married', neither the spouses nor their families have a simple definition of an in-between state: they are neither old nor young, adult nor child, married nor single. Lacking such a specification, the divorced spouse is subject to criticism by some, no matter what she or he does. Behavior and emotion may seem inappropriate to some members of the family or to some friends. In particular, the proper relationship *between the divorced spouses* is not clearly defined.

These ambiguities do not necessarily create great emotional distress and, as we shall see later on, many women may adjust to divorce with relatively little anguish. However, social behavior is simplified in all societies by roled definitions, accepted and known to almost all participants, and morally approved. When these definitions are lacking, the necessary decisions must be made on a more individual basis, and the people concerned can not count on general social approval, whether or not their previous behavior has been proper.

27 Mirra Komarovsky

Blue-Collar Marriage

Excerpt from Mirra Komarovsky, *Blue-Collar Marriage*, Random House, 1962, pp. 336–44.

The value of companionship has been frequently cited by sociologists as the distinctive feature of modern marriage. Many writers have described the evolution of the modern family that brought about a specialization in its functions. The remaining functions have been variously described as affectional or expressive and child-rearing or socialization. 'We have argued above', concludes one recent discussion, 'that the nuclear family is specialized far over in the expressive tension-management and socialization directions.'

If Glenton families are at all typical of comparable classes in other communities, then for considerable segments of our population these writings are more prescriptive than descriptive. They define the appropriate functions of marriage in modern society. But the logic of the analysis does not unfortunately bring the required patterns into existence automatically. Possibly even for the unhappy one-third of the Glenton couples, marriage entails some satisfactions. But these men and women do not turn to one another for emotional support, and it is uncertain whether the net effect of the marital relationship is to relieve or to increase personal tension.

Changes in patterns of socialization and improvement in interpersonal skills would go far towards strengthening marriage. But the root of the difficulty lies deeper. Shortening of the work day, smaller families and the withdrawal of many economic functions from the home have given these couples long evenings and week-ends together. But life in general is impoverished, and marriage assumes a saliency by default. It is questionable whether any relationship can fill so great a void. Even the middle-class suburbanite, who has reputedly forsaken the world for the family nest, bristles with outside interests in comparison with our respondents. Status-seeking, the elaboration of living standards, the social life, to say nothing of civic and cultural interests, fill life with tension and struggle but also with emotional involvement and rewards. As for Glenton couples, those in their twenties still enjoy social life and other forms of recreation. The birth of children and the striving to purchase a home and to furnish it still give life a sense of movement. But many couples in their late thirties, especially among the less-educated, seem almost to have withdrawn from life. There they sit in front of the television set: 'What's there to say? We both see it.' 'If you had two extra hours every day, how would you like to spend them?' asked the interviewer, and one man mused: 'This would make the evening awfully long and tiring if you're watching TV.'

The social isolation, especially of the older men, has been repeatedly noted. We have described the relatively low involvement of the men, as compared with their wives, in the lives of their married children. Social life with friends also declines with age. Only infrequently do the men appear to enjoy emotionally significant ties with work-mates. They lack even the kind of segmented, though intense, relationships that professional and businessmen frequently have with co-workers. If this social isolation is characteristic of working-class men of other ethnic, religious and regional groups, it may play a role in explaining the relatively lower level of mental health in blue-collar strata as compared with the middle and upper classes. In any event, this social isolation, we believe, tends to strain the marriage relationship. It robs life and therefore marriage of stimulation and novelty and it closes outlets that might siphon off marital irritations.

We were slow to perceive the problem brought about by a drab existence and constant 'togetherness', for a reason that illustrates anew how tacitly held values can distort perception. We approached the study with the image of the East London working-class marriage in mind. Will the American working-class marriages, we asked, show the same estrangement between the sexes? Do husbands and wives in Glenton, as in London, lead their separate lives in work and in leisure? The English pattern fell short of our own ideal of friendship in marriage.

Glenton families were found to differ significantly from the East London ones. Most wives know to the penny what their husbands earn, and economic decisions are made jointly. There is no lack of togetherness in the sense of time spent in each other's physical presence. Indeed, these couples probably spend more time together as a family (and probably more time together as a pair, without children, relatives or friends) than middle-class couples with their more active social and club life. Our own moral set led us to approve these deviations from the East London patterns, and we were temporarily blinded to the problem that togetherness entailed for our respondents. We mistakenly assumed that the greater association between the spouses automatically brought about a deeper relationship than in East London.

The difficulties that hinder a fuller realization of the ideal of companionship illustrate a familiar mode of social disorganization, that arising out of the discrepancy between aspirations and opportunities for their attainment. With respect to marital communication, our data enabled us to compare the magnitude of this discrepancy for men and women at each educational level. The older high school women experience the widest gap between their expectations, on the one hand, and the actual quality of the marital dialogue, on the other. They are consequently more dissatisfied with marital communication than the less-educated wives at the same stage of life, despite the fact that they enjoy a higher level of sharing and companionate interchange. The less-educated women accept their lot with amazing fortitude and, occasionally, even with good cheer.

The gulf between desired goals and means available for their attainment is wide in other areas of life, with unfavorable consequences for marriage [resulting in] occupational, financial and status frustrations. Not only the poorest fourth of the families, but others also live from one pay envelope to the next, with no savings or insurance to cushion a possible crisis. This explains the undercurrent of anxiety which repeatedly comes to the surface in such remarks as 'He worked good last year. I hope he will this year' and 'I hope we'll stay healthy'. Public relief is too humiliating to contemplate for these people, and in moments of panic they are much more likely to think of their relatives as a possible source of assistance.

For the man, the economic difficulties have a special emotional significance – they undermine his self-esteem. For example, he is concerned about his parental responsibilities. Our question, 'Would you like your son to follow you in your line of work?' was generally answered negatively: 'No, I would like him to do a lot better'. But at the same time the fathers doubted their ability to provide for their children the necessary means of advancement.

The husbands experience some other characteristic strains. Their actual power in the family frequently falls short of their patriarchal aspirations. In contrast, successful professional husbands may occasionally enjoy more power in marriage than is sanctioned by their egalitarian ideals. The twinges of guilt which this latter discrepancy produces are less painful than the workingman's problem. Our respondents thought that 'men should have the final say-so in family decisions'. However, they found themselves pitted against resourceful wives who held paid jobs prior to marriage and could hold their own in marriage. This is especially true of the women high school graduates. One young wife told the interviewer that her husband's current weekly wages were only $10 higher than her own pay before marriage. Even the good providers lack the halo of prestige that high achievement and high community status bestow on a successful business or professional man.

Not all of Glenton families experience these difficulties with equal intensity. The high school graduates, on the whole, are happier in marriage than the less-educated. This is especially true in the first years of marriage. The better-educated marry later and delay childbearing in comparison with the less-educated couples. Consequently, fewer of the former suffer from the syndrome of problems of some young couples: too many infants, parenthood too soon after marriage under difficult economic conditions and in the absence of companionship between the mates. Moreover, the high school men (perhaps because they are younger) do not include the completely defeated men whose sense of failure has such unhappy consequences for marriage.

While high school graduates also believe in the traditional division of labor between the sexes, in practice the husbands help more frequently with the care of infants and with shopping than in less-educated families. Equally significant is their fuller marital communication. They have more faith in the possibility of friendship between men and women. One young high school graduate explained why women have more need of heart-to-heart talk than men: 'The husband's job is an outlet for him and her days are more routine and so she needs to sit down and feel the closeness with her husband'. When depressed, this wife finds that 'a good heart-to-heart talk can do a lot for her morale'. A value endorsed so explicitly must surely affect behavior. In contrast, the less-educated tend to feel, as was indicated in an earlier chapter, that friendship is more likely to exist between persons of the same sex and that the principal marital ties are sexual union, mutual devotion and complementary tasks.

But the better-educated have some typical problems of their own. Status frustration is one of them. Generally, status-seeking is not a prominent drive among these families. There is an order of priorities in goals and many are preoccupied with sheer survival. Even the more prosperous families do not live with gazes fixed on their reflected image, and with the constant comparative self-appraisal allegedly so characteristic of our society. This is no 'other-directed' group. Many a middle-class couple who have to cultivate the 'right' people for the sake of the husband's career would envy the freedom these families enjoy to entertain only the people they like. Their social life, such as it is, is pure sociability. Nevertheless, some pressures for upward mobility do exist and some high school couples exhibit strain because their aspirations for higher status are frustrated.

We found no difference between the two educational groups in the prevalence of sexual problems or in psychological sources of marital strains. No personality tests were employed in this study, and observations about psychological factors in marital maladjustment here appear inconclusive. But some speculation is aroused by the higher proportion of hostile sons and daughters among the less-educated couples, caused apparently by a number of social factors in their early lives. An unhappy childhood and hostile parent–child relationships tend to affect adversely the marital adjustment of the individual. If this excess of parent–child conflict among the less-educated is confirmed by future studies it will offer another possible explanation of their lower marital happiness.

We limited our summary to problems in marriage, brought about, directly or indirectly, by socio-economic and cultural conditions. But there is hardly a case history cited in this book which does not suggest psychological factors involved in marital strain. Sharing a home with in-laws need not necessarily create an in-law problem, but it requires, as we have seen, a closer emotional dovetailing of personalities if trouble is to be avoided. Given the same degree of congeniality, those residing in separate households will experience less strain. Given a common residence, variations in psychological factors will also produce variations in the outcome. Similar interplay of psychological and social factors is illustrated in every chapter of this book. Maintaining the fiction of her husband's supremacy in public is, for example, an accepted stratagem of a dominant wife. But this adaptation to a deviant situation is not available to some personalities. We encountered a wife whose competitiveness with her husband, more or less dormant in the privacy of the home, is aroused by the presence of an audience.

This study did not include any middle- or upper-class respondents, and it contains no data on broad class differences in marital adjustment. Recent evidence shows that divorce rates tend to decrease with higher socio-economic and educational status. The data on marital satisfaction are consistent; satisfaction appears to go up with the rise in the class hierarchy. We have no information about the rates of divorce or desertion among the general population of Glenton's Protestant blue-collar families from which we drew our respondents. Nevertheless, our comparison of the two educational categories of blue-collar families has some pertinence to the question of broad class differences in marital happiness.

Current analyses of this problem seek to ascertain the peculiarly stressful experiences of the working classes in comparison with the upper strata. But it is not certain whether the extent of stress does in fact decline as one ascends the occupational or the educational ladder. The economic and occupational frustrations were indeed more prevalent among our less-educated respondents as they are, no doubt, in a comparable stratum in the society at large. But offsetting these and other difficulties of these workers is their freedom from a number of allegedly typical problems of the higher and better-educated classes. Ambiguous definitions of mutual rights and duties and the resulting ethical inconsistencies, mental conflict produced by an abundance of choices, conflicting loyalties and standards, strain produced by the sheer volume of stimuli – all these are relatively rare in Glenton. Glenton couples are also free from the self-conscious scrutiny of relationships that, some writers claim, robs marriage of its spontaneity among many highly educated persons.

Are we to assume then, *ex post facto*, that these problems, more prevalent among the higher classes, are somehow less disturbing than those typical of the workingman?[1]

The interpretation of this problem may require a shift in emphasis. It is an open question whether life is less stressful for the higher classes. But it must surely contain richer rewards. The sense of satisfaction with marriage, as with life in general, may depend not so much upon an absence of stress as upon the presence of rewards – a momentary feeling of closeness with one's mate, the occasional excitement of hope, even a fleeting triumph of achievement. True, a low level of expectations inflates the rewards of minor attainments ('I had myself a ball once when I came out two dollars over the budget that we didn't have to pay out all at once'). But even with their modest aspirations, too many Glenton couples find life drab and unrewarding.[2]

The reader must be reminded that this dark portrait is not the total picture of Glenton families. It is an analysis of their problems. For the happiest third of the group, life contains many satisfactions, and satisfactions appear to outweigh the pain. The birth of a child ('I get real set up when one of them gets born'); the down payment of a home; a good carpentry job and a compliment from a visiting relative; a husband's unexpected gift ('a real classy box of candy'); a child's good report card; sexual satisfaction ('sex is a big thing with us'); a family reunion of relatives in church, followed by a good meal; playing with the children ('they are really comical'); beer in the tavern with congenial buddies; a

1. It is possible that the Glenton sample is too stable to be typical of working-class strata that are generally included in the class comparisons of marital adjustment. But the insulation from intellectual currents of the larger society and absence of group affiliation have been demonstrated in numerous working-class studies in other communities.

2. The theory that higher socio-economic classes may experience both more happiness and more tension in marriage is no mere conjecture. The more highly-educated respondents in one study rated their marital happiness higher than people of less education, but they also expressed more sense of inadequacy and more self-questioning.

new spring outfit; a good bowling score; a new bedroom set; a new car; a good TV show and a companionable snack afterwards; the baby's first word; a drive to the shore; a picnic with relatives – these and others have been mentioned by our respondents as sources of pleasure and happiness. And of course there is the underlying satisfaction of men and women who feel that they have fulfilled honorably their basic roles of provider, mate and parent.

Life at its best is economically comfortable and rewarding, but for the great majority life is narrowly circumscribed. A spotlight outlines a small circle of ground around each family, with the relatives, a few friends, the boss and some work-mates, the tavern keeper, the church and the union. Visible also are the top movie stars, baseball players and other athletes, TV performers and top national office holders. But beyond that circle extends a vast darkness. These English-speaking, well-dressed, well-mannered, responsible persons do not enjoy full membership in their society. They lack even such bridges to the larger society as may be provided by membership in a women's club or a Chamber of Commerce. The union occasionally (but from what could be ascertained, only infrequently) provides such a channel of information and sense of participation. Verbal and intellectual limitations curtail reflection even about the immediate environment. In the words of Beatie, the working-class rebel of *Roots*: 'Ever since it began the world's bin growin' hasn't it? Things have happened, things have bin discovered, people have bin thinking and improving and inventing but what do we know about it all?' Economically poorer racial and ethnic minorities are no doubt still more deprived, but this does not make the exclusion of Glenton families any less wasteful and disturbing.

This is not merely the judgement of the author. In considerable measure, this is also the respondents' self-appraisal. Why, otherwise, would a father exclaim with such feeling: 'No, I want my children to go a lot farther.' But for all their fervent hopes and the struggle, these parents cannot provide for their children the environment enjoyed by the average middle-class child. Unless school and society find ways to improve the life chances for all citizens, a proportion of Glenton's children will grow up to live as do their parents, on the fringes of their society.

28 Herbert J. Gans

The Negro Family

Excerpts from Herbert J. Gans, 'The Negro family: reflection on the Moynihan Report', in Lee Rainwater and William L. Yancey (eds.), *The Moynihan Report and the Politics of Controversy*, MIT Press, 1967, pp. 446–57.

The breakdown of the negro family: the 'Moynihan Report' and its implications for federal civil rights policy

Last March, the US Department of Labor published 'for official use only' a report entitled *The Negro Family: The Case for National Action*. Written by Daniel Patrick Moynihan and Paul Barton just before the former resigned as Assistant Secretary of Labor to run unsuccessfully for President of New York's City Council, it was soon labeled the 'Moynihan Report' by the Washington officials who were able to obtain copies.

Although not apparent from its title, the report called for a bold and important change in federal civil rights policy, asking the federal government to identify itself with the Negro Revolution, and to shift its programs from an emphasis on liberty to one on equality. 'The Negro Revolution,' says Moynihan, 'like the industrial upheaval of the 1930s, is a movement for equality as well as liberty', but the Supreme Court decision for school desegregation, the Civil Rights Act of 1964 and 1965 and other legislation have only provided political liberty. The War on Poverty, which Moynihan describes as the first phase of the Negro revolution, makes opportunities available, but job training programs which promise no jobs at their conclusion cannot produce equality. Held back by poverty, discrimination and inadequate schooling, Negroes cannot compete with whites, so that 'equality of opportunity almost insures inequality of results'.

Federal policies must therefore be devised to provide equality, 'distribution of achievements among Negroes roughly comparable to that of whites,' for otherwise, 'there will be no social peace in the United States for generations.'

But according to Moynihan, a serious obstacle stands in the way of achieving equality, the inability of Negroes 'to move from where they are now to where they want and ought to be'. This inability he ascribes to the breakdown of Negro social structure, and more particularly, to the deterioration of the Negro family. The remainder of the report is devoted to an analysis of that deterioration.

Soon after the report was published, President Johnson drew extensively on it for a commencement address at Howard University. He placed himself firmly behind Moynihan's proposal for a policy of equality of results, describing it as 'the next and more profound stage of the battle for civil rights', and pointed to the breakdown of the Negro family as a limiting factor. He called for programs to strengthen the family, and announced that a White House conference would be assembled in the fall for this purpose.

During the summer, public interest in both the report and the speech declined as new speeches and reports made the headlines, but after the Los Angeles riots, the Moynihan report suddenly achieved new notoriety, for its analysis of Negro society seemed to provide the best and the most easily available explanation of what had happened in Watts. Demand for copies increased, and now the government has released it to the press. Consequently, it is worth looking more closely at its findings and their implications.

From a variety of government and social science studies, Moynihan concludes that the principal weaknesses of the Negro family are its instability, its proclivity for producing illegitimate children, and its matriarchal structure. Nearly a quarter of married Negro women are divorced or separated, and 35 per cent of all Negro children live in broken homes. Almost a quarter of Negro births are illegitimate, and nearly one-fourth of all Negro families are headed by a woman. As a result, 14 per cent of all Negro children are being supported by the Aid for Families of Dependent Children (AFDC) program.

Although these figures would suggest that a smaller proportion of the Negro community is in trouble than is often claimed, they also underestimate the extent of the breakdown, for more families are touched by it at one time in their lives than at the given moment caught by the statistics. Thus, Moynihan estimates that less than half of all Negro children have lived with both their parents by the time they reach the age of eighteen, and many legitimate children grow up without their real fathers. As L. Rainwater has pointed out, lower class Negro women often marry the man who fathers their first or second child in order to obtain the valued status of being married, but thereafter they live in unmarried unions with other men. Also, many households in which a man is present are nevertheless headed by women, for Moynihan indicates that in a fourth of Negro families in which a husband is present, he is not the principal earner. Perhaps the best illustration of the way in which available figures understate the problem comes from unemployment statistics which show that while the average monthly unemployment rate for Negro males in 1964 was 9 per cent, fully 29 per cent were unemployed at one time or another during that year. Moreover, the rates of family instability among whites are considerably lower and still decreasing, while they are on the rise among the Negro population.

The population which bears the brunt of these instabilities is of course the low-income one. Although the proportion of stable two-parent Negro families is probably increasing, 'the Negro community is ... dividing between a stable middle class group that is steadily growing stronger ... and an increasingly disorganized and disadvantaged lower class group'.

In that group, a significant minority of the families are broken, headed by women, and composed of illegitimate children. The Negro woman can either obtain employment or welfare payments to support her children, while the Negro man, saddled with unstable jobs, frequent unemployment and short-term unemployment insurance, cannot provide the economic support that is a principal male function in American society. As a result, the woman becomes the head of the family, and the man a marginal appendage, who deserts or is rejected by his wife when he can no longer contribute to the family upkeep. With divorce made impossible by economic or legal barriers, the woman may then live with a number of men in what W. Miller calls 'serial monogamy', finding a new mate when the inevitable quarrels start over who should support and head the family. And because the women value children, they continue to have them, illegitimately or not.

This family structure seems to have detrimental effects on the children, and especially on the boys, for they grow up in an environment which constantly demonstrates to them that men are troublesome good-for-nothings. Moynihan's data show that Negro girls do better in school and on the labor market than the boys, and that the latter more often turn to delinquency, crime, alcohol, drugs, and mental illness in order to escape the bitter reality of a hopeless future. The girls are not entirely immune from ill-effects, however, for many become pregnant in their teens, but since the girls' mothers are quite willing to raise their grandchildren, the girls do not become a public and visible social problem.

The fundamental causes of family instability Moynihan properly traces to slavery and unemployment. Drawing on the researches of F. Tannenbaum and S. Elkins, he points out that American slave-owners treated their slaves as mere commodities and, unlike their Latin American counterparts, often denied them all basic human rights, including that of marriage. More important, the structure of Southern slave economy also placed the Negro man in an inferior position. He was needed only when the plantation economy was booming, and his price on the slave market was generally lower than that of the woman. Her services were always in demand around the household – or in the master's bed – and until her children were sold away from her, she was allowed to raise them. This established her in a position of economic and familial dominance which she has maintained, willingly or not, until the present day. All the available evidence indicates that since the Civil War, Negro male unemployment has almost always been higher than female. The gap has been widened further in recent years, especially in the cities, as job opportunities increased for women, while decreasing for men due to the ever shrinking supply of unskilled and semiskilled work and the continuing racial discrimination in many trades. Since Negroes are still moving to the cities in large numbers, the trends which Moynihan reports are likely to continue in the years to come.

Slavery made it impossible for Negroes to establish a two-parent family, and its heritage has undoubtedly left its mark on their descendants. Even so, slavery is only a necessary not a sufficient cause of the problem. Histories of the nineteenth century European immigration, anthropological studies of the Caribbean matriarchal family, and observations among Puerto Ricans in American cities indicate that whenever there is work for women and serious unemployment among men, families break up as the latter desert or are expelled. The most impressive illustration of this pattern is a chart in the Moynihan Report which shows that between 1951 and 1963, increases in the Negro male unemployment rate were followed, a year later, by a rise in the proportion of separated women.

Underemployment, being stuck in a dead-end job, and low wages may have similar consequences. The HARYOU report on Harlem, *Youth in the Ghetto*, reported that social pathology is as high among those holding inadequate jobs as among the unemployed, and Moynihan points out that the minimum wage of $1.25 an hour, which is all that too many Negroes earn, can support an individual but not a family.

In short, Moynihan's findings suggest that the problems of the Negro family which he sees as holding back the achievement of equality are themselves the results of previous inequalities, particularly economic ones that began with slavery and have been maintained by racial discrimination ever since. The report's concluding proposal, that 'the policy of the United States is to bring the Negro American to full and equal sharing in the responsibilities and rewards of citizenship' and that 'to this end, the programs of the federal government ... shall be designed to have the effect, directly or indirectly, of enhancing the stability and resources of the Negro American family', therefore requires a drastic change of direction in federal civil rights activities.

The Moynihan Report does not offer any recommendations to implement its policy proposal, arguing that the problem must be defined properly first in order to prevent the hasty development of programs that do not address themselves to the basic problem. While this argument was perhaps justified as long as the report remained confidential, it may have some negative consequences now that the contents have been released to the press. The vacuum that is created when no recommendations are attached to a policy proposal can easily be filled by undesirable solutions, and the report's conclusions can be conveniently misinterpreted.

This possibility is enhanced by the potential conflict between the two major themes of the report, that Negroes must be given real equality, and that because of the deterioration of the family, they are presently incapable of achieving it. The amount of space devoted to the latter theme, and the inherent sensationality of the data make it possible that the handicaps of the Negro population will receive more attention than Moynihan's forthright appeal for an equality of outcomes.

Thus, the findings on family instability and illegitimacy can be used by right-wing and racist groups to support their claim that Negroes are inherently immoral and therefore unworthy of equality. Politicians responding to more respectable white backlash can argue that Negroes must improve themselves before they are entitled to further government aid, and so can educators, psychologists, social workers, and other professionals who believe that the Negro's basic problem is 'cultural deprivation' or 'ego inadequacy' rather than lack of opportunities for equality. This in turn could lead to a clamor for pseudo-psychiatric programs that attempt to change the Negro family through counseling and other therapeutic methods. Worse still, the report could be used to justify a reduction of efforts in the elimination of racial discrimination and the War on Poverty, watering down programs which have only recently been instituted and have not yet had a chance to improve the condition of the Negro population, but are already under concerted attack from conservative white groups and local politicians.

Of course, the deterioration of Negro society is due both to the lack of opportunity and to cultural deprivation, but the latter is clearly an effect of the former, and is much more difficult to change through government policies. For example, poor Negro school performance results both from inadequate, segregated schools and from the failure of the Negro home to prepare children for school, as well as from low motivation on the part of Negro children who see no reason to learn if they cannot find jobs after graduation. Even so, however difficult it may be to improve and desegregate the schools and to provide jobs, it is easier, more desirable and more likely to help Negro family life than attempts to alter the structure of the family or the personality of its members through programs of 'cultural enrichment' or therapy, not to mention irresponsible demands for Negro self-improvement.

In addition, it must be stressed that at present, we do not even know whether the lower-class Negro family structure is actually as pathological as the Moynihan Report suggests. However much the picture of family life painted in that report may grate on middle-class moral sensibilities, it may well be that instability, illegitimacy, and matriarchy are the most positive adaptations possible to the conditions which Negroes must endure.

Moynihan presents some data which show that children from broken homes do more poorly in school and are more likely to turn to delinquency and drugs. Preliminary findings of a study by B. Mackler of the Center for Urban Education show no relationship between school performance and broken families, and a massive study of mental health in Manhattan, reported by T. Langner and S. Michaels in *Life Stress and Mental Health*, demonstrated that among whites at least, growing up in a broken family did not increase the likelihood of mental illness as much as did poverty and being of low status.

Families can break up for many reasons, among them cultural and personality differences among the parents, economic difficulties, or mental illness on the part of one or both spouses. Each of these reasons produces different effects on the children, and not all are likely to be pathological. Indeed, if one family member is mentally ill, removing him from the family and thus breaking it up may be the healthiest solution, at least for the family.

Likewise, the matriarchal family structure and the absence of a father has not yet been proven pathological, even for the boys who grow up in it. Sociological studies of the Negro family have demonstrated the existence of an extended kinship system of mothers, grandmothers, aunts, and other female relatives that is surprisingly stable, at least on the female side. Moreover, many matriarchal families raise boys who do adapt successfully and themselves make stable marriages. The immediate cause of pathology may be the absence of a set of emotional strengths and cultural skills in the mothers, rather than the instability or departure of the fathers. A family headed by a capable if unmarried mother may thus be healthier than a two-parent family in which the father is a marginal appendage. If this is true, one could argue that at present, the broken and matriarchal family is a viable solution for the Negro lower-class population, for given the economic and other handicaps of the men, the family can best survive by rejecting its men, albeit at great emotional cost to them.

Similar skepticism can be applied to premature judgements of Negro illegitimacy. Since illegitimacy is not punished in the lower class as it is in the middle class, and illegitimate children and grandchildren are as welcome as legitimate ones, they may not suffer the pathological consequences that accompany illegitimacy in the middle class. Moreover, even the moral evaluation of illegitimacy in the middle class has less relevance in the Negro lower class, particularly when men cannot be counted on as stable family members.

Finally, illegitimacy and the bearing of children generally has a different meaning in this population than in the middle-class one. Rainwater suggests that adolescent Negro girls often invite pregnancy because having children is their way of becoming adults and of making sure that they will have a family in which they can play the dominant role for which they have been trained by their culture. Although many older Negro women have children because they lack access to birth control methods they can use or trust, I suspect that others continue to have them because in a society in which older children are inevitably a disappointment, babies provide a source of pleasure and of feeling useful to their mothers. If having children offers them a reason for living in the same way that sexual prowess does for Negro men, then alternate rewards and sources of hope must be available before illegitimacy can either be judged by middle-class standards, or programs developed to do away with it. Until more is known about the functioning and effects of lower-class Negro family structure, the assumption that it is entirely or predominantly pathological is premature.

It would thus be tragic if the findings of the Moynihan Report were used to justify demands for Negro self-improvement or the development of a middle-class family structure before further programs to bring about real equality are set up. Consequently, it is important to see what conclusions and recommendations emerge from the forthcoming White House conference and how the assembled experts deal with the two themes of Moynihan's Report. It is also relevant to describe some recommendations which seem to me to be called for by the findings of that report.

The fundamentally economic causes of the present structure of the Negro family indicate that programs to change it must deal with these causes, principally in the areas of employment, income, and the provision of housing and other basic services. The history of the Negro family since the time of slavery indicates that the most important single program is the elimination of unemployment. If Negro men can obtain decent and stable jobs, then many – and far more than we think – can at once assume a viable role in the family and can raise children who will put an end to the long tradition of male marginality and inferiority [. . .]

The insistence on equality of results in the Moynihan Report is therefore the most effective approach to removing the instabilities of the Negro family. Whether or not Moynihan's plea – and that made by President Johnson at Howard University – will be heeded remains to be seen. The economic, social, and political changes required to provide equality are drastic, and both the white and the Negro middle class – not to mention the white lower class – have a considerable investment in the *status quo* which condemns the poor Negro to membership in a powerless, dependent and deprived underclass. President Johnson's success in achieving his legislative program in Congress suggests that some change can be initiated through federal action, but the implementation of civil rights legislation and antipoverty programs also indicates that much of the federal innovation is subverted at the local level and that a significant portion of the new funds are drained off to support the very political and economic forces that help to keep the lower-class Negro in his present position.

Federal and local officials must do all they can to prevent this from happening in the future, but they must be supported – and pressured – by professional, religious, and civic groups dedicated to racial equality. Also, the civil rights movement must begin to represent and speak for the low-income Negro population more than it has done in the past, for if the Negro revolution and the social peace of which Moynihan speaks are to be won, they must be won by and for that population.

Yet inescapably, the Negro problem is primarily a white problem, for the ultimate source of change must be the white population. Of the twin ideals of American democracy which Moynihan describes, it has traditionally opted for Liberty rather than Equality, including the liberty to keep the less equal in their place. It would be hard to imagine a sudden ground swell for equality from the white population, but if it really wants to prevent the spreading of violent protest through race riots, and the proliferation of the less visible but equally destructive protest expressed through delinquency and drug addiction, it must allow its political leaders to make the changes in the American social, economic, and political structure that are needed to move toward equality. Unfortunately, so far most whites are less touched than titillated by riots and family breakdown, and more driven to revenge than to reform when Negro deprivation does reach into their lives. In this desert of compassion, the Moynihan Report is a tiny oasis of hope, and if properly interpreted and implemented, a first guide to the achievement of equality in the years to come.

29 Political and Economic Planning

Women and Top Jobs

Excerpt from *Women and Top Jobs: An Interim Report*,
Political and Economic Planning, 1967, pp. 15–21.

Few today would defend the idea that women are both different from men and inferior. The commonest idea is rather that women are equal but different, and that their priorities in family life, work, and the community should reflect this. The Robbins Commission on Higher Education noted that 'It is generally held that no significant differences exist between the innate potential of men and women. There may be differences of kind – for example, as between linguistic and mathematical aptitudes – but no differences in level'. The affirmation of equality of level is characteristic, but so is the hint at 'differences of kind'.

'Differences of kind' and the practical consequences drawn from them tend to be seen today as less sharply marked than in the past. There is a general trend, though with variations from one class and group to another, towards greater equality between husband and wife and more sharing of tasks and interests both outside the family and in it. Social surveys have consistently shown a trend towards fathers helping with the children and the housework. Husbands and wives more often than not go out together. When they do not, it can well be the husband, not the wife, who baby-sits. In nearly all families both partners have a voice in the financial decisions. Conversely, wives as well as husbands expect to work outside the home, at least when there are no children below school age.

But this convergence of conjugal roles has hitherto had firm limits, and these limits have been an effective barrier to many women who might otherwise have made the commitments needed for a career, especially at top level. The norm is still that for a wife, and especially for a mother, the internal needs of the family come first, whereas for a husband and father work comes first. It is the wife who is expected to move to the place most convenient for the husband's career and to drop her own career to support his, not *vice versa*. It is most likely to be the wife who must take time off in family emergencies. She is very likely to drop work altogether when the children are small, and may do so at other times when extra help is needed in the home even if it would be financially possible to employ someone else for this. It is the girl who is commonly expected not to outshine her prospective husband in work or work-related activities, and not the other way round. A man of working age who does not work is likely to be looked at askance even if he has plenty of capital to live on, while the woman with young children is likely to be looked at askance if she works even if she has adequate domestic help. Among graduate wives, though they are the most work-prone group of women, the British Federation of University Women found that the proportion working dropped from 81 per cent where the husband's income was £1000 a year or less to 46 per cent where the income was over £3000. The proportion working full-time dropped even more steeply. In traditionally-minded families even today the fact that a wife works is seen as a public reflection on the husband's capacity to support his family.

A husband who does not help in the home is likely today to meet at best with tolerance and often with resentment, but still not with the same contempt as the malingerer who neglects his work and lives off social security or his wife's earnings. The husband's help in the home is an extra to be fitted in as his career permits. For a wife it is her career that has to be fitted into the interstices of duties at home. Though high career achievement by a wife may be greatly admired, it will be accepted only partly as an excuse for 'unfeminine' behaviour or a sloppily kept home, and not at all for neglect of the children. When American women graduates are asked what type of women they admire most, they refer chiefly to women who receive awards for scientific, scholarly, literary and artistic work. But the kind of success they want most for themselves is to be 'mother of several highly accomplished children' and 'the wife whose husband becomes very prominent'.

In recent years this well-established pattern has been challenged in terms of both theory and policy by writers in a number of countries – Sweden, France and the United States among others – in the name of a different, more open-ended approach.

Let me present the utopia that I would like to see in which girls would not be discriminated against in education or elsewhere. This would be a world in which the actual bio-cultural distinctions between the sexes would be seen as large, overlapping curves in which many boys would be in their temperaments more like most girls than like most boys; and so, too, with girls the differences would be group differences that would permit individuals to pursue their own native endowment irrespective of sex.

This approach does not, or at any rate need not, deny differences between the average or typical aptitudes and interests of men on the one hand and women on the other. As Riesman adds 'I would like to see more women in science . . . for the sake of science, because it would present a different face to society if the women in it were sufficiently numerous and confident not to follow the male models or definitions.'

What an approach like Riesman's does challenge is the tendency to press men and women (although less strongly than in the past) into standard moulds which may suit the average or modal member of each sex, but do not suit that large proportion of both sexes whose interests and aptitudes diverge from the average. There are plenty of men whose interest is in politics, or social service, or sport, or simply in their homes and family life, rather than in their careers. They make a living to their employers' satisfaction, but their heart is elsewhere. Equally there are women who may be successful wives and mothers, but wish without necessarily giving this up to commit themselves whole-heartedly to church work, social or political work, or a career.

In a husband–wife relationship, Riesman implies, any combination of patterns of career, voluntary service, and family life is possible and should be socially accepted. One is the present conventional pattern in which the husband is fully committed to his career while the wife has a career but is primarily committed to her family. In another both partners could be committed first and foremost, with the help of domestic service and of nursery schools and other forms of non-domestic child care, to a career or other interests outside the home. They might pursue these either in their separate individual ways or jointly; as Bernard Shaw said of the marriage of Sidney and Beatrice Webb, 'two typewriters beating as one'. In another pattern again, though both partners might contribute to the family income, neither would be specially interested in a career. Both would concentrate on the home, the family, and leisure or social service interests centred on it. Another possible pattern is for both husband and wife to be strongly interested both in their family and in a career, but to distribute their activities and responsibilities between them in other than the traditional way. In another case again the conventional pattern might be reversed. The wife would put her primary effort into her career, while the husband took over the role of host. The wife's career, not the husband's, would decide the location of the family home. In other cases again men or women could continue as now to decide that their commitment to a career or to social service was inconsistent with any commitment to family life at all. For many men it has always been true that 'my profession is my only true wife' (Brunel). J. Bernard offers similar advice to women who wish to get to the top in science, 'The going will be rough . . . you might do well not to encumber yourself with any other kind of husband than your work.' The experience of religious orders underlines that many women as well as men have been ready to heed such advice. Any of these choices might be appropriate in the light of the special interests and aptitudes of individual men and women. The suggestion is that once reasoned choices have been made in this light, society should give its equal approval to all of them.

How readily are views like these likely to be accepted in future? Will men's and women's roles in our society converge to the point where, apart from the irreducible biological minimum, differences between the sexes as such disappear and only differences between individuals of either sex remain? The answer to this question is important to women and men at any level of ability, for questions about commitment to a career or other outside interests may arise for any of them. But it is specially important for those women with the ability to go through to the highest posts, for it is here that the career commitment which is needed for success is usually most intense and can most easily clash with stereotypes of what a feminine role should be. There is less and less difficulty today for a woman to include in her life cycle marriage, a family, and a career of interest and some responsibility. There can still be very considerable difficulty in combining marriage and a family with a career leading to the top. To make such combinations more usual and possible involves issues of family and community organization as well as of motivating women and using their talents as individuals.

It is useful to consider the issues bearing on highly qualified women and their careers as they are affected by three sets of forces. Each of these makes up a sub-system of society in which women are directly or indirectly involved. Each of these sub-systems influences the functioning of the others.

1. *Occupational aspects.* Suppose that the number of either men or women with the abilities, training, and experience needed for senior posts in management and the professions were suddenly doubled, would the British economy have an economic use for them? The answer is more doubtful than it might seem. Employers also see a number of difficulties about employing specifically women in senior posts. These difficulties arise both from employers' assessment of the contribution that women can make (the demand side) and, on the supply side, from women's readiness or lack of it to enter into the commitments needed to reach and hold a top job. They concern such things as interrupted careers, part-time work, and doubts of women's ability to manage, and have to be overcome, compensated, or shown to be unreal if employers are to see the promotion of more women into these posts as an economic proposition.

2. *The family and social network.* These are alternative claims on women's time and interest. Able women have open to them many ways of using their lives, and could have more. Sometimes one option reinforces another; a mother who takes a job may find that she has a stronger and better influence on her children than before. Sometimes one has to be sacrificed to another. The value placed on commitment to a career – its opportunity cost – is measured by the other options given up for its sake. Its benefit includes not only the advantages arising directly out of it but any favourable repercussions in other areas. Different options are likely to be valued in different ways in different groups and cultures. The manager of a home and children is for some 'just a housewife', for others engaged in a work of education and culture which can use the highest grade of ability.[1] How is the balance of profit and loss (not only, of course, in the cash sense) from choosing different life patterns or combinations of patterns likely to be seen over the next generation by women themselves, in the light of their different individual interests and abilities; by their husbands and children; by their employers, who are influenced by wider social considerations as well as by the immediate needs of their firms; and by society as a whole, which has an interest in maximizing not only the national income but the welfare of families and individuals, women as well as men? The way in which the gain or loss from various options is seen by all these parties – not only by women themselves – influences the decisions reached by all of them at key points in women's life and career cycles, and so both the number of able women who are willing to come forward for top level careers and the readiness of employers to make a place for them.

3. *The agencies of change.* The timing of change, its channels, strategies, and agents are agencies of change. The process by which a major social change such as the admission of more women to senior jobs takes place can be described in more than one language. It is a social process, a decision system, in which, in part non-logically and in part through deliberate action, individuals and groups become aware of problems, discover new solutions, unfreeze their traditional preconceptions, fight out their conflicts, reach decisions, and consolidate the new social arrangements

1. One of the most striking illustrations is the experience of the Soviet Union, where to be a housewife at home has become a matter for apology. Soviet higher education policy in recent years has discriminated at least marginally against women. The degree of discrimination can be explained by a model which relates readiness to admit any person to higher education to that person's prospective contribution to the money national income, attributing no corresponding value to the work of a wife at home. N. T. Dodge, *Women in the Soviet Economy,* Johns Hopkins Press, 1966, p. 48–51, 53, 112–118.

resulting from them. Economically it is a marketing process, in the wide sense of a process for creating and satisfying a customer on terms also satisfactory to the other parties concerned. The object of this particular marketing operation is to attract into economic circulation a valuable resource, the services of able and qualified women, and to press it on to the occupational market, whether through scattered initiatives and competition or by deliberately organizing the market. A variety of agencies are engaged in doing this for varied motives. What are these agencies? How do they operate and relate to one another, and what is effective in their practice?

Among the agents who have a hand, knowingly or unknowingly, in the decisions that affect a woman's career are parents, teachers, peer-groups, career and marriage counsellors, employers, political and public opinion agencies (for instance the churches), owners and producers of the mass media, and of course a woman's own husband and herself. The influences going out from these decision centres interweave, reinforcing or contradicting one another. No one centre controls the whole process. This means on the one hand that rapid and successful change needs leverage at many points and from many centres at once,[2] on the other the risk that individuals and groups, seeing how limited is their own power to change the situation as a whole, may contract out of their responsibility for action and adapt to things as they are. In any case the process of change must be spread over time. It is likely at different times to have different short-term goals and to be carried forward by different agencies, each with its own changing ideology and strategy. Whatever changes may be likely for the future, by what stages and strategies are they likely to come about? Over what length of time will they be spread? What agencies, promoting what conception of men's and women's roles in and out of work, will be involved and take the lead at each stage?

2. For an outstanding illustration of the interweaving process see A. M. Greeley and P. H. Rossi, *The Education of Catholic Americans*, Aldine (for National Opinion Research Center), 1966. The influence of a school, for example, may be almost imperceptible in itself, except in the very shortest run, but very substantial where it cumulates with that of the university on the one hand and parents and the community on the other. None of these, in turn, would have as much impact as they do were it not for the (in itself often barely perceptible) reinforcement of the school. None of these agencies, including the school, can exert maximum or even, often, any influence until their mutually reinforced impact builds up to a certain threshold or breakthrough point.

Part Six Education: Inequality and Change

The analysis of social inequalities in education is a part of an enduring controversy about the relative importance of heredity and environment in explaining differences in educational achievement (Reading 30). In emphasizing the importance of environment, sociologists do not discount the importance of heredity but they observe that inherited ability is always affected by social background. The effects of material deprivations such as low income, inadequate housing or broken families, reduce a child's educational opportunities irrespective of his genetic endowment. Increasingly, however, greater importance has been attributed to less tangible environmental factors such as the values, modes of behaviour and patterns of speech that a child develops to cope with the demands of family and neighbourhood. These emerge from a particular experience of socialization and become part of a child's personality that instil in him persisting modes of reacting to and interpreting his environment. This socialization, which begins before going to school and continues during a child's schooldays, provides a frame with which a child interprets the learning situation.

Bernstein indicates the difficulties of communication that emerge in the classroom from differences in the speech codes used by children and by teachers or in textbooks. Bernstein's point is that this difficulty is not simply one of poor speech on the one hand, or too great sophistication on the other, but that speech patterns reflect patterns of socialization: the problem of classroom communication is thus one of adjusting different frames of reference. A child may come to school, for example, expecting direct authoritative instructions and a neatly-organized environment with everything in its place, but instead finds that pupils are expected to make their own decisions and are left to themselves to order their environment. Under such circumstances, children find it difficult to understand what they are expected to learn, or to see the reasons for it.

In emphasizing the importance of environment a sociologist is only to a limited extent concerned with cognitive development, that is the processes through which mental capacity is enlarged and qualitatively changed. The social environment he grows up in crucially affects this development. Much research has been concerned with the uses to which a child's abilities are put. He may have the inherited potential for an ample cognitive development, but because of his environmental experiences not be motivated to develop this potential, or may choose to use it in organizing a street gang rather than in mathematics.

The sociologist thus claims that it is educationally more relevant to ask *how* we learn, and *what* is learnt, than to search for an inherited educational capacity that is anyway difficult to identify. He sees it as more important, and also less invidious, to look at means of more adequately utilizing and developing the educational potential of all children rather than to emphasize persisting differences in genetic endowment. Whatever the extent to which intelligence is a matter of endowment, the more efficiently a person's capacities are exploited and stimulated, the less relevant any genetic differences are likely to be for carrying out all but a very few jobs in contemporary society.

In this respect, we must be careful in using the concept of compensatory education. Although a child's home experiences often handicap his intellectual development, it is an error to think that the solution is simply to provide experiences that compensate for such presumed deficiencies. As we noted above, the way a child orders his environment is developed in the context of family and neighbourhood experiences, and any compensatory education needs to be integrated with these if it is to have meaning for the child. Thus visits to places of culture, and special classes or informal study groups that seek to develop verbal skills, will have no enduring effect on the educationally-deprived child if they are divorced from his habitual environment. The idea of compensatory education is also misleading if it is taken to imply that there is a fixed set of educational skills which must be instilled into a child. Education is essentially an interactive process in which a child learns, through gradually adjusting his own perceptions, at successively rising levels of complexity, to those of teachers and fellow pupils, and to the paraphernalia of formal education. In this way, the basic processes of education are interaction and mutual accommodation, and are neglected in the one-way traffic between teacher and taught implied in much of compensatory education. This line of argument raises the more fundamental point that since home environment reflects the way society is organized, compensatory education is in effect attempting to compensate for the inequalities in society. Since these persist beyond and outside the educational process, such attempts will be unsuccessful and will generate new strains because they involve exposing a child more intensively to an alien cultural milieu. After such exposure a child may feel the inequalities in the distribution of wealth, education and information that exist around him even more acutely. Effective change in education thus needs to be linked to those changes in the economic and social organization of society that improve the general quality of working and leisure activities. Along with such changes, there is a continuing need to devise means of developing curricula, home–school relations and school-based activities that encourage children to consciously examine and make use of their experiences.

This discussion leads us, then, to the familiar problem of the effect of social class on education. Social class is undoubtedly an important and persisting factor in educational inequality; it affects not only the ability of a family to provide material resources and encouragement, but also the way a child is treated in school by peers and teachers. To concentrate exclusively on such inequalities would, however, over-simplify contemporary problems in education, because the environment includes factors that cannot be directly related to economic situations. To take just one aspect of this problem, the content of interaction between children and the adults in their environment is influenced by factors such as size of class or family, the presence or absence of emotional problems, and the competing demands on their time that parents experience. Economic deprivation may, of course, underlie each or all of these factors, but coming from middle and upper class background may also create difficulties for other children exposed to certain types of educational experiences. Differences among and between arts and science subjects, performance in creative projects and reaction to unstructured as well as structured learning-situations, are all examples of aspects of education that can be negatively affected by differences in socialization within as well as between social classes.

This argument means that we must re-examine the familiar contention that the basic problem faced by working-class children in education is the contrast between their home experiences and teaching that is geared to the values and behavioural norms of the middle classes. Such a contrast is not even factually the case in a period of considerable social mobility within and through education. Not all teachers come from backgrounds where their fathers were middle class, and even those who do come from such backgrounds do not have common values or patterns of behaviour. Regional differences, the particular careers of the teachers, and the precise nature of the social relationships into which they enter, also lead different teachers to approach the teaching situation in different ways.

Indeed, we obtain a better understanding of the problem of the teacher's relationship to pupil and parents if we recognize that schools and higher educational institutions are large-scale organizations involving defined career patterns for their staff. Apart from the business of teaching, they have to account for their activities to parents, fellow-teachers, principals and administrators; they have also to visibly demonstrate that they are doing an effective job if they wish to secure advancement in their career. These pressures are often conflicting ones, and a teacher's behaviour towards his pupils can often be understood in terms of his attempts to resolve such conflicting pressures. Furthermore, for teachers with large classes, the basic problem that they face is to maintain control rather than to transmit academic class-based values. Depending on their social origins, the subject they teach and the types of schools that they teach in, teachers develop differing expectations of the satisfaction they receive from teaching. Some treat their school merely as a means to make a living and devote their energies to leisure activities, while others dedicate themselves to their pupils and the life of the school. These differences in orientation among teachers are not accidental but reflect the way education is organized and the patterns of recruitment into it. The problem of communication within the classroom thus becomes one of fitting the priorities and patterns of behaviour encouraged by particular types of organization among those who work in these organizations, to the needs of children who are accustomed to more intimate relationships at home and who are, to differing degrees, unused to the range of values and priorities which they encounter at school.

A major problem in education is thus the nature and extent of its organization. This, of course, is a severe problem in those areas in which socially disadvantaged children live. For example, children living in inner-city slums attend schools that are peripheral parts of a large educational bureaucracy and suffer from considerable turnover of teachers and principals. Under these conditions there is a less continuing stimulus to experimentation than is desirable, given the characteristics of the children it teaches. Janowitz (in Street's *Innovation in Mass Education*, Wiley, 1969) for example, has compared unfavourably the administration and practice of inner-city slum schools with other 'people-changing' institutions such as correctional institutions or mental hospitals. He argues that such schools still operate as custodial institutions and have not devised new forms of organization aimed at retaining the interest of students over longer periods, as well as the good faith of parents and employers. Concern with bureaucratization and with lack of experimentation in education has led to discussion by writers such as Goodman and Kohl (see Readings 32 and 33 respectively) of means of 'creatively disrupting' existing administrative arrangements so as to produce a more flexible teaching environment. Such discussion is made more urgent because rigid organization in the school reinforces the effect of home environments which do not motivate children to learn easily from books or to compete in traditional academic terms. Thus, in Hargreaves' account (Reading 31) it is the combination of streaming within a 'secondary modern' school with home and neighbourhood backgrounds which orientate the pupils to activities outside the school that results in pronounced anti-school and delinquent subcultures.

Underlying our discussion is a problem that goes beyond that of social deprivation; it is the extent to which education, when successful, is disruptive of existing social and economic organization. We commonly stress the need for children to be creative in school and to learn to think for themselves, as if the opportunities were present for them in society to exercise this creativity and critical thought. For many, they are not: society is rigidly organized in terms of social and economic inequalities and job careers are heavily routinized. Under such conditions education becomes potentially a disruptive force. Many regard this as a necessary and desirable aspect of education; but it also means that others are likely to see the gravest social problems in education not as those of social inequality but those of the spirit of discontent fostered by education. Confronted by student political radicalism over national and international issues, and by student attempts to radically and often violently reform educational institutions, they commonly emphasize the paradox of students being at one and the same time the most privileged and the most discontented members of society. Students are, however, members of organizations that have grown larger and more complex, in which personal contact between teachers and taught has diminished because of increased demands made on staff time. Impersonality has been accompanied by the routinization of the educational process, with emphasis on record-keeping, examinations and tests, and computer-based timetabling of academic classes. These developments are not necessarily educationally undesirable, but they create an environment in which students feel the impact of bureaucratic rigidity directly, while being expected to develop their own potential for critical thought. Since they are relatively unencumbered by domestic responsibilities and have time to think, it is not surprising that they are vocal critics of social injustices both within and without education. Their activities point to the contradictions between a highly complex and organized economy, requiring the services of peoples who have been trained to think for themselves, and the awareness, fostered by education, of the disadvantages of social and educational rigidity, inequality and hierarchy.

30 D. F. Swift

Educational Psychology, Sociology and the Environment:
a Controversy at Cross-Purposes

Excerpt from D. F. Swift, 'Educational psychology, sociology and the environment: a controversy at cross-purposes', *British Journal of Sociology*, vol. 16, 1965, no. 4, pp. 336–41.

Douglas [has recently] attempted to clarify the association between completed family size and tested intelligence. In doing this, he inevitably found himself seeking 'heredity' and 'environment' explanations:

It is indeed difficult to believe that large families in the professional classes owe their existence to inefficiency or ignorance of family planning – it seems more likely that the considerable differences observed at this social level in the average measured ability of children from small and large families are of environmental origin. This is to be interpreted in its broadest sense to include deficiences of parental care as well as the material background of the home.

Thus the material background plus the effects of parental care constitutes 'the environment' in its *widest sense* for Douglas. But these represent the environment in almost the narrowest sense for the sociologist. And further, to the sociologist interested in the mechanisms by which social experience influences cognition, it represents the least important part of it. There appears to be a basic difference in the conception of 'the environment' held by British educational psychologists and medical researchers on the one hand, and sociologists on the other. Whereas the sociologist is particularly concerned about the social process as the environment of the individual, the educational psychologist tends not to perceive the normative order as a social fact. Since it is principally in this part of the environment that we must look for influences on cognitive and motivational skills, there is little wonder that sociologists and educational psychologists have had so little time for each other's conclusions.

From a sociological point of view, the crucial problem is, what do we mean by relevant differences in cultural experience? Here, sociology is lacking in specific answers. It is not, however, lacking in techniques of analysis which might begin to arrive at some answers; nor is it lacking in an intuitive understanding which appears not to be specially valued in statistical psychology. One example of differences in intuitive understanding of the social process, which also might indicate a very different conception of it, may be drawn from a comment by Warburton.

But we don't want to run away from the facts (and they seem to be true) that some are born with greater intellectual endowment than others, or that environmental differences can be so great that they blot out hereditary factors altogether or *that environmental differences of this magnitude are rarely found* within Western society (italics added).

The third assertion is an unwarrantable conclusion for three major reasons. Firstly, it is something which can be said with scientific conviction only after the incredibly complex relationships between sub-cultural experience and the structure of the mind have been charted, not as a prelude to it. Secondly, it simplifies culture to a caricature by concentrating upon the physical artifacts and patterns of action to the exclusion of the normative order and the symbolizing process which lies behind all three elements of the culture. Thirdly, it pays too little attention to the function of the educational system as a self-fulfilling prophecy which imposes culturally based evaluations of intellectual processes upon the self-concepts of children.

The first reason for the unacceptability of Warburton's assumption is a purely academic one which derives from different evaluations of data and different conceptions of the complexity of the problem. The second reason may be portrayed starkly by a further example which (one hopes) takes the conception of culture held by many educational psychologists to the point of caricature. This example is taken from a debate between Conway and Burt on the one hand, and Halsey on the other. It was plain that when the disputing parties in this debate were using the notion 'social environment', it carried with it such different meanings for those involved that very little in the way of communication took place. Conway was presenting a piece of evidence in support of her belief that the personal and political prejudices of an 'environmentalist' were preventing him from comprehending the facts which any unbiased scientist would at once recognize.

In discussing the effects of environmental 'improvements' Conway pointed out that from 1922 onwards the researches of Burt and his associates have revealed marked differences between the average intelligence scores in the different social classes for both adults and children. These differences, she points out, are of the same order today. However:

During the last thirty years, the environmental differences have greatly diminished. Both the economic and cultural conditions prevailing in the humbler classes have undergone vast improvement. If the environment was the chief source of the difference between one class and another, we would naturally expect that the IQ difference would likewise have diminished.

Given the perception of what is important to learning which we must assume to be implicit in this statement, Conway's annoyance is understandable. The complaint of the sociologist, however, is that this is a quite inadequate way of conceptualizing the cultural environment when one wishes to deal with the development of intellective skills.

What Conway would need to show, for the purposes of her argument, is that an increased proportion of the lower class were now living in accordance with the cognitive, cathectic and evaluative requirements of the higher. Particularly important in this respect, she would have to show that the effect of the social class system upon the development of self-concepts of ability has been changed. These are all requirements which could not be met in the present stage of social research. Certainly it can be shown that the working class own more consumer goods, but there is little justification, these days, for assuming that crude economic indicators have any causal relation with intellective ability. The nearest we can come to this idea has been suggested by Floud where a within-class relationship between wealth and academic success in Middlesbrough was explained *ex post facto* as a result of the operation of economic forces. However, this could equally well be explained in terms of sub-cultural differences which themselves related to the economic indicators. For example, in a strongly Roman Catholic Local Education Authority area, Swift found that, within the middle class, material wealth associated negatively with the likelihood of success in the 11+.

Similarly, the 'cultural' changes which Conway assumes are also arguable. Presumably, by 'cultural' here is meant high culture in the sense of personal refinement in intellectual pursuits. Research in this sphere is almost non-existent. Writings of the sort stimulated by Hoggart would tend to argue that from the point of view of the intellectual literary aspect of culture there has been a regression in the working class.

Finally, it would have been impossible for Conway to have spoken of cultural 'improvement' and at the same time to have meant what sociologists mean by culture. The sociologist would be much more likely to talk of a higher degree of social organization, that is, greater homogeneity in the normative order and behaviour patterns. To impose one's own feelings that this change was an 'improvement', as opposed to a 'change', would represent a fairly crude sort of cultural parochialism which social analysts usually try to avoid.

The most recent example of the gulf between the two conceptions of 'the environment' is a book [by S. Wiseman, *Education and Environment* (1964)] which maintained the traditional point of view of British educational psychology in claiming that the research it reports has dealt with the environment. Instead of this, the book reports some ecological analysis supported by intuitive reasoning which repeatedly falls into the trap known as the aggregative fallacy.

A problem of inter-disciplinary communication

There is no earthly reason why educational psychologists should have to recapitulate the history of the development of sociology before they are able to analyse the mechanisms by which environmental factors influence cognitive and motivational development. How, therefore, can sociologists make available some of the fruits of their work to educational psychologists and why has the dialogue been gladiatorial rather than dialectical?

Part of the blame must be laid at the feet of the sociologists for putting their case badly. The problem is that it is more or less impossible to put the case at all if it has to be in terms of the naïvely restrictive canons of scientific work which psychologists tend to trust as the only possible bridge between themselves and 'truth'. The principal difficulty lies in the fact that, in psychology, these canons have become enshrined in methods of research which were developed in aid of the individual perspective on human behaviour. Satisfying the psychologist, that is, employing research strategies which he would find acceptable, commits the researcher to a level of analysis and statistical tools, which the sociologist would consider to be inappropriate. For their part, the psychologists not only do not speak the same language but would feel that they were prejudicing the scientific status of their discipline if they were to try.

Several times, over the years, educational psychologists have been forced to point out erroneous statements relating to test meanings and construction which have been made by sociologists whose disrespect for some of the findings of the research on intelligence has led them into misrepresenting the psychological perspective. From the writer's point of view, the present meagre state of knowledge of intellectual processes and the dangers in an infant science of mistaking an arithmetical approach for a scientific one, are sufficiently serious to make such iconoclastic intrusions more than welcome. They are more than welcome, that is, provided that they encourage new thinking and do not simply stimulate the educational psychology establishment to close ranks in defence of the sacred word.

It is to be hoped that the potential contributions of the sociologists will not be discounted simply because of an occasional statistical or psychological *faux pas*. For there is reason behind their anxiety to rush in where psychological angels fear to tread. This reason lies not so much with 'left-wing' bias, but with the vastly improved insights into social interaction which have been forthcoming in sociology and anthropology. The need for a more satisfactory understanding of the social process is the clearest requirement which emerges for the sociologist in reading the literature on intelligence and educational achievement. That is, the blunderings of the sociologist in the psychological area are well matched by those of the psychologist in his approach to the social process.

Having suggested that a psychologist's approach to the 'environment' is inadequate, we have to face the task of suggesting ways in which an inter-disciplinary approach would be an improvement. Before doing this we should do some elementary division of labour. The question of the development of intellectual skills is primarily a psychological one. However, there are two aspects of it. On one hand, we have the structure of intellect. This is either a psychological or a neurological problem. On the other hand, we must consider the environment, in interaction with which the structure develops. It is in this second area that an interdisciplinary approach is needed. The sociologist can help the psychologist in the analysis of the environment. Basically, the sociologist complains that a pscyhologist's treatment of the environment tends to be a simple extension of his approach to the rat in the laboratory maze. That is the environment is treated principally as if it consisted of physical artifacts. It is something against which the individual barks his shins. On the other hand, the sociologist wishes to suggest that the vital aspect of the environment is its presence in the mind of the individual who imposes meaning upon the world around him through a process of symbolizing. This process is learned, and is carried on, in interaction with other people.

One example of the sociologist's dissatisfaction has been dealt with earlier in Miss Conway's concentration upon economic wealth as a factor in the development of school skills. Another example from the other direction is the unhappiness of psychologists with the use which sociologists have made of the concept, social class. Sociologists have tended to use this as a criterion for grouping children without making fully explicit their assumptions about the different arrangement of symbolizing experiences for which the social class criterion is believed to be a useful indicator. To the psychologist it was little more than the construction of not very meaningful aggregates. Why, they ask, should the work which the father does mean something for the cognitive skills which his child develops? The great deal of theorizing and research which is relevant to this question may be summarized in the words of M. Kohn:

Social class has proved to be so useful a concept because it refers to more than simply educational level, or occupation, or any of the large number of correlated variables. It is so useful because it captures the reality that the intricate interplay of all these variables creates different basic conditions of life at different levels of the social order. Members of different social classes, by virtue of enjoying (or suffering) different conditions of life, come to see the world differently – to develop different conceptions of social reality, different aspirations and hopes and fears, different conceptions of the desirable.

The point of view makes sense to the sociologist for two reasons. Firstly, it is important to perceive the socio-cultural environment as a configuration of elements each one of which derives its meaning for the developing consciousness from its context in that configuration. Secondly, analysis from this point of view provides a link between social structure and individual behaviour.

Further Reading

CONWAY, J. (1951), 'Class differences in general intelligence, part 2', *British J. of Stat. Psychol.* May, pp. 5–14.
DOUGLAS, J. W. B. (1964), *The House and the School*, MacGibbon & Kee.
WARBURTON, F. W. (1962), 'Education psychology', *Annual Rev. of Psychol*, vol. 13, pp. 371–414.

31 David Hargreaves

Streaming and the Peer Group

Excerpts from David Hargreaves, *Social Relations in a Secondary School*,
Routledge & Kegan Paul, 1967, pp. 182–92.

Perhaps the main consequence of this study has been to affirm the
fundamental importance of the social system of the school, and especially the structure of peer groups, in relation to the educative process.
One of the tasks of future educational research will be to investigate the
ways in which home and other external influences interact with those
internal to the school. Yet it is these in-school forces which have been
neglected by teachers and researchers alike. The teachers at Lumley
Secondary Modern School for Boys constantly under-estimated or were
ignorant of the power of the peer group in regulating the behaviour of
pupils. It was common practice for the teachers to shed the blame for
many difficulties which might be caused or reinforced by the school itself
on to the home environment. Yet the belief that children are 'difficult' in
school *because* they come from 'difficult' homes is a convenient oversimplification. At Lumley, the misbehaviour of low stream boys was
often 'explained' by the teachers in terms of a popular psychology or
sociology. A teacher once remarked to me, 'Well, what can you expect?
That lad's got no father' – but he failed to appreciate that the most hard-
working member of the 'intellectual' clique in 4A was also fatherless.

Once in school children become part of a social system and are subjected to a variety of influences. Most important of all, they become
members of a group of age-mates, most often from the same stream.
These groups have values, norms and status hierarchies which every
member must take into account. These pressures towards conformity to
the peer group will be especially powerful after the third year in secondary school with the onset of the 'adolescent syndrome'. We know
from many other studies that the mid-teens is a period when many young
people begin to reject the authority of parents and teachers; when they
begin to emancipate themselves from adults in their desire to liberate
themselves from childhood dependency. The adolescent is in transition
from childhood to adulthood; being no longer a child but not yet an
adult, he has no valid autonomous status in the eyes of his elders. It is at
this point that young people tend to fall back on the peer group, for it is

with their age-mates that they most interact and from whom independent status may be derived. Moreover, adolescence is a period in which the search for a self-identity is most marked, and in which many basic social attitudes are acquired. Personality is not a static but a dynamic and changing process to which peer group membership may make a fundamental contribution.

It is within this general framework that subcultural differentiation takes place: for boys in low streams the onset of the adolescent syndrome is concomitant with the perception of status deprivation within school and its extension into their future careers. The association between low stream and delinquency at Lumley may be as much the result of school and peer group influence on personality development as of the fact that the school tends to select certain personality types into different streams.

A central aim of education is to organize the school in such a way that *all* the pupils are educated to the full extent of their potentialities. An equally important educational goal is the integration of the pupils into the social life of the school. That is, the school should provide opportunities for, and stimulate motives conducive to, the development of satisfying and cooperative relationships between pupils and teachers and between pupils in different streams. Neither of these goals was achieved at Lumley School. The boys in the lower streams seem to have become progressively retarded by the fourth year, and their relationships with both teachers and high stream boys were hostile. It is tragic that often an A stream boy was not on speaking terms with a D stream boy, even though both may have been pupils in the same class in Junior School and both may live in the same street [. . .]

One of the principal reasons for the progressive retardation and the development of a delinquescent subculture among the low streams is the fact that they are unlikely to be motivated to work hard at school because they cannot see any useful or tangible reward for their labours.

A similar process is at work among the teachers. We have already noted the differential allocation of teachers to the various streams and need not repeat it here. The point is that none of the teachers feels under the same pressure to motivate or stimulate the low stream pupils because the lack of an external examination as a goal means that there is no way in which their achievement can be externally checked. The problem is most acute for those teachers who devote the majority or all of their timetable to the low streams. They have neither the satisfaction of preparing high stream boys for the examinations, nor have they a measure of their own competence and effort through the externally assessed examination results. These teachers of low streams may, like their pupils, feel status deprived. Their motivation to strive must be entirely self-induced. Moreover the unrelenting demands made by low stream, delinquescent pupils on the strength and patience of such teachers must in many cases be almost unbearable. It is hardly surprising that many of them treat their job as a routine custodial task and thus fail to inspire and motivate their pupils. The result is that they begin to *expect* little of their pupils, who adapt to this reduced expectation with a lowered level of aspiration. This is one of the roots of progressive retardation [. . .]

One of the most important results of the segregation of the pupils into streams at Lumley School is that the boys in one subculture perceive the other subculture as a negative reference group. This does, of course, promote a fear of 'demotion' in high stream boys, but it also tends to undermine the assumptions teachers make about the 'promotion' system in that low stream boys often do not desire, and sometimes actively avoid, promotion into a higher stream. The subcultures are expanded as boys of the appropriate orientation are drawn to the poles. The hostility and lack of communication which exists between the two subcultures is disturbing. The evidence in this research does not offer support to the view that the neighbourhood ('one-class') Comprehensive School will solve many of our educational problems. It may be true that the working class boy is deprived in our middle-class-dominated Grammar Schools, but it is clear that an analogous class warfare is at work in this working class Secondary Modern School [. . .]

It is possible that more progress could be made if the teachers identified the boys of high informal status and used them as a means of entry to the peer group, for unless the leaders are 'converted' first, there is little hope of effecting any extensive attitude change. When the teacher finds himself locked in permanent combat with the informal leaders, he has forsaken his only chance of directing the behaviour of these boys into the channels he considers desirable. Attempts to compel these boys by force of threat of punishment into an academic orientation are self-defeating and have the reverse effect. It may seem unrealistic to treat 'bad' pupils as if they were 'good' pupils, but if the teacher is to achieve his ends he needs to transform the role conception of the pupils; and to do this he must obtain the loyalty and cooperation of the informal leaders [. . .]

The most radical way in which the formation of the subcultures could be suppressed at Lumley is through the complete abolition of the streaming system. There is no doubt that the vast majority of teachers in this country regard streaming as basic to the organization of schools and the staff at Lumley were no exception. Only one of the teachers of senior forms was in favour of non-streaming. Some did feel that the introduction of non-streaming would improve the general behaviour level of the school, but they opposed the idea on the grounds that non-streaming would reduce the general level of academic performance. Although some of the less able boys might improve their academic performance, they argued, the progress of the A stream pupils would be restrained. They also believed that it would be impossible, or at least very difficult, to teach a class of boys with a wide variation in intelligence.

The research on streaming is far from conclusive. Some studies claim that pupils in unstreamed schools acquire better social adjustment and more favourable attitudes to school. Daniels found that in unstreamed conditions pupils made gains in IQ and in attainment in Arithmetic and English. He has claimed further that streaming slightly lowers the general level of attainment, slightly reduces the attainment of the 'bright' pupils, markedly retards the 'slower' pupils, and artificially increases the range of attainment. Douglas has shown that at each IQ level children placed in the upper streams improve their score on his test between the ages of eight and eleven years, whereas those assigned to lower streams show a deterioration in test score during the same period. This is true *within* each social class, even though middle class children are disproportionately represented in the upper streams, as documented by Jackson and others. Thus, despite some non-supportive studies, there is a growing body of evidence which indicates that the streaming system is self-validating in that it to some extent *manufactures* the differences on which it is justified by teachers. This evidence is supported by the claims of many teachers that de-streaming has led to enormous academic and social benefits.

It appears that at Lumley School, and presumably at other similar schools, the development of opposing subcultures is an extreme form of this differentiation process, which is accentuated by, if not actually caused by, the streaming system. The abolition of streaming at Lumley might thus impede the formation of the subcultures and in part the acquisition of delinquent attitudes by low stream boys. Yet if such a policy were adopted, some fundamental re-thinking about teaching methods would have to be made. The supporters of non-streaming have emphasized the need for a committed and convinced staff who want to make non-streaming work and who are prepared to experiment with new teaching methods. A superficial change in the formal organization of the school cannot be expected to create major academic or social changes. At present the staff at Lumley, with one exception, do not believe that de-streaming would contribute to a solution of some of their problems, and this is partly because they do not fully appreciate the far-reaching effects of the streaming system as indicated by this research. Moreover they are convinced that it would be impossible, or at least very difficult, to teach groups of mixed ability.

This belief is based on at least two important assumptions. The first is that their present teaching methods are relatively immutable. The second is their conviction that the forms under a streamed system are indeed homogeneous in terms of ability. In fact the degree of heterogeneity in the fourth year forms was far greater than the teachers realized, for they tended to regard attainment and a positive orientation to the school's values as synonymous with ability. They believed that the A streams contained the 'brightest' boys and the D streams the 'dullest' and from this concluded that over the four years the promotion-demotion transfer system intensified this selection by ability. This is not substantiated by an examination of the IQ scores. In terms of IQ (from the eleven-plus examination) the homogeneity of the streams had declined, not increased, by the fourth year. The fourth year comprised boys with a range of forty-two IQ points (71–113). In the A stream the range in IQ scores changed from 18 points when the boys were in the second year to 33 points by the fourth year. The equivalent change in the D stream was from a range of twenty-two to thirty-one IQ points. Alternatively we may say that in the second year the A stream contained 94 per cent of the boys with IQ scores above the median, but by the fourth year this figure had declined to 78 per cent.

In a word, the overlap between the streams in terms of the IQ scores of the boys in this study increased over the four-year period. This is so because membership of a high stream is a function not simply of ability but of positive orientation to academic values, the reverse being true of low streams. It seems that the subcultural formation, especially the development of anti-academic values and the progressive retardation in the low streams, misled the teachers into believing that within the fourth year as a whole there existed a greater variation in ability range than was really the case, and secondly that each stream contained a group that was homogeneous in terms of IQ rather than orientation. The teachers' support for the streaming system, and their opposition to non-streaming, thus rests in part on the subcultural divergence which is itself to some extent a product of the streaming system.

It is, of course, impossible to assess the extent to which subcultural formation is the direct result of streaming. In this exploratory study we have found that subcultural development is generated by a number of mutually reinforcing factors, of which the organization of pupils into streams is the basic structural component. In other streamed schools these additional factors may or may not be present and there may be further important factors which do not obtain at Lumley. This research cannot be taken as general evidence against streaming, for under different conditions, whether streamed or unstreamed, subcultural development might not take place. In middle class schools, for instance, it may be that there exists a low stream subculture which is far from delinquescent. Yet on the basis of this exploratory study, and on the assumption that Lumley is not atypical of schools in 'problem areas', we would imagine that there are many schools in Britain with similar problems of a similar genesis which may be diagnosed in a similar way. It is the task of future research to examine the distribution and nature of subcultural formation in our schools.

If these research findings are valid for other schools, especially those in 'problem areas', they indicate that major reforms are necessary if their pupils are to be adequately educated and the school is to be a force which draws children away from delinquent values and behaviour. Ultimately the possibility of some reform lies in the hands of the teachers themselves. The *status quo* is based on an elitist view of education, whereby children are educated and socialized to fit into certain preconceived social strata of life in the modern world. If we are to educate all these children to develop and maintain cooperative and satisfying human relationships, to lead useful and constructive adult roles in society, to attain a degree of personal integrity and self-realization, many of the assumptions about education we make as parents, teachers, administrators and legislators must be urgently challenged and reformulated.

32 Paul Goodman

The Universal Trap

Excerpt from Paul Goodman, *Compulsory Miseducation*, Horizon Press, 1962, Penguin, 1971, pp. 25–34.

Let us examine realistically half a dozen aspects of the school that is dropped out *from*.

1. There is widespread anxiety about the children not learning to read, and hot and defensive argument about the methods of teaching reading. Indeed, reading deficiency is an accumulating scholastic disadvantage that results in painful feeling of inferiority, truancy and drop-out. Reading is crucial for school success – all subjects depend on it – and therefore for the status success that the diploma is about. Yet in all the anxiety and argument, there is no longer any mention of the freedom and human cultivation that literacy is supposed to stand for.

In my opinion, there is something phony here. For a change, let us look at this 'reading' coldly and ask if it is really such a big deal except precisely in the school that is supposed to teach it and is sometimes failing to do so.

With the movies, TV and radio that the illiterate also share, there is certainly no lack of 'communications'. We cannot say that as humanities or science, the reading-matter of the great majority is in any way superior to the content of these other media. And in the present stage of technology and economy, it is probably *less* true than it was in the late nineteenth century – the time of the great push to universal literacy and arithmetic – that the mass teaching of reading is indispensable to operate the production and clerical system. It is rather our kind of urbanism, politics and buying and selling that require literacy. These are not excellent.

Perhaps in the present dispensation we should be as well off if it were socially acceptable for large numbers not to read. It would be harder to regiment people if they were not so well 'informed'; as Wiener used to point out, every repetition of a cliché only increases the noise and *prevents* communication. With less literacy, there would be more folk culture. Much suffering of inferiority would be avoided if youngsters did not have to meet a perhaps unnecessary standard. Serious letters could only benefit if society were less swamped by trash, lies and bland verbiage. Most important of all, *more* people might become genuinely literate if it were understood that reading is not a matter of course but a *special useful art with a proper subject-matter, imagination and truth,* rather than a means of communicating top–down decisions and advertising. (The advertising is a typical instance: when the purpose of advertising was to give information – 'New shipment of salt fish arrived, very good, foot of Barclay Street' – it was useful to be able to read; when the point of advertising is to create a synthetic demand, it is better not to be able to read.)

2. Given their present motives, the schools are not competent to teach authentic literacy, reading as a means of liberation and cultivation. And I doubt that most of us who seriously read and write the English language ever learned by the route of 'Run, Spot, Run' to *Silas Marner.* Rather, having picked up the rudiments either in cultured homes or in the first two grades, we really learned to read by our own will and free exploration, following our bent, generally among books that are considered inappropriate by school librarians!

A great neurologist tells me that the puzzle is not how to teach reading, but why some children fail to learn to read. Given the amount of exposure that any urban child gets, any normal animal should spontaneously catch on to the code. What prevents? It is almost demonstrable that, for many children, it is precisely going to school that prevents – because of the school's alien style, banning of spontaneous interest, extrinsic rewards and punishments. (In many underprivileged schools, the IQ steadily falls the longer they go to school.) Many of the backward readers might have had a better chance on the streets.

But let me say something, too, about the 'successful' teaching of reading and writing in the schools. Consider, by contrast, the method employed by S. Ashton-Warner in teaching little Maoris. She gets them to ask for their *own* words, the particular gut-word of fear, lust or despair that is obsessing the child that day; this is written for him on strong cardboard; he learns it instantaneously and never forgets it; and soon he has an exciting, if odd, vocabulary. From the beginning, writing is by demand, practical, magical; and of course it is simply an extension of speech – it is the best and strongest speech, as writing should be. What is read is what somebody is importantly trying to tell. Now what do our schools do? We use tricks and mechanical conditioning. These do positive damage to spontaneous speech, meant expression, earnest understanding. Inevitably, they create *in the majority* the wooden attitude toward 'writing', as entirely different from speech, that college teachers later try to cope with in Freshman Composition. And reading inevitably becomes a manipulation of signs, e.g., for test-passing, that has no relation to experience.

(Until recently, the same discouragement by school teachers plagued children's musical and plastic expression, but there have been attempts to get back to spontaneity – largely, I think, because of the general revolution in modern art and musical theory. In teaching science, there is just now a strong movement to encourage imagination rather than conditioned 'answers'. In teaching foreign languages, the emphasis is now strongly on vital engagement and need to speak. Yet in teaching reading and writing, the direction has been the contrary; even progressive education has gone back to teaching spelling. These arts are regarded merely as 'tools'.)

3. The young rightly resist animal constraint. But, at least in New York where I have been a school-board visitor, most teachers – and the principals who supervise their classes – operate as if progressive education had not proved the case for noise and freedom of bodily motion. (Dewey stresses the salutary alternation of boisterousness and tranquility.) The seats are no longer bolted to the floor, but they still face front. Of course, the classes are too large to cope with without 'discipline'. Then make them smaller, or don't wonder if children escape out of the cage; either into truancy or baffled daydream. Here is a typical case: an architect replacing a Harlem school is forbidden by the board to spend money on soundproofing the classrooms, even though the principal has called it a necessity for the therapy of pent-up and resentful children. The resentment, pent-up hostility, is a major cause of reactive stupidity; yet there is usually an absolute ban on overt expression of hostility, or even of normal anger and aggression.

Again, one has to be blind not to see that, from the onset of puberty, the dissidence from school is importantly sexual. Theoretically, the junior high school was introduced to fit this change of life; yet astoundingly, it is sexless. My own view, for what it's worth, is that sexuality is lovely, there cannot be too much of it, it is self-limiting if it is satisfactory, and satisfaction diminishes tension and clears the mind for attention and learning. Therefore, sexual expression should be approved in and out of season, also in school, and where necessary made the subject of instruction. But whether or not this view is correct, it certainly is more practical than the apparent attempt of the schools to operate as if sexual drives simply did not exist. When, on so crucial an issue, the schools act a hundred years out of date, they are crucially irrelevant.

But the following *is* something new.

Trenton, 24 May (AP) – A state health official believes some over-anxious New Jersey parents are dosing their children with tranquilizers before sending them to school ... the Health Department pediatrician assigned to the State Education Department said the parents apparently are trying to protect the children from cracking under pressure for good grades.

4. Terrible damage is done to children simply by the size and standardization of the big system. Suppose a class size of twenty is good for average purposes, it does *not* follow that thirty-five is better than nothing. Rather, it is likely to be positively harmful, because the children have ceased to be persons and the teacher is destroyed as a teacher. A teacher with a ten-year-old class reading at seven-year-old level will have to use the content as well as the vocabulary of *Dick and Jane* since that is the textbook bought by the hundred thousands. The experience of a wise principal is that the most essential part of his job is to know every child's name and be an available 'good father', so he wants a school for 400. Yet the city will build the school for 2000, because only that is practical, even though the essence is entirely dissipated. The chief part of learning is in the community of scholars, where classwork and social life may cohere; yet social engineers like Dr Conant will, for putative efficiencies, centralize the high schools – the 'enriched' curriculum with equipment is necessary for the national needs.

A programme – e.g., to prevent drop-out – will be, by an attentive teacher, exquisitely tailored to the children he works with; he will have a success. Therefore his programme must be standardized, watered down, for seventy-five schools – otherwise it cannot be financed – although now it is worthless. But here is an unbeatable anecdote: An architect is employed to replace a dilapidated school but is forbidden to consult the principal and teachers of the school about their needs, since his building must conform to uniform plans at headquarters, the plans being two generations out of date. As a functionalist, the architect demurs, and it requires an *ad hoc* assembly of all the superintendents to give him special permission.

Presumably all this is administratively necessary, but then it is also necessary for bruised children to quit. Our society makes a persistent error in metaphysics. We are so mesmerized by the operation of a system with the appropriate name, for instance 'Education', that we assume that it *must* be working somewhat, though admittedly not perfectly, when perhaps it has ceased to fulfill its function altogether and might even be preventing the function, for instance, education.

5. Especially today, when the hours of work will sharply diminish, the schools are supposed to educate for the satisfaction of life and for the worthwhile use of leisure. Again, let us try to be realistic, as a youngster

is. For most people, I think, a candid self-examination will show that their most absorbing, long and satisfactory hours are spent in activities like friendly competitive sports, gambling, looking for love and love-making, earnest or argumentative conversation, political action with signs and sit-ins, solitary study and reading, contemplation of nature and cosmos, arts and crafts, music and religion. Now none of these requires much money. Indeed, elaborate equipment takes the heart out of them. Friends use one another as resources. God, nature and creativity are free. The media of the fine arts are cheap stuff. Health, luck and affection are the only requirements for good sex. Good food requires taking pains more than spending money.

What is the moral for our purposes? Can it be denied that in some respects the drop-outs make a wiser choice than many who go to school, not to get real goods but to get money? Their choice of the 'immediate' – their notorious 'inability to tolerate delay' – is not altogether impulsive and neurotic. The bother is that in our present culture, which puts its entire emphasis on the consumption of expensive commodities, they are so nagged by inferiority, exclusion and despair of the future that they cannot enjoy their leisure with a good conscience. Because they know little, they are deprived of many profound simple satisfactions and they never know what to do with themselves. Being afraid of exposing themselves to awkwardness and ridicule, they just hang around. And our urban social arrangements – e.g., high rent – have made it impossible for anybody to be decently poor on a 'low' standard. One is either in the rat-race or has dropped out of society altogether.

6. As a loyal academic, I must make a further observation. Mainly to provide Ph.D.s, there is at present an overwhelming pressure to gear the 'better' elementary schools to the graduate-universities. This is the great current reform, genre of Rickover. But what if the top of the ladder is corrupt and corrupts the lower grades? On visits to seventy colleges everywhere in the country, I have been appalled at how rarely the subjects are studied in a right academic spirit, for their truth and beauty and as part of humane international culture. The students are given, and seek, a narrow expertise, 'mastery', aimed at licences and salary. They are indoctrinated with a national thoughtlessness that is not even chauvinistic. Administrators sacrifice the community of scholars to aggrandizement and extramurally sponsored research.

Conversely, there is almost never conveyed the sense in which learning is truly practical, to enlighten experience, give courage to initiate and change, reform the state, deepen personal and social peace. On the contrary, the entire educational system itself creates professional cynicism or the resigned conviction that Nothing Can Be Done. If this is the university, how can we hope for aspiring scholarship in the elementary schools? On the contrary, everything will be grades and conforming, getting ahead not in the subject of interest but up the ladder. Students 'do' Bronx Science in order to 'make' MIT and they 'do' MIT in order to 'make' Westinghouse; some of them have 'done' Westinghouse in order to 'make' jail.

What then? The compulsory system has become a universal trap, and it is no good. Very many of the youth, both poor and middle class, might be better off if the system simply did not exist, even if they then had no formal schooling at all. (I am extremely curious for a philosophic study of Prince Edward County in Virginia, where for some years schooling did not exist for Negro children.)

But what would become of these children? For very many, both poor and middle class, their homes are worse than the schools, and the city streets are worse in another way. Our urban and suburban environments are precisely not cities or communities where adults naturally attend to the young and educate to a viable life. Also, perhaps especially in the case of the overt drop-outs, the state of their body and soul is such that we must give them refuge and remedy, whether it be called school, settlement house, youth work or work camp.

There are thinkable alternatives. Here are half a dozen alternative proposals directly relevant to the subject we have been discussing, the system as compulsory trap. In principle, when a law begins to do more harm than good, the best policy is to alleviate it or try doing without it.

1. Have 'no school at all' for a few classes. These children should be selected from tolerable though not necessarily cultured, homes. They should be neighbours and numerous enough to be a society for one another so that they do not feel merely 'different'. Will they learn the rudiments anyway? This experiment cannot do the children any academic harm, since there is good evidence that normal children will make up the first seven years school-work with four to seven months of good teaching.

2. Dispense with the school building for a few classes; provide teachers and use the city itself as the school – its streets, cafeterias, stores, movies, museums, parks and factories. Where feasible, it certainly makes more sense to teach using the real subject matter than to bring an abstraction of the subject matter into the school-building as 'curriculum'. Such a class should probably not exceed ten children for one pedagogue. The idea – it is the model of Athenian education – is not dissimilar to youth-

gang work but not applied to delinquents and not playing to the gang ideology.

3. Along the same lines, but both outside and inside the school building, use appropriate *unlicensed* adults of the community – the druggist, the storekeeper, the mechanic – as the proper educators of the young into the grown-up world. By this means we can try to overcome the separation of the young from the grown-up world so characteristic in modern urban life, and to diminish the omnivorous authority of the professional school-people. Certainly it would be a useful and animating experience for the adults. (There is the beginning of such a volunteer programme in the New York and some other systems.)

4. Make class attendance not compulsory, in the manner of A. S. Neill's Summerhill. If the teachers are good, absence would tend to be eliminated; if they are bad, let them know it. The compulsory law is useful to get the children away from the parents, but it must not result in trapping the children. A fine modification of this suggestion is the rule used by F. Brown in Florida: he permits the children to be absent for a week or a month to engage in any worthwhile enterprise or visit any new environment.

5. Decentralize an urban school (or do not build a new big building) into small units, twenty to fifty, in available storefronts or clubhouses. These tiny schools, equipped with record-player and pin-ball machine, could combine play, socializing, discussion and formal teaching. For special events, the small units can be brought together into a common auditorium or gymnasium, so as to give the sense of the greater community. Correspondingly, I think it would be worthwhile to give the Little Red Schoolhouse a spin under modern urban conditions, and see how it works out: that is, to combine all the ages in a little room for twenty-five to thirty, rather than to grade by age.

6. Use a *pro rata* part of the school money to send children to economically marginal farms for a couple of months of the year, perhaps six children from mixed backgrounds to a farmer. The only requirement is that the farmer feed them and not beat them; best, of course, if they take part in the farmwork. This will give the farmer cash, as part of the generally desirable programme to redress the urban rural ratio to something nearer to 70 per cent to 30 per cent. (At present, less than 8 per cent of families are rural.) Conceivably, some of the urban children will take to the other way of life, and we might generate a new kind of rural culture.

I frequently suggest these and similar proposals at teachers' colleges, and I am looked at with an eerie look – do I really mean to *diminish* the state-aid grant for each student-day? But mostly the objection is that such proposals entail intolerable administrative difficulties.

Above all, we must apply these or any other proposals to particular individuals and small groups, without the obligation of uniformity. There is a case for uniform standards of achievement but they *cannot* be reached by uniform techniques. The claim that standardization of procedure is more efficient, less costly, or alone administratively practical, is often false. Particular inventiveness requires thought, but thought does not cost money.

33 Herbert R. Kohl

The Open Classroom

Excerpts from Herbert R. Kohl, *The Open Classroom*,
Methuen, 1970, pp. 15–32, 63–75, 82–97.

It is difficult to say exactly what an open classroom is. One almost has to
have been in one and feel what it is. However there are certain things
that it is not. It is important not to equate an open classroom with a
'permissive' environment. In an open classroom the teacher must be as
much himself as the pupils are themselves. This means that if the teacher
is angry he ought to express his anger, and if he is annoyed at someone's
behavior he ought to express that, too. In an authoritarian classroom
annoying behavior is legislated out of existence. In a 'permissive' classroom the teacher pretends it isn't annoying. He also permits students to
behave only in certain ways, thereby retaining the authority over their
behavior he pretends to be giving up. In an open situation the teacher
tries to express what he feels and to deal with each situation as a communal problem [. . .]

Teachers' expectations have a tendency to become self-fulfilling. 'Bad'
classes tend to act badly, and 'gifted' classes tend to respond to the
special consideration that they expect to be given to them if they perform
in a 'superior' way [. . .]

A teacher in an open classroom needs to cultivate a state of *suspended
expectations*. It is not easy. It is easy to believe that a dull class is dull, or
a bright class is bright. The words 'emotionally disturbed' conjure up
frightening images. And it is sometimes a relief to discover that there are
good pupils in the class that is waiting for you. Not reading the record
cards or ignoring the standing of the class is an act of self-denial; it
involves casting aside a crutch when one still believes one can't walk
without it. Yet if one wants to develop an open classroom within the
context of a school which is essentially totalitarian, such acts of will are
necessary.

What does it mean to suspend expectations when one is told that the
class one will be teaching is slow, or bright, or ordinary? At the least it
means not preparing to teach in any special way or deciding beforehand
on the complexity of the materials to be used during a school year. It
means that planning does not consist of finding the class's achievement

level according to the record cards and tailoring the material to those levels, but rather preparing diverse materials and subjects and discovering from the students as the year unfolds what is relevant to them and what isn't.

Particularly it means not reading IQ scores or achievement scores, not discovering who may be a source of trouble and who a solace or even a joy. It means giving your pupils a fresh chance to develop in new ways in your classroom, freed from the roles they may have adopted during their previous school careers. It means allowing children to become who they care to become, and freeing the teacher from the standards by which new pupils had been measured in the past.

There are no simple ways to give up deeply rooted expectations. There are some suggestions, however:

– talk to students outside class
– watch them play and watch them live with other young people
– play with them – joking games and serious games
– talk to them about yourself, what you care about
– listen

In these situations the kids may surprise you and reveal rather than conceal, as is usual in the classroom, their feelings, playfulness, and intelligence [. . .]

The concept of order in an open classroom is not the same as that current in the schools where rules and routines are developed to avoid disagreements. In most classrooms there is no place for argument or conflict, nor is there time for teachers and pupils to learn how to live with and listen to each other. There is no give-and-take. The students direct their talk to the teacher, and obey the teacher's rules. Conflict, defiance, or disagreement are disciplinary problems and offenders must be punished. In an open classroom there is considerable give-and-take, argument, disagreement, even conflict. These are organic elements in the life of the group, to be dealt with and resolved by the group and arbitrated by the teacher. The teacher is a mediator and not a judge or executioner.

Students may have disputes about where they want to sit, or how to line up. It may take a while for them to learn to talk or listen to each other or to the teacher. But in the classroom – as in life – it is more dangerous to legislate disagreement out of existence than to accept and integrate it into the whole [. . .]

The classroom not only segregates young people from society. It segregates them from each other. We have elementary schools, junior high schools, high schools – six year olds never meet ten or fifteen or seventeen year olds in school. It is absurd. Not only do we not let children of the same age teach each other by insisting upon silence in the classroom, we make it impossible in the context of school for older children[1] to teach younger ones [. . .]

Interactions can be looked upon as a study of the relationships between physical objects. It can also be looked upon as a study of the relationship between individuals (psychology), groups (sociology), nations (history), ideas (?). Interactions can be danced out, developed in improvizational drama, or studied in literature or the mass media. Interactions in the scientific sense can be looked at as a subclass of all the systems of interactions that man is involved in.

Relativity need not be confined to relativity physics. One can study moral principles and values, examine the relativity of cultures, listen to alternate musical systems (8 tone, 5 tone, 12 tone), even create musical instruments and systems that have their value relative to other musical systems. One can also study relatives (I'm his cousin, he's my cousin, but I'm his uncle and he's my nephew) and then kinship systems. One can also talk about looking at the world through other eyes and trying to understand the experience of other people and creatures. One can dance out the movement of two independent systems moving with relationship to each other.

Systems and Subsystems. Think of a jazz combo as a system with several subsystems, one, for example, the rhythm section and another (within the rhythm section) the subsystem of drums and cymbals. Listen to the musical group as a whole and then listen to the subsystems. Or, again, take a game like football – think of the whole team, the offense, the defense, the linemen, the quarterback, the running backs. Play the game and look at films of the game the way you would look at a physical system to be studied in physics. Then look at the game as a dance. Move from one mode of perception and thought to another. The free play of imagination and intellect is certainly one of the components of creative thought in any discipline.

Environments. One can study physical environment. One can also create environments. Recently I worked with a group of youngsters who created a suburb out of cardboard tubes, string, and paper. As we

1. I feel uneasy about this word. It makes some sense when applied to kindergarten or first grade people but none whatever when applied to high school students.

developed the suburb we became the residents of our environment and acted out the lives of people we created. Using the simplest and cheapest materials one can recreate the world in the classroom. One can look at contemporary art, at the environments of Andy Keinholtz, Claes Oldenburg, Allan Kaprow, or study theater as a means of creating a simulated environment. One can look at the magic of storytelling and fiction where at their best convincing worlds are spun out of words [...]

One way to begin a change is to devote ten minutes a day to doing something different. There is never any problem of finding ten minutes to play with, since what the pupils 'must cover' is usually padded in order to fill up time. During that ten minutes present the class with a number of things they can choose to do. Present them with options you feel may interest them. Allow them the option of sitting and doing nothing if they choose. Moreover, make it clear that nothing done during that period will be graded, and nothing need to be shown or explained to the teacher. That ten minutes is to be their time and is to be respected as such. Step out of the way and observe the things your pupils choose to do.

Step out of the way, but don't disappear. Make it clear that you won't tell people what to do or how to do it, but that you will be available to help in any way you can, or just to talk. For ten minutes cease to be a teacher and be an adult with young people, a resource available if needed, and possibly a friend, but not a dictator, a judge, or an executioner. Also try to make it possible for the ten minutes to grow to fifteen, twenty, so long as it makes sense to you and your pupils. It is not unlikely that those ten minutes may become the most important part of the day, and after a while may even become the school day [...]

Schools are afraid to let their students go into the world away from the critical eye of the teacher. It won't be easy to leave the school several times a week with the class, much less develop apprenticeships for individual students away from the school building. However, you can move slowly, and should get as much help from the kids' parents as possible. Visit where they work, get to know the neighbourhood you teach in. Ask the kids to tell you what's happening and to take you places. If there are places they feel you shouldn't know about, don't press.

The whole community ought to be the school, and the classroom a home base for the teachers and kids, a place where they can talk and rest and learn together, but not the sole place of learning. The classroom ought to be a communal center, a comfortable environment in which plans can be made and experiences assessed. However one can open up the classroom as much by moving out of it as by changing the life within it [...]

A non-authoritarian public school is rare, and an authoritarian school with much tolerance for non-authoritarian teaching may be rarer. An open classroom is a threat in a school where the maintenance of control is a central concern. It is a threat to teachers who may find their pupils demanding rights and freedom not acceptable in their classes. It is a threat to supervisors who have a stake in carefully ordered curriculum or who feel the need to know what the teachers and pupils in their school are doing at every moment. It is a threat to parents who are fearful for their children's future and are anxious about their final grades and test results. It is also a threat, at first, to students who have been in school too long and are frightened by freedom. Initially, teaching in an open class-room can be a lonesome, difficult experience, and the teacher has to be strong and believe it is worth it to himself and to his students.

Survival is always an issue for an innovator and it is no different for the radical teacher than for any other revolutionary. Compromises will have to be made with other teachers, administrators, with one's own principles, in order to survive, and it will always be problematic whether they are worth it. Survival in a given school is not always desirable or possible. There are times to quit or to be fired, to oppose, defy, and confront people ...

Troubles with teachers
Noise

An open classroom with many activities going on simultaneously is not a silent place. Students talk to each other. They also talk to the teacher and move around from group to group. The noise in the classroom is not harsh or hysterical, but it often fills the room and can upset other teachers who insist upon silence in their rooms. I have seen teachers become irrationally upset by a noisy classroom, even when they are convinced that the noise was productive and not chaotic. Perhaps noise suggests lack of control and thus activates the authoritarian's fear of his not being in command.

Noise can be modulated but not eliminated. If other teachers are upset you can mention that to the class and together you can decide how to control the volume. If a particular teacher becomes threatening and your supervisors also disapprove of noise then you may be able to find a way to calm the teacher down and negotiate a truce. Perhaps you can find that teacher's weakness and complain about it, instead of being defensive about the noise in one's own room. But the students' right to talk to one another cannot be withdrawn without destroying the openness of your classroom.

Dirt

Dirt upsets many teachers as much as noise. Everything must be clean and antiseptic as well as quiet in their classrooms. The students can't mess around, they can't decorate the walls without supervision, or drop things on the floor without being corrected. The teacher fears loss of control of the physical environment and in order to maintain power sterilizes it.

An open classroom should not be filthy but is often messy because many things are happening in it. Students can experiment with things and leave unfinished experiments about the room. They can decorate the walls, use the library, move the furniture about, and generally live comfortably in the room.

Many teachers cannot stand the apparent disorder of an open classroom, but the problem is not so serious as it is with noise. They needn't see disorder if it upsets them. Often it is useful to place a drawing over the window looking into one's room and invite only sympathetic teachers to visit your class. So long as the freedom of your class doesn't spill out of your room many authoritarian teachers will let you go your own way. This is a melancholy fact, and one that some people can't put up with. The degree to which one pretends or refuses to conform is a matter for each teacher's conscience.

Students as threats

The students in an open classroom can become threats to other teachers. As information spreads through the student underground that interesting things are happening in your room, you may find curious students passing by and looking in. Welcome them and tell them what is going on. Invite them to poke around and speak to your students. There is no better way to spread the idea throughout the school that there is a different way of teaching. Encourage your students to tell their friends what they are doing, to be living examples of the fact that your people can be people and not merely disenfranchised 'children' within the setting of a school. And remember when you receive the hostile stares of teachers you've never met before that your pupils have become 'bad examples' for the rest of the school.

There is no direct way I know of to deal with this hostility, but it is important not to be surprised by it. Many people in a school do not speak honestly to others. They bear grudges, spread rumors, are capable of much pettiness. If at a moment of confrontation many enemies emerge, do not be surprised or disarmed. Though it may never be explicit; it is covertly acknowledged in schools that any teachers and students who manage to get away with free and open behavior are threats to the survival of the educational system as it now exists [. . .]

Possibly the most important thing to remember is that supervisors who allow teachers to experiment, and support them, are rare; few are interested in helping teachers cope with problems that arise in the classroom. They judge teachers primarily according to how they fit into the social structure of the school. It is important for young teachers to realize this and not be surprised if their inability to get along with a colleague who has tenure is weighed more heavily against them than success in the classroom is weighed for them. There is little that can be done about this short of changing the people and the structure of the school. That is certainly one long-term objective of developing open classrooms in public school situations. However, the question of survival must be dealt with before the question of victory ever arises. In this respect, there are many different things one might have to do, such as:

1. Keep two sets of lesson plans, one for the supervisor that follows the curriculum and another for oneself that deals with the reality of one's classroom.

2. Create a set of authoritarian lessons to use when supervisors observe.

3. Be polite and silent at faculty meetings.

4. Seem to comply with administrative directives.

There are problems with making hypocritical concessions in order to survive. That is what all teachers do anyway, and unless one makes the concessions in the service of change and is willing on occasion to confront people, the openness of one's classroom will be a lie. It is possible to become another scared teacher talking to students about their freedom and autonomy yet afraid to fight for one's own [. . .]

The position of a teacher can be difficult. In some ghetto communities parents may want a rigid authoritarian education for their children so that a teacher who wants to create an open classroom may find himself at odds with people he politically agrees with. There is no general way out of such a dilemma. I suppose the best he can do is explain his work as fully as possible to the parents and ask them to speak to their children about what goes on in his classroom. Also he should show people his students' work. If people are still not convinced, there may be times a teacher has to leave a school voluntarily because political control may be at that point more crucial than non-authoritarian teaching.

One further note: keep a diary that documents your experiences. The document will be invaluable in assessing your own work and in case of crisis will be your strongest weapon.

On becoming indispensable

There is a way a teacher can experiment with nonauthoritarian teaching and be free of other teachers and supervisors. That way is to work with problem students – those students the school system has given up on. Disturbed and retarded and disruptive and delinquent students are in a special category. They are often considered 'troubled' simply because they refuse to conform to the authoritarian structure of the school and refuse to acknowledge the totalitarian power of the teacher. They don't have to go through the curriculum and don't have to take tests. Nothing is expected of them and all that is expected of their teachers is to get them off the backs of the rest of the staff in the school. Many extraordinary teachers have accepted this situation and created free and open classrooms for their 'special' students. The main problem one has to worry about when such a class works well is whether by handling the school's problems one isn't indirectly helping the system by reducing conflicts created by the system itself.

34 David Adelstein

Roots of the Crisis in British Universities

Excerpts from David Adelstein, 'Roots of the British crisis', in A. Cockburn and R. Blackburn (eds.), *Student Power*, Penguin, 1969, pp. 61–79. Originally published in *New Left Review*.

To understand the significance and potential of student action it is essential to examine the nature of higher education through its historical development and in its immediate structure. Higher education only reflects, as do other branches of education, the society within which it functions. Hence conflicts in higher education at the same time mirror wider social conflicts. The prime function of higher education used to be the recruiting and cultural buttressing of the social elite. Nowadays it has an added dimension – the fundamental role it plays in the economy. For skilled manpower is the scarcest resource of a modern capitalist society. It is this fact that collective student action can exploit.

Because of its history, Britain is the last industrial country to begin to technocratize its higher education. This makes the conflict between the older, traditional style of higher education and the new technocratic model more extreme than has been experienced elsewhere. It also engenders particular intellectual characteristics in the various disciplines, making the resolution of the conflict all the more difficult.

Such an abrupt confrontation, with students as its main victims, is bound to provoke student awareness of their situation. In this possibility lies the potential for students to assault all that is rotten in both the old and the new forms of education. For the arousal of student consciousness confronts us with the opportunity of obtaining a more authentic education.

Higher education is divided into three sectors, neatly piled in a prestige pyramid. At the top are the universities and below them the colleges of education and further education (the technical, commercial and art colleges). How did this structure develop, and what are the main features of each sector? [. . .]

Symptoms of the crisis

By looking at higher education historically one can begin to see the foundations of the crisis. Highly qualified manpower is now an increasingly essential asset of neo-capitalist society, best attained through the democratization of education plus the operation of a selection process. While the selection process operates very strongly in Britain, democratization resisted at every point by the class structure is a long way off A consistent pattern emerges from numerous investigations: a Ministry of Education Report in 1954, the Crowther Report 1959–60, Kelsall on University Application 1957, the Robbins Report 1963, and the Plowden Report 1967 all confirm the deep-seated inequality of opportunity in British education. Epitomizing this situation is the public schools – Oxbridge nexus which retains as its essence an unspecialized, gentlemanly elitism.

There are two very commonly discussed symptoms of this crisis. The most prominent of course is the severe shortage of scientific and technologically trained people. This is not entirely due to inadequate training facilities. It is partly caused by insufficient applicants for these subjects, and partly by the 'brain drain'. Recent estimates suggest that the numbers of qualified engineers required by industry, government and education must increase by 24 per cent every three years. Yet the Dainton Committee, investigating this problem, predicts that in 1971 there will only be 30,000 to 35,000 applicants for such places, compared to 40,000 in 1964. Not only will the rapid increase not be forthcoming – there will actually be a drop. That there are many more places than applicants for degrees in applied science subjects, is a function of the uncritical and anti-intellectual presentation of science and its associate disciplines in most schools and university departments, an approach deeply embedded in the country's tradition. It is a sad paradox that theology is nowadays taught in an enlightened spirit of critical inquiry, while scientific knowledge is leadenly imparted as though it were theological dogma. Students interested in more stimulating study know from their school experience not to apply for science. On the other hand the 'brain drain' affects those in the science side partly through lack of internationally competitive salaries, but mainly because of inadequate research facilities. Because the gap between science and humanities, the 'two cultures' phenomenon, manifest in early schooldays, has its origins in the intellectual and social history of the country, the educational structure at the higher level cannot hope to be altered without a profound shake-up of the entire system.

In addition there is an increasingly critical shortage of teachers. An optimistic figure from the Economist Intelligence Unit estimated that Britain will be short of 36,000 teachers in 1972. Wastage rates amongst teachers are high and the National Union of Teachers has up till now miserably failed to better the salaries and status of teachers. A trained teacher at twenty-one takes home less than £15 a week. When one compounds this with the conditions in colleges of education it is not hard to understand why the country finds it difficult to provide enough teachers. Many students go to training college because they have failed to get into university. Here they are usually isolated from social and cultural centres, and are subject to the most archaic disciplinary rules. No wonder it takes new ideas and teaching methods so long to penetrate the schools. Once again the problem requires not only a complete reallocation of governmental expenditure priorities, in itself an immense political task, but also a revolution in the intellectual climate of teaching education.

This, briefly, is the general situation which has existed in higher education for some time. What 'solutions' have been offered, what are the likely trends and how might students play a part in these affairs? Firstly it is necessary to consider the implications of the Robbins Report, the most significant landmark in the growth of higher education.

The Robbins report: a liberal technocracy?

The Robbins Report with its numerous appendices appeared in October 1963, more than two years after it was commissioned. It is the only major and coherent work on higher education, yet its recommendations have been, in effect, entirely negated. Almost every basic argument contained in the Report has been subsequently discarded by the Government; all that remains is a mass of statistics. Why has this central work been so thoroughly jettisoned?

The Report fully documented the state of full-time higher education, showing how very backward we might soon be in terms of numbers of trained students. It showed the expansion that had taken place in higher education. At the turn of the century, 1 per cent of the nineteen-year-old age group attended university (universities were then the only full-time colleges), whereas in 1962, 7 per cent of the age group were in full-time education. In sixty years the student numbers had gone up by more than eight times and doubled since the war. On the basis of the numbers likely to be qualified for full-time courses, the committee recommended that the availability of places be drastically increased to avail 558,000 students (17 per cent of the age group) of the opportunity of higher education in 1980–81. These estimates, the committee recognized, were biased on the conservative side and in fact the number of qualified school-leavers has greatly exceeded the Robbins estimates.

The Report did not attempt to reach its recommendations on the basis of the needs of the economy (perhaps because it didn't know how), but based them purely on estimates of the number of qualifying sixth formers – the so-called 'pool of ability'. This is not to say that an economic case was not made for expansion. It was, but only in the general sense that higher education helps the economy and that in order to maintain our place in relation to other countries it was necessary to expand student numbers. In this sense the Robbins Report was 'student oriented' – it catered for apparent student demand. In so far as it based its case on the inherent value of expansion rather than upon economic demands, the Report represents possibly the last 'liberal' document that a government commission will produce for some time. Indeed, Robbins as an educationalist is very much a liberal heir to Newman. Both favour universities as cosy, intimate communities. Although Newman viewed knowledge as man's most fundamental relationship with God and Robbins views it as man's relationship with man, both conclude that there must exist some overriding 'spirit of universality'. Robbins says that universities 'must emphasize the common element in civilizations rather than the minor variations', that the most important value is the 'transcendence of values'. Thus, despite his 'modernity', the essence of Robbins's concept of a university community is very similar to the aristocratic tradition which Newman extolled: it is the fostering of a common identity that is all important in higher education, i.e., the socializing process. This explains one of the main problems with the Robbins recommendations: their university orientation. One of the deliberate intentions of the committee was to abolish rigid structural differences between the sectors of higher education. It thus recommended that all institutions be given the potential to become universities and that as many as possible form links with existing universities. Expansion of the university sector was to be greater than the other sectors. It posed the university style of education as the ultimate, envisaging technical colleges and training colleges beneath this umbrella. Unfortunately there was a problem here. The further education sector is inextricably tied to large numbers of part-time courses, so, unless part-timers are to be included in the system, a line has to be drawn somewhere. Furthermore, the Robbins committee naïvely assumed the Government would be prepared to pay for its proposals, which would have involved an increase in real costs from £206 million in 1962–3 to £506 million in 1980–81. With a matching naïvety the committee thought that more scientists and technologists could be provided by merely increasing the number of places. The significant decisions are made in school at about the age of fourteen but the school system went unchallenged in this respect, as indeed it was in most others. The Report revealed that 45 per cent of the children of fathers in the higher professional groups enter higher education compared with 4 per cent of the children of skilled manual workers and 2 per cent of the semi- and unskilled workers. Yet, how was this problem to be solved? – the committee had no idea. Finally it might have been argued that a corollary of basing student numbers on student demand should have been a recommendation that the content of courses be determined by student demand. There is, however, no such recommendation in the Report, nor in any of its appendices. In fact the Report ignores the content of education in favour of organizational proposals designed to preserve the buoyancy of the universities.

To summarize: the Robbins Report attempted to direct old liberal notions into a new technocratic programme. It recommended substantial changes in the structure of higher education and indeed in society at large: 'The expansion we recommend will bring with it a very extensive transformation of the social and economic picture.' Such a transformation could hardly occur without at least a vast change in the school system, let alone in the political climate of the country.

The binary system: divide and rule

How did the Labour Government respond to the problems in higher education? The Government's policy was enunciated in a speech by Anthony Crosland, then Secretary of State for Education and Science, at Woolwich polytechnic on the 27 April 1965. In it he outlined what quickly became known as the Binary System, the implications of which involved an absolute reversal of the Robbins philosophy. Where the supreme principle of the Robbins Report was that there should be no rigid distinctions between types of institution in higher education, the Binary System, as its name suggests, involved the segregation of institutions into two completely discrete compartments: the autonomous sector and the public sector. The autonomous sector comprises the universities, including colleges of advanced technology which had become universities by that date, all receiving their finance from the Universities Grants Committee and accountable only to themselves in their spending. The public sector is all the rest: polytechnics, technical colleges, other colleges in further education such as art colleges and colleges of commerce, as well as the colleges of education. These receive their money from local education authorities and are directly responsible to them in their spending [...]

The Government's real problem is how to encourage a technocratic ethos of sufficient status to rival the university tradition, how to break the old liberal stranglehold of the universities and replace it with a new managerial-technological culture. Yet the Secretary of State consciously devised a policy which has not the slightest hope of doing this. It might have had the glimmering of a chance if the colleges of advanced technology, the only potential spearhead of the new technocracy, had not immediately prior to the announcement of the policy been absorbed (in keeping with tradition) into the universities.

Again, as with Robbins, the sort of social change demanded by the Binary System is not something that occurs merely by the Government's recommending it [. . .]

A structural device cannot, by virtue of being officially decreed, change the present relations. Any contemplated change must take account of the interest groups behind, and the differentials dividing, the two sectors. It is worth looking into these.

There were 184,000 students in forty-three universities in 1967; 202,000 full-time and sandwich course students in over 300 technical and other colleges and 87,000 students in 200 colleges of education. In fact there are about three million students of different sorts in further education. In what sense is there 'healthy rivalry' or 'parity of esteem' between the universities and the rest? An average of £581 is spent per year on a university student's academic facilities compared with £249 for a trainee teacher. The average union fee for universities is £8 per head; in the public sector it is £3. Living accommodation hardly exists for technical college students. The size and location of colleges in the public sector make them both more physically and more intellectually isolated. Staff–student ratios are more equal in universities whilst university staff enjoy greater sums of money for research. In fact a tidy picture of financial privilege emerges.

Oxford and Cambridge, of course, are the most endowed. In St Catherine's College, Oxford, each student has in his room a new chair costing eighty guineas to cushion him against life and student radicalism. The Robbins Report found that 29 per cent of university undergraduates came from manual working families as opposed to 44 per cent of the full-timers in technical colleges of education. The prestige of the universities, the low educational image of technology and the lower status of teaching, ensure that there are many more applicants for university places; those attending a non-university college have often failed to gain admission to a university. To complete the pattern, university graduates have in general higher social destinies than those from non-university colleges.

Underlying the Binary System is the fundamental gulf between theoretical and applied subjects, between the abstract and the practical, such that the one side veers towards dilettantism and the other towards mechanical specialism. This is the profound cultural schism that the Binary System creates and reinforces.

This aspect indicates how the Government is using the Binary System: to provide as cheaply as possible middle-and lower-grade technicians for the economy and teachers for schools. The infusion of thirty polytechnics as academic focal points into the public sector does not change this a bit. The system is such that even Robbins could say:

I can sincerely say that nothing has astonished me more than that a Government with an egalitarian background and actively engaged at the school level in an attempt to reduce unnecessary and invidious distinctions, should be energetically supporting, in the field of higher education, a separation which must have exactly the opposite effect.

Robbins is right. The logic of the Government's case is of course the same as the 1944 Education Act which it so strenuously attacked in opposition. Parity of prestige, each section pulling its weight, is as much bunk in the higher education system in 1967 as it was in the lower in 1944 [. . .]

Contradictions within the system

It is now possible to describe more precisely the conflict that exists within higher education. It is basically a conflict, embodied in the Binary System, between social forces, in which neo-capitalist economic demands are pitted against the power structure and culture of existing society. The old education trained the unspecialized person to apply himself, with managerial qualities, to non-standard situations. The new requires the specialist to do the same. But the old education belongs to a previous century whilst the 'new' produces universities and colleges which one critic has called 'battery factories for broiler technicians'.

By isolating the inherent shortcomings in the whole structure and seeing how these problems inflict themselves on student existence, it is possible to define a third and alternative model to the two competing currently. There are three interrelated contradictions affecting students:

1. *The contradiction between the economically necessary expenditure to ensure output of trained personnel and the Government's persistent failure to meet its responsibility for this investment.* The economic system requires the Government to limit severely spending on the social services and education. Education, the third largest sector of public spending, cost about £1936 million in 1967. The Government's meagre projections expect educational expenditure to rise in real terms at about 5 per cent per year. Yet even this rate of growth will be impossible to obtain. For although education is an urgent social and economic investment it is argued that the rate of increase of spending on the social services cannot exceed the rate of growth of the economy (and we all know the latter is

not bounding along), a view which implicitly accepts that the alignment of priorities of Government spending is static and unchangeable. Here the Binary System displays its latent utility: to economize – the move to obtain more student places without more money. Expansion of student places is to be concentrated in the public sector which is financed through the local authorities from rates, a source hardly sufficient for an expanding sector of expenditure. And so we find the comparatively extravagant university finance being contrasted against that of the public sector and 'healthy rivalry' resulting in the literal impoverishment of our education.

Education on the cheap hits students in many ways. Facilities, teaching and living accommodation are bad, whilst the size of the institutions increases. All sorts of measures are now presented or discussed to reduce student income. These range from the introduction of loans, or increasing the parental contribution in the means test to the freezing of student grants by withholding the customary compensation for inflation. To foster such policies numerous myths about the irresponsibility of students, living idly off the State and the taxpayer, are publicly encouraged. Making the student's financial life harder ties him more to the *status quo*. Hence, in opposing measures to worsen his financial lot the student adopts a position of challenge to the *status quo*. He is forced to argue in terms of socially necessary investment and to think in terms of his social, rather than individual, existence. Hence there develops a student consciousness as a particular type of skilled worker and this must produce a total challenge to the Government's spending priorities and economic policies.

2. *The contradiction between the stratifying functions of the educational system and the need to make opportunity really equal.* Educational progress has always been hindered by this conflict. In the nineteenth century the great fear of the reactionaries was that compulsory elementary education would encourage the working class to mistake its social place. This apprehension proved unfounded and it is now gradually being learnt how to practise supposedly egalitarian policies yet maintain fairly rigid social stratification. Comprehensive secondary schooling is meaningless whilst streaming persists and class differentials begin in early primary school.

It is in school that the individualizing competitiveness of the whole education system is instilled in the most obviously authoritarian manner. From school the fittest go on to university or college where the authoritarianism manifests itself less physically and more academically. The prime instrument of this process is the examination system. Its function is to atomize and stratify, to produce with a label so that prospective employers know the value of the product. Yet because the examination system embodies the most invidious element of the system, rejection of it opens up to students a very powerful tactic: the threat of refusing to sit examinations which would jeopardize substantial sections of the economy.

In higher education the specific thrust comes from the inchoate technocratic education challenging the old liberal form for supremacy. The classical tradition, ensconced as it is in the entire social structure, will not easily be budged. But although at present the universities control the intellectual heights, the expansion of higher education makes the foundations more irrational, and thereby gives the further education sector an interest in making its students aware of their own inferior situation. Hence the student demand for a truly comprehensive structure of higher education develops, coupled with an attack on all stratifying procedures.

3. *The contradiction between the collective and autonomous nature of productive work and the individualist and authoritarian structure of contemporary education.* This contradiction pervades most work situations. The conflict is particularly active, though, in higher education as it is in this sphere that the technocratic capitalist society demands its greatest changes. Consumer society has one characteristic dimension: that only the products of work should be regarded as gratifying. Work itself must remain only a means to an end. Intellectual work must be motivated by individual careerism. Never can the process of productive work become meaningful in itself for as soon as this happens its structures may be challenged on a different basis. In the France of 1968 it was the students and the young, especially skilled, workers who were in the forefront of the rebellion, their demands being not for better material rewards but for control over their work situations. Furthermore, consumer society requires trained people for the unproductive tasks of promoting consumption which in turn heightens the contradictions.

There are two contradictory pressures increasingly exerted upon students. The examination system requires students to show themselves solely as individuals, but at the same time students and young graduates are more and more frequently being required to work together as teams, although quality of this sort is untrained and untested; collective work involves an appreciation of other disciplines yet interfering in another's subject is strictly frowned upon. Students are expected to examine critically the first principles of their own disciplines whilst remaining entirely impervious to important intellectual questions outside their own spheres.

Their minds are required to be pungent and penetrating in one direction and totally blunted in all others. No wonder more students are wishing to study sociology which at least touches on the implications of all other disciplines and attempts a synthesis, than the natural sciences which are so often intellectually one-dimensional.

This inner contradiction permeates our education. The Binary System calls on some students to study abstract, theoretical disciplines and others applied and practical subjects, but the economy demands productivity, which in turn demands the combination of these two extremes. The System categorically segregates them yet simultaneously requires a fusion.

It is in this context that the demand for student power arises. For students cannot question critically and at the same time blindly accept what their educators say. The teachers have a vested interest in preserving the compartments in their disciplines; the students are interested in removing this atomization. The staff are bent on moulding the students to their own image; the students are concerned with deciding for themselves what the crucial questions are and how they should combine to study them. In this conflict, then, is the embryo of the demand for students to participate in, or even control the decisions affecting their academic lives [. . .]

The problem with the present system is not that it mixes the ingredients in the wrong ratios: the theoretical with the applied: the sciences with the humanities: the vocational with the intellectual. The fault is that the intermediate and connecting areas, what C. Wright Mills called 'sensibilities' are lacking. Wright Mills wrote:

Skills and values cannot be so easily separated as the academic search for supposedly neutral skills causes us to assume. And especially not when we speak seriously of liberal education. . . . To train someone to operate a lathe or to read and write is pretty much the education of a skill; to evoke from people an understanding of what they really want from their lives or to debate with them Stoic, Christian and humanist ways of living is pretty much a clear-cut education of values. But to assist in the birth among a group of people of those cultural and political and technical sensibilities which would make them members of a genuinely liberal public, this is at once a training in skills and an education in values. It includes a sort of therapy in the ancient sense of clarifying one's knowledge of one's self; it includes the imparting of all those skills of controversy with one's self, which we call thinking; and with others, which we call debate. And the end product of such liberal education of sensibilities is simply the self-educating, self-cultivating man and woman.

Thus what is required is a new education for the whole man; one which rejects the compartments of the technocratic model and transcends its functional requirements, but at the same time exposes the false sense of independence of the classical tradition and redirects its theoretical heritage, one which does not inflict its values from above but consciously adopts them through independent and critical study, intimately entwined with practical activity.

Such a position is most likely to be properly assumed only by students. The government, we have seen, has its own economic masters. The staff have, to a greater or lesser degree, invested their careers in the *status quo*. Students on the other hand are less career bound and generally less tied to established institutions. Moreover, because the contradictions of the system tend to concentrate on students and because students are undergoing such a formative period in their lives it is highly probable that the most combative force will be the students.

Student power

At its base 'student power' must mean the ability of the students' bloc to inflict, if necessary, sanctions of sufficient economic, social, or political magnitude to force its opinions to be heeded. At a more operative level it implies the participation of students in, or the joint control by students and staff of, the internal authority structure. 'Student power' is a difficult concept to use, linked, as it currently is, to all the other power slogans on the scene. 'Student control' might have been more appropriate but it excludes the defensive aspect of the power concept.

It is necessary to consider initially the way in which national developments affect students in their local environments. Here there are two main factors: the expansion of higher education itself, and the actual direction of the change, i.e., from a traditional–liberal model to a technocratic–managerial one.

The rapid expansion of a higher education automatically brings about a change in the students' view of the process. Whereas higher education was previously seen as a privilege, it is now taken as a right.

Because the ideology of expansion is based on social need and equality, even though this is not the objective case, students respond as though it were. The ideological 'structure' of expansion inevitably constitutes a determinant of behaviour in its own right. Nor are students' career prospects as secure as before.

This transformation of student attitudes takes place even though students are still, despite the vast expansion in numbers, a relative elite. Previously, as only a tiny element of the national elite, graduates were assured of automatic status and self-enhancement through the possession of a degree, no matter what its quality.

No longer is this the case. A good or a higher degree is now the deciding factor for social status and the possibility of irrational rejection by the system is thus greater. The student who regards his study as a privilege or a means of social mobility is likely to be very passive towards the system, to assiduously learn what he is told, never questioning its validity. In contrast, the student who takes higher education as a right will respond much more assertively. He will demand his 'rights', adopting a generally critical approach to all he is taught or expected to know. Methods of teaching, the content of courses, the entire system of examinations will all be called into question.

The second factor is the direction of the expansion towards a technocratic-managerial society. The old system educated the whole man; the new processes only that part of him which is economically functional. The rest must remain dormant because whole-man education is now too expensive. With this, the cushy surroundings of student life necessarily dwindle and it becomes harder to chloroform students with their former luxury. It is, moreover, no longer possible to control the student's social life as before. In return for the privilege of the old whole-man education the student had to endure strict hierarchical social relationships between himself and the staff. But with social and informal relationships now much more egalitarian, the actual disparities in formal relationships are highlighted, resulting in the student's demand for equality on a formal level as well. By illuminating the actual power differentials between staff and student, and even between staff, the debate focuses upon those who make decisions in the college. Here the students might often encounter the staff as the enemy. For, although there are often contradictions within the staff's own ranks, especially between the junior and the senior staff, power invariably lies in the hands of the senior staff. Academics are essentially conservative in relation to affairs within their own institution even though they might be well-known progressive figures externally. Staff interests, in research and teaching require security and stability. Hence student demands sometimes assume menacing proportions in the eyes of the teachers.

Before any demands can be seriously launched, there are a number of prerequisites in the form of student rights. The first is the right of the students' union to be completely self-governing. Very few unions are fully autonomous at the moment but it is obvious that if students do not at least have full control over their own organization the strength of any other control they might have is likely to be gravely weakened. Similarly the rights of free speech, discussion and expression are essential. For if the student voice is to carry any significant weight, it must have absolute freedom to raise whatever matters it wishes. (At LSE not only were students forbidden to discuss a particular matter but they were even forbidden to discuss whether or not they should discuss this matter.) Finally there are disciplinary rights. The old education, aimed at moulding the whole personality, inflicted a complete social range of disciplinary strictures on the student. But students will be prepared to submit to the semi-legality of *in loco parentis* only so long as they feel higher education to be a privilege. The fact is that students ought to come neither above nor below the ordinary law of the land – there is no ounce of justification for academic authorities to have non-academic disciplinary powers.

35 Howard S. Becker

The Career of the Chicago Public Schoolteacher

Howard S. Becker, 'The career of the Chicago public schoolteacher', *American Journal of Sociology*, vol. 57, March 1952, pp. 470–77.

The concept of *career* has proved of great use in understanding and analyzing the dynamics of work organizations and the movement and fate of individuals within them. The term refers, to paraphrase Hall, to the patterned series of adjustments made by the individual to the 'network of institutions, formal organizations, and informal relationships' in which the work of the occupation is performed. This series of adjustments is typically considered in terms of movement up or down between positions differentiated by their rank in some formal or informal hierarchy of prestige, influence, and income. The literature in the field has devoted itself primarily to an analysis of the types, stages, and contingencies of careers, so conceived, in various occupations. We may refer to such mobility through a hierarchy of ranked positions, if a spatial metaphor be allowed, as the *vertical* aspect of the career.

By focusing our attention on this aspect of career movement, we may tend to overlook what might, in contrast, be called the *horizontal* aspect of the career: movement among the positions available at one level of such a hierarchy. It need not be assumed that occupational positions which share some characteristics because of their similar rank in a formal structure are identical in all respects. They may, in fact, differ widely in the configuration of the occupation's basic problems which they present. That is, all positions at one level of a work hierarchy, while theoretically identical, may not be equally easy or rewarding places in which to work. Given this fact, people tend to move in patterned ways among the possible positions, seeking that situation which affords the most desirable setting in which to meet and grapple with the basic problems of their work. In some occupations more than others, and for some individuals more than others, this kind of career movement assumes greater importance than the vertical variety, sometimes to such an extent that the entire career line consists of movement entirely at one level of a work hierarchy.

The teachers of the Chicago public schools are a group whose careers typically tend toward this latter extreme. Although it is possible for any educationally qualified teacher to take the examination for the position of principal and attempt ascent through the school system's administrative hierarchy, few make the effort. Most see their careers purely in teaching, in terms of movement among the various schools in the Chicago system.[1] Even those attempting this kind of vertical mobility anticipate a stay of some years in the teacher category and, during that time, see that segment of their career in much the same way. This paper will analyse the nature of this area of career movement among teachers and will describe the types of careers found in this group. These, of course, are not the only patterns which we may expect to find in this horizontal plane of career movement. It remains for further research in other occupations to discern other career varieties and the conditions under which each type occurs.

The analysis is based on interviews with sixty teachers in the Chicago system. The interviewing was unstructured to a large extent and varied somewhat with each interviewee, according to the difficulty encountered in overcoming teachers' distrust and fear of speaking to outsiders. Despite this resistance, based on anxiety regarding the consequences of being interviewed, material of sufficient validity for the analysis undertaken here was secured through insisting that all general statements of attitude be backed up with concrete descriptions of actual experience. This procedure, it is felt, forced the interviewees to disclose more than they otherwise might have by requiring them to give enough factual material to make their general statements plausible and coherent.

I

The positions open to a particular teacher in the system at a given time appear, in general, quite similar, all having about the same prestige, income, and power attached to them. This is not to deny the existence of variations in income created by the operation of seniority rules or of differences in informal power and prestige based on length of service and length of stay in a given school. The fact remains that, for an individual with a given amount of seniority who is about to begin in a school new to her, all teaching positions in the Chicago system are the same with regard to prestige, influence, and income.

Though the available teaching positions in the city schools are similar in formal characteristics, they differ widely in terms of the

---

1. The Chicago system has a high enough salary schedule and sufficient security safeguards to be safe as a system in which a person can make his entire career, thus differing from smaller school systems in which the teacher does not expect to spend her whole working life.

configuration of the occupation's basic work problems which they present. The teacher's career consists of movement among these various schools in search of the most satisfactory position in which to work, that being the position in which these problems are least aggravated and most susceptible of solution. Work problems arise in the teacher's relations with the important categories of people in the structure of the school: children, parents, principal, and other teachers. Her most difficult problems arise in her interaction with her pupils. Teachers feel that the form and degree of the latter problems vary considerably with the social-class background of the students.

Without going into any detailed analysis of these problems, I will simply summarize the teacher's view of them and of their relation to the various social-class groups which might furnish her with students. The interviewees typically distinguished three class groups: firstly a bottom stratum, probably equivalent to the lower-lower and parts of the upper-lower class, and including, for the teacher, all Negroes; secondly an upper stratum, probably equivalent to the upper-middle class; and thirdly a middle stratum, probaby equivalent to the lower-middle and parts of the upper-lower class. Three major kinds of problems were described as arising in dealings with pupils: the problem of *teaching*, producing some change in the child's skills and knowledge which can be attributed to one's own efforts; the problem of *discipline*, maintaining order and control over the children's activity; and the problem of what may be termed *moral acceptability*, bringing one's self to bear some traits of the children which one considers immoral and revolting. The teacher feels that the lowest group, 'slum' children, is difficult to teach, uncontrollable and violent in the sphere of discipline, and morally unacceptable on all scores, from physical cleanliness to the spheres of sex and 'ambition to get ahead'. Children of the upper group, from the 'better neighbourhoods', were felt to be quick learners and easy to teach but somewhat 'spoiled' and difficult to control and lacking in the important moral traits of politeness and respect for elders. The middle group was considered to be hard-working but slow to learn, extremely easy to control, and most acceptable on the moral level.

Other important problems arise in interaction with parents, principal, and colleagues and revolve primarily around the issue of authority. Parents of the highest status groups and certain kinds of principals are extremely threatening to the authority the teacher feels basic to the maintenance of her role; in certain situations colleagues, too, may act in such a way as to diminish her authority.

Thus, positions at the teaching level may be very satisfactory or highly undesirable, depending on the presence or absence of the 'right' kind of pupils, parents, principal, and colleagues. Where any of these positions are filled by the 'wrong' kind of person, the teacher feels that she is in an unfavorable situation in which to deal with the important problems of her work. Teachers in schools of this kind are dissatisfied and wish to move to schools where 'working conditions' will be more satisfactory.

Career movement for the Chicago teacher is, in essence, movement from one school to another, some schools being more and others less satisfactory places in which to work. Such movement is accomplished under the Board of Education's rules governing transfer, which allow a teacher, after serving in a position for more than a year, to request transfer to one of as many as ten other positions. Movement to one of these positions is possible when an opening occurs for which there is no applicant whose request is of longer standing, and transfer takes place upon approval by the principal of the new school.

The career patterns which are to be found in this social matrix are not expected to be typical of all career movements of this horizontal type. It is likely that their presence will be limited to occupational organizations which, like the Chicago school system, are impersonal and bureaucratic and in which mobility is accomplished primarily through the manipulation of formal procedures.

II

The greatest problems of work are found in lower-class schools and, consequently, most movement in the system is a result of dissatisfaction with the social-class composition of these school populations. Movement in the system, then, tends to be out from the 'slums' to the 'better' neighborhoods, primarily in terms of the characteristics of the pupils. Since there are few or no requests for transfer to 'slum' schools, the need for teachers is filled by the assignment to such schools of teachers beginning careers in the Chicago system. Thus, the new teacher typically begins her career in the least desirable kind of school. From this beginning two major types of careers were found to develop.

The first variety of career is characterized by an immediate attempt to move to a 'better' school in a 'better' neighborhood. The majority of interviewees reporting first assignment to a 'slum' school had already made or were in the process of making such a transfer. The attitude is well put in this quotation:

When you first get assigned you almost naturally get assigned to one of those poorer schools, because those naturally are among the first to have openings because people are always transferring out of them to other schools. Then you go and request to be transferred to other schools nearer your home or in some nicer neighborhood. Naturally the vacancies don't come as quickly in those schools because people want to stay there once they get there. I think that every teacher strives to get into a nicer neighborhood.

Making a successful move of this kind is contingent on several factors. First, one must have fairly precise knowledge as to which schools are 'good' and which are not, so that one may make requests wisely. Without such knowledge, which is acquired through access to the 'grapevine', what appears to be a desirable move may prove to be nothing more than a jump from the frying pan into the fire, as the following teacher's experience indicates:

When I put my name down for the ten schools I put my name down for one school out around —— ('nice' neighborhood). I didn't know anything about it, what the principal was like or anything, but it had a short list. Well, I heard later from several people that I had really made a mistake. They had a principal there that was really a terror. She just made it miserable for everyone. . . .

But I was telling you about what happened to me. Or almost did. After I had heard about this principal, I heard that she was down one day to observe me. Well, I was really frightened. If she had taken me I would have been out of luck, I would have had to stay there a year. But she never showed up in my room. . . . But, whatever it was, I was certainly happy that I didn't have to go there. It just shows that you have to be careful about what school you pick.

Second, one must not be of an ethnic type or have a personal reputation which will cause the principal to use his power of informal rejection. Though a transferee may be rejected through formal bureaucratic procedure, the principal finds it easier and less embarrassing to get the same result through this method, described by a Negro teacher:

All he's got to do is say, 'I don't think you'll be very happy at our school'. You take the hint. Because if the principal decides you're going to be unhappy, you will be, don't worry. No question about that. He can fix it so that you have every discipline problem in the grade you're teaching right in your room. That's enough to do it right there. So it really doesn't pay to go if you're not wanted. You can fight it if you want, but I'm too old for that kind of thing now.

This has the effect of destroying the attractive qualities of the school to which transfer was desired and of turning choice in a new direction.

Finally, one must be patient enough to wait for the transfer to the 'right' school to be consummated, not succumbing to the temptation to transfer to a less desirable but more accessible school:

When I got assigned to —— (Negro school) for instance, I went right downtown and signed on ten lists in this vicinity. I've lived out here for twenty-five years and I expect to stay here, so I signed for those schools and decided I'd wait ten years if necessary, till I found a vacancy in the vicinity.

The majority of teachers have careers of this type, in which an initial stay in an undesirable 'slum' school is followed by manipulation of the transfer system in such a way as to achieve assignment to a more desirable kind of school.

Thirteen of the interviewees, however, had careers of a different type, characterized by a permanent adjustment to the 'slum' school situation. These careers were the product of a process of adjustment to the particular work situation, which, while operating in all schools, is seen most clearly where it has such a radical effect on the further development of the career, tying the teacher to a school which would otherwise be considered undesirable. The process begins when the teacher, for any of a number of possible reasons, remains in the undesirable school for a number of years. During this stay changes take place in the teacher and in the character of her relations with other members of the school's social structure which make this unsatisfactory school an easier place in which to work and which change the teacher's view of the benefits to be gained by transferring elsewhere. Under the appropriate circumstances, a person's entire career may be spent in one such school.

During this initial stay changes take place in the teacher's skills and attitudes which ease the discomfort of teaching at the 'slum' school. First, she learns new teaching and disciplinary techniques which enable her to deal adequately with 'slum' children, although they are not suited for use with other social-class groups:

Technically, you're not supposed to lay a hand on a kid. Well, they don't, technically. But there are a lot of ways of handling a kid so that it doesn't show – and then it's the teacher's word against the kid's, so the kid hasn't got a chance. Like dear Mrs G –. She gets mad at a kid, she takes him out in the hall. She gets him stood up against the wall. Then she's got a way of chucking the kid under the chin, only hard, so that it knocks his head back against the wall. It doesn't leave a mark on him. But when he comes back in that room he can hardly see straight, he's so knocked out.

Further, the teacher learns to revise her expectations with regard to the amount of material she can teach and learns to be satisfied with a smaller accomplishment; a principal of a 'slum' school described such an adjustment on the part of her teachers:

Our teachers are pretty well satisfied if the children can read and do simple number work when they leave here. . . . They're just trying to get these basic things over. So that if the children go to high school they'll be able to make some kind of showing and keep their heads above water.

She thus acquires a routine of work which is customary, congenial, and predictable to the point that any change would require a drastic change in deep-seated habits.

Finally, she finds for herself explanations for actions of the children which she has previously found revolting and immoral, and these explanations allow her to 'understand' the behavior of the children as human, rather than as the activity of lunatics or animals:

I finally received my permanent assignment at E –. That's that big colored school. Frankly, I wasn't ready for anything like that. I thought I'd go crazy those first few months I was there. I wasn't used to that kind of restlessness and noise. The room was never really quiet at all. There was always a low undertone, a humming, of conversation, whispering, and shoving. . . . I didn't think I would ever be able to stand it. But as I came to understand them, then it seemed different. When I could understand the conditions they were brought up in, the kind of family life and home background that they had, it seemed more natural that they should act that way. And I really kind of got used to it after awhile.

At the same time that these changes are taking place in the teacher's perspectives, she is also gradually being integrated into the network of social relations that make up the school in such a way as to ease the problems associated with the 'slum' school. In the first place, the teacher, during a long stay in a school, comes to be accepted by the other teachers as a trustworthy equal and acquires positions of influence and prestige in the informal colleague structure. These changes make it easier for her to maintain her position of authority *vis-à-vis* children and principal. Any move from the school would mean a loss of such position and its advantages and the need to win colleague acceptance elsewhere.

Second, the problem of discipline is eased when the teacher's reputation for firmness begins to do the work of maintaining order for her: 'I have no trouble with the children. Once you establish a reputation and they know what to expect, they respect you and you have no trouble. Of course, that's different for a new teacher, but when you're established that's no problem at all.'

Finally, problems of maintaining one's authority in relation to parents lessen as one comes to be a 'fixture' in the community and builds up stable and enduring relationships with its families: 'But, as I say, when you've been in that neighbourhood as long as I have everyone knows you, and you've been into half their homes, and there's never any trouble at all.'

The 'slum' school is thus, if not ideal, at least bearable and predictable for the teacher who has adjusted to it. She has taken the worst the situation has to offer and has learned to get along with it. She is tied to the school by the routine she has developed to suit its requirements and by the relationships she has built up with others in the school organization. These very adjustments cause her, at the same time, to fear a move to any new school, which would necessitate a rebuilding of these relationships and a complete reorganization of her work techniques and routine. The move to a school in a 'better' neighborhood is particularly feared, desirable as it seems in the abstract, because the teacher used to the relative freedom of the 'slum' school is not sure whether the advantages to be gained in such a move would not be outweighed by the constraint imposed by 'interfering' parents and 'spoiled' children and by the difficulties to be encountered in integrating into a new school structure. This complete adjustment to a particular work situation thus acts as a brake on further mobility through the system.

III

Either of these career patterns results, finally, in the teacher's achieving a position in which she is more or less settled in a work environment which she regards as predictable and satisfactory. Once this occurs, her position and career are subject to dangers occasioned by ecological and administrative events which cause radical changes in the incumbents of important positions in the school structure.

Ecological invasion of a neighborhood produces changes in the social-class group from which pupils and parents of a given school are recruited. This, in turn, changes the nature and intensity of the teacher's work problems and upsets the teacher who has been accustomed to working with a higher status group than the one to which she thus falls heir. The total effect is the destruction of what was once a satisfying place in which to work, a position from which no move was intended:

I've been at this school for about twenty years. It was a lovely school when I first went there. ... Of course, the neighborhood has changed quite a bit since I've been there. It's not what it used to be.

The neighborhood used to be ninety, ninety-five per cent Jewish. Now I don't think there are over forty per cent Jews. The rest are Greek, Italian, a few Irish, it's pretty mixed now. And the children aren't as nice as they used to be.

Ecological and demographic processes may likewise create a change in the age structure of a population which causes a decrease in the number of teachers needed in a particular school and a consequent loss of the position in that school for the person last added to the staff. The effect of neighborhood invasion may be to turn the career in the direction of adjustment to the new group, while the change in local age structure may turn the career back to the earlier phase, in which transfer to a 'nicer' school was sought.

A satisfactory position may also be changed for the worse by a change in principal through transfer or retirement. The departure of a principal may produce changes of such dimension in the school atmosphere as to force teachers to transfer elsewhere. Where the principal has been a major force upholding the teachers' authority in the face of attacks by children and parents, a change can produce a disastrous increase in the problems of discipline and parental interference:

I'm tempted to blame most of it on our new principal. . . (the old principal) kept excellent order. Now the children don't seem to have the same feeling about this man. They're not afraid of him, they don't respect him. And the discipline in the school has suffered tremendously. The whole school is less orderly now.

This problem is considered most serious when the change takes place in a 'slum' school in which the discipline problem has been kept under control primarily through the efforts of a strict principal. Reactions to such an event, and consequent career development, vary in schools in different social-class areas. Such a change in a 'slum' school usually produces an immediate and tremendous increase in teacher turnover. A teacher who had been through such an experience estimated that faculty turnover through transfer rose from almost nothing to 60 per cent or more during the year following the change. Where the change takes place in a 'nicer', upper-middle-class school, teachers are reluctant to move and give up their hard-won positions, preferring to take a chance on the qualities of the new incumbent. Only if he is particularly unsatisfying are they likely to transfer.

Another fear is that a change in principals will destroy the existing allocation of privilege and influence among the teachers, the new principal failing to act in terms of the informal understandings of the teachers with regard to these matters. The following quotations describe two new principals who acted in this fashion:

He knows what he wants and he does it. Several of the older teachers have tried to explain a few things to him, but he won't have any part of it. Not that they did it in a domineering way or anything, but he just doesn't like that.

He's a goodhearted man, he really means well, but he simply doesn't know anything about running a school. He gets things all mixed up, listens to people he shouldn't pay any attention to. . . . Some people assert themselves and tell him what to do, and he listens to them when he shouldn't.

These statements are the reaction of more strongly intrenched, 'older' teachers who depend greatly for their power on their influence with the principal. Their dissatisfaction with a new principal seldom affects their careers to the point of causing them to move to another school. On the other hand, the coming of a new principal may be to the great advantage of and ardently desired by younger, less influential teachers. The effect of such an event on the career of a younger teacher is illustrated in this quotation:

I was ready to transfer because of the old principal. I just couldn't stand it. But when this new man came in and turned out to be so good, I went downtown and took my name off the transfer list. I want to stay there now. . . . Some of those teachers have been there as long as thirty years, you see, and they feel like they really own the place. They want everything done their way. They always had things their way and they were pretty mad when this new principal didn't take to all their ideas.

Any of these events may affect the career, then, in any of several ways, depending on the state of the career development at the time the event occurs. The effect of any event must be seen in the context of the type of adjustment made by the individual to the institutional organization in which she works.

IV

This paper has demonstrated the existence, among Chicago schoolteachers, of what has been called a 'horizontal' plane of career strivings and movements and has traced the kind of career patterns which occur, at this level, in a public bureaucracy where movement is achieved through manipulation of formal procedures. It suggests that studies of other occupations, in which greater emphasis on vertical movement may obscure the presence and effects of such horizontal mobility, might well direct their attention to such phenomena.

Further research might also explore in detail the relations between the horizontal mobility discussed here and the vertical mobility more prominent in many occupations. Studies in a number of occupations might give us answers to questions like this: To what extent, and under what circumstances, will a person forego actions which might provide him with a better working situation at one level of an occupational hierarchy in the hope of receiving greater rewards through vertical mobility? Hall notes that those doctors who become members of the influential 'inner fraternity' undergo a 'rigorous system of selection, and a system of prolonged apprenticeship. The participants in the system must be prepared to expect long delays before being rewarded for their loyalty to such a system.' We see that the rewards of eventual acceptance into this important group are attractive enough to keep the fledgling doctor who is apprenticed to it from attempting other ways of bettering his position. Turning the problem around, we may ask to what extent a person will give up possible vertical mobility which might interfere with the successful adjustment he has made in terms of horizontal career movement. A suggestion as to the kinds of relationships and processes to be found here comes from the following statement made by a high-school teacher with regard to mobility within the school system:

That's one reason why a lot of people aren't interested in taking principal's exams. Supposing they pass and their first assignment is to some school like M – or T –. And it's likely to be at some low-class colored school like that, because people are always dying to get out of schools like that. ... Those schools are nearly always vacant, so that you have a very good chance of being assigned there when you start in. A lot of people I know will say, 'Why should I leave a nice neighborhood like Morgan Park or South Shore or Hyde Park to go down to a school like that?' ... These guys figure, 'I should get mixed up with something like that? I like it better where I am.'

Finally, we have explored the phenomenon of adjustment to a particular work situation in terms of changes in the individual's perspectives and social relationships and have noted the way in which such adjustment acted to tie the individual to the particular situation and to make it difficult for him to consider movement to another. We may speculate as to the importance and effects of such a process in the vertical mobility prominent in many occupations. One further research problem might be suggested: what are the social mechanisms which function in occupations where such adjustment is not allowed to remain undisturbed, to bridge the transition between work situations, to break the ties binding the individual to one situation, and to effect a new adjustment elsewhere?

Part Seven Crime and Deviance

The choice of readings we have made in this part does not attempt to deal systematically with all the angles from which the study of crime and deviance may be approached. There are many theories which aim to account for the distribution of deviant behaviour, and many empirical studies not represented here.

Our aim has been to concentrate attention on a particular way of conceiving of crime and deviance which may be rather different from commonsense approaches to the emotionally and politically loaded subject of what is commonly described as 'criminal', 'anti-social', or 'deviant' behaviour. The common thread running through the extracts is the attempt to understand deviance not merely from the point of view of those who observe and possibly condemn it, but also from the point of view of those who participate in it.

Matza (Reading 36) shows, indeed, how difficult it is to arrive at a hard and fast definition of what is to count as 'deviance'. Behaviour which is tolerated in one generation, may not be tolerated in the next. Behaviour which is *required* in one cultural context, is *unacceptable* in another. There is thus a very large degree of cultural variability in norms. Even if we agree with Aubert that deviance is 'conduct contrary to the prevailing norms of a group or system', many issues remain to be clarified. We need to ask questions like, 'What *are* the norms of a group?', 'How are these norms discovered, enacted, and enforced?', 'What sanctions are available for the group to use in enforcing these norms?', 'Who decides what is to count as deviant and what as normal?', 'If behaviour occurs which appears to violate a norm, what criteria are used in order to determine whether it actually does?'

As Matza remarks 'one man's deviation may be another's custom', and it may be that a nominal definition is, initially at any rate, the most useful. For deviance occurs within any society: it is, as Matza points out, a 'normal and inevitable part of social life'. Whenever and wherever laws are made by society, the possibility of deviance is thereby created. Moreover, laws are enacted to deal with forms of behaviour which are defined as deviant, but once this unacceptable behaviour is brought under control or becomes acceptable, society discovers *new* forms of behaviour to stigmatize as deviant.

Deviant and correctional behaviour are often much closer than we often realize. As Matza shows, the two kinds of behaviour overlap. He further observes that deviant behaviour itself is essentially normal – 'deviation [. . .] needs no extraordinary accounting. Straying from a path need be regarded as no less comprehensible nor more bewildering than walking it. Given the moral character of social life, both *naturally* happen, and thus are pondered and studied by sociologists and others.'

This approach to deviance obviously requires a clear statement of exactly how, and by using what kind of methods, the phenomena are to be identified and studied. Matza quotes Becker with approval when the latter asserts that 'if [the researcher] is to get an accurate and complete account of what deviants do [. . .] he must spend at least some time observing them in their natural habitat as they go about their ordinary activities'. By looking at the deviant culture with the eyes of an anthropologist studying an alien non-literate society, Matza argues, the student can become familiar with the way of life that is actually *lived* by his subjects, and may avoid the temptation to categorize their behaviour in advance as pathological. 'We ought not,' Becker declares 'to view [deviant behaviour] as something special, as depraved, or in some magical way better than other kinds of behaviour. We ought to see it simply as a kind of behaviour some disapprove of and others value, studying the processes by which either or both perspectives are built up and maintained. Perhaps the best surety against either extreme is close contact with the people we study' (p. 176).

This way of studying deviance is by no means new: it was practised, for example, in the classic works of the Chicago School of the 1920s, and by W. F. Whyte later, who immersed himself in the life of a slum area of a large American city. This led him to appreciate that slum life, contrary to the popular view of it, was not characterized by 'social disorganization'. Although the standards of behaviour were different from those obtaining in 'middle-class' society, none the less the slum dwellers had a very clear, if not rigid code of morality, which their behaviour conformed with in practice (Reading 37).

In relations with the opposite sex, for instance, they differentiated between the 'lays' and the 'good girls'. This categorization of women is closely related to basic values and understandings about the institution of marriage and the marriageability of the 'good girls'. It was these internalized sentiments, rather than the fear of being 'found out', which regulated the sexual activities of Whyte's informants. These norms provided standards of conduct which differed according to the particular category in which a girl had been placed. Thus, although one man – Danny – feels he can gain status by telling a story about an incident in which he takes advantage of a prostitute by a rather mean trick, the same man also feels he has acted correctly by refusing to take advantage of a virgin even when a most favourable opportunity presents itself.

Thus Whyte makes us see that behaviour which may appear to be 'deviant' or 'without standards' according to the norms of 'middle-class' morality, is in fact very closely, almost minutely, controlled by a moral code.

Bensman and Gerver report (Reading 38) from another area of social life – the factory. This analysis is in part a critique of simple-minded functionalist explanations which assume that deviant behaviour must essentially be inimical to a social system. They discuss a type of industrial 'crime' which is, in a sense, intrinsic to the system. Deviant actions are not therefore a separate and readily identifiable category of actions and indeed many actions cannot be unambiguously defined as deviant. The authors discuss the way a special tool – the 'tap' – is used to cut new threads into nuts used in aircraft assembly. The object of this – 'illegal' – exercise is to bring the nut and its corresponding bolt (and thereby two sections of the wing) into a forced alignment. This is done because these components had been incorrectly aligned previously.

This action was 'deviant' in two senses. Firstly, there was a management rule explicitly forbidding the use of the 'tap', because the practice introduced strain into the wing and hence made it more liable to give way. The management were supported in this by the customer, in this case the Air Force, who introduced their own team of inspectors to detect instances of 'tapping'. Secondly, the practice ran counter to the values of good craftsmanship among the workers.

Yet the researchers found that the 'tap' was widely used on the shop-floor, although its use was closely restricted by the operation of informal understandings. For instance, only workmen who had attained a certain level of competence and seniority – craftsmen – were permitted to use it, and new recruits were not allowed to do so until they had demonstrated sufficient skill and ability. To account for this, Bensman and Gerver introduce the concept of 'institutional schizophrenia' by which they mean that the institution's goals are in conflict, and consequently the means of attaining these ends also in conflict. There is a conflict also between ends which are 'public' and those which are 'private'. For instance, although the management publicly outlawed tapping, they nonetheless supplied workers with instruments – tap extractors – so that they could extract taps which broke off inadvertently.

Again, if the management were inconsistent so were workers: as craftsmen, they defined the practice of tapping as 'bad workmanship' but as wage-earners interested in maximizing production and income by meeting quotas, they treated the same practice as both 'reasonable' and 'efficient'. In the same way the foreman, whose job it was to 'get the work out', and who were subject to considerable pressures from above to get it out, were in the same ambivalent position about evading the publicly declared rules.

Thus, whether or not 'tapping' appears to be 'deviant' or 'normal' depends on which hat the participant is wearing at the particular time. Hence employees *at all levels in the organization* developed an informal system of controls which served to reduce the visibility of their 'deviance' to the Air Force inspectorate which was attempting to enforce a rule which the employees themselves fundamentally agreed with.

Once the nature of the goals and interests of those concerned in deviant activity and the pressures upon them is appreciated, a greater understanding of their behaviour is acquired and the vendor, like the rule-breakers themselves, feels less confident in labelling such behaviour as 'deviance'. Geis (Reading 39) brings home this realization with reference to law-breaking, the violation of enacted legislation, in this case the crime of conspiracy, committed by large organizations, or rather by executives employed in large organizations. This is a crime so massive in its intent and its implications that it seems almost misleading to discuss it in the same terms as the individual deviations we have examined so far. However, the lawyer defending those accused of acts in violation of the anti-trust statutes attempted to excuse his clients by pointing out that their high social status meant that they were not 'real criminals'.

Geis interprets the behaviour, without excusing it, in terms of the conflicts of values; between the free enterprise ethic of competition and the free movement of prices, on the one hand, and the organization's belief, on the other, that collusion was the only way to maintain a 'balanced' market situation, ensuring each company a share of the market proportional to that which it had achieved previously.

One executive crystallized this ambivalent attitude by pointing out with nice irony 'It is the only way business can be run. It's free enterprise.' This remark illustrates the offenders' need to 'rationalize their behaviour in a manner in keeping with their image of themselves as law-abiding, decent and respectable persons'. Thus Geis shows how this 'deviant' behaviour is guided by motives which are generally rewarded in industry and which are associated with an attempt to create the conditions of market security and predictability. Many forms of 'respectable' bureaucratic organization are established precisely to achieve these goals. Here Geis illustrates how the cardinal virtues of initiative, enterprise and competition can encourage not only praiseworthy performance but also illegal activities.

This research strategy of adopting the 'inside' perspective on deviance depends a great deal on the researcher's willingness to empathize or feels his way into the positions of those who do break the rules. Becker has complained about many studies of delinquency that:

Very few tell us in detail what a juvenile delinquent does in his daily round of activity and what he thinks about himself, society, and his activities [. . .] One consequence is the construction of faulty or inadequate theories. Just as we need precise anatomical description of animals before we can begin to theorise and experiment with their physiological and biochemical functioning, just so we need precise and detailed descriptions of social anatomy before we know just what phenomena are present to be theorised about.

One of the main concerns of sociology, ever since the days of the Chicago School, has been to build up basic ethnographic descriptions of 'deviant' groups and their members, such as those Goffman mentions, when he refers to sub-communities of 'prostitutes, drug addicts, criminals, jazz musicians, bohemians, gypsies, fairground workers, hobos, winos, show people, full-time gamblers, beach-dwellers, homosexuals, and the urban unrepentant poor'.

One of the earliest and most influential accounts of the career of a young criminal was Clifford Shaw's *The Jack-Roller*. This study had its starting-point in the relationship revealed by statistical research between high rates of delinquency and the slum milieux in which delinquents lived. But the factors which are associated statistically with the high delinquency rates – the problem family, the unstable home, the lower-class culture, the influence of poor-groups – are interpreted by Shaw in terms of their operation in the life-experiences of one person – Stanley, the jack-roller (Reading 40).

In Shaw's transcription of the young criminal's own account of his transition from truancy, through youthful delinquency, to capture, prison, recidivism, and subsequent graduation as a fully-fledged criminal, we follow the typical development of the 'career' of a deviant which has been repeated by thousands. We see the successive stages in the development of the social identity which society labels as 'criminal', and the way in which, in a sense, the criminal is *produced* by the society which abhors and fears criminality. And the career of this young man reveals him to be essentially 'normal' and 'ordinary' in a psychological sense.

This attempt to portray Stanley's life-experiences leads Shaw to examine the role of law-enforcement agencies in developing the deviant's attitues towards the wider society and towards the behaviour he is being punished for committing. To understand the career-pattern of the deviant we have to understand the way others react to him, once his rule-breaking is publicly revealed; how, in other words, he becomes stigmatized and what consequences follow from this.

The extract from Goffman (Reading 41) deals at greater length with the process of stigmatization. Central to his development of this concept is his account of the distinction between 'virtual' and 'actual' social identity. He argues that we can ascribe to any individual a set of expectations about the kind of person he may turn out to be. Thus we would commonly expect someone described to us as 'a doctor' in upper-class society in the United States to be White, Anglo-Saxon, and Protestant. It *should* follow that, for instance, he has also been to an 'Ivy League' university. Attributes which we ascribe to an individual, as Goffman puts it, 'in potential retrospect', form his *virtual social identity*. But in any particular case, the individual in question possesses a specific set of attitudes, which constitute his *actual* social identity. If we return to the example of the doctor, what are the likely consequences of our discovering that the doctor, although Anglo-Saxon, Protestant and Ivy League, is also Black? What is the first thing we notice about him? It is his *blackness*. In others words there is a discrepancy between his *virtual* social identity and his *actual* social identity. And this particular sort of discrepancy is such as in some way to reduce some people's valuation of the individual. It is incongruous with the stereotype they have previously held of what a person of that particular type *should* be, in order to qualify as a *proper, whole*, and *complete* person of that particular type. This discrepancy is what Goffman refers to as a *stigma*.

Goffman goes on to distinguish two separate classes of problem. One refers to those who have already been *discredited*: their stigma has been, as it were, publicly announced. The other refers to the *discreditable*, whose stigma is, in a sense, latent. The latter are vulnerable to becoming discredited, to the damaging disclosure that they possess a stigma.

Goffman argues that around each such attribute and its possession there develops a set of beliefs which constitute a 'stigma theory'. These theories have the function of justifying the practice of treating stigmatized individuals differently from others and of castigating them as outsiders. Thus around the possession of a black skin, in a racialist society, there are a set of beliefs which constitute the ideology of racism.

Similarly societies which rate individual achievement very greatly, and which see 'intelligence' as a significant factor in that achievement, are likely to develop theories which justify treating *stupidity* as a stigma. Thus 'stupid' becomes a term of abuse, and those who believe themselves to be stupid go to great lengths to hide the fact.

People who possess a stigma may become aware of this knowledge in different ways at different points of their lives. The implications of such a discovery will therefore also be different in each case. Thus the problem for the 'normal' person who *subsequently* acquires a stigma is a different one from that of the child who has been sheltered from the realization of what he now sees to be the 'truth'.

Such a realization marks the first stage in the moral career of the stigmatized individual. By referring to the 'moral career', Goffman is emphasizing certain crucial experiences of those who are stigmatized. These are the experiences which lead him to change his conception of himself. He must now reject the stigma theory if he is to develop a new identity and a new relationship with those in the same boat as himself.

The consequence of this 'unlearning' of the stigma theory is a positive identification with the 'sympathetic others' who form a new 'in-group'. For the stigmatized individual becomes aware of them as normal persons in every other way. Thus he 'learns who it is that he must now accept as his own', although he may still feel some ambivalence about his newfound associates initially. This ambivalence may persist, and he may oscillate in his attachment to his stigmatized fellows, or, at first, even reject them. But the process of learning that the members of such a group possess many 'normal' qualities which the stigma had previously overshadowed is important if he is to be in a position to receive moral support from the group.

For those whose status is 'discreditable', who have not yet been discredited, different problems are involved. This individual has to guard against the disclosure of the shameful secret, either deliberately or inadvertently. Consequently he has to attempt to manage the information about his social identity which he presents to others so that the risks of such a disclosure are minimized. Thus the major problem for the discreditable, who possess a stigma which he has been able to hide at all times, is to manage his appearance and maintain a front when in the company of normals. The discreditable person has to be constantly on his guard, and managing his problem may become a major preoccupation. Thus in a society with severe legal sanctions against homosexual behaviour, the 'discreditable' homosexual, who to all intents and purposes leads a 'normal' life, perhaps even to the extent of being married with children, may in fact be more preoccupied with managing his situation and concealing his stigma than the overt 'queer', who is visibly 'discredited'.

Goffman, throughout, emphasizes the crucial role played by others, and their reactions to those who possess a stigma. One implication for the study of deviance in general is that being labelled as a deviant implies a change of position and status for the person who is so labelled. This change may be a dramatic one, or it may be gradual. For many kinds of deviance, the labelling may be, to all intents and purposes, *irreversible*. It is the conceptions and actions of certain significant others which are central in this change of status.

This last point emerges very clearly from Sudnow's article (Reading 42) on 'normal' crimes. In this analysis, Sudnow investigates the meanings and definitions of deviant activities which are used by those who operate within the formal machinery of justice. His attention is focused on American criminal courts, the pivotal institution of the whole process by which people are labelled as 'deviant'.

Sudnow starts from the recognition that the vast majority of cases appearing before the law courts never 'go to trial' in the generally accepted sense of the term. In fact, the defendant is commonly found guilty of the offence with which he is charged, *on his own admission*. But the formally constituted machinery of criminal justice is based on the assumption that the defendant will plead his innocence of the offence, and that a *contest* will then ensue. Such a high incidence of guilty pleas might be explained by arguing that those who operate the court system have a vested interest in persuading people to plead guilty because it makes their work easier. Certainly if each and every defendant were to exercise his right to enter a plea of 'not guilty', an intolerable burden would be thrown on the court system.

In examining these processes, Sudnow argues that certain inducements are offered to the defendant to plead guilty. These consist typically of an offer to reduce the original charge to one which carries a lesser penalty. But charges cannot of course be reduced to just any other charge: these reductions operate within a regular pattern of precise, even if informal, understandings between the major parties to the court-room drama. The Public Defender, who represents clients who could not afford an attorney of their choice, and the District Attorney, who appears for the prosecution, operate a system of negotiated 'guilty' pleas. It is the informal understandings between them which explain the kinds of criteria according to which charges are *typically* reduced. In fact, there are quite explicit legal criteria based on the notions of 'necessary' and 'situational' inclusion (described below) of one crime in another which could provide a *rational* basis for the reductions. But these criteria are insufficient in themselves to enable the observer to predict what reductions are actually made in practice.

The Public Defender and the District Attorney in practice operate with conceptions of 'normal crimes'. They believe that certain legally-defined acts *typically* occur under certain specific circumstances, and that those who commit such acts possess certain *typical* attributes. This whole set of attributes, characteristics and situations are summarized into a shorthand formula – the concept of the 'normal crime'. If a particular offender and the offence with which he is charged can be included in the relevant category of normal crime, the Public Defender and the District Attorney will be willing to negotiate a guilty plea. Conversely, if a particular case cannot be seen as falling within a class of such cases of normal crime, the attempt to organize a reduction of the charge in return for a plea of 'guilty' will not be made.

One inference which we can draw from this kind of analysis is that an understanding of the processes which underlie formal legal proceedings is essential. If they are ignored, quite misleading conclusions about the incidence and frequency of 'crime' of various types can be drawn from official statistics relating to detected offenders.

Sudnow's article emphasizes the need to study those who activate and operate the process of labelling other people as deviants or criminals. Unless we do this we will never fully understand deviance, and neither will we be able to assess the significance of rates of deviance, such as crime statistics, or arrest or suicide rates. We must not, as many people do, take these at face value. They may not reveal the 'real' volume and types of crime and suicide. Nor will those who are detected and labelled as criminals necessarily be a representative cross-section of all law-breakers.

Before we can really make any sense of such statistics it is necessary, as Sudnow's article demonstrates, to focus our attention on the decisions and activities of those who produce them. As our first selection by Lemert (Reading 43) explains, it is not always as simple as we imagine to decide whether or not someone has broken a rule and whether we should treat that person thereafter as a deviant. The meaning of other people's actions may be ambiguous and the appropriate response consequently difficult to determine at first. As Lemert argues, 'it is impossible to determine what is regarded as normal or deviant behaviour merely by inspecting its external features'. A man who pats the knee of another male several times during the course of a conversation is more likely to be suspected of having homosexual tendencies if he is a confirmed bachelor with an effeminate appearance, than is the tough rugby-playing type who does *the same thing*.

What we have to study therefore, is the total situation where the parties meet and the rules and understandings which form the background to the encounter between the person who is acting 'strangely' and the observer.

It does not follow necessarily that when the behaviour of the other person is not in keeping with the observer's expectations he will define that person as a deviant. The observer may prefer to alter his definition of that behaviour, placing a new interpretation upon it. For example, in one case studied, a wife did not initially accept that her husband was mentally ill when he started to act in bizarre ways. Instead she 'normalized' his behaviour by interpreting it in the light of his war experience, the job he did which led him to 'live on his nerves', and in terms of the fact that he had always been a 'nervous' person.

Lemert raises these points on 'normalization' and the problematic response to others' actions, in the context of his discussion of primary and secondary deviation. Perhaps the most useful aspect of this distinction is the fact that it draws our attention to what happens to someone after he has been labelled as an Outsider, i.e., after being stigmatized.

Such a person may well go on to act in ways which deviate even further from the expectations of others. He may *compound* his deviance. In other words, in responding to the conditions society has created in its reactions to his original 'failings'. The irony of the situation is clear. His continued deviance only confirms the view of those who originally branded him as 'untrustworthy', 'criminally disposed' or 'mentally ill'. Moreover it justifies the continued treatment of him as that sort of person. In this way the stigma-theory (the rationalizations and ideologies which 'justify' society's response) is validated. But the pathos lies in the fact that the behaviour which validates society's response, was created by that self-same response!

It is essential that we try to distinguish the original rule-breaking and its consequences, from later deviance which is a reaction to the way society has dealt with the deviant in the first place. The last two sections make this point forcefully.

Lemert (Reading 44) explains why stuttering has been found among the Pacific Coastal Indians, when earlier researchers had been unable to find any evidence of this type of speech disorder among other tribes of North American Indians. Lemert suggests that the reason for this is to be found in the cultural emphasis which was put, in the Pacific Coastal tribes only, upon performance at feasts and other ritual ceremonies. Performers had to demonstrate their competence on such occasions if they wished to win public approval and maintain their status in society. Parents were extremely concerned that their offspring should prove capable of learning the appropriate behaviour and become skilled performers. Anything which detracted from this became a source of anxiety and attempts were made to correct it.

Lemert argues that stuttering arises as a consequence of these preoccupations and attempted remedies. What might well have been treated as 'normal' variations of speech patterns in other societies, were severely stigmatized and became a source of shame for the child and his immediate family. The effects of parental concern and anxiety and the reactions of others such as teasing, were often recognized by members of these tribes themselves. 'It seems to make them worse: they do more and more funny things', one man remarked.

Stuttering represents a secondary response to this social climate; according to Lemert it is not a manifestation of, or even caused by, the original speech defect.

Our last selection, which deals with drug addiction, was chosen because it demonstrates how the ideas we have been discussing could be useful in developing more informed policies for dealing with drug addiction.

Schur (Reading 45) begins by challenging the stigma theory, the 'dope-fiend myth', which so often influences the way we think about addicts. On the basis of the medical evidence, he suggests that various patterns of behaviour commonly believed to be typical of addicts are in fact extremely unlikely to occur, because of the effect of these drugs on the body's metabolism. For example, addicts are unlikely to be 'sex-fiends' because the drug inhibits the sexual appetite. Moreover, by empathizing with the addict and understanding the way he uses and experiences the drug, Schur challenges the view that persons who are addicted, take drugs for the thrills these provide. Once the addict has learned that withdrawal from the drug is a terrible experience, he comes to define the drug as something he needs in order 'to keep well' – i.e., it is seen as contributing to his health balance, not as an extreme or exotic experience.

Keeping in mind the meaning of drug-use to the addict himself, and his desperate need for drugs, we can trace the consequences of a policy which makes unauthorized possession of drugs illegal. A black market situation is created, the price of drugs is maintained at a high level and consequently addicts are forced to compound their deviance, for instance by stealing to finance their addictions. To maintain a fairly regular source of supply, they are forced to win the confidence of those who traffic in drugs, and have to organize their lives so as to ensure that they are around when a supply becomes available.

Owing to the legal penalties and the black market situation, the addict is drawn into a sub-culture which provides him with a new self-conception and new justifications for his behaviour and thus further removes him from conventional society. This sense of alienation is likely to be reinforced by a feeling of injustice created by the knowledge, and perhaps the experience, of police malpractices which can arise due to the difficulties of enforcing this kind of legislation.

When we look at the problem of drug addiction, therefore, Schur, like Lemert, reminds us that we must separate the original effects of the drug from those characteristics displayed by addicts which are not caused by the action of the drug, but by the reactions of society to drugs and to drug-users. Although Schur's article refers, in the main, to the American situation, the reader might consider how far Britain has recently moved away from a relatively benign policy to one which is closer to the American approach to drug addiction.

Given the fact that there is a very high relapse rate, and that present attempts at cure are largely unsuccessful, how many of us would be prepared to support the addict and allow him to persist in his addiction? Are we prepared to forsake the ideal of *curing* him?

The answers one gives to such questions about this particular form of deviant behaviour will depend in part upon wider attitudes to deviance in general. The following excerpts have been selected in order to help the reader arrive at his own conclusions in the light of some of the more thoughtful contributions in this field.

36 David Matza

Becoming Deviant

Excerpt from David Matza, *Becoming Deviant*, Prentice-Hall, 1969, pp. 10–14.

One may make a fetish of definitions. Except when needing a term that has been used otherwise, I prefer to make little of them, at least in the beginning when a *nominal* definition will suffice. A nominal definition is one that is not too outlandish, one that will facilitate and not hamper meaningful discourse. Since no further use, such as 'generating propositions', is contemplated, premature elaboration or esoteric usage serves little purpose. Indeed, such elaboration or usage would discourage the reader because his capacity to survive conceptual discussion depends on whether he has first been exposed to the concrete.

According to any standard dictionary – still the best source of clearly stated nominal definitions – to deviate is to *stray*, as from a path or standard. If one delights in such a pursuit, he may classify the forms of straying according to a number of ready-made criteria: the clarity of the path, the distance from the path, the auspices under which the path is constructed or commended, whether one strays from the path in isolation or in company, the penalty, the motives commonly imputed for straying, or (what usually comes to the same thing) the academic discipline currently claiming learned jurisdiction over the souls of those who stray. But when all is said and done, we inevitably return to the wise observation that there are many kinds of deviation and that deviation is in some measure a matter of degree. At the nominal level, nothing more can be said, though that much can be said in surprisingly extended detail.

Whatever the conception of standard or path, occasional phenomena existing at the border are readily observable. When these lie at the margin of deviant or conventional realms, the very designation, *deviant*, is dubious. Such uncertainty is troublesome for those who abhor sloppiness, but, in truth, the difficulty resides in the nature of society not in the conception of deviation. Cultural definitions, especially in contemporary society, tend toward ambiguity. Since standards shift, members of society may respond to marginal phenomena with open ambiguity, or, if there is reason to be guarded, with a certain shiftiness.

Students of society must tolerate such ambiguity. Finely drawn and strictly operational conceptions leaving no place for ambiguity may be a source of satisfaction for the analyst, but he will find that ordinary subjects of inquiry have the capacity to subvert such conceptions and render them useless. Whether the phenomenon personified, say, by a waitress in topless attire is deviant is a question that will yield a clear-cut answer if our concept of deviation is sufficiently rigorous and operational. But the clear-cut yes or no will be gained only by suppressing, and thus denying, the patent ambiguity of this novel phenomenon and the easily observable tentative, vacillating, and shifty responses to it. Accordingly, the cost of rigor may be deemed excessive since certainty in classifying the phenomenon as deviant or not is accomplished through the dubious expedient of restricting our view of compelling and relevant social facts – ambiguity and shift.

There is another aspect of this problem. In a pluralistic society, one man's deviation may be another's custom. Or as Parsons puts its:

There is a certain relativity in the conceptions of conformity and deviance. ... It is not possible to make a judgment of deviance ... without specific reference to the system ... to which it applies. The structure of normative patterns in any but the simplest sub-system is always intricate and usually far from fully intergrated; hence singling out one such pattern without reference to its interconnections in a system of patterns can be very misleading.

Moreover, libertine and puritan traditions may divide even those segments of the population for whom the activity is not customary, yielding enormous differences in the level of toleration. In such societies, some phenomena will be sensed as morally complicated, defying easy classification. In short, there may be differences of opinion among ordinary members of society; that social fact affects even the most nominal of definitions. The social fact of pluralism, like that of ambiguity, must be lived with and appreciated. It cannot be evaded simply to expedite a rigorous definition of deviation. Shift, ambiguity, and pluralism are implicated in the very idea of deviation; their net effect is to make even our nominal conception inexact and blurred at the edges. The uncertainty cannot be liquidated; it can only be observed and reported.

When there is no authoritative resolution of differences regarding the moral status of a phenomenon, it is presumptuous, and perhaps even useless, to say anything more than that the point is moot. But often there *is* authoritative resolution. When there is, as in civil or criminal law, we may observe either laboriously or simply that the issue, the difference of opinion, has been painfully and tentatively resolved – though not to everyone's satisfaction. Thus, for instance, the moral status of waitresses in topless attire was tentatively and joyfully resolved in San Francisco, at least with respect to legality, but the ambiguity of the phenomenon remains, as do the plural and shifty responses to it. Both the authoritative resolution and the continuing disagreement are consequential and thus worth noting.

The appreciation of shift, ambiguity, and pluralism need hardly imply a wholesale repudiation of the idea of common morality. Such an inference is the mistake of a rampant and mindless relativism. Plural evaluation, shifting standards and moral ambiguity may, and do, coexist with a phenomenal realm that is *commonly sensed* as deviant. The very meaning of pluralism, the very possibility of shift and ambiguity depend on a wider consensus, founded in common understandings, regarding the patently deviant nature of many none the less ordinary undertakings. Thus, the deviant nature of many phenomena is hardly problematic, the best evidence being that no operative member of society bothers to develop a position one way or the other. Except for those who conjure a path whenever they see a company of strayers, it is clear to everyone – including the strayers – that commonly understood and commonly held deviations have occurred. Thieves – except perhaps for Genet and he who sanctified him – do not believe in stealing, though they engage in it, defensively justify it, and even develop a measure of expertise and sense of craft. Bullies do not believe in assaulting people though they, too, may cultivate, justify, and develop their special skill. Bastards are frowned on and derogated despite the fact that they are regularly spawned and variably tolerated. Thus there is little need to choose abstractly between a common, and perhaps natural, human morality and what has come to be known as cultural relativism.

Beyond this brief consideration of a nominal and simple conception of deviation and the inevitable difficulties in applying it to empirically problematic phenomena, elaboration would be misleading. To labor long is to imply inadvertently that there is something mysterious and slippery about the concrete phenomena to which the nominal conception points – and that is precisely the stance I wish to avoid. Instead, I want to assume that deviant phenomena are common and natural. They are a normal and inevitable part of social life, as is their denunciation, regulation, and prohibition. Deviation is implicit in the moral character of society: 'To give oneself laws and to create the possibility of disobeying them come to the same thing'.

That deviation is implicit in the idea of society was well-stated by Durkheim and has since been a matter of general consensus among sociologists. No matter what the measure of moral rectitude, deviation will occur. Moral improvement of a citizenry will not of itself diminish deviation since the very fact of moral uplift will suggest new and more demanding standards of conduct.

Imagine a society of saints, a perfect cloister of exemplary individuals. Crimes, properly so called, will there be unknown; but faults which appear venial to the laymen will create there the same scandal that the ordinary offense does in the ordinary consciousness. ... For the same reason, the perfect and upright man judges his smallest failings with a severity that the majority reserves for acts more truly in the nature of an offense. Formerly, acts of violence against persons were more frequent than they are today, because respect for individual dignity was less strong. As this has increased, these crimes have become more rare; and also, many acts violating this sentiment have been introduced into the penal law which were not included there in primitive times (e.g., calumny, insults, slander, fraud, etc.).

Thus, according to Durkheim, deviation is implicit in social and moral organization. When specific deviations are brought under control and reduced or obliterated, the category of deviation nonetheless survives. The demise of the specific deviation is coincident with the general elevation of the standards it violated. Consequently, phenomena that are more refined violations of the same general standards will emerge as new deviations. Durkheim's point here is not merely the thesis of relativism. It is more subtle, and more universal. His thesis rests on a coincidence between the decline in the prevalence of gross violations of the sentiment of individual dignity and the heightened morality of society experiencing that decline. A population experiencing heightened morality – a society of saints – will gradually come to see that insults and slander, too, are serious and actionable violations of individual dignity. Other precepts – minimality, for instance – may serve to limit or check the insatiable morality postulated by Durkheim. But even if checked and hampered by others, the lifting of standards and the survival of categories of deviation are tendencies, none the less.

Since deviation is a common feature of society, since it is implicit in social and moral organization, it needs no extraordinary accounting. Straying from a path need be regarded as no less comprehensible nor more bewildering than walking it. Given the moral character of social life, both *naturally* happen, and thus are pondered and studied by sociologists and others.

37 William Foote Whyte

A Slum Sex Code

Excerpt from W. F. Whyte, 'A slum sex code', *American Journal of Sociology*, vol. 49, July 1943, no. 1, pp. 24–31.

Respectable middle-class people have very definite standards of sex behavior. They are inclined to assume that behavior which does not conform to these standards is unorganized and subject to no set of ethics. It is my purpose to point out that, in one particular area commonly thought to be characterized by laxness of sex behavior, there is an elaborate and highly developed sex code. A study of the social and sex life of the slum will also yield certain clues as to the nature of the process of assimilation of an alien people into American society.

My information is based upon a three-and-a-half-year study of the Italian slum district of 'Cornerville' in 'Eastern City'. By discussions with a number of men in corner gangs, in which I was a participant observer, I was able to learn the sex code of the slum, as it appears to the corner boys.

The story must be told against a background of local social life. In peasant Italy, as in other peasant societies, the family group undertook to regulate the social and sexual relations of the children. Marriages were arranged by the parents of the couple, and no young man was allowed to visit a girl's home unless he had been accepted as her suitor. The influence of this system is still to be observed in Cornerville. Parents try to keep a strict watch upon their daughters. In most cases they are unable to arrange the marriage for their children, but they retain control over the home. The corner boy knows that if he once visits a girl in her home it will be assumed by her parents (and by everyone else) that he intends to marry her. Consequently, until he is completely sure of his own intentions, the corner boy remains outside of the house. He even hesitates to make a date with a girl for if he does take her out alone it is assumed that he is her 'steady'.

Dances given by local clubs mark the high point of the social activities. Except for those who are 'going steady', groups of men and groups of girls go separately to the dances. The man chooses his girl for each dance and, at the conclusion of the number, leaves her with her friends. There is no cutting in. When the dance is over, the men and women go home separately. Parties in a girl's home, picnics, evenings at the bowling alleys, and other social activities all tend to take this group form.

When a man centers his attention upon one girl, he arranges to meet her on the street corner. Good girls are not expected to 'hang' on the corner, but the men consider it perfectly respectable for them to keep appointments on the corner. Most parents object to this practice more or less strongly and try to insist that the man shall come to the home. The insistence of the parents and the reluctance of the corner boy place the girl in a difficult position. Of course, she herself may not wish to give the relationship the permanent form which a visit to the home would involve. If they work outside of the home, most girls are able to insist upon some right to govern their social relations; but this always involves friction with the parents, its seriousness depending upon the strength of parental control and the strenuousness of the daughter's efforts to gain independence.

The sex life of the corner boy begins when he is very young. One of them writes:

In Cornerville children ten years of age know most all the swear words and they have a good idea of what the word 'lay' means. Swearing and describing of sex relations by older people and by the boys that hang on the corner are overheard by little children and their actions are noticed and remembered. Many of the children when they are playing in the streets, doorways and cellars actually go through the motions which pertain to the word 'lay.' I have seen them going through these motions, even children under ten years of age.

Most all the boys that I know and all my friends carry safes [condoms]. Most boys start carrying safes when they are of high school age.

Safes are purchased from necktie salesmen as cheap as a dozen for fifty cents. Some boys buy them and then make a profit by selling them to the boys at school. You can get them in some of the stores around here.

The sex play of young boys is relatively unregulated. The code of sex behavior crystallizes only as the corner boys reach maturity.

Relations between corner boys and women cannot be described in uniform terms, since there are tremendous variations in behavior, depending upon the category in which the woman is placed and the man's qualifications for access to women of various categories. The local classification of women which is explicit or implicit in corner-boy attitudes and behavior may be represented in the three categories shown in the accompanying tabulation. The most highly valued type of woman is placed at the top of each category.

Sex experience	Physical attractiveness	Social- and ethnic-group position
1. 'Good' girls	Beautiful	1. Superior groups
2. 'Lays'		2. Italian nonslum
(a) One-man girls	to	3. Italian slum
(b) Promiscuous		
(c) Prostitutes	ugly	

One evening the corner boys were discussing a beautiful girl in the neighborhood. Danny said that he would take three months in any jail in the country, even Alcatraz, for the privilege of being in bed with her for eight hours. Doc said that Danny felt this was because the girl was a virgin. Danny agreed but added: 'I would take one week in any jail even if she was a lay; that's how good I think she is.' The difference between three months and one week strikingly illustrates the different valuations placed upon 'good girls' and 'lays'. Doc explained the desirablity of a virgin in this way: 'No one has been there before. You are showing her the way. It's a new discovery. . . . We all say we would like to lay a virgin, but we really wouldn't.'

The corner-boy code strongly prohibits intercourse with a virgin. Thus the most desirable of women is also the most inaccessible. A good girl may submit to a limited amount of kisses and caresses without compromising her reputation. She must not be a 'teaser' (one who attempts to excite the man as much as possible without granting him sexual access). The virginity of a 'teaser' is thought to be only a technicality, and if she is raped it serves her right. Otherwise a girl's virginity must be protected.

'Good girls' are the kind that one marries. A man who takes her virginity from a 'good girl', seriously affecting her marriageability, will marry her because he is responsible. The man who seeks to evade his responsibility, especially if he has made the girl pregnant, may be forced into marriage by the priest and the girl's parents. The alternative is going to jail and being held liable for the support of the child to the age of twenty-one.

While strong legal and institutional sanctions uphold virginity, corner boys do not abide by the code simply from fear of the consequences of violation. They have strong sentiments supporting the sanctity of virginity. It is felt that only the lowest type of man would have intercourse with a virgin.

If the ban on intercourse with virgins were never violated, the only nonvirgins would be girls who had had sex relations with men outside of the district. This is obviously not the case. Several stories indicate that some early-adolescent boys and girls introduce each other to sex activity.

William Foote Whyte 353

The young boy who has never had intercourse himself does not feel so strongly the protective attitude toward virgins that he will assume later. There are a few local men who break the rule, but the danger of entanglements within the district is so great that most such activity must be confined to outsiders. In any case a corner boy cannot admit having 'laid' a virgin without incurring the scorn of his fellows.

The corner boys believe that a man's health requires sexual intercourse at certain intervals. 'Good girls' are not available for this purpose, and even casual social relations with them are likely to lead to commitments and responsibilities that the man is not prepared to assume. The corner boy has much more freedom, and much less responsibility in dealing with 'lays'; freedom increases and responsibility decreases as he establishes relations lower down in this class.

From the standpoint of prestige and social advantage, the ideal girl in the 'lay' class is the one who will have sexual relations with only one man in one period, but there are great risks involved in such a relationship. As one corner boy said: 'If you go with a girl too long, even if she lays, you're bound to get to like her. That's human nature. I was going out with a girl, and I was banging her every date. After about four months, I saw I was really getting fond of the girl so I dropped her just like that.' While a man should marry only a good girl, he may become attached to the one-man girl and allow his emotions to override his judgment. Furthermore, if it is not widely known that the girl is a 'lay' and she consequently enjoys a good reputation, her family will be able to exert a good deal of pressure to force a marriage. If he makes her pregnant, marriage is hardly to be avoided.

The promiscuous girl is less desirable socially, but there is also less risk in having relations with her. Only pregnancy can impose a responsibility; and, since the identity of the father is difficult to prove, such entanglements may frequently be avoided.

In practice it is hard to distinguish between these two types of 'lays' because the promiscuous girl usually tries to pass herself off as a one-man 'lay' and one-man girls are constantly slipping into the lower category. Nevertheless, there is a real distinction in the mind of the corner boy and he acts differently according to his conception of the girl's sexual status. He talks freely about the promiscuous girl and is glad to share her with his friends. He keeps the higher type of 'lay' to himself, says little about his relations with her, and treats her with more respect. The reputation of the one-man 'lay' is not, however, permanently protected. If she breaks off with the corner boy and takes up with another man, the corner boy is likely to boast openly that he had her first.

The professional prostitute or 'hustler' is the least desirable of women.

I have heard some men advocate having relations with prostitutes on the ground that no social risk is involved; but generally the corner boys feel that to go to a house of prostitution would be to admit that they could not 'pick up' any girls. One corner boy expressed his opinion in this way:

I never go to a whore house. What do you get out of that? It's too easy. You just pay and go in and get it. Do you think the girl gets any fun out of that? ... I like to take a girl out and bull her into it [persuade her]. Then when you lay her, you know she's enjoying it too. ... And after you're through, you feel that you have accomplished something.

Another had this to say:

You might pay a hustler a dollar and that's all there is to it, it's a business proposition. If you pick up a girl, you may spend three to five dollars on food and drinks, but I'd rather do that any time. ... You figure, the other way, it's just a business proposition. When you go out with a girl that ain't a hustler, you figure, she must like you a little anyway or she wouldn't go out with you. A hustler will take any man she can get, but this girl is just for you tonight anyway. You take her out, have something to eat and drink, and you go for a ride, you begin muggin' her up, then you get in there. ... That's the way I like to do it. You're staking out new territory. You get the feeling you really done something when you get in there.

The corner boys make a distinction between a house of prostitution and a 'line-up'. In a line-up one of the men brings a prostitute to some room in the district and allows his friends to have intercourse with her, each man paying the girl for the privilege. While this is a commercial arrangement, nevertheless, it is handled by the boys themselves, and some who would not think of going to a house of prostitution are willing to participate with their friends in a line-up.

The code not only differentiates different types of women in corner-boy attitudes; it also involves strikingly different behavior with women of the different categories, as the following stories indicate.

Danny had picked up a 'hustler' and taken her to his gambling joint on the understanding that she would receive a dollar a man. When she was finished, he handed her an envelope containing the bills. She had counted the bills when he pretended to be alarmed and snatched the envelope away from her, replacing it in his pocket. She protested. Danny handed her another envelope of the same size which contained only slips of paper. She was satisfied and went away without looking into the envelope. Danny felt that he had played a clever trick upon the girl.

Doc told me another story about Danny:

There are some noble things down here, Bill. ... You take Danny's wife, as we call her. She goes to church all the time – what a good kid she is, and she's nice looking too. She goes for Danny. She wants to marry him. Now she goes for him so much that he could probably belt her if he wanted to. But he doesn't want to marry her. He hasn't a job to support a wife. So he stays away from her. . . . Then take Al Mantia. He was a hound. He was after women all the time. One time he and Danny went out with a girl – she said she was a virgin. She had one drink, and she was a little high. They were up in a room, and they had her stripped – stripped! She still said she was a virgin, but she wanted them to give her a belt. But they wouldn't do it. . . . Can you imagine that, Bill? There she was stripped, and they wouldn't do anything to her. . . . The next day she came around and thanked both of them. They can't be such bad fellows if they do that.

The Danny who spared the virgin is the same Danny who cheated the 'hustler'. In one case the code imposed a strong responsibility; in the other case no responsibility was involved.

38 Joseph Bensman and Israel Gerver

Crime and Punishment in the Factory:
The Function of Deviancy in Maintaining the Social System

Excerpts from Joseph Bensman and Israel Gerver, 'Crime and punishment in the factory: the function of deviancy in maintaining the social system', *American Sociological Review*, vol. 28, 1963, no. 4, pp. 588–98.

Since social life involves acceptance and rejection of proffered norms or expectancies, 'deviancy', i.e., deviant actions, are the expectable actions of individuals who have divergent ends, and of individuals who do not comply exclusively to others or those in authority but who sometimes comply to their self-expectancies.

Deviant actions thus are not a separate category of actions, defiant of the central ends of a total system, but are simply part of the totality of actions that make up the hundreds of individual transactions in an organization. With such a conception of 'social systems' it is unnecessary to have a 'clear definition' of the system or its parts. It is only necessary to describe the actions and interrelations of persons with respect to a common enterprise. Analytical description thus results in a different type of functionalism.

This Reading is a case study in the internal law of one organization [. . .] The violation of 'law' is specifically a rule of workmanship. For the sake of simplicity, the rules and their violations relevant to one instrument – the tap – are the subject of study. This is because the study of the tap summarizes an entire area of rules of workmanship and their violations. One could also have selected other violations of workmanship rules such as counter-sinking dimples, rolling of edges in fairing, stretching of metal skins, or greasing and waxing screw threads. The tap was selected as a major example because of its frequent usage, and because it is the most serious violation of rules of workmanship.

While suggesting the engineering complexity of the data, our theoretical interest is in the social function of crime, particularly violations of private organizational law.

The research was carried out in an airplane factory employing 26,000 people in the New York metropolitan area. One of the authors was a participant observer from September 1953 through September 1954. He gathered his data in the daily course of work while working as an assembler on the aileron crew of the final wing line. No special research instruments were used; the ordinary activities of workers along the line were observed and noted as they occurred, and recorded daily. All aspects involved in the use of the tap were discussed in the context of the work situation when they were relevant and salient to the personnel involved, and without their realizing that they were objects of study.

The tap and its functions

The tap is a tool, an extremely hard steel screw, whose threads are slotted to allow for the disposal of the waste metal which it cuts away. It is sufficiently hard so that when it is inserted into a nut it can cut new threads over the original threads of the nut.

In wing assembly work bolts or screws must be inserted in recessed nuts which are anchored to the wing in earlier processes of assembly. The bolt or screw must pass through a wing plate before reaching the nut. In the nature of the mass production process alignments between nuts and plate-openings become distorted. Original allowable tolerances become magnified in later stages of assembly as the number of alignments which must be coordinated with each other increase with the increasing complexity of the assemblage. When the nut is not aligned with the hole, the tap can be used to cut, at a new angle, new threads in the nut for the purpose of bringing the nut and bolt into a new but not true alignment. If the tap is not used and the bolt is forced, the wing plate itself may be bent. Such new alignments, however, deviate from the specifications of the blueprint which is based upon true alignments at every stage of the assembly process. On the basis of engineering standards true alignments are necessary at every stage in order to achieve maximum strength and a proper equilibrium of strains and stresses.

The use of the tap is the most serious crime of workmanship conceivable in the plant. A worker can be summarily fired for merely possessing a tap. Nevertheless, at least one-half of the work force in a position to use a tap owns at least one. Every well-equipped senior mechanic owns four or five of different sizes and every mechanic has access to and, if need be, uses them. In fact, the mass use of the tap represents a widespread violation of this most serious rule of workmanship.

The tap is defined as a criminal instrument, primarily because it destroys the effectiveness of stop nuts. Aviation nuts are specifically designed, so that, once tightened, a screw or bolt cannot back out of the nut under the impact of vibration in flight. Once a nut is tapped, however, it loses its holding power and at any time, after sufficient vibration, the screw or bolt can fall out and weaken the part it holds to the wing and the wing itself [...]

The tap, then, is an illegal tool, the use or possession of which carries extreme sanctions in private organizational law, but which is simultaneously widely possessed and used despite its illegal status. The problem of such a pattern for the meaning of private organizational law is to account for the wide acceptance of a crime as a means of fulfilling work requirements within a private organization, the aircraft plant.

The socialization of the worker

To most workers entering an aircraft plant the tap is an unknown instrument. Dies which thread bolts, i.e., the process opposite to tapping, are relatively well known and are standard equipment of the plumbing trade. The new worker does not come into this contact with the tap until he finds it impossible to align the holes in two skins. In desperation and somewhat guiltily as if he had made a mistake, he turns to his partner (a more experienced worker) and states his problem. The experienced worker will try every legitimate technique of lining up the holes, but if these do not succeed, he resorts to the tap. He taps the new thread himself, not permitting the novice to use the tap. While tapping it he gives the novice a lecture on the dangers of getting caught and of breaking a tap in the hole, thereby leaving tell-tale evidence of its use.

For several weeks the older worker will not permit his inexperienced partner to use a tap when its use is required. He leaves his own work in order to do the required tapping and finishes the job before returning to his own work. If the novice demonstrates sufficient ability and care in other aspects of his work he will be allowed to tap the hole under the supervision of a veteran worker. When the veteran partner is absent, and the now initiated worker can use the tap at his own discretion he feels a sense of pride. In order to enjoy his new found facility, he frequently uses the tap when it is not necessary. He may be careless in properly aligning perfectly good components and then compensate for his own carelessness by using the tap.

He may forego the easier illegal methods (which are also viewed as less serious crimes) of greasing and waxing bolts or enlarging the misaligned holes and indulge himself in the more pleasurable, challenging and dangerous use of the tap. Sooner or later he inevitably runs into difficulties which he is technically unprepared to cope with. When his partner and mentor is not available, he is forced to call upon the assistant foreman. If the situation requires it, the foreman will recommend the tap. If he has doubts about the worker's abilities, he may even tap the hole himself. In doing this, he risks censure of the union, because as a foreman he is not permitted to handle tools.

At the time the research was conducted, there were four levels of foremen. These were: assistant foreman (one star); foreman (two stars); assistant general foreman (three stars), and general foreman (four stars).

The stars are on the foremen's badges and are their insignia of rank. The assistant foreman is the immediate supervisor of a work crew. The four-star is the shop supervisor. The two and three star foremen have authority over increasingly larger sections of the assembly line. In the following discussion the foreman refers to the one-star assistant foreman, unless otherwise noted.

While the foreman taps the hole, he also lectures on the proper and technically workmanlike ways of using the tap: 'The tap is turned only at quarter turns . . . never force the tap . . . it has to go in easy or it's likely to snap . . . if it snaps, your ass is in a sling and I won't be able to get you out of it.'

The foreman warns the worker to make sure 'not to get caught, to see that the coast is clear, to keep the tap well hidden when not in use, and to watch out for inspectors while using it.' He always ends by cautioning the worker, 'It's your own ass if you're caught.'

When the worker feels that he is experienced and can use the tap with complete confidence, he usually buys his own, frequently displaying it to other workers and magnanimously lending it to those in need of it. He feels himself fully arrived when a two star foreman or, even higher, an assistant general foreman borrows his tap or asks him to perform the tapping. The worker has now established his identity and is known as an individual by the higher ups.

Once the right to use the tap is thus established, the indiscriminate use of it is frowned upon. A worker who uses a tap too often is considered to be a careless 'botcher'. A worker who can get his work done without frequently using a tap is a 'mechanic', but one who doesn't use the tap when it is necessary does not get his own work done on time. Proper use of the tap requires judgement and etiquette. The tap addict is likely to become the object of jokes and to get a bad work reputation among workers, foremen and inspectors.

Agencies of law enforcement

The enforcement of the plant rules of workmanship devolves upon three groups: foremen, plant quality control and Air Force quality control. The ultimate and supreme authority resides in the latter group. The Air Force not only sets the blue-print specifications, but also and more importantly, can reject a finished airplane as not meeting specifications.

Furthermore, the Air Force inspectors re-inspect installations which have been previously 'bought' by plant quality control. If these installations do not meet Air Force standards they are 'crabbed', i.e., rejected. When this happens, the plant inspectors who bought the installations are subject to 'being written up', i.e., disciplinary action for unintentional negligence which may lead to suspensions, demotions or in extreme cases loss of jobs. The Air Force inspector has the absolute right to demand that any man be fired for violating work rules.

There were only two Air Force inspectors to a shop at the time of these observations, so that it was almost impossible for Air Force inspectors to police an entire shop of over 2000 men. As an Air Force inspector walks up the line, it is standard procedure for workers to nudge other workers to inform them of the approach of the 'Gestapo'. When tapping is essential and when it is known that Air Force inspectors are too near, guards of workers are posted to convey advance notice of this approach to any one who is actively tapping. This is especially true when there are plant drives against the use of the tap.

In all instances, when the Air Force inspector is in the vicinity, workers who have a reputation for open or promiscuous use of the tap are instructed by the assistant foreman to 'disappear'. Such types can return to work when the 'coast is clear'.

Despite the Air Force inspectors' high authority and the severity of their standards, they are not sufficiently numerous to be considered the major policing agency for detecting and apprehending violators of the rules of workmanship. Plant quality control is the actual law enforcement agency in terms of the daily operations of surveillance. There are approximately 150 plant inspectors to a 2000 man shop. They work along the assembly line along with the workers. In some cases a panel of inspectors is assigned to inspect the work done by a number of crews who are supervised by a two-star foreman. In this system a call book which guarantees the equal rotation of inspections is kept. When a worker has completed a job and requests an inspection, he enters his wing number and the requested inspection in the call book. The inspector, after completing an inspection, marks the job as completed and takes the next open inspection as indicated in the call book.

A result of either type of inspection setup is the free and intimate intermingling of inspectors, and workers. In off moments, inspectors and workers gather together to 'shoot the breeze and kill time'. Inspectors, unlike workers, may have long waiting periods before their next assignment. During such periods out of boredom and monotony they tend to fraternize with workers. This causes conflict between the role of 'good eggs' and the role of policeman. A cause of leniency on the part of inspectors is intrinsic to the relationship between mechanics and themselves in circumstances not involving the tap. There is a sufficient amount of mechanical work which is not easily and immediately accessible to inspectors. This is particularly true if the inspector does not want to spend several hours on a fairly simple inspection. In order for the inspector to complete his work and make sure that the work he 'buys' will be acceptable to later inspectors, he must rely on the workmanship of the mechanic. In brief he must have faith not only in the mechanic's workmanship but also in his willingness not to 'louse him up'. If the inspector gets the reputation of being a 'bastard', the mechanic is under no obligation to do a good job and thus protect the inspector. Since the penalties for the use of the tap are so severe, no inspector feels comfortable about reporting a violation. A number of suberterfuges are resorted to in an effort to diminish the potential conflict.

There is a general understanding that workers are not supposed to use a tap in the presence of plant inspectors. At various times this understanding is made explicit. The inspector frequently tells the workers of his crew: 'Now fellas, there's a big drive now on taps. The Air Force just issued a special memo. For God's sakes, don't use a tap when I'm around. If somebody sees it while I'm in the area, it'll be my ass. Look around first. Make sure I'm gone.'

At other times the verbalization comes from the worker. If a worker has to use a tap and the inspector is present, he will usually wait until the inspector leaves. If the inspector shows no signs of leaving, the worker will tell him to 'Get the hell outa here. I got work to do and can't do it while you're around.'

If the worker knows the inspector he may take out the tap, permitting the inspector to see it. The wise inspector responds to the gesture by leaving. Of course, a worker has already 'sized up' the inspector and knows whether or not he can rely upon him to respond as desired.

When there is an Air Force-inspired drive against the tap, the inspectors will make the rounds and 'lay the law down': 'I want no more tapping around here. The next guy caught gets turned in. I can't cover you guys any more. I'm not kidding you bastards. If you can't do a decent job, don't do it at all. If that s.o.b. foreman of yours insists on you doing it, tell him to do it himself. He can't make you do it. If you're caught, it's your ass not his. When the chips are down, he's got to cover himself and he'll leave you holding the bag!'

For about three or four days thereafter, taps disappear from public view. The work slows down, and ultimately the inspectors forget to be zealous. A state of normal haphazard equilibrium is restored.

Other types of social relations and situations between workers and inspectors help maintain this state of equilibrium. An inspector will often see a tap in the top of a worker's tool box. He will pick it up and drop it into the bottom of the box where it cannot be seen easily. Perhaps he will tell the worker that he is a 'damned fool for being so careless'. The inspector thus hopes to establish his dependability for the worker, and creates a supply of good will credit, which the worker must repay in the form of protecting the inspector.

Another typical worker–inspector situation occurs when a mechanic is caught in the act of tapping, and the inspector does not look away. The inspector severely reprimands the mechanic, 'throws the fear of God into him', holds him in suspense as to whether he will turn him in, and then lets him go with a warning. This, generally, only happens to new workers. Occasionally when a worker has a new inspector and no previously established trust relationship, the same situation may arise. In both cases they are an integral part of the socialization of the worker to the plant or, rather, to a specific phase of its operation.

The role of the foreman

Another type of ceremonial escape from law enforcement through pseudo-law enforcement involves the foreman. In rare cases an inspector will catch a worker using the tap, reprimand him and turn him over to his foreman. The foreman then is forced to go through the procedure of reprimanding the errant worker. The foreman becomes serious and indignant, primarily because the worker let himself get caught. He gives the worker a genuine tongue lashing, and he reminds him once again that he, as foreman, has to go to bat so save the worker's neck. He stresses that it is only because of *his* intervention that the worker will not lose his job. He states, 'Next time be careful. I won't stick my neck out for you again. For God's sakes don't use a tap, *unless it's absolutely necessary.*'

The worker is obliged to accept the reprimand and to assume the countenance of true penitent, even to the extent of promising that it won't happen again. He will say, 'Awright, awright. So I got caught this time. Next time I won't get caught.' Both the foreman and worker play these roles even though the worker tapped the hole at the specific request of the foreman. The most blatant violation of the mores in such a situation is when the worker grins and treats the whole thing as a comic interlude. When this happens, the foreman becomes truly enraged, 'That's the trouble with you. You don't take your job seriously. You don't give a dam about nothing. How long do I have to put up with your not giving a dam.'

The public ritual therefore conceals an entirely different dimension of social functions involved in the use of the tap [. . .]

At a moment's glance, top supervision can single out foremen who are not pulling their weight. In aviation assembly, since the work cycle for a particular team is relatively long (four to eight hours) and since a foreman has relatively few teams (usually three) all doing the same job, any slow-down which delays one team damages the foreman's production record in the immediate perceivable terms of the report card. Moreover, delay caused by the inability of one crew to complete its task prevents other crews from working on that wing. The foremen of these crews will complain to the two- or three-star foremen that they are being held up and that their production records will suffer because of another foreman's incompetence.

As a result of these considerations, the pressures 'to get work out' are paramount for the foreman. There is a relatively high turnover among foremen, even at the two-star level. In the last analysis, production records are the major consideration in supervisory mobility. All other considerations – e.g., sociability, work knowledge, personality, etc. – are assumed to be measured by the production chart.

In this context the foreman, *vis à vis* the ticklish question of the tap, is compelled to violate some of the most important laws of the company and the Air Force. Crucial instances occur at times when the Air Force institutes stringent anti-tap enforcement measures. When key holes do not line up it may be necessary, as an alternative to using the tap, to disassemble previous installations. The disassembling and reassembling may take a full eight hours before the previously reached work stage is again reached. The production chart for that eight-hour period will indicate that no work has been done. In such a situation the worker may refuse to tap a hole since he risks endangering his job. The foreman also may be reluctant to request directly that the worker tap a hole. To get the work done he therefore employs a whole rhetoric of veiled requests such as 'Hell, that's easy ... you know what to do ... you've done it before.' 'Maybe you can clean out the threads,' or 'Well, see what you can do.'

If the worker is adamant, the foreman will practically beg him to do the *right* thing. He will remind him of past favors, he will complain about his chart rating and of how 'top brass doesn't give a damn about anything but what's on the chart'. He usually ends his plea with: 'Once you get this done, you can take it easy. You know I don't work you guys too hard most of the time.'

If the veiled requests and pitiful pleadings don't produce results, the foreman may take the ultimate step of tapping the hole himself. He compounds the felony, because he not only violates the rules of workmanship but also violates union rules which specifically state that no foreman can use a tool. To add insult to injury, the foreman furthermore has to borrow the tap in the midst of an anti-tap drive when taps are scarce.

From the viewpoint of production the use of the tap is imperative to the functioning of the production organization, even though it is one of the most serious work crimes. This is recognized even at official levels, although only in indirect ways.

Taps, being made of hard steel, have the disadvantage of being brittle. If not handled carefully, they may break within the nut. This not only makes further work impossible, but makes for easier detection of the crime. To cope with such a problem, the tool crib is well equipped with a supply of tap extractors. Any worker can draw an appropriately sized tap extractor from the tool crib. All these are official company property. He can do this even amidst the most severe anti-tap drives without fear of the danger of punishment.

Crime and the social system

Deviancy, in the sense that it implies a rejection of the norms of a social system or behaviour outside of a system, is not a useful concept for analyzing this type of crime. Rather, the use of the tap is literally a major crime which is intrinsic to the system. The conception of a social system as a tightly knit series of interlocking fuctions, mutually supporting each other and contributing to the support and continuance of the system, is not at all applicable to an understanding of this case.

Crime as defined by the use of the tap (and the other crimes of workmanship subsumed under our discussion of the tap) supports in its own way the continuance of the system, just as the avoidance of the use of the tap contributes to the perfection of the system. The motion of deviancy or of 'patterned deviancy' as a residue of systemic analysis – i.e. action not conforming to the demands of the system, or resulting in dysfunctions of the system – does not adequately describe the system. One reason for this inadequacy is that deviance as thus understood derives from a prior postulation of some primary but not specifically located end, which the analyst himself attributes to the system. The 'deviant' action may be as central to the system as is the norm it allegedly deviates from.

On the other hand, if one considers the actions called 'deviant behaviour' as intrinsic to the system, deviant behavior contributes to and supports the system just as does conformity, simply because the system is composed of its interrelated parts. From the standpoint of the past, any change is dysfunctional; that is, it represents a disruption of the system as it was. From the standpoint of the present, those same changes when adopted, can be viewed as functions, since they become for the moment intrinsic parts of system [. . .]

For the Air Force the major end is a high rate of production of high quality planes at low cost. Reducing costs and maintaining quality are secondary ends, or if one wishes to so describe it, means to the primary end of producing efficient aircraft. For the individual foreman, maintaining his job, gaining a promotion or staying out of trouble may be his primary private ends. The maintaining or exceeding of his production quota, while a major end for the 'company' as a whole and as defined by the executives, are the means of attaining the private goals of the foreman.

Similarly the primary ends of plant inspectors are to get along with workers, to avoid buying jobs which will be rejected in later inspection, and in some cases to achieve a supervisory position. Again, the actions of inspectors in developing a mutual trust situation, and in protecting themselves and workers in the tap situation, represents a compromise between different private ends. Similarly the ends of workers are to get their work done with a minimum of effort, to get along at least minimally with foremen and inspectors, to stay out of trouble and to avoid being fired. The semi-secret use of the tap, then, represents a compromise between these complexes of ends.

Taking these means–ends situations together, we find that what are means for one group are ends for another. In all cases, means and ends can be defined as either public or private attributes. Public ends are means to private ends, and private ends are in some cases limited by 'public', i.e., organizationally sanctioned, ends and means. In brief the empirical situation is extremely complex, and not analyzable in *a priori* terms. The complex of public and private means and ends constitutes a specific research problem insofar as it accounts for an overall operation of the organization.

In terms of the specific problem of the tap as an instrument, and its relationship to means-and-ends relationships within the organization, we find that the use of the tap is a private means to publicly stated ends. But those ends to which the use of the tap is oriented are, from both the standpoint of that abstraction 'the company' and from the standpoint of its members, only one of a number of possible ends. It is the plurality of ends that accounts for 'deviant behavior' rather than the conflict between means and ends. Production is a major end, and quality is a necessary condition for the attainment of that end. Moreover, as individuals are distributed at different levels and in different lines of the status hierarchy, different ends become more salient to individuals occupying different positions. The relationship of means to ends at both the public and private levels is different (in fact is sometimes reversed) for individuals in different positions in the organization. The statement of 'public ends' attached to the organization or the social system describes the ends of a limited number of particular and publicly accessible or visible positions in the system.

Thus any theoretical model which accepts as an initial postulate the dominance of an ultimate end, and which conceptualizes disorganization as a conflict between means and ends, overlooks the possibility that conflicting means and ends are actually conflicts between the means to one end with the means to another end.

Moreover, in any complex organization where plural ends are distributed in different ways among office holders, the conflict of ends and the conflicts between means and ends, are institutionalized as conflicts between various departments or segments in the organization. Thus from the point of view of production supervision, quality control is a major obstacle to the achievement of its ends. From the standpoint of quality control, sloppy workmanship is a major crime which may result in sanctions to the inspector. The tolerance of the tap is a means by which workers, inspectors and production supervisors attempt to achieve their respective ends in a mutually tolerable manner in a situation where they are forced to work together according to directives, which if closely followed would result in mutual frustration. For the worker, the inspector and the foreman, the development of a satisfactory social environment, the minimization of conflict, and the development of tolerable social relations become a major end. Crime, and the toleration of crime within the limits of avoiding extreme sanctions, becomes a means to these social ends, as well as a means to the publicly recognized ends of the organization.

In sum, a large part of behavior, visible to an insider or to a sophisticated observer, is 'criminal', i.e., it violates publicly stated norms. But since such behavior is accepted – in fact often stimulated, aided and abetted by the effective on-the-spot authorities – the criminality of such behavior has limited consequences.

39 Gilbert Geis

White-Collar Crime: The Heavy Electrical Equipment
Antitrust Cases of 1961

Excerpts from Gilbert Geis, 'White-collar crime: the heavy electrical equipment
antitrust cases of 1961' in M. B. Clinard and R. Quinney (eds.), *Criminal Behaviour
Systems: A Typology*, Holt, Rinehart & Winston, 1967, pp. 139–51.

An inadvertent bit of humor by a defense attorney provided one of the
major criminological motifs for 'the most serious violations of the antitrust laws since the time of their passage at the turn of the century'. The
defendants, including several vice-presidents of the General Electric
Corporation and the Westinghouse Electric Corporation – the two
largest companies in the heavy electrical equipment industry – stood
somberly in a federal courtroom in Philadelphia on 6 February 1961.
They were aptly described by a newspaper reporter as 'middle-class men
in Ivy League suits – typical business men in appearance, men who
would never be taken for lawbreakers'. Several were deacons or vestry-
men of their churches. One was president of his local chamber of commerce, another a hospital board member, another chief fund raiser for
the community chest, another a bank director, another a director of the
taxpayer's association, another an organizer of the local little league.

The attorney for a General Electric executive attacked the
government's demand for a jail sentence for his client, calling it 'cold-
blooded'. The lawyer insisted that government prosecutors did not
understand what it would do to his client, 'this fine man', to be put
'behind bars' with 'common criminals who have been convicted of embezzlement and other serious crimes'.

The difficulty of defense counsel in considering antitrust violations
'serious crimes', crimes at least equivalent to embezzling, indicates in
part why the 1961 prosecutions provide such fascinating material for
criminological study [. . .]

Though much of the data regarding them is tantalizingly incomplete,
unresponsive to fine points of particular criminological concern, the antitrust offenses nonetheless represent extraordinary case studies of white-
collar crime, that designation which, according to Sutherland, applies to
behavior by 'a person of high socioeconomic status who violates the
laws designed to regulate his occupational activities' and 'principally
refers to business managers and executives'. In particular, the antitrust
cases provide the researcher with a mass of raw data against which to test

and to refine earlier hunches and hypotheses regarding white-collar crime.

Facts of the antitrust violations

The most notable characteristic of the 1961 antitrust conspiracy was its wilful and blatant nature. These were not complex acts only doubtfully in violation of a highly complicated statute. They were flagrant criminal offenses, patently in contradiction of the letter and to the spirit of the Sherman Antitrust Act of 1890, which forbade price-fixing arrangements as restraints upon free trade [. . .]

Techniques of the conspiracy

The *modus operandi* for the antitrust violations shows clearly the awareness of the participants that their behavior was such that it had better be carried on as secretly as possible. Some comparison might be made between the antitrust offenses and other forms of fraud occurring in lower economic classes. It was one of Sutherland's most telling contentions that neither the method by which a crime is committed nor the manner in which it is handled by public agencies alters the essential criminal nature of the act and the criminal status of the perpetrator. Selling faucet water on a street corner to a blind man who is led to believe that the product is specially prepared to relieve his ailment is seen as no different from selling a $50 million turbine to a city which is laboring under the misapprehension that it is purchasing the product at the best price possible from closed competitive bidding. The same may be said in regard to methods of treatment. Tuberculosis, for example, remains tuberculosis and its victim a tubercular whether the condition is treated in a sanatorium or whether it is ignored or even condoned by public authorities. So too with crime. As Miss Stein might have said: A crime is a crime is a crime.

Like most reasonably adept and optimistic criminals, the antitrust violators had hoped to escape apprehension. 'I didn't expect to get caught and I went to great lengths to conceal my activities so that I wouldn't get caught', one of them said. Another went into some detail concerning the techniques of concealment:

It was considered discreet to not be too obvious and to minimize telephone calls, to use plain envelopes if mailing material to each other, not to be seen together on traveling, and so forth . . . not to leave wastepaper, of which there was a lot, strewn around a room when leaving.

The plans themselves, while there were some slight variations over time and in terms of different participants, were essentially similar. The offenders hid behind a camouflage of fictitious names and conspiratorial codes. The attendance roster for the meetings was known as the 'Christmas card list' and the gatherings, interestingly enough, as 'choir practice'. The offenders used public telephones for much of their communication, and they met either at trade association conventions, where their relationship would appear reasonable, or at sites selected for their anonymity. It is quite noteworthy, in this respect, that while some of the men filed false travel claims, so as to mislead their superiors regarding the city they had visited, they never asked for expense money to places more distant than those they had actually gone to – on the theory, apparently, that whatever else was occurring, it would not do to cheat the company.

At the meetings, negotiations centered about the establishment of a 'reasonable' division of the market for the various products. Generally, participating companies were allocated essentially that part of the market which they had previously garnered. If Company A, for instance, had under competitive conditions secured 20 per cent of the available business, then agreement might be reached that it would be given the opportunity to submit the lowest bid on 20 per cent of the new contracts. A low price would be established, and the remainder of the companies would bid at approximately equivalent, though higher, levels.

Explanations of the conspiracy

Attempts to understand the reasons for and the general significance of the price-fixing conspiracy have been numerous. They include re-examinations of the antitrust laws as well as denunciations of the corporate ethos and the general pattern of American life and American values. For example, 'This is the challenge of the grim outcome in Philadelphia. Can corporations outgrow the idea that employees must produce, whatever the moral cost, or lose their prerequisites? Is it possible to create a business ethic favoring honesty even at the expense of profit? Can our society get away from its pervasive attitude that a little cheating is harmless? The electrical cases raise those questions not only in the antitrust field, but in others, especially taxation. And they are questions not only for large corporations and not only for business but for all of us.'

A not inconsiderable number of the defendants took the line that their behavior, while technically criminal, had really served a worthwhile purpose by 'stabilizing prices' (a much-favored phrase of the conspirators). This altruistic interpretation almost invariably was combined with an attempted distinction among illegal, criminal, and immoral acts, with the offender expressing the view that what he had done might have been designated by the statutes as criminal but either he was unaware of such a designation or he thought it unreasonable that acts with admirable consequences should be considered criminal. The testimony of a Westinghouse executive during hearings by the Senate Subcommittee on Antitrust and Monopoly clearly illustrates this point of view:

Committee Attorney: Did you know that these meetings with competitors were illegal?
Witness: Illegal? Yes, but not criminal. I didn't find that out until I read the indictment. ... I assumed that criminal action meant damaging someone, and we did not do that. ... I thought that we were more or less working on a survival basis in order to try to make enough to keep our plant and our employees.

This theme was repeated in essentially similar language by a number of witnesses. 'It is against the law', an official of the Ingersoll-Rand Corporation granted, but he added: 'I do not know that it is against public welfare because I am not certain that the consumer was actually injured by this operation.' A Carrier Corporation executive testified that he was 'reasonably in doubt' that the price-fixing meetings violated the antitrust law. 'Certainly, we were in a gray area. I think the degree of violation, if you can speak of it that way, is what was in doubt.' Another offender said: 'We were not meeting for the purpose of getting the most that traffic could bear. It was to get a value for our product.' Some of these views are gathered together in a statement by a former sales manager of the I-T-E Circuit Breaker Company:

One faces a decision, I guess, at such times, about how far to go with company instructions, and since the spirit of such meetings only appeared to be correcting a horrible price level situation, that there was not an attempt to actually damage customers, charge excessive prices, there was no personal gain in it for me, the company did not seem actually to be defrauding, corporate statements can evidence the fact that there have been poor profits during all these years. ... So I guess morally it did not seem quite so bad as might be inferred by the definition of the activity itself.

For the most part, personal explanations for the acts were sought in the structure of corporate pressures rather than in the avarice or lack of law-abiding character of the men involved. The defendants almost invariably testified that they came new to a job, found price-fixing an established way of life, and simply entered into it as they did into other aspects of their job. This explanatory scheme fit into a pattern that Senator Hart of Michigan, during the subcommittee hearings, labeled *imbued fraud* [. . .]

Westinghouse and General Electric differed considerably in their reactions to the exposure of the offenses, with Westinghouse electing to retain in its employ persons involved in the conspiracy, and General Electric deciding to dismiss the employees who had been before the court. The reasoning of the companies throws light both on the case and on the relationship between antitrust offenses and the more traditionally viewed forms of criminal behavior.

Westinghouse put forward four justifications for its retention decision. First, it declared, the men involved had not sought personal aggrandizement: 'While their actions cannot in any way be condoned, these men did not act for personal gain, but in the belief, misguided though it may have been, that they were furthering the company's interest.' Second, 'the punishment incurred by them already was harsh' and 'no further penalties would serve any useful purpose'. Third, 'each of these individuals is in every sense a reputable citizen, a respected and valuable member of the community and of high moral character.' Fourth, there was virtually no likelihood that the individuals would repeat their offense.

General Electric's punitive line toward its employees was justified on the ground that the men had violated not only federal law but also a basic company policy, and that they therefore deserved severe punishment. The company's action met with something less than wholehearted acclaim; rather, it was often interpreted as an attempt to scapegoat particular individuals for what was essentially the responsibility of the corporate enterprise and its top executives. 'I do not understand the holier-than-thou attitude in GE when your directions came from very high at the top,' Senator Kefauver said during his committee's hearings, while Senator Carroll of Colorado expressed his view through a leading question: 'Do you think you were thrown to the wolves to ease the public relations situation ... that has developed since these indictments?' he asked a discharged General Electric employee. The witness thought that he had.

Perhaps most striking is the fact that though many offenders quite clearly stressed the likely consequences for them if they failed to conform to price-fixing expectations, not one hinted at the benefits he might expect, the personal and professional rewards, from participation in the criminal conspiracy. It remained for the sentencing judge and two top General Electric executives to deliver the harshest denunciations of the personal motives and qualities of the conspirators to be put forth during the case.

The statement of Judge J. Cullen Ganey, read prior to imposing sentence, received widespread attention. In it he sharply criticized the corporations as the major culprits, but he also pictured the defendants in a light other than that they chose to shed upon themselves in their subsequent discussions of the offenses:

They were torn between conscience and an approved corporate policy, with the rewarding objective of promotion, comfortable security, and large salaries. They were the organization or company man, the conformist who goes along with his superiors and finds balm for his conscience in additional comforts and security of his place in the corporate set-up.

The repeated emphasis on 'comfort' and 'security' constitutes the basic element of Judge Ganey's view of the motivations of the offenders. Stress on passive acquiescence occurs in remarks by two General Electric executives viewing the derelictions of their subordinates. R. Paxton, the retired company president, called antitrust agreements 'monkey business' and denounced in vitriolic terms one of his former superiors who, when Paxton first joined General Electric, had put him to work attempting to secure a bid on a contract that had already been prearranged by a price-fixing agreement. R. Cordiner, the president and board chairman of General Electric, thought that the antitrust offenses were motivated by drives for easily acquired power. Cordiner's statement is noteworthy for its dismissal of the explanations of the offenders as 'rationalizations':

One reason for the offenses was a desire to be 'Mr Transformer' or 'Mr Switchgear' . . . and to have influence over a larger segment of the industry. . . . The second was that it was an indolent, lazy way to do business. When you get all through with the rationalizations, you have to come back to one or the other of these conclusions.

There were other explanations as well. One truculent offender, the sixty-eight-year-old president of a smaller company who had been spared a jail sentence only because of his age and the illness of his wife, categorically denied the illegality of his behavior. 'We did not fix prices,' he said. 'I can't agree with you. I am telling you that all we did was recover costs.' Some persons blamed the system of decentralization in the larger companies, which they said placed a heavy burden to produce profit on each of the relatively autonomous divisions, particularly when bonuses – 'incentive compensation' – were at stake, while others maintained that the 'dog-eat-dog' business conditions in the heavy electrical equipment industry were responsible for the violations. Perhaps the simplest explanation came from a General Electric executive. 'I think,' he said, 'the boys could resist everything but temptation' [. . .]

Various analytical schemes and theoretical statements in criminology and related fields provide some insight into elements of the price-fixing conspiracy. Galbraith's caustic observation regarding the traditional academic view of corporate price-fixing arrangements represents a worth-while point of departure:

> Restraints on competition and the free movement of prices, the principal source of uncertainty to business firms, have been principally deplored by university professors on lifelong appointments. Such security of tenure is deemed essential for fruitful and unremitting thought.

It seems apparent, looking at the antitrust offenses in this light, that the attractiveness of a secure market arrangement represented a major ingredient drawing corporate officers to the price-fixing violations. The elimination of competition meant the avoidance of uncertainty, the formalization and predictability of outcome, the minimization of risks. It is, of course, this incentive which accounts for much of human activity, be it deviant or 'normal', and this tendency that Weber found so pronounced in bureaucracies in their move from vital but erratic beginnings to more staid and more comfortable middle and old age.

For the conspirators there had necessarily to be a conjunction of factors before they could participate in the violations. First, of course, they had to perceive that there would be gains accruing from their behavior. Such gains might be personal and professional, in terms of corporate advancement toward prestige and power, and they might be vocational, in terms of a more expedient and secure method of carrying out assigned tasks. The offenders also apparently had to be able to neutralize or rationalize their behavior in a manner in keeping with their image of themselves as law-abiding, decent, and respectable persons. The ebb and flow of the price-fixing conspiracy also clearly indicates the relationship, often over-looked in explanations of criminal behavior, between extrinsic conditions and illegal acts. When the market behaved in a manner the executives thought satisfactory, or when enforcement agencies seemed particularly threatening, the conspiracy desisted. When market conditions deteriorated, while corporate pressures for achieving attractive profit-and-loss statements remained constant, and enforcement activity abated, the price-fixing agreements flourished.

More than anything else, however, a plunge into the elaborate documentation of the antitrust cases of 1961, as well as an attempt to relate them to other segments of criminological work, points up the considerable need for more and better monographic field studies of law violators and of systems of criminal behavior, these to be followed by attempts to establish theoretical guidelines and to review and refine current interpretative viewpoints. There have probably been no more than a dozen, if that many, full-length studies of types of criminal (not delinquent) behavior in the past decade. The need for such work seems overriding, and the 1961 antitrust cases represent but one of a number of instances, whether in the field of white-collar crime, organized crime, sex offenses, personal or property crimes, or similar areas of concern, where we are still faced with a less than adequate supply of basic and comparative material upon which to base valid and useful theoretical statements.

40 Clifford R. Shaw

From Delinquent to Criminal

Excerpts from Clifford R. Shaw, *The Jack-Roller*, University of Chicago Press, 1930, pp. 49-56, 102-5.

My stepmother favored her own children in every way. They received what luxuries were to be had, while my brother and sister and I had crumbs to pick off the table. She let her children eat at the table, and made us wait. Whenever one of her children would do a wrong they would tell her that I did it, and then I, instead of the culprit, would get the beating. My father couldn't interfere, because if he did the step-mother would threaten to leave. That would have been the best thing for his children, but of course he didn't want her to go.

Things went on this way. We fought with her because she favored her children at meals and beat us for their misdemeanors. Hard indeed it was for me to get enough to eat. Often when I would go to the store to buy food for the family, I would take a little biscuit or anything I could without my stepmother knowing it. So that much was I ahead when I got my portion at mealtime. My father worked steady and received good wages, so there was no good reason why we could not have enough to eat. But the stepmother was saving and fed her own children and let us go starved and half-naked on the street.

The stepmother also made us (brother, sister, and myself) do all the hard work in the house. And then she would beat us if we complained. That is what embittered me against her and her children. I developed a hatred against her that still lasts; a hatred that was so burning that when she would look into my eyes she would read it there, and in that way she knew my feeling. The Lord knows I tried to love her, but my nature could not stand her caresses in one of those sympathetic moods which she seldom had. Occasionally she would seem to feel sorry for her abuses and cruelty, and would ask me to kiss her; but my feelings protested. My fear and hatred made me avoid her and resent her caresses. Then she would get angry and beat me.

So I grew old enough to go out on the street. The life in the streets and alleys became fascinating and enticing. I had two close companions that I looked up to with childish admiration and awe. One was William, my stepbrother. The other one was Tony, a dear friend of my stepbrother,

William. They were close friends, four years older than me and well versed in the art of stealing.

To my child-seeing eyes, I visioned Tony as a great leader in the neighborhood, and he directed his gang around with much bravado. He and William were always stealing and talking about stealing and I fell in with them as soon as I began to play around in the neighborhood.

Tony was a squatty boy, rough features, closely set eyes, and a body that bespoke strength and ruggedness. With his strength and fighting ability, he maintained leadership over his gang. He was also daring and courageous. I remember vividly how awed I was by his daring in stealing and fighting. These things made him a guy to be looked up to and respected in the neighborhood.

Tony liked his whiskey and in our neighborhood one could find as many as four or five saloons in one block in those days. He would dare me to drink and I would, although it burned my throat. I was what they call 'game' and I just swallowed it without a word, to maintain that high distinction which I was openly proud of.

Tony had two sisters who always played with us and went on our stealing adventures. They could steal as good as any boy. Also they had sex relations openly with all the boys in the neighborhood. I remember how the boys boasted that they had had sex relations with each of them. All the boys talked about it and the girls didn't care; they seemed to be proud of it and expect it. The funny thing about it was that Tony knew all about his sisters and their behavior and only made merry about it.

The boys in the gang teased me about Tony's sisters, asking me how many times I had had sex relations with them. Even the girls would talk to me about sex things, put their arms around me, and touch my body. At first I was too young to know what it all meant, but I soon learned and developed many sex habits, like masturbation and playing with girls.

Tony didn't work, but made his money by stealing, and he made lots of it for a boy of his age.

My stepmother sent me out with William (my stepbrother) to pick rags and bottles in the alleys. She said that would pay for my board and make me more useful than fretting and sulking at home. I did not mind that in the least. In fact, I enjoyed it, because I was at least out of the old lady's reach. I began to have a great time exploring the whole neighborhood – romping and playing in the alleys and 'prairies', gathering rags, bones, and iron, and selling them to the rag peddlers. This romping and roaming became fascinating and appealed to my curiosity, because it was freedom and adventure. We played 'Indian' and other games in the alleys, running through the old sheds and vacant houses. Then we gathered cigarette 'buttses' along the street and took them to the shed, where we smoked and planned adventure. I was little and young, but I fell in with the older guys. Outside, in the neighborhood, life was full of pleasure and excitement, but at home it was dull and drab and full of nagging, quarreling, and beating, and stuffy and crowded besides.

On the trips with William, I found him to be a rather chummy companion. I regarded him, not as a brother, but rather as a boy friend from another home. He was five years my senior. He sort of showed it in his obvious superiority. But I didn't seem to notice that fault. He was a 'mamma's boy' at home, but oh, Lord, how he changed on our trips! He taught me how to be mischievous; how to cheat the rag peddler when he weighed up our rags. He would distract the peddler's attention while I would steal a bag of rags off the wagon. We would sell the rags back to the victimized peddler. He also took me to the five-and-ten cent store on Forty-seventh Street, and would direct me to steal from the counter while he waited at the door. I usually was successful, as I was little and inconspicuous. How I loved to do these things! They thrilled me. I learned to smile and to laugh again. It was an honor, I thought, to do such things with William. Was he not the leader and I his brother? Did I not look up to him? I was ready to do anything William said, not because of fear, but because he was my companion. We were always together, and between us sprang up a natural understanding, so to speak.

One day my stepmother told William to take me to the railroad yard to break into box-cars. William always led the way and made the plans. He would open the cars, and I would crawl in and hand out the merchandise. In the cars were foodstuffs, exactly the things my stepmother wanted. We filled our cart, which we had made for this purpose, and proceeded toward home. After we arrived home with our ill-gotten goods, my stepmother would meet us and pat me on the back and say that I was a good boy and that I would be rewarded. Rewarded, bah! Rewarded with kicks and cuffs.

After a year of breaking into box-cars and stealing from stores, my stepmother realized that she could send me to the market to steal vegetables for her. My stealing had proved to be very profitable to her, so why not make it even more profitable? I knew it was for my own good to do what she wanted me to do. I was so afraid of her that I couldn't do anything but obey. Anyway, I didn't mind stealing, because William always went with me, and that made me feel proud of myself, and it gave me a chance to get away from home.

Every Saturday morning we would get up about three o'clock and prepare for the venture. William, Tony, and his two sisters and I would always go. We would board a street car, and the people on the car would always stare at us and wonder where such little kids were going so early in the morning. I liked to attract the attention of people and have them look down upon me with curiosity. The idea of my riding in a street car at that early hour appealed to my adventurous spirit and keyed me up to stealing. In the street car, William would give me orders on what to steal and how to go about it. I listened to him with interest and always carried out his orders. He had me in the palm of his hand, so to speak. He got the satisfaction of ordering me, and I got the thrill of doing the stealing. He instructed me on how to evade peddlers and merchants if they gazed at me while I was stealing. After arriving at the market, William would lay out the plan of action and stand guard while I did the stealing. He knew what the stepmother wanted, and he always filled her orders to overflowing. All in all, I was a rather conceited little boy who thought himself superior to the other boys of his age; and I didn't miss impressing that little thing upon their minds. I was so little that the peddlers were not suspicious of me, and it didn't take long to fill our baskets and be ready for the journey home. All spring, summer, and fall did we go to the market, and never did I get caught and never did we go home with empty baskets.

Stealing in the neighborhood was a common practice among the children and approved by the parents. Whenever the boys got together they talked about robbing and made more plans for stealing. I hardly knew any boys who did not go robbing. The little fellows went in for petty stealing, breaking into freight cars, and stealing junk. The older guys did big jobs like stick-up, burglary, and stealing autos. The little fellows admired the 'big shots' and longed for the day when they could get into the big racket. Fellows who had 'done time' were big shots and looked up to and gave the little fellows tips on how to get by and pull off big jobs [. . .]

Freedom now possessed me. I felt that I could get along some way on my own hook. But soon I learned that Fate was still master of my destiny. I was supposed to go to school, but it never appealed to me. To sit in a schoolroom all day was like being confined to prison. I would sit in school and think of traveling and roaming without a care. I always wanted to play hookey, so finally I was arrested and taken to the Juvenile Detention Home, where I learned the first law of nature – self-preservation [. . .]

In prison

We reached Pontiac and were herded into a waiting truck like so much livestock going to the market. As we turned into a main street the front of the institution glared out before me, and on its top floated an American flag, as if to give an air of respectability to the sordid hole. Arriving at the door of the institution, we were herded into the main office, and the clerk looked us over as if appraising us at our market value. He asked each of us our age, and hesitated when he came to me. I supposed he thought I was rather young, but I was taken in. We were then led to the vestibule, where we had a view of the whole institution, to wait for the guard who was to admit us. It was noontime, and the prisoners were coming from the shops to eat dinner. Being November, the day was hazy, and the gray uniforms of the prisoners struck me as the worst glaring scene I ever saw. The scene dazed me and I felt sick at heart; but I had more serious setbacks coming [. . .]

The guard led me, along with the other prisoners, to the receiving and discharging department, where I was stripped of my civilian clothes and ordered to take a bath. Then I was given my prison uniform and led to the Bertillon Room, where my photographs and measurements were taken, and identification marks recorded. After having my hair shaved off, given a number for a name, and a large tablespoon to eat with, I was assigned to a cell.

The cell was bare, hard, and drab. As I sat on my bunk thinking, a great wave of feeling shook me, which I shall always remember, because of the great impression it made on me. There, for the first time in my life, I realized that I was a criminal. Before, I had been just a mischievous lad, a poor city waif, a petty thief, a habitual runaway; but now, as I sat in my cell of stone and iron, dressed in a gray uniform, with my head shaved, small skull cap, like all the other hardened criminals around me, some strange feeling came over me. Never before had I realized that I was a criminal. I really became one as I sat there and brooded. At first I was almost afraid of myself, being like a stranger to my own self. It was hard for me to think of myself in my new surroundings. That night I tried to sleep, but instead I only tossed on my bunk, disturbed by my new life. Not one minute was I able to sleep.

When the whistle blew for breakfast the next morning I was heartsick and weak, but after visiting with my cell mate, who took prison life with a smile and as a matter of course, I felt better. He said, 'You might as well get used to things here; you're a "convict" now, and tears won't melt these iron bars.' He was only seventeen, but older than me, and was in for one to ten years for burglaries. He delighted in telling about his exploits in crime, to impress me with his bravery and daring, and made me look up to him as a hero. Almost all young crooks like to tell about their accomplishments in crime. Older crooks are not so glib. They are hardened, and crime has lost its glamor and become a matter of business. Also, they have learned the dangers of talking too much and keep their mouths shut except to trusted friends. But Bill (my cell partner) talked all the time about himself and his crimes. I talked, too, and told wild stories of adventure, some true and some lies, for I couldn't let Bill outdo me just for lack of a few lies on my part [. . .]

I found Pontiac to be a very clean and sanitary prison, compared to the County Jail. But like St Charles, the way of the transgressor of the prison rules was hard there. For even a minor infraction of the rules, a prisoner would be sent to the 'screens' or 'hole'. That is the solitary confinement. It is just a dark, barren cell. It has a toilet and bowl and a dark screen in front of it, so the prisoner cannot see out or have anything to eat or smoke pushed through to him. My God! it is solitary, all right. You might just as well be confined in the bowels of the earth, beyond the reach of human beings. I cannot describe the horrors of loneliness and mental stagnation that I felt many times in the black, bottomless pit.

41 Erving Goffman

Stigma and Social Identity

Excerpts from Erving Goffman, *Stigma: Notes on the management of spoiled identity*, Prentice-Hall, 1963, Penguin, 1970, pp. 11–19 and 45–58.

Preliminary conceptions

Society establishes the means of categorizing persons and the complement of attributes felt to be ordinary and natural for members of each of these categories. Social settings establish the categories of persons likely to be encountered there. The routines of social intercourse in established settings allow us to deal with anticipated others without special attention of thought. When a stranger comes into our presence, then, first appearances are likely to enable us to anticipate his category and attributes, his 'social identity' – to use a term that is better than 'social status' because personal attributes such as 'honesty' are involved, as well as structural ones, like 'occupation'.

We lean on these anticipations that we have, transforming them into normative expectations, into righteously presented demands.

Typically, we do not become aware that we have made these demands or aware of what they are until an active question arises as to whether or not they will be fulfilled. It is then that we are likely to realize that all along we had been making certain assumptions as to what the individual before us ought to be. Thus, the demands we make might better be called demands made 'in effect', and the character we impute to the individual might better be seen as an imputation made in potential retrospect – a characterization 'in effect', a *virtual social identity*. The category and attributes he could in fact be proved to possess will be called his *actual social identity*.

While the stranger is present before us, evidence can arise of his possessing an attribute that makes him different from others in the category of persons available for him to be, and of a less desirable kind – in the extreme, a person who is quite thoroughly bad, or dangerous, or weak. He is thus reduced in our minds from a whole and usual person to a tainted, discounted one. Such an attribute is a stigma, especially when its discrediting effect is very extensive; sometimes it is also called a failing, a shortcoming, a handicap. It constitutes a special discrepancy between virtual and actual social identity. Note that there are other types of discrepancy between virtual and actual social identity, for example the kind that causes us to reclassify an individual from one socially anticipated category to a different but equally well-anticipated one, and the kind that causes us to alter our estimation of the individual upward. Note, too, that not all undesirable attributes are at issue, but only those which are incongruous with our stereotype of what a given type of individual should be.

The term stigma, then, will be used to refer to an attribute that is deeply discrediting, but it should be seen that a language of relationships, not attributes, is really needed. An attribute that stigmatizes one type of possessor can confirm the usualness of another, and therefore is neither creditable nor discreditable as a thing in itself. For example, some jobs in America cause holders without the expected college education to conceal this fact; other jobs, however, can lead the few of their holders who have a higher education to keep this a secret, lest they be marked as failures and outsiders. Similarly, a middle class boy may feel no compunction in being seen going to the library; a professional criminal, however, writes:

I can remember before now on more than one occasion, for instance, going into a public library near where I was living, and looking over my shoulder a couple of times before I actually went in just to make sure no one who knew me was standing about and seeing me do it.

So, too, an individual who desires to fight for his country may conceal a physical defect, lest his claimed physical status be discredited; later, the same individual, embittered and trying to get out of the army, may succeed in gaining admission to the army hospital, where he would be discredited if discovered in not really having an acute sickness. A stigma, then, is really a special kind of relationship between attribute and stereotype, although I don't propose to continue to say so, in part because there are important attributes that almost everywhere in our society are discrediting.

The term stigma and its synonyms conceal a double perspective: does the stigmatized individual assume his differentness is known about already or is evident on the spot, or does he assume it is neither known about by those present nor immediately perceivable by them? In the first case one deals with the plight of the *discredited*, in the second with that of the *discreditable*. This is an important difference, even though a particular stigmatized individual is likely to have experience with both situations. I will begin with the situation of the discredited and move on to the discreditable but not always separate the two.

Three grossly different types of stigma may be mentioned. First there are abominations of the body – the various physical deformities. Next there are blemishes of individual character perceived as weak will, domineering or unnatural passions, treacherous and rigid beliefs, and dishonesty, these being inferred from a known record of, for example, mental disorder, imprisonment, addiction, alcoholism, homosexuality, unemployment, suicidal attempts, and radical political behaviour. Finally there are the tribal stigma of race, nation, and religion, these being stigma that can be transmitted through lineages and equally contaminate all members of a family. In all of these various instances of stigma, however, including those the Greeks had in mind, the same sociological features are found: an individual who might have been received easily in ordinary social intercourse possesses a trait that can obtrude itself upon attention and turn those of us whom he meets away from him, breaking the claim that his other attributes have on us. He possesses a stigma, an undesired difference from what we had anticipated. We and those who do not depart negatively from the particular expectations at issue I shall call the *normals*.

The attitudes we normals have towards a person with a stigma, and the actions we take in regard to him, are well known, since these responses are what benevolent social action is designed to soften and ameliorate. By definition, of course, we believe the person with a stigma is not quite human. On this assumption we exercise varieties of discrimination, through which we effectively, if often unthinkingly, reduce his life chances. We construct a stigma theory, an ideology to explain his inferiority and account for the danger he represents, sometimes rationalizing an animosity based on other differences, such as those of social class. We use specific stigma terms such as cripple, bastard, moron in our daily discourse as a source of metaphor and imagery, typically without giving thought to the original meaning. We tend to impute a wide range of imperfections on the basis of the original one, and at the same time to impute some desirable but undesired attributes often of a supernatural cast, such as 'sixth sense', or 'understanding'.

For some, there may be a hesitancy about touching or steering the blind, while for others, the perceived failure to see may be generalized into a gestalt of disability, so that the individual shouts at the blind as if they were deaf or attempts to lift them as if they were crippled. Those confronting the blind may have a whole range of belief that is anchored in the stereotype. For instance, they may think they are subject to unique judgement, assuming the blinded individual draws on special channels of information unavailable to others.

Further, we may perceive his defensive response to his situation as a direct expression of his defect, and then see both defect and response as just retribution for something he or his parents or his tribe did, and hence a justification of the way we treat him.

Now turn from the normal to the person he is normal against. It seems generally true that members of a social category may strongly support a standard of judgement that they and others agree does not directly apply to them. Thus it is that a businessman may demand womanly behaviour from females or ascetic behaviour from monks, and not construe himself as someone who ought to realize either of these styles of conduct. The distinction is between realizing a norm and merely supporting it. The issue of stigma does not arise here but only where there is some expectation on all sides that those in a given category should not only support a particular norm but also realize it.

Also, it seems possible for an individual to fail to live up to what we effectively demand of him, and yet be relatively untouched by this failure; insulated by his alienation, protected by identity beliefs of his own, he feels that he is a full-fledged normal human being, and that we are the ones who are not quite human. He bears a stigma but does not seem to be impressed or repentant about doing so. This possibility is celebrated in exemplary tales about Mennonites, Gypsies, shameless scoundrels, and very orthodox Jews.

In America at the present, however, separate systems of honour seem to be on the decline. The stigmatized individual tends to hold the same beliefs about identity that we do; this is a pivotal fact. His deepest feelings about what he is may be his sense of being a 'normal person', a human being like anyone else, a person, therefore, who deserves a fair chance and a fair break. (Actually, however phrased, he bases his claims not on what he thinks is due *everyone,* but only everyone of a selected social category into which he unquestionably fits, for example anyone of his age, sex, profession, and so forth.) Yet he may perceive, usually quite correctly, that whatever others profess, they do not really 'accept' him and are not ready to make contact with him on 'equal grounds'. Further, the standards he has incorporated from the wider society equip him to be intimately alive to what others see as his failing, inevitably causing him, if only for moments, to agree that he does indeed fall short of what he really ought to be. Shame becomes a central possibility, arising from the individual's perception of one of his own attributes as being a defiling thing to possess, and one he can readily see himself as not possessing.

The immediate presence of normals is likely to reinforce this split between self-demands and self, but in fact self-hate and self-derogation can also occur when only he and a mirror are about:

When I got up at last ... and had learned to walk again, one day I took a hand glass and went to a long mirror to look at myself, and I went alone. I didn't want anyone ... to know how I felt when I say myself for the first time. But there was no noise, no outcry; I didn't scream with rage when I saw myself. I just felt numb. That person in the mirror *couldn't* be me. I felt inside like a healthy, ordinary, lucky person – oh, not like the one in the mirror! Yet when I turned my face to the mirror there were my own eyes looking back, hot with shame ... when I did not cry or make any sound, it became impossible that I should speak of it to anyone, and the confusion and the panic of my discovery were locked inside me then and there, to be faced alone, for a very long time to come.

Over and over I forgot what I had seen in the mirror. It could not penetrate into the interior of my mind and become an integral part of me. I felt as if it had nothing to do with me; it was only a disguise. But it was not the kind of disguise which is put on voluntarily by the person who wears it, and which is intended to confuse other people as to one's identity. My disguise had been put on me without my consent or knowledge like the ones in fairy tales, and it was I myself who was confused by it, as to my own identity. I looked in the mirror, and was horror-struck because I did not recognize myself. In the place where I was standing, with that persistent romantic elation in me, as if I were a favoured fortunate person, to whom everything was possible, I saw a stranger, a little, pitiable, hideous figure, and a face that became, as I stared at it, painful and blushing with shame. It was only a disguise, but it was on me, for life. It was there, it was there, it was real. Every one of those encounters was like a blow to the head. They left me dazed and dumb and senseless every time, until slowly and stubbornly my robust persistent illusion of well-being and of personal beauty spread all through me again, and I forgot the irrelevant reality and was all unprepared and vulnerable again.

The central feature of the stigmatized individual's situation in life can now be stated. It is a question of what is often, if vaguely, called 'acceptance'. Those who have dealings with him fail to accord him the respect and regard which the un-contaminated aspects of his social identity have led them to anticipate extending, and have led him to anticipate receiving; he echoes this denial by finding that some of his own attributes warrant it [...]

Moral career

Persons who have a particular stigma tend to have similar learning experiences regarding their plight, and similar changes in conception of self – a similar 'moral career' that is both cause and effect of commitment to a similar sequence of personal adjustments. (The natural history of a category of persons with a stigma must be clearly distinguished from that natural history of the stigma itself – the history of the origins, spread, and decline of the capacity of an attribute to serve as a stigma in a particular society, for example, divorce in American upper middle class society.) One phase of this socialization process is that through which the stigmatized person learns and incorporates the stand-point of the normal, acquiring thereby the identity beliefs of the wider society and a general idea of what it would be like to possess a particular stigma. Another phase is that through which he learns that he possesses a particular stigma and, this time in detail, the consequence of possessing it. The timing and interplay of these two initial phases of the moral career form important patterns, establishing the foundation for later development, and providing a means of distinguishing among the moral careers available to the stigmatized. Four such patterns may be mentioned.

One pattern involves those with an inborn stigma who become socialized into their disadvantageous situation even while they are learning and incorporating the standards against which they fall short. For example, an orphan learns that children naturally and normally have parents, even while he is learning what it means not to have any. After spending the first sixteen years of his life in the institution he can later still feel that he naturally knows how to be a father to his son.

A second pattern derives from the capacity of a family, and to a much lesser extent a local neighbourhood, to constitute itself a protective capsule for its young. Within such a capsule a congenitally stigmatized child can be carefully sustained by means of information control. Self-belittling definitions of him are prevented from entering the charmed circle, while broad access is given to other conceptions held in the wider society, ones that lead the encapsulated child to see himself as a fully qualified ordinary human being, of normal identity in terms of such basic matters as age and sex.

The point in the protected individual's life when the domestic circle can no longer protect him will vary by social class, place of residence, and type of stigma, but in each case will give rise to a moral experience when it occurs. Thus, public school entrance is often reported as the occasion of stigma learning, the experience sometimes coming very precipitously on the first day of school, with taunts, teasing, ostracism, and fights. Interestingly, the more the child is 'handicapped' the more likely he is to be sent to a special school for persons of his kind, and the more abruptly he will have to face the view which the public at large takes of him. He will be told that he will have an easier time of it among 'his own', and thus learn that the own he thought he possessed was the wrong one, and that this lesser own is really his. It should be added that where the infantilely stigmatized manages to get through his early school years with some illusions left, the onset of dating or job-getting will often introduce the moment of truth. In some cases, merely an increased likelihood of incidental disclosure is involved:

I think the first realization of my situation, and the first intense grief resulting from this realization, came one day, very casually, when a group of us in our early teens had gone to the beach for the day. I was lying on the sand, and I guess the fellows and girls thought I was asleep. One of the fellows said, 'I like Domenica very much, but I would never go out with a blind girl.' I cannot think of any prejudice which so completely rejects you.

In other cases, something closer to systematic exposure is involved, as a cerebral palsy victim suggests:

With one extremely painful exception, as long as I was in the protective custody of family life or college schedules and lived without exercising my rights as an adult citizen, the forces of society were kindly and unruffling. It was after college, business school, and innumerable stretches as a volunteer worker on community projects that I was often bogged down by the medieval prejudices and superstitions of the business world. Looking for a job was like standing before a firing squad. Employers were shocked that I had the gall to apply for a job.

A third pattern of socialization is illustrated by one who becomes stigmatized late in life, or learns late in life that he has always been discreditable – the first involving no radical reorganization of his view of his past, the second involving this factor. Such an individual has thoroughly learned about the normal and the stigmatized long before he must see himself as deficient. Presumably he will have a special problem in re-identifying himself, and a special likelihood of developing disapproval of self:

When I smelled an odor on the bus or subway before the colostomy I used to feel very annoyed. I'd think that the people were awful, that they didn't take a bath or that they should have gone to the bathroom before traveling. I used to think that they might have odors from what they ate. I used to be terribly annoyed; to me it seemed that they were filthy, dirty. Of course, at the least opportunity I used to change my seat and if I couldn't it used to go against my grain. So naturally, I believe that the young people feel the same way about me if I smell.

While there are certainly cases of individuals discovering only in adult life that they belong to a stigmatized tribal group or that their parents have a contagious moral blemish, the usual case here is that of physical handicaps that 'strike' late in life:

But suddenly I woke up one morning, and found that I could not stand. I had had polio, and polio was as simple as that. I was like a very young child who had been dropped in to a big, black hole, and the only thing I was certain of was that I could not get out unless someone helped me. The education, the lectures, and the parental training which I had received for twenty-four years didn't seem to make me the person who could do anything for me now. I was like everyone else – normal, quarrelsome, gay, full of plans, and all of a sudden something happened! Something happened and I became a stranger. I was a greater stranger to myself than to anyone. Even my dreams did not know me. They did not know what they ought to let me do – and when I went to dances or to parties in them, there was always an odd provision or limitation – not spoken of or mentioned, but there just the same. I suddenly had the very confusing mental and emotional conflict of a lady leading a double life. It was unreal and it puzzled me, and I could not help dwelling on it.

Here the medical profession is likely to have the special job of informing the infirm who he is going to have to be.

A fourth pattern is illustrated by those who are initially socialized in an alien community, whether inside or outside the geographical boundaries of the normal society, and who then must learn a second way of being that is felt by those around them to be the real and valid one.

It should be added that when an individual acquires a new stigmatized self late in life, the uneasiness he feels about new associates may slowly give way to uneasiness felt concerning old ones. Post-stigma acquaintances may see him simply as a fated person; pre-stigma acquaintances, being attached to a conception of what he once was, may be unable to treat him either with formal tact or with familiar acceptance:

My task [as a blind writer interviewing prospective clients for his literary product] was to put the men I'd come to see at their ease – the reverse of the usual situation. Curiously, I found it much easier to do with men I'd never met before. Perhaps this was because with strangers there was no body of reminiscences to cover before business could be gotten down to and so there was no unpleasant contrast with the present.

Regardless of which general pattern the moral career of the stigmatized individual illustrates the phase of experience during which he learns that he possesses a stigma will be especially interesting, for at this time he is likely to be thrown into a new relationship to others who possess the stigma too.

42 David Sudnow

Normal Crimes

Excerpts from David Sudnow, 'Normal crimes: sociological features of the penal code in a public defender office', *Social Problems*, vol. 12, Winter 1965, no. 3, pp. 255–68.

Two stances toward the utility of official classificatory schema for criminological research have been debated for years. One position, which might be termed that of the 'revisionist' school, has it that the categories of the criminal law, e.g., 'burglary', 'petty theft', 'homicide', etc., are not 'homogeneous in respect to causation'. From an inspection of penal code descriptions of crimes, it is argued that the way persons seem to be assembled under the auspices of criminal law procedure is such as to produce classes of criminals who are, at least on theoretical grounds, as dissimilar in their social backgrounds and styles of activity as they are similar. The entries in the penal code, this school argues, require revision if sociological use is to be made of categories of crime and a classificatory scheme of etiological relevance is to be developed. Common attempts at such revision have included notions such as *'white collar* crime', and *'systematic* check forger', these conceptions constituting attempts to institute sociologically meaningful specifications which the operations of criminal law procedure and statutory legislation 'fail' to achieve.

The other major perspective toward the sociologist's use of official categories and the criminal statistics compiled under their heading derives less from a concern with etiologically useful schema than from an interest in understanding the actual operations of the administrative legal system. Here, the categories of the ciminal law are not regarded as useful or not, as objects to be either adopted, adapted, or ignored; rather, they are seen as constituting the basic conceptual equipment with which such people as judges, lawyers, policemen, and probation workers organize their everyday activities. The study of the actual use of official classification systems by actually employed administrative personnel regards the penal code as data, to be preserved intact; its use, both in organizing the work of legal representation, accusation, adjudication, and prognostication and in compiling tallies of legal occurrences, is to be examined as one would examine any social activity. By sociologically regarding, rather than criticizing, rates of statistics and the categories employed to assemble them, one learns, it is promised, about the 'rate producing agencies' and the assembling process.

While the former perspective, the 'revisionist' position, has yielded several fruitful products, the latter stance (commonly identified with what is rather loosely known as the 'labelling' perspective), has been on the whole more promissory than productive, more programmatic than empirical [. . .]

I will address the question: what of import for the sociological analysis of legal administration can be learned by describing the actual way the penal code is employed in the daily activities of legal representation? First, I shall consider the 'guilty plea' as a way of handling criminal cases, focusing on some features of the penal code as a description of a population of defendants. Then I shall describe the Public Defender operation with special attention to the way defendants are represented. The place of the guilty plea and penal code in this representation will be examined [. . .]

Guilty pleas, inclusion and normal crimes

It is a commonly noted fact about the criminal court system generally, that the greatest proportion of cases are 'settled' by a guilty plea. In the county from which the following material is drawn, over 80 per cent of all cases 'never go to trial'. To describe the method of obtaining a guilty plea disposition, essential for the discussion to follow, I must distinguish between what shall be termed 'necessarily-included-lesser-offenses' and 'situationally-included-lesser-offenses'. Of two offenses designated in the penal code, the lesser is considered to be that for which the length of required incarceration is the shorter period of time. *Inclusion* refers to the relation between two or more offenses. The 'necessarily-included-lesser offense' is a strictly legal notion.

Whether a lesser offense is included in the crime charged is a question of law to be determined solely from the definition and corpus delicti of the offense charged and of the lesser offense. . . . If all the elements of the *corpus delicti* of a lesser crime can be found in a list of all the elements of the offense charged, then only is the lesser included in the greater.

Stated alternatively: 'The test in this state of necessarily included offenses is simply that where an offense cannot be committed without necessarily committing another offense, the latter is a necessarily included offense.'

The implied negative is put: could Smith have committed A and not B? If the answer is yes, then B is not necessarily included in A. If the answer is no, B is necessarily included. While in a given case a battery might be committed in the course of a robbery, battery is not necessarily included in robbery. Petty theft is necessarily included in robbery but not in burglary. Burglary primarily involves the 'intent' to acquire another's goods illegally (e.g., by breaking and entering); the consummation of the act need not occur for burglary to be committed. Theft, like robbery, requires that some item be stolen.

I shall call *lesser* offenses that are not necessarily but 'only' *actually* included, 'situationally-included-lesser-offenses'. By statutory definition, necessarily included offenses are 'actually' included. By actual here, I refer to the 'way it occurs as a course of action'. In the instance of necessary inclusion, the 'way it occurs' is relevant. With situational inclusion, the 'way it occurs' is definitive. In the former case, no particular course of action is referred to. In the latter, the scene and progress of the criminal activity would be analyzed.

The issue of necessary inclusion has special relevance for two procedural matters.

1. *A man cannot be charged and/or convicted of two or more crimes any one of which is necessarily included in the others, unless the several crimes occur on separate occasions.*
If a murder occurs, the defendant cannot be charged and/or convicted of both 'homicide' and 'intent to commit a murder', the latter of which is necessarily included in first degree murder. If, however, a defendant 'intends to commit a homicide' against one person and commits a 'homicide' against another, both offenses may be properly charged. While it is an extremely complex question as to scope and definition, in most instances the rule is easily applied.

2. *The judge cannot instruct the jury to consider as alternative crimes of which to find a defendant guilty, crimes that are not necessarily included in the charged crime or crimes.*
If a man is charged with 'statutory rape' the judge may instruct the jury to consider as a possible alternative conviction 'contributing to the delinquency of a minor', as this offense is necessarily included in 'statutory rape'. He cannot however suggest that the alternative 'intent to commit murder' be considered and the jury cannot find the defendant guilty of this latter crime, unless it is charged as a distinct offense in the complaint.

It is crucial to note that these restrictions apply only to (1) the relation between several charged offenses in a formal allegation, and (2) the alternatives allowable in a jury instruction. At any time before a case 'goes to trial', alterations in the charging complaint may be made by the district attorney. The issue of necessary inclusion has no required bearing on (1) what offence(s) will be charged initially by the prosecutor, (2) what the relation is between the charge initially made and 'what happened', or (3) what modifications may be made after the initial charge and the relation between initially charged offenses and those charged in modified complaints. It is this latter operation, the modification of the complaint, that is central to the guilty pleas disposition.

Complaint alterations are made when a defendant agrees to plead guilty to an offense and thereby avoid a trial. The alteration occurs in the context of a 'deal' consisting of an offer from the district attorney to alter the original charge in such a fashion that a lighter sentence will be incurred with a guilty plea than would be the case if the defendant were sentenced on the original charge. In return for this manipulation the defendant agrees to plead guilty. The arrangement is proposed in the following format: 'If you plead guilty to this new lesser offense, you will get less time in prison than if you plead not guilty to the original, greater charge and lose the trial.' The decision must then be made whether or not the chances of obtaining complete acquittal at trial are great enough to warrant the risk of a loss and higher sentence if found guilty on the original charge. As we shall see below, it is a major job of the Public Defender, who mediates between the district attorney and the defendant, to convince his 'client' that the chances of aquittal are too slight to warrant this risk.

If a man is charged with 'drunkenness' and the Public Defender and Public Prosecutor (hereafter PD and DA) prefer not to have a trial, they seek to have the defendant agree to plead guilty. While it is occasionally possible, particularly with first offenders, for the PD to convince the defendant to plead guilty to the originally charged offense, most often it is felt that some 'exchange' or 'consideration' should be offered, i.e., a lesser offense charged.

To what offense can 'drunkenness' be reduced? There is no statutorily designated crime that is necessarily included in the crime of 'drunkenness'. That is, if any of the statutorily required components of drunk behavior (its corpus delicti) are absent, there remains no offense of which the resultant description is a definition. For drunkenness there is, however, an offense that while not necessarily included is 'typically-situationally-included', i.e., 'typically' occurs as a feature of the way drunk persons are seen to behave – 'disturbing the peace'. The range of possible sentences is such that, of the two offenses, 'disturbing the peace' cannot call for as long a prison sentence as 'drunkenness'. If, in the course of going on a binge, a person does so in such a fashion that 'disturbing the peace' may be employed to describe some of his behavior, it would be considered as an alternative offense to offer in return for a guilty plea. A central question for the following analysis will be: in what fashion would he have to behave so that disturbing the peace would be considered a suitable reduction?

If a man is charged with 'molesting a minor', there are not any necessarily included lesser offenses with which to charge him. Yet an alternative charge – 'loitering around a schoolyard' – is often used as a reduction. As above, and central to our analysis the question is: what would the defendant's behavior be such that 'loitering around a schoolyard' would constitute an appropriate alternative?

If a person is charged with 'burglary', 'petty theft' is not necessarily included. Routinely, however, 'petty theft' is employed for reducing the charge of burglary. Again, we shall ask: what is the relation between burglary and petty theft and the *manner in which the former occurs* that warrants this reduction?

Offenses are regularly reduced to other offenses the latter of which are not necessarily or situationally included in the former. As I have already said the determination of whether or not offense X was situationally included in Y involves an analysis of the course of action that constitutes the criminal behavior. I must now turn to examine this mode of behavioral analysis.

When encountering a defendant who is charged with 'assault with a deadly weapon', the PD asks: 'What can this offense be reduced to so as to arrange for a guilty plea?' As the reduction is only to be proposed by the PD and accepted or not by the DA, his question becomes 'what reduction will be allowable?' (As shall be seen below, the PD and DA have institutionalized a common orientation to allowable reductions.) The method of reduction involves, as a general feature, the fact that the particular case in question is scrutinized to decide its membership in a class of similar cases. But the penal code does *not* provide the reference for deciding the correspondence between the instant event and the general case; that is, it does not define the classes of offense types. To decide, for purposes of finding a suitable reduction, if the instant case involves a 'burglary', reference is not made to the statutory definition of 'burglary'. To decide what the situationally included offenses are in the instant case the instant case is not analyzed as a *statutorily* referable course of action; rather, reference is made to a *non-statutorily* conceived class 'burglary' and offenses that are typically situationally included in it, taken as a class of behavioral events. Stated again: in searching an instant case to decide what to *reduce it to*, there is no analysis of the statutorily referable elements of the instant case; instead, its membership in a class of events, the features of which cannot be described by the penal code, must be decided. An example will be useful. If a defendant is charged with burglary and the PD is concerned to propose a reduction to a lesser offense, he might search the elements of the burglary at hand to decide what other offenses were committed. The other offenses he might 'discover' would be of two sorts: those necessarily and those situationally included. In attempting to decide those other offenses situationally included in the instant event, the instant event might be analyzed as a statutorily referable course of action. Or, as is the case with the PD, the instant case might be analyzed to decide if it is a 'burglary' in common with other 'burglaries' conceived of in terms other than those provided by the statute.

Burglaries are routinely reduced to petty theft. If we were to analyse the way burglaries typically occur, petty theft is neither situationally or necessarily included; when a burglary is committed, money or other goods are seldom illegally removed from some person's body. If we therefore analysed burglaries, employing the penal code as our reference, and then searched the PD's records to see how burglaries are reduced in the guilty plea, we could not establish a rule that would describe the transformation between the burglary cases statutorily described and the reductions routinely made (i.e., to 'petty theft'). The rule must be sought elsewhere, in the character of the non-statutorily defined class of 'burglaries', which I shall term *normal burglaries*.

Normal crimes

In the course of routinely encountering persons charged with 'petty theft', 'burglary', 'assault with a deadly weapon', 'rape', 'possession of marijuana', etc., the PD gains knowledge of the typical manner in which offenses of given classes are committed, the social characteristics of the persons who regularly commit them, the features of the settings in which they occur, the types of victims often involved, and the like. He learns to speak knowledgeably of 'burglars', 'petty thieves', 'drunks', 'rapists', 'narcos', etc., and to attribute to them personal biographies, modes of usual criminal activity, criminal histories, psychological characteristics, and social backgrounds. The following characterizations are illustrative:

Most ADWs (assault with deadly weapon) start with fights over some girl.

These sex fiends (child molestation cases) usually hang around parks or schoolyards. But we often get fathers charged with these crimes. Usually the old man is out of work and stays at home when the wife goes to work and he plays around with his little daughter or something. A lot of these cases start when there is some marital trouble and the woman gets mad.

I don't know why most of them don't rob the big stores. They usually break into some cheap department store and steal some crummy item like a $9.95 record player you know.

Kids who start taking this stuff (narcotics) usually start out when some buddy gives them a cigarette and they smoke it for kicks. For some reason they always get caught in their cars, for speeding or something.

They can anticipate that point when persons are likely to get into trouble:

Dope addicts do OK until they lose a job or something and get back on the streets and, you know, meet the old boys. Someone tells them where to get some and there they are.

In the springtime, that's when we get all these sex crimes. You know, these kids play out in the schoolyard all day and these old men sit around and watch them jumping up and down. They get their ideas.

The PD learns that some kinds of offenders are likely to repeat the same offense while others are not repeat violators or, if they do commit crimes frequently, the crimes vary from occasion to occasion:

You almost never see a check man get caught for anything but checks – only an occasional drunk charge.

Burglars are usually multiple offenders, most times just burglaries or petty thefts

Petty thefts get started for almost anything – joy riding, drinking, all kinds of little things.

These narcos are usually through after the second violation or so. After the first time some stop, but when they start on the heavy stuff, they've had it.

I shall call *normal crimes* those occurrences whose typical features, e.g. the ways they usually occur and the characteristics of persons who commit them (as well as the typical victims and typical scenes), are known and attended to by the PD. For any of a series of offense types the PD can provide some form of proverbial characterization. For example, *burglary* is seen as involving regular violators, no weapons, low-priced items, little property damage, lower class establishments, largely Negro defendants, independent operators, and a non-professional orientation to the crime. *Child molesting* is seen as typically entailing middle-aged strangers of lower class middle-aged fathers (few women), no actual physical penetration or severe tissue damage, mild fondling, petting, and stimulation, bad marriage circumstances, multiple offenders with the same offense repeatedly committed, a child complainant, via the mother, etc. *Narcotics* defendants are usually Negroes, not syndicated, persons who start by using small stuff, hostile with police officers, caught by some form of entrapment technique, etc. *Petty thefts* are about fifty-fifty Negro–White, unplanned offenses, generally committed on lower class persons and don't get much money, don't often employ weapons, don't make living from thievery, usually younger defendants with long juvenile assaultive records, etc. *Drunkenness* offenders are lower class white and Negro, get drunk on wine and beer, have long histories of repeated drunkenness, don't hold down jobs, are usually arrested on the streets, seldom violate other penal code sections, etc.

Some general features of the normal crime as a way of attending to a category of persons and events may be mentioned:

1. The focus, in these characterizations, is not on particular individuals, but offense types. If asked 'What are burglars like?' or 'How are burglaries usually committed?', the PD does not feel obliged to refer to particular burglars and burglaries as the material for his answer.

2. The features attributed to offenders and offenses are often not of import for the statutory conception. In burglary, it is 'irrelevant' for the statutory determination whether or not much damage was done to the premises (except where, for example, explosives were employed and a new statute could be invoked). Whether a defendant breaks a window or not, destroys property within the house or not, etc., does not affect his statutory classification as a burglar. While for robbery the presence or absence of a weapon sets the degree, whether the weapon is a machine gun or pocket knife is 'immaterial'. Whether the residence or business establishment in a burglary is located in a higher income area of the city is of no issue for the code requirements. And, generally, the defendant's race, class position, criminal history (in most offenses), personal attributes, and particular style of committing offenses are features specifically not definitive of crimes under the auspices of the penal code. For deciding 'Is this a "burglary" case I have before me', however, the PD's reference to this range of non-statutorily referable personal and social attributes, modes of operation, etc., is crucial for the arrangement of a guilty plea bargain.

3. The features attributed to offenders and offenses are, in their content, specific to the community in which the PD works. In other communities and historical periods the lists would presumably differ. Narcotics violators in certain areas, for example, are syndicated in dope rackets or engage in systematic robbery as professional criminals, features which are not commonly encountered (or, at least, evidence for which is not systematically sought) in this community. Burglary in some cities will more often occur at large industrial plants, banking establishments,

warehouses, etc. The PD refers to the population of defendants in the county as 'our defendants' and qualifies his prototypical portrayals and knowledge of the typically operative social structures, 'for our county'. An older PD, remembering the 'old days', commented: 'We used to have a lot more rapes than we do now, and they used to be much more violent. Things are duller now in —'.

4. Offenses whose normal features are readily attended to are those which are routinely encountered in the courtroom. This feature is related to the last point. For embezzlement, bank robbery, gambling, prostitution, murder, arson, and some other uncommon offenses, the PD cannot readily supply anecdotal and proverbial characterizations. While there is some change in the frequences of offense-type convictions over time, certain offenses are continually more common and others remain stably infrequent. The troubles created for the PD when offenses whose features are not readily known occur and whose typicality is not easily constructed, will be discussed in some detail below.

5. Offenses are ecologically specified and attended to as normal or not according to the locales within which they are committed. The PD learns that burglaries usually occur in such and such areas of the city, petty thefts around this or that park, ADWs in these bars. Ecological patterns are seen as related to socio-economic variables and these in turn to typical modes of criminal and non-criminal activities. Knowing where an offense took place is thus, for the PD, knowledge of the likely persons involved, the kind of scene in which the offense occurred, and the pattern of activity characteristic of such a place: almost all of our ADWs are in the same half a dozen bars. These places are Negro bars where laborers come after hanging around the union halls trying to get some work. Nobody has any money and they drink too much. Tempers are high and almost anything can start happening.

6. One further important feature can be noted at this point. Its elaboration will be the task of a later section. As shall be seen, the PD office consists of a staff of twelve full time attorneys. Knowledge of the properties of offense types of offenders, i.e., their normal, typical, or familiar attributes, constitutes the mark of any given attorney's competence. A major task in socializing the new PD deputy attorney consists in teaching him to recognize these attributes and to come to do so naturally. The achievement of competence as a PD is signalled by the gradual acquisition of professional command not simply of local penal code peculiarities and courtroom folklore, but, as importantly, of relevant features of the social structure and criminological wisdom. His grasp of that knowledge over the course of time is a key indication of his expertise. Below, in our

brief account of some relevant organizational properties of the PD system, we shall have occasion to re-emphasize the competence-attesting aspects of the attorney's proper use of established sociological knowledge. Let us return to the mechanics of the guilty plea procedure as an example of the operation of the notion of normal crimes.

Over the course of their interaction and repeated 'bargaining' discussions, the PD and DA have developed a set of unstated recipes for reducing original charges to lesser offenses. These recipes are specifically appropriate for use in instances of normal crimes and in such instances alone. 'Typical' burglaries are reduced to petty theft, 'typical' ADWs to simple assault, 'typical' child molestation to loitering around a schoolyard, etc. The character of these recipes deserves attention.

The specific content of any reduction, i.e., what particular offense class X offenses will be reduced to, is such that the reduced offense may bear no obvious relation (neither situationally nor necessarily included) to the originally charged offense. The reduction of burglary to petty theft is an example. The important relation between the reduced offense and the original charge is such that the reduction from one to the other is considered 'reasonable'. At this point we shall only state what seems to be the general principle involved in deciding this reasonableness. The underlying premises cannot be explored at the present time, as that would involve a political analysis beyond the scope of the present report.

Both PD and DA are concerned to obtain a guilty plea wherever possible and thereby avoid a trial. At the same time, each party is concerned that the defendant 'receive his due'. The reduction of offense X to Y must be of such a character that the new sentence will depart from the anticipated sentence for the original charge to such a degree that the defendant is likely to plead guilty to the new charge and, at the same time, not so great that the defendant does not 'get his due'.

In a homicide, while battery is a necessarily included offense, it will not be considered as a possible reduction. For a conviction of second degree murder a defendant could receive a life sentence in the penitentiary. For a battery conviction he would spend no more than six months in the county jail. In a homicide, however, 'felony manslaughter', or 'assault with a deadly weapon', whatever their relation to homicide as regards inclusion, would more closely approximate the sentence outcome that could be expected on a trial conviction of second degree murder. These alternatives would be considered. For burglary, a typically situationally included offense might be 'disturbing the peace', 'breaking and entering' or 'destroying public property'. 'Petty theft', however, constitutes a reasonable lesser alternative to burglary as the sentence for petty theft will often range between six months and one year in the county jail and burglary regularly does not carry higher than two years in the state prison. 'Disturbing the peace' would be a thirty-day sentence offense.

While the present purposes make the exposition of this calculus unnecessary, it can be noted and stressed that the particular content of the reduction does not necessarily correspond to a relation between the original and altered charge that could be described in either the terms of necessary or situational inclusion. Whatever the relation between the original and reduced charge, its essential feature resides in the spread between sentence likelihoods and the reasonableness of that spread, i.e., the balance it strikes between the defendant 'getting his due' and at the same time 'getting something less than he might so that he will plead guilty' [. . .]

When a PD puts questions to the defendant he is less concerned with recording nuances of the instant event (e.g., how many feet from the bar were you when the cops came in, did you break into the back gate or the front door), than with establishing its similarity with 'events of this sort'. That similarity is established, not by discovering statutorily relevant events of the present case, but by locating the event in a sociologically constructed class of 'such cases'. The first questions directed to the defendant are of the character that answers to them either confirm or throw into question the assumed typicality. First questions with ADWs are of the order: 'How long had you been drinking before this all started?'; with 'child molestation cases': 'How long were you hanging around before this began?'; with 'forgery' cases: 'Was this the second or third check you cashed in the same place?'

We shall present three short excerpts from three first interviews. They all begin with the first question asked after preliminary background data is gathered. The first is with a 288 (child molestation), the second with a 459 (burglary) and the last with 11530 (possession of marijuana). Each interview was conducted by a different Public Defender. In each case the PD had no information about the defendant or this particular crime other than that provided by the penal code number.

288
PD: OK, why don't you start out by telling me how this thing got started?
Def: Well, I was at the park and all I did was to ask this little girl if she wanted to sit on my lap for awhile and you know, just sit on my lap. Well, about twenty minutes later I'm walkin' down the street about a block away from the park and this cop pulls up and there the same little girl is, you know, sitting in the back seat with some dame. The cop asks

me to stick my head in the back seat and he asks the kid if I was the one and she says yes. So he puts me in the car and takes a statement from me and here I am in the joint. All I was doin was playin' with her a little. . . .

PD: (interrupting) . . .OK I get the story, let's see what we can do. If I can get this charge reduced to a misdemeanor then I would advise you to plead guilty, particularly since you have a record and that wouldn't look too well in court with a jury.

(The interview proceeded for another two or three minutes and the decision to plead guilty was made.)

459

PD: Why don't you start by telling me where this place was that you broke into?

Def: I don't know for sure . . . I think it was on 13th street or something like that.

PD: Had you ever been there before?

Def: I hang around that neighborhood you know, so I guess I've been in the place before, yeah.

PD: What were you going after?

Def: I don't know, whatever there was so's I could get a little cash. Man, I was pretty broke that night.

PD: Was anyone with you?

Def: No, I was by myself.

PD: How much did you break up the place?

Def: I didn't do nothing. The back window was open a little bit see and I just put my hand in there and opened the door. I was just walking in when I heard police comin' so I turn around and start to run. And, they saw me down the block and that was that.

PD: Were you drunk at the time?

Def: I wasn't drunk, no, I maybe had a drink or two that evening but I wasn't drunk or anything like that.

11530

PD: Well Smith, why don't you tell me where they found it (the marijuana)?

Def: I was driving home from the drugstore with my friend and this cop car pulls me up to the side. Two guys get out, one of them was wearing a uniform and the other was a plain clothes man. They told us to get out of the car and then they searched me and then my friend. Then this guy without the uniform he looked over into the car and picked up this thing from the back floor and said something to the other one. Then he asked me if I had any more of the stuff and I said I didn't know what he was talking about. So he wrote something down on a piece of paper and made me sign it. Then he told my friend to go home and they took me down here to the station and booked me on possession of marijuana. I swear I didn't have no marijuana.

David Sudnow 401

PD: You told me you were convicted of possession in 1959.

Def: Yeah, but I haven't touched any of the stuff since then. I don't know what it was doing in my car, but I haven't touched the stuff since that last time.

PD: You ought to know it doesn't make any difference whether or not they catch you using, just so as they find it on your possession or in a car, or your house, or something.

Def: Man, I swear I don't know how it got there. Somebody must have planted it there.

PD: Look, you know as well as I do that with your prior conviction and this charge now that you could go away from here for five years or so. So just calm down a minute and let's look at this thing reasonably. If you go to trial and lose the trial, you're stuck. You'll be in the joint until you're twenty-eight years old. If you plead to this one charge without the priors then we can get you into jail maybe, or a year or two at the most in the joint. If you wait until the preliminary hearing and then they charge the priors, boy you've had it, it's too late.

Def: Well how about a trial?

(After ten minutes, the defendant decided to plead guilty to one charge of possession, before the date of the preliminary hearing.)

43 Edwin M. Lemert

Primary and Secondary Deviation

Excerpt from Edwin M. Lemert, 'Human Deviance, Social Problems and Social Control', in Marshall Chinard (ed.) *Anomie and Deviant*, Free Press, 1964, pp. 17–20.

There is a processual aspect to deviation, whose acknowledgement is forced on us by the fact that with repetitive, persistent deviation or invidious differentiation, something happens 'inside the skin' of the deviating person. Something gets built into the psyche or nervous system as a result of social penalties, or 'degradation ceremonies', or as a consequence of having been made the subject of 'treatment' or 'rehabilitation'. The individual's perception of values, means, and estimates of their costs undergoes revision in such ways that symbols which serve to limit the choices of most people produce little or no response in him, or else engender responses contrary to those sought by others.

Primary and secondary deviation

Considerations of this sort led the present writer, in an earlier paper, to pose a theoretical distinction between primary and secondary deviation. This was devised to bring attention to two different kinds of research problems, the second of which is untouched in Merton's discussions of deviation: firstly, how deviant behavior originates; secondly, how deviant acts are symbolically attached to persons and the effective consequences of such attachment for subsequent deviation on the part of the person.

Primary deviation is assumed to arise in a wide variety of social, cultural, and psychological contexts, and at best has only marginal implications for the psychic structure of the individual; it does not lead to symbolic reorganization at the level of self-regarding attitudes and social roles. Secondary deviation is deviant behavior, or social roles based upon it, which becomes means of defense, attack, or adaptation to the overt and covert problems created by the societal reaction to primary deviation. In effect, the original 'causes' of the deviation recede and give way to the central importance of the disapproving, degradational, and isolating reactions of society. The distinction between primary and secondary deviation is deemed indispensable to a complete understanding of deviation in modern, pluralistic society. Furthermore, it is held that the second research problem is pragmatically more pertinent for sociology than the first:

In modern society it is difficult or impossible to derive theoretically a set of specific behavioral prescriptions which will in fact be normatively supported, uniformly practised, and socially enforced by more than a segment of the total population. Under such conditions it is not the fact that individuals engage in behavior which diverge from some theoretically posited 'institutional expectations', or even that such behaviors are defined as deviant by the conventional and conforming members of society. A sociological theory of deviance must focus specifically on the interactions which not only define the behavior as deviant but also organize and activate the application of sanctions by individuals, groups and agencies. For in modern society the socially significant differentiation of deviants from non-deviants is increasingly contingent upon circumstances of situation, place, social and personal biography and bureaucratically organized agencies of social control.

Social control and deviation

We can move now from a kind of revisionist critique of Merton's paradigm to the major theoretical issue between a purely structural conception of deviation and the view of deviation as a consequence of the extent and form of social control. The latter rests upon the assumption that social control must be taken as an independent variable rather than as a constant, or merely reciprocal, societal reaction to deviation. Thus conceived, social control becomes a 'cause' rather than an effect of the magnitude and variable forms of deviation.

Facts are readily marshaled to give body to this conception. Firth, in the previously cited study of suicide in Tikopia, brought out the importance of the organization and dispatch of rescue fleets among other factors determining the lethal probabilities in suicide behavior. In our own society differences in crime rates between communities can be related to variations in available means for policing, as measured, for example, by a ratio of police to population. The differing efficacy of families as supervisory agencies similarly can be shown to have a notable effect on rate differences in juvenile delinquency. Finally, the presence of absence of a 'compliance section' in corporations undoubtedly has something to do with frequency with which antitrust laws are violated.

However, it is necessary to proceed beyond these obvious implications of social control for the incidence of deviation to those more closely connected with its operation in modern pluralistic society. In so doing we would like to note that new ways of thinking can be opened up by assuming that, in the absence of pressures to conform, people will deviate, or more precisely, express a variety of idiosyncratic impulses in overt behavior. When this assumption is joined with our earlier one, that our society increasingly shows fluid and open structuring of situations, categorically different ideas about deviation follow.

An equally flexible conception of norms is required to supplement these assumptions. So considered, norms become little more than a reference point for action, or, following F. Cohen, a set of probabilities that in some situations certain unpleasant things will happen to people either at the hands of associates or from actions of legal or other tribunals. When these probabilities are high we can assume that behavior of an individual and of those reacting to it express patterned values. When they are low we must make other assumptions about the outcome of the individual's actions and of the actions of those who react to him; we must, in so doing, adopt a social-interactional rather than a relationship perspective.

Constitutive norms

Garfinkel has originated an intriguing set of notions revolving around what he designates as 'constitutive rules of social interaction', which appear to be promising concepts for research on behavior in unstructured situations. These are less specifications of substantive behavior than they are criteria of the possible locale, numbers of participants, and order of action an individual assumes must be chosen by himself and others in social interaction. These most nearly resemble ground rules or basic rules of a game. Thus, in a bridge game there are no rules requiring that a given card be played, only rules as to who should play it. Furthermore, players do not respond so much to the act as they do to its meaning in relation to the emerging strategy of the game. It is assumed that constitutive rules are discoverable as interactional guides in the course of daily events as well as in games.

The germane conclusion is that in certain situations it is impossible to determine what is regarded as normal or deviant behavior merely by inspecting its external features. It must be known what rules are the basis of social interaction and at what point the participants are in an interactional sequence. In the course of such interaction, individuals may unilaterally change the rules or the rules may, by group interaction, be shifted to a new ground. In some cases this may take the form of a sliding scale of norms, as at a cocktail party where behavior which would not be allowable at the beginning may become so after 'things get going'. Courtship and sex behavior in general would seem to fall into the category of game-like interaction, in which rules are progressively changed by variety of subtle cues, dress, or sententious silence. Often this applies not only to the courting pair but also to parents and the community.

When constitutive rules are breached, the situation becomes 'confused', which may either lead to withdrawal of persons from interaction or to a redefinition of the unexpected behavior in terms of alternative meanings of what is constitutively 'normal' or acceptable. The interim interaction which culminates in mutual acceptance of new constitutive rules is one of 'normalization'. Normalization takes place between persons who 'trust' one another, or who are bonded together by mutual claims, as in family, friendships, reciprocal business and professional relationships, or by informal ties which grow up within formal organizations. It also may occur in what Goffman calls 'encounters', when they are governed by some criteria of politeness or courtesy, or by humanitarian solicitude for physically handicapped persons.

From the point of view of valuational choice, normalization will persist so long as the value satisfactions contingent on the interactional bond are of a higher order than those sacrificed by continued normalization. In such a context anomie becomes the state of confusion during which social interactors are unable to discover alternately acceptable meanings for the departure from the rules. Deviant behavior and the possibility of control action arise from the assignment of unacceptable meanings to behavior in interaction which results in high costs or sacrifices of values to those associated with the bond of trust who have access to means of social control.

Normalization is readily perceived in family interaction where a wide variety of idiosyncratic behavior becomes acceptable by virtue of esoteric rules which evolve out of social interaction. A great deal of behavior which in another context would be defined as 'delinquent' is normalized because the rules of interaction are different. Even more impressive is the normalization of behavior which, when projected against the diagnostic criteria of formal psychiatry, would be looked upon as 'neurotic' or 'psychotic'. Equally revealing is the diversity of meaning of intoxication in courtship, marriage, and family settings, or even in occupational situations. One position established by research, as well as theory, in the field of speech disorders is that there is no such thing as abnormal speech among children, and that speech problems are a function of parental perception and evaluation.

There are pressing reasons why primary groups go to what might be thought of as extreme lengths in normalizing the behavior of members. When confronted by a breach of constituted rules, voluntary withdrawal or 'leaving the field' often is impossible for interacting members. Excluding the person who breaches the rules is a drastic step, for it betokens a betrayal of trust, which must be justified to group members as well as to others. The problem is even more critical if the group turns to formal or legal agencies of social control, or when the primary group is forced to interact with such formal agencies due to violation of formal rules by a member.

44 Edwin M. Lemert

Stuttering among the North Pacific Coastal Indians

Excerpts from Edwin M. Lemert, 'Stuttering among the North Pacific coastal Indians', *South-Western Journal of Anthropology*, vol. 8, Winter 1952, pp. 429–41.

The following is a report and tentative interpretation of research findings of a field investigation into the incidence and cultural aspects of stuttering among a number of Indian tribes in the North Pacific coastal area of British Columbia. The project was part of a larger enterprise to gather comparative materials on deviant behavior but more specifically followed certain lines of inquiry initiated by clinical psychologists working on the problem of speech disorders in American Indian societies, who were unable to find evidence of stuttering in these groups [. . .]

Attitudes toward stutterers

The attitudes of the coastal Indians in the North Pacific toward stutterers range from mild to serious disapproval, through humorous tolerance, to pity and condescension. Members of the three mainland tribes, the Homalthko, Sliammon, and Tlahoose were easily moved to laughter by mention or discussion of the subject. Their reaction is best summed up by the statement of one man who said: 'Oh, we laugh at such people at first but then we get used to them.' Another man interviewed on the Nanaimo reserve expressed essentially the same attitude, adding the observation that 'outsiders' continued to laugh at stutterers even though their immediate associates came in time to accept them without comment. Several of the undirected, freely associated stories which we had children of the Port Alberni residential school write on the subject of 'A person who couldn't talk right or who stuttered' conveyed ideas that in the Bella Bella and Tsimshian areas parents tended to be shamed by their children if they stuttered. This is not unexpected in the light of the high standards of decorum for children, especially of high-ranking parents, held in the old Tsimshian culture, in which, among other stringencies, children were forbidden to run in their play lest they accidentally fall and thus shame their parents.

A more specific demonstration of negative attitudes toward stutterers came from our case history of a Tsimshian stutterer. His father severely criticized him as a child for his faulty speech, invoking the native term for 'acting crazy' (in contradistinction to insanity) to express his strong disapproval of his son's verbal failures. This concept was generally applied to anyone deviating in disapproved ways from the norms of the culture. This man's father also had told him disapprovingly that in former days boys with speech defects had to take a back seat in the 'potlatch' ceremonies and could not actively participate in them. A Haida woman confirmed that this was also the case in her tribe in former times. A Kwakiutl spokesman said he had known of stutterers but had never known of one who took part in a potlatch. However, all of this does not mean that anyone in these tribes was free to insult a person because of his speech difficulties, for there was always the threat that the family of the offended man or woman would give a potlatch to shame the person or clan responsible for the insult.

It is from the Nootka that we get the most abundant evidence of social penalization of persons with physical and speech defects. In this culture fat persons, very small persons, sore-eyed, squinting, cock-eyed, hunchbacked, lame, circumcized, left-handed people and those with different speech disorders became the object of pity, mockery, satirization, humor, and patronage of the sort shown small children. This is most apparent in the myths of the Nootka, but emerges with equal clarity in associations of animals, mythological characters, and defective persons with various linguistic and stylistic processes involving the symbolic use of sounds. Thus when a person who had a speech defect was addressed or talked about, his defect was imitated or mocked, with changes in word forms – such as suffix changes – which carried implications of smallness, childishness, animal quality, or of some physical defect.

The analysis of myths occurring throughout the broader culture area of the Northwest reveals much the same social rejection and social isolation of such child deviants as orphans, crippled, blind, stupid, dirty, lazy, weak, and those with scabs or skin diseases. Most of these myths are analogues of the success stories of our own culture and have been specifically analyzed as variants of the Cinderella theme in Grimms' fairy tales. It is perhaps significant that the Swaixwe mask, whose mythological origin concerns a boy who gets cured of a bad skin disease and is enabled to invent and use a new dance ceremony, has the widest distribution of any mask in the Northwest. While stutterers are not mentioned in any of these myths, we found in several of the stories written for us by the residential school children there were equivalents of Horatio Alger-like stutterers who overcome their defect to go on and become famous. Since the analysis of the myths was a content analysis and not a stylistic or linguisitic one, we do not know whether abnormal speech forms were used in telling the myths as was found by Sapir in Nootka.

With the Nootka these abnormal speech forms could have varying meanings of mere smallness, contempt, or even pitying affection depending upon the nature of the relationship between the speaker and the person addressed or discussed. Imitation of the defects of one person might be done in a friendly spirit, whereas the same mimicry of another would be an insult. Furthermore, it seems that some restraint was exercised in mocking adults when they were present, although this was not the case for children. An expression of this qualified attitude toward persons with speech disorders is seen in the application of special names by the Nootka. Our informant recalled, for example, one lame man who was known as 'rotten foot', another known as 'the man whose wound healed with skunk cabbage in it', and lastly, of more direct interest, one called the 'stuttering man'. He said that such names could be given the person either by himself or by close relatives. However, it would be insulting for unrelated persons to impose the name, and only such a man's close friends were free to address him in this fashion.

Insofar as our data permit us to say, the Nootka differed from the Tsimshian in respect to the more formal discrimination against persons with speech disorders. Being a stutterer did not bar one from giving a potlatch if he were otherwise able and entitled to do so. A stutterer who formerly lived at Barclay Sound was the head man of one of the four clans there and took part in and gave numerous potlatches. It might be added that this man was exceptionally well-liked for his personal characteristics. It should be borne in mind that while a high-ranking Nootka might make his own speeches at potlatch ceremonies, still it was culturally permissible to hire professional speakers for this purpose. However, doing this to show a person's wealth would be quite different from doing it because the person was an ineffective speaker.

The relation of stuttering to cultural factors

With the time and resources available our research could not result in the collection of data which would permit testing of any considerable number of the current theories of stuttering. Some isolated facts may be taken as bearing upon one or two of these theories. For example, there seems to have been very little mental disorder among the Nootka, which may be interpreted to mean that speech disorders there were unlikely to have been the function of neurotic or personality disorders. The theory that stuttering is related to dysphemia and changed-handedness gets some oblique support from the recorded aversion of the Nootka to left-handedness and their rather painful method used to discourage children from using their left hands. However, the limited nature of our knowledge of these things can permit little beyond speculation.

The particular data we secure and those available in ethnographies of the Northwest coastal culture areas lend themselves far more readily to testing socio-psychological theories of stuttering which make room for the interplay of cultural factors. Here we have in mind the explicit recognition of the importance of such factors in Johnson's 'evaluational' theory of stuttering and their implicit emphasis in Van Riper's formulation of the growth of stuttering as a process. Both theories, which have been widely influential in the study and treatment of stuttering, lay stress upon:

1. The penalizing reactions of others, especially those of anxious parents, critical siblings, and ridiculing playmates, toward the speech of the young child.

2. The internalization of these reactions or negative evaluations by the child.

3. The growth of anxiety in the child about his own speech.

4. The pathological disruption of the child's speech rhythms by this anxiety.

The main difference in the two views regarding the development of stuttering concerns the appearance of the initial symptoms of stuttering, with Van Riper holding that disorganization of the child's immediate social invironment can produce generalized conflict or anxiety, of which the stuttering is an expression. At this stage of the 'primary symptoms' the reactions of others enter by the above indicated process to create the exaggerated blocks we commonly recognize as stuttering. Johnson apparently believes that early as well as late stuttering is entirely due to the way in which mothers *define* (evaluate) the normally variable speech of children.

Our data can best be cited to test the more general socio-psychological proposition upon which there seems to be agreement in the theories of the two writers to whom we have referred. Insofar as it is possible we will examine data which bear upon the second, perhaps less important, point on which there is divergence of viewpoints. The most significant socio-cultural factors, of course, are those which affect parent–child interaction, for there seems to be a consensus that practically all stuttering begins in childhood. Consequently a consideration of child-rearing practices in relation to stuttering among the Northwest coastal Indians is directly relevant.

No trait of primitive society, particularly in North America, has been more widely commented upon than that of parental indulgence of children. The primitive cultures of the North Pacific prove to be no exception with respect to this characteristic. In general the reconstructed picture of primitive practice in this area is one in which corporal punishment plays a minor part or is absent entirely in the discipline of children. One exception we discovered, in recounts of the old culture of the mainland Homalthko, Tlahoose, and Sliammon, serves to emphasize the generalization. Here a child, if extremely recalcitrant, might be spanked with a beaver tail in front of other children of the band. However, this was always done by two persons especially designated for the job, never by the parents. The socialization of the child generally seems to have been brought about through teaching by example, long moral lectures and morality stories – often repeated – given by the grandparents, and private scoldings heavily laced with the shame motif. Threats seldom if ever entered into these.

Granting what seem to be obvious similarities between the childrearing methods of the northern Pacific Indian cultures and those in the rest of North America, it does not follow that the standards of childhood decorum, aspiration, and expectations of the child's ultimate participation in the formal rituals of the culture which served as goals of the educational process were comparable. Indeed it is precisely here, in the rich ceremonial solo drama and theatricality of feasts and potlatches captioning the life crises of the individual, that we perceive the differentiation of the Northwest coastal Indian cultures from those broadly conceived as North American. The importance of the ceremonial vindication of the individual's position in society was impressed quite early, with the indoctrinaton of adult values and goals beginning almost at birth. Parents in the Nootka tribes often began their discourses on mores while the infant was still cradle-bound, with high ranking fathers seriously lecturing sons at this time on the merits of giving feasts and potlatches. Most Nootka children while still quite young were expected to learn their privileged dances and sacred songs, and adults worked continuously with them to achieve the necessary competence in their performances. At very tender ages they were required to perform alone before assemblies of their own and other tribesmen. The Nootka ordinarily initiated children into the Shaman's dance at the age of seven or eight years; a chief might have his one-year-old son inducted as a novice, or even have his pregnant wife treated as a 'novice' as a means of initiating his unborn child into the adult ceremonial life.

This ritual, more or less central to the whole ceremonial complex of the Nootka, by its rough nature was undoubtedly a traumatic experience to many of the small children who were necessarily spectators and participants. On this point Drucker says:

Small children were usually frightened during the performance . . . the hulla-baloo and running about, the rough practical jokes (carried to the point of throwing people bodily into the sea), kidnapping and purported slaying of siblings and playmates all combined to make small children the least enter-tained and most perturbed of the spectators.

By the time children were old enough to become active participants in the Shaman's dance it is true that their fears inspired by it tended to disappear, but in their place came anxieties as to whether they would 'remember their instructions' and whether they would perform ade-quately. This anxiety, when it occurred, clearly seems to have been a reciprocal of socially invidious distinctions and the praise-rewards reac-tions of adults in terms of competency in performing rituals. In this connection it is informatve to read of an Ehetisaht Shaman's dance in which the 'wolves' going through the village announced that they wanted only those novices who could sing their songs and sing them well. An observer as far back as 1868 tells how Nootka boys in their evening play on the beach frequently mimicked famous orators of the tribes and recited parts of legendary speeches before an audience of old men who pointed out this boy or that boy as destined to do great things. That parents of the Nootkan tribes had anxieties concerning the future verbal facility of their children seems demonstrated by the custom of putting a finger far down in the infant's throat to insure his becoming a good singer.

It is to be noted that Nootka culture admitted of little or no deviation from ordinary rules of inheritance of songs or rituals, private or public, simply because the proper heir could not learn them. But along with this a person did not automatically gain acceptance in his rank purely by inheritance; it was necessary to show his right to social position by his personal traits, proper conduct, and ritualistic versatility. From the standpoint of the child the standards of the culture were not only rigor-ous and exacting but also inexorable; and their early imposition in-dubitably played a significant part in creating a very shame-conscious person, highly sensitive to his own behavior deviations and to those of other persons, including members of his own family. That this sensitivity extended to speech behavior is emphasized by Sproat's early remarks on the 'standard of correct speech' held by the Nootka and the extreme care with which they pronounced names and words they heard for the first time.

The competitive, rank-conscious stress of the culture undoubtedly made the deviant person especially vulnerable to mimicry, humorous anecdotes, and gossip, and, although the cultural ideal specified that the deviant accept all of this in good grace, it seems unlikely that he was able to do so. Thus, in speaking of persons who are *o'ucshaid* (bunglers, clumsy ones), the Nootka say they are teased without malice and that they tell stories on themselves, but also insightfully add that the teasing 'seems to make them worse; they do more and more funny things'. In the case of the stutterers it seems clear that they would be at the additional disadvantage of not being able to tell stories on themselves or to use effectively verbal aggressions when goaded beyond endurance.

While the general adult population of these Northwestern Indian tribes may have been partly restrained in criticizing the stuttering child, in all likelihood this was not true for his immediate family. It is also probable that in play groups the stutterer aboriginally encountered much open ridicule from other children – especially away from the presence of adults. The only deterrent here seems to have been cautions from parents to their children to be careful what they said to sons of chiefs. We guess that such cautions were ignored as frequently by, say, Nootka children in early times as comparable injunctions are by children in our society today.

The potlatch, of course was the main defense of the deviant against insult, but it is questionable whether the speech deviant was free to avail himself of the device, for by its very nature it would lead to a public display of the behavior occasioning the insult. Even if relatives or a friendly chief gave the potlatch for the insulted person, his defect would still be publicized. Indeed potlatches of this order seem to have been used more for wiping out shame related to incidental deviations from norms and accepted practices rather than that associated with a permanent or continuing social inadequacy.

Conclusion

There is fair to good evidence that stuttering is present among the people of the northwest coastal Indian tribes and for the probabilities of its aboriginal incidence. The cultural setting in these Indian societies in the past as well as in the present seems favorable to the development of stuttering. The facts indicate that aboriginally stuttering was culturally defined, that stutterers were and still are socially penalized, that parents tended to be specifically concerned or anxious about the speech development of children, that children were anxious about ritual performances involving solo verbal behavior, and that Indian stutterers showed and still show 'secondary' symptoms of the defect, which are ordinarily interpreted as distortions of the speech induced by internationalizations of anxiety about the speech.

We have no particular reason for questioning the authenticity of Johnson's and Snidecor's reports of an absence of stuttering and con-

comitant cultural definitions of the defect among the Bannock and Shoshone, inasmuch as their sample was large and as specialists in their field
they presumably knew what they were looking for. Consequently we are
left with the possibility that a real differentiation exists between these
cultures and Northwest Coast Indian cultures in these respects. However,
such differences are not incompatible with general nature of the theory
which we have been interested in testing. Indeed one study of child
development among the Wind River Shoshone gives much evidence that
the culture differs sharply from the cultures we have described with
respect both to degree of pressure on children and treatment of defective
persons.

45 Edwin M. Schur

Drug Addiction

Excerpts from Edwin M. Schur, *Crimes without Victims*,
Prentice-Hall, 1965, pp. 120–25, 130–52.

In recent years there has been considerable repudiation of the once prevalent 'dope fiend' myth – which depicted the drug addict as a degenerate and vicious criminal much given to violent crimes and sex orgies. More and more people are coming to understand the nature of opiate drugs and the meaning of addiction. This discussion will be concerned primarily with that class of pain-killing and soothing drugs derived from or equivalent to opium. Morphine and heroin are the best known of these drugs; others include codeine, meperidine (Demerol), and methadone (Amidone, Dolophine). Such pain-killers are the drugs of choice of most persons who are fully addicted in the sense described below. This is an important point, because the continued use of these opiate-type drugs (to which the term *narcotics* may also be applied) produces characteristics and behavior quite at odds with stereotyped conceptions of the dope addict.

Effect of opiates

Central to the various common misconceptions is the belief that the addict is dangerously 'hopped up'. Actually, opiates are depressants – that is, they produce a general lowering of the level of nervous and other bodily activity. The effects of these drugs have been summarized in this way: the depressant actions include analgesia (relief of pain), sedation (freedom from anxiety, muscular relaxation, decreased motor activity), hypnosis (drowsiness and lethargy), and euphoria (a sense of well-being and contentment).

Although the relation between addiction and criminality will be examined, there is nothing about the operation of these drugs which would incline a user to commit criminal offenses. In fact, the specific effects of opiates serve to decrease the likelihood of any violent antisocial behavior. Similarly, opiates produce a marked diminishing of the sexual appetite – long-term addiction producing impotence, among most male addicts; hence, concern about 'dope fiend sex orgies' is quite unfounded. Indeed, perhaps the most striking characteristic of addicts is their general inactivity – on the basis of which they might be considered unproductive or withdrawn but hardly fearsome.

It has also been widely believed that opiates produce definite and extreme organic disturbance and deterioration in the users. Yet, as an authoritative report recently emphasized, there are no known organic diseases assocated with chronic opiate addiction – such as are produced by alcohol addiction, regular cigarette-smoking, and even chronic over-eating. Although opiate use does produce such effects as pupillary constriction, constipation, and sexual impotence, none of these conditions need be fully disabling, nor are they permanent. Similarly many charac-teristics and ailments, such as unkempt appearance and symptoms of malnutrition, which often are exhibited by addicts in our society, are attributable to the difficulties they experience in obtaining drugs rather than to the drugs' direct effects.

There is also considerable misunderstanding about the supposedly pos-itive feelings the addict receives from the drugs. As noted above, a sense of well-being and contentment is often produced by opiates. As a young female addict has put it:

You simply do not worry about things you worried about before. You look at them in a different way. . . . Everything is always cool, everything is all right. It makes you not feel like fighting the world. . . . I mean it's that sort of a thing, you know, when you're *not* hooked.

Some discussions of addiction have exaggerated the positive nature of these euphoric effects, and this has led to the widespread belief that addicts take drugs solely for 'kicks'. The crucial misunderstanding is suggested by the addict's express limitation of the above description of euphoria to when you're *not* hooked. In most cases positive feelings about the drug are largely restricted to the early stages of addiction. In the later stages, a reversal of effects occurs in which the drug is no longer taken primarily to obtain positive pleasure but rather to avoid the nega-tive effects of withdrawal. As the addict just quoted goes on to say, the user's feeling about the drug changes drastically once real dependence upon it is reached: 'Suddenly, the character of taking off [injecting the drug] changes ... all you're trying to do is keep from getting ill, really. ...' Indeed, the theory of 'kicks' may be inadequate even when applied to the early stages of addiction. As one major research report has noted, the 'kicks' adolescent addicts seek may reflect their overwhelming general unhappiness. To the extent that the drug combats this un-happiness, it primarily offers relief rather than positive pleasure. The same report also refers to interesting laboratory findings of wide varia-tion in individual responses to an initial injection of opiates. These data suggest that even if such drugs tend to produce some euphoria, the nature and extent of this feeling may be greatly affected by the user's personality characteristics.

The addiction process

The process of becoming addicted involves a developing bondage to the drug. According to a World Health Organization definition:

Drug addiction is a state of periodic or chronic intoxication produced by the repeated consumption of a drug (natural or synthetic). Its characteristics include: (1) an overpowering desire or need (compulsion) to continue taking the drug and to obtain it by any means; (2) a tendency to increase the dose; (3) a psychic (psychological) and generally a physical dependence on the effects of the drug; (4) an effect detrimental to the individual and to the society.

The term *intoxication* may not be the most appropriate to use in describing the effects of opiates, and there is at least some dispute about the nature and extent of detriment necessarily associated with addiction. However, the rest of the definition does highlight the crucial features of the addiction process. Tolerance and dependence are the characteristics which distinguish the confirmed addict from other drug users. *Tolerance* refers to the process through which the body adapts to the effects of a drug. Because of such adaptation, the dose must increase in size if the same effects are to be produced; likewise, with the growth of tolerance the drug user becomes able to safely take doses which might be dangerous or even fatal if taken by a nonuser. It is important to note that addiction exhibits a *tendency to increase the dose*. As will be seen, there is considerable dispute about whether this tendency is virtually unalterable or whether it is possible for some addicts to be maintained on a stabilized dose.

Once tolerance to opiates reaches a certain level, a distinct physiological (as well as psychological) dependence on the drug is produced. When this dependence has developed addiction is complete and the user is properly referred to as an addict (although the term *addict* sometimes has been used more broadly to cover regular use even of non-dependence-producing drugs). The user's bodily system now, in effect, requires the drug to function smoothly, and if it is withdrawn the addict experiences acute symptoms of distress, known as the 'abstinence syndrome'. This syndrome includes a variety of both somatic and psychological symptoms, the severity of which is directly related to

The nature of the narcotic, the daily dosage used and the intervals, the duration of the addiction, the rapidity with which the drug is withdrawn, and the intensity of psychic and somatic dependence. It is inversely related to the resistance, vigor, and well-being of the addict.

As this same report notes, despite the likely variations just indicated, 'all recent authorities agree that the withdrawal syndrome has an organic basis'. It also seems clear that withdrawal of the confirmed addict from drugs is always at least an extremely unpleasant experience. Although in some cases the physical symptoms (which reflect disturbance of the neuromuscular, gastrointestinal, and respiratory systems) may be no more severe than a bad case of the flu, in other instances the addict may be acutely and violently ill. And the psychological impact of the experience should not be overlooked:

I thought I would go mad. I was on the verge of insanity. I prayed for help, for relief, for death. My clothes must have been wet with sweat. I cursed the habit. If anyone could have seen me they would have thought I was a raving maniac.

The phenomena of physical dependence and withdrawal distress are important to an understanding of the addiction problem. However, it would be a mistake to think that physical dependence fully explains the confirmed addict's need for drugs. Any individual administered opiates in sufficient dosages over a long enough time will, when administration is stopped, experience withdrawal distress. Thus many persons receiving such drugs in the course of medical treatment for the relief of pain become addicted to them. Yet not all such individuals revert to drugs after withdrawal. The term *drug addict* is ordinarily applied to those persons who, over some period of time, feel the 'overpowering desire or need (compulsion)' mentioned in the WHO definition; a recent study has employed the term *craving* in discusssing this important aspect of addiction.

At the same time, the fact that the long-term addict has a physiological as well as psychological need for his drugs helps to put his condition and his behavior in proper perspective. Dependence also provides a basis for distinguishing truly addictive drugs from those which may be said to be only habit-forming – or to which users ordinarily develop merely a psychological habituation or dependence. Tobacco and coffee would be good examples of such habituating drugs. Stimulants such as cocaine, marihuana, and peyote (mescaline and LSD are similar) may produce striking effects on the users and sometimes strong psychological habituation, but they are not truly addicting. Amphetamines (such as Benzedrine) also fall into this category. Barbiturate drugs, can, in prolonged use, lead to actual tolerance and physical dependence, but despite the danger of such addiction the medical use of barbiturates (primarily to treat insomnia) is widespread and socially approved in our society. Similarly, social approval of alcohol exists in the face of the well-known dangers of excessive drinking. Many experts insist that the condition of alcoholism is far more harmful to the individual than is opiate addiction. The unhappy lessons of the Prohibition experiment point up the key role negative social sanctions on drug use may play in creating secondary problems [. . .]

Drug laws and enforcement
Narcotics legislation

The practical effect of American narcotics laws is to define the addict as a criminal offender. This result has stemmed largely from the interpretation given the Harrison Act passed by Congress in 1914. This law requires registration of all legitimate drug-handlers and payment of a special tax on drug transactions. It thus establishes a licensing system for the control of legitimate domestic drug traffic. In this respect the Harrison Act has been extremely successful, and it seems clear that originally the statute was intended merely to serve this function. It specifically provided that the restrictions would not apply to dispensing of narcotics to a patient by a physician 'in the course of his professional practice' and 'for legitimate medical purposes'. As a recent and authoritative report concludes: 'Clearly, it was not the intention of Congress that government should interfere with medical treatment of addicts.' Yet, through a combination of restrictive regulations, attention only to favorable court decisions, and harassment, the Narcotics Division of the US Treasury Department (and its successor, the Federal Bureau of Narcotics) has effectively and severely limited the freedom of medical practitioners to treat addict-patients as they see fit – in particular, to provide addicts with drugs when that is believed medically advisable [. . .]

The failure of enforcement

What have these legal policies accomplished? Law enforcement officials often assert that addiction is being kept under control, yet even government estimates have placed the number of addicts between 45,000 and 60,000, and almost all non-governmental experts feel these figures greatly understate the problem. In any case, it is certain that these laws have not come anywhere close to eliminating addiction. They have, however, greatly influenced the narcotics problem. Cut off from legal supplies of narcotics, the addict naturally seeks illicit drug sources. The strong demand of addicts for their drugs means that there are huge profits to be made in the black market and this in turn makes the risks involved in such an endeavor worthwhile. According to one account, the retail value of one thousand dollars worth of heroin may surpass three million dollars. It is understandable, then, that the endless circle of supply and demand alluded to in a discussion of abortion should also be in evidence here. The addict's position in this exchange is so vulnerable that not only must he pay exorbitant amounts but typically he must settle for a highly diluted product; the repeated adulteration of narcotics as they go down the line from the original importer to the various distributors and ultimately to the addict is well-known. Many experts contend that no amount of law enforcement effort could reasonably be expected to stifle the black market in narcotics. Such observers believe that, given the extreme and continuous demand of addicts, some way always will be found to make the drugs available illegally. For, as Merton has suggested: 'In strictly economic terms, there is no relevant difference between the provision of licit and of illicit goods and services.'

Most enforcement officials admit that the task of significantly curbing the smuggling of narcotics into the US is a pretty hopeless task. The former US Commissioner of Narcotics himself has been quoted as saying that the combined efforts of the Army, the Navy, the Narcotics Bureau and the FBI could not eliminate drug smuggling. As a customs agent has pointed out, discussing his agency's operations in New York City:

On normal passenger arrival days it is the policy of the collector of customs at the Port of New York to examine baggage 100 per cent, but when the passenger arrivals are heavy, a spot-check of baggage is performed. Under these circumstances it is not difficult to understand how a passenger using a false-bottom trunk or a suitcase with a false compartment might be able to conceal narcotics and get by the examining inspector; searches of persons are infrequently made and then only as a last resort and only based on substantial reasons.

Again, as in the case of abortion, there occurs the competitive development of enforcement and anti-enforcement techniques.

But, basically, it is the supply-and-demand element and the lack of a complaining victim, rather than the cleverness of the law violators, that render the drug laws so largely unenforceable. Predictably in such a situation law enforcers must resort to special investigative techniques. A major source of evidence in narcotics cases is the addict-informer. Though the addict-informer faces grave danger of underworld reprisal, their eagerness to stay out of jail (and avoid sudden withdrawal from drugs) or simply their need for funds with which to purchase drugs impels many addicts to assume this role. The Bureau of Narcotics is authorized to pay the 'operating expenses' of informants whose information leads to the seizure of drugs in illicit traffic: hence, the Bureau at least indirectly supports the addiction (and the 'crime') of some addicts in order to uncover others. Despite this fact, and the questionable legal aspects involved in trapping suspects through informers, enforcement spokesmen insist on the propriety and even the necessity of such practices [. . .]

Often the informer or even the narcotics agent himself will directly attempt to obtain a prescription or a supply of drugs from a suspected doctor or peddler or through an addict. Thus narcotics investigations frequently tread the fine line between detection and entrapment [. . .]

In short, it is evident that the police face an impossible task in seeking to enforce current drug laws. The laws are inherently self-defeating. Even to approximate efficiency in their administration would require the wholesale violation of legal rights, which the courts will not permit. Likewise, judges are often unwilling to impose maximum sentences on addicted drug violators, and even prosecutors sometimes proceed against them under the less stringent of several possible charges. At the same time, enforcement personnel are under considerable pressure from segments of the public and from higher officials to produce results. It is not surprising, under these circumstances, that they exhibit strong hostility toward the addict, and view themselves as engaged in a 'war' against addiction. With a sharp attitudinal dividing line separating the 'good guys' (law enforcers) from the 'bad guys' (those involved in the world of drugs), important distinctions such as that between the addict and the nonaddicted drug violator, blur or disappear. These punitive attitudes, in turn, lead to increasingly brutal treatment of the addict, without any corresponding increase in the effectiveness of antinarcotic measures.

Addict crime and subculture

These laws do not merely fail to curb addiction, they also vitally influence addict behavior. The issue of crime by addicts has long concerned students of addiction. (The criminal behavior being considered here, of course, is not the mere possession and use of drugs – which may or may not be defined as criminal). One point alluded to at the beginning of this chapter must be underscored here: there is no evidence suggesting that crime results from the direct effects of the drugs themselves. Also, the addict is much more likely to commit nonviolent crimes against property than violent crimes against persons. This is to be expected from the depressant nature of the drugs. In an early study, psychiatrist L. Kolb suggested even that 'one is led to believe violent crime could be much less prevalent if all habitual criminals were addicts who could obtain sufficient morphine or heroin to keep themselves fully charged with one of these drugs at all times.' There is strong evidence that most crimes committed by addicts are undertaken in order to obtain funds with which to purchase illicit drugs. The statements and records of individual addicts amply corroborate the relationship between drug use and 'crime for profit'. Furthermore, the New York studies have shown that in high drug use areas there are relatively high rates of cash-producing delinquencies (robbery, burglary, procuring, and the like) and relatively low rates of violent crimes and other non-profit offenses. Similarly, a study of arrest data for Chicago in 1951 (comparing cases handled in the Narcotics Bureau with those processed by the municipal police department) indicated that 'the number of arrests for nonviolent property crimes was proportionately higher among addicts. In contrast, however, the number of arrests of addicts for violent offenses against the person, such as rape and aggravated assault, was only a fraction of the proportion constituted by such arrests among the population at large' [. . .]

Repression breeds subculture

Addict subculture also reflects the pressures produced by anti-addiction policies. That is brought out in an analysis of addict life prepared by S. Fiddle, a sociologist working with the East Harlem Protestant Parish in New York:

While certain patterns of addict life may have been in existence before the Harrison Act, the conversion of addiction into a mass criminal activity appears to have given special form and meaning to addiction, so that we may speak reasonably about an addict culture operating as a system.

Fiddle cites the existence of two major aspects of this subculture: the 'circulatory system' and the 'survival system'. The former term refers to the system of roles and interrelationships through which addicts secure illegal drugs. With the exception of physician-addicts and some other well-to-do addicts who may obtain narcotics (illegally, but with slight risk) from 'legitimate' sources (such as doctors and pharmacists), all addicts in the United States must enter into the complex underworld network distributing illicit drugs. The addict, then, is of necessity thrown into contact with drug peddlers or pushers, he may very likely become a pusher himself in order to support his habit, he invariably comes to engage in frequent interaction with other drug-users as well as with distributors. It is to his practical as well as psychological advantage to engage himself in every aspect of the drug-distributing and drug-consuming world. Fiddle makes this clear in discussing key features and functions of the 'survival system', which he lists as follows:

1. Ideology of justification.
2. The 'reproductive' process.
3. Defensive communication.

4. Neighborhood warning systems.
5. Ritualistic, magical and cyclical patterns.
6. The attractiveness of personal relations.

Like other oppressed minorities, drug addicts adopt a justifying ideology to support their morale and lessen their feeling of isolation. Although this might be true even in the absence of legal repression, it is all the more important in the face of such repression. By 'reproductive' process, Fiddle refers to the fact that the system continually requires new members in order to maintain itself. The considerable involvement of addicts in the drug-distribution process has led some observers to assert that it is basically the addicts themselves who spread the habit, and that therefore elimination of the 'professional' peddler would not appreciably alter the problem of addiction. In this view, the subculture and the addict-pusher are seen almost as causes of the addiction problem. Yet the evidence indicates that they are at least partly caused, in turn, by the supply-demand cycle and the pattern of legal repression. In any case, it is obvious that behind whatever distribution addicts themselves engage in are professional illicit suppliers who are motivated solely by the desire for profit. As one addict has put it: 'The trail always leads back to the same direction, to the peddler who was originally around to turn somebody on (introduce him to drug-taking)'.

Addict argot and special speech and gestural habits may serve practical as well as morale-enhancing functions. The need for cohesive ties in the face of strong adverse reaction is especially conducive to the development of such argot among deviants. But defensive communication means more than just a special addict jargon. Another aspect is the 'grapevine system':

Information about the coming of the police, or about the kind of heroin being sold, in different parts of the city, are said to pass rapidly and accurately, with what is said to be greater safety than that furnished by the telephone. ... Information is sifted out according to a consensus concerning the reliability of different individuals. In particular, there is a belief that informers can be spotted so that they can be excluded from the grapevine or sent on to a fake grapevine. In some periods, information can be so valuable that it is paid for by the addicted.

It is also reported that in some neighborhoods (particularly where there is an ethnic or other communal bond) even nonaddicts may be more or less willing to protect addicts from police interference. Despite the usually strained relations between addicts and their nonaddicted neighbors, 'a residue of loyalty may continue to keep the local populace from any active cooperation with the police'. As part of the 'ritual, magical, and cyclical patterns' Fiddle discusses the addict's use of time – which reflects the bondage of addiction and the need for addicts in our society to devote almost all their energy to the search for illicit supplies.

There is a time, or some time, for getting money; a time, or some time, for getting drugs; a time, or some time, for using the drugs. (An interesting point is the way in which the term *scoring* (purchasing) has been inflated to cover all the phases of the process.) This triadic pattern may be repeated several times a day, or may be abbreviated according to the skill and fortunes of the addicted person. But whatever the combination, the day is ordered according to a detectable perspective.

Through police intervention this perspective may well lose its clarity, so that the day is increasingly freighted with despair, bitterness, and confusion. These experiences themselves act as secondary sources for drug use as the drug is called upon to perform sedative functions.

Finally Fiddle notes that addict 'life' serves a general function (presumably more psychological than practical or defensive) in fostering intense interpersonal relationships between addicted individuals.

It should not be thought that the addict subculture engulfs everyone coming into contact with it. In all high drug-use neighborhoods nonusing 'squares' live alongside the addicts. Although drug distribution is closely related to the underworld, delinquent gangs as such are not a key factor in the promotion of addiction. In New York it was found that although some gangs provided 'an arena in which the use of narcotics can develop', generally the gangs not only discouraged and inhibited drug use but also satisfied needs 'which may otherwise lead to earlier use. ...' Another type of misapprehension about the addict subculture may be inadvertently created by 'inside' accounts of addict life in America. It is not true that addiction to narcotics automatically makes the individual a member of an addict subculture. This is shown, for example, by one study of American physician-addicts. Those interviewd 'almost never associated with other physician-addicts, or did not do so knowingly. They did not have any occasion for doing so, either for the purpose of getting drugs or for passing time, or for emotional support.' As might be expected, it was similarly found that the physicians in question did not make use of the special addict jargon. Thus, although there may be some psychological pressures working to bring addicts together, the addict's overall social and legal status and his relation to drug sources seem to be the overriding factors determining subcultural membership. This point is borne out by the experience in Britain, where the availability of drugs eliminates the need for addicts to involve themselves in underworld distribution processes and thus prevents the significant development of an addict subculture.

The gradual immersion of most American addicts in a world of their own is inextricably connected with the general process by which they have been cast out of respectable society. The social definition of the addict as a criminal not only vitally influences his behavior but also significantly affects his self-image. Certainly the knowledge that one has become fully addicted must in itself have a profound impact on this self-image. At the same time it is noteworthy that although the physician-addict and the subcultural-type addict are addicted in precisely the same physiological sense, their self-images are likely to be strikingly different. Both may recognize themselves as addicts, yet the physican is most unlikely to consider himself a criminal. On the other hand, the addict who is driven to underworld connections and to crime in order to support his habit cannot help but begin to feel that he is an enemy of society (or at least that society is *his* enemy). A self-fulfilling-prophecy cycle is set in motion from which it is very difficult for such an addict to extricate himself. He is aware that respectable people view him as a criminal, and he sees that he is beginning to act like one. Increasingly he must turn to the drug world for interpersonal support as well as for drug supplies. As the need to finance his habit occupies more and more of his time and energy, and as other worlds (such as those of work, family, and so on) recede into the background or fade away completely, addiction becomes a way of life [. . .]

Key treatment issues

Most general discussions of the treatment of addiction have indicated dispute about three central and interrelated issues. The first involves institutional versus out-patient treatment. Experts generally agree that a hospital provides the most appropriate setting for the withdrawal of the addict from drugs. At the same time, some observers emphasize that specialized treatment facilities for addicts have certain drawbacks. One authority states: 'My opinion, borne out by experience, is that any treatment center which brings active drug addicts together in large numbers is bound to fail of its purpose.' One addict's account of her stay in Lexington emphasized the fact that conversation among the patients was almost entirely about narcotics. Rather than being weaned away from the world of drugs, the patient may thus experience a strengthening and reinforcement of his identification with that world. As this girl went on to say, it was only on release from Lexington that she became convinced she was an incurable addict: 'I felt beaten when I got out of there, really beaten.' The very process of treatment, then, if it occurs in a compulsory context, may promote and reinforce the addict's deviant self-image.

Officially, American policy has sanctioned only institutional treatment of addicts. Out-patient treatment has persistently been repudiated in material distributed by the Bureau of Narcotics – which frequently cites a 1924 pronouncement of the American Medical Association opposing such treatment. Insistence on the need to hospitalize addicts may prevent useful exploration of other treatment approaches. One project in New York has indicated that some addicts can be successfully withdrawn on an out-patient basis, and suggested that the difficulties of dealing with addicts as voluntary out-patients have sometimes been exaggerated. The ability of this project to keep thirteen addicts in voluntary out-patient treatment for a full year was attributed to its nonpunitive and non-moralizing orientation.

Closely related to the out-patient-institutional dispute are strong differences of opinion about the value of compulsory treatment. Under present policies, most institutionalization of addicts is more or less compulsory. Addicts are directly committed by courts, given the option of commitment instead of prison, or else forced into treatment by the pressures of maintaining the drug habit illegally (for example, many addicts undergo withdrawal treatment in order that they can resume their drug use at a lower dosage level and hence at lower cost). The extremely high relapse rate has convinced some observers that compulsory treatment simply will not work. When the compulsion is blatant, it will make little difference that the institution is called a *treatment center* or *hospital*, and that the addict is labeled a *patient* rather than an *offender*. As Szasz and Goffman have suggested in their discussions of commitment to mental institutions, the facts of deprivation of liberty and of involuntary immersion in the life of a 'total institution' will often overshadow in the committed individual's view any appreciation he might have of efforts by the treatment staff to help him. This may be particularly true in the addict's case since ordinarily he will be fully capable of understanding just what is happening to him. In any case, apart from how the patient views a specific institutional program, there is the basic problem that without the addict's cooperation in a genuine effort at prolonged abstinence no cure can be expected. Although some therapists have stated that addict-patients require compulsion to help them develop the self-discipline necessary for a cure, others stress that the success of any treatment program has been the result of its voluntary character. They urge that it may be necessary to recognize that one simply cannot cure an addict, in the long term, against his will.

This brings up a third major issue in addiction treatment: are the terms *cure* and *treatment* synonymous? All specialists agree that addition is undesirable and that the ultimate goal should be its elimination – insofar as that is possible. Some believe, however, that a preoccupation with the total elimination of addiction and with the cure of individual addicts has unnecessarily limited efforts at more general medical management of the addiction problem. Thus it has been widely argued that any treatment program under which some addicts might receive medically prescribed drugs would involve doctors in the perpetuation of disease and amount to an abandonment of the effort to cure addiction. This argument conveniently ignores the fact that addiction is actually being perpetuated under the present arrangements, even if doctors play no direct part in its perpetuation. As the author of the New York Academy of Medicine's 1955 proposal for narcotics clinics pointed out:

We are not saying to give the addicts more drugs. We are simply advising a different method of distribution ... every addict gets his drug right now ... why not let him have his minimum requirements under licensed medical supervision, rather than force him to get it by criminal activities, through criminal channels?

Increasingly, proposals for narcotics reform urge placing as many addicts as possible under some kind of medical management. Treatment should depend on the particular addict's problems and prognosis. If medical administration of drugs is necessary even for a prolonged period – during efforts to enlist cooperation in a cure, or in a case in which cure seems unlikely – then such administration (occurring as part of an overall treatment program) should be considered a legitimate aspect of medical practice in this area. These proposals involve recognizing that different types of addicts may require varying treatment approaches. Even more significantly, perhaps, they offer a major advantage conspicuously absent from all crash programs to cure individual addicts. Medical administration of low-cost legal drugs could drastically undercut the economic incentives underlying the illicit traffic and could largely eliminate various secondary aspects of addiction as a social problem.

Part Eight Sickness and Health

In the previous Part we emphasized the fact that the same experiences and actions could be interpreted in many different ways. The meanings imposed upon what appear to be identical phenomena may differ according to time and place. Drug addicts may be seen as patients in need of support and sympathy or as criminals deserving punishment. Behaviour which is taken as normal in one society is abnormal in the eyes of another.

Surely, however, the same ambiguities do not arise in the case of experiences such as pain, disease and illness? Moreover, surely everyone would agree that such states and conditions are highly undesirable, unpleasant and to be feared because they represent a threat both to the individual and to society. However the extracts which follow demonstrate that the problems of sickness and disease are not always as clear-cut as such views would seem to indicate. Zola, for instance, points out that many studies have revealed that the 'true' distribution of sickness and symptoms of disease is more widespread than is generally imagined. If we are to account for this fact we must recognize that cultural factors enter even into the definitions of the symptoms of physical illnesses.

The Italian and Irish patients in Zola's study (Reading 46) differed markedly in the way they perceived and reacted to the same illness. The Irish patients tended to play down the discomfort and inconvenience resulting from their illness. They also tended to perceive their trouble as some specific localized disorder, and to feel that it was not inconveniencing their social relationships. But the Italians differed in all these respects.

Physiological factors cannot account for these discrepancies. Cultural values led the Italians to adopt dramatization as a means of coping with the anxieties caused by the illness. The Irish, whose cultural values emphasize understatement and restraint, tended to believe that 'the less said the better'.

Zborowski (Reading 47) focuses more specifically on the patient's responses to spontaneous pain and the effect of social and cultural factors on these responses. The patients in his study – of Jewish, Italian, and old-American stock – differed in their interpretation of the experience of pain. The manifest behaviour of the Jewish and Italian patients revealed them to be uninhibited in reacting to their sufferings, by groaning, moaning and crying. The Jewish patients were concerned, however, about what the pain really meant in terms of *their future capacity* to meet obligations and commitments to the family and at work. For this reason, the administration of pain-relieving drugs did not relieve the anxieties of these patients. The Italians, who were more concerned about the *immediacy* of the pain, were encouraged by the alleviation of their discomfort. Both sets of patients, however, were less popular with the doctors and nurses than the old-American patients, who adopted a stoical attitude and cooperated with the medical staff by describing in objective and unemotional terms the nature of their symptoms. Unlike the Jewish patients, the old-Americans tended to have a good deal of faith in their doctors. This confidence represents one aspect of a generalized belief of American culture in the omnipotence of Science.

Mumford's work (Reading 48) on the training of medical students illustrates that the medical profession *itself* does not have the same faith in its knowledge of disease and in its ability to cure. This introduces another area of *uncertainty* within the social organization of illness and its treatment. As Mumford explains, it is of tremendous importance for the future performance and satisfaction of the young doctor, that he learns to cope with these ambiguities. The patient expects to obtain from the doctor clear, unambiguous and concrete information about the matter which concerns him most deeply, namely what is wrong with him and what are his chances of recovery. In the face of such demands from the patient, the well-trained doctor is able to offer a seemingly confident diagnosis, despite his own awareness of the fact that his knowledge of the disease in question may be limited.

Davis (Reading 49) distinguishes between two aspects of uncertainty. There is the 'real' uncertainty which is a clinical and scientific thing, and there is the 'functional' uncertainty which may be used by the physicians as a strategy in their management of social relations with patients and their relatives. Davis studied fourteen families which had a child in hospital, suffering from polio. He points out that, at each stage of treatment, what the doctors knew and understood of the child's condition was different from what the parents knew. The parents' knowledge was largely communicated to them by the doctors and they were thus dependent on the doctors for forming a judgement about their child's progress.

In the early stages of the treatment, because there is 'real', that is *clinical,* uncertainty, neither parents nor doctors *could* be in a position to form an accurate judgement and make a realistic prognosis. But after six weeks to three months the element of clinical uncertainty is very much removed *for the doctor.* However, the doctors did not share this information with the parents, who were thus kept in the dark about the likely outcome of their child's treatment. Thus, at this stage, 'functional' uncertainty becomes more important.

Davis argues that this functional uncertainty 'serves the purely managerial ends of the treatment personnel in their interaction with parents'. One of these ends is the reduction of time, effort, and involvement in the case, which an admission of the doctor's prognosis to the child's parents might involve. The doctor wishes to avoid being drawn into a possibly awkward or distasteful situation with parents who find it hard to accept the complete loss of expectations of a full and natural recovery for their child. This device for avoidance is supported by the doctor's 'convenient rationalization' that the child's parents could not or would not understand what the doctor had to tell them. Moreover, the doctor could argue that the continuance of uncertainty might be the means of maintaining a climate of hope among the parents. If hope cannot be maintained, then the doctor may argue that the uncertainty is of assistance in managing a difficult period of status transition for the child and its parents.

Earlier we referred to the rather startling fact that several studies had discovered a large amount of illness which went undetected. In the following extract – the first from Goffman's *Asylums* (Reading 50), a rather similar point is made with reference to those who suffer from 'mental illness'. For Goffman argues 'in the degree that the "mentally ill" outside hospitals numerically approach or surpass those inside hospitals, one could say that mental patients distinctively suffer not from mental illness, but from contingencies'. What Goffman seems to be saying here is that we cannot say with any degree of certainty that someone who has those symptoms which appear to mark him out as 'mentally ill' will in fact eventually end up in a mental hospital. This is uncertain because there are numerous unpredictable factors which may intervene to determine what happens in the career of such a person. Goffman identifies those parties who can play an important role in shaping this career. The first is the 'next-of-relation' who will usually be the patient's next of kin, and whom the patient normally appears to depend on in time of trouble. Secondly is the 'complainant' whose action starts the person on his way to the hospital. Finally there are the 'mediators', who relay and process the person towards the hospital. One consequence of the collusion between these sets of parties, in having the person hospitalized, is to create in him a profound sense of betrayal. And as he reflects on the events which led up to his confinement, the mental patient feels that he was conned all the way along the line. Goffman suggests that this may be a very realistic interpretation of what happened. The person's next-of-relation may have invented some pretext for having him visit the psychiatrist. The psychiatrist, police and other 'mediators' may have pretended that the situation was not as bad as it appeared to him at the time, to avoid his making a scene.

But once the person enters the institution he is faced by a new situation. He perceives himself for the first time as a *mental patient*. This new conception of himself appears to be confirmed by his reviewing in retrospect the sequence of events which has led him there (see Reading 51).

The end of one mental career is the beginning of another: the 'prepatient' is now the 'inpatient'. As he settles down in his new role, he finds that the 'total institution' demands that he subject himself to it in a number of ways. These may not necessarily be physically unpleasant, but are nonetheless damaging to the conceptions of himself which he has previously operated with.

It is the business of the institution to change these conceptions because the patients 'failure' at the business of living has proved the inadequacy of his attitudes to life and his ways of dealing with people. But such a new conception cannot be taken over wholesale by the inpatient. He has to construct what Goffman calls an 'apologia' or a 'sad tale' which embodies a more acceptable account of how he comes to be in a mental hospital. The inpatient's apologia may also refer to the likelihood that he will be released shortly, to take up the threads of a career that only the *contingencies* of life have interrupted.

But to the hospital administration such apologias become further evidence of the inpatient's incapacity. They may even become incorporated in case-notes and records relating to the patient. These records, Goffman points out, may contain material which is damaging and discrediting to the patient. The practice of recording and using such information in ways which may appear to be against the patient's interests is supported by psychiatric theories which regard mental illness as a *generalized* disorder, with its roots in the distant past. This belief justifies the hospital's collecting information about any and every area of the patient's life.

Goffman does not attempt to offer any easy answer to questions about whether patients suffering from mental illness are 'really' ill, and if so, in what sense. But he indicates that the regime in many mental hospitals may be counter-productive of the aim of preparing the patient for a speedy return to the outside world. For instance, the mental hospital by originally defining 'unacceptable' behaviour within narrow limits may produce a form of secondary deviation. The patient who reacts as a 'normal' person might do, and rebels against the institutionalized regime, may find his behaviour used by the authorities as proof of his *essential* madness.

Throughout this section, the emphasis has not been on the distribution and incidence of illness and sickness behaviour. Rather we have tried to indicate that even behaviour which apparently derives from physical or organic causes is associated with underlying social processes. This perspective is basic to our interpretation of sickness and health as a 'social problem'.

46 Irving Kenneth Zola

Culture and Symptoms:
An Analysis of Patients' Presenting Complaints

Excerpts from Irving Kenneth Zola, 'Culture and symptoms: an analysis of patients' presenting complaints', *American Sociological Review*, vol. 31, 1966, pp. 615–29.

The conception of disease

In most epidemiological studies, the definition of disease is taken for granted. Yet today's chronic disorders do not lend themselves to such easy conceptualization and measurement as did the contagious disorders of yesteryear.

Usually the issue of life without disease has been dismissed as a philosophical problem – a dismissal made considerably easier by our general assumptions about the statistical distribution of disorder.

Yet studies have increasingly appeared which note the large number of disorders escaping detection. Whether based on physicians' estimates or on the recall of lay populations, the proportion of untreated disorders amounts to two-thirds or three-fourths of all existing conditions. The most reliable data, however, come from periodic health examinations and community 'health' surveys. At least two such studies have noted that as much as 90 per cent of their apparently healthy sample had some physical aberration or clinical disorder. Moreover, neither the type of disorder, nor the seriousness by objective medical standards, differentiated those who felt sick from those who did not. In one of the above studies, even of those who felt sick, only 40 per cent were under medical care. It seems that the more intensive the investigation, the higher the prevalence of clinically serious but previously undiagnosed and untreated disorders.

Such data as these give an unexpected statistical picture of illness. Instead of it being a relatively infrequent or abnormal phenomenon, the empirical reality may be that illness, defined as the presence of clinically serious symptoms, is the statistical *norm*. What is particularly striking about this line of reasoning is that the statistical notions underlying many 'social' pathologies are similarly being questioned. A number of social scientists have noted that the basic acts or deviations, such as law breaking, addictive behaviors, sexual 'perversions' or mental illness, occur so frequently in the population that were one to tabulate all the deviations that people possess or engage in, virtually no one could escape the label of 'deviant'.

Why are so relatively few potential 'deviants' labelled such or, more accurately, why do so few come to the attention of official agencies. Perhaps the focus on how or why a particular deviation arose in the first place might be misplaced; an equally important issue for research might be the individual and societal reaction to the deviation once it occurs. Might it then be the differential response to deviation rather than the prevalence of the deviation which accounts for many reported group and subgroup differences? A similar set of questions can be asked in regard to physical illness. Given that the prevalence of clinical abnormalities is so high and the rate of acknowledgment so low, how representative are 'the treated' of all those with a particular condition? Given further that what *is* treated seems unrelated to what would usually be thought the objective situation, i.e., seriousness, disability and subjective discomfort, is it possible that some selective process is operating in what gets counted or tabulated as illness?

The interplay of culture and 'symptoms'

Upon surveying many cross-cultural comparisons of morbidity, we concluded that there are at least two ways in which signs ordinarily defined as indicating problems in one population may be ignored in others. The first is related to the actual prevalence of the sign, and the second to its congruence with dominant or major value-orientations.

In the first instance, when the aberration is fairly widespread, this, in itself, might constitute a reason for its not being considered 'symptomatic' or unusual. Even within our own society, Koos has noted that, although lower back pain is a quite common condition among lower-class women, it is not considered symptomatic of any disease or disorder but part of their expected everyday existence. For the population where the particular condition is ubiquitous, the condition is perceived as the normal state. This does not mean that it is considered 'good' (although instances have been noted where not having the endemic condition was considered abnormal) but rather that it is natural and inevitable and thus to be ignored as being of no consequence. Because the 'symptom' or condition is omnipresent (it always was and always will be) there simply exists for such populations or cultures no frame of reference according to which it could be considered a deviation.

In the second process, it is the 'fit' of certain signs with a society's major values which accounts for the degree of attention they receive. For example, in some non-literate societies there is anxiety-free acceptance of and willingness to describe hallucinatory experiences. Wallace noted that in such societies the fact of hallucination *per se* is seldom disturbing; its content is the focus of interest. In Western society, however, with its emphasis on rationality and control the very admission of hallucinations is commonly taken to be a grave sign and, in some literature regarded as the essential feature of psychosis. In such instances it is not the sign itself or its frequency which is significant but the social context within which it occurs and within which it is perceived and understood. Even more explicit workings of this process can be seen in the interplay of 'symptoms' and social roles.

Also illustrative of this process are the divergent perceptions of those bodily complaints often referred to as 'female troubles'. Nausea is a common and treatable concomitant of pregnancy yet Margaret Mead records no morning sickness among the Arapesh; her data suggest that this may be related to the almost complete denial that a child exists, until shortly before birth. In a Christian setting, where the existence of life is dated from conception, nausea becomes the external sign, hope and proof that one is pregnant. Thus in the United States, this symptom is not only quite widespread but is also an expected and almost welcome part of pregnancy. A quite similar phenomenon is the recognition of dysmenorrhea. While Arapesh women reported no pain during menstruation, quite the contrary is reported in the United States. Interestingly enough the only consistent factor related to its manifestation among American women was a learning one – those that manifested it reported having observed it in other women during their childhood.

From such examples as these, it seems likely that the degree of recognition and treatment of certain gynecological problems may be traced to the prevailing definition of what constitutes 'the necessary part of the business of being a woman'.

The patient and his illness

The data are based on a comparison between sixty-three Italians (thirty-four female, twenty-nine male) and eighty-one Irish (forty-two female, thirty-nine male), who were new admissions to the Eye, the Ear, Nose and Throat, and the Medical Clinics of the Massachusetts General Hospital and the Massachusetts Eye and Ear Infirmary, seen between July 1960, and February 1961.

With regard to general medical coverage, there were no apparent differences between the ethnic groups.

Location and quality of presenting complaints

In the folklore of medical practice, the supposed opening question is,

'Where does it hurt?' This query provides the starting-point of our analysis – the perceived location of the patient's troubles. Our first finding is that more Irish than Italians tended to locate their chief problem in either the eye, the ear, the nose, or the throat (and more so for females than for males). The same tendency was evident when all patients were asked what they considered to be the most important part of their body and the one with which they would be most concerned if something went wrong. Here, too, significantly more Irish emphasized difficulties of the eye, the ear, the nose or the throat. That this reflected merely a difference in the conditions for which they were seeking aid is doubtful since the two other parts of the body most frequently referred to were heart and 'mind' locations, and these represent only 3 per cent of the primary diagnoses of the entire sample. In the re-testing of these findings on diagnostically matched pairs, while there were a great many ties, the general directions were still consistent. Thus even when Italians had a diagnosed eyes or ear disorder, they did not locate their chief complaints there, nor did they focus their future concern on these locations.

Pain, the commonest accompaniment of illness, was the dimension of patients' symptoms to which we next turned. Pain is an especially interesting phenomenon since there is considerable evidence that its tolerance and perception are not purely physiological responses and do not necessarily reflect the degree of objective discomfort induced by a particular disorder or experimental procedure. In our study not only did the Irish more often than the Italians deny that pain was a feature of their illness but this difference held even for those patients with the same disorder. When the Irish were asked directly about the presence of pain, some hedged their replies with qualifications. ('It was more a throbbing than a pain . . . not really pain, it feels more like sand in my eye.') Such comments indicated that the patients were reflecting something more than an objective reaction to their physical conditions.

While there were no marked differences in the length, frequency or noticeability of their symptoms, a difference did emerge in the ways in which they described the quality of the physical difficulty embodied in their chief complaint. Two types of difficulty were distinguished: one was of a more limited nature and emphasized a circumscribed and specific dysfunctioning; the second emphasized a difficulty of a grosser and more diffuse quality. When the patients' complaints were analyzed according to these two types, proportionately more Irish described their chief problem in terms of specific dysfunction while proportionately more Italians spoke of a diffused difficulty. Once again, the findings for diagnostically matched pairs were in the predicted direction.

Diffuse versus specific reactions

What seems to emerge from the above is a picture of the Irish limiting and understating their difficulties and the Italians spreading and generalizing theirs. Two other pieces of information were consistent with this interpretation: first, an enumeration of the symptoms an individual presented – a phenomenon which might reflect how diffusely the complaint was perceived; second, the degree to which each patient felt his illness affected aspects of life other than purely physical behavior.

The first measure of this specific-diffuse dimension – number of distinguishable symptoms – was examined in three ways:

1. The total number presented by each patient;
2. The total number of different bodily areas in which the patient indicated he had complaints, e.g., back, stomach, legs;
3. The total number of different qualities of physical difficulty embodied in the patient's presenting complaints. The ethnic differences were consistent with the previous findings. Compared to the Irish, the Italians presented significantly more symptoms, had symptoms in significantly more bodily locations, and noted significantly more types of bodily dysfunction.

The second analysis, the degree to which a patient felt his illness affected his more general well-being, was derived from replies to three questions:

1. Do you think your symptoms affected how you got along with your family?
2. Did you become more irritable?
3. What would you say has bothered you most about your symptoms? The Irish were more likely than the Italians to state that their disorders had not affected them in this manner. Here again the asides by the Irish suggested that their larger number of negative responses by the Irish reflected, considerable denial rather than a straightforward appraisal of their situation.

To examine these conclusions in a more rigorous manner, we turned to our subsample of matched diagnostic pairs. In general, the pattern and direction of the hypotheses were upheld (see Table 1). Thus, even for the same diagnosis, the Italians expressed and complained of more symptoms, more bodily areas affected, and more kinds of dysfunctions, than did the Irish, and more often felt that their symptoms affected their interpersonal behavior.

The following composite offers a final illustration of how differently these patients reacted to and perceived their illnesses.

Table 1

Diagnosis	Question of interviewer	Irish patient	Italian patient
Presbyopia and hyperopia	What seems to be the trouble?	I can't see to thread a needle or read a paper.	I have a constant headache and my eyes seem to get all red and burny.
Pharyngitis	Is there any pain?	No, maybe a slight headache but nothing that lasts.	Yes, I have had a headache a few days. Oh, yes, every time I swallow it's annoying.
Presbyopia and hyperopia	Do you think the symptoms affected how you got along with your family? your friends?	No, I have had loads of trouble. I can't imagine this bothering me.	Yes, when I have a headache, I'm very irritable, very tense, very short-tempered.
Deafness, hearing loss	Did you become more irritable?	No, not me ... maybe everybody else but not me.	Oh, yes ... the least little thing aggravates me ... and I take it out on the children.

Sociocultural communication

What has so far been demonstrated is the systematic variability with which bodily conditions may be perceived and communicated. Until now the empirical findings have been presented without interpretation. Most of the data are quite consistent with those reported by other observers. Although no data were collected in our investigation on the specific mechanics of the interplay between being a member of a specific subculture and the communication of 'symptoms' some speculation on this seems warranted.

In theorizing about the interplay of culture and symptoms particular emphasis was given to the 'fit' of certain bodily states with dominant value orientations. The empirical examples for the latter were drawn primarily from data on social roles. Of course, values are evident on even more general levels, such as formal and informal societal sanctions and the culture's orientation to life's basic problems. With an orientation to problems usually goes a preferred solution or way of handling them. Thus a society's values may also be reflected in such preferred solutions. One behavioral manifestation of this is defense mechanisms – a part of the everyday way individuals have of dealing with their everyday stresses and strains. We contend that illness and its treatment (from taking medicine to seeing a physician) is one of these everyday stresses and strains, an anxiety-laden situation which calls forth coping or defense mechanisms. From this general reasoning, we would thus speculate that Italian and Irish ways of communicating illness may reflect major values and preferred ways of handling problems within the culture itself.

For the Italians, the large number of symptoms and the spread of the complaints, not only throughout the body but into other aspects of life, may be understood in terms of their expressiveness and expansiveness so often in sociological, historical, and fictional writing. And yet their illness behavior seems to reflect something more than lack of inhibition, and valuation of spontaneity. There is something more than real in their behavior, a 'well-seasoned, dramatic emphasis to their lives'. In fact, clinicians have noted that this openness is deceptive. It only goes so far and then. . . . Thus this Italian overstatement of 'symptoms' is not merely an expressive quality but perhaps a more general mechanism, their special way of handling problems – a defense mechanism we call dramatization. Dynamically dramatization seems to cope with anxiety by repeatedly overexpressing it and thereby dissipating it [. . .] Through many works on the southern Italian there seems to run a thread – a valued and preferred way of handling problems shown in the tendency toward dramatization. The experience of illness provides but another stage.

But if the Italian view of life is expressed through its fiestas, for the Irish it is expressed through its fasts. Their life has been depicted as one of long periods of plodding routine followed by episodes of wild adventure, of lengthy postponement of gratification of sex and marriage, interspersed with brief immediate satisfactions like fighting and carousing. Perhaps in recognition of the expected and limited nature of such outbursts the most common Irish outlet, alcoholism, is often referred to as 'a good man's weakness'. Life was black and long-suffering, and the less said the better.

It is the last statement which best reflects the Irish handling of illness. While in other contexts the ignoring of bodily complaints is merely descriptive of what is going on, in Irish culture it seems to be the culturally prescribed and supported defense mechanism – singularly most appropriate for their psychological and physical survival. When speaking of the discomfort caused by her illness, one stated, 'I ignore it like I do most things.' In terms of presenting complaints this understatement and restraint was even more evident. It could thus be seen in their seeming reluctance to admit they have any symptoms at all, in their limiting their symptoms to the specific location in which they arose and finally in their contention that their physical problems affected nothing of their life but the most minute physical functioning.

While there has long been recognition of the subjectivity and variability of a patient's reporting of his symptoms, there has been little attention to the fact that this reporting may be influenced by systematic social factors like ethnicity. Awareness of the influence of this and similar factors can be of considerable aid in the practical problem of diagnosis and treatment of many diseases, particularly where the diagnosis is dependent to a large extent on what the patient is able and willing, or thinks important enough, to tell the doctor. The physician who is unaware of how the patient's background may lead him to respond in certain ways, may, by not probing sufficiently, miss important diagnostic cues or respond inappropriately to others.

The documentation of sociocultural differences in the perception of and concern with certain types of 'symptoms' has further implications for work in preventive medicine and public health. It has been found in mental health research that there is an enormous gulf between lay and professional opinion as to when mental illness is present, as well as when and what kind of help is needed. If our theorizing is correct, such differences reflect not merely something inadequately learned (that is, wrong medical knowledge) but also a solidly embedded value system.

47 Mark Zborowski

Cultural Components in Responses to Pain

Excerpts from Mark Zborowski, 'Cultural components in responses to pain',
Journal of Social Issues, no. 4, 1952, pp. 16–30.

In human society, pain, like so many other physiological phenomena, acquires specific social and cultural significance, and, accordingly certain reactions to pain can be understood in the light of this significance. As Hardy, Wolff and Goodell state in their recent book, 'The culture in which a man finds himself becomes the conditioning influence in the formation of the individual reaction patterns to pain. ... A knowledge of group attitudes toward pain is extremely important to an understanding of the individual reaction [. . .]'

Pain among patients of Jewish and Italian origin

Attitudes of Italian and Jewish patients toward pain-relieving drugs can serve as an indication of their attitude toward pain. When in pain the Italian calls for pain relief and is mainly concerned with the analgesic effects of the drugs which are administered to him. Once the pain is relieved the Italian patient easily forgets his sufferings and manifests a happy and joyful disposition. The Jewish patient, however, often is reluctant to accept the drug, and he explains this reluctance in terms of concern about the effects of the drug upon his health in general. He is apprehensive about the habit-forming aspects of the analgesic. Moreover, he feels that the drug relieves his pain only temporarily and does not cure him of the disease which may cause the pain. Nurses and doctors have reported cases in which patients would hide the pill which was given to them to relieve their pain and would prefer to suffer. These reports were confirmed in the interviews with the patients. It was also observed that many Jewish patients after being relieved from pain often continued to display the same depressed and worried behavior because they felt that though the pain was currently absent it may recur as long as the disease was not cured completely. From these observations it appears that when one deals with a Jewish and an Italian patient in pain, in the first case it is more important to relieve the anxieties with regard to the sources of pain, while in the second it is more important to relieve the actual pain.

Another indication as to the significance of pain for Jewish and Italian patients is their respective attitudes toward the doctor. The Italian patient seems to display a most confident attitude toward the doctor which is usually reinforced after the doctor has succeeded in relieving pain, whereas the Jewish patient manifests a skeptical attitude, feeling that the fact that the doctor has relieved his pain by some drug does not mean at all that he is skillful enough to take care of the basic illness. Consequently, even when the pain is relieved, he tends to check the diagnosis and the treatment of one doctor against the opinions of other specialists in the field. Summarizing the difference between the Italian and Jewish attitudes, one can say that the Italian attitude is characterized by a present-oriented apprehension with regard to the actual sensation of pain, and the Jew tends to manifest a future-oriented anxiety as to the symptomatic and general meaning of the pain experience.

It has been stated that the Italians and Jews tend to manifest similar behavior in terms of their reactions to pain. As both cultures allow for free expression of feelings and emotions by words, sounds and gestures, both the Italians and Jews feel free to talk about their pain, complain about it and manifest their sufferings by groaning, moaning, crying, etc. They are not ashamed of this expression. They admit willingly that when they are in pain they do complain a great deal, call for help and expect sympathy and assistance from other members of their immediate social environment, especially from members of their family. When in pain they are reluctant to be alone and prefer the presence and attention of other people. This behavior, which is expected, accepted and approved by the Italian and Jewish cultures, often conflicts with the patterns of behavior expected from a patient by American or Americanized medical people. Thus they tend to describe the behavior of the Italian and Jewish patient as exaggerated and over-emotional. The material suggests that they do tend to minimize the actual pain experiences of the Italian and Jewish patient, regardless of whether they have the objective criteria for evaluating the actual amount of pain which the patient experiences. It seems that the uninhibited display of reaction to pain as manifested by the Jewish and Italian patient provokes distrust in American culture instead of provoking sympathy.

To summarize the description of the reactive patterns of the Jewish and Italian patients, the material suggests that on a semi-conscious level the Jewish patient tends to provoke worry and concern in his social environment as to the state of his health and the symptomatic character of his pain, while the Italian tends to provoke sympathy toward his suffering. In one case the function of the pain reaction will be the mobilization of the efforts of the family and the doctors toward a complete cure, while in the second case the function of the reaction will be focused upon the mobilization of effort toward relieving the pain sensation.

On the basis of the discussion of the Jewish and Italian material two generalizations can be made: first, similar reactions to pain manifested by members of different ethno-cultural groups do not necessarily reflect similar attitudes to pain; second, reactive patterns similar in terms of their manifestations may have different functions and serve different purposes in various cultures.

Pain among patients of 'Old American' origin

There is little emphasis on emotional complaining about pain among 'Old American' patients. Their complaints about pain can best be described as reporting on pain. In describing his pain, the 'Old American' patient tries to find the most appropriate ways of defining the quality of pain, its localization, duration, etc. When examined by the doctor he gives the impression of trying to assume the detached role of an unemotional observer who gives the most efficient description of his state for a correct diagnosis and treatment. The interviewees repeatedly state that there is no point in complaining and groaning and moaning, etc., because 'it won't help anybody'. However, they readily admit that when pain is unbearable they may react strongly, even to the point of crying, but they tend to do it when they are alone. Withdrawal from society seems to be a frequent reaction to strong pain.

There seem to be different patterns in reacting to pain depending on the situation. One pattern, manifested in the presence of members of the family, friends, etc., consists of attempts to minimize pain, to avoid complaining and provoking pity; when pain becomes too strong there is a tendency to withdraw and express freely such reactions as groaning, moaning, etc. A different pattern is manifested in the presence of people who, on account of their profession, should know the character of the pain experience because they are expected to make the appropriate diagnosis, advise the proper cure and give the adequate help. The tendency to avoid deviation from certain expected patterns of behavior plays an important role in the reaction to pain. This is also controlled by the desire to seek approval on the part of the social environment, especially in the hospital, where the 'Old American' patient tries to avoid being a 'nuisance' on the ward. He seems to be, more than any other patient, aware of an ideal pattern of behavior which is identified as 'American', and he tends to conform to it. This was characteristically expressed by a patient who answered the question how he reacts to pain by saying, 'I react like a good American'.

An important element in controlling the pain reaction is the wish of the patient to cooperate with those who are expected to take care of him. The situation is often viewed as a team composed of the patient, the doctor, the nurse, the attendant, etc., and in this team everybody has a function and is supposed to do his share in order to achieve the most successful result. Emotionality is seen as a purposeless and hindering factor in a situation which calls for knowledge, skill, training and efficiency. It is important to note that this behavior is also expected by American or Americanized members of the medical or nursing staff, and the patients who do not fall into this pattern are viewed as deviants, hypochondriacs and neurotics.

As in the case of the Jewish patients, the American attitude toward pain can be best defined as a future-oriented anxiety. The 'Old American' patient is also concerned with the symptomatic significance of pain which is correlated with a pronounced health-consciousness. It seems that the 'Old American' is conscious of various threats to his health which are present in his environment and therefore feels vulnerable and is prone to interpret his pain sensation as a warning signal indicating that something is wrong with his health and therefore must be reported to the physician. With some exceptions, pain is considered bad and unnecessary and therefore must be immediately taken care of. In those situations where pain is expected and accepted, such as in the process of medical treatment or as a result of sports activities, there is less concern with the pain sensation. In general, however, there is a feeling that suffering pain is unnecessary when there are means of relieving it.

Though the attitudes of the Jewish and 'Old American' patients can be defined as pain anxiety they differ greatly. The future-oriented anxiety of the Jewish interviewee is characterized by pessimism or at best, by skepticism, while the 'Old American' patient is rather optimistic in his future-orientation. This attitude is fostered by the mechanistic approach to the body and its functions and by the confidence in the skill of the expert which are so frequent in the American culture. The body is often viewed as a machine which has to be well taken care of, be periodically checked for disfunctioning and eventually, when out of order, be taken to an expert who will 'fix' the defect. In the case of pain the expert is the medical man who has the 'know-how' because of his training and experience and therefore is entitled to full confidence. An important element in the optimistic outlook is faith in the progress of science. Patients with intractable pain often stated that though at the present moment the doctors do not have the 'drug' they will eventually discover it, and they will give the examples of sulpha, penicillin, etc.

The anxieities of a pain-experiencing 'Old American' patient are greatly relieved when he feels that something is being done about it in terms of specific activities involved in the treatment. It seems that his security and confidence increases in direct proportion to the number of tests, X-rays, examinations, injections, etc. that are given to him. Accordingly 'Old American' patients seem to have a positive attitude toward hospitalization, because the hospital is the adequate institution which is equipped for the necessary treatment. While a Jewish and an Italian patient seem to be disturbed by the impersonal character of the hospital and by the necessity of being treated there instead of at home, the 'Old American' patient, on the contrary, prefers the hospital treatment to the home treatment, and neither he nor his family seems to be disturbed by hospitalization.

To summarize the attitude of the 'Old American' toward pain, he is disturbed by the symptomatic aspect of pain and is concerned with its incapacitating aspects, but he tends to view the future in rather optimistic colors, having confidence in the science and skill of the professional people who treat his condition.

48 Emily Mumford

The Norm of the Open Mind

Excerpts from Emily Mumford, *Interns: from Students to Physicians*,
Harvard University Press, 1970, pp. 155–63.

Since the physician must at times face situations where two equally
relevant norms conflict, he is forced to choose, by action or inaction, and
his direction can have significant consequences. He cannot, at each decision point, go back over the whole route of consciously weighing the
validity of each norm in the light of larger social issues and the profession – as well as in relation to himself, the particular patient, and
situation. To keep the whole route open would not only subject him to
intolerable stress, he could not act for trying to decide. What seems to
happen is that through successive acts and experiences some special
weight gets attached to certain norms – the norms that receive the most
consistent reinforcement from the people whom house-staff members respect in their learning environment. The young physicians build their
own way of handling dilemmas until the way becomes established. Some
may ultimately become desensitized to the extent of contradiction in
norms that apply to performance in one area. Some will become less
acutely aware of how much choice they actually have.

Conflicts between pairs of norms are frequently made explicit in poig-
nant life situations in the hospital, and the maturing physician is likely to
have special needs for development of priorities. For example, the physician's commitments to prolong life and also to relieve suffering often
come into conflict. Indeed, this is a subject that medical students and
house-staff physicians frequently worry about, discuss, and debate with
considerable feeling [. . .]

Through his training, the physician is helped and encouraged to live with
uncertainty, and his training for acknowledgment of uncertainty continues longer and more effectively in some hospitals than in others. For
some physicians, 'Medicine is a science of uncertainty and an art of
probability.' This is an area of stress, for in the nature of the patient's
position of anxiety, possible pain, and fear he 'develops an insatiable
desire for information of the kind that would be supplied by definite
diagnosis and firm prognosis'. Training for uncertainty also generates

anxiety among students. One faculty member reported, 'My students are dismayed when I say to them, "Half of what you are taught as medical students will in ten years have been shown to be wrong, and the trouble is, none of your teachers knows which half." '

Running through many conversations and conferences at University Hospital are affirmations of the norm of the open mind and acceptance of uncertainty in medical findings – a readiness to admit that no amount of knowledge is ever final. Two interns and a resident seemed to express a common value when they said, 'You have to admire him for saying he doesn't know.' On one service, discussion on rounds, formal and informal, offered frequent comments such as 'Can't be certain, but . . . '. On grand rounds for this service, the chief of service cautioned: 'You *really* could be certain that that is the reason for it?' And an attending physician challenged a resident: 'Are you prepared to prove that was *the* reason?' In an interview, a resident stressed his conviction that 'In medicine you can *never* say something will always be.' One resident said the kind of person he admired was 'Somebody who realizes he does not know everything. We all have to realize how much we do not know.' Other comments at University Hospital: 'If they do not admit they don't know, or they might be mistaken when they first arrive, they do in a short time.' 'No one seems to mind talking about his mistakes.' 'You can never say what something will always be; you must say it is *probably* such and such.' 'This hospital teaches you to be a little bit skeptical about what other people say.' 'When you have been doing a thing a certain way for a while, you need to stop and ask yourself if you are really right.' Some negative comments carry the same message: 'He sure didn't like being wrong!' 'He is not forging into new discoveries or exploring.' People in both University Hospital and Community Hospital appear aware that a conscientious intern or resident may be apprehensive at times. However, University Hospital seems to extend medical-school 'training for uncertainty' relatively farther than does Community Hospital.

In one study of 507 attending physicians at University Hospital, 'only 4 per cent expressed any degree of disapproval' when they were asked how they would feel if a physician in their speciality were to admit uncertainties with respect to a diagnostic problem. 'Eighty-six per cent definitely approved of admitting uncertainty when it existed.'

We do not know at what point physicians in each of the hospitals may become aware of limits of their certain knowledge. However, it may be that where admission of uncertainty is accepted and approved more readily – and where cases are frequently complex, and colleagues are often around to remind about uncertainty – limits to knowledge are more readily perceived. But irrespective of the actual limitations of knowledge, what is important here is the desirability that it be acknowledged over and over again and that this acknowledgement becomes one of the criteria that physicians use to judge colleagues' performance.

Many factors at University Hospital seem to provide some of the comfort and reassurance to interns and residents that contributes to their ability to live up to the expectation for admitting mistakes, and gaps in knowledge. The chief of one service told his house-staff members there was no one who couldn't learn something. Throughout the year, the intern and resident can hear renowned experts discussing their own uncertainty of findings. The prestige of a University Hospital internship, won over applicants from numerous schools, and occasional invidious comparison between their own performance in such areas as chartwork, and the people not 'of the hospital', may also be reassuring. The house-staff member in the major teaching center sometimes seems to say, 'We know enough to know when we don't know'. The tendency for house-staff members to give much time and energy to pursuing problems of diagnosis – and to tell each other how much they have worked – may also give some comfort. They can say, 'At least we tried very hard'. The creed of limited knowledge does not give immunity to ignorance, but the University Hospital environment encourages admission of uncertainty coupled with much information about what the latest literature has to say on related problems, and what multiple diagnostic results on the case reveal and suggest. Rounds characteristically included an abundance of specific information, many references to findings, and results from extensive diagnostic work.

The possibilities at University Hospital for 'disguised consultations' also provide some comfort and reassurance on behalf of uncertainty and the 'open mind'. Statements like, 'We overlooked that', 'We are not certain', take some of the onus away from the individual physician's admission of either a mistake or uncertainty. Face-saving assistance and support from the group also provides a cushion that protects high standards in high-risk areas. The intern can 'stick his neck out' with a question, be reassured enough to pursue investigation and tests, in spite of counter-pressure from a patient and his family.

Group activity and the visibility it implies also contribute to reinforcement of the norm of the open mind by increasing the probability that the intern will be forced to awareness of some limits to his knowledge. Replication of histories and chartwork on ward patients provide his peers with ample opportunity to 'call' him, should he be disposed to slip over any evidence of knowledge limits. There is always someone who may question an assumption not backed by test results.

A degree of tolerance for going around some hospital regulations confirms the priority of an open inquiring uncertainty. In ordering tests and laboratory work for patients, interns and residents presented evidence of some patterned evasion of formal regulations in favor of commitments to careful diagnostic work-ups and the norms of the open, inquiring mind. One assistant resident described how one situation was handled where the group had worked out a means of sustaining its own values by 'getting around' an opposing norm in some hospital regulations. The central laboratory once had attempted to 'set a limit' for diagnostic tests for each floor. The resident described how his speciality 'managed' the quota: 'We would go around to another floor (on the same service) and see if they had any unfilled quota and if they did, we would enter the lab request through them.' Although the laboratory had set the quota at a generous maximum, the regulation did not stay in force very long. The resident explained: 'That lab will think an intern is ordering tests which he doesn't need to make his diagnosis. He may just be curious about something, but really that is his privilege. He doesn't get paid much in a hospital like this, but in exchange for that he should get more lab work done. ... It is a teaching hospital. ... A few people lose their heads and do order unnecessarily, but if they learn something by it, *it doesn't bother me.*'

In University Hospital obtaining knowledge, whether or not it benefits the patient, is legitimized by the value placed on teaching and learning. In contrast, an intern at Community Hospital described having learned *not* to order as many tests as she had thought necessary when a medical student.

The questioning attitude also stimulates the intern to challenge many objective 'findings'. When a resident at University Hospital was asked whether he often re-ran laboratory tests when he got a positive finding, he said: 'Yes, it is good practice to do that'. One resident said about checking laboratory results that show abnormality: 'That is the only thing to do.' Other house-staff members frequently talked about their own reruns of some laboratory tests. In the more research-oriented environment, findings were often replicated before they were accepted.

This differs markedly from the pattern in the smaller, more practice-oriented hospital, where findings were more readily accepted as accurate when they came from the laboratory. In contrast to some statements by University Hospital house-staff members about re-running test results as 'the only thing to do', a Community Hospital intern said: 'Heavens, no!' when she was asked whether she had results re-run, or often checked slides herself.

The tendency of some Community Hospital physicians to discourage what they refer to as 'excessive preoccupation with diagnostic testing' is consistent with the practice orientation of the hospital. It is expensive for patients and time consuming for them to have many tests run, and at times also physically and emotionally taxing. Comments at Community Hospital about ordering tests are in contrast to the University Hospital resident's affirmation of the intern's 'privilege' to have tests run.

The norm of uncertainty fits the scientific orientation of University Hospital and it fits the pattern of colleague orientation of physicians there. Knowledge is conditional and to be replaced.

In science, each of us knows that what he has accomplished will be antiquated in ten, twenty, fifty years. That is the fate to which science is subjected: it is the very meaning of scientific work, to which it is devoted in a quite specific sense . . . Every scientific 'fulfilment' raises new 'questions'; it asks to be 'surpassed' and outdated. Whoever wishes to serve science has to resign himself to this fact.

Innovation within science represents a special type of conformity, and may require, therefore, some special social support. The scientist is expected to investigate and introduce new findings. He must move beyond existing knowledge, providing that he satisfies the criteria of evidence and procedure. Even within proper procedure, however, the innovator may encounter some resistance from time to time.

Risk is implicit in innovation and exploration. The experimenter at the very least risks being wrong, with all that may imply for his self-esteem, his personal, social, and sometimes professional and financial security. In refusing to abide by accustomed ways the innovator in medicine carries an additional burden of risk over that of the physician who abides by accepted ways. He 'sticks his neck out' beyond the already unavoidable risk of working with human life.

What fellow physicians at University Hospital reward as admirable admission of uncertainty can seem less than laudable to an anxious patient and his family. Most patients would enjoy a confident assurance that their doctor knew the source of their medical problem – and had in mind the specific treatment of choice. This balm of reassurance may be an enjoyment that patients at Community Hospital receive more often than do patients on the University Hospital teaching wards.

In his advice to the young practitioner, Oliver Wendell Holmes wrote, 'Let me recommend you, as far as possible, to keep your doubts to yourself and give the patient the benefit of your decision.' The patient benefits from faith in the outcome and faith that this physician is very concerned, or knows for certain what to do and what will happen. The extent of benefit from the patient's trust in his doctor is repeatedly suggested in 'placebo effects'. But the physician's education suffers when a closed mind and too much certainty replaces doubt.

It may be that some patients in teaching hospitals become socialized at least to an appearance of accepting uncertainty just as their physicians are socialized to admitting it. In case presentations in seminars for nurses in a large, university-affiliated hospital similar to University Hospital, I have been struck by the apparently accepting attitude toward uncertainty expressed by some patients who have long histories of repeated admissions to a teaching center. These are the 'interesting patients', and some of them do seem to take on attitudes that complement and facilitate the physician's ability to conform to some expectations of the teaching and research center. Patients on University Hospital wards can be heard to say with some pride, 'They are going to try . . . now.' 'We don't know whether this will help, but . . .'. Thus, even the sector that might otherwise challenge the norm of the open mind – the patient population – sometimes offers the University Hospital intern some reassurance about the legitimacy of his commitment.

49 Fred Davis

Uncertainty in Medical Prognosis

Excerpts from Fred Davis, 'Uncertainty in medical prognosis, clinical and functional', *American Journal of Sociology*, vol. 66, July 1960, no. 1, pp. 41–7.

The present Reading examines the scope and significance of uncertainty as evidenced in the treatment of a particular disease. Specifically, it seeks to distinguish between 'real' uncertainty as a clinical and scientific phenomenon and the uses to which uncertainty – real or pretended, 'functional' uncertainty – lends itself in the management of patients and their families by hospital physicians and other treatment personnel. By extrapolation this distinction suggests a fourfold typology of patterns of communication from doctor to patient, analysis of which highlights important sources of strain other than uncertainty.

The disease in question is paralytic poliomyelitis, and the subjects are fourteen Baltimore families, in each of which a young child had contracted the disease [. . .] It was possible to compare and contrast, at successive stages of the disease and its treatment, what the parents knew and understood of the child's condition with what the doctor knew and understood. One must assume that the doctor's knowledge of the disease and its physical effects is more accurate, comprehensive, and profound than that of the parents. The problem, then, could be stated: How much information was communicated to the parents? How was it communicated? And what consequences did this communication have on the parents' expectations of the child's illness and prospects for recovery? And, since in paralytic poliomyelitis (as in many other diseases and illnesses) uncertainty does affect the making of diagnoses and prognoses, an attempt was made to assess the scope, significance, and duration of uncertainty for the doctor. This then provided some basis for inferring the extent to which the parents' knowledge and expectations, or lack thereof, could also be attributed ultimately to uncertainty.

For purposes of simplicity, the discussion that follows is restricted to uncertainty only as it impinges on the prognosis of residual disability expected as a result of the poliomyelitic attack. This subsumes questions of such relatively great moment to child and parent as: Would he be permanently handicapped? Would he require the aid of braces and other supportive appliances? Would his handicap be so severe as to prevent him from engaging in a wide range of normal motor activities or be barely detectable?

Now the pathological course of paralytic poliomyelitis is such that, during the first weeks following onset, it is difficult in most cases for even the most skilled diagnostician to make anything like a definite prognosis of probable residual impairment and functional disability. During the acute phase of the disease and for a period thereafter, the examining physician has no practical way of directly measuring or indirectly inferring the amount of permanent damage or destruction sustained by the horn cells of the spinal cord as a result of the viral attack. (It is basically the condition of these cells, and not that of the muscles neurologically activated by them, that accounts for the paralysis.) Roughly, a one- to three-month period for spontaneous recovery of the damaged spinal cells – a highly unpredictable matter in itself – must first be allowed for before the effects of the disease are sufficiently stabilized to permit a clinically well-founded prognosis.

During this initial period of the child's hospitalization, therefore, the physician is hardly ever able to tell the parents anything definite about the child's prospects of regaining lost muscular function. In view of the very real uncertainty, to attempt to do so would indeed be hazardous. To the parents' insistent questions, 'How will he come out of it?' 'Will he have to wear a brace?' 'Will his walk be normal?' and so on, the invariable response of treatment personnel was that they did not know and that only time would tell. Thus during these first weeks the parents came to adopt a longer time perspective and more qualified outlook than they had to begin with.

By about the sixth week to the third month following onset of the disease, however, the orthopedist and physiotherapist are in a position to make reasonably sound prognoses of the amount and type of residual handicap [. . .]

By this time, therefore, the element of clinical uncertainty regarding outcome, so conspicuously present when the child is first stricken, is greatly reduced for the physician, if not altogether eliminated. Was there then a commensurate gain in the parents' understanding of the child's condition after this six-week to three-month period had passed? Did they then, as did the doctors, come to view certain outcomes as highly probable and others as improbable?

On the basis of intensive and repeated interviewing of the parents over a two-year period, the answer to these questions is that, except for one case in which the muscle check pointed clearly to full recovery, the parents were neither told nor explicitly prepared by the treatment personnel to expect an outcome significantly different from that which they understandably hoped for, namely, a complete and natural recovery for the child. This does not imply that the doctors issued falsely optimistic prognoses or that, through indirection and other subtleties, they sought to encourage the parents to expect more by way of recovery than was possible. Rather, what typically transpired was that the parents were kept in the dark. The doctors' answers to their questions were couched for the most part in such hedging, evasive, or unintelligibly technical terms as to cause them, from many such contacts, to expect a more favorable recovery than could be justified by the facts then known. As one treatment-staff member put it, 'We try not to tell them too much. It's better if they find out for themselves in a natural sort of way.'

Indeed, it was disheartening to note how, for many of the parents, 'the natural way' consisted of a painfully slow and prolonged dwindling of expectations for a complete and natural recovery. This is ironical when one considers that as early as two to three months following onset the doctors and physiotherapists were able to tell members of the research team with considerable confidence that one child would require bracing for an indefinite period; that another would never walk with a normal gait; that a third would require a bone-fusion operation before he would be able to hold himself erect; and so on. By contrast, the parents of these children came to know these prognoses much later, if at all. And even then their understanding of them was in most instances partial and subject to considerable distortion.

But what is of special interest here is the way in which uncertainty, a *real* factor in the early diagnosis and treatment of the paralysed child, came more and more to serve the purely managerial ends of the treatment personnel in their interaction with parents. Long after the doctor himself was no longer in doubt about the outcome, the perpetuation of uncertainty in doctor-to-family communication, although perhaps neither premeditated nor intended, can nonetheless best be understood in terms of its functions in the treatment system. These are several, and closely connected.

Foremost is the way in which the pretense of uncertainty as to outcome serves to reduce materially the expenditure of additional time, effort, and involvement which a frank and strightforward prognosis to the family might entail. The doctor implicitly recognizes that, were he to tell the family that the child would remain crippled or otherwise impaired to some significant extent, he would easily become embroiled in much more than a simple, factual medical prognosis. Presenting so unwelcome a prospect is bound to meet with a strong – and, according to many of the treatment personnel, 'unmanageable' – emotional reaction from parents; among other things, it so threatens basic life-values which they cherish for the child, such as physical attractiveness, vocational achievement, a good marriage, and, perhaps most of all, his being perceived and responded to in society as 'normal, like everyone else'. Moreover, to the extent to which the doctor feels some professional compunction to so inform the parents, the bustling, time-conscious work milieu of the hospital supports him in the convenient rationalization that, even were he to take the trouble, the family could not or would not understand what he had to tell them anyway. Therefore, in hedging, being evasive, equivocating, and cutting short his contact with the parents the doctor was able to avoid 'scenes' with them and having to explain to and comfort them, tasks, at least in the hospital, often viewed as onerous and time-consuming.

Second, since the parents had been told repeatedly during the first weeks of the child's illness that the outcome was subject to great uncertainty, it was not difficult for them, once having accepted the idea, to maintain and even to exaggerate it, particularly in those cases in which the child's progress fell short of full recovery. For, equivocally, uncertainty can be grounds for hope as well as despair, and when, for example, after six months of convalescence the child returned home crippled, the parents could and characteristically did interpret uncertainty to mean that he still stood a good chance of making a full and natural recovery in the indefinite future. The belief in a recuperative moratorium was held long after there was any real possibility of the child's making a full recovery, and with a number of families it had the unfortunate effect of diverting them from taking full advantage of available rehabilitation procedures and therapies. In fact, with few exceptions the parents typically mistook rehabilitation for cure, and, because little was done to correct this misapprehension, they often passively consented to a regimen prescribed for the child which they might have rejected had they known that it had nothing to do with effecting a cure.

Last, it must be noted that in the art (as opposed to the science and technique) of medicine, a sociologically inescapable facet of treatment – often irrespective of how much is clinically known or unknown – is frequently that of somehow getting the patient and his family to accept, 'put up with', or 'make the best of' the socially and physically disadvantageous consequences of illness. Both patient and family are understandably reluctant to do this at first, for no other reason than that it usually entails a dramatic revaluation in identity and self-conception. Not only in paralytic poliomyelitis but in numerous other chronic and long-term illnesses, such as cardiac disease, cancer, tuberculosis, mental illness, and diabetes, such is usually the case. Depending on a number of variables, not the least of which are those of personality, the cultural

background of the family, and the treatment setting, a number of strata-
gems besides that of rendering a full and frank diagnosis and prognosis
(even when clinically known) are open to the physician who must carry
the family through this difficult period. Whereas the evasiveness and
equivocality of hospital treatment staff described here may not have
been as skilled or effective a means for accomplishing this as others
which come to mind, it must in fairness be recognized that there is still
little agreement within medical circles on what practice should be in
these circumstances. (The perennial debate on whether a patient and his
family should be told that he is dying of cancer, and when and how
much they should be told, is an extreme though highly relevant case in
point.) And perhaps the easiest recourse of the hospital practitioner –
who, organizationally, is better barricaded and further removed from
the family than, for example, the neighborhood physician – is to avoid it
altogether.

Clearly, then, clinical uncertainty is not responsible for all that is not
communicated to the patient and his family. Other factors, interests, and
circumstances intrude in the rendering of medical prognoses, with the
result that what the patient is told is uncertain and problematic may
often not be so at all. And, conversely, what he is made to feel is quite
certain may actually be highly uncertain.

50 Erving Goffman

The Road to the Mental Hospital

Excerpts from Erving Goffman, 'The moral career of the mental patient' in *Asylums: Essays on the Social Situation of Mental Patients and Other Inmates*, Doubleday, 1961, Penguin, 1968, pp. 124–35. Originally published in *Psychiatry*, 1959, vol. 22.

For the person who has come to see himself – with whatever justification – as mentally unbalanced, entrance to the mental hospital can sometimes bring relief, perhaps in part because of the sudden transformation in the structure of his basic social situation: instead of being to himself a questionable person trying to maintain a role as a full one, he can become an officially questioned person known to himself to be not so questionable as that. In other cases, hospitalization can make matters worse for the willing patient, confirming by the objective situation what has theretofore been a matter of the private experience of self.

Once the willing prepatient enters the hospital, he may go through the same routine of experiences as do those who enter unwillingly. In any case, it is the latter that I mainly want to consider, since in America at present these are by far the more numerous kind. Their approach to the institution takes one of three classic forms: they come because they have been implored by their family or threatened with the abrogation of family ties unless they go 'willingly'; they come by force under police escort; they come under misapprehension purposely induced by others, this last restricted mainly to youthful prepatients.

The prepatient's career may be seen in terms of an extrusory model: he starts out with relationships and rights, and ends up, at the beginning of his hospital stay, with hardly any of either. The moral aspects of this career, then, typically begin with the experience of abandonment, disloyalty, and embitterment. This is the case even though to others it may be obvious that he was in need of treatment, and even though in the hospital he may soon come to agree.

The case histories of most mental patients document offences against some arrangement for face-to-face living – a domestic establishment, a work place, a semi-public organization such as a church or store, a public region such as a street or park. Often there is also a record of some *complainant*, some figure who takes that action against the offender which eventually leads to his hospitalization. This may not be the person who makes the first move, but it is the person who makes what turns out to be the first effective move. Here is the *social* beginning of the patient's career, regardless of where one might locate the psychological beginning of his mental illness [. . .]

Separating those offences which could have been used as grounds for hospitalizing the offender from those that are so used, one finds a vast number of what students of occupation call career contingencies. Some of these contingencies in the mental patient's career have been suggested, if not explored, such as socio-economic status, visibility of the offence, proximity to a mental hospital, amount of treatment facilities available, community regard for the type of treatment given in available hospitals, and so on. For information about other contingencies one must rely on atrocity tales: a psychotic man is tolerated by his wife until she finds herself a boy friend, or by his adult children until they move from a house to an apartment; an alcoholic is sent to a mental hospital because the jail is full, and a drug addict because he declines to avail himself of psychiatric treatment on the outside; a rebellious adolescent daughter can no longer be managed at home because she now threatens to have an open affair with an unsuitable companion; and so on. Correspondingly there is an equally important set of contingencies causing the person to by-pass this fate. And should the person enter the hospital, still another set of contingencies will help determine when he is to obtain a discharge – such as the desire of his family for his return, the availability of a 'manageable' job, and so on. The society's official view is that inmates of mental hospitals are there primarily because they are suffering from mental illness. However, in the degree that the 'mentally ill' outside hospitals numerically approach or surpass those inside hospitals, one could say that mental patients distinctively suffer not from mental illness but from contingencies.

Career contingencies occur in conjunction with a second feature of the prepatient's career – the circuit of agents – and agencies – that participate fatefully in his passage from civilian to patient status. Here is an instance of that increasingly important class of social system whose elements are agents and agencies which are brought into systemic connection through having to take up and send on the same persons. Some of these agent roles will be cited now, with the understanding that in any concrete circuit a role may be filled more than once, and that the same person may fill more than one of them.

First is the *next-of-relation* – the person whom the prepatient sees as the most available of those upon whom he should be able to depend most in times of trouble, in this instance the last to doubt his sanity and the first to have done everything to save him from the fate which, it transpires, he has been approaching. The patient's next-of-relation is usually his next of kin; the special term is introduced because he need not be. Second is the *complainant*, the person who retrospectively appears to have started the person on his way to the hospital. Third are the *mediators* – the sequence of agents and agencies to which the prepatient is referred and through which he is relayed and processed on his way to the hospital. Here are included police, clergy, general medical practitioners, office psychiatrists, personnel in public clinics, lawyers, social service workers, schoolteachers, and so on. One of these agents will have the legal mandate to sanction commitment and will exercise it, and so those agents who precede him in the process will be involved in something whose outcome is not yet settled. When the mediators retire from the scene, the prepatient has become an inpatient, and the significant agent has become the hospital administrator [. . .]

In the prepatient's progress from home to the hospital he may participate as a third person in what he may come to experience as a kind of alienative coalition. His next-of-relation presses him into coming to 'talk things over' with a medical practitioner, an office psychiatrist, or some other counsellor. Disinclination on his part may be met by threatening him with desertion, disownment, or other legal action, or by stressing the joint and exploratory nature of the interview. But typically the next-of-relation will have set the interview up, in the sense of selecting the professional, arranging for time, telling the professional something about the case, and so on. This move effectively tends to establish the next-of-relation as the responsible person to whom pertinent findings can be divulged, while effectively establishing the other as the patient. The prepatient often goes to the interview with the understanding that he is going as an equal of someone who is so bound together with him that a third person could not come between them in fundamental matters; this, after all, is one way in which close relationships are defined in our society. Upon arrival at the office the prepatient suddenly finds that he and his next-of-relation have not been accorded the same roles, and apparently that a prior understanding between the professional and the next-of-relation has been put in operation against him. In the extreme but common case, the professional first sees the prepatient alone, in the role of examiner and diagnostician, and then sees the next-of-relation alone, in the role of adviser, while carefully avoiding talking things over seriously with them both together. And even in those non-consultative cases where public officials must forcibly extract a person from a family that wants to tolerate him, the next-of-relation is likely to be induced to 'go along' with the official action, so that even here the prepatient may feel that an alienative coalition has been formed against him.

The moral experience of being third man in such a coalition is likely to embitter the prepatient, especially since his troubles have already probably led to some estrangement from his next-of-relation [. . .]

I am suggesting that the prepatient starts out with at least a portion of the rights, liberties, and satisfactions of the civilian and ends up on a psychiatric ward stripped of almost everything. The question here is how this stripping is managed. This is the second aspect of betrayal I want to consider.

As the prepatient may see it, the circuit of significant figures can function as a kind of betrayal funnel. Passage from person to patient may be effected through a series of linked stages, each managed by a different agent. While each stage tends to bring a sharp decrease in adult free status, each agent may try to maintain the fiction that no further decrease will occur. He may even manage to turn the prepatient over to the next agent while sustaining this note. Further, through words, cues, and gestures, the prepatient is implicitly asked by the current agent to join with him in sustaining a running line of polite small talk that tactfully avoids the administrative facts of the situation, becoming, with each stage, progressively more at odds with these facts. The spouse would rather not have to cry to get the prepatient to visit a psychiatrist; psychiatrists would rather not have a scene when the prepatient learns that he and his spouse are being seen separately and in different ways; the police infrequently bring a prepatient to the hospital in a strait-jacket, finding it much easier all around to give him a cigarette, some kindly words, and freedom to relax in the back seat of the patrol car; and finally, the admitting psychiatrist finds he can do his work better in the relative quiet and luxury of the 'admission suite' where, as an incidental consequence, the notion can survive that a mental hospital is indeed a comforting place. If the prepatient heeds all of these implied requests and is reasonably decent about the whole thing, he can travel the whole circuit from home to hospital without forcing anyone to look directly at what is happening or to deal with the raw emotion that his situation might well cause him to express. His showing consideration for those who are moving him towards the hospital allows them to show consideration for him, with the joint result that these interactions can be sustained with some of the protective harmony characteristic of ordinary face-to-face dealings. But should the new patient cast his mind back over the sequence of steps leading to hospitalization, he may feel that everyone's current comfort was being busily sustained while his long-range welfare was being undermined. This realization may constitute a moral experience that further separates him for the time from the people on the outside [. . .]

The final point I want to consider about the prepatient's moral career is its peculiarly retroactive character. Until a person actually arrives at the hospital there usually seems no way of knowing for sure that he is destined to do so, given the determinative role of career contingencies. And until the point of hospitalization is reached, he or others may not conceive of him as a person who is becoming a mental patient. However, since he will be held against his will in the hospital, his next-of-relation and the hospital staff will be in great need of a rationale for the hardships they are sponsoring. The medical elements of the staff will also need evidence that they are still in the trade they were trained for. These problems are eased, no doubt unintentionally, by the case-history construction that is placed on the patient's past life, this having the effect of demonstrating that all along he had been becoming sick, that he finally became very sick, and that if he had not been hospitalized much worse things would have happened to him – all of which, of course, may be true. Incidentally, if the patient wants to make sense out of his stay in the hospital, and, as already suggested, keep alive the possibility of once again conceiving of his next-of-relation as a decent, well-meaning person, then he, too, will have reason to believe some of this psychiatric work-up of his past.

Here is a very ticklish point for the sociology of careers. An important aspect of every career is the view the person constructs when he looks backward over his progress; in a sense, however, the whole of the prepatient career derives from this reconstruction. The fact of having had a prepatient career, starting with an effective complaint, becomes an important part of the mental patient's orientation, but this part can begin to be played only after hospitalization proves that what he had been having, but no longer has, is a career as a prepatient.

51 Erving Goffman

Inside the Asylum

Excerpts from Erving Goffman, 'The moral career of the mental patient', *Asylums: Essays on the Social Situation of Mental Patients and Other Inmates*, Doubleday, 1961, Penguin, 1968, pp. 136–46. Originally published in *Psychiatry*, 1959, vol. 22.

The last step in the prepatient's career can involve his realization – justified or not – that he has been deserted by society and turned out of relationships by those closest to him [. . .]

Once the prepatient begins to settle down, the main outlines of his fate tend to follow those of a whole class of segregated establishments – jails, concentration camps, monasteries, work camps, and so on – in which the inmate spends the whole round of life on the grounds, and marches through his regimented day in the immediate company of a group of persons of his own institutional status.

Like the neophyte in many of these total institutions, the new inpatient finds himself cleanly stripped of many of his accustomed affirmations, satisfactions, and defences, and is subjected to a rather full set of mortifying experiences: restriction of free movement, communal living, diffuse authority of a whole echelon of people, and so on. Here one begins to learn about the limited extent to which a conception of oneself can be sustained when the usual setting of supports for it are suddenly removed.

While undergoing these humbling moral experiences, the inpatient learns to orient himself in terms of the 'ward system'. In public mental hospitals this usually consists of a series of graded living arrangements built around wards, administrative units called services, and parole statuses [. . .]

The ward system, then, is an extreme instance of how the physical facts of an establishment can be explicitly employed to frame the conception a person takes of himself. In addition, the official psychiatric mandate of mental hospitals gives rise to even more direct, even more blatant, attacks upon the inmate's view of himself. The more 'medical' and the more progressive a mental hospital is – the more it attempts to be therapeutic and not merely custodial – the more he may be confronted by high-ranking staff arguing that his past has been a failure, that the cause of this has been within himself, that his attitude to life is wrong, and that if he wants to be a person he will have to change his way of dealing with people and his conceptions of himself. Often the moral value of these verbal asaults will be brought home to him by requiring him to practise taking this psychiatric view of himself in arranged confessional periods, whether in private sessions or group psychotherapy.

Now a general point may be made about the moral career of in-patients which has bearing on many moral careers. Given the stage that any person has reached in a career, one typically finds that he constructs an image of his life course – past, present, and future – which selects, abstracts, and distorts in such a way as to provide him with a view of himself that he can usefully expound in current situations. Quite generally, the person's line concerning self defensively brings him into appropriate alignment with the basic values of his society, and so may be called an apologia. If the person can manage to present a view of his current situation which shows the operation of favourable personal qualities in the past and a favourable destiny awaiting him, it may be called a success story. If the facts of a person's past and present are extremely dismal, then about the best he can do is to show that he is not responsible for what has become of him, and the term sad tale is appropriate [. . .]

In the mental hospital, the setting and the house rules press home to the patient that he is, after all, a mental case who has suffered some kind of social collapse on the outside, having failed in some over-all way, and that here he is of little social weight, being hardly capable of acting like a full-fledged person at all. These humiliations are likely to be most keenly felt by middle-class patients, since their previous condition of life little immunizes them against such affronts, but all patients feel some downgrading. Just as any normal member of his outside subculture would do, the patient often responds to this situation by attempting to assert a sad tale proving that he is not 'sick', that the 'little trouble' he did get into was really somebody else's fault, that his past life-course had some honour and rectitude, and that the hospital is therefore unjust in forcing the status of mental patient upon him. This self-respecting tendency is heavily institutionalized within the patient society where opening social contact typically involve the participants' volunteering information about their current ward location and length of stay so far, but not the reasons for their stay – such interaction being conducted in the manner of small talk on the outside. With greater familiarity, each patient usually volunteers relatively acceptable reasons for his hospitalization, at the same time accepting without open immediate question the lines offered by other patients. Such stories as the following are given and overtly accepted.

I was going to night school to get a M A degree, and holding down a job in addition, and the load got too much for me.

The others here are sick mentally but I'm suffering from a bad nervous system and that is what is giving me these phobias.

I got here by mistake because of a diabetes diagnosis, and I'll leave in a couple of days. (The patient had been in seven weeks.)

I failed as a child, and later with my wife I reached out for dependency.

My trouble is that I can't work. That's what I'm in for, I had two jobs with a good home and all the money I wanted [. . .]

But the patient's apologia is called forth in a unique setting, for few settings could be so destructive of self-stories except, of course, those stories already constructed along psychiatric lines. And this destructiveness rests on more than the official sheet of paper which attests that the patient is of unsound mind, a danger to himself and others – an attestation, incidentally, which seems to cut deeply into the patient's pride, and into the possibility of his having any.

Certainly the degrading conditions of the hospital setting belie many of the self-stories that are presented by patients, and the very fact of being in the mental hospital is evidence against these tales. And of course there is not always sufficient patient solidarity to prevent patient discrediting patient, just as there is not always a sufficient number of 'professionalized' attendants to prevent attendant discrediting patient. As one patient informant repeatedly suggested to a fellow patient, 'If you're so smart, how come you got your ass in here?'

The mental-hospital setting, however, is more treacherous still. Staff have much to gain through discreditings of the patient's story – whatever the felt reason for such discreditings. If the custodial faction in the hospital is to succeed in managing his daily round without complaint or trouble from him, then it will prove useful to be able to point out to him that the claims about himself upon which he rationalizes his demands are false, that he is not what he is claiming to be, and that in fact he is a failure as a person. If the psychiatric faction is to impress upon him its views about his personal make-up, then they must be able to show in detail how their version of his past and their version of his character hold up much better than his own. If both the custodial and psychiatric factions are to get him to cooperate in the various psychiatric treatments, then it will prove useful to disabuse him of his view of their purposes, and cause him to appreciate that they know what they are doing, and are doing what is best for him. In brief, the difficulties caused by a patient are closely tied to his version of what has been happening to him, and if cooperation is to be secured, it helps if this version is discredited. The patient must 'insightfully' come to take, or affect to take, the hospital's view of himself.

The staff also have ideal means – in addition to the mirroring effect of the setting – for denying the inmate's rationalizations. Current psychiatric doctrine defines mental disorder as something that can have its roots in the patient's earliest years, show its signs throughout the course of his life, and invade almost every sector of his current activity. No segment of his past or present need be defined, then, as beyond the jurisdiction and mandate of psychiatric assessment. Mental hospitals bureaucratically institutionalize this extremely wide mandate by formally basing their treatment of the patient upon his diagnosis and hence upon the psychiatric view of his past.

The case record is an important expression of this mandate. This dossier is apparently not regularly used, however, to record occasions when the patient showed capacity to cope honourably and effectively with difficult life situations. Nor is the case record typically used to provide a rough average or sampling of his past conduct. One of its purposes is to show the ways in which the patient is 'sick' and the reasons why it was right to commit him and is right currently to keep him committed; and this is done by extracting from his whole life course a list of those incidents that have or might have had 'symptomatic' significance. The misadventures of his parents or siblings that might suggest a 'taint' may be cited. Early acts in which the patient appeared to have shown bad judgement or emotional disturbance will be recorded. Occasions when he acted in a way which the layman would consider immoral, sexually perverted, weak-willed, childish, ill-considered, impulsive, and crazy may be described. Misbehaviours which someone saw as the last straw, as cause for immediate action, are likely to be reported in detail. In addition, the record will describe his state on arrival at the hospital – and this is not likely to be a time of tranquillity and ease for him. The record may also report the false line taken by the patient in answering embarrassing questions, showing him as someone who makes claims that are obviously contrary to the facts:

Claims she lives with oldest daughter or with sisters only when sick and in need of care; otherwise with husband, he himself says not for twelve years.

Contrary to the reports from the personnel, he says he no longer bangs on the floor or cries in the morning.

Where contrary facts are not known by the recorder, their presence is often left scrupulously an open question:

Even with considerable pressure she was unwilling to engage in any projection of paranoid mechanisms.

No psychotic content could be elicited at this time.

And if in no more factual way, discrediting statements often appear in descriptions given of the patient's general social manner in the hospital:

When interviewed, he was bland, apparently self-assured, and sprinkles high-sounding generalizations freely throughout his verbal productions.

Armed with a rather neat appearance and natty little Hitlerian mustache this 45 year old man who has spent the last five or more years of his life in the hospital, is making a very successful hospital adjustment living within the role of a rather gay liver and jim-dandy type of fellow who is not only quite superior to his fellow patients in intellectual respects but who is also quite a man with women. His speech is sprayed with many multi-syllabled words which he generally uses in good context, but if he talks long enough on any subject it soon becomes apparent that he is so completely lost in this verbal diarrhea as to make what he says almost completely worthless.

The events recorded in the case history are, then, just the sort that a layman would consider scandalous, defamatory, and discrediting. I think it is fair to say that all levels of mental-hospital staff fail, in general, to deal with this material with the moral neutrality claimed for medical statements and psychiatric diagnosis, but instead participate, by intonation and gesture if by no other means, in the lay reaction to these acts. This will occur in staff–patient encounters as well as in staff encounters at which no patient is present.

Part Nine Race Relations

Most people see problems arising in the field of race relations as some of the most desperate of our time. Amongst those who reject segregation as an answer, there are deep differences of opinion as to what kind of action would be effective in breaking down racial barriers. Some feel that 'no policy' is the best policy, that action merely exacerbates racial tension. For example N. Lawson argued recently in the *Sunday Times* that 'the simplest way of improving race relations in Britain today would probably be to wind up the whole existing race relations industry, lock, stock and barrel'. Others put their faith in programmes of education; yet others in legal controls. Finally, there are those who see no hope of a tolerant multi-racial society coming about through anything short of large-scale revolution.

Before we consider what light sociology might throw on possible courses of action, we need to examine what we mean by 'race'; what racialism means both to those who suffer from its effects and to those who support it; and what responses have been made by oppressed racial minorities to their condition.

A definition of 'race relations'

The term 'race relations' refers to relations among members of two groups between whom physical differences have social meaning attached to them. In a society consisting of people with 'white' and 'black' skins, but where such physical differences were in no way relevant in determining how the members related to each other, there would be no race relations. Black (or white) skin, like hair colour, height and similar features, would simply be a characteristic of occasional interest, but no social importance. Race relations arise when significant and different values are put on physical characteristics. Hence the question as to whether or not there are significant bio-genetic differences between people with 'white' or 'black' skins respectively is usually not the issue at stake. What is important is that people *believe* these differences to exist and behave in ways that are the expression of that belief. They use physical differences to mark themselves off as separate from others.

Secondly, sociologists conventionally distinguish between 'racism', that is, the holding of inflexible beliefs about other groups which are physically different, and 'racialism', which is the systematic unequal treatment of other racial groups. In other words, racist beliefs support racialist policies and practices.

Thirdly, there are many similarites between the situation of those who are discriminated against because they are physically different, and those who are discriminated against because they have different cultures – different religions, different languages, different nationalities, different ways of living – even though they may be of the same physical stock. Thus Jews in the USSR or Catholics in Northern Ireland have much in common with Negroes in the USA. This wider field of 'ethnic' relations, based on cultural differences, is not explicitly discussed here, but frequent parallels can be drawn, in studying the meaning of discrimination, the origin of prejudice, and ways of resolving inter-group conflict, between situations where physical differences are the basis of discrimination and those where cultural differences are uppermost.

We may conclude that we have a race relations situation when a group of people who are physically distinct:

1. Hold rigid beliefs about their social superiority to another group (prejudices).
2. Regularly behave towards them in a way which denies them equal access to such resources as jobs, houses, transport and social facilities (discrimination).
3. Thereby maintain an unequal distribution of power in the society (stratification) (compare, Rex's *Race Relations in Sociological Theory*, Weidenfeld & Nicolson, 1970).

In the next section we examine each of these factors in turn.

The meaning of racialism

Racialism has quite different implications in the three societies covered most fully in the selections in this chapter: the USA, South Africa and Brazil. However, one common factor is that whatever the manifestations of racialism, they cannot be fully understood by the Whte Man, simply because he is white. In this respect, our first selection, Reading 52 (Griffin), constitutes the outstanding exception. The extracts presented from the diary he kept while his skin was artificially 'blackened' so as to give the appearance of a Negro, clearly describe the humiliations he had to endure from people who, if only they had known he was *really* white, would have treated him with courtesy and respect. What stands out is that his relations with Whites were not *personal* (as between friends); nor were they *structural* (as between employer and employee, or bus conductor and passenger); they were consistently *categorical*. That is, people treated him not as an individual, nor in terms of the role he was playing at the time (or attempting to play), but on the basis of the category 'Black' which he represented, regardless of his personal characteristics or the relationship in which he was involved.

In the second extract, Kuper (Reading 53) shows how such categorical treatment of black-skinned people by the dominant White racial group in South Africa is not something which can be avoided by keeping clear of certain special situations. Rather, everyone, even those who oppose racial laws, is drawn on the one hand into practising or conniving at racialism, or, on the other, breaking the law through maintaining forbidden contacts in the course of 'marriage, sex, living in a home, trading, working, studying, healing, welfare work, going to a cinema, eating, playing golf [or] attending a meeting' (Kuper, p. 34). That is, the racial criterion is the dominant one in the basic routine of everyday living. Black are committed by its effects, and most Whites are committed to its practice.

Where low status roles are systematically ascribed to black people on account of their physical characteristics, the distribution of power within the society is weighted heavily in favour of the White. This remains broadly true for Brazil, despite its reputation for being racially equalitarian, as well as for South Africa and the USA. In Britain, too, while there are distinguished individuals and a few high status occupational groups, such as Indian and Pakistani doctors, who deviate from this pattern, in general 'coloured' people are concentrated in the lower socio-economic groups and even more concentrated in areas of inferior housing.

Various mechanisms help to justify such systems of oppression. Prejudiced beliefs, that is, beliefs about the general characteristics of a group which prejudge the characteristics of particular people with whom one comes into contact, mean that those who practise racial discrimination regard it as quite legitimate, and even in the interests of the victims. Thus not only do White people in racially-mixed societies hold pejorative views of the Black population, which are maintained by careful selection or 'manufacturing' of appropriate 'facts' (Rex), they also tend to justify the application of different standards in various ways: they are upholding 'White Christian civilization', 'allowing each group to develop its own destiny,' putting some White blood into the Black race by sexual exploitation of Black women. At the same time, individual courtesies to Black people (who are treated as exceptional), the fact that racial discrimination may be rewarding to the dominant group, and that White people cannot appreciate what it is like to be Black, all help to justify discriminatory behaviour and to maintain prejudiced attitudes.

Responses to racialism

Victims of racialism have produced a variety of responses. One response, exemplified by the extracts from Malcolm X (Reading 55) and Segal (Reading 58), is militancy: the struggle to replace the system which institutionalizes racialism against Blacks with one in which physical differences will be irrelevant to social behaviour. Kuper argues that it is the racialism of the Whites in South Africa which provokes the counter-racialism of the Blacks. Similarly, Malcom X talks of the growing recognition among Black Americans that they must treat White America on its own terms: 'Brotherhood is a two-way street', 'violence is a two-way street', 'killing is a two-way street': you must talk in the language that people understand, and that may be the language of violence. The newly-won independence of Black African states is only a precursor of liberation for internal Black colonies in places like the USA.

Not all Black minorities, however, have reacted to oppression with militancy. One of the classical responses of Black people has been to seek refuge in special forms of religion which allow them to compensate for their disprivileges in other spheres. More recently, however, the religious orientations adopted by Black Americans have concentrated not so much on providing a different system of values in which 'the first shall be last', as in uniting Black people by focusing their attention on changing their position of disprivilege in this world, whether through Martin Luther King's Southern Christian Leadership Conference or the Black Muslim movement described by Malcolm X. A parallel non-religious development among ghetto Negroes has been the effort to generate a distinctive cultural nationality, expressing the 'essence of Negroness', and summed up in the term 'soul'. The extract from Hannerz (Reading 56) shows how this culture comes to protect Negroes who might otherwise become the victims of self-doubt. Not being able to live up to the mainstream achievements or to convince themselves that the barriers to achievement in White society are in fact impenetrable, 'soul brothers' react by idealizing their own way of life, which labels them 'successful' rather than failures.

Finally, Bastide (Reading 57) describes a third direction: the tendency among Brazilian Negroes not to work for the overthrow of society, or to develop a cultural nationalism which would dignify them in the face of racialist oppression, but to strive to achieve higher positions within the racialist society on an individual basis. That is, as with Caribbean societies, for example, Black people have accepted the racist values of the society, but tried to achieve what they could within that system.

A future for racialism

The contribution sociology might make to the resolution of racial conflicts is limited in various ways. First, as Rex points out (Reading 54), social scientists are just as likely to have strongly ideological views on appropriate courses of action as reactionary politicians. While sociologists clearly recognize in the abstract the difference between being committed to a set of beliefs and being biased by ideological factors in their analysis, in practice 'arguments about facts conceal arguments about values' and the two cannot always be clearly separated. Secondly, sociologists are not able to make precise predictions about future states of race relations. Too many variables are involved in the analysis; much of the basic data that would be necessary to attempt such an undertaking is not available; and in any case sociological theory is not well-geared to conceptualizing changes on such a large scale. A third point is that sociologists make no claim to be able to explain the whole of behaviour in the terms of their discipline. Parallel investigations by, for example, psychologists, geneticists and economists, also help us to understand relations between racial groups. Each discipline applies its own methods and techniques in an effort to understand elements of society, and while their findings are often complementary, none of them has a monopoly of the truth.

A further factor is that South African, American and Brazilian society have institutionalized racism to different degrees. Prospects for the resolution of racial conflict, and appropriate strategies, are therefore also likely to differ. Kuper stresses the 'chain-reaction of racialization' in South Africa, which forces relationships between Black and White to be largely categorical, by virtue of the *apartheid* laws which ensure that the White Man plays the superior role and the Black Man the inferior role. He concludes that revolutionary change is the only way of radically altering the racialism of South African society.

Segal offers much the same diagnosis of the USA, though Hannerz points out that the ghetto-dwellers who are developing 'soul culture' have not yet joined up with those who are reacting to their disadvantaged position more militantly. Williams (Reading 59), indeed, argues that as a result of changes on the international scene, the development of mass production systems and markets, and the effects of urbanization and rising aspirations, the cultural patterns of White and Black Americans have become more alike and that racial discrimination is increasingly under strain. The concurrent rise in racial tension can even support this thesis, for racial conflict can be conceived of as the result of Black expectations and demands rising faster than Whites are prepared to make concessions.

Brazil offers a contrast to both South Africa and the USA. Whites are similarly concentrated among the higher socio-economic strata, and Negroes amongst the working class, yet Negroes have been successfully incorporated into the heterogeneous mass of the urban-industrial working class along with Whites, so that in work-related matters at least, they are the object of class prejudice rather than race prejudice.

We noted earlier on that racialist behaviour, that is, the regular allocation of inferior roles to people on the basis of physical differences which have been given social meaning, tends to be associated with two other factors, a set of racist interpretations of other groups and a relative monopoly of power in the hands of White people – whether economic power, higher social status, or the capacity to enforce one's will, whether through normal political channels or not. Any assessment of strategies for changing the pattern of race relations in society must therefore recognize the interdependence of these two factors, the objective differences in power between Black and White people, and the racist ideas which White people use to decide on appropriate behaviour.

Sociologists have argued that historically it was the brutal political domination and economic exploitation of Black people by White during the period of Western European imperialism which led to the intensification of racism, and that while slavery has been abolished, the inequalities of power persist. Basic changes in racial attitudes and behaviour require a real redistribution of power between White and Black. For example, Kuper argues strongly that it is the near-monopoly of economic and political power which Whites still hold that reinforces their racist attitudes towards Blacks; they cannot *afford* to ignore skin colour if they wish to protect their standard of living.

On the other hand, racist ideas are powerful in themselves, and race relations is one of the most important fields in which we can observe the operation of what Merton called the 'self-fulfilling prophecy', that is, the prediction which comes true because people have come to believe in it rather than because it was bound to happen in any case. Thus, if White families in a residential area feel sufficiently strongly that if Black families move in property values will drop, a natural reaction will be to anticipate this by moving out before it happens. But by so doing they are creating the very conditions which will make the depreciation of property values certain: they are increasing the supply of houses for sale without increasing the demand for them. Thus, whether or not their initial assumptions were justified, they have been 'proved' correct by the consequences. Racist interpretations of situations, and racialist inequalities in the distribution of power, then, reinforce each other, and a programme for reducing racialist behaviour which ignores either of these dimensions is likely to be ineffective.

Programmes for reducing racialism are also limited in other ways. While sociologists may be able to identify prejudiced attitudes and discriminatory behaviour, frequently these factors are not easily changed. Those who control the levers of change may well not be interested in developing racial tolerance at all, or may have other priorities. Bastide's discussion of industrialization in Brazil shows that it was undertaken for purely economic reasons, not in order to diminish racialism in Brazilian society. In the short run, indeed, it had precisely the opposite effect, in that it intensified prejudice by increasing competition for jobs. Nor is the pace of industrialization today governed by the desire to create racial harmony, though the tendency to treat workers in a standardized way, whatever their colour, may be one result of the change from small, family businesses to the large bureaucratically-organized factories which typify modern industry (see Patterson's *Immigrants in Industry,* Oxford University Press, 1968). Sociologists have observed that the changing pattern of industry, if other things were equal, would be likely to benefit race relations. Other factors, however, such as periodic economic recessions which diminish the supply of jobs, do continue to obtrude, and entrenched racialism, as in South Africa, is quite compatible with modern industry.

A further factor whose overall effect appears to be to inhibit racialism, is the expansion of education. The growth of modern mass education is not due to belief in the virtues of education 'in itself', or to the spread of notions of social equality, so much as to the growing belief that an educated workforce is a necessity for modern industry. Nor does education always have the effect of softening racial attitudes. It may enable people to rationalize their prejudice in a more sophisticated fashion, or, as Williams suggests, lead to a switch in the focus of their prejudices. His own research suggests that education only reduces prejudice when it is combined with personal contact with members of the group against whom prejudice is expressed. But steps can be taken to deliberately and successfully foster more equal opportunities and to inhibit racial prejudice. Thus legislation can be used to prohibit racial discrimination. Even so, the law has its limits: the passage from Malcolm X shows that Civil Rights laws have not been the answer to the problems of the Black minority in America and Segal notes that they certainly did not stop ghetto riots. There remains a broad divide between 'equality of opportunities' and 'equality of outcomes'. However, while legislation has not radically transformed the economic prospects of Black Americans, overall it has probably been of benefit, particularly where it was framed and its administration financed in such a way as to allow effective enforcement of the law, and reliance was not placed simply on moral pressure. But in the absence of other measures designed to ensure equal opportunities for members of oppressed minorities, the law by itself is likely to be of little value.

Such supporting measures have taken widely differing forms, in accordance with different local circumstances. But Williams identifies two related factors which help account for some of the more successful initiatives. He stresses the value of joint action by members of different racial groups towards shared objectives. Thus the recognition of common interests not directly relevant to racial status is likely to bring members of different racial groups to relate to each other on equal terms, and provides a social context in which they can see each other in terms of their personal qualities rather than in a purely categorical fashion. Sport and popular music are fields in which this has been most common. But the identification of shared interests and common objectives is equally important in the designing of personnel policies in industry, or in allocating local authority housing. Again, governmental measures are more politically acceptable and more likely to be effective when they are not specifically addressed to improving the position of a particular racial minority, but when they seek to remove social disadvantages which are shared by other groups as well. Thus it may be that, alongside a legal framework designed to secure equal opportunities, appropriately-conceived and administered urban aid programmes will be more effective in overcoming the handicaps of, for example, educational disadvantages or substandard housing, than direct measures of 'positive discrimination' in the interests of a singled-out disadvantaged group.

Secondly, Williams argues that rather than concentrating on trying to reduce racial conflict in a way that will leave inequalities of power largely unchanged, a more useful strategy might be to learn how to use conflict constructively. That is, as well as learning what conditions tend to produce cooperation rather than conflict at an interpersonal level as well as between groups, sociologists should urgently be trying to discover 'how conflict can be used to enhance understanding and social growth'. Movements of protest and threats to the stable maintenance of a discriminatory system – for example in access to housing resources – should not automatically be seen as a 'threat to public order', but more importantly as a prelude towards a more equalitarian system.

The global system of racial prejudice and discrimination nourished by centuries of imperialism and economic exploitation has produced vested interests of power and privilege among White people too great to be sacrificed without a struggle. That this struggle will continue to be fought is not in doubt. The great majority of sociologists would be glad if their expertise were used to enable the inevitable conflict to be constructively directed towards the development of genuinely tolerant multi-racial societies.

52 J. H. Griffin

The Experience of Being Black

Excerpts from J. H. Griffin, *Black Like Me*, Panther Books, 1964, pp. 50–65, 95–121, 142–4.

I went to the Y café next door for breakfast of grits and eggs. The elderly gentleman who ran the café soon had me talking – or rather listening. He foresaw a new day for the race. Great strides had been made, but greater ones were to be made still. I told him of my unsuccessful job-hunting. He said it was all part of the pattern of economics – economic injustice.

'You take a young white boy. He can go through school and college with a real incentive. He knows he can make good money in any profession when he gets out. But can a Negro – in the South? No, I've seen many make brilliant grades in college. And yet when they come home in the summers to earn a little money, they can't get jobs according to their education or capabilities. No, they have to do the most menial work. And even when they graduate it's a long hard pull. Most take postal jobs, or preaching or teaching jobs. *This is the cream.* What about the others, Mr Griffin? A man knows no matter how hard he works, he's never going to *quite* manage . . . taxes and prices eat up more than he can earn. He can't see how he'll ever have a wife and children. The economic structure just doesn't permit it unless he's prepared to live down in poverty and have his wife work too. That's part of it. Our people aren't educated because they either can't afford it or else they know education won't earn them the jobs it would a white man. Any kind of family life, any decent standard of living seems impossible from the outset. So a lot of them, without even understanding the cause, just give up. They take what they can – mostly in pleasure, and they make the grand gesture, the wild gesture, because what have they got to lose if they do die in a car wreck or a knife fight or something else equally stupid'.

'Yes, and then it's these things that cause the whites to say we're not worthy of first-class citizenship.'

'Ah . . .' he dropped his hands to his sides in hard frustration. 'Isn't it so? They make it impossible for us to earn, to pay much in taxes because we haven't much in income, and then they say that because they pay most of the taxes, they have the right to have things like they want. It's a vicious circle, Mr Griffin, and I don't know how we'll get out of it. They put us low, and then blame us for being down there and say that since we are low, we can't deserve our rights' [. . .]

After a week of wearying rejection, the newness had worn off. My first vague, favourable impression that it was not as bad as I had thought it would be came from courtesies of the whites towards the Negro in New Orleans. But this was superficial. All the courtesies in the world do not cover up the one vital and massive discourtesy – that the Negro is treated not even as a second-class citizen, but as a tenth-class one. His day-to-day living is a reminder of his inferior status. He does not become calloused to these things – the polite rebuffs when he seeks better employment; hearing himself referred to as nigger, coon, jigaboo; having to by-pass available rest-room facilities or eating facilities to find one specified for him. Each new reminder strikes at the raw spot, deepens the wound. I do not speak here only from my personal reaction, but from seeing it happen to others, and from seeing their reactions.

The Negro's only salvation from complete despair lies in his belief, the old belief of his forefathers, that these things are not directed against him personally, but against his race, his pigmentation. His mother or aunt or teacher long ago carefully prepared him, explaining that he as an individual can live in dignity, even though he as a Negro cannot. 'They don't do it to you because you're Johnny – they don't even know you. They do it against your Negro-ness.'

But at the time of the rebuff, even when the rebuff is impersonal, such as holding his bladder until he can find a 'Coloured' sign, the Negro cannot rationalize. He feels it personally and it burns him. It gives him a view of the white man that the white can never understand; for if the Negro is part of the black mass, the white is always the individual, and he will sincerely deny that he is 'like that', he has always tried to be fair and kind to the Negro. Such men are offended to find Negroes suspicious of them, never realizing that the Negro cannot understand how – since as individuals they are decent and 'good' to the coloured – the whites as a group can still contrive to arrange life so that it destroys the Negro's sense of personal value, degrades his human dignity, deadens the fibres of his being.

Existence becomes a grinding effort, guided by belly-hunger and the almost desperate need to divert awareness from the squalors to the pleasures, to lose oneself in sex or drink or dope or gut-religion or gluttony or the incoherence of falsity; and in some instances in the higher pleasures of music, art, literature, though these usually deepen perceptions rather than dull them, and can be unbearable; they present a world that is ordered, sane, disciplined to felicity, and the contrast of that world to theirs increases the pain of theirs [. . .]

In the bus station lobby, I looked for signs indicating a coloured waiting-room, but saw none. I walked up to the ticket counter. When the lady ticket-seller saw me, her otherwise attractive face turned sour, violently so. This look was so unexpected and so unprovoked I was taken aback.

'What do you want?' she snapped.

Taking care to pitch my voice to politeness, I asked about the next bus to Hattiesburg.

She answered rudely and glared at me with such loathing I knew I was receiving what the Negroes call 'the hate stare'. It was my first experi-ence with it. It is far more than the look of disapproval one occasionally gets. This was so exaggeratedly hateful I would have been amused if I had not been so surprised.

I framed the words in my mind: 'Pardon me, but have I done some-thing to offend you?' But I realized I had done nothing – my colour offended her.

'I'd like a one-way ticket to Hattiesburg, please,' I said and placed a ten-dollar bill on the counter.

'I can't change that big bill,' she said abruptly and turned away, as though the matter were closed. I remained at the window, feeling strangely abandoned but not knowing what else to do. In a while she flew back at me, her face flushed, and fairly shouted: 'I *told* you – I can't change that big bill.'

'Surely,' I said stiffly, 'in the entire Greyhound system there must be some means of changing a ten-dollar bill. Perhaps the manager – '

She jerked the bill furiously from my hand and stepped away from the window. In a moment she reappeared to hurl my change and ticket on the counter with such force most of it fell on the floor at my feet. I was truly dumbfounded by this deep fury that possessed her whenever she looked at me. Her performance was so venomous, I felt sorry for her. It must have shown in my expression, for her face congested to high pink. She undoubtedly considered it a supreme insolence for a Negro to dare to feel sorry for her.

I stooped to pick up my change and ticket from the floor. I wondered how she would feel if she learned that the Negro before whom she had behaved in such an unlady-like manner was habitually a white man.

With almost an hour before bus departure, I turned away and looked for a place to sit. The large, handsome room was almost empty. No other Negro was there, and I dared not take a seat unless I saw some other Negro also seated.

Once again a 'hate stare' drew my attention like a magnet. It came from a middle-aged, heavy-set, well-dressed white man. He sat a few yards away fixing his eyes on me. Nothing can describe the withering horror of this. You feel lost, sick at heart before such unmasked hatred, not so much because it threatens you as because it shows humans in such an inhuman light. You see a kind of insanity, something so obscene the very obscenity of it (rather than its threat) terrifies you. It was so new I could not take my eyes from the man's face. I felt like saying: 'What in God's name are you doing to yourself?'

A Negro porter sidled over to me. I glimpsed his white coat and turned to him. His glance met mine and communicated the sorrow, the understanding.

'Where am I supposed to go?' I asked him.

He touched my arm in that mute and reassuring way of men who share a moment of crisis. 'Go outside and around the corner of the building. You'll find the room.'

The white man continued to stare, his mouth twisted with loathing as he turned his head to watch me move away [. . .]

Gandy bent double with laughter and outrage. He asked P D how the voting situation was in Mississippi and P D told the story of the Negro who went to register. The white man taking his application gave him the standard literacy tests.

'What is the first line of the thirty-second paragraph of the United States Constitution?' he asked.

The applicant answered perfectly.

'Name the eleventh President of the United States and his entire cabinet.'

The applicant answered correctly.

Finally, unable to trip him up, the white man asked 'Can you read and write?'

The applicant wrote his name and was then handed a newspaper in Chinese to test his reading. He studied it carefully for a time.

'Well, can you read it?'

'I can read the headline, but I can't make out the body text.'

Incredulous, the white man said: 'You can read *that* headline?'

'Oh, yes, I've got the meaning all right.'

'What's it say?'

'It says this is one Negro in Mississippi who's not going to get to vote this year' [. . .]

I walked what – ten, fifteen miles? I walked because one does not just simply sit down in the middle of a highway, because there was nothing to do but walk.

Late in the afternoon, my mind hazed with fatigue. I concentrated all my energy in putting one foot in front of the other. Sweat poured down into my eyes and soaked my clothes and the heat of the pavement came through my shoes. I remember I stopped at a little custard stand and bought a dish of ice-cream merely to have the excuse to sit at one of the tables under the trees – none of which were occupied. But before I could take my ice-cream and walk to one of them some white teenagers appeared and took seats. I dared not sit down even at a distant table. Wretched with disappointment I leaned against a tree and ate the ice-cream.

Behind the custard stand stood an old unpainted privy leaning badly to one side. I returned to the dispensing window of the stand.

'Yes, sir,' the white man said congenially. 'You want something else?'

'Where's the nearest rest room I could use?' I asked.

He brushed his white, brimless cook's cap back and rubbed his forefinger against his sweaty forehead. 'Let's see. You can go on up there to the bridge and then cut down the road to the left ... and just follow that road. You'll come to a little settlement – there's some stores and gas stations there.'

'How far is it?' I asked, pretending to be in greater discomfort than I actually was.

'Not far – thirteen, maybe fourteen blocks.'

A locust's lazy rasping sawed the air from the nearby oak trees.

'Isn't there any place closer?' I said, determined to see if he would not offer me the use of the dilapidated outhouse, which certainly no human could degrade any more than time and the elements had.

His seamed face showed the concern and sympathy of one human for another in a predicament every man understands. 'I can't think of any ...' he said slowly.

I glanced around the side towards the outhouse. 'Any chance of me running in there for a minute?'

'Nope,' he said – clipped, final, soft, as though he regretted it but could never permit such a thing. 'I'm sorry.' He turned away.

'Thank you just the same,' I said [. . .]

I hitch-hiked up towards the swamp country between Mobile and Montgomery. A magnificent cool day.

I walked some miles before a large, pleasant-faced man halted his light truck and told me to get in. When I opened the door I saw a shotgun propped against the seat next to his knee. I recalled it was considered sport among some elements in Alabama to hunt 'nigs' and I backed away.

'Come on,' he laughed. 'That's for hunting deer.'

I glanced again at his florid face, saw he looked decent and climbed into the leather seat beside him.

'Do you have any luck getting rides through here?' he asked.

'No, sir. You're my first ride since Mobile.'

I learned he was a married man, fifty-three years old, father of a family now grown and grandfather of two children. He was certainly, by the tone of his conversation, an active civic leader and respected member of his community. I began to hope that I had encountered a decent white.

'You married?' he asked.

'Yes, sir.'

'Any kids?'

'Yes, sir – three.'

'You got a pretty wife?'

'Yes, sir.'

He waited a moment and then with lightness, paternal amusement, 'She ever had it from a white man?'

I stared at my black hands, saw the gold wedding band and mumbled something meaningless, hoping he would see my reticence. He overrode my feelings and the conversation grew more salacious. He told me how all of the white men in the region craved coloured girls. He said he hired a lot of them both for housework and in his business. 'And I guarantee you, I've had it in every one of them before they ever got on the payroll.' A pause. Silence above humming tyres on the hot-top road. 'What do you think of that?'

'Surely some refuse,' I suggested cautiously.

'Not if they want to eat – or feed their kids,' he snorted. 'If they don't put out, they don't get the job.'

I looked out of the window to tall pine trees rising on either side of the highway. Their turpentine odour mingled with the soaped smells of the man's khaki hunting clothes.

'You think that's pretty terrible don't you?' he asked.

I knew I should grin and say, 'Why no – it's just nature,' or some other disarming remark to avoid provoking him.

'Don't you?' he insisted pleasantly.

'I guess I do.'

'Why, hell – everybody does it. Don't you know that?'

'No, sir.'

'Well, they sure as hell do. We figure we're doing you people a favour to get some white blood in your kids' [. . .]

I decided to try to pass back into white society. I scrubbed myself almost raw until my brown skin had a pink rather than a black undertone. Yes, looking into the mirror, I felt I could pass. I put on a white shirt, but by contrast it made my face and hands appear too dark. I changed to a brown sports shirt which made my skin appear lighter.

This shift was nerve-racking. As a white man I could not be seen leaving a Negro home at midnight. If I checked into a white hotel and then got too much sun, it would, in combination with the medication still in my system, turn me too dark and I would not be able to return to the hotel.

I waited until the streets were quiet outside and I was sure everyone in the house slept. Then, taking my bags, I walked to the door and out into the night.

It was important to get out of the neighbourhood and into the white sector as quickly and inconspicuously as possible. I watched for police cars. Only one appeared in the distance and I dodged down a side street.

At the next intersection a Negro teenager strode by. I stepped out and walked behind him. He glanced at me and then kept his eyes to the front. Obviously thinking I might harass him, he pulled something from his jacket and I heard a click. Though I could not see what he held in his hand, I have no doubt it was a switch-blade knife. To him I was nothing more than a white stranger, a potential source of harm against whom he must protect himself.

He stopped at the corner of a wide street and waited to cross. I came up beside him.

'It's getting cold, isn't it?' I said, seeking to reassure him that I had no unfriendly intentions.

He stood like a statue, unresponsive.

We crossed the street into a brighter downtown section. A policeman strolled towards us and the boy quickly dropped his weapon into his jacket pocket.

The policeman nodded affably to me and I knew then that I had successfully passed back into white society, that I was once more a first-class citizen, that all doors into cafés, rest rooms, libraries, movies, concerts, schools and churches were suddenly open to me. After so long I could not adjust to it. A sense of exultant liberation flooded through me. I crossed over to a restaurant and entered. I took a seat beside white men at the counter and the waitress smiled at me. It was a miracle. I ordered food and was served, and it was a miracle. I went to the rest room and was not molested. No one paid me the slightest attention. No one said, 'What're you doing here, nigger?'

Out there in the night I knew that men who were exactly as I had been these past weeks roamed the streets and not one of them could go into a place and buy a cup of coffee at this time of night. Instead of opening the door into rest rooms, they looked for alleys.

To them as to me, these simple privileges would be a miracle. But though I felt it all, I felt no joy in it. I saw smiles, benign faces, courtesies – a side of the white man I had not seen in weeks, but I remembered too well the other side. The miracle was sour.

53 Leo Kuper

The Compulsions of Racialism

Excerpts from Leo Kuper, *An African Bourgeoisie*,
Yale University Press, 1965, pp. 32–41.

The early Calvinists carried out the rationalization of life for the greater glory of God. Not desiring the world, they none the less conquered it. The latter-day Calvinists of South Africa have substituted the comprehensive racialization of life, though hardly, it would seem, for the glory of God. Profoundly desiring to conquer their world, they appear to be losing it.

Superficially, the South African policy of racialization (apartheid) seems rationally enough adjusted to the ends of Afrikaner nationalism. I am assuming the not unnatural desire of Afrikaner nationalists to maintain their political power, and to convert it into wealth and prestige. Of course, this is not the expressed aim of apartheid. Political parties rarely acknowledge their concern with power, and they propagate the belief that it is indecent, cynical, and Machiavellian to analyze their activities in these terms. The Afrikaner nationalists are no exception. Racialization is presented in the somewhat curious altruism of a mission to preserve White civilization against Black barbarism, Christian capitalism against atheistic communism, and the God-given differences between races and nations against the miscegenating lusts of integration. Material self-interest happily coincides with both the will of God and the duty of self-preservation.

The maintenance of Afrikaner power obviously depends on the maintenance of the separate identity of Afrikaners as a political group. They are a majority of the White population, and hence of the voters. Monopoly of constitutional power requires the continued supply of voting fodder, bearing the nationalist cross to the ballot paper. The solution lies between the sheets for numbers – though this is hardly necessary during the next generation – and in the insemination of racial solidarity by the Afrikaner churches and schools in an alliance sanctified by the rituals of nationalism: the basis of Afrikaner power thus rests on the racialization of the Afrikaners [. . .]

The presence of a large non-White majority in a ratio of about four-to-one, drives the nationalists toward the comprehensive racialization of the society. They control the constitutional power to legislate the social pattern, and are thus able to relegate non-Whites to an apolitical category; non-Whites are objects of bureaucratic regulation, not agents of legitimate political action. Compliance with the prescribed legislative pattern is enforced by an increasing armory of penal sanctions and other, more lethal weapons; but there remains the danger of non-White unity, and a revolutionary challenge to the whole structure of power. If, however, barriers could be maintained between White and non-White, and equalizing processes aborted; if non-Whites could be fragmented into racial and tribal groups; and if each non-White group could be imbued with ethnic pride and exclusiveness, by much the same devices as succeeded with the Afrikaners, then Afrikaner power would rest on a sucral self-perpetuating process of racialization, and everyone, not least the Afrikaners, would live happily ever after – at any rate, for a while.

At the same time, the policy can be administered in a moral capsule. The main ingredient is the supreme value of the ethnic group. Each group is endowed with its own unique quality, its own soul, its own destiny. The greatest fulfillment for the individual lies in subordination to the group, and the greatest fulfillment of the group in the realization of its destiny. The Afrikaners are therefore offering each non-White group a revelation of its destiny; they are freely offering what the Afrikaners themselves desire most fervently. The destinies are different, that is all: – the cities, industry, commerce, the developed areas of South Africa, and some four-fifths of its land for the Whites, and the rural, underdeveloped, and periurban areas for the non-Whites; a modern, Western, wealthy democracy for the Afrikaners, and an Afrikaner tribal revivalism and modernization for the Africans.

The difficulty about all this predestination is that it rests not on the inscrutable and incomprehensible will of God, but on the all too obvious and comprehensible material self-interest of the Afrikaner. For some strata in African society, the ideology may be persuasive; for many, it is too transparent to beguile, and they reject it totally. For others, it becomes a means of political maneuver to be cynically manipulated for personal gain, or indeed for the subversion of the system.

This contradictory strand, this boomerang from one's own weapons, affects not only the ideology but the whole policy of racialization. The underlying conception of society appears to be superficial. Enacted law does not automatically become custom. Society is not plasticine, to be pummeled into crude shapes; there are limits to its remodeling by fiat. Rule by Saracen and machine gun may exact too high a price and provoke counterviolence. Racialization is not a Calvinist Bible, which can be opened and closed as the spirit moves. It is not a process which can be arrested at any moment and petrified into a monumental pattern, like Lot's wife, head turned to the past. It is not a sluggish stream, to be canalized for the irrigation of the White man's vineyards, maize fields, or orchards. Racialization is turbulent, intractable, and passionate. The humiliation may still devour, the bitterness still corrode, when the insults have been avenged a thousandfold.

The fuel for racialization is a heightened consciousness of race, shaped by the apartheid laws. These laws impose racial separation, or provide for control of racial contact, in almost every conceivable human relationship, from physical intimacy to shared religious or intellectual experience. Recent racial legislation affects marriage, 'illicit carnal intercourse', proximity between neighbors and traders, inclusion on a common electoral roll, the reservation of work opportunities, industrial conciliation and trade unions, school and university education, occupation of premises for homes, worship, and medical care, or even briefly, for recreation, refreshment, and public assembly. In consequence, the racial concept becomes increasingly weighted with social and cultural connotations.

Race consciousness is given an intense emotional quality by a system of punishments and rewards. The control of race relations is enforced by penal sanctions. Marriage, sex, living in a home, trading, working, studying, healing, welfare work, going to a cinema, eating, playing golf, and attending a meeting are not in themselves criminal offenses in South Africa, but they may become so if they involve forbidden race relations. The primacy of the racial criterion is thus emphasized in the daily indispensable routine of living under the threat of punishment as a criminal.

On the positive side, rewards provide additional incentives. Racial separation in South Africa is highly discriminatory, and, with few exceptions, immediately rewarding to those who impose it. Moreover, such laws as the Group Areas Act, providing for residential and commercial segregation, offer new and handsome dividends in the racial partitioning of South Africa, and the reservation of occupations provides a systematic basis for favored treatment in employment. Race and an aggressive consciousness of race may be as valuable an asset as entrepreneurial skill and technical training.

As the range of racially defined situations extends, more and more persons are involved. Most Whites are committed in one way or another – as participants in plans for the racial redistribution of property and opportunities for unearned wealth under the Group Area Act, as employers of non-White labor, domestic and other, and so on, in many of the contexts described above. New occupational opportunities are opened in state and local administration, and rewards of office stimulate conscientious devotion to racialism. Outside of administration, organizations providing services on an interracial basis are obliged to re-examine, and perhaps modify, their policies in the light of the new racial laws, and even those who oppose these laws become more racially conscious under conditions where interracial contact savors of deliberate defiance.

Non-Whites are equally affected with Whites. Administration and legislation relates not only to broad categories of non-Whites but also to their subdivisions – Colored, Malay, Chinese, Indian, and, in the case of Africans, linguistic and tribal subdivisions. Increasingly, the linguistic or ethnic group is the unit of administration for Africans, as for example in the revival of tribal authority in the rural areas and in the settlement by segregated linguistic groups in the towns and in the new universities. Reward and punishment reinforce the system. Penal sanctions inevitably fall more heavily on the non-Whites, and their punishment is augmented indirectly by the redistribution of resources, as in the Group Areas Act. But there are rewards too – not only fictitious as in the lavish promise of separate development but real also, as in the opening of new occupational opportunities in tribal administration, in social services, in the economic expansion of the country, and in the development of the reserves.

Inevitably, political activity follows the lines of racial cleavage, expressed in legislation and propagated by it. The Government virtually represents the Afrikaner people and the interests of Afrikaner domination, and derives its dynamic force from racial conflict. The official opposition represents English-speaking White people and a minority of Afrikaners, and the interests of the English-speaking in an equal share in White domination. The non-White political groups are largely confined to extraparliamentary activities directed against White domination. Political activity, pressure towards conservatism or towards revolution, is largely racial and serves to heighten racial consciousness.

In these circumstances, there is little likelihood that the people of South Africa will lose their 'sense of color', as members of the Government sometimes phrase it. Race has become a primary, immediate element of perception. Race consciousness proliferates throughout the society, and a vast bureaucracy transforms it into the routine of office [. . .]

The racial ideology of the dominant group, in one of its most general formulations, rests on the basic incompatibility of the races and the inevitability of conflict between them when in contact. A race must dominate or be dominated; or, to express the theory in less general terms, the non-Whites will use their numbers to dominate the Whites if given the opportunity. The survival of the White man and his way of life depends, therefore, on White paramountcy in areas where they live together (which is to say, discrimination against non-Whites in all material respects) or on territorial separation.

These laws, policies, and ideologies presumably encourage conflict in racial contact, since there is an ideological expectation of conflict. Race consciousness is canalized in a sharply antagonistic form by both the concept and the reality of races in competition for power and wealth, while discrimination is invited, since self-preservation is assumed to depend on withholding from the subordinate races, as far as possible, any opportunities which might contribute to their power as competing groups.

Discrimination itself serves to heighten racial prejudices. The main apartheid laws seek to eliminate primary contacts as far as possible, excluding, however, the master and servant relationship. Secondary contacts, that is to say, formal, remote contacts, are confined to discriminatory situations, or a highly impersonal and fleeting. In consequence the White man finds himself consistently in a position of superiority. This routine experience may be expected to reinforce sentiments of superiority. Moreover, a realistic basis for these sentiments of superiority is ensured by discrimination itself, which severely limits the opportunities for development of members of the subordinate races. It is natural that, in these circumstances, the White man should seek to maintain his social superiority, and perhaps to enhance it, by further discrimination.

Apartheid therefore sets in motion a self-perpetuating process, the chain reaction of racialization. Race consciousness in the White group is heightened by increasing emphasis on the criterion of race in the routine of living. It is molded into racial prejudice and racial discrimination by official legislated encouragement in the form of rewards and punishments. Increasing racial prejudice seeks expression in an intensified discrimination, and the extension of discriminatory practices stimulates racial prejudice. Prejudice feeds on discrimination, and discrimination feeds on prejudice, unleashing a racial arrogance which threatens the society.

There are further consequences, of a dehumanizing nature. Apartheid rests on the preponderance of a single idea. Salvation, but in this world, is to be sought in the separation of the races. Weber argued, in his discussion of the Protestant ethic, that the preoccupation of the early Calvinists with the salvation of their souls developed in them a ruthless self-confident, self-righteous personality and a lack of sympathy for the poor and unfortunate, whose sufferings were regarded as evidence of a lack of grace. So, too, in apartheid, there is an indifference to the sufferings of the non-Whites. Sacrifices are imposed and justified because they serve the ends of racial separation, which is to provide the opportunity for each God-created ethnic group to fulfill its own unique mission. While the early Calvinists derived their self-righteousness from the doctrine of predestination, the Afrikaner nationalists find it in the sanctification of the group, the moral elephantiasis of nationalism, and in the crusade for self-preservation and the preservation of White civilization.

The routine and continuous exercise of extensive powers over the lives of others may also be dehumanizing. What were the effects on the personality of the Nazi official who, in the course of his duties, decided the fate of the many thousands of inmates in the concentration camps? And what stamp is laid on the personalities of South African influx control officials who decide whether Africans are to be given the opportunity to work in the urban areas, or whether they are to be returned to their rural poverty and despair? And how are the police molded by the routine of mass raids, the magistrates by the administration of discriminatory laws, and the general White population by habituation to non-White suffering? It is possible that a warm sympathy within one's group may be combined with a callous indifference to the human qualities of others, but it seems more likely that there will be a general brutalization, an undermining of the concept of justice and of the feeling for humanity.

The dominance of the apartheid idea results in the pervasiveness of racialism throughout the society. The same patterns ramify. The Government relies on the Group Areas Act, providing for racial segregation, to control interracial activities. So too, some of the White English-speaking members of the Methodist Church Conference sought to rely on the Group Areas Act when faced with a challenge by Africans for leadership of the Church, as did the South African Golf Union when a leading Indian golfer first wished to compete in the South African Open Golf Championship. The Government considers that in principle Africans should largely finance their own social services. Even English ministers of religion may justify unequal salaries on the ground that African congregations should support their own ministers. There is a general discrimination in salaries against non-Whites. There is also discrimination in English-speaking churches.

Issues quite remote from race are invaded by racialism. If a nurse behaves irresponsibly, it becomes immediately relevant that she is African, and evidence that Africans cannot be entrusted with responsibility. Much as crystals form around a foreign body dropped into a saturated solution, so racialism crystallizes in South Africa around seemingly irrelevant issues. The society is saturated in racialism. The overwhelming importance of race impedes the perception of a common humanity.

Economic interests accentuate the racial divisions, and reinforce the denial of a common humanity. Racial separation is not an end in itself, but a means for conserving and promoting racial privilege. Specific laws (such as the Group Areas Act and the reservation of types of employment for a particular racial group), function to enrich the White man, while the whole structure of apartheid laws serves to maintain his dominant position, both economically and politically.

Two important consequences for race relations flow from this. First, the groups which impose and support apartheid or White domination, and which wield political power – i.e. the Afrikaner nationalists and to some extent the Whites in general – are numerous, and their economic interests must first be satisfied. Pareto writes: 'The more numerous that [ruling] class is, the greater the evils resulting from its domination, because a large class consumes a larger portion of wealth than does a class restricted in size.' It therefore becomes impossible to allocate sufficient resources to non-Whites, and in this way to win from them extensive support for the system. Even though Africans are sometimes accorded opportunity for wealth, their earnings mostly fall below a modest subsistence level. Really substantial inducements in the form of a redistribution of wealth, or of opportunities for wealth, are inconceivable without revolutionary change in the structure of power. Apartheid sets the material interests of the racial groups in sharp conflict. Only if nations friendly to the South African Government could be persuaded to finance the development of the African reserves would it be possible to allocate significant resources to Africans within the framework of apartheid.

A second consequence is that a certain ferocity is injected into race relations by the innumerable economic interests of the White settlers. This appears to be a characteristic of White settler societies. It is especially marked in South Africa where the National Party represents the numerous descendants of a large poor White population; small men entering the civil service, industry, and commerce; workers paid at civilized rates and protected from non-White competition. The system offers them privilege and opportunity. High rewards are within their grasp. But precisely at this turn of most favorable fortune, they are beset with fear. The growth of independent African states, the events in Kenya, Congo, Angola, and Algeria give a realistic basis for insecurity. This is a crucial combination – uncertainty about the future at the moment of fulfillment. And the Whites may be expected to defend their material interest with the same violent aggression as the colons in Algeria.

The system of apartheid has stimulated, among the Whites, a racialism which moves to extremes, and provokes a counterracialism among the non-Whites. The apartheid laws create a systematic discrimination against non-Whites in almost every sphere of life. Discrimination may be based on consent. Our picture of traditional Hindu caste society is oversimplified, but there were certainly elements in Hindu thought which facilitated the acceptance of inequality – such as the religious sanctions for social differentiation and the doctrine of moral responsibility for one's social situation in society (the doctrine of Karma). Religious beliefs also gave hope for the future, rendering inequality more acceptable. By fulfillment of duties in this life, a man might improve his position in the next. In other societies, too, for a variety of reasons and social philosophies, discrimination and inequality were regarded as the natural or divine order of things.

None of these philosophies, which might mold consent to inequality, is, however, accepted in South Africa. Whatever its practice may be, the Government does not justify inequality in its propaganda. On the contrary, it proclaims a policy of creating independent African states. Bantu States are offered as a solution by which equality, self-determination, and independence may be secured to Africans in carefully defined and regulated linguistic subgroups.

Nor do the churches justify discrimination. The English-speaking churches increasingly attack the imposition of social inequality as 'un-Christian'. Even the Nederduitse Gereformeerde Kerk, which stands in a more intimate relationship with apartheid than the early Calvinists with capitalism, does not offer scriptural sanctification for the policy of legally enacted inequality. In its statements, the discriminations of apartheid are regarded as an interim and regrettable necessity in the realization of ultimate justice.

The Nederduitse Gereformeerde Kerk has made it clear by its policy and by synod statements in the past that it can justify and approve of the policy of independent distinctive development (i.e., apartheid), provided it is carried out in a just and honourable way, without impairing or offending human dignity. The Church has also accepted that this policy, especially in its initial stages, would necessarily cause a certain amount of disruption and personal discomfort and hardship, for example in connection with the clearing of slums. The whole pass system must be seen in this light (*Dutch Reformed Church Monthly Newsletter*, mid-April, 1960).

From a religious point of view, this means the sanctification of sinful means for the sake of an uncertain future [...] From a social point of view, the issue is not simply that of a temporary personal discomfort occasioned by such desirable programs as slum clearance, as suggested by the quotation, but the uprooting of hundreds of thousands of people under Group Areas and Black Spot removals, and a massive burden of discrimination.

There is thus no ideology which nourishes systematic inequality, save as a temporary expedient, to be judged by the speed with which it is discarded. Separation is justified, but not inequality. And the rejection of racial discrimination by non-Whites is shown clearly in the campaigns against Unjust Laws and in the vast numbers of statutory offenses committed by Africans. It is evasive to place responsibility, as the Government does, on agitators, whether communists, liberals, progressives, Anglican churchmen, English newspapermen, or interfering busybodies from overseas. There are many other sources of the desire for freedom. Respect for human dignity and the concept of the equality of all persons, irrespective of race, color, or creed, are part of the contemporary world ethos, proclaimed in the policies of non-White peoples. They will not be eliminated in South Africa by shock therapy in the form of treason trials, mass arrests, banishments, bannings, house arrests, torture, routine midnight raids, states of emergency, and Bantu education. Indeed, local experience suggests that these sufferings merely heighten the determination to achieve equality. Nor can the treatment of members of a racial group be confined within the boundaries of a single nation. Why should Africans in South Africa accept discrimination as Africans when members of their racial group are governing independent states?

Important consequences flow from the fact that the ideal of human equality is firmly established in the consciousness of large numbers of non-Whites, and that discrimination does not rest on their consent. Discrimination is imposed on racial grounds. It is imposed by one race on another race. Hence each act of discrimination constitutes a direct racial aggression, and the resentment against the discriminations is inevitably expressed in racial terms.

Discrimination by Whites provokes the reaction of non-White racialism, more particularly African racialism. And thus the self-feeding mechanism of racialization is completed. Apartheid stimulates a heightened racial consciousness among Whites and channels it in the direction of racial prejudice. This racial prejudice expresses itself in discrimination and is in turn intensified by discrimination. Prejudice and discrimination feed on each other, engendering extremism. Since the system does not rest on consent, Africans increasingly react with a counterracialism. The more extreme the racial actions of Whites, the more embittered the racial reactions of non-Whites. As the non-Whites move from mass murmurings and protest to organized revolt, insecurity besets the White group, aggravating the racial antagonism. The Whites respond with increasing repression, and the struggle moves into a revolutionary phase. Racialization has ceased to be an instrument of policy, and now threatens the structure of Afrikaner domination.

54 John Rex

The 'Facts' in Race Relations

Excerpt from John Rex, *Race Relations in Sociological Theory*, Weidenfeld & Nicolson, 1970, pp. 147–50.

Everyone who has participated in the debate about the rights of coloured people, Jews or other minority groups knows that commonly the debate amongst non-sociological laymen and amongst practical politicians takes the form of an argument about what the facts of the case are. But the experienced debater of these issues will also be aware that any final demonstration of and agreement about what facts exist is impossible. The argument twists and turns, and, whenever one of the contenders is apparently pinned down on one logical level, he quickly changes his ground so that the issue is taken up on a new level. This may best be illustrated by examples.

The campaign to secure a cessation of coloured immigration into Britain, and, indeed, the repatriation of established immigrants, is supported by what claim to be factual assertions about individual cases and by statistical generalizations. But immediately these assertions are challenged new questions open up about how such facts are to be evaluated anyway.

Thus a well-known Conservative politician, who has for some time been advocating the cessation of coloured immigration, adduces in support of his policy proposals 'evidence' to the effect that he has been told that there is a street in his constituency where there is only one white person left, and that she, an old lady, has been terrorized by immigrants, who amongst other things have put their excreta through her letter box. Investigations by journalists show that there is only one old lady who lives in anything like the situation described, that she likes and is liked by her immigrant neighbours, that she has not had excreta put through her letter box and that she is distressed that the politician concerned might have created hostility between herself and her neighbours.

As this argument proceeds the Conservative politician and his supporters question whether the old lady interviewed by the journalists is the one in question, and argue that whether or not the original old lady exists in the conditions described, the fact that people believe she does is the important thing. Hence, if interracial hostility is not to increase, it would be best if coloured immigrants did not exist. So the argument changes its ground, and will change it again, as soon as it appears to be finally pinned down to a purely factual question.

Again the issue of the presence of large numbers of coloured children in certain schools might be represented as a threat to the education of the native white children and the reason given for this is that coloured children are unable to speak the language in which instruction is normally given. When it is pointed out that West Indian coloured children speak English, whereas many Cypriot or Italian children do not, either we are told that West Indian children do not speak English properly, or the ground of the argument shifts, and we are told 'it isn't only a question of language'.

On the level of statistics the grounds for manoeuvre in the argument are even easier to come by. Thus, if it is argued that statistics show that the number of immigrants is less than is widely supposed, arguments might be produced to show that there are possibilities of illegal entry, or that births to the immigrants are not adequately and separately recorded. The number of coloured immigrant mothers occupying maternity beds is quoted as compelling evidence which is not easily shaken by estimates of what would happen if coloured immigration ceased and the coloured immigrants' places were taken by others. The argument more generally about the charge represented by the immigrants on the social services readily passes to an argument about whether or not it is right that every penny spent on immigrants should be treated as a dead loss. And so it seems every argument about statistics is likely to develop. We are not, of course, concerned with the question of how the problem might be resolved by competent statisticians (though they too will usually be found to be capable of finding reasons for disagreement amongst themselves). The important thing is which arguments can be made to hold water in the actual practical and political conditions in which the debate is conducted. Here it would seem the argument can be made to go on *ad infinitum*, and the mere continuance of the argument serves to mark out the group whose rights are being discussed and to bring those rights into question. Thus, if anyone wished as a matter of deliberate policy to increase hostility towards a group a possible guiding rule might be 'Get the argument going by whatever assertions you can muster. Once it is going you will find that the facts don't speak for themselves. With skill you can make them speak for you.'

It should not be imagined from what we have just said that conscious or unconscious distortion is the prerogative of the 'reactionary' side of this argument. In political debate the 'liberals' will also deploy their arguments and statistics in a way which leads to the conclusions which they want accepted. Even the man who tries to be as honest as possible finds it difficult to produce a finally compelling argument when any of his logical methodological, theoretical or factual assumptions might be called into question at any time. He is thus very often driven into a kind of dogmatism by the very conditions of the debate and once this has happened it can very readily be said that there is no way of deciding between alternative views.

It is obvious to the sociologist of knowledge or the sociologist of politics that what purport to be arguments about fact in this debate often conceal arguments about values. The reactionaries and the liberals have taken up their positions in advance and use facts selectively to support their positions. Moreover, as Myrdal has pointed out, when there is some kind of strain between the society's ultimate value system and its actual behaviour toward certain ethnic minorities, there may be a positive compulsion to invent facts.

In the American situation Myrdal argued that a value system like the 'American creed' was so explicit that it was not possible to allow extensive racial discrimination without the support of some intervening beliefs, which would justify the apparent departure from principles. Thus a general proposition in the American creed might take the form 'all men are entitled to equal opportunity in employment according to their ability'. The belief that negroes do not have equal intellectual ability with white people is therefore necessary to make the creed compatible with discriminatory practice.

55 Malcolm X

The Philosophy of Black Nationalism

Excerpts from Malcolm X, *The Speeches of Malcolm X at Harvard*, edited by
Archie Epps, Morrow, Apollo edition, 1968, pp. 140–42, 164–75.

Self-respect for the black man

In New York we have recently founded the Muslim Mosque
Incorporated, which has as its base the religion of Islam, the religion of
Islam because we have found that this religion creates more unity among
our people than any other type of philosophy can do. At the same time,
the religion of Islam is more successful in eliminating the vices that exist
in the so-called Negro community, which destroy the moral fiber of the
so-called Negro community [. . .]

For when a politician in the so-called Negro community is controlled
by a political machine outside, seldom will that politician ever do what is
necessary to bring up the standard of living or to solve the problems that
exist in that community. So our political philosophy is designed to bring
together the so-called Negroes and to re-educate them to the importance
of politics in concrete betterment, so that they may know what they
should be getting from their politicians in addition to a promise. Once
the political control of the so-called Negro community is in the hands of
the so-called Negro, then it is possible for us to do something towards
correcting the evils and the ills that exist there.

Our economic philosophy of Black Nationalism means that instead of
our spending the rest of our lives begging the white man for a job, our
people should be re-educated to the science of economics and the part
that it plays in our community. We should be taught just the basic
fundamentals: that whenever you take money out of the neighborhood
and spend it in another neighborhood, the neighborhood in which you
spend it gets richer and richer, and the neighborhood from which you
take it gets poorer and poorer. This creates a ghetto, as now exists in
every so-called Negro community in this country. If the Negro isn't
spending his money downtown with what we call 'the man', 'the man' is
himself right in the Negro community. All the stores are run by the white
man, who takes the money out of the community as soon as the sun sets.
We have to teach our people the importance of where to spend their
dollars and the importance of establishing and owning businesses. Thereby

we can create employment for ourselves, instead of having to wait to boycott your stores and businesses to demand that you give us a job. Whenever the majority of our people begin to think along such lines, you'll find that we ourselves can best solve our problems. Instead of having to wait for someone to come out of your neighborhood into our neighborhood to tackle these problems for us, we ourselves may solve them.

The social philosophy of Black Nationalism says that we must eliminate the vices and evils that exist in our society, and that we must stress the cultural roots of our forefathers, that will lend dignity and make the black man cease to be ashamed of himself. We have to teach our people something about our cultural roots. We have to teach them something of their glorious civilizations before they were kidnapped by your grandfathers and brought over to this country. Once our people are taught about the glorious civilization that existed on the African continent, they won't any longer be ashamed of who they are. We will reach back and link ourselves to those roots, and this will make the feeling of dignity come into us; we will feel that as we lived in times gone by, we can in like manner today. If we had civilizations, cultures, societies, and nations hundreds of years ago, before you came and kidnapped us and brought us here, so we can have the same today. The restoration of our cultural roots and history will restore dignity to the black people in this country. Then we shall be satisfied in our own social circles; then we won't be trying to force ourselves into your social circles. So the social philosophy of Black Nationalism doesn't in any way involve any anti-anything. However, it does restore to the man who is being taunted his own self-respect. And the day that we are successful in making the black man respect himself as much as he now admires you, he will no longer be breathing down your neck every time you go buy a house somewhere to get away from him [. . .]

Brotherhood is a two-way street

Despite being a Muslim, I can't overlook the fact that I'm an Afro-American in a country which practices racism against black people. There is no religion under the sun that would make me forget the suffering that Negro people have undergone in this country. Negroes have suffered for no reason other than that their skins happen to be black. So whether I'm Muslim, Christian, Buddhist, Hindu, atheist or agnostic, I would still be in the front lines with Negro people fighting against the racism, segregation, and discrimination practiced in this country at all levels in the North, South, East, and West.

I believe in the brotherhood of all men, but I don't believe in wasting brotherhood on anyone who doesn't want to practice it with me. Brotherhood is a two-way street. I don't think brotherhood should be practiced with a man just because his skin is white. Brotherhood should hinge upon the deeds and attitudes of a man [. . .]

Europeans created and popularized the image of Africa as a jungle, a wild place where people were cannibals, naked and savage in a countryside overrun with dangerous animals. Such an image of the Africans was so hateful to Afro-Americans that they refused to identify with Africa. We did not realize that in hating Africa and the Africans we were hating ourselves. You cannot hate the roots of a tree and not hate the tree itself. Negroes certainly cannot at the same time hate Africa and love themselves. We Negroes hated the African features: the African nose, the shape of our lips, the color of our skin, the texture of our hair. We could only end up hating ourselves. Our skin became a trap, a prison; we felt inferior, inadequate, helpless. It was not an image created by Africans or by Afro-Americans, but by an enemy.

Since 1959 the image has changed. The African states have emerged and achieved independence. Black people in this country are crying out for their independence and show a desire to make a fighting stand for it. The attitude of the Afro-American cannot be disconnected from the attitude of the African. The pulse beat, the voice, the very life-drive that is reflected in the African is reflected today here among the Afro-Americans. The only way you can really understand the black man in America and the changes in his heart and mind is to fully understand the heart and mind of the black man on the African continent; because it is the same heart and the same mind, although separated by four hundred years and by the Atlantic Ocean. There are those who wouldn't like us to have the same heart and the same mind for fear that that heart and mind might get together. Because when our people in this country received a new image of Africa, they automatically united through the new image of themselves. Fear left them completely. There was fear, however, among the racist elements and the State Department. Their fear was of our sympathy for Africa and for its hopes and aspirations and of this sympathy developing into a form of alliance. It is only natural to expect us today to turn and look in the direction of our homeland and of our motherland and to wonder whether we can make any contact with her [. . .]

Not a single white person in America would sit idly by and let someone do to him what we black men have been letting others do to us. The white person would not remain passive, peaceful, and nonviolent. The day the black man in this country shows others that we are just as human as they in reaction to injustice, that we are willing to die just as quickly to protect our lives and property as whites have shown, only then will our people be recognized as human beings. It is inhuman, absolutely sub-human, for a man to let a dog bite him and not fight back. Let someone club him and let him not fight back, or let someone put water hoses on his women, his mother and daughter and babies and let him not fight back ... then he's subhuman. The day he becomes a human being he will react as other human beings have reacted, and nobody [in humanity] will hold it against him [...]

Of course the Civil Rights Bill was designed supposedly to solve our problem. As soon as it was passed, however, three civil rights workers were murdered. Nothing has been done about it, and I think nothing will be done about it until the people themselves do something about it. I, for one, think the best way to stop the Ku Klux Klan is to talk to the Ku Klux Klan in the only language it understands, for you can't talk French to someone who speaks German and communicate. Find out what language a person speaks, speak their language, and you'll get your point across. Racists know only one language, and it is doing the black man in this country an injustice to expect him to talk the language of peace to people who don't know peaceful language. In order to get any kind of point across our people must speak whatever language the racist speaks. The government can't protect us. The government has not protected us. It is time for us to do whatever is necessary by any means necessary to protect ourselves [...]

The Negro problem has ceased to be a Negro problem. It has ceased to be an American problem and has now become a world problem, a problem for all humanity. Negroes waste their time confining their struggle to civil rights. In that context the problem remains only within the jurisdiction of the United States. No allies can help Negroes without violating United States protocol. But today the black man in America has seen his mistake and is correcting it by lifting his struggle from the level of Civil Rights to the level of human rights. No longer does the United States government sit in an ivory tower where it can point at South Africa, point at the Portuguese, British, French, and other European colonial powers. No longer can the United States hold twenty million black people in second-class citizenship and think that the world will keep a silent mouth. No matter what the independent African states are doing in the United Nations, it is only a flicker, a glimpse, a ripple of what this country is in for in the future, unless a halt is brought to the illegal injustices which our people continue to suffer every day.

The Organization of Afro-American Unity (to which I belong) is a peaceful organization based on brotherhood. Oh yes, it is peaceful. But I believe you can't have peace until you're ready to protect it. As you will die protecting yours, I will die protecting mine [...] We believe that the

O A A U should provide defense units in every area of this country where workers are registering or are seeking voting rights, in every area where young students go out on the battlefront (which it actually is). Such self-defense units should have brothers who will not go out and initiate aggression, but brothers who are qualified, equipped to retaliate when anyone imposes brutally on us, whether it be in Mississippi, Massachusetts, California, or New York City. The O A A U doesn't believe it should permit Civil Rights workers to be murdered. When a government can't protect Civil Rights workers, we believe we should do it. Even in the Christian Bible it says that he who kills with the sword shall be killed by the sword, and I'm not against it. I'm for peace, yet I believe that any man facing death should be able to go to any length to assure that whoever is trying to kill him doesn't have a chance. The O A A U supports the plan of every civil rights group for political action, as long as it doesn't involve compromise. We don't believe Afro-Americans should be victims any longer. We believe we should let the world know, the Ku Klux Klan know, that bloodshed is a two-way street, that dying is a two-way street, that killing is a two-way street [. . .]

56 Ulf Hannerz

Soul

Excerpts from Ulf Hannerz, 'The rhetoric of soul: identification in Negro society', *Race*, vol. 9, 1968, pp. 454–65.

What is 'soul'? As the concept has come to be used in urban ghettos over the last number of years, it stands for what is 'the essence of Negroness' and, it should be added, this 'Negroness' refers to the kind of Negro with which the urban slum dweller is most familiar – people like himself. The question whether a middle-class, white-collar suburban Negro also has 'soul' is often met with consternation. In fact, 'soul' seems to be a folk conception of the lower-class urban Negro's own 'national character'. Modes of action, personal attributes, and certain artifacts are given the 'soul' label. Typically, in conversations, one hears statements such as, 'Man, he got a lot of soul'. This appreciative opinion may be given concerning anybody in the ghetto, but more often by younger adults or adolescents about others of their own categories. In particular, speaking in terms of 'soul' is common among younger men [. . .]

When it comes to 'soul' music, there are a couple of themes in style and content which I would suggest are pervasive in ghetto life and which probably make them appear very close to the everyday experience of ghetto inhabitants.

One of these is the lack of control over the social environment. There is a very frequent attitude among 'soul brothers' – that is, the ghetto's younger males – that one's environment is somewhat like a jungle where tough, smart people may survive and where a lot happens to make it worth while and enjoyable just to 'watch the scene' if one does not have too high hopes of controlling it. Many of the reactions in listening to 'progressive jazz' seem to connect to this view; 'Oooh, man, there just ain't nothing you can do about it but sit there and feel it goin' all the way into you.' Without being able to do much about proving it, I feel that exposure to experiences – desirable or undesirable – in which one can only passively perceive events without influencing them is an essential fact of ghetto life, for better or for worse; thus it is 'soul'.

Related to this is the experience of unstable personal relationships. Among lower-class urban Negroes there are many 'broken' families (households without a husband and father), many temporary common-law unions, and in general relatively little consensus on sex roles. Thus, it is not much of an exaggeration to speak of a constant 'battle of the sexes', and the achievement of success with the opposite sex is a focal concern in lower-class Negro life. From this area come most of the lyrics of contemporary rock-and-roll music. It may be objected that this is true of white rock-and-roll as well; to this it may be answered that this is very much to the point. For white rock-and-roll is predominantly adolescent music, thus reaching people with similar problems of unstable personal relationships. In the case of lower-class urban Negroes, such relationships are characteristic of a much wider age-range, and music on this theme also reaches this wider range [. . .]

My thesis here is that recent changes in race relations in the United States have indeed made the social barriers to achievement at least seem less impermeable than before to the ghetto population. One often hears people in the ghetto expressing opinions such as, 'Yeh, there are so many programs, job-training and things, going on, man, so if you got anything on the ball you can make it'. On the other hand, there are also assertions about the impossibility of getting anywhere which contradict the first opinion. Obviously, the clear-cut exclusion from mainstream American culture is gradually being replaced by ambivalence about one's actual chances. This ambivalence, of course, seems to represent an accurate estimate of the situation; the lower-class Negro continues to be disadvantaged, although probably his chances of moving up and out are somewhat better than earlier – people do indeed trickle out of the ghetto.

It is in this situation that the ethnocentric vocabulary of 'soul' has emerged, and I want to suggest that it is a response to the uncertainty of the ghetto dweller's situation. This uncertainty is particularly strong for the younger male, the 'soul brother'. While women have always been able to live closer to mainstream culture norms, as homemakers and possibly with a type of job keeping them in touch with the middle-class world, men have had less chance to become competent in mainstream culture as well as to practice it. Older men tend to feel that current social changes come too late for them but put higher expectations on the following generation. Thus the present generation of young men in the Negro ghettos of the United States are placed in a new situation to which it is making new responses, and much of the unrest in the ghettos today is perhaps the result of these emerging pressures.

I will suggest here that this new situation must be taken into account if we are to understand the basis of the emergence of the 'soul' vocabulary. The increasing ambivalence in conceptions of one's opportunities in the changing social structure may be accompanied by doubts about one's own worth. Earlier, the lack of congruence between mainstream culture norms and the lower-class Negro's achievements could easily be explained by referring to the social barriers. Under-achievement with respect to mainstream norms was an ascribed characteristic of lower-class Negroes. However, when as at present the suspicion arises, which may very well be mistaken, that under-achievement is not ascribed but due to one's own failure, self-doubt may be the result. Such doubt can be reduced in different ways. Some, of course, are able to live up to mainstream norms of achievement, thereby reducing the strain on themselves (but at the same time increasing that on others). Higher self-esteem can also be arrived at by affirming that the boundaries are still impermeable. A third possibility is to set new standards for achievement, proclaiming one's own achievements to be the ideals. It is not necessary, of course, that the same way of reducing self-doubt is always applied. In the case of 'soul', the method is that of idealizing one's own achievements, proclaiming one's own way of life to be superior. Yet the same 'soul brother' may argue at other times that they are what they are because they are not allowed to become anything else.

In any case, 'soul' is by native public definition 'superior', and the motive of the 'soul' vocabulary, I believe, is above all to reduce self-doubt by persuading 'soul brothers' that they are successful. Being a 'soul brother' is belonging to a select group instead of to a residual category of people who have not succeeded [. . .]

At least at present, I think that there is little basis for connecting the majority of 'soul brothers' with militant black nationalism – there is hardly a 'soul movement'. 'Soul' became publicly associated with black militancy as the term 'soul brother' made its way to international prominence during recent ghetto uprisings – Negro businessmen posted 'soul brother' signs in their windows, it was noted by mass media all over the world. However, it is worth noting that this was an internal appeal to the ghetto moral community by black shopkeepers, not a sign of defiance of the outside world by the participants. It may be said that the outsiders merely caught a glimpse of an internal ghetto dialogue. Yet organized black nationalism may be able to recruit followers by using some kind of transformed 'soul' vocabulary, and I think there are obviously attempts on its side to make more of 'soul' than it is now. Certainly, there is seldom any hostility to black militants among the wider groups of self-defined 'soul brothers', although the vocabulary of 'soul' has not been extensively employed for political purposes. If it is so used, however, it could possibly increase the ghetto dwellers' identification with political nationalism. Thus, if at present it is not possible to speak of more than a 'rhetoric of soul', it may be that in the future we will find a 'soul movement'. If that happens, of course, 'soul' may become a more controversial concept, as 'black power' is now.

57 Roger Bastide

Industrialization and Race in Brazil

Excerpts from Roger Bastide, 'The development of race relations in Brazil', in Guy Hunter (ed.), *Industrialization and Race Relations*, Oxford University Press for Institute of Race Relations, 1965, pp. 14–26.

Let us try to define the 'traditional' racial relations which defined non-industrialized Brazil, before its economic revolution.

These were paternalist relations in a society of multi-racial classes, where coloured people occupied the lowest positions in the hierarchy. Slavery had disappeared, but the consequence was not that the mass of Negroes rose into the global community; the Negroes remained just where they were before, not forming a competitive group. It is precisely because they did not constitute a danger to the traditional social structure, because they did not threaten the whites' status, that the latter did not feel fear, resentment or frustration towards coloured people. Personal, emotional relationships could thus come about between whites and blacks.

But, naturally, this paternalism only operated within a climate of domination and patronage. One of its manifestations was the system, Catholic in origin, by which coloured families of a neighbourhood were bound to some prominent white person. The white owed protection and financial aid; he could also promote the education of his coloured godchildren; in return, the Negro owed material aid (and his wife owed domestic service): he constituted the 'clientele' of the white man (rather in the Roman sense of the word). He was part of the electoral mass who would vote according to the white's recommendations. The passage to town from country did not necessarily carry with it the disintegration of the custom of patronage as a matter of course – the great families still had 'protégés', descendants of their former slaves; but patronage tended to pass from the family to the political party, as the white leader increasingly replaced the patriarch.

Paternalism prevented tensions and softened the relations between races. But, at the same time, it strengthened the domination of one coloured group over another; and it institutionalized the subordination of the Negroes, who could only benefit from the protection of the whites, or from a certain familiarity in the whites' treatment of them, on condition that they 'knew their place' and proved their deference, gratitude and respect. It was therefore an instrument of political and economic control, which, by avoiding the competitive relations which are possible in an individualistic society like ours, by preventing a struggle, and by rendering useless any wish for collective mobility on the part of the Negroes, assured supremacy and security to the white class. Under these conditions, one can understand why prejudices are at a minimum in a paternalist society, or, at least, why they remain latent rather than finding external expression. The reason is that they are unnecessary. Their functions of controlling and damming up are fulfilled by paternalism. But prejudice appeared every time this social order was in danger of being attacked, for example, by a mulatto wanting to gain access to the upper class.

In the same way, paternalism today serves to put a brake on the ambitions towards advancement of the black group as such; the Brazilian Negro does not try to improve his economic or social condition in a group but individually, as a member of the lower classes. This is why educated mulattoes or Negroes are found in the intermediate classes, even if in small numbers, and even a few light-skinned mulattoes, whose ancestry has been more or less forgotten, are found in the upper classes. It is this possibility of individual advancement which defines the Brazilian 'racial democracy' as much as, if not more than, paternalism, which would more exactly define the *homme cordial* trait of the basic personality of the Brazilian. But this mobility itself still remained controlled, in such a way that it would not become a danger to a society created by whites for the benefit of whites; on the contrary, it constituted a safety valve and diminished interracial tension. In other words, the flood-gates were only half open, the ways were guarded, the tests for exit were fixed, and the white could shut the doors at any moment. The chosen tests were colour of skin, financial means, type of profession, education and moral upbringing. From this we get the famous formula: 'A rich black is white: a poor white is black'. Also from this we get the different behaviour of the white Brazilian towards mulattoes and dark Negroes [. . .]

The fact is that the mulattoes and Negroes accepted the ideologies of the natural inequality of races which the whites built up for themselves in the course of time, and which took on their final forms at the end of the epoch of slavery. Taking as his starting point the formula often heard when Brazilians are questioned about their ideas on race, 'We are one people, we are all Brazilians', Pierson has defined these ideologies as an ideology of 'integration'. Unfortunately, the term only brings out the positive aspects of the formative process in Brazilian society. There are also negative aspects. These appear better in Smith's formula: the ideology of 'whitening' (*blanchiment*). This whitening is due, first of all to the greater morbidity and mortality of the poorer – therefore black – classes in comparison with that of the mulattoes; and, secondly, to the acceptance on the part of the blacks of the superiority of the white colour and therefore of the ideology, prejudices and values of the dominant class. From this we get the policy on the part of the Negroes, since the times of slavery, of 'purging one's blood' – that is to say, of sleeping with whites in order to have children of lighter skin; I shall come back to this in a moment. But there exists another formula still in the south of Brazil, which emphasizes even better the negative elements of this policy or ideology: that of the 'progressive arianization' of the country. Indeed, the policy of European immigration in the central and southern States was not just instituted to permit the development of productivity, by substituting contingents of free workers used to differentiated tasks for a mass of slaves lacking professional training; it was also designed to submerge the descendants of Africans into a more prolific white population, and, in the last analysis, to change the ethnic composition of the population of the country. This, of course, implies the myth of the superiority of the white race [. . .]

What was to be the effect of industrialization on these traditional forms of racial relations?

Theoretically, industrialization marks the transition from status to contract. It suppresses the inequality of conditions which are attached to external attributes, like the colour of the skin, or ethnic origin, in order to consider only a man's productive skill, physical strength or professional knowledge. Compared to the pre-industrial, agricultural regime, it multiplies and differentiates jobs, thus permitting a wider social mobility. The industrial regime, at least in capitalist countries, is at the same time individualist (all workers with equal qualifications are interchangeable) and competitive (the struggle of the labour market, where the best man wins). Finally, by causing the concentration of men in large towns, it favours the enlargement of the tertiary sector and permits the constitution of a middle class. On the other hand, the slave regime rested on the predominance of status, prevented competition by the so-called legislation of castes, and curbed the development of the tertiary sector. All these effects of industrialization acted in Brazil and tended to pull the Negro into the productive circuit, to shatter the barriers of race in the competition and vertical social mobility of educated Negroes, and, finally, to permit the appearance of a small coloured middle class.

But at the same time these effects were slowed down by the survival of former patterns of racial relations and stereotypes of the Negroes, inherited from slavery. Thus we shall find simultaneously in Brazil two systems of contradictory attitudes; the one founded on status traditionally bound to colour, and the other imposed by economic development. From these causes sprang tensions, conflicts and frustrations, perhaps taking their gravest forms on the level of the small mulatto middle class. One may, of course, wonder why the former paternalist and segregationist concepts of 'cordiality' were able to survive in a competitive and individualistic regime. First, it was because Abolition only dates from 1888. But it was also because the social system of Brazil was still based on the family, and the wife was the guardian of the integrity and purity of the family. The white man could therefore encounter the black man on equal terms in the sphere of work relations, and participate in strikes or social claims with him. But, under the influence of his wife, he closed the intimacy of his family to the Negro and even refused him entry to the dances of his class, dances being the ante-room to marriage. Again, urbanization tended to separate the working-class groups from the other groups by the establishment of 'working districts', and these districts were inhabited by former rural *émigrés*, side by side with workers already born in the town, among whom there were many coloureds. The migrants, and especially their wives, if they do not work, and remain in the home, have not yet changed their mentality, and it is for this reason that the former patterns are perpetuated right through until today [...]

It is now the positive factors of industrialization which are coming into play. Why? First of all, under the pressure of poverty, the immigration of peasants from the arid zones of the north-west into the towns of the centre has intensified. These peasants, often small landowners, are not motivated by any wish for social advancement and they certainly do not expect to be definitively integrated into industrial life. They therefore constitute a mass of unskilled labour, of unqualified and unspecialized workers, indispensable most of all to the building industry and for work where the demand is only for physical strength. This was, of course, the former position of the Negroes. There are, indeed, some Negroes among these migrants ('the Bahianians') but the whites are dominant. The collective image which is given to this mass, the unfavourable judgements it gives rise to, and the stereotypes which define it, do not separate these whites from the Bahianians. There is, therefore, a displacement of prejudice from an individual's colour to his function in the economic development; from his racial origin to his position in a functional hierarchy. The Negro, who is already engaged in the industrial process, profits from this. Thus the black group is displaced from the sub-proletariat to the proletariat proper.

Secondly, although the number of small factories does not decrease, the phenomenon of concentration tends to carry the day; and a large factory, unlike the small workshop, facilitates the development of class consciousness. The aspiration towards social equality cannot merely be the aspiration of the Negroes alone; it is the common objective of the whole proletariat. The rise in prices following on inflation with which wages never manage to catch up, determines the tensions which affect all the workers, whatever the colour of their skin. There are more common problems than problems particular to such and such a racial or ethnic sector of the working population.

Finally, the trade union movement, which was originally the creation of the State, and which served rather to control the population than to be a voice for it, has changed its nature in the course of the last six years. There is a growing group of workers, black and white, sometimes directed by a black leader (although the heads of the unions are still usually white), 'for whom labour conditions define the whole future perspective' (Cardoso). All these positive effects of industrialization have only been possible because Brazil is in full spate of economic expansion. If a recession were to occur, bringing with it a contraction of the labour market, it is possible that the prejudices, stereotypes and discriminations which remain latent would again be aroused and would tear the proletariat apart. But even under those circumstances, victories which have been won can never entirely disappear.

One of the effects of these changes appears in sexual relationships. Certainly, the ideology of *blanchiment* is not disappearing, and inter-racial marriages are still made according to the rule of feminine hypergamy. But whereas a few years ago the most numerous couples, though still not legally married, were those of white men and black women, one now sees an increasing number of couples of black men and white women.

In spite of everything, I cannot state that prejudice is dead. The rapidity of industrial and urban growth is such that the situation is extremely complex and it still offers a mixture of new and old social structures, without some gaining definitively over others. I have mentioned the rural exodus and the formation of working-class suburbs in which the traditional patterns of racial relations are dominant, which means that the two systems of attitudes still coexist, one in the sphere of work, the other in the sphere of family life. The coloured *petit bourgeois* is more isolated than the worker; yet here too a change can be discerned. Formerly, it was the man who felt and suffered from this isolation. Today it is the woman who suffers from it most, because it is not always possible for her to find a coloured husband of the same economic and cultural level as herself, for this perfect partner prefers a lighter-skinned woman. On the other hand, the law of interracial marriages being the hypergamy of the man, not of the woman, she will always see herself refused by the white men. In the industrial sphere itself, a distinction must be made between the large factories and the little family businesses. Rationalization wins in the former, where what counts is efficiency. Discriminations continue in the latter, especially if they are run by foreigners, because these bosses will give preference in the jobs to compatriots or their immediate descendants.

To sum up, industrialization has played a double role in Brazil. On the one hand, it has intensified prejudice and given sharper forms to discrimination at the beginning of industrial growth, when the Negroes first became competitors with the whites. On the other hand, in periods of prosperity and rapid economic development, it has tended to make social tensions predominate over racial tensions. This is, of course, only in the single sphere of work relations. The rest of life – neighbourhood relations, amusement relations and friendships – continues to be regulated by the traditional models which still co-exist with the new models born from industrialization.

58 Ronald Segal

A Revolutionary Cure for Racial Violence

Excerpts from Ronald Segal, *The Race War*, J. Cape, 1966, Penguin, 1967, pp. 290–99.

A sign of what race violence could mean to the American city significantly appeared at the same time that members of the government and senior leaders of the civil rights movement were celebrating the successful passage of Johnson's Voting Rights Act, with its promise to extend through the South the formal equality possessed by Negroes elsewhere in the nation. Suddenly in August 1965 Los Angeles, which had long congratulated itself on its excellent race relations, was swept by five days of Negro revolt that made the rioting of the previous summer in New York or Rochester or Philadelphia seem a mere skirmish in comparison. As usual, the apparent provocation was the arrest of a Negro by white police, and as usual the centre of insurrection was a ghetto, the slum suburb of Watts, 98 per cent Negro, with rotting houses and schools, and with the streets seething under the sullen surface of unemployment. Of 600,000 Negroes in the city, some 30 per cent were workless, most of them unskilled and many of them illiterate, while almost a third of those under the age of eighteen came from broken homes. The alienation felt by many of these, not only from the traditional Negro leadership of constitutional advance but from any community outside that of race, was only too predictable.

The command of rioting was held from the first by gangs of young Negroes, whose leaders met at the end of the first day in what they themselves called a 'war council' to distribute assignments and coordinate assaults. Their attacks were directed at white property, and Negro shops, whose owners hastily scrawled 'Blood Brother' on the windows or walls, were generally safe. From street to street the devastation spread, reaching far beyond the ghetto to penetrate the city's commercial centre and, in the end, encompass more than forty square miles. Whites who entered Negro-held territory were commonly attacked, and even those in distant suburbs armed themselves for defence. It was less a riot than, indeed, guerrilla warfare of race. The Government moved troops into the city, restored a smouldering order, and Americans began assembling the statistics: 34 killed, most of them Negroes; over 800 treated at hospitals (and how many of the injured were not?); some 3800 arrested; and damages assessed at $175,000,000. The impact on relations between white and black throughout the country was less easy to assess.

Such violence is not, and cannot be, contained within the rim of struggle between white and black Americans alone. It must affect the relations of white with white Americans and black with black, as well as the relations of each with the outside world. The growing violence of American thought, language and action, the mounting acceptance of apocalyptic possibilities, are in significant measure the outcome of racial tension and turbulence within America itself. The racial struggle is a disease of the American system, and the failure to treat it properly and in time may have overwhelming consequences for all humanity.

Certainly there can be no cure, no longer even much relief, in the patent medicines of Civil Rights laws and civic commissions. While America is economically two segregated races, it must be socially and politically so. And that is why America needs not another dose of reform, but a revolution. The traditional structure of American society, for all the neon signs of rewarded enterprise on its façade, confines Negroes to the basement, and the commandments of free competition keep them there. How many Negroes can reach the board-rooms, when one in five cannot even find unskilled work? How many Negroes are equipped in their decaying slum schools to satisfy the demands of an increasingly technical appetite? How fitted for effort and enterprise at all are those who grow up in rat-infested tenements, along streets of broken bottles and discarded lives, where the buildings cage the very air and the gutter seems the only escape?

If there is any prospect at all of a lasting racial peace in the United States, it rests in the recognition by Negroes and an ever-growing number of whites, the more vigorous of them among the young, that American society needs reshaping, at its roots. After the long grey conformity of the McCarthyite era and its pale aftermath, a surge of discovery and dissent is sweeping not only the whole Civil Rights movement, but the mainly white universities of America. SNICK and CORE have drawn their activities from white students and teachers as well as from Negro ones, and among the jailed in Mississippi towns or the assaulted in Alabama streets have been white lawyers and doctors, clergymen and housewives searching not just for a method of furthering Negro rights but for the outline of a new society. As Abolitionism a century ago was a movement of emancipation not from slavery alone, but, inevitably, if often unsuspectedly, from the clutch of plantation feudalism as well, so the Civil Rights struggle today is and must be concerned with an emancipation from poverty and the totalitarianism of wealth [. . .]

The increasing identification of coloured America with the coloured world has implications which neither white America nor the white world can reasonably expect to escape. The Moynihan Report acknowledged one aspect.

It was in no way a matter of chance that the nonviolent tactics and philosophy of the [Negro] movement, as it began in the South, were consciously adapted from the techniques by which the Congress Party undertook to free the Indian nation from British colonial rule. It was not a matter of chance that the Negro movement caught fire in America at just that moment when the nations of Africa were gaining their freedom. Nor is it merely incidental that the world should have fastened its attention on events in the United States at a time when the possibility that the nations of the world will divide along color lines seems suddenly not only possible, but even imminent.

(Such racist views have made progress within the Negro American community itself – which can hardly be expected to be immune to a virus that is endemic in the white community. The Black Muslim doctrines, based on total alienation from the white world, exert a powerful influence. On the far left, the attraction of Chinese Communism can no longer be ignored.)

It is clear that what happens in America is being taken as a sign of what can, or must, happen in the world at large. The course of world events will be profoundly affected by the success or failure of the Negro American revolution in seeking the peaceful assimilation of the races in the United States.

It is also clear, however, that what happens in the world at large is being taken as a sign of what can, or must, happen in America. Negroes are less and less indifferent to the striving of coloured peoples on three continents. Harlem and Watts and the Black Belt of the South see the dispatch of American marines to the Dominican Republic and, above all, the American military effort in Vietnam rather differently on the whole from the way that the white suburbanites of Connecticut and Illinois do. It was not a matter of chance either that one of the eight Negroes recently elected to the lower house of the Georgia legislature publicly associated himself with an anti-war statement issued by the Student Nonviolent Coordinating Committee. The Georgia legislature in consequence denied him his seat, and African diplomats at the United Nations honoured him at a luncheon. This spreading deafness within the Civil Rights movement to the demands of pure patriotism has already alienated some whites who gave their support in the past to the struggle against racial segregation. The militant Negroes are quick to reply that such whites understand neither the content nor the purpose of the Negro revolt.

The protests and initiatives of this revolt are likely to grow in number and effect. The ghettoes of the North are being daily strengthened in the force of their disaffection by the rising political influence of the Negro millions still in the South. The Voting Rights Act has been adding to the electorate a new Negro multitude, whose leadership and temper have been made revolutionary by the long and violent intransigence of white authority. Any further intransigence, any display of timidity or caution or indifference by the federal government, will only increase the impatience of the black South for a different America. Any further advance in electoral power will increase the political pressures throughout the country for a different America. And the prospect of an alliance between the black poor and the white poor for the achievement of equality, if wildly improbable still in the North, has a Southern precedent at least in the populism of the last century. It is the one chance, if seemingly now a slight one, of extending the Negro revolution beyond the militants of race.

But alone or in some new alliance, the Negro revolution is unlikely to be deflected from its course. And the course involves a new commitment by America no less to the world at large than to itself. Certainly, the abandonment of the old standards becomes relentlessly more and more vital and urgent. The policy of white America towards the poor non-white peoples of the world is as purblind and clumsy as its policy towards the poor non-white population at home. There is racial violence in the fields of Africa and Asia as well as in the streets of America itself, and the struggle is as likely to be won by planes in the world beyond as by police in New York or Chicago. If white America as a whole does not see this, black America does. And so in the end, perhaps, the Negro may yet save white America from itself.

59 Robin M. Williams, Jr

Forces Reducing Racial Conflict

Excerpts from Robin M. Williams, Jr, *Strangers Next Door: Ethnic Relations in American Communities*, Prentice-Hall, 1964, pp. 378–91.

Nearly all of the most distinctive and definitive characteristics of the emerging twentieth-century American society are such as to place under strain the systems of racial and ethnic discrimination and segregation that had developed earlier. The international role of the nation renders arbitrary discrimination politically embarrassing, creates a considerable disadvantage in international persuasion and propaganda, and represents an economic liability and a military vulnerability. The needs of mass production for trained, reliable, and interchangeable labor-force units are to some extent inconsistent with racial discrimination, as are the needs of mass markets. The only principles upon which a political democracy can base and defend itself make it difficult to justify denial of political liberties, political rights, or civil rights to any segment or class of the citizenry. Urbanization throws members of different racial, ethnic, and religious collectivities into unavoidable relationships. High levels of aspiration spread through the whole population in response to education, mass communication, advertising, and the experience of rising actual levels of consumption. Increasing commonality of culture and behavior patterns remove much of the previously accepted rationales for segregation and discrimination [. . .]

The role of education warrants special comment. Our own data have shown that level of education stands in complex relations to ethnic prejudice and interaction. Analysis of data from a large number of other studies indicates that better-educated white persons, as compared with the less well educated, are somewhat more often willing to give such tolerant or liberal responses as these: to accept Negroes as co-workers, to favor integration in the Armed Forces, to accept a Negro as a nurse, and to eat in a restaurant that serves Negroes. On the whole, however, the better educated are *less* willing to accept Negroes either as individual neighbors or as a substantial element in their residential area, and often fail to take a liberal position on the most highly controversial questions of interracial relations. The relationships between education and prejudices are quite complex, although the main effect appears to be the development of a more positive, accepting attitude. The effects are highly contingent upon general socioeconomic status and history of status mobility, upon initial ideology, and upon experience of interaction with members of minority groups, for example:

The finding that education has more impact among those who have had contact with Negroes of their own status needs no special elucidation. We should note, however, that in the absence of such contact, schooling has little effect – a fact which points up how severely its potential is limited where segregation, formal or informal, continues to exist [. . .]

It is likely that increased levels of formal education will, in the long run, serve to reduce ethnic/racial prejudice and discrimination. The effectiveness, however, will be crucially dependent upon the balance of gratifications in the stratification system, and upon all those events and processes that reduce a sense of threat in the movement toward the elimination of arbitrary segregation and discrimination. Thus, the reactions toward Negroes on the part of persons in the lower income strata in the white population are powerfully influenced by their own sense of integrity and well being. For example, the more these low-status white people themselves are disparaged and brought to feel that they are regarded as subordinate and of low worth, the greater will tend to be their demands for differential deference and prestige *vis à vis* racial and ethnic minorities, their resistance to equal interaction, and their resistance to changing stereotyped beliefs [. . .]

It has been maintained in many quarters that intergroup adjustments had best be left exclusively to the informal, natural processes of interpersonal dealings. It now seems quite evident that existing strains, tensions, and conflicts – that press imperatively for remedial action – cannot be contained or resolved by interpersonal contacts, private propaganda and education, voluntary groups, and informal negotiation and mediation.

Paramount factors are these:

1. The fact of increased aspirations and claims on the part of previously less articulate and less well-organized racial and religious minorities.

2. The increased acknowledgement by the majority group, especially by its leadership, of the legitimacy of these aspirations and claims.

3. The increased political power and economic importance of these minorities (or of some segments of them).

4. The continuing and increasing massive segregation of the urban Negro

population, North and South, with attendant frustrations, resentments, fears, and blocked communication between Negro and white citizens (interpersonal understanding ceases to be even a potential solvent of intergroup tension when no interpersonal communication is occurring).

5. Continuing differences of beliefs and values in matters that are inherently objects of public policy.

6. Continuing large-scale differentials in economic returns and social rewards, differentials attributed by many minority-group persons to systems of categorical discrimination [. . .]

One of the great symptoms of impending social change is a shift in the respectability of dominant attitudes, beliefs, and values. When naïve ethnocentrism prevails in a society or a community, the support of existing patterns of discrimination and segregation takes the form of reference to unquestionable beliefs and values of the kind that everybody knows. These beliefs will be accepted and indorsed by the most prestigeful and respectable elements of the society – its leaders and pillars-of-normality in economic, religious, educational, and political affairs. It is always a sign of the possibility of important changes when there is a break in the interlocking chain of consensus and support. The shift of a portion of the intellectual leaders and articulate commentators from full support to the expression of questions, doubts, and criticisms will, if long continued, spread a certain measure of alienation among the more highly educated, articulate – and often politically active – people. If the doubts and criticisms touch upon real vulnerabilities of inconsistency, maladaptations, and irreality – as judged in terms of *other* accepted values and beliefs – it may rather quickly happen that the criticized beliefs and values become divested of sanctity and prestige. A very great deal has already happened, for example, when people begin to refer to their own ethnocentric beliefs and feelings as prejudices, and their secure commitment to the old system has largely disintegrated by the time they say, 'I can't help it, but I'm just prejudiced' [. . .]

Conflict among men will continue to arise from time to time so long as there is not a more acceptable way of resolving disagreements. Disagreements will continue to arise, so long as men differ in their interests, values, and beliefs. We foresee no way of totally avoiding disagreements, even should that outcome be thought desirable. But there are many disagreements that do not lead to conflict. If conflict does arise, it is not always violent. And whether or not it is violent, it does not have to be of a group character. If it is of a group character, it does not have to be polarized along ethnic lines.

Robin M. Williams, Jr 521

Our conclusion, then, has to be that ethnic conflict is not inevitable. This means that we can conceive of realistic conditions under which ethnic conflict would be at such a low level of prevalence and intensity as to be of no serious concern in a given community or society at a particular time [. . .]

We would regard legal action through the courts and administrative action in business, education, government, and religious organizations as major avenues of realistic efforts to alter systems of discrimination and prejudice. These avenues are congruent with the dominant value systems and with the character of the complex social structure that has developed. And law and law enforcement are great agencies of public education.

The slowness of change put up against the moral claims of minorities for equality of rights necessarily maintains high tension. Furthermore, it cannot be assumed that any and all types of industrialization and urbanization will lead to a decrease in discrimination or to a narrowing of occupational and income differentials between whites and Negroes. For instance, under conditions of plentiful labor and weak unions (or with segregated monopoly-oriented white unions), differential job and wage opportunities may be maintained even with large industrial growth [. . .]

Great pressures exist to move the society toward social integration of ethnic minorities. Great resistances are thereby aroused. One key to the understanding of resistance on the part of dominant ethnic groupings is the recognition that resistance derives from a sense of threat. One key to understanding a sense of threat is to be found in answers to the questions: what is threatened? And how? We would propose as especially important the following hypothetical propositions:

1. The extent and intensity of resistance to increased rights (or privileges) of any ethnic (racial, religious) segment of the society will increase directly with the degree to which the present or prospective change is perceived by persons in other ethnic categories as a direct threat to their own long-term future prestige ranking, as determined by the evaluations of other persons who are in a position to importantly affect that ranking.

In short, resistance will increase directly with perceived threat to prestige status.

2. More specifically, resistance will vary directly with the perceived threat from the reactions of others within the dominant ethnic segment who have economic or political power, religious authority, or other indirect sanctioning power (for example, the ability to influence com-

munity evaluations of the person). That is, anticipated sanctions from persons of power and authority are especially threatening.

3. Whatever the perceived threat to status, it will be the more powerful, the less possibility there is for alternative ways of maintaining status, once the prospective change has occurred. Feeling trapped tends to produce panic [. . .]

Finally, we believe that the total body of evidence we have reviewed overwhelmingly supports the view that cooperation and solidarity among persons who differ in ethnic membership is fostered by any arrangements that produce joint action toward shared objectives. From a variety of approaches and theoretical suppositions one finds suggestions that social solidarity among individuals or groups *is enhanced* by recognition of the sharing of a positive and noncompetitive regard for a common object of concern [. . .]

Personal association of members of different groups is most effective in reducing hostility and increasing understanding when the focus of interaction is upon a common interest, goal, or task rather than upon intergroup association as such. . . . Prejudice is reduced by arranging for personal, intimate contacts of members of different groups who share important tastes and interests in common.

There seems little doubt that in the communities we studied it was interaction with awareness of a congruent community of interest that minimized ethnic prejudice and encouraged the reduction of discrimination. As American society in the second half of the century experiences the struggle of minorities to end categorical ethnic discrimination and forced segregation, it will be a matter of urgency to determine what conditions, specifically, tend to produce cooperative rather than conflictful interaction, both at the level of person-to-person and of collectivity-to-collectivity. It will further be of great urgency to discover how conflict can be used to enhance understanding and social growth.

Part Ten Religion and Social Problems

At first glance it might appear strange that a section on religion should appear in a book of Readings on social problems. Surely, it might be argued, one can conceive of poverty and over-population, crime and sexual deviance, urban congestion and pollution as 'social problems', but is it not a purely personal matter whether a person goes to church or not? Paradoxically, the asking of this question may be the best justification for the inclusion of a section on religion. For some feel that the growth of these problems is a consequence of the declining influence of religion; others will argue that it is the persistence of religious sentiments that inhibits a rational solution to many of these problems, over-population for example. Thus there is still a debate about the kind of influence religion has or does not have on individual life, on the nature of society itself, and about the kind of influence that religion *ought* to have on social and personal life. Nor is this debate merely an academic one: it is part and parcel of the lives and concerns of many people. The extract from Brothers (Reading 62) illustrates some of the dilemmas and confusions. Is it true that many of the public issues which are debated in the mass media – the use of drugs, the 'permissive society', racial violence, 'drop-outs' – reflect the fact that religion no longer has the integrative power it once had? Or is it the case that 'young people are more religious today than they have ever been' and that the religion of the future will be something completely outside the orthodox thinking and practice of existing churches and denominations? Is it true that Communism is a religion? Such questions are being asked and sociologists can help to formulate answers.

Sociologists do not only study contemporary society: hence studies of the role of religion in quite other cultures and other eras can throw light on current social issues. Our first selection, by Eisenstadt (Reading 60), is a commentary on the classic exposition by Weber of the relationship between the 'Protestant Ethic' and the 'spirit of capitalism'. Weber argued that Protestant doctrines and the effects they had on conduct were vital elements in the development of Western capitalism. The argument is not just of interest in studying past history, however; it has contemporary relevance in two ways. It shows that religious changes occur in response to other changes in society, and that changes in belief and in religious organization conversely have their effects in changing secular society. Thus Weber stressed the role of Protestant beliefs in the development of industrial capitalism in Western societies. However, we may now ask whether some similar sort of doctrine, some ethic preaching the rational accumulation and use of resources and the necessity of disciplined, regular work-habits, is not a necessary condition for the development of today's underdeveloped societies. The extract from Roberts (Reading 65) shows how Protestantism is still a belief-system which enables some groups striving to improve their economic position to come to terms with urban life in Guatemala. For many others, the atheistic ethic of Communism has an analogous 'mobilizing' significance.

Religion in 'secular' society

We have said that religion remains a major problem for many: there are those who are *wholly committed* to a religion, and who feel that its decline is distressing and has damaging consequences for men and society as a whole; there are those who are *opposed* to some or all religions, who feel that where decline occurs it does not take place quickly enough, and who are eager to root out the last vestige of superstition and magic; and finally, there are those who are *uncertain* as to whether we are witnessing the decline of religion or only the decline of some particular form, notably traditional Christianity, and who feel that there is a general need for religion that must be met and that will encourage the development of new religious attitudes, beliefs and practices. The central focus of this debate is the extent to which society has become 'secular', whether 'secularization', if this can be demonstrated, is really synonymous with the decline of religion, and what it means for the churches. Thus the passage from Brothers shows the effects of education – one of the forces which has tended to 'secularize' society – on the traditional life of a Roman Catholic parish in Liverpool.

As with other controversial issues, the debate about facts conceals a debate about values. Indeed, this leads Martin (Reading 61) to question whether there is any virtue in using such terms as 'secular' and 'secularization' at all, in view of the range of meaning and ambiguities that they conceal. Thus the fact that, in the past, the church wielded considerable political power, and that this is no longer the case, may to some indicate the increasing secularization of society; to others it may indicate the growth of a 'purer' form of religion untainted by temporal wealth or power. Again the gradual transfer of responsibility for education and social welfare from the Church to the State is taken by some to indicate the declining role of the church, and thus the secularization of society. To others, however, it denotes the progressive incorporation of Christian values into the surrounding society. Or consider the often-quoted fact that fewer people go to church today than did in 1851, when the only official religious census in Britain was carried out. Whether or not one interprets this as a measure of secularization depends upon firstly whether one is satisfied that church attendance is an adequate index of religious belief, practice and influence, and secondly, whether in fact the high level of church attendance of Victorian times was wholly religious in motivation.

We may in fact agree with Martin that the term 'secularization' is not so much a tool of scientific analysis as a symbol or a complex set of symbols through which people attempt to interpret some aspects of social change and in relation to which people take up different and often opposed positions. The sociologist, therefore, can contribute to the debate by examining the ambiguities and implications inherent in the lay and professional uses of the word 'secular', and study the way these varying interpretations are used, by whom, for what purposes. The sociologist is interested, for example, not merely in collecting data about the trends in church attendance or in church weddings, baptisms and funerals, but also in examining the ways in which these trends are understood and expounded by those defending conflicting ideological positions.

Religious bodies have responded to secularizing influences in society in different ways. Some churches have preferred to maintain their traditional beliefs in an undiluted form, regardless of any loss in size or influence which resulted. Other bodies have tried to maintain their size and influence by diluting their distinctive beliefs, and identifying with cultures, goals and styles of life found in secular society, perhaps stressing involvement in social or political affairs. This has made the differences between denominations which once competed for clients both less real and less apparent. Berger, indeed, argues, in Reading 63, that if we want to understand the reaction of churches to changes in society we can borrow the economist's 'market models' and treat churches like firms, which, for example, develop cartels so as to control competition between 'products' which they 'market': basically similar 'products', only marginally differentiated from each other. Churches have tended to explain their declining role in quite other ways: for example, by reference to factors which imply that the decline is not irreversible (it has been put down, for example, to the effects of two world wars, to sloppy forms of worship, or to irrelevant social ethics).

Religion and the integration of society

Whatever position one takes in the secularization debate, it is clear that the model which Durkheim gave us in *The Elementary Forms of the Religious Life* of a closed system of mutually reinforcing elements – religious practice, religious symbols and beliefs, and social integration – no longer obtains for society as a whole. For one thing, society is more complex and differentiated. We still have local and national ceremonials and symbols, but these tend to be temporary and short-lived affairs, and may be the occasion for division as much as for unity. The American or British flag may be saluted or it may be burnt. It is true that there are religious and political sects which conform closely to Durkheim's model of a highly integrated community, but, significantly enough, these groups often define themselves *in opposition to* the wider society in which they exist. Thus the relationship between religion and other aspects of social life – particularly its role in the integration of society – becomes problematic. Simple statements such as 'religion holds society together' or religion provides 'the basis for our moral values' cannot be taken for granted, for society itself is highly differentiated. Religion may unite society or it may divide society, it may be conservative or revolutionary, it may assist social change, inhibit social change or enable individuals to cope with social change. All these statements have been true at some place or at some time. Sociologists can normally show that, whatever the society being analysed at whatever period of history, in some ways religion is influencing other aspects of the structure of society (i.e., it has a relative degree of autonomy), while in other ways it reflects the economic interests, the life-styles and the overall power-position of groups within that society.

Thus religion is not tied to any one political system. It has been used to legitimate totalitarian societies of both the Left and the Right, as well as more democratic forms of political control. The extract from Lewy's account of the Catholic Church in Nazi Germany (Reading 64) illustrates the ways in which religion may give legitimacy to a totalitarian, in this case, Fascist regime. Thus the German Catholic Church tended to view the early manifestations of National Socialism sympathetically as a defence against the kind of Communist society which had developed in Russia. Churches have in any case learnt to become adept at 'fitting in' with whatever political party is in power in order to preserve their sphere of influence, and Biblical ordinances to respect temporal authority have given divine sanction to the indifference of the Church to the forms of government. Again, Lewy points out that the Catholic Church may prefer religious freedom, even under a Catholic dictator such as Franco, to a democratically-elected government eager to secularize the State.

But this is not to say that the Church is inevitably right-wing. In Communist societies too, religious bodies have to reflect, at least partially, the interests of the ruling class, as well as the interests of minorities who are at odds with the political regime. Conversely, where the church has traditionally supported right-wing regimes, as in say Latin America, we see both a growing support for revolutionary movements on the part of individual priests and laymen and the mushrooming of sectarian bodies which stress their opposition to the secular world and the Catholic Church. The passage from Roberts describes such a sect in Guatemala City, and shows how in the developing societies of Latin America sectarian religion helps some sections of the population to cope with problems of rapid social change.

It seems likely that the stable, not to say static, system of interdependence between a single church and secular authority that is characteristic of, for example, feudal societies, is gone for ever. There have been radical changes in the structure of religious bodies (in England, the Anglican Church as well as sectarian groups such as the Seventh Day Adventist Church and the various Pentecostal Churches, increasingly take on the form of denominations). Again, the content of religious beliefs has changed substantially. But despite secularization of society, there is no evidence of any decline in religious or quasi-religious beliefs of one kind or another. In a supposedly scientific age, we witness the popularity of, for example, astrology, horoscopes, Scientology, and the Exclusive Brethren. At the same time many people continue to be married by a religious ceremony, have their children baptized and regularly attend Sunday worship.

Religion may comfort the lowly, providing them with a supplementary set of values in which their 'true' self is cognized. But people located in the higher ranks of society, too, have personal and social problems to face, and often still look to religion in some form as a justification of their right to enjoy their privileged position. At the same time, these religious perspectives may prevent the adoption of other solutions to problems confronting people. Thus the power of religion is still a force to be reckoned with if we are to understand the social issues and problems which are an equally distinctive element of the contemporary world.

60 S. N. Eisenstadt

The Protestant Ethic

Excerpt from S. N. Eisenstadt, *The Protestant Ethic and Modernization*, Basic Books, 1968, pp. 9–19.

The shift of focus from an analysis of the direct causal links between Protestantism and capitalism (or other types of modern institutions) to an analysis of the broader transformative tendencies of Puritanism gives our discussion a broader perpective of the totality of Weber's work. As Mommsen has recently put it so succinctly:

To Max Weber the exemplar among such religious movements that 'change the world' was the Puritans. Although he investigated other variants of Christianity and other great world religions from the standpoint of the social consequences of their teaching, none in his opinion had influenced the course of human development in quite such a revolutionary manner as had Puritanical religiosity.

The shift also gives the discussion a broader general comparative and analytical perspective.

The major emphasis in Weber's work on the sociology of religion in general and on the Protestant ethic in particular is not on direct religious injunctions about different types of economic behavior but on the more general *Wirtschaftsethik* of each religion – that is, on those broader attitudes inherent in the ethos of each which influence and direct economic motives and activities. The shift to an analysis of the transformative capacities of different religions contains an additional element – namely, the possibility that, under certain conditions, a given religion may foster new types of activities which go beyond its original *Wirtschaftsethik* (economic ethic). That is, there may take place a transformation of the original religious impulses which may in its turn lead to the transformation of social reality.

It is necessary to reformulate the problem for the general purposes of analysis and particularly for the consequent re-examination of the Weberian thesis – albeit within the context of Weber's over-all work. In addition to identifying and examining the *Wirtschaftsethik* of different religions, or the religious orientations of different social groups (a central aspect of Weber's work which is fully analysed by Andreski), it is necessary to follow him further and to analyse the *transformative* capacities of different religions (or, for that matter, of secular ideologies). By transformative capacity is meant the capacity to legitimize, in religious or ideological terms, the development of new motivations, activities, and institutions which were not encompassed by their original impulses and views.

Here several problems stand out. The first is: what is it within any given religion (or ideology) that creates or may account for the existence of such transformative capacities? The second problem is: in what directions may such transformative capacities develop? Finally: what are the conditions in the society within which such religious or ideological groups develop which facilitate or impede the institutionalization of such transformative capacities? Only preliminary and very tentative answers can be given to these questions. But even such preliminary answers may indicate some of the latent possibilities of such an analytic and comparative approach.

With regard to the first question – what it is in the nature of a given religion that creates such a transformative potential – the answer has been given by many scholars with reference to Protestantism. The answer probably needs further elaboration and systematization. All the scholars who have dealt with the matter seem to agree that the transformative potential seems not to be connected to a single tenet of the Protestant faith but rather may be inferred from several aspects of its basic religious and ethical outlook. The most important of these are its strong combination of 'this-worldliness' and transcendentalism. Such a combination orients individuals toward activities *of* this world but at the same time does not ritually sanctify them – either through a mystic union or ritual activity – as final proofs of religious consummation or worthiness. Second is the strong emphasis on individual activism and responsibility. Third is the direct relationship of the individual to the sacred and to the sacred tradition. This relationship, while strongly emphasizing the importance and relevance of the sacred tradition, yet minimizes the extent to which individual commitment is mediated by any institution, organization, or textual exegesis. Hence it opens up the possibility of continuous redefinition and reformation of the nature and scope of such a tradition, a possibility which is further enhanced by the strong transcendental emphasis that minimizes the sacredness of any 'here and now'.

These Protestant and especially Calvinist tendencies were not, however, confined to the realm of the sacred. They were closely related to and manifest in the conception most Protestant groups had of the social world and of their own place in it – that is, in what may be called their status images and orientations. Most Protestant groups developed a combination of two such orientations. First was their 'openness' toward the wider social structure. This was rooted in their 'this-worldly' orientation which was not limited to the economic sphere but which also, as we shall see, encompassed other social fields. Second, they were characterized by a certain autonomy and self-sufficiency. They evinced but little dependence – in crystallizing their own status symbols and identities – on existing political and religious centers.

With regard to the second question, in what directions such transformative capacities can be effective, the picture is much more complicated – certainly more so than as Weber presented it. The first institutional aspect – and probably the one not dealt with by Weber – which Protestantism tended to transform was the central symbols, identities, and institutions of the political sphere. Because of the nature of the totalistic reformatory impulses of the Protestants, these institutions constituted natural focuses of their interest and activities. The basic theological tenets of Luther, Zwingli, and Calvin themselves – however marked were the differences in their attitudes toward political institutions – contained some very strong reformulations of the relationships between state and 'society', between rulers and ruled, and of the scope and nature of the political community.

The initial failure of their totalistic attempts did not abate or nullify these impulses. On the contrary, the structural roots of the various crises of European society in the sixteenth and seventeenth centuries, and especially of the crisis of the 'state versus society' as well as the political exigencies of the Protestant communities in various European states, have facilitated and even reinforced this continuous orientation toward the political sphere.

And indeed the Protestant Reformation did have a great initial impact on the central political institutions and symbols. This effect was not necessarily intended by the rulers who adopted Protestantism. Yet their adoption of the reform did have important structural effects which greatly facilitated the further development of a more flexible and dynamic social system. Two factors are relevant here. The first was the need of the Protestant rulers to find new sources of legitimation. The second was their need to forge new symbols of national identity. On both levels there developed, initially through the religious impact of the major Protestant groups and then through their transformation, the possibility of a reformation of relations between rulers and ruled, of patterns of political participation, and of the scope and nature of the political community.

The activities of the Protestant rulers also led to a restructuring of central legal institutions. This restructuring was based on the idea of covenant and contract and on the reformulation of many concepts of natural law. Its results were a more differentiated view of the law and the freeing of voluntary and business corporations from the more restricted view of the political sphere inherent in the traditional understanding of natural law. And, indeed, both in the first Protestant societies (in England, Scandinavia, and the Netherlands) and later in the United States, there occurred, through the incorporation of Protestant thought into law, a transformation of the basic interrelationship between the political and social spheres. The change took place perhaps even before new economic motivations and scientific activities fully evolved. It has not only reinforced the relative autonomy of these spheres but created new, more flexible political symbols, new bases of political obligation, and more flexible political institutions.

Here a comparison with Catholic countries, especially during and after the Counter Reformation, is extremely instructive. The seeds for almost all the changes – new bases of legitimation, new national symbols, and autonomy of religious institutions (as evident, for instance, in the Gallican Church) – existed in most of these countries on the eve of the Reformation and even to some extent throughout the Counter Reformation. And yet in the Catholic countries – in Spain, France, and even earlier in the Italian states of the Renaissance in which modern statecraft first developed – these potentially diversifying tendencies were stifled. Here at least two factors played a part. First were various external exigencies, such as the warfare among the small Italian principalities and the deflection of trade routes from them. Second was the fact that the older Catholic symbols of legitimation were maintained, as were the traditional relations between Church and state. Both were viewed as natural or preordained mediators between the individual and the larger community on the one hand and the sacred and natural orders on the other.

The transformative effects of Protestantism were not limited to central institutions and symbols but were seen in other modern institutions. They were evident particularly in the development of new types of roles, role structures, and role sets and in the motivations required for the adoption and performance of such roles. The core of Weber's Protestant ethic thesis, as distinct from his discussion of the wider effects of Protestantism, is contained in his analysis of the development of the role of economic entrepreneur and of the new type of labor and of the specific setting in which this role could become institutionalized.

Again it is obvious that many of the elements necessary for this development existed before and even after the Counter Reformation to some extent in Catholic countries. But it is also true that in the period after the Counter Reformation these elements – no matter how similar quantitatively to factors that favored economic growth in the Protestant countries – could not be freed, as Lüthy's work on the bank shows, from their dependence, in terms both of goal orientation and legitimation, on the political center. It was largely in Protestant countries or in Protestant (Calvinist) communities that the economic entrepreneur acquired a new type of autonomy which in turn fostered the development of relatively independent and more differentiated economic organization. It was also largely in the Protestant communities that another crucial change took place – namely, the development of intense motivation for undertaking the new roles and goals and for identifying with them.

Thus the transformative potential of Protestantism had at least three specific economic effects in terms of role development. First was the definition of new economic roles and new economic goals and collectivities not tied to existing economic or political frameworks. Second was the provision of broader institutional, organizational, and legal normative settings which gave the new roles both legitimacy and the necessary resources and frameworks with which their continuous operation was facilitated. Last was the development of new types of motivation for the understanding of such roles and for identifying with them. Although these three aspects of the development of new roles and role complexes are very closely interwoven (and were perhaps not fully distinguished by Weber), yet they must be kept distinct, because to some extent at least they may develop to different degrees.

Whatever the exact nature of these new developments, however, it must be emphasized that they occurred not only in the economic sphere but in a great variety of institutional spheres. New roles in fact evolved in the political sphere proper, giving rise to new types of active political participation and organizations, in the form of parties, community organizations, and public services (in Scotland, the Netherlands, and France). They also evolved in the cultural, and especially the scientific and educational, realm. In the economic sphere itself they could develop in other ways distinct from capitalist-mercantile or industrial entrepreneurship. The transformation of the economic activities of the gentry is a case in point. In all these spheres the beginnings of such new roles existed before Protestantism, but in the Protestant countries the roles achieved more autonomy in terms of goals, organizational structure, and legitimation than in the Catholic countries.

We may now pass very briefly to the third question – namely, to the conditions under which the transformative capacities of Protestantism (or of other religions) could become 'absorbed' or institutionalized. In very broad terms it would seem that the possibility of such institutionalization is greater the stronger are the seeds within any society for autonomy in the social, cultural, and political orders. The existence of autonomy in the cultural realm facilitated the development of new symbols which could support and legitimize the building of new central institutions. The existence of autonomy in the sphere of social organization facilitated the development of some viable new institutions without disrupting the whole fabric of the pre-existing order and thus enabled the new order to build to some extent on elements of the old.

It was the European, and especially the western European Christian, countries whose cultural, political, and social institutions had the strongest tradition of autonomy; and it was those countries that had the greatest impetus to modernization. The course of modernization was not, of course, even, continuous, or the same in all countries, including those of western and central Europe. The specific transformative potentials of Protestantism are seen in the way in which the new religion took up the elements of autonomy and pluralism and helped recrystallize them in a more differentiated setting. In Catholic countries such as Spain and France the potentially pluralistic impact of various modern trends, including Protestantism itself, was inhibited by the formation of the Catholic state during the Counter Reformation.

Even within the Protestant countries, however, there was great variation. The transformative tendency of Protestantism did not necessarily develop fully or in the same direction among all Protestant groups in all countries, though to some minimal extent it probably existed in most of them. The concrete development and institutionalization of such tendencies depended to no small extent on the interaction between the attitudes and influence of the major Protestant groups on the one hand and, on the other, the pre-existing social structure, especially on the potential openness or flexibility of political and cultural centers and of the broader groups and strata, and on their initial reaction to religious innovation. The exact scope of such institutionalization varied greatly in accordance with the nature of the groups (that is, whether aristocracy, urban patriciate, various 'middle' groups, urban proletariate, or peasantry) who were the bearers of Protestantism as well as their placement within the broader social structure, with particular regard to the political and cultural center.

The transformative capacities of the Protestant groups were smallest in those cases in which they attained full powers (as, for instance, in the extreme case of South Africa) – when their more totalistic and therefore restrictive impulses became dominant – and in situations in which they became down-trodden minorities. Conversely, the scope of the new activities and the extent to which they were successful in transforming society were most far-reaching in those cases in which the various Protestant groups were in a position of what may be called very broadly 'secondary' elites, close to, but not identified with, the central elites. They were also successful insofar as they became integrated into wider national communities which developed on the basis of the prior autonomy of the estates without becoming the only bearers of such new political or national identity.

Interaction between various transformative potentialities and existing structures might lead to paradoxically similar – or divergent – results. For example, the influence of Lutheranism – allegedly more conservative than Calvinism – was felt in a variety of ways. In the German principalities Lutheranism had a very restrictive effect, because the existing political framework was appropriate for the development of a new national identity and community or for the development of more autonomous and flexible status orientations among the broader strata. The 'traditional' or autocratic rulers of the small principalities adopted the new religious beliefs, and in this context the more conservative of these religious orientations became predominant and often restricted further institutional development. In the Scandinavian countries the new religious beliefs were integrated into wider national communities and developed on the basis of the prior autonomy of the Estates. While they certainly did not impede the development of an absolutist state in Sweden, they did help make possible their subsequent political development in a more pluralistic direction.

Similarly paradoxical results, also demonstrating the significance of restrictive prior situations, are evident in the institutionalization of Calvinism. Of special importance is the Prussian case; the institutionalization of Calvinist attitudes by the absolutist, autocratic Hohenzollerns did *not* facilitate the development of a flexible, pluralistic political framework, though it did support the development of more activist collective political goals.

The juxtaposition of the transformative capacities of the various Protestant groups in different institutional settings accounts for the great variety of new symbols, activities, and institutions among the Protestant countries and communities. Only a full comparative analysis of the development of European society during the sixteenth and seventeenth centuries – obviously beyond the scope of the present chapter – could do full justice to this topic and enable us to test more systematically the various indications presented above.

Whatever may be the validity of the hypotheses concerning the transformative capacities of Protestantism presented in the preceding sections, they point in the direction of their wider comparative application. The main upsurge of a broader interest came in conjunction with studies of modernization and development in non-Western countries. It is true that the direction of social change in general and of religious change in particular differed in these countries greatly from the initial processes of modernization in Europe. All these countries were latecomers to modernization, in many cases being at the outset on the periphery of the modern European political and cultural centers, or their provinces. The process of modernization developed in them at first largely under the impact of external forces and only to a smaller degree through internal initiative. In each of them the institutional centers which were developed in the first stage were almost always incapable of coping with the growing problems of more intensive social mobilization. As a result, some of the major problems these societies faced arose because of the necessity for developing almost entirely new centers under the impact of relatively intensive social mobilization of broader strata. The new centers evolved very often without a concomitant change in internal regulative mechanisms or in values among the groups caught up in these processes.

Because of the central need in these societies to set up new centers, there developed in all of them a relative primacy of political and power considerations during the entire process of modernization. Similarly, because of their relative 'traditionalism' and the relative weakness of the internal modernizing impulses of the broader strata, the policies undertaken by the centers both for fostering and for regulating social mobilization were of special importance in the structuring of the process of modernization. Within this context the problem of finding some continuous 'dialogue' between tradition and modernity has been of focal importance, and in this regard developments in the religious field may become very significant.

The initial situation in the religious sphere in these societies also differed from that of late medieval Europe. It is true that in all these societies the process of modernization undermined the older religious systems – including those of the great world religions such as Eastern Christianity, Islam, Buddhism, Hinduism, and Confucianism as well as some of the small tribal religions abounding in Africa – and gave rise to widespread movements of religious reform on the one hand and of religious revivalism on the other. But whatever reformative tendencies developed within these religions, they had from the very beginning to fight, as it were, on two fronts. They had first to effect changes within their own fold and second to maintain some continuity of identity in the face of modernization and Westernization. In particular they had to defend themselves against secular ideologies such as nationalism, liberalism, and socialism, which claimed to have the panacea for all the problems created by modernization. Moreover, the changes in the religious sphere, connected as they were in all these societies with the erosion of traditional patterns of culture, gave rise – to a much greater degree than in either pre-Reformation or Reformation Europe – to new aspirations, some of which became entirely disconnected from broader commitments.

Because of the nature of all these processes, most of the religious – and to some extent the ideological – movements were set in potentially transformative settings. In only a few cases could they fully implement a new social order in terms of their own tenets. Rather they had the difficult choice of either adjusting to the new order or of finding within themselves some forces which, while perhaps necessitating some change in their initial orientation, could transform the new order.

It is because of all these characteristics of non-Western modernization that the problem of the transformative capacities of these religious ideologies (and of secular ideologies which became predominant within them) becomes even more critical. Their success or failure in developing such transformative potential may provide the key to the difference between purely structural or demographic change on the one hand and the ability to force new institutions capable of absorbing continuous, sustained change on the other. Thus the broader application of the Weberian thesis to an analysis of the transformative capacities of these religions and of their impact on institutional development in these countries becomes even more salient.

The search for equivalents of the Protestant ethic in non-Western countries has led in several directions. The relationships that have been studied are to some extent parallel, but not identical, with factors pertaining to the Protestant ethic thesis proper. The first step was to re-examine various religious beliefs and practices in terms of the degree to which they facilitate or sanction the undertaking of continuous 'systematic' economic activities. Two aspects of non-Western religions were usually given prominence. One was the extent to which any religious system focuses on 'a multitude of very concretely defined and only loosely ordered sacred entities' which emphasize discrete ritual or magical activities that could become involved in an independent, segmented, and immediate 'manner' with almost any sort of actual event. Such a system would preclude any sustained effort on the part of its adherents that encouraged, as it were, a continuous dissipation of energies and resources in such immediate situations.

The other, more 'rationalized' religious beliefs are not so thoroughly intertwined with the concrete details of ordinary life. They are 'apart', 'above', or 'outside' them; and the relationship of the system of 'ritual' and belief in which they are embodied to secular society is not intimate and unexamined but distant and problematic. They are logically coherent, more abstract, and more generally 'phased'.

It has been claimed that the more 'magical' or 'discrete' a religious system is, the less it is likely to facilitate the development of more continuous secular activities. The multitude of dispersed religious rituals found in most 'primitive' religions were shown to inhibit the development of such sustained effort. But it has also been shown that such nonrationalized religious emphasis is found not only in so-called 'primitive' or 'simple' religions but also to some extent in many of the peripheral areas of the 'higher' religions – Buddhism, Hinduism, Islam, and Eastern Christianity. There have also been numerous illustrations of the ways in which many of the customs of such otherworldly higher religions as Moslem Ramadan are inimical to sustained economic efforts. Of these two factors the first – the extent of the 'rationality' of a given religion – seems to be more crucial from the point of view of its potential influence on the 'encouragement' of economic or other secular activities.

Religions which have in principle a positive orientation to worldly activities may yet, insofar as discrete, magical rituals are important in them, give little support to more continuous systematic efforts in any field of activity. On the other hand, religions whose main stress is otherworldly may yet exhibit a positive attitude to certain types of secular activities. Such an attitude may be demonstrated in two ways. Certain religions enjoin their adherents to perform their 'secular' duties. Second, insofar as such religions have developed a certain level of 'rationality' they may also encourage some continuous systematic effort in various secular spheres. The extent to which these religions encourage such activities depends not so much on their *general* this-worldly or otherworldly emphasis but more, as Weber's classical analysis of the great religions showed, on their differential evaluation of various sacred and secular spheres in terms of their more generalized and 'rationalized' orientations.

However, although such rationalization constitutes a basic prerequisite for the encouragement of more sustained activity in various secular fields, it does not in itself reveal the extent to which there may also develop within these religions more varied transformative orientations to secular spheres of life. As Pieris shows, the existence of some broad, generalized support for economic or other secular activity does not in itself demonstrate the extent to which these religions give *religious legitimation* and sanction for continuous secular activities. It does not tell us the extent to which they endow various activities in the secular world with direct religious meaning or the extent to which such activities become the focus of religiosity.

Religious legitimation of secular activities is a relatively rare phenomenon in the major world religions, whatever their concrete attitudes to this world, so long as they arose within relatively 'traditional' settings. This does not necessarily preclude the possibility that, once they are set in the less 'congenial' environment in which modernization is taking place, there may develop from within them some transformative tendencies. Such tendencies are not necessarily always positively related to an initial worldly outlook or negatively related to an initial otherworldly outlook. Overtly otherworldly religions may contain within themselves transformative potentials for a growing religious legitimation of worldly activities and for making these activities an active focus of their religiosity. There are necessarily great differences between the various religions as well as between the ability of the settings in which they operate to absorb such transformative potentials. Ames's analysis of some recent religious movements in Buddhist Ceylon and Geertz's of potential 'internal conversion' in Bali, as well as several developments in Islamic Indonesia, are cases in point.

Because of the special circumstances in which modernity was thrust upon most of the great non-Western European religions, an additional aspect of their reactions to modernity becomes very important, namely, the extent of their permissiveness. By this we mean the extent to which they do not oppose the new goals, institutions, and activities which modernity brings with it but rather show receptiveness to them. Hinduism on the one hand and the Japanese religious congeries or system on the other are probably the most far-reaching examples of such permissiveness.

Permissiveness need not, however, go hand in hand with a transformative capacity. It seems quite possible that to some degree the two may be opposed to each other. While the permissiveness may indeed facilitate the acceptance of new goals and organization, it cannot provide the new institutional settings with religious legitimation and therefore it cannot effect far-reaching transformation on the institutional or motivational levels. Paradoxical as it may sound, it seems probably true that the more nonpermissive religions may, under certain conditions, develop greater transformative capacities.

61 David Martin

Secularization: The Range of Meaning

Excerpt from David Martin, *The Religious and the Secular*,
Routledge & Kegan Paul, 1969, pp. 48–55.

In the semantic riches of [the word] 'secular' and therefore of 'secularization' two broad areas of interest suggest themselves. Firstly, the area of religious institutions and customs, and secondly the area of thought and attitude. These two are appropriately divided respectively into the institutional sphere and the customary sphere, and thought and attitude may similarly be separated off. So this essay consists of four sections in the order just indicated, including some remarks on the paradoxes of meaning which have been uncovered.

The first group of meanings encapsulated in 'secularization' are concerned with the ecclesiastical institution, and specifically with any decline in its power, wealth, influence, range of control and prestige. Hence it is peculiarly appropriate to discussions which are concerned with the changing place of the church in western society since, say, Innocent III. In this respect the word 'secularization' is largely restricted to those cultures where the ecclesiastical institution stands in close relation to the wider society and its power structure, but nevertheless remains separate. This specificity in turn gives rise to a contradiction, equally specific, whereby this same intimate relation is regarded as a betrayal of true religion, i.e. as the essence of secularization. It is necessary to underline this contradiction right from the outset since those items about to be listed which refer to losses of power and of establishment by the church *vis-à-vis* the wider society have to be seen both as secularization and as desecularization.

The areas over which ecclesiastical institutions can lose power and influence are primarily the State apparatus and the professions. Of course this whole process is sociologically set under the heading of the differentiation of spheres. The church may be separated from the State, and the wider society may repudiate any explicit association with a particular religious body or with religion as such. At the extreme it may explicitly associate itself with irreligion. Areas of life may be removed from ecclesiastical patronage and control, for example, the arts, administration, medicine and welfare. A parallel development is the laicization of the professions, notably teaching. The net result of these various changes is generally the replacement of the religious legitimation of a society by a secular legitimation (such as some myth of the nation or the revolution), as well as the removal of areas of thought from religious control, and from the dominanace of religious notions and symbolism. Religion becomes a private matter in a pluralist society where different perspectives and metaphysics compete on equal terms; or a private matter where perspectives emphatically do *not* compete on equal terms.

Alongside these changes but not in any necessary association with them may go the secularization of church lands and of buildings, in that they are removed from ecclesiastical control and given over to non-religious uses, e.g., where churches become museums. The secularization of land in the sixteenth century was of peculiar economic importance. The dissolution of monasteries in the same period in a sense 'secularized' the Church: where it occurred all clergy became secular clergy.

The second sphere of concern is the secularization of religious customs, practices and rituals. Generally this means diminution in their frequency, number and intensity, and in the estimate of their importance and efficacy. It also involves a diminishing range and proportion of contexts in which they are thought appropriate. They are considered or treated in practice as marginal to life's prime concerns.

At the simplest level secularization in this sphere means that there is less frequent attendance at church services of all kinds and less religious observance in the home. People pray less frequently, show no interest in appeals to the Deity, even when in danger, and make no reference to Him. Religious sanctuaries and sacred names and objects are treated as equivalent. Religious formulae (e.g., in legal documents) become increasingly rare. In the performance of all such rites there occurs greater conventionality and insincerity, and motivation is less religious than social, in the sense that religious values are less salient than (say) public opinion. Conversion becomes less frequent and less lasting.

By extension from the above there is a decreased number of religious personnel relative to population available to conduct ceremonies, solemnities and rites of passage. Vocations are less valued in the specific form of calls to the ministry or priesthood and the whole concept of vocation becomes generalized or disappears. Plainly the generalization of this concept as, for example, to the professions, involves a paradox in that such a change can also be seen as an *extension* of religious concepts. A certain form of Protestantism may be involved here, whereby a cult centred on church, priest and ritual is devalued on religious grounds, in which case some losses in the overall estimate of the churchly and rituallistic would count as desecularization. This point runs parallel to the point made about the separation of Church and State. It also relates to conceptions of the Church as the invisible body of the friends of God, and for religious attitudes of this kind decreases in conventional prayers and socially-motivated observance is no loss to religion. In other words, from the viewpoint of some religions mass observance and conventionality can often be associated together,[1] and by implication the reverse may also be true that little observance and genuine faith go together. Or true religion and observance may be seen as having no connection, not even negatively. Hence 'real' secularization is not susceptible to measurement. The point is important since quite apart from any religious viewpoint about the value of ritual and of the visible church it is probably empirically the case that mass observance where it occurs contains strong elements of the conventional, so that a 'religious' aspect goes along with a secular aspect, thus making declines in 'conventional' religion difficult to interpret.

It is perhaps important here to note two other dimensions which hardly come under the heading of ritual, but which scarcely come anywhere else. These are religious knowledge and conduct: aspects also regarded as important by Glock. Conduct is notoriously difficult to estimate in terms of secularization, particularly when religion lays stress on the motive or on contrition, neither of which can be measured. Or indeed the religious emphasis may be on an underlying attitude of faith and trust rather than outward moral observance: this poses the same problem for secularization as outward ritual observance. In any case standards change, moral emphases change, circumstances change (e.g. opportunity for crime) making comparisons over time in the same society (whatever 'same' may mean) almost impossible, even with regard to conduct apparently susceptible to statistics, such as crime, divorce and use of contraceptives.[2] There is in any case the additional problem that conduct considered wrong by one religious tradition, like artificial contraception, is not so regarded by another. One cannot overcome this by simply regarding one religious tradition as more secularized than another. On

1. By mystics, for example. I doubt if there is much possibility of sign-posting secularization by the differential occurrences of mystical illumination. There are notorious difficulties of defining illumination, though one can chart certain historical variations in its form and contents, as, for example, in histories of quietism. Actual measurement of the incidence of various types of illumination is probably impossible. Conceivably one might estimate over a period of time phenomena like appearances of the Virgin.

2. The 'apparently' needs to be underlined. With regard to divorce statistics, for example, one cannot use legal indices as an index of family breakup. The difficulties of interpreting criminal and divorce statistics are well-known to sociologists but not to moralists.

the other hand religious knowledge, involving understanding of religious symbols, comprehension of religious issues and ability to pick up references to religious stories, scriptures, doctrine, church history, etc., is fairly easy to estimate, at least in principle.

The intellectual dimension of secularization is very important simply because so many notions of secularization are artefacts of the history of ideas. Such histories are often conceived in a simple linear fashion and emphasize new developments without reference to continuities which may still command a large scale assent not considered worthy of note. Even secularization in the intellectual sphere is not some form of linear development moving towards Baconian empiricism, Humean scepticism and Cartesian rationalism.

The intellectual sphere of secularization is not simply a matter of epistemological position, but this is clearly very important. The adoption of a rationalistic, empirical or sceptical viewpoint is normally regarded as a secular tendency, though it probably needs to be emphasized that this adoption must be exclusive in temper, since there are plenty of examples of religious rationalism and scepticism, even of empiricism. Sceptical positions notoriously leave more room for faith; and rationalism of a particularly all-embracing and internally consistent kind has until recently been the philosophical norm of Christendom's largest body.

If, however, stress is laid on an *exclusively* rationalistic or empiricist framework then secularization can be seen as the adoption of this framework. This involves an emphasis on observables, and although concept formation and some of the principles of modern science may require non-observables, they are not of the type involved in notions like the Unmoved Mover. At any rate mysteries and the mysterious are rejected. The dominant perspective is naturalistic and monistic, requiring no supramundane principles or notions; and it is usually suspicious of teleology. No 'purposes' are predicated beyond observable functions in natural science; and in social science there are no purposes outside human purposes.

This complex of secular attitudes rejects appeals to ontologically privileged authorities or to tradition and substitutes falsifiable empirical likelihoods adumbrated by appropriate experts within the controls operated by the scientific community. These experts claim no contact or communion with transcendental powers or occult agencies. Though they may have flashes of creative imagination, they do not appeal to Revelation or revelations. Nor are the results of such imaginative inquiry total in their range, as are most ideologies and religions.

There are some aspects related to the above which do not come precisely under epistemological position or scientific methodology. For example, the adoption of a nominalistic attitude to categories (holding that such categories are merely names rather than substantial entities), is sometimes associated with a rejection of the archetypical and the generalized in favour of what is individualized. This might involve a historical movement away from the syndrome of the impersonal, monumental, hieratic and sacred best illustrated by Egypt and Byzantium. (There have, of course, been notable recoveries of elements in these intellectual and cultural styles during recent times). Allied to a decline in the hieratic syndrome there is an emphasis on the sensuous and textural, even the sensual; or alternatively on the functional. Sensualism can be regarded as the affective, aesthetic aspect of empiricism and there can be a further extension into the moral sphere in terms of either a stress on situational experience as the basic moral criterion or a preference for hedonism, particularly of the short-run variety.

It is perhaps worth noting that an *exclusive* reliance on the empirical mode violates its own prescriptions insofar as the principle of exclusiveness is not itself verifiable or falsifiable. Hence the use of a term like 'scientism' to indicate an incipiently religious and dogmatic approach within the scientific attitude itself. It is also noteworthy that the concepts utilized by anti-religious elements supposedly within the ambit of genuine science use notions like 'false-consciousness', 'rationalization', etc. which are rooted in systems of metaphysical privilege, albeit of a naturalistic variety, which suggest a propriety in the notion of secular religion – particularly when the main mode of proof becomes dogmatic deduction from the positions of metaphysical privilege, the 'defining out' of all alternatives and persistent scriptural citation.[3] In other words anti-religion often paradoxically involves elements normally predicted of religion.[4]

One further secularization not easily fitted in with the elements delineated above might be the kind of demystification and translation which relocates religious concepts and symbols within a human and temporal reference, e.g., explanations of the real 'inner' human meaning of the cult of the Virgin, or interpretations of original sin as a poetic way of describing man as a 'Yahoo'. Alternatively there is the psychoanalytic translation.

The final dimension is concerned with attitudes. In particular secularization involves the increase in any attitude which rejects the reverent-

3. Text-swapping, particularly by rival sects.
4. It is not particularly germane to this particular discussion but surely of interest that transcendental metaphysics by definition interfere less with science than naturalistic metaphysics, which often advance their claims under the banner of science.

ial, or which is indifferent to charismatic appeals, halo effects, awe, or the numinous. There is a decrease in any sense of something beyond, deeply interfused, underlying. By extension this can be seen as leading to a lack of deep seriousness, dedication, and ultimate concern, and by a further extension as manipulative, cynical, even unprincipled.

The world is as accepted for what it is, especially as regards disease and death, in the sense that there are no sources of compensation or transfiguration other than human ones, but *not* in the sense that the mundane order is ineluctably set in its present state by divine decree or unalterable natural limits. The world is also seen as disenchanted, neutral, and maybe as therefore quantifiable in most important aspects.

The secular attitude of the psyche is claimed to be free, flexible, not obsessive or ritualistic, and indifferent to totems and taboos unless they have defensible social functions in terms of human benefit. Human or social needs are made the measure of all things. However, this leads on to a basic problem which provides the major paradox in the attitudinal sphere: the definition of needs and appropriate human activity in terms of some concept of natural. Either *anything* is 'natural', which includes religion, or only certain things are natural, which, because it cannot be empirically established, involves metaphysical preference. (The problem of 'natural' is of course peculiarly intense in the sphere of sexual behaviour and its institutional regulation.) Thus secular attitudes either propose a metaphysically privileged definition of 'natural' equivalent to the religious definition of natural, or deny the whole concept. As has just been pointed out, if they take the latter option then there is no criterion for defining the religious preferences for certain types of conduct as *un*natural. The adjective 'secular' is appropriately predicated of both options.

Thus far I have attempted to suggest four main spheres of secularization, within each of which there are notable paradoxes: the problem of the 'natural' just mentioned, the unavoidable presence of religious elements in anti-religious positions, the difficulty of interpreting declines in religious practices when these practices can be viewed as either religiously indifferent, or religiously negative or else as empirically rooted in conventionality. And finally, to arrive at the point where I began, there is the fact that the height of ecclesiastical power can be seen either as the triumph of the religious or its more blasphemous secularization.[5]

5. There is, of course, a long-standing controversy between those who see the elimination of all totems and taboos as beneficial and those who see some totems and taboos as assisting human happiness.

62 Joan Brothers

Church and School

Excerpt from Joan Brothers, *Church and School: A Study of the Impact of Education on Religion*, Liverpool University Press, 1964, pp. 158–63.

An investigation was carried out concerned with the effect in the religious sphere of a deliberate plan to alter the educational system, a plan which has resulted in new patterns of social mobility. The gradual disappearance of the social homogeneity of Roman Catholicism in Liverpool has been sharply accelerated in recent years. The sons and daughters of working-class families now attend universities in increasing numbers. A single family may experience in a few years changes which were previously accomplished over several generations. What consequences have these changes in the social structure of Catholicism had for the social organization of the Church? How far has a uniform social grouping, centred on the parish, persisted in spite of changes in the class system? What has been the overall effect on the religious and social life of those who have borne the brunt of these changes?

It can be seen that the educational system has operated as an agent of change in that it has given similar experiences to young people of widely differing social class, and has thus made them conscious of having a great deal in common with one another. For many from working-class homes, the ideas and ways of behaving they learn in the grammar schools from their teachers and school fellows become more important and more real than those of their families. The findings of this study indicate how acceptable most of these young people found the focus on the school community, and the extent to which their social relationships, both as pupils and later in life, were influenced by it.

The old devotion and loyalty to the parochial settings have come to have little meaning to most of these young people who have attended grammar schools. Although allegiance to their families and former classmates still holds a few in parochial communities, the majority feel themselves removed from the old context, but not in the sense of being uprooted; on the contrary, they have shed the old ties in the parish with ease. Grammar school education has led the former pupils to regard the parish as part of a cultural way of living in which they themselves have no part. This is because their concept of the Church is more abstract than that accepted by previous generations of Catholics in the city, and their identification with Catholicism goes beyond the local setting; the parish is no longer the all-important centre of their religious lives. Their education, and the experiences which this has either given them or led them towards, have removed them into a social sphere which is unrelated to the neighbourhood. They acknowledge the value of the parish as a means of social interaction for others, but they do not see themselves as 'that sort of person'. For themselves, they demand from the parish little more than the adequate provision of religious services.

The findings of this research reveal the inability of the parochial structure, as it is currently understood by clergy and people in Liverpool, to absorb the impact of new attitudes and ideas. The parish has assimilated many changes in an urban setting, but the latest has proved beyond its powers, perhaps because it has been confronted here, not with individual desires, but with a fundamental reconstructing of the institutional framework which is associated with the increase in grammar-school education. The ideas and attitudes which established the social life of the parish in the past, and adapted and sustained its organization in an urban environment, have little place in the lives of the former pupils of grammar schools. They do not even see the parish as something against which to react, but as something which is simply irrelevant, of limited importance. Even their criticisms of the parochial clergy, for instance, explosive though they may be at times, contain none of the calculated bitterness which can characterize intellectuals on the Continent of Europe. An individual priest might annoy them with his conservative approach, certain aspects of his role in the parish might be considered ill adapted to contemporary circumstances, but for the priesthood itself, respect is retained. However, in a parochial setting, the former pupils of grammar schools are simply not at ease, and they acknowledge this lack of familiarity and interest willingly, without any sense of obligation or shame.

With the extension of grammar school education, the social systems which have developed round the schools have grown in strength. It is these and not the parish which play the most important part in the lives of the pupils. The increasing emphasis upon the school, and the ways it is taking on more and more of the functions of the parish, have brought about a situation in which it has come to rival the traditional institution. It is hardly surprising, therefore, that the former pupils do not want to fit into the parish, an institution which many among them may never have really experienced or appreciated. In any case, it can be argued that the schools and organizations encountered later at universities and colleges, are better able to meet the spiritual and social needs of pupils and students than the parochial structure as it now exists.

But the continued emphasis which is placed upon the parish both legally, and in the formal policies of the Church in regions such as Liverpool, means that the attitudes and behaviour of those who have been to Catholic grammar schools may often be viewed with disapproval, especially by pastors. The results of this inquiry show how strongly some of the parish priests lamented the reluctance of the former pupils of grammar schools to take an active part in the parish; and such priests felt that in this way the institution of the grammar school has failed to fulfil one of its major functions, one which the teachers often do not consider to be their task at all. It is not surprising, therefore, that the parish priests regard education in grammar schools with mixed feelings. Further research, examining the factors involved more precisely than has been possible in this preliminary investigation, should reveal how far these attitudes are related to education in non-parochial schools, and how far they are directed towards the consequences of higher education itself. The pastors are glad at their parishioners' success, but grieve because experience has taught them that in this step some of the children are 'lost' to their care. To some priests, these young Catholics represent the Christian parable of the talents in reverse – they are seen as being like the man who received the most, yet wasted them instead of using them to the full. However one may evaluate the situation, it seems that, by and large, the educated section of parishioners are, in fact, being 'lost' to the parish at the present time.

At the same time as the structural changes are taking place, new values and ways of looking at the Church and the world are communicated through the schools, which result in different relationships within the Catholic community. The most noticeable change is that which has occurred in the role system between pastor and parishioner. The roles which tradition regulated so carefully have been disturbed by changing attitudes and behaviour on the part of the laity. Some priests may still tend to expect from these new kinds of parishioners the approach and behaviour to which tradition has accustomed them. But the former pupils of grammar schools have not learned to think or behave in the ways transmitted through the parochial schools. Although some have previously attended such schools, it is the later experiences in the grammar schools which make the greater impact. Familiar with the approach of specialist non-parochial clergy, perhaps at the university, the demands of the parish priest often appear authoritarian to these young people. The pastor's advice is not sought because he is not expected to know how to cope with their problems. The parish priest, on the other hand, has grown accustomed to the fact that as far as his parishioners are concerned, the responsibility for taking the initiative lies with him. He is now confronted with lay people who seem to him argumentative and disrespectful, who criticize the way the services are conducted, or deplore the fact that he may find Bingo the only way of meeting the enormous debt he has incurred on the parish school.

The confusion which has arisen between pastor and parishioners is perhaps one of the most striking facts which this inquiry has brought to light. It is highly probable that some reading this would feel angry at the attitude of these young Catholics, and others would criticize the parish priests' approach as outdated. But the purpose of this research was not to show how far one set of people or another was at fault, but to discover the crises and tensions, as well as the hopes and enthusiasms, which surround a new development in the religious life. This situation between pastor and parishioner has not arisen out of individual ill will or indifference, but because a whole institutional framework and the relationships within it have been disturbed by changes in the wider social structure. The earlier familiarity has disappeared, and people are unaware of what to expect from one another.

Adaptation to the changing concepts of role behaviour between priests and people is unlikely to be a simple process. It does not only represent problems with regard to the pastor's responsibility and authority, for it also involves at the present time complicated attitudes on the part of the laity. It can be observed that many young Catholics, ready to voice criticisms amongst themselves about the attitudes of parochial clergy, find it so difficult to discover a new relationship which is satisfactory to both sides that, on the rare occasions when they encounter their pastors, they tend to accept the traditional relationship as the only possible one; the comments of university students upon such situations reveal how often they despise themselves for doing so afterwards. Thus, when they would most like to be articulate in communicating their views, they may find themselves unable to do so. As a result, the situation may appear at times to remain unchanged, yet underneath new attitudes are developing towards the clergy.

It would seem, therefore, that one of the major pastoral problems in this country is not, as in many Continental countries, to understand the ideas and behaviour of the working classes, for the background and experiences of the parochial clergy already assures this sympathy; nor yet to come to grips with the emerging 'intellectuals', for specialist clergy of similar education and views already exist. It is the rapidly expanding sections of the population which fall between the two which are likely to produce the biggest pastoral difficulties in the next few years, and it is these which are least well provided for in the institutional life of the Church. For their ways of thinking and behaving fall into neither of the two categories already described; the failure of schemes in provincial University Catholic Societies modelled upon traditional Oxbridge patterns indicates that young people who are emerging into the middle classes as a result of educational innovations think very differently from those whose place in the social class hierarchy is simply maintained by university education.

The relationships between parishioners are changing, too. The investigation has described how grammar school education has divided people who were once class mates at the parochial school, not simply because of the time lapse, for this was overcome in the case of those who shared a private primary education, but through social divisions. No longer is there the same degree of social equality among parishioners as there was in earlier generations in Liverpool parishes. 'We're not the same sort', the former pupils of grammar schools say awkwardly of themselves, sometimes ashamed of the underlying sentiments. But they are thus acknowledging a social fact. In the parish club, the young graduate finds he can contribute little to the conversation, and the sad phrase, 'We have nothing to say to one another', is heard yet again.

In extreme cases, as with some university students and graduates, this breakdown in communication can lead to intolerance over matters such as traditional pieties and phrases, or popular art forms. At times, criticisms of this kind fail to distinguish between superstitions, which are in themselves inimical to the development of Christian beliefs, and practices which are simply associated with the expression of Catholicism in a particular environment. Rapid changes leave some young people unable to understand that while such aspects of folk Catholicism do not help them, they may fulfil a valuable function for others who are accustomed to a different social *milieu*; for Christianity does not seek to isolate the individual from the cultural forms of the society in which he lives, but rather inspires him to develop his values in such a way that they will permeate social life and 'restore all things in Christ'. Moreover, criticisms of this nature, especially with regard to aesthetic judgements, are culturally produced in precisely the same manner as the practices they are deploring.

In sum, it seems that the educational system has been instrumental in bringing about a vast amount of social change. In the first place, it has accelerated the processes of social mobility, transcending social barriers in making children from working-class families feel a part of the middle-class way of living. But at the same time, it has created new social distinctions between individuals, former class mates, even families. Religious affiliation does not seem to be a strong enough link in social situations to overcome these divisions. As far as ordinary social relationships are concerned, it seems that education in the present context is as powerful an influence as religion.

63 Peter Berger

Religion on the Market

Excerpts from Peter Berger, *The Social Reality of Religion*, Faber, 1969, pp. 137–49.

The key characteristic of all pluralistic situations, whatever the details of their historical background, is that the religious ex-monopolies can no longer take for granted the allegiance of their client populations. Allegiance is voluntary and thus, by definition, less than certain. As a result, the religious tradition, which previously could be authoritatively imposed, now has to be *marketed.* It must be 'sold' to a clientele that is no longer constrained to 'buy'. The pluralistic situation is, above all, a *market situation*. In it, the religious institutions become marketing agencies and the religious traditions become consumer commodities. And at any rate a good deal of religious activity in this situation comes to be dominated by the logic of market economics.

It is not difficult to see that this situation will have far-reaching consequences for the social structure of the various religious groups. What happens here, quite simply, is that the religious groups are transformed from monopolies to competitive marketing agencies. Previously, the religious groups were organized as befits an institution exercising exclusive control over a population of retainers. Now, the religious groups must organize themselves in such a way as to woo a population of consumers, in competition with other groups having the same purpose. All at once, the question of 'results' becomes important. In the monopolistic situation the socio-religious structures are under no pressure to produce 'results' – the situation itself predefines the 'results'. Medieval France, for instance, was Catholic by definition. Contemporary France, however, can be so defined only in the teeth of overwhelmingly contrary evidence. It has become, indeed, a *pays de mission*. Consequently, the Catholic church must raise the question of its own social structure, precisely in order to make possible the achievement of missionary 'results'. The confrontation with this question accounts in large measure for the turmoil through which French Catholicism has passed in recent years.

The pressure to achieve 'results' in a competitive situation entails a rationalization of the socio-religious structures. However these may be legitimated by the theologians, the men charged with the mundane welfare of the various religious groups must see to it that the structures permit the rational execution of the groups' 'mission'. As in other institutional spheres of modern society, such structural rationalization expresses itself primarily in the phenomenon of bureaucracy.

The spread of bureaucratic structures through the religious institutions has the consequence that these, irrespective of their various theological traditions, increasingly resemble each other sociologically. The traditional terminology pertaining to matters of 'polity' usually obfuscates this fact. Thus a certain position, A, may carry out the same bureaucratic functions in two different religious groups, but it may be legitimated by theological formula B in one group and by formula C in the other, and indeed the two theological legitimations may be directly contradictory without affecting the functionality of the position in question. For instance, the control over investment funds may be in the charge of a bishop in one group and of the chairman of a laymen's committee in another, yet the actual bureaucratic activities necessitated by this position will have little if any connection with the traditional legitimations of the episcopate or of lay authority. To be sure, there are different models or *Leitbilder* of bureaucracy involved in this process. Thus European Protestant churches, with long experience in state–church situations, will tend toward political models of bureaucracy, while American Protestantism tends to emulate the bureaucratic structures of economic corporations. The central administration of the Catholic church, on the other hand, has its own bureaucratic tradition, which so far has shown itself highly resistant to modernizing modifications. But the demands of rationality are very similar in all these cases and exercise similarly strong pressure on the respective socio-religious structures.

The contemporary situation of religion is thus characterized by a progressive bureaucratization of the religious institutions. Both their internal and their external social relations are marked by this process. Internally, the religious institutions are not only administered bureaucratically, but their day-to-day operations are dominated by the typical problems and 'logic' of bureaucracy. Externally, the religious institutions deal with other social institutions as well as with each other through the typical forms of bureaucratic interaction. 'Public relations' with the consumer clientele, 'lobbying' with the government, 'fund raising' with both governmental and private agencies, multi-faceted involvements with the secular economy (particularly through investment) – in all these aspects of their 'mission' the religious institutions are compelled to seek 'results' by methods that are, of necessity, very similar to those employed by other bureaucratic structures with similar problems.

Very importantly, the same bureaucratic 'logic' applies to the dealings of the several religious institutions with each other.

Bureaucracies demand specific types of personnel. This personnel is specific not only in terms of its functions and requisite skills, but also in terms of its psychological characteristics. Bureaucratic institutions both *select* and *form* the personnel types they require for their operation. This means that similar types of leadership emerge in the several religious institutions, irrespective of the traditional patterns in this matter. The requirements of bureaucracy override such traditional differentiations of religious leadership as 'prophet' versus 'priest', 'scholar' versus 'saint', and so forth. Thus it does not matter very much whether a certain bureaucratic functionary comes out of a Protestant tradition of 'prophetic' ministry or a Catholic tradition of 'priestly' one – in either case, he must above all adapt himself to the requirements of his bureaucratic role. Where possible, the traditional formulas will be retained to legitimate the new social-psychological types; where this is no longer possible, they will have to be modified in order to permit such legitimation. For example, theological scholarship was traditionally central to the role of the Protestant minister; it has become increasingly irrelevant to the roles of the minstry both in 'wholesale' (bureaucratic administration) and 'retail' (local marketing) operations; Protestant educational institutions for the ministry have been accordingly modified, with concomitant modifications in their legitimating rationales. The social-psychological type emerging in the leadership of the bureaucratized religious institutions is, naturally, similar to the bureaucratic personality in other institutional contexts – activist, pragmatically oriented, not given to administratively irrelevant reflection, skilled in interpersonal relations, 'dynamic' and conservative at the same time, and so forth. The individuals conforming to this type in the different religious institutions speak the same language and, naturally, understand each other and each other's problems. In other words, the bureaucratization of the religious institutions lays a social-psychological foundation for 'ecumenicity' – an important fact to understand, we would contend.

'Ecumenicity', however, in the sense of an increasingly friendly collaboration between the different groups engaged in the religious market, is demanded by the pluralistic situation as a whole, not just by the social-psychological affinities of religio-bureaucratic personnel. These affinities ensure, if nothing else, that religious rivals are regarded not so much as 'the enemy' but as fellows with similar problems. This, obviously, makes collaboration easier. But the necessity to collaborate is given by the need to rationalize competition itself in the pluralistic situation. The competitive market is established once it has become impossible to utilize the political machinery of the society for the elimination of religious rivals. The forces of this market then tend toward a system of free competition very similar to that of *laisser-faire* capitalism. Such a system however, requires further rationalization as it develops. Free competition between the different marketing agencies, without any restraints imposed from without or agreed upon by these agencies themselves, becomes irrational at the point where the cost of such competition begins to jeopardize the gains to be derived from it. This cost may, first of all, be political and in terms of 'public image'. Thus it may be easier to extract favors from a religiously neutral government by different churches acting in concert than by their trying to undercut each other. Also, overly savage competition for consumer patronage may be self-defeating inasmuch as it may have the effect of alienating various classes of potential 'customers' from the religious market altogether. But untrammeled competition also tends to become irrational, that is, too costly, in purely economic terms. The marketing of any commodity, material or otherwise, to a modern mass public is an exceedingly complex and expensive operation. Thus any new venture on the part of the churches (particularly what is called 'church expansion' in America) necessitates the expenditure of substantial capital. The bureaucrats in charge of these operations must calculate rationally, which in turn forces them to reduce the risks as much as possible. The training of religious personnel, the construction and upkeep of religious edifices, the output of promotional materials, the rising overhead of bureaucratic administration – all these entail vast sums of money, for the rational use of which the religious bureaucrats are responsible. The responsibility increases to the extent that the supply of funds for these purposes is subject to exigency. This may be because the sources of income have become uncertain – the 'giving' habits of un-coerced clients and/or of governmental funding agencies may be hard to predict accurately, thus introducing elements of risk into the calculations. Or it may be because of inflation in the economy at large, making all expenditures a more risky undertaking (an important element in all 'church expansion' programs in America). One obvious way of reducing risks is to come to various kinds of understanding with one's competitors – to 'fix prices' – that is, to rationalize competition by means of cartelization ...

Cartelization, here as elsewhere in competitive market situations, has two facets: the number of competing units is reduced through mergers; and the remaining units organize the market by means of mutual agreements. 'Ecumenicity', in the contemporary situation, is, of course, characterized by both of these two facets. At any rate within Protestantism, churches have merged at an increasing rate and negotiations looking forward to further mergers are continuing apace. Both within and beyond Protestantism, there has been increasing consultation and collaboration between the large bodies 'surviving' the merger process. It is important to see that this process of cartelization does *not* tend toward the re-establishment of a monopoly situation – in other words, the notion of an eventual 'world church' is very unlikely to be realized empirically. Rather, the tendency is clearly oligopolistic, with mergers in prospect only to the extent that these are functional in terms of rationalizing competition. To go beyond this extent, quite apart from the strain this would put on the theological legitimations, would actually be irrational in terms of the institutional interests of the several religious bureaucracies. Nor is it easily imaginable that this would meet consumer demand (which, ironically, is frequently more traditional in its denominational loyalties than the thinking of the religious bureaucrats).

The pluralistic situation thus entails a network of bureaucratic structures, engaged in rational dealings with the society at large and with each other. The pluralistic situation, inasmuch as it tends toward cartelization, tends toward 'ecumenicity' in its social, political and economic dynamics. The quotation marks should indicate that this tendency need not be related *a priori* to any particular theological conceptions about the term. It is very likely that something like the present-day ecumenical movement would have resulted from the pluralistic situation in any case, even if there had not been the particular theological developments now used to legitimate it. Indeed, it seems plausible, to the sociologist at any rate, to see the theological developments as consequences rather than cause of the pluralistic infrastructure, without thereby denying their capacity to 'act back' upon that infrastructure. It goes without saying, of course, that seeing the matter in this way does not in the least impugn the sincerity of the theological motives of anyone engaged in the ecumenical movement. 'Conspiracy theories' are rarely convincing when it comes to large-scale social phenomena, but they are particularly unsatisfying when the phenomena have a religious character.

The effects of the pluralistic situation are not limited to the social-structural aspects of religion. They also extend to the religious contents, that is, to the product of the religious marketing agencies. It should not be difficult to see why this should be so, in view of the preceding discussion of structural changes. As long as religious institutions occupied a monopoly position in society, their contents could be determined in accordance with whatever theological lore seemed plausible and/or convenient to the religious leadership. This does not mean, of course, that the leadership and its theological decisions were immune to forces originating in the larger society, for instance within the power centers of the latter. Religion has always been susceptible to highly mundane influences, extending even to its most rarified theoretical constructions. The pluralistic situation, however, introduces a novel form of mundane influences, probably more potent in modifying religious contents than such older forms as the wishes of kings or the vested interests of classes – the dynamics of consumer preference.

To repeat, the crucial sociological and social-psychological characteristic of the pluralistic situation is that religion can no longer be imposed but must be marketed. It is impossible, almost *a priori,* to market a commodity to a population of un-coerced consumers without taking their wishes concerning the commodity into consideration. To be sure, the religious institutions can still count on traditional ties holding back certain groups of the population from too drastic liberty in religious choice – in terms of the market, there still is strong 'product loyalty' among certain groups of 'old customers'. Furthermore, the religious institutions can to a certain extent restrain disaffection among the same groups by means of their own promotional activities. All the same, the basic necessity of taking on a soliciting stance *vis-à-vis* a public means that consumer controls over the product being marketed are introduced.

This means, furthermore, that a dynamic element is introduced into the situation, a principle of changeability if not change, that is intrinsically inimical to religous traditionalism. In other words, in this situation it becomes increasingly difficult to maintain the religious traditions as unchanging verity. Instead, the dynamics of consumer preference is introduced into the religious sphere. Religious contents become subjects of 'fashion'. This need not necessarily imply that there will be rapid change or that the principle of unchangeability will be surrendered theologically, but the *possibility* of change is introduced into the situation once and for all. Sooner or later, the chances are that the possibility will be realized and that the possibility will eventually be legitimated on the level of theological theorizing. This is obviously easier to admit for some religious groups than for others (for instance, for the Protestants than for the Catholics), but no group can escape this effect completely.

The dynamics of consumer preference does not, in itself, determine the substantive contents – it simply posits that, in principle, they are susceptible to change, without determining the direction of change. However, there are some other factors in the contemporary situation that have substantive influence on the character of this change. Insofar as the world of the consumers in question is secularized, their preference will reflect this. That is, they will prefer religious products that can be made consonant with secularized consciousness over those that cannot.

This will, of course, vary with the strata that serve as clienteles for different religious institutions. Consumer demand in upper-middle-class suburbia in America, for instance, is different in this respect from consumer demand in the rural South. Given the variability in the degree of secularization of different strata, the secularizing influence of these strata as religious consumers will vary. But inasmuch as secularization is a global trend, there is a global tendency for religious contents to be modified in a secularizing direction. In the extreme cases (as in liberal Protestantism and Judaism) this may lead to the deliberate excision of all or nearly all 'supernatural' elements from the religious tradition, and a legitimation of the continued existence of the institution that once embodied the tradition in purely secular terms. In other cases it may just mean that the 'supernatural' elements are de-emphasized or pushed into the background, while the institution is 'sold' under the label of values congenial to secularized consciousness. For example, the Catholic church is obviously less ready to 'de-mythologize' its contents than most of its Protestant competitors, but *both* traditional Catholicism *and* 'progressive' Protestantism can be effectively advertised as strengthening the moral fiber of the nation or as supplying various psychological benefits ('peace of mind' and the like).

Another substantive influence comes from the institutional 'location' of religion in contemporary society. Since the socially significant 'relevance' of religion is primarily in the private sphere, consumer preference reflects the 'needs' of this sphere. This means that religion can more easily be marketed if it can be shown to be 'relevant' to private life than if it is advertised as entailing specific applications to the large public institutions. This is particularly important for the moral and therapeutic functions of religion. As a result, the religious institutions have accommodated themselves to the moral and therapeutic 'needs' of the individual in his private life. This manifests itself in the prominence given to private problems in the activity and promotion of contemporary religious institutions – the emphasis on family and neighborhood as well as on the psychological 'needs' of the private individual. It is in these areas that religion continues to be 'relevant' even in highly secularized strata, while the application of religious perspectives to political and economic problems is widely deemed 'irrelevant' in the same strata. This, incidentally, helps to explain why the churches have had relatively little influence on the economic and political views of even their own members, while continuing to be cherished by the latter in their existence as private individuals.

The pluralistic situation, then, has, not surprisingly, coincided with a new emphasis on the laity in the religious institutions. The 'age of the laity', as defined by a number of theologians, is grounded in the character of this laity as a population of consumers. In other words, the theological propositions about the role of the laity may be understood as *post hoc* legitimations of developments rooted in the infrastructure of the contemporary religious market. Again, some religious traditions have been easier to modify in this direction than others. Thus Protestants in the free church tradition have been able to legitimate the dominance of consumer demand and controls in terms of venerable theological propositions (despite the fact that, of course, these propositions originally referred to an entirely different situation – the Puritan covenant, for instance, hardly referred to a consumers' cooperative). It is all the more interesting to see how the same 'rediscovery of the laity' has been taking place in religious traditions previously bereft of such legitimations, as even within Catholicism.

Two other effects of consumer controls over religious contents are standardization and marginal differentiation – once more replications of the general dynamics of a free market. Insofar as the religious 'needs' of certain strata of clients or potential clients are similar, the religious institutions catering to these 'needs' will tend to standardize their products accordingly. For example, all religious institutions oriented toward the upper-middle-class market in America will be under pressure to secularize and to psychologize their products – otherwise, the chances of these being 'bought' diminish drastically. Thus even the Catholic priest in suburbia is much less likely to talk about Fatima than to engage in a 'dialogue' with some available psychiatrist on 'religion and mental health'. His Protestant and Jewish colleagues, of course, are likely to have legitimated their whole operations as some kind of family psychotherapy long ago. This standardization of religious contents, brought about by consumer pressures, tends to de-emphasize traditional confessional cleavages. As a result, it facilitates the cartelization necessitated by the structural features of the pluralistic situation. Group A may merge or 'fix prices' with group B simply as a result of the pragmatic problems faced by the two bureaucracies in question, but the operation is easier to accomplish when, in fact, contents A and B have become close to being indistinguishable.

The pluralistic situation, however, has engendered not only the 'age of ecumenicity' but also, apparently in contradiction to it, the 'age of the rediscovery of confessional heritages'. This has often been observed and simply noted as some sort of 'countervailing movement', welcomed or deplored as the case may be. It is important to see, we would contend, that the renewed emphasis on denominational identities (specifically, those identities that survive the cartelization process) is actually part of the same process of the rationalization of competition. The 'counter-vailing movement' is brought about by the need for marginal differentiation in an over-all situation of standardization. Put simply, if group A decides *not* to merge with group B, despite the fact that their products have become highly standardized, something must be done to enable consumers to distinguish between the two products and to be able to make a choice between them. Emphasizing the 'confessional heritage' of each group is one obvious way of doing this. It may happen that this will actually arrest or even reverse the process of standardization. It may also happen (probably more frequently) that the differentiation is one of 'packaging' only – inside the package there may still be the same old standardized product. In either case, it is likely that marginal differentiation will go only as far as is necessitated by the dynamics of consumer demand in any particular market. This will vary, then, not so much in accordance with specific confessional traditions but rather with the variations of consumer 'needs' in terms of general social stratification. The 'rediscovery of confessional heritages', therefore, is not very aptly described as a 'countervailing movement' to 'ecu-menicity', but is rather to be understood as a structurally required counterpart to the latter. The differentiation of religious products in these terms will then have a social-psychological correlate. That is, once group A has been 'profiled' in terms of its 'rediscovered' tradition, represen-tatives of group A will have to define themselves as standing in this tradition as they confront the representatives of other groups. This goes far to explain the dynamics of identification and self-identification in the 'who's who' of contemporary ecumenism – by definition, every par-ticipant in the latter must be something – all the social-psychological pressures of the situation then push him toward becoming what he is supposed to be, namely a representative of the religious tradition to which he has been assigned.

64 Guenther Lewy

The Catholic Church and Nazi Germany

Excerpts from Guenther Lewy, *The Catholic Church and Nazi Germany*, Weidenfeld & Nicolson, 1964, pp. 325–36.

The behaviour of the Catholic Church under Nazi rule was related to a number of specifically German conditions. The Church shared the widely prevailing sense of nationalism and patriotism; she was affected by the same excessive respect for authority that did so much to hinder the Resistance. More importantly, the bishops, many of the lower clergy and their parishioners concurred in certain Nazi aims. They welcomed the Nazis' anti-Communism as a counterpoise to the liberal, anti-clerical and atheistic currents of the Weimar republic. They were attracted by the National Socialist call for a strong state, a new German Reich that would again be a world power and able to solve the country's pressing economic and social problems. Some churchmen expected that the increase in the power of the state and the introduction of the leadership principle would result also in a strengthening of the authority of the Church.

In a mood of naïve trust and wishful thinking about Hitler's promises of religious peace, and anxious to protect the Church's organizations, schools and newspapers, the German bishops supported the signing of the Concordat. After this pact had been concluded the course of accommodation was fixed. In order not to jeopardize those provisions of the Concordat which the Nazi regime chose to honor it was regarded as imperative to placate the Nazis.

Had Hitler pursued a policy similar to that of Mussolini's peaceful coexistence with the Church, it is more than likely that the German episcopate, like its counterpart in Italy, would have become even more identified with the Nazi government and movement than they actually did. But German National Socialism was truly totalitarian in its aspirations, intent upon dominating all aspects of life, and hence ill-inclined to accept partners. The conflict between Church and State was therefore probably unavoidable no matter what the policy of the hierarchy and the Holy See.

Only very gradually and rather late did the bishops begin to realize that Hitler's regime was intent upon destroying the Church. Even then they thought that they could ward off the encroachments of the Nazis by protesting against violations of the Concordat and combining these protests with affirmations of loyalty to the state. The Church's opposition was carefully circumscribed; it was rooted in her concern for her institutional interests rather than in a belief in freedom and justice for all men. In this the German episcopate followed a policy very much in keeping with the Church's traditional mode of operation and thought.

With this summary we leave behind the specific German elements underlying the conduct of the German Church. We turn to our concluding task, an explanation on a higher level that involves the Catholic Church as a world-wide institution, and its political and moral theories.

The church and democracy

'In any crucial situation', Sidney Hook once observed, 'the behavior of the Catholic Church may be more reliably predicted by reference to its concrete interests as a political organization than by reference to its timeless dogmas.' One may go a step further and say that these dogmas are sufficiently flexible and ambiguous so that the Church can accommodate a variety of political conditions running the gamut from democracy to totalitarian dictatorship. Some of this ambiguity can be attributed to the highly abstract theological and metaphysical foundations of Catholic political theory, but much is a matter of design that serves to pave the way for the Church's adjustment to different situations [. . .]

The adaptation to authoritarian and dictatorial regimes was facilitated by the Church's hierarchical constitution and the affinity for authoritarian ideas produced by its make-up. Catholicism, wrote the historian Christopher Dawson in 1936, 'is by no means hostile to the authoritarian ideal of the State. Against the liberal doctrines of the divine right of majorities and the unrestrained freedom of opinion the Church has always maintained the principles of authority and hierarchy and a high conception of the prerogatives of the State.' Catholic social ideals set forth in the encyclicals of Leo XIII and Pius XI, Dawson argued, 'have far more affinity with those of Fascism than with those of either Liberalism or Socialism.' Catholic political ideas 'correspond much more closely, at least in theory, with the Fascist conception of the functions of the "leader" and the vocational hierarchy of the Fascist State than they do with the system of parliamentary democratic party government. . . .'

As long as Fascist movements served as a bulwark against Communism, the Church was willing to accept the loss of political liberties that followed their accession to power. Atheistic Communism has for a century been the Church's number one enemy. This uncompromising hostility drew strength from the personal experiences of Popes Pius XI and XII. At the end of World War I, as Papal Nuncios in Poland and Germany, respectively, the two men had had experience with the anti-religious fervor of Communist regimes, and what they saw and heard in Warsaw, Munich and Berlin colored their political outlook and influenced their subsequent policies as heads of the Church. Both of these Popes were preoccupied with the threat of Communism, and therefore showed considerable benevolence to both Fascist Italy and Nazi Germany. The French Fascist movement, *Action Française,* was eventually condemned by the Vatican, but, in the words of one Catholic writer, this was done 'not merely because there was ground for condemnation, but because it estimated that the degree of success possible for the movement was great enough permanently to damage the essential Catholic interests in democratic France, but not great enough to protect them in the long run'. On 7 July 1939, soon after the election of Pacelli to the Papacy, the ban was lifted. Pius XII, even more than his predecessor, was convinced of the usefulness of anti-Communist right-wing movements.

At the end of World War II, cognizant of the fact that the support of dictatorial, if not outright criminal regimes such as those of Mussolini and Hitler, had done much to injure the moral prestige of Catholicism, the Church began to assume a more sympathetic attitude toward democracy. Pius XII, who throughout World War II had steered a course of careful neutrality, in December 1944, when the defeat of the Axis powers was imminent, acknowledged 'that a democratic form of government is considered by many today to be a natural postulate of reason itself'. After the downfall of the Nazi regime, Pope Pius in October 1945 declared that totalitarianism cannot satisfy 'the vital exigencies of any human community' since 'it allows the state power to assume an undue extension' and forces 'all legitimate manifestations of life – personal, local and professional – into a mechanical unity or collectivity under the stamp of nation, race or class'. Short of totalitarianism, even the so-called authoritarian regimes, the Pope went on, pervert the essential nature of state power by splitting the nation into rulers and ruled, and by excluding the citizens from effective participation in forming the will of society. True democracy, on the other hand, holding the Christian faith as the principle of civil life, satisfies the requirements of a sound community, though 'the same applies, or could apply, under the same conditions, also to the other legitimate forms of government [monarchy, aristocracy, etc.]'.

The benevolence toward popular forms of government became even more pronounced under Pius' successor, Pope John XXIII. In his encyclical *Pacem in Terris* (Peace on Earth) issued on 10 April 1963, Pope John, like Leo XIII seventy years earlier, reaffirmed that even though authority comes from God, men have the right to choose their rulers. 'It is thus clear that the doctrine which we have set forth is fully consonant with any truly democratic regime.' The old neutrality toward the forms of government was not yet repudiated, but John XXIII did proclaim that the rule of law and the principle of constitutionalism were preferred modes of government. The separation of the state's functions into legislative, judicial and executive branches, the Pope declared, is 'in keeping with the innate demands of human nature'. Pope John's lengthy discussion of human rights, including 'the right to take an active part in public affairs', also pointed toward an eventual acceptance of democracy by the Church as the form of government judged best for all who have reached a degree of political maturity.

The timing of this gradual political reorientation is significant; it shows that the Church is following rather than leading. As a perceptive Catholic sociologist has noted in connection with the social encyclicals of the modern popes, the Church respects 'the majesty of facts', she ratifies the gains scored by others. Once a liberating movement has broken certain chains, the Church will incorporate the newly gained liberties into her ethic of natural law. She will then recognize them, as previously she had recognized the validity of the chains. Whereas in earlier centuries monarchy was held to be the best and most natural form of government, now the rule of law and the separation of functions are viewed as consonant with the demands of human nature.

The indifference of Catholic political philosophy to the forms of government has been justified by the abuses to which all political systems are exposed and 'because the political form of government as such does not actually guarantee the best realization of the common good'. One can readily assent to this proposition. It shows the same realism, reminiscent of Aristotle, as is displayed in Pope John's statement in *Pacem in Terris* that 'it is impossible to determine, once and for all, what is the most suitable form of government, or how civil authorities can most effectively fulfil their respective functions... great weight has to be given to the historical background and circumstances of given political communities, circumstances which will vary at different times and in different places.' But the validity of one premise does not prove a conclusion. While it may be impossible to substantiate the assertion that democracy, as practiced for example in the United States or Great Britain, represents an ideal form of government to be followed by all other nations everywhere and at any time, it is certainly possible, negatively, to rule out some forms of government from consideration. The

Nazi regime's policies of genocide, for example, were an integral part of National Socialist doctrine; these policies represented a logical outgrowth of a system of government refusing to recognize human equality and dignity. Quite apart from the question of what is the best mode of government, it is therefore not at all difficult to show that certain totalitarian regimes by their very nature are in open violation of the basic moral principles of the Judaeo-Christian tradition. This judgement the Church avoided making until Nazi and Fascist totalitarianism, containing and supported by large numbers of Catholics, had disappeared from the map of history.

As soon as one of these totalitarian regimes attacks the rights of the Church, the Church will protest. But until these regimes are actually overthrown, the Church will hesitate to utter the ban and she will seek an accommodation to protect her own interests as an institution. In such situations, of which the encounter with the Third Reich was a good example, the doctrine of the Church's indifference to the forms of government is highly useful. Thus the German bishops were able to assert that the Catholic religion was no more opposed to the Nazi form of government than to any other. And when the Hitler government reacted with anger to the statement of *L'Osservatore Romano* in July 1933, that the conclusion of the Concordat between Germany and the Holy See did not entail the recognition of a specific political doctrine, the bishops were able to explain: 'The assertion of *L'Osservatore Romano* that the conclusion of the Concordat did not express assent to the National Socialist state does by no means signify a basic rejection of that state. Otherwise the Concordat would never have been concluded. It merely represents the intentional suspension of an evaluation, [a suspension] made necessary by the relations of the Holy See to all other states.'

The neutrality of the Church toward the various forms of government is thus an ideological adjunct of church diplomacy; neutrality is necessitated by the wide-flung interests of the Church. These interests demand flexibility. On the other hand, and more basically, this neutrality derives from the fact that the chief concern of the Church is with the supernatural aspects of human existence. The Church regards herself as the divinely appointed means of man's redemption; to protect her pastoral mission the Church will work with all types of government, and these acts of accommodation, in the form of a concordat or without such a formal tie, rule out ideological intransigence. Given a sufficient *quid pro quo*, the Church will even close an eye to the violation of the common good by such a regime, for the interests of religion are her paramount concern. Or to put it differently: since religion is 'the general and supreme good' of the community to which all else must yield, the welfare of the state is measured by the freedom enjoyed by religion. From the standpoint of the Church, as a prominent English Catholic has observed correctly, 'political and civil liberties . . . are secondary and only favored in so far as they seem to give some guarantee for the higher liberties'. It is for such reasons that Catholic dictators like Franco and Salazar, despite the oppressive character of their regimes, can be considered more valuable by the Church than democratic statesmen, eager to secularize the state, no matter how much the latter may contribute to other areas of public life.

The Church, insisted Lord Acton, must be attached to a spirit making for good government: 'a country entirely Protestant may have more Catholic elements in its government than one where the population is wholly Catholic.' This enlightened point of view has never yet been shared by those guiding the destiny of the Church.

The challenge of tyranny

The attitude of the contemporary Church to the problem of resistance to tyrannical regimes is marked by the same ambivalence of doctrine and the acceptance of accomplished facts as she shows toward forms of government [. . .]

The ambiguity of the Church's position on the legitimacy of resistance to constituted authority is of considerable advantage, for with it she can sail a flexible course adaptable to the ebb and flow of the tides of circumstances. But such cautious helmsmanship, such waiting on the sidelines of history, leaves the individual Catholic burdened with a decision in the making of which he should have moral guidance from his Church. Often, moreover, his bishops will seek to conform his thinking to what they consider the long-range interests of the Church, and these interests may or may not coincide with those of the people involved. During the time of the Algerian rebellion the French episcopate could not agree upon a common evaluation of the insurrection. 'We cannot positively affirm that it is legitimate,' stated one bishop, 'neither can we condemn it as if it were illegitimate.' In the face of such circumspection one is left wondering about the relevance of Catholic political teaching to the dilemmas of modern man.

The Church's political doctrine, in line with the scriptural injunctions to obey the powers that be, grants the presumption of legitimacy to all types of government provided they are firmly in possession of power. The decision on whether and how far to oppose a regime that is or becomes tyrannical will be made by the episcopate of that country primarily in terms of that state's attitude to the rights of religion. If the

Church, as in Fascist Italy and essentially also in Nazi Germany, is allowed to pursue her pastoral mission, the bishops will exhort their followers to render willing obedience to the State. But if the Church's rights are assaulted, as happened in Mexico between 1917 and 1936 and in Spain under the republican regime at the outbreak of the Spanish Civil War, if churches are burnt and priests killed, the Church will support even an insurrection, provided the rebels promise to protect her interests and seem to have a chance to prevail against the legitimate government.

65 B. R. Roberts

Protestant Groups and Coping with Urban Life in Guatemala City

Excerpt from B. R. Roberts, 'Protestant groups and coping with urban life in Guatemala City', *American Journal of Sociology*, vol. 73, 1967–8, pp. 762–7.

Joining a Protestant group brings an individual into frequent social inter-action with other members of a congregation. In both neighborhoods, Protestants attend their churches or meeting houses about three times a week, with services lasting two or more hours. In the three Pentecostal churches in the ravine neighborhood [of Guatemala City], services are held almost every night of the week and last from about 7.30 p.m. to after 10.0 p.m. In addition, North American missionaries attached to the cen-tral churches of almost all these groups have attempted to introduce Guatemalans to North American standards of behavior. Consequently, many of these groups provide recreational and educational associations designed to educate members in household budgeting, social com-portment, and table manners. These activities and the compulsory social visiting among members of a church take up another one or two even-ings of a Protestant's week.

The above social relationships also secure material aid and advice for neighborhood Protestants. To counter the political and economic uncer-tainties of Guatemala City, the various Protestant groups in the two neighborhoods have developed a complete system of aid among members. Funds attached to the central headquarters of these groups pay for funeral expenses when a family member of a believer dies. When a Protestant in one of the neighborhoods is sick, members of his con-gregation join together to provide money for the affected family and frequently visit the sick person. Should a Protestant in one of the neigh-borhoods need help to improve or repair his house, install drainage, or obtain a loan, other members of his congregation join together to give help. If a Protestant is out of a job or wants to change his work, other members of his congregation help him to find work.

The size of the individual Protestant groups reflects their secular as well as religious purposes. Most congregations number about thirty active adult members. The relative smallness of the congregations makes it possible for all members of a congregation to interact with each other, take an active part in church affairs, and help each other when necessary. In the ravine neighborhood, one Pentecostal group had split after a period of rapid expansion. Indeed, while Pentecostals in the ravine neighborhood are active in missionary activity outside their neighborhood, they make little effort to convert new members within the neighborhood, and they wait for converts to approach them. Yet the neighborhood contains many non-active Protestants and Catholics. In fact, the Pentecostals are content with their present size. It is a size that best caters to the social and economic needs of members of these groups.

The identity of these Protestant groups is reinforced by the minority status of Protestantism in Guatemala. Protestants in both neighborhoods are not only religious dissenters but a highly visible group of dissenters. This is more pronounced in the ravine neighborhood where homes are thin-walled shacks. In this neighborhood, Protestants are easily recognizable by their radios loudly broadcasting religious services many hours of the day, by the sound of their guitars and hymns emanating from their chapels, and by their abstention from drinking and smoking. In the other neighborhood also, Protestants with Bible in hand or singing loudly in their churches are also a visible group. This visibility has entailed hostility and mild forms of persecution from some Catholics. In the early days of the foundation of the ravine neighborhood, storekeepers refused to serve Protestants. To this day, stones are thrown onto the roofs of Protestants and neighbors turn their radios even louder to interrupt a Protestant gathering. To Protestantism, such annoyances are signs of a corrupt environment where the majority of people are not yet saved. These features of their minority status help Protestants to maintain the boundaries of their neighborhood groups. It gives them a means of selecting those with whom they interact. In fact, these groups concentrate on the economic and social needs of their own members and limit their obligations to neighbors, relatives, or acquaintances inside and outside the neighborhood.

Membership in the Protestant groups in the two neighborhoods also provides an extensive, as well as intensive, network of personal contacts. And in Guatemala City, individual survival and betterment depend on an extensive network of relationships to provide contacts for jobs or information about other economic opportunities.

There are few full-time professionals to organize linkages among the various churches of a sect and to concern themselves with over-all expansion and organization. Consequently, this work is done, to a great extent, by individual members of a congregation. In the three Pentecostal churches of the ravine neighborhood, church members go out in groups to visit a church in another part of the city. Similarly, missionary work is conducted through the personal contacts of individual members. In the ravine neighborhood, there are Protestants who have converted relatives in rural villages to Protestantism. Once every fortnight one of these Protestants journeys to his relatives' village accompanied by members of his congregation. The distance is about twenty miles. There the group holds Protestant services to help start a Pentecostal church in the village.

A second Protestant in the ravine neighborhood who has Protestant relatives in a village visits less often because the distance is greater. When he does go he takes with him a group from his congregation with their guitars and accordions. Still another Protestant, who travels a great deal to sell his wares in rural areas, often makes contact with Protestants in a distant village. Then, on a weekend, he and a group of Protestants from the ravine neighborhood will visit this village and hold a service.

Visits between Protestant churches within and outside the city are also encouraged through messages on the radio. Protestants have religious programs on one of the city radio stations every day and all day. These programs not only provide sermons and hymns but also relay news and invitations to visit from one church to another, giving exact addresses and times of services.

The contacts that Protestants develop in the course of their travels serve as useful sources of information with respect to jobs and other economic opportunities. In one case, a fellow Pentecostal arrived from across the city to tell a shoemaker in the ravine neighborhood about the possibility of work in a shoe factory. The two had met at religious meetings about a year or so before and had kept up infrequent contact since. A Protestant who had lost a factory job soon found another good job through a religious contact elsewhere in the city. Likewise in their trips to rural areas, neighborhood Protestants discuss the land situation, possibilities for trade, and economic changes in the village.

From the preceding analysis we can see that Protestant groups in these two neighborhoods are groups that encompass the lives of church members. Their social organization effectively diminishes contact between Protestants and Catholics. Protestants in the two neighborhoods emphasize that, apart from passing acquaintances, they no longer have time to form friendships with Catholics.

I conclude this section by suggesting that joining a Protestant group in these two neighborhoods is not an act of withdrawal in the face of difficult urban problems but an active attempt to cope with these problems through an available and suitable form of association.

The consequences of membership in Protestant groups

I now want to assess the significance of these Protestant groups for urban life in Guatemala City. I take two aspects of this general problem: the effect of membership in these neighborhood Protestant groups on an individual's economic and social position, and the relation of Protestant groups to politics in Guatemala City.

From my data in the two neighborhoods, there is little evidence that membership in a Protestant group involves considerable personal economic improvement. The average income of Protestants is higher than that of Catholics ($64 and $58, respectively), but the difference is small. Protestants have no more education than Catholics, and in both groups approximately 70 per cent of heads of family are literate. Protestants do not have better material possessions than Catholics. In the ravine neighborhood, only one Protestant has improved his hut with concrete floors and adobe walls, in contrast to more than twenty Catholic families who have made similar improvements. In this ravine neighborhood, not one Protestant has a child who is in secondary education. Yet, many Protestants have children of secondary school age and want them to get jobs requiring a secondary education. Only in two or three cases have Protestants improved their jobs since their conversion.

Those Protestants who are economically better off than most inhabitants of the two neighborhoods have improved their situation through work and contacts that owe little to their membership in a Protestant group. Despite the cohesion of Protestant groups in the two neighborhoods, individual Protestants do vary in the intensity of their participation. Approximately one-third of all Protestants in the sample have ceased to attend a Protestant church regularly, and they confine their religion to Bible reading in their own homes. These non-active Protestants are, in many cases, economically more successful than other Protestants. They ceased to be active participants in their churches when they developed social relationships outside their churches. Of all Protestants, they are the only ones belonging to associations such as a chess club, a social club, or a political party. For most of these non-active Protestants, intense religious activity had conflicted with opportunities to improve their position through devoting more time to work or through utilizing non-religious ties.

These findings are at first sight surprising, since I have stressed how Protestant social organization helps individual members to cope actively with the economic and social problems of living in Guatemala City. Also, other studies of similar Protestant groups in Guatemala and other developing countries have shown that membership in these groups is associated with economic improvement. Nash, studying a village in

Guatemala, found that Protestants derive practical advantages from their membership. They avoid drinking and the expenses involved in the traditional religious organization. N. Long, working among Jehovah's Witnesses in rural Zambia, argues that the network of contacts developed by the Witnesses through their religious activities becomes a useful basis for trading activities. He finds that, along with a change in religious beliefs, converts to the Witnesses are also economically mobile. Thus, a group with a religious ethic similar to the groups in the two Guatemalan neighborhoods, has a more pronounced effect on its members' economic position.

Both Long's and Nash's studies show that a Protestant group helps an individual to improve economically by providing a break with a traditional system of social organization which prevents individuals from making use of new economic opportunities. In Guatemala City, however, few people are constrained by traditional values from seizing economic opportunities. The constraint on economic improvement is a static economic situation, as a high failure rate of small businesses in the city attests.

In Guatemala City, Protestants are too few and most are too poor to provide the network of contacts that would be of considerable help in improving a member's material position. Few of the neighborhood Protestants are able to use their missionary contacts in rural areas to further their own businesses. One Protestant shoemaker, who travels often to do missionary work, carries out his sales work in rural areas through a neighborhood Catholic woman who has extensive family and friendship contacts in these areas. Indeed their contacts with rural areas often lead Protestants to emphasize values antagonistic to urban industrial civilization. They talk favorably of the countryside, claiming that it is easier to be a true Christian there in the absence of urban amusements and without the temptation of too much money to spend. In the city, there are few Protestant merchants or professionals who are accessible to neighborhood Protestants through religious ties. As noted, richer Protestants often cease to be active members of their churches, and consequently the expansion in the numbers of Protestants does not substantially add to the number of useful contacts that poorer Protestants can develop.

Furthermore, Protestant groups are recent organizations, and members are highly involved in the extensive activities of their group. These activities impose a drain on Protestants' income. Mutual aid involves the outlay of money as well as possible aid in emergencies. Also, contributions to church building, financing visits to other churches in the city or country, and helping to maintain a pastor consumes as much as 15 to 20 per cent of a family's budget. In terms of time, the religious activities of these Protestant groups preclude a member from devoting himself to the incessant business activity required for economic success in Guatemala. The organization of their churches and missionary activities often requires individuals to find time in a working day to devote to such concerns. Consequently, many Protestants say that they do not get better-paid and steadier work because it interferes with their religious activities. Thus, because these Protestant groups encompass the lives of their members, economic and social betterment of members is limited by the resources within a group and the commitments it demands. In this respect, joining a Protestant group aids an individual in maintaining himself in the city and slowly improving his social and economic situation until new opportunities and non-religious relationships gradually become available through his work or chance contacts. From an economic and social point of view, joining a Protestant sect is thus a stage in an individual's urban life career. It is a stage that not all will leave.

The social and economic benefits that Protestants accrue from their membership in a Protestant group are of a subtle kind. No Protestant is as economically poor as are several Catholics in the two neighborhoods. Out-of-work Protestants soon find jobs through religious contacts, and consequently the economic position of Protestants is less precarious than that of many Catholics. This is an important advantage to Protestant workers, the majority of whom are self-employed. Protestants dress their children well and are beginning to make slow but steady improvements to their houses. The many activities of these Protestant groups completely provide for the recreational needs of members and give them a defined social position. The whole family of Protestants is involved in these activities, strengthening family bonds in an urban situation where family breakup is a common phenomenon. It is in these broader social benefits that neighborhood Protestants are investing their surplus wealth.

The self-sufficient social relationships among Protestants also determine their political behavior. They do so because they diminish effective contact with Catholics and because they withdraw these neighborhood Protestants from overt participation in urban politics and community organization. Thirty-three per cent of eligible Protestants in my sample voted in the last national elections of Guatemala as against 52 per cent of eligible non-Protestants. In my interviews, even those Protestants who had voted stated that they had only done so because they thought fines would be levied on those who did not vote. Protestants' lack of concern with national politics is reflected in their attitudes to the organization and improvement of their neighborhoods. Protestants in both neighborhoods have generally refused to take part in community betterment organizations even when these have been of a non-political nature. In the ravine neighborhood, not one Protestant has served on a community betterment committee. This has occurred despite attempts of Catholics to persuade Protestants to serve on such committees. These findings cannot be explained by the occupational status of most Protestants. Self-employed Catholics are the most active community and political leaders in both neighborhoods. Likewise in these two neighborhoods, younger age and more recent migration are associated with more active participation in the communities' political life.

Protestants' lack of political participation is due to their enclosed social organization, which leads them to act as a self-contained society within the larger society. Thus they are active as pressure groups in local politics. Neighborhood Protestants have acted as blocking groups against attempts to organize neighbors to improve the community. They refuse to maintain contact with community improvement councils and yet fear that improvement projects will harm their interests by exploiting them financially or taking away their property. They seek to diminish such alleged threats to their well-being by actively sabotaging community-wide organizations. They are sources of unfounded rumors about the financial dishonesty of the improvement committees elected by the neighborhoods. In the last national elections, the various Protestants in the two neighborhoods allied themselves with political groups opposed to existing community improvement organizations. When these opposition political groups gained power and formed new improvement committees, Protestants continued their opposition.

Protestants in these two neighborhoods are thus unsettling forces that add to the divisions within their society. They are so because their social organization keeps them from being dependent on Catholics, and they act as an isolated group with few interests in common with other inhabitants of the city.

Conclusions

I have interpreted the attraction of Protestant groups in the two neighborhoods in terms of the advantages, both moral and practical, that they offer to those without stable contacts in the city and who are exposed to economic and social insecurity. The visible presence of wealth in the city, the accessibility of mass media, and the availability of educational institutions stimulate the aspirations of low-income groups to improve their own and their children's positions. These aspirations are in most cases blocked by a social and economic system which denies opportunities for advancement to the mass of Guatemala's population. Membership in Protestant groups of the type found in these two neighborhoods is one of the few means in Guatemala City by which isolated and aspiring individuals can readily obtain a community of personal contacts, activities, and beliefs that enables them to cope with the problems of urban life. Consequently, these sects serve social as well as religious ends and recruit for secular as well as religious reasons.

It is the social relationships and social organization made available by membership in one of these groups that explains their effects on an individual's economic position and public behavior. The social relationships associated with membership in a particular Protestant group are likely to be useful in, and extendable to, secular activities, whether economic or social. The social range of these relationships and the opportunities available in a given urban situation determine the effect of membership in a Protestant group on an individual's social and economic position. The formal doctrine of these religious groups is, in this respect, less important; for, in Guatemala City, there is an active attempt among most low-income workers to better their position. The will to change their position is there; it is the means that are lacking.

Part Eleven The Future

The immediate prospects for the development of society present a growing concern to many sociologists: these researchers no longer share the confidence of nineteenth-century social scientists who thought that their work would contribute to the rational organization of the enormously expanding powers of man and society, for men today suffer from a sense that there are crucial and pressing dilemmas confronting us, and, in some cases, feel that the time for choice may already be past. There is a deep uncertainty about the future; man seems to have attained, at once, both the power to liberate himself from material scarcity and the capacity to destroy himself and his fellows. It is not even certain that these two abilities are more than the opposite sides of the same coin, for some feel that material abundance can only be a short-term achievement, won at the cost of the destruction of the environment.

Public and private bureaucracies have encouraged the growth of research into the field of social prediction. The military, government and industry must, if they are to work at all, commit themselves to policies for the next several years and must commit human and economic resources to the implementation of these policies: in the face of heavy investment of this kind they seek to render the future calculable so that they may take the likely developments in relevant areas of life into account in decision making. The estimation of demand for goods, the electoral consequences of policies, the results of administrative policies and the shape of military strategy, all provide fields within which professional specialists in the arts and sciences of prediction may find work. Such professionals are increasingly common as the need for more precise characterization of possibilities is more widely felt. They employ more or less elaborate practices in order to divine the prospects for change: through the use of sophisticated mathematical procedures, the exploitation of the expanding capacities of the computer, and the involvement of specialist intellectuals, they attempt to extrapolate present tendencies, simulate contemporary problem situations and depict the most probable consequences of innovation in policy. The work of committees of experts, of 'think-tanks', and of corporations specializing in the study of policy and the future becomes, increasingly, an important factor in the formulation of policies and the making of decisions in, at least, the larger organizations. (The kind of work done by committees of specialists employing such techniques in an investigation of the prospects for disarmament is satirized in J. Doe's *Report from Iron Mountain,* edited by C. Lewin, Macdonald, Penguin, 1968.)

It is, however, coming to be thought that the work of such specialists is too important to be left in their hands, that the thinking behind their work may be imaginative and expert but that it is, fundamentally, the thought of desiccated calculators, lacking human values, sympathies and, even, reason. The specialist in prediction is apt to accept the mandate that he is given; and is likely to bring his talents to bear upon the most absurd, inhumane and distorted ambitions of bureaus and bureaucrats and to search hard for evidence to justify them or ways to effect them. In his attempts to develop his profession and his techniques the specialist in this field is prone to substitute technical considerations, where, his critics feel, moral matters should be. The very language of such experts calls forth criticism; they devise terms like 'megadeath' and 'overkill' which are designed to describe in neutral and unemotional ways the most hideous human situations, involving the death of millions of men, women and children; language of this sort obscures the fact that governments and other agencies are actively considering projects that some find monstrous and it also enables the persons involved in the review of policy to detach and distance themselves from the real nature of the projects they are evaluating. Basically, it is being argued, the specialist treatment of the prospects for the future involves a treatment of the choices before men and their governments as though they were purely technical choices between more or less efficient and effective ways of doing things rather than as the moral choices between basic values that they more usually are. The specialist, in a vital sense, is seen to be irresponsible, for he sacrifices the interests and obligations arising from his citizenship in a society in favour of the narrow pursuit of whatever ends are assigned to him by the organizations for which he works.

The critics do not, of course, suggest that we abandon all concern with the future but, rather, demand that we consider the future in the proper way; instead of allowing experts to work within the framework of ends set by their masters and within the cloak of secrecy that the employing organizations increasingly draw around their employees, we should bring debate into the open where we may consider not just the best means to a particular end but also call the ends themselves into question. The critics demand, too, that the choices be presented to us in such a way that we may see exactly what the choices are, what effects the pursuit of any end will have on the life, death, freedom and well-being of other human beings and, eventually, upon the fate of humanity as a whole.

The kinds of predictions that have been made, even within the last few years, about the future have been very varied indeed, ranging along a scale from extreme optimism to the deepest pessimism, encompassing within their scope the narrowest, policies and the fate of mankind, stretching across long and short spans of time, and focusing upon people as items within a total human population, as consumers of particular goods and as consumers of the total resources of the earth, as victims and survivors of nuclear war, as electors, users of medical and social services and so on. An exhaustive list of predictions numbering only those made by social scientists would be an enormous task and we can only include a very small sampling of writings here. We have chosen to begin with an excerpt from the work of Kahn (Reading 66), whose writings have come to stand as a paradigm of the approach of the professional predictor. Kahn is prepared to 'think about the unthinkable', is willing to examine the possible consequences of any social, political or military strategy and to calculate the cost of each strategy in terms of the likelihood that it will result in a greater or lesser loss of human life; he is convinced that any problem can and should be approached in a rational way and that when we are faced with an appalling set of possibilities we should nonetheless attempt to analyse them with a view to choosing the most advantageous of them. His critics feel that Kahn's emphasis upon 'realism', upon facing realistically the situation and its possibilities, is of the kind that C. Wright Mills called 'crackpot realism'. Kahn seems to be committed to acceptance of the ends specified by governments and bureaucracies, and seems unable to recognize that moral issues are deeply involved in the problems that he considers and that the pursuit of a narrow, national interest may not be the most effective strategy from a broader point of view. De Kadt (Reading 67) presents some arguments about nuclear war that are intended as a critique of the kind of thinking that Kahn and others like him are prepared to engage in.

The likelihood of nuclear war is no longer the matter of intense concern that it was only a few years ago; the Campaign for Nuclear Disarmament in Britain is almost defunct, and there are no analogous movements elsewhere in the world, even though nuclear weapons development continues apace. The threat of nuclear war is present and presumably in the back of people's minds, but it does not command the centre of attention at the present time: happenings *inside* the more advanced and less developed societies are more immediately involving.

The possibility that revolutionary changes might take place in highly industrialized society, a possibility that was considered almost wholly unlikely at the time of the campaigns against the Bomb, is now seriously considered. Hall (Reading 68) examines the Hippie Movement as an omen for the future, examining it as a response by some of society's members to the inadequate quality of life in a society that is able to provide material security.

Perhaps more than any other work, Herbert Marcuse's *One-Dimensional Man: The Ideology of Industrial Society*, (Beacon Press), from which we are unfortunately unable to make an excerpt, has encouraged us to think positively about the potential available in industrialized societies for the liberation of man from the restriction imposed by limitations of material resources and, consequently, for an expansion of human creative activity. Yet this potential is so far denied because our technology is so often used in anti-human ways. In one sense, Marcuse, then, is an optimist; in another – since he sees no serious or immediate agency in advanced capitalist society likely to achieve such changes – he is pessimistic.

Turning to the under-developed world, Worsley in Reading 69 examines the condition of the Third World in the post-war period during which time there has been as emphasis upon the modernization and industrialization of the post-colonial society: he is doubtful that programmes for development have been as sincerely devoted to their explicit aim as they might have appeared, is sure that they have not succeeded, and is not hopeful that they will have any great success in the future. It may be that efforts to model the Third World after the examples of the other two capitalist and Communist worlds are destined to fail because they are based on the wrong strategies and assumptions. Endogenous solutions, such as the Chinese Communists achieved, may be the only solutions.

In the last few years a concern with ecological systems has been growing and the interconnection of all societies within a single world ecological system has been stressed: we include a deeply pessimistic scenario describing the social and natural disasters that might be expected within the next few years as population growth, the increasingly rapid consumption of natural resources, and increasing pollution, discussed by Mitchell, plus growing political tensions, generate an explosive situation. Ehrlich's grim sketch of development (Reading 70) is fictional, but as he notes 'is firmly based on fact and, in a sense, we're already a long way into this scenario. Everything mentioned as happening before 1967 has actually occurred; much of the rest is based on projection of trends already appearing' (see

Ehrlich's book *The Population Bomb*, Pan Books, 1971).

Finally, we include a discussion by Chomsky (Reading 71) of the responsibility of the intellectual within society, an essay in which Chomsky denies that one can separate one's social responsibilities from one's scholarly analyses of socio-political situations.

66 Herman Kahn

On Thermonuclear War

Excerpt from Herman Kahn, *On Thermonuclear War*, Princeton University Press; reprinted by Oxford University Press, 1960, pp. 558–64.

Thermonuclear war seems so horrible that it is difficult for most people to imagine that such events can – and do – occur. People have a belief, conscious or unconscious, that an all-out war is impossible – *inconceivable* would be a more accurate word. Peace-loving people believe, in effect, that the invention of fission and fusion bombs has abolished war. (One only wishes he could agree.) They believe this because they desperately want to believe it. I suspect that any moderately prudent man who examined the situation objectively would conclude that it is extremely optimistic to ignore the possibility of war or threat of war; at the same time this moderately prudent man might ignore many things which are possible but extremely unlikely – that is to say, the possibilities we are talking about are not 'worst cases' which only pedants or narrow professionals worry about.

We should also remember that historically we did not acquire this large military establishment to deter a direct attack on the United States, but to defend Europe and Asia. Even if we have adequate Type 1 Deterrence and Counterforce as Insurance we still need Type 2 and Type 3 Deterrence. Even if one accepts the balance-of-terror theory and believes that we do not have to worry about a deliberate Soviet attack on the United States, we are still faced with important strategic problems. In 1914 and 1939 it was the British who came to feel they had to declare war – not the Germans. The Germans would have been delighted to see the British sit the war out. Such a circumstance might arise again. If the balance of terror were totally reliable we would be as likely to be deterred from striking the Soviets as they would be from striking us. We must still be able to fight and survive wars just as long as it is possible to have such a capability. Not only is it prudent to take out insurance against a war occurring unintentionally, but we must also be able to stand up to the threat of fighting or, credibly, to threaten to initiate a war ourselves – unpleasant though this sounds and is. We must at least make it risky for the enemy to force us into situations in which we must choose between fighting and appeasing. We must have an 'alternative to peace', so long as there is no world government and it is technologically and economically possible to have such an alternative. This 'alternative to peace' must include a general war capability as well as a limited war capability.

Under current programs the United States may in a few years find itself unwilling to accept a Soviet retaliatory blow, no matter what the provocation. To get into such a situation would be equivalent to disowning our alliance obligations by signing what would amount to a nonaggression treaty with the Soviets – a nonaggression treaty with almost 200 million American hostages to guarantee performance. Before drifting into such an 'alliance', we should ask ourselves: What does it mean to live with this nonaggression treaty? Can we prevent it from being 'signed'? Can we delay its 'ratification'? Those who would rely on limited means to control possible Soviet provocations must ask themselves the question, What keeps the enemy's counteraction to acceptable limits if there are no credible Type 2 Deterrence capabilities?

Those who think of very limited capabilities or mutual-homicide threats either separately or in combination as being sufficient to meet our Type 3 Deterrence problems are ignoring the dynamics of bargaining and conflict situations. When two men or two nations are arguing over something that both feel to be important it is common for things to get out of control, for prestige to become committed, and for threats and counterthreats and actions and counteractions to increase in almost limitless intensity – that is, unless there are internal or external sanctions to set and enforce limits.

These remarks will distress all who very properly view the thought of fighting a war with so much horror they feel uneasy at having even a high-quality deterrent force, much less a credible capability for initiating, fighting, and terminating all kinds of wars. I can sympathize with this attitude. But I believe it borders on the irresponsible.

The threat of force has long been an important regulatory factor in international affairs; one cannot remove or greatly weaken this threat without expecting all kinds of unforeseen changes – not all of them necessarily for the better. It is true that many of the measures that preserve our ability to fight and survive wars may turn out to be temporary expedients. They may not solve our long-run security problems. But this hardly means they are not important. You cannot reach 1970 or 1975 if you do not successfully pass through 1960 and 1965. If we neglect our short-term problems, we are bound to run serious risks of a disastrous deterioration in the international situation or in our own posture. This in turn may make it impossible to arrive at a reasonable, stable state.

In fact, insofar as the balance-of-terror theory is correct, if any nation actually becomes militarily provocative, then no matter what our previous threats have been we must meet that behavior by using limited means, or we will simply allow that nation to get away with whatever it is trying to do. The aggressor will realize this too, and he will gain confidence from the realization. For this reason any attempt to use threats of mutual homicide to control an aggressor's behavior (short of trying to deter him from an attack on one's own country) is ill-advised. Even if one intends his threat seriously, it will still not be credible to the enemy or ally – particularly if the challenge is ambiguous in any way. If this view of the mutual homicide threat is correct, then we need other external controls to coerce the Soviets in any conflicts that may arise. To depend on their exercising internal controls when there is a conspicuous gap in the range of our capabilities seems to me to be wishful thinking. To be able to take only very limited action or steps leading to mutual annihilation does leave a conspicuous gap which the Soviets may try to exploit – either in a crisis or even in cold blood.

There is another problem that arises if we should not have the ability to fight and survive a war. Insofar as the mutual homicide view is not correct and only one of us believes that it is, or insofar as it should prove correct but one or both of us have not fully assimilated the meaning of this notion, we are still likely to stumble into war as the result of miscalculation – much as World War I started. In either case, it seems to be very dangerous to assume away some of our most important military problems by placing excessive faith in the quality and capabilities of existing and programmed Type 1 Deterrence forces and the range of situations that such forces will be able to handle, arguing that the important problems now lie in the nonmilitary or limited war arenas and saying that other preparations can be neglected.

It is of some importance to comprehend the complete range of our military problems before they reach the crisis stage – in some cases years before they reach that stage. This Reading is dedicated to an attempt to anticipate such crises and, more importantly, to create an intellectual environment in which potential and hypothetical crises are seriously and critically examined while there is still time to program corrective measures.

I have conceded that as technology advances it is quite possible that technical validity may be given the common picture of a war in which both sides can easily be destroyed – irrespective of the preparations that are made before the war. Doomsday Machines may be built (but it is most unlikely that they will be connected up to a high-speed computer). Even then, unless we are willing to surrender we must at least make preparations to fight wars carefully. If a war occurs it might be the desire of both parties to fight it 'carefully'. Even the *façade* of being able and willing, under duress, to fight a war might produce enough uncertainty in a potential aggressor's mind of our intentions or behaviour that he would not be able to afford to make the most unambiguous and provocative types of challenges.

Many people seem to have adopted the following rather curious set of views. They are perfectly willing to concede that if there were no H-bombs or atomic bombs in the world we might then expect the Russians to behave very badly; they admit that we or our allies might then be called upon to use violence in order to restrain Russian behavior. Many of these same people believe that the chance of being called on to use violence somehow gets smaller as the credibility that it will be used gets smaller. This belief is based upon a notion (imprecisely formulated, but influential) that the risks of violence are symmetrical and that the Russians will inevitably be deterred from misbehaving. This does not take into account the fact that over the years both nations are going to learn that acts of provocation get safer and safer. (The nations will learn it even more than did the Europeans from 1871 to 1914, because there will exist a theory that this is, after all, a correct view of the world.)

Many people think it important to emphasize the horror and impracticability of thermonuclear war. Then they instill a sense of urgency that we must settle our survival problem by peaceful means. Temptation will be removed from any adventurers. But a problem immediately arises. If this program of deterrence-by-exaggeration is to be successful, it must be mutual and reliable. If the West alone is subjected to a continuous barrage of the automatic mutual annihilation theory, this cannot help but tempt us to drop our guard. Insofar as the mutual annihilation theory is correct – and understood to be so by both sides – this is not serious; but insofar as the theory is not correct, it can be dreadfully dangerous for us to be negligent. In addition, as I keep pointing out, mutual belief in the automatic annihilation theory is an open invitation to Munich-type blackmail. Therefore, to the extent that the theory may not be true, we should avoid deliberately weakening ourselves to the point where we cannot withstand such tactics.

We must take the military problem seriously, treating it as a military problem rather than one whose primary importance lies in the prewar impact on budgets, foreign relations, domestic politics, international prestige, the business cycle, and the like – that is, we must begin thinking of thermonuclear war as something which may have to be fought or deterred by an objective capability, rather than as a sort of nightmare which is banished by the possession in peacetime of a system which can deliver bombs (the Minimum Deterrence position). It is almost incredibly difficult for even planners and experts to do so. Most of us simply do not believe in war, or at least in *deliberate* thermonuclear war, and most people also find it hard to worry concretely about accidents and miscalculations. However, it is my belief that our almost complete reliance on deterrence working is probably an example of frivolity or wishful thinking.

In any geographical area where it became known that there was one chance in a hundred of a hurricane or an earthquake, one would find that many concessions would be made, affecting almost all activities, to meet the risk presented by these potential hurricanes and earthquakes. Inhabitants take out insurance; they build their houses to make them more resistant; they build special cellars; they put up warning systems. All these things are done without any notion of deterring this hypothetical event, but in the hope of actually alleviating it and being in a reasonable position after the situation has occurred. Some will try various forms of prayer or incantation to deter or avert, but even the most religious or superstitious will know that such preparations are incomplete. While one can presumably put more faith in the notion of deterrence in the military field, even an imprudent person should be unwilling to place all bets on deterrence working, so long as there are reasonable ways to hedge the bet. The race with the enemy involves much more than prestige and a sort of polite make-believe bluffing. The competition is deadly serious, simply because the equipment that is being bought may be used, and because it makes a world of difference how it is used.

Even those who are bemused with the intellectual simplicity and logic of pure deterrence as a solution to our military problems and have very few qualms about our current position should be willing to hedge their bets by buying what I have called a Pre-attack Mobilization Base. This would enable our country to obtain very rapidly the capabilities it will need if the international situation ever deteriorates. Very few – even of the more optimistic – would be willing to depend upon our current posture (or our future posture as indicated by current programs) as an adequate means of handling a Hitler-type of opponent. But even Hitler took about four or five years to move from relatively innocuous challenges to ones that put the issue of major appeasement or fighting a war squarely up to his opponents. It is not likely that we will again have four or five years of relatively unambiguous warning. But if the international situation does take a serious turn for the worse we may have one or two years, and it would seem to be simple prudence to have the capability to use such warning. I have already discussed the possibility that having this capability could in itself have a decided deterring effect on potential Hitlers or other types of gamblers. Many suggestions [. . .] are partly or wholly concerned with preparations for a part of such a Pre-attack Mobilization Base. It is hard for me to believe that any person who takes a serious long-range view would be unwilling to see our government spend hundreds of millions of dollars a year on such preparations for survival. The future peaceful course of international relations is just not that certain. However, the Pre-attack Mobilization Base should not be relied on for Type 1 Deterrence except to provide additional insurance.

It should supplement our Type 2 Deterrence and our capability to fight either limited or general wars. Type 1 Deterrence is too important to depend on strategic warning or on wishful thinking.

67 Emanuel J. de Kadt

The Bomb: Uncertainty and Disaster

Excerpt from Emanuel J. de Kadt, *British Defence Policy and Nuclear War*, Cass, 1964, pp. 25–9.

In academic circles discussion has already moved beyond the conception of general nuclear war. The latest answer to the problem of the use of nuclear weapons (as opposed to their function as deterrents) has been sought in the doctrine of Limited Strategic War. This is a very different strategy from the tactical use of nuclear weapons. The basic idea of limited strategic war is the following. Under certain circumstances of Soviet (or American?) provocation or aggression the US (USSR) would direct a very small number of nuclear weapons (perhaps only one) in a first strike against the Soviet Union, (United States). The object of such a strike would not be to gain a military advantage, such as would be gained by eliminating all or a substantial part of its opponent's nuclear capability. The strike would be launched in order to gain a political advantage. It would be an attempt to strengthen one's bargaining position by showing resolve to react to the provocation and by indicating one's willingness to raise the stakes further should the opponent retaliate. But the very object would be to attempt to prevent the other side from responding in kind. On the contrary it would be hoped that the strike would make him lower the stakes on his part by retreating from the provocative position. The fact that vast nuclear power lies behind the probing shot is an important element of the strategy.

Limited nuclear war is thus essentially part of a bargaining process in which blows and counter-blows are exchanged. It postulates as the first blow in such a process a provocation by one's opponent. The counter-blow is essentially a warning signal, a symbol of one's determination not to accept the opponent's attempt to change the *status quo*. Such a bargaining strike may take a number of forms. At one end of the scale one could conceive of the detonation of a small nuclear weapon on an unpopulated Soviet island somewhere in the Arctic. Next the suggestions go that a missile might be directed at an isolated dam or air-base, or possibly at a gaseous diffusion plant. Or one could shoot a missile off at Moscow with a small nuclear warhead and explode it at great altitude, perhaps merely breaking a few windows, or the warhead could be replaced by a container filled with leaflets.[1] Finally such a limited strategy could 'take out a city', presumably after an ultimatum had been delivered to the opponent to 'back down, or else . . .'. This ultimatum would serve as a warning, enabling him to evacuate his city in case he preferred not to back down but to see what would happen, possibly after uttering a counter-ultimatum of his own. Limited strategic war, then, is essentially in the eyes of its analysts a war of risk-taking and of intimidation. It attempts to counter the provocations of an opponent by biting into his resolve, rather than by attrition of his military forces.[2] It searches for a way to overcome the strategic nuclear stalemate and to find a use for nuclear weapons much in the classic sense meant by von Clausewitz when he spoke of war as an extension of policy by other means.

The crucial question with limited strategic strikes is, obviously, whether they succeed in actually lowering the stakes involved, or whether escalation will occur early and quickly. A situation in which there is only one strike, the original show of resolve, is certainly not impossible. But neither is it inconceivable that the opponent responds. In that case he, in turn, is likely to raise the stakes a little in order to show *his* resolve, or he may even promise to raise the stakes as soon as he receives the ultimatum: the first party is then faced with the dilemma whether to strike at all. This limited raising of the stakes, say from one air-base to two, or from a small city to a large one, and then to two large ones, cannot go on for long. It may come to an early end, while the parties search for a political settlement. It may also soon escalate, in which case a spasm response seems more likely than a controlled response: a full-scale pre-emptive strike may suddenly look terribly attractive.

Limited strategic war, then, more than any other strategy, depends on and appeals to the inherent rationality of the opponents. It attempts, as Kaplan points out, to induce the opponents to think in cooperative rather than in competitive ways. Unless they do so, unless they find some common interest in limiting the exchange, they will almost certainly destroy each other. So far past experience has given us no reasons to assume with Goldstein and Miller that 'the men at the panic-buttons'

1. The effects of a high altitude burst may not be as harmless as is here suggested, particularly in respect to the possibility of serious eye damage.
2. Recently Schelling has suggested that even the *tactical* use of nuclear weapons should be regarded in this manner. There too the focus should be, in terms of timing, target selection and control, on the bargaining effect – not on the military effect. The introduction of tactical nuclear weapons should be seen as conveying a message, the message namely that we are willing to risk general nuclear war.

have the temperament of 'paranoic poker addicts' rather than of 'shrewd chess players'. But the assumptions of rationality and cold-bloodedness figure so prominently in limited strategic war, that to call them into question at all degrades the 'attractiveness' of this posture considerably. Many of the close students of the strategy stress, after concluding that it is nonetheless preferable to all-out nuclear war, the enormous uncertainties and risks with which it is fraught.

The problems of communication are also quite formidable. It is far from certain that the actual *intent* of the strike can be adequately conveyed to the opponent or that he will believe the statements made. Instead of accepting the strike as a bargaining counter he may see it in fact as a prelude to all-out war, and respond in terms of his own, very different, definition of the situation. A sobering thought of Schelling's is further that it pays to seem less rather than more rational in the 'game', for your opponent will be all the more circumspect if you appear to be 'flying off the handle'. A similar idea is expressed by Kahn in his discussion of the 'game of nuclear chicken'.

There is, of course, an additional consideration. Strategies and strategic studies modelled on some type of interpersonal relationship, be it game or conflict, assume that in the model we may substitute 'players' – rational individuals – for states. In our own discussion this practice has often been followed. It is hard not to succumb to the frame of reference imposed by an on-going discussion. But one must recognize the limitations of such a frame of reference, however convenient it may be to continue using it in many circumstances. One of these limitations exists in respect to the indivisibility of the national poker players. States are not like persons; they are made up of many individuals and groups who attempt to influence events in one way or another. Even the behaviour of governments is in many respects hardly comparable to that of individuals. The more the actions flowing from our nuclear strategies must be considered as tests of nerves, or as exercises in risk taking, bargaining or brinkmanship, the greater becomes the importance of extraneous influences on the decision makers. This is particularly the case in democratic societies, where the free expression of dissent with government policy is possible. The limited strategic war 'players' just cannot afford to ignore what Abt and Pool call the constraint of public attitudes, and they might well find their position substantially weakened *vis-à-vis* a determined autocratic adversary.

One can hardly conclude that this latest attempt at formulating a nuclear strategy has been a success. Limited strategic war is slightly less riddled with logical inconsistencies than its predecessors. But although perhaps less *illogical* and more internally consistent than some of the earlier options it is hardly more *workable*. The rules of the game are not hard and fast, while the opponents may well not be playing the same game in the first place. The uncertainties remain, with their possibly disastrous consequences.

68 Stuart Hall

The Hippies: Dissent in America

Excerpts from Stuart Hall, 'The hippies: An "American" moment', in Julian Nagel (ed.), *Student Power*, Merlin Press, 1969, pp. 173–89, 200–201.

Most sub-cultures tend to dramatize the gap between their own 'worlds' and the worlds of 'others' in language. Hippie phrases constitute a complex *argot,* drawn eclectically from Negro culture, from the jazz and pop worlds, from homosexual and hip slang, from the addict sub-cultures, from the idiomatic language of the street, the city and Bohemia. The slogans are striking, linguistically, especially for two aspects: their emphasis on the continuous-present tense – 'grooving', 'balling', 'tripping', 'mind blowing', etc., and their prepositional flavour – 'turn *on*', 'freak-*out*', 'be-*in*', 'love-*in*', 'cop-*out*', 'put-*on*', '*up*tight', 'where it's *at*'. The style of phrasing appears to be *existential* and *situational*.

One can explore this matter of language further by looking at one slogan which came as near as anything to symbolizing the Hippie way of life: that is the phrase coined by Dr Timothy Leary, *'Turn on, tune in and drop out'.* Each phrase in that slogan is both a direct injunction and a submerged metaphor. To 'turn on', literally invites the Hippie to switch to the use of mind-expanding drugs, and to turn on as many other members of the straight society as he can reach. But, metaphorically, it means to switch (in the sense of turning the dials on a TV set) to a more authentic mode of experience, to leave the safe routes of middle class society, for more private, apocalyptic channels. To 'tune in' means, literally, to 'attune' oneself to another way of life: but it is also, like the first phrase, a submerged metaphor drawn from the mass media. There is, the phrase suggests, more than one 'channel of perception' through which we experience the world. The trouble with straight society is that it is tuned in to the 'wrong station' and thus getting the wrong message or signal. If we were to switch wavelengths we might begin to receive messages from 'underground', intimations from unexplored inner spaces. 'Drop out' is perhaps the most complex message of all in its associative meaning. Again, it means, literally, that the Hippie should reject the structures of middle class experience, the way of life oriented towards work, power, status, consumption – goals which have been discredited within the counter-value system of Hippie sub-culture. The Hippie is a 'drop out' from the system for which family, education and socialization have been grooming him: he actively 'opts in' to the 'deviant' round of life. But the phrase 'drop out' has a more precise social and political reference. Drop-outs are also early school and college-leavers, rejects of the school system or self-absentees from college, who find the whole system of education and training meaningless. In the first instance, 'drop outs' were early-leavers, Goodman's 'absurds', who felt alienated from school or couldn't meet the grades or didn't choose to keep up the pace. Leary's phrase therefore tries to establish an identification between the hippies and this rejected social group. The identification is largely symbolic, of course, since by and large the Hippies are recruited, *not* from educational rejects but from the brighter, academically more promising, middle-class students. If they have given up on formal education, it is not because they were alienated by the school's tasks or because their home environment was poor or their learning situation unsupported, but because, in some more symbolic sense, they find the whole 'educational bit' irrelevant [. . .] The association with educational rejects is only one of a complex series of identifications with groups of the deprived or disadvantaged celebrated in Hippie sub-culture. If we were to compare American hippies with their British counterparts, the most striking fact would be the degree of, and emphasis upon, *assumed* poverty among the Americans, the identification with 'the poor' [. . .]

The poor are only the most obvious group in a wider circle of the disadvantaged with whom the Hippies emotionally identify. In part, this is a matter of shared or overlapping life-experiences. In their escape from middle-class suburbia, in their search for cheaper places to live and areas of the city where social controls are less rigidly exercised, Hippies are driven to share those locales where other groups and sections of the so-called 'disorganized' have already clustered. More important, however, is the identity which Hippies feel with all those whom 'straight society' has labelled 'deviant', outside the norms and expectations of respectability. To be labelled 'deviant' is to accept a social identity and the possibilities of a social career which passes beyond the rules and conventions of 'the system'. Those situations, identities and careers which the society has labelled 'deviant' are precisely those which the Hippies value most highly. This is one of the many symbolic ways in which Hippies attempt to subvert and reverse the conventional legitimations of society [. . .]

Even the poor are not far down or far out enough. The poor are disadvantaged socially, but they are often respectable they are rarely exotic. An even more powerful identification, therefore, is made with the culture, costume and spirit of the American Indian. Serapes, bells, beads, headbands, moccasins – these are central features of Hippie costume. The lines of connection between Indian culture and Hippie sub-culture are really very complex. American Indians stand, of course, as an emblem of the simple, a primitive survival on the continent of affluence and technological sophistication. They also represent the way white outsiders exploited the native peoples of the American continent. American Indians are therefore one among the several deprived and exploited social groups with whom young people in general, and Hippies in particular, tend to identify. (Even before the rise of the Hippies, Mexico stood to the itinerant student generation in a strong symbolic relation.) The disadvantaged groups include, as we have suggested, social deviants of all sorts – addicts, educational rejects and the poor. There is one striking omission to that list: the blacks. This is all the more striking if, for a moment, we look back to that group of premature hippies of an earlier period, the Original Beat Generation [. . .] Mailer called the hip generation 'white negroes'. My case is that the American Negro is no longer 'available' in these terms to the Hippie. He is no longer living out his life in some submerged night-time suburb of the imagination of white America. The ghettoes still stand, of course: but through Civil Rights, the Black Muslim movement, Afro-American nationalism, the ghetto rebellions, the rhetoric of Malcolm X, Elijah Muhammed, Stokeley Carmichael and Rap Brown, and finally, Black Power, the Negro has reached for and achieved, it not a real, then certainly a potential imaginative liberation from the cultural imperialism of white racist and white fellow-traveller alike. The remaining lines of contact between black and white society have been severely ruptured. The Hippies cannot, then, find a sympathetic counter-culture in the orbit of black ghetto life: and any attempt to do so would be regarded by most black militants as another of the multiple forms of cultural patronage which white society still pays to black. Hippie society is, therefore, strikingly, a part of white America [. . .]

The theme of withdrawal from the active to the passive mode (with or without the use of drugs) is to be traced, not only in the Hippie feel for Indian culture, but also in their interest in the more mystical philosophies and art of the 'other' Indians and peoples of the Orient.

The themes of mysticism and contemplation overlap with the implicit pastoral-arcadian spirit of Hippie culture. The move to the West Coast and San Francisco – the land of the never-ending surf-ride – is itself an aspect of this pastoralism, though one should not forget the Hippie enclaves of Toronto, the East Village in New York and elsewhere. So is the attempt to set up utopian communities which has attracted so many

Hippies, and led to the founding of truly separatist, functioning agricultural communities of California kibbutzim. So too is the fondness for Tolkien's Hobbits and the fairyland of Cockayne. But despite the retreat to pastoral settings, I would suggest that this motif is better understood as [. . .] an attempt to build up an arcadian enclave within the heart of city life, thereby combining two powerful cultural impulses: rural simplicity and modernity. Hippie pastoralism is the dream of urban arcadia.

There is, of course, another aspect to arcadianism and that is communal sharing. The Hippie group which has taken this arcadian communism to its most extreme lengths is the group known as the Diggers, who operate a Free Store where clothes, food and furniture is freely available, who run a number of free 'pads' for itinerant hippies and distribute free food in the afternoon in San Francisco's Panhandle district [. . .] But on the whole, the pastoral/arcadianism of the Hippies marks a return to the self-sufficient simplicty of the separate community which has made its appearance so strongly from time to time in American culture; a view that life in its simpler forms and settings can be pared back to the bare essentials, and thus is counter-posed to the frenzy, the stimulated wants and consumer anxieties of a modern technological civilization; the desire to recreate within industrial and urban America the peace and gentle cohesiveness of the tribal community. No wonder the issue, in summer 1967, of a stamp bearing the head of David Thoreau was an occasion for celebration in Hippie circles.

It is difficult to use the phrase 'tribal community' without thinking of that other phrase, 'the global village'. And although most Hippies are in revolt against the pseudo-psychic-togetherness of the mass media, there is no doubt that deep in the value structure of Hippie life is the desire to counterpose to the individualism and competitiveness of American life a new kind of togetherness. Hippie scenes openly express this loosely organized communalism. So do the interest in Eastern philosophies, which has at its centre the notion of the all-embracing unity which underlies the varied multiplicity of life, the resolution of the Many in the One [. . .]

It is in this context that I raise the question of Love – in some ways the central motif of Hippie immanent philosophy. The Love being spoken of implies more than the lowering of sexual constraints, the so-called sexual permissiveness of Hippie life. It goes without saying that Love, where it exists, is not only not repressed – it is freely and openly celebrated. But in the Hippie alphabet, Love stands for something wider and more inclusive than sex. It is a complex affirmation. It has a widening circle of resonances. First, it is a liberation from the repressive taboos of middle-class life, which surround sexual experience. Secondly, Love stands for the physical and spiritual community between men and men. Thirdly, Love stands for an inclusive and receptive tenderness to others, a sacred respect for personal relationships (in a world where personal relationships are fragile and contingent). Fourthly, there is the all-embracing love for mankind, naïve and vulnerable in its apparent simplicity, but transformed, in Hippie philosophy, into a sort of silent power. It is hard to define the resonance of this word accurately, since it both includes sexual relations between and within the sexes, but, at the same time, transcends – even, critics would say, evades – the fully developed genital sexuality common to post-Freudian generations. It is a commonplace that young Hippie couples, holding hands in that open and disarming way, remind one most of children guiding one another through the woods – though, admittedly, they are children who are sleeping with one another. It has long been a standing joke that young men and women are steadily coming to look more and more like one another, an observation interpreted by those attached to more virile and aggressive models of sexual identity as a trend, among young men, towards effeminacy. What seems closer to the truth is that there is a change in the definitions of, and a greater fluidity between, 'masculine' and 'feminine'; a fluidity which comes to rest, temporarily, in a curiously pre-pubertal or pre-genital stasis. Certainly the aggressive, activist, dominant, instrumental virtues attached to the established cultural definitions of the male identity are undermined in this world. But certain aspects of the commonly accepted definitions of 'adulthood' seem also to be sloughed off along with certain definitions of 'masculinity' [. . .]

The word Love, then, connects with the other themes – with simplicity and innocence, with togetherness and tribalism. But it also has a different inflection, a wider reach. Only the Hippies and their generational counterparts could have coined the phrase 'Zap Them With Love'. The phrase stands opposed to one of the most brutally flip phrases to emerge from the Vietnam war – the game of picking off VC guerrillas from the air, known familiarly as 'Zapping the Cong'.

In strong contrast to the purposive, instrumental, goal-driven and emotionally-controlled way of managing the self and social relations in a modern technological society, the Hippies celebrate open expressiveness and the gratification of wishes and desires in the here and now. Their emphasis on expressiveness is a counter-thrust to the bottling up of emotions and the role-doubling which they feel to be so central a part of the dominant personality types of modern American society. The immediate gratification of desires – the injunction to 'do your own thing – now' – is a latent attempt to deny the historicity and the causality of human society. Just as the past can be sloughed off – we can learn to free ourselves from anxious routines and controls – so very little can be postponed to the future, since the future, too, is open-ended and undefined. Hippies are 'drop-outs from history' (as Fiedler comments) – but also, dropouts from the long future. What is left, what is real, is total self-expression and authenticity in the here and now. Life is a loosely-organized series of unplanned 'happenings', with the stress on the immediacy, the spontaneous participation and the free-form expressiveness of the response [. . .]

Love, I suggested, is a certain kind of power. Its emblem in the world is the flower. Love is 'flower power'. The flower carries with it the multiple associations which we have seen to be common to other Hippie symbols. It stands for the colourful, the gay, the pleasurable. It stands for the natural, the wild, the primitive. It stands for the pastoral, the utopian, the Arcadian. It stands for the beautiful. It stands for the senses against the reign of intellect. It stands for the rich colour spectrum of psychedelic art. It stands for the flowering cannabis, the sacred plants and roots from which the hallucinogens are distilled. 'God', the Hippies remind us, 'grows his own.' But it also stands for the tenderness, the openness, the gentleness and receptivity with which Hippies hope to confront and unmask the power and authority structures of civil society. When the police – the Hippies' inveterate foe – turn nasty, find, they say, a little love in your heart for them. Love is the symbol of a new kind of passive resistance. It may be too much even in the Hippie code of ethics to ask anyone to love the cops; but it helps to give them a bunch of daffodils. The state, the police, the military-industrial complex, war, brutality, authority, civil order – all these structures, Hippies argue, are sanctioned by violence. And those who try to challenge 'the System' directly and overthrow it, counterpose one type of violence to another: they get caught in a collective trap. The Hippies mean, not to conquer but to transcend the confrontation, by smothering all *that* sort of power in a riot of blooms [. . .]

There are many observers of the Hippie scene who believe that all the talk about 'blowing the mind' is an elaborate rationalization for a depraved and dangerous social habit. No doubt there is some element of rationalization. For many Hippies, drug-taking probably carries no deep philosophic implication: it is simply the insignia of entry into the group, a sort of required conformity. There is also an element of contrived confrontation, since not only does widespread drug-taking bring in its wake the police and the narcotics squad – thereby ritualizing the gulf between the Hippies and the rest and confirming their position 'outside' society, but it has a way of bringing middle class taboos out into the open. Middle-class society has its own tolerated drugs – alcohol and tobacco – but denies even cannabis, which has never been proved to be more harmful than smoking, to the Hippies. Thus drug-taking as an element in the Hippie way of life has the added attraction of demonstrating how artificial are the established boundaries to that moral code which society takes to be 'right' and 'natural'.

But essentially, the case for the use of mind-expanding drugs in Hippie culture has to be understood in different terms. The greatest damage perpetrated by the middle-class way of life upon American people, in their view, is that it has constrained and confined them to a narrow, inauthentic spectrum of feeling and perception. We cut off and repress all those modes of experiencing the world – dream, fantasy, hallucination, trance, exaltation, vision, madness – which we cannot incorporate into the (in Blakean terms) 'single vision' of our work-driven, task-orientated, problem-solving, goal-oriented world. But beyond these strict and patrolled confines of the modern versions of the Protestant Ethic, lie ways of experiencing the self and others 'in depth', ways of achieving rapport with nature, colour, sound, of communicating with 'inner space'. There is only one way to recover this rich, hidden utopia within the self: through the medium of mind-expanding drugs. Others by long discipline and the practice of asceticism have managed to enter these forbidden realms of feeling: hence the interest in meditation and the mystical religions of the East. But Hippies are in too much of a hurry, and disciplined asceticism too alien, for more than a very dedicated minority to take the long route to inner space through contemplation, when there is available the short trip via LSD or the other hallucinogens [. . .]

Having spoken of the elements of tribalism within Hippie culture, it may seem paradoxical to speak of its extreme individualism. Yet behind the collective withdrawal, the fraternal arcadianism, the spontaneous community of Hippie culture lies buried an extreme variant of American individualism. This individualism has many roots. In part it springs from the idealization of the spontaneous, the fluid, unstructured, unsequential quality to experience – the approximation of life to 'the happening' – which is so characteristic of Hippie styles of action. In part, it is a protest against the over-managed, over-directed, over-routinized character of middle class life – a revolt against the model of the 'organization man' and the 'organized life' which is the archetype or paradigm of success in the square world. In part, it springs from an assertion of the primacy of the imperatives of self as against the claims of society. But in part Hippie individualism is also rooted in the same soil as the American Constitution and the manifold myths of the free-enterprise, every-man-his-own-President society. From these roots many wild and contradictory variants have flowered – populism, agrarian utopianism, frontierism, free enterprise capitalism, resistance to the gun law, and the cowboy, to name but a few. The Hippies are yet another, even wilder, blossoming of the same secret ideal: the essentially American dream of innocence: free and single men in the open air [. . .]

The Hippies are voyagers, explorers, adventurers of the under-soul, the subterranean caverns, the unconscious sub-life of the revolutionary moment [. . .] In their present form then, they are doomed to disappear. So long as the dialectical trajectory of the movement lasts, these two poles, the expressive and the activist, will continue to appear and disappear, absorbing and taking forward those things incompletely defined in one 'moment' into the next. The subtle mutation of the pure Hippie style into the 'mixed' Yippie style in the year of the Presidential election is a regressive-progressive movement of just this kind. There will be more reversals to follow. The 'meaning' of the Hippies for the movement is *not* defined by their capacity to survive intact as a separate formation, but precisely their capacity to flow back into and through the fluid forms which revolutionary activity continues to take in this pre-revolutionary ferment. But, despite their tendency to break up under the pressure of events, they 'project' for the whole movement some future forms even from within and through the negative distortions and experience of the present [. . .] These 'possible solutions' are, of course, as yet *utopian*, for the societal context in which real solutions could be offered to real, emergent problems is precisely what, in the confrontation between the movement and the system, is being contested. Yet it is in Utopia that future possibilities are rehearsed. Hippie life is precisely such a negative rehearsal for the future [. . .]

69 Peter Worsley

Aid or Revolution?

Excerpt from Peter Worsley, 'Problems of the have-not world', in M. Cunliffe (ed.), *The Times History of Our Times*, Weidenfeld & Nicolson, 1971, pp. 43–61.

The sixties was the decade of the most significant failure of all in terms of collective efforts on an international scale to abolish world poverty without radical transformation of established political and social structures, for this was the 'development decade' that never took place. Nor is there any good reason to assume that the second 'development decade' will be any more effective.

In so far as this failure has been a failure of aid policy, some examination of the philosophy and practice of aid is called for. It is no vulgar cynicism to observe that aid is not philanthropy. It is a form of social exchange, to understand which the economists' way of working out the costs and benefits is quite inadequate. What is exchanged certainly includes capital, material goods and services; what is much more crucial is the maintenance or creation of an interdependence, both economic and political, that has consequences for the future. In the extreme, grants may be given to poor countries, free of interest, with no conditions imposed that they be spent in purchasing goods of the donor country; here, the crucial exchange may be a flow of material aid in one direction, and a flow of quite immaterial political support, a sense of obligation, even gratitude, in the other direction, all of which constitute powerful political gains for the donor country.

Aid generates economic as well as political dependence. More aid is now taking the form of grants, not loans (at the end of 1970 grants made up about 60 per cent of official aid; loans 40 per cent). Those loans which are given at rates of interest below normal commercial rates of course contain a 'grant' element to that extent. But most do not. Loans have to be repaid; they are no more charity than is money-lending. And they have to be repaid with interest. The result is that interest charges on past loans have accumulated over time to the extent that under-developed countries are now spending the equivalent of 10 per cent of their export earnings in servicing loan-debts.

The 'donor' country further exercises politico-economic influence over the recipient in so far as some or all of the credits have to be expended in the donor country, thus providing a powerful stimulus to the export trade of that country. Some 60 per cent of official aid is 'tied' aid of this kind. About half of the aid in official statistics, too, is made up of private investment. A good deal of direct or indirect influence is also exercised in the very process of implementing the loan. The donor country does not simply hand over a cheque: it insists on feasibility studies to see if the moneys that it is being asked to provide will be put to good use: pre-investment surveys are usually carried out to examine the economic and social viability of a set of specified projects, rather than a merely general indication that the loan will be expended on 'agricultural development'. Such surveys are particularly meticulous where the operation proposed is a large-scale one, such as the building of a hydro-electric dam, the setting up of a medical school or a family-limitation campaign. The negotiation of a general loan between an underdeveloped country and a rich one may involve an 'opening of the books' of the poor country to an extent which seems degrading to countries supersensitive about their newly found independence, but which now find themselves visited by experts from the very powers, often, whose direct rule they have escaped from. In mounting pre-investment surveys (usually with some – often quite token – representation of experts from the country whose projects are being studied), and because they are in a position to approve or disapprove of the proposed investment in the end, the donor power obviously exercises considerable influence over crucial economic decisions, whatever the constitutional or *de facto* internal political strength of the government seeking the aid.

It is common for loans to cover a long list of named projects. It is equally common to label such a list of projects a 'Plan'. A 'Plan', however, may be anything from a mere putting together on paper of dozens of separate projects, to an interrelated set of projects, deliberately designed to be launched together so as to take the economy and society in a specified direction. Again, 'Plans' vary according to the degree to which they are, at one pole, merely 'indicative' – either indicating the areas in which the government would *like* to see investment or in which concessions (e.g., in the form of tax concessions) or inducements are used to encourage the desired kind of investment – or, at the other, highly centralized, rigidly planned specifications of production-targets for every branch of industry and each unit of production. The latter type of planning, of course, was characteristic of the Stalin era in the Soviet Union. It has not been imitated in the new communist countries outside Europe, since these turned to communism largely after the Stalin era and were well aware of the shortcomings of this over-bureaucratized mode of economic organization, as well as the unacceptable social, political and human consequences entailed. Thus Cuba found Czech methods of running a planned economy to be disastrous and rapidly terminated the experiment.

But non-communist underdeveloped countries have still been faced with the same need to modernize quickly; this spells state planning, for they are attracted by the 'demonstration effect' of the USSR and of China as agrarian countries which have lifted themselves up by their own bootstraps. However much many of the new regimes have feared, even abhorred, communist society, they could not fail to be impressed by the emergence of the Soviet Union as the second greatest power in the world in just over thirty years, and the even more relevant emergence of agrarian China as a major power in only twenty years.

In the immediate post-independence period, a set of short-term crises occurs. A major one arises because there are usually too few nationals capable of filling gaps left by expatriate administrators.

To people in the developed countries, the presence of British nationals working in the inner sanctums of Nigerian or Malawian ministries is taken to be quite unremarkable: it is merely a continuation of a tradition that goes back into the history of the colonial era. But it is precisely this connection that rankles. The British would be unlikely to accept, without twinges of suspicion or wounded pride, Greeks or Turks, let alone Malawians or Nigerians, working on contract in their sacred ministries in Whitehall. And where an 'unacceptable' country provides the Third World with precisely similar services – as with the Chinese on the Tanzania-Zambia Railway – indignant allegations of political influence and photographs of those foreign nationals at work in Africa are to be found in all the newspapers. To the nationals of the states in question, of course, Chinese are not more or less 'foreign' than are Canadians or Israelis. The training of hundreds of indigenous future higher civil servants thus becomes an early priority. But short-term answers have been found to these short-term problems: the shortfall has usually been met by swallowing national pride and hiring expatriates on contract or by recruiting them from countries other than that of the former colonial power.

Once trained, such administrators have usually been engaged in laying the foundations, on paper at least, for planned development, and specialized planning machinery is set up. Where costly capital-intensive projects are called into being, as with the Volta River Dam Project in Ghana, many different branches of government, and the lives of large numbers of people, are affected in many different ways. Thus dam-construction – a large enough operation in itself – further involves electricity generating and the rational economic use of such energy (whether industrial or domestic); the use of water to irrigate unused arid lands; the relocation of population from the flooded areas and the moving of other populations to newly usable land; the building of access and feeder roads, and a thousand and one other major and minor operations.

Whether the project be large-scale or small-scale, however, the donor country remains a significant force even when the investment has actually taken place, for the equipment will normally come from the donor country and will continue to be serviced from there. It makes sense in terms of economics of scale and cutting overhead costs to buy more of the same, if the equipment is technically satisfactory. Military *matériel* is the most obvious case, where weapons are not standardized internationally, and Russian tanks will not take American shells. Personnel are further required to do servicing or maintenance on the spot. These countries whose supply of modern machinery spares and replacements gets cut off – notably the case of Cuba, a country formerly heavily dependent on American suppliers – experience acute problems of substitution.

The reference to military supplies should remind us that the greater part of aid has not contributed seriously to maximizing either production or consumption directly. World aid figures usually exclude or conceal the flow of purely military aid. But a whole vocabulary of motives needs to be spelt out before we accept the assumptions lying behind the very distinction between 'military' and 'non-military' or 'political' aid and 'aid without strings', for quite humane programmes to improve the health or the food-consumption of the civilian population may, at one level, be part of a general strategy of winning over such a country as an ally, or, by enabling it to put its house in order internally, to make it a more effective political or military ally. Finally, there is usually a direct connection between the provision of aid and the geopolitical strategic interests of the disbursing countries. Conversely, there is no coherent relationship between the pattern of aid-flow and the extent to which the internal political and social systems of the recipient countries coincide with that of the donor. In the game of international patronage, hard cash is exchanged for political support, and ideals are treated as subsidiary variables, something with which political romantics can afford to delude themselves, but not politicians. Western aid has by no means gone to the more democratic states in the Third World: it has flowed strongly towards such authoritarian regimes as South Korea, Thailand, and South Vietnam in Asia; in Latin America, to Brazil and Argentina, where military regimes have displaced parliamentary-democratic ones; and even in Europe, to Greece and Spain. Equally cynically the Chinese People's Republic has supported 'feudal' or military regimes in Burundi and Pakistan, and the USSR has poured money and armaments into the UAR, where indigenous Communists languish in gaol.

Revolution

Aid programmes of this kind are unlikely to diminish the social inequalities that give rise to political protest. For the poor countries, faced with an ever-widening gap between themselves and the rich countries, the prospects for revolution might appear to be as bright as Chou En-lai declared them to be for Africa in 1964. Subsequent events have not borne out his predictions. In most of Black Africa, military regimes have displaced single-party states. If the political swing has been unmistakably to the right, the difference on the ground has not been remarkably great. Despite the weakening of non-alignment and of the UN, despite the failure of the 'development decade' and the arrival of the military, no corresponding sharpening of revolutionary resistance can be chalked up on the other side of the account. There has been one very good reason for this, well expressed by one in a strategic position to reflect on revolutionary mis-estimates, for it was Régis Debray himself who declared that 'Cuba has raised the material and ideological level of imperialist reaction in less time than that of the revolutionary vanguard'.

Outside Africa, military regimes have been much more overtly counter-revolutionary, particularly in Indonesia, where the largest communist movement in the non-communist world was cut to ribbons in the slaughter of several hundred thousand communists which followed the *coup d'état* in 1965.

Since the Second World War though, 'revolution' has been a much more inclusive term than the term 'Communist'. Not a single one of the armed revolutionary movements in Africa in the past two decades – with the exception perhaps of that in Portuguese Guinea – has been either Socialist or Communist either in ideology or leadership. Algeria, Mau Mau, the guerrilla movements in Angola and Mozambique, and lesser movements operating against South Africa, have predominantly been nationalist movements. Like non-revolutionary independence movements, they have often used left-wing rhetoric and vocabulary, but when they have arrived in power, have created precious little Socialism or Communism in practice. 'Nationalization', for instance, has generally meant the replacement of expatriate *local* executives of state enterprises, new and old, by indigenous nationals: the presence of representatives of the state on the boards of 'mixed', public/private, national/foreign enterprise, or a 'token' indigenous director or two on the boards of international companies, means little in terms of hard power, however striking the symbolism.

The language of revolution in our time is Marxism, as it was once the language of the Bible. Nearly all radical movements, therefore, even those simply seeking political power without any accompanying social transformation, have used this language (and hence provided their enemies with a stick with which to beat them). It is hard to recall now that Nkrumah and Kenyatta were once seriously labelled 'Communist'. There have been socially Conservative and anti-Communist nationalists, too, like the early Chiang Kai-shek or Algeria's Boumédienne, as well as anti-communist *radical* nationalists, like Gamal Abdul Nasser, who did not simply secure the final exodus of the British, but who also carried through a land-reform programme, nationalized a great deal of industrial and commercial enterprise, and allied his country with the USSR. It is too early to judge whether the new Peruvian left-wing military regime, or the advent of a democratically elected (Russian-type) Marxist as president of Chile, are the first examples of novel forms of revolutionary innovation. Nor can the potential demonstration effect of Tanzanian Socialism be evaluated at this stage.

There is one exception to the record of revolutionary setback, however, that outweighs all these failures. For the tiny agrarian society of revolutionary Vietnam has provided an extraordinary example to the rest of the world's revolutionaries and potential revolutionaries that, given the will and some external help, it can be done.

The effects of revolution are not just demonstations of how to seize power. Once the revolutionary state is established it becomes a model of development also. Inimitable as the history of Russia or China may be for the population of small-scale peasant societies, they constitute 'utopias', to use Mannheim's term, which are powerful sources of inspiration, but are sources of material assistance as well.

Revolutionary models of development are particularly powerful because they are composed of several overlapping elements, each one of which would be powerful enough if it occurred separately. Taken together, they seem to provide decisive answers to a set of related problems. Firstly, the revolutionary doctrine provides an intellectual map of the world, an explanation of the way it works, and a specification of its principal components: it tells men that they are victims of 'imperialism'. Secondly, the revolutionary ideology locates the actor or potential actor within this world: it provides him with an identity which he shares with others like him: he belongs to a 'class'. Further, it tells him who he is, not simply in structural terms, but also in ethical terms: he is a 'downtrodden worker' or an 'exploited peasant'. The identity he is thus provided with is new and disturbing, even exciting: 'he is no longer simply a "Thai", a member of the X clan, a "Buddhist" or a "villager"'. Next, the identity of his friends and enemies is pointed out to him (the 'middle peasantry' and the 'Soviet people', or the 'rich peasants' and the 'American imperialists', respectively). The evolutionary ideology also provides a set of goals: the alternative society towards which one should aim, and a programme to be followed in order to reach these goals. Finally, above all, ideology and programme do not simply float around in some disembodied form. They are communicated, and the agency that does the communicating is the party itself. But the party has not been merely an agency of communication; it has also been the organization which translates that ideology into action, by mobilizing people.

70 Paul Ehrlich

Eco-Catastrophe!

Paul Ehrlich, 'Eco-Catastrophe!', in Harry Harrison and Brian W. Aldiss (eds.), *The Year's Best Science Fiction, No. 3*, Sphere Books, 1970, pp. 66–78.

The end of the ocean came late in the summer of 1979, and it came even more rapidly than the biologists had expected. There had been signs for more than a decade, commencing with the discovery in 1968 that DDT slows down photosynthesis in marine plant life. It was announced in a short paper in the technical journal, *Science*, but to ecologists it smacked of doomsday. They knew that all life in the sea depends on photosynthesis, the chemical process by which green plants bind the sun's energy and make it available to living things. And they knew that DDT and similar chlorinated hydrocarbons had polluted the entire surface of the earth, including the sea.

But that was only the first of many signs. There had been the final gasp of the whaling industry in 1973, and the end of the Peruvian anchovy fishery in 1975. Indeed, a score of other fisheries had disappeared quietly from over-exploitation and various eco-catastrophes by 1977. The term 'eco-catastrophe' was coined by a California ecologist in 1969 to describe the most spectacular of man's attacks on the systems which sustain his life. He drew his inspiration from the Santa Barbara offshore oil disaster of that year, and from the news which spread among naturalists that virtually all of the Golden State's seashore bird life was doomed because of chlorinated hydrocarbon interference with its reproduction. Eco-catastrophes in the sea became increasingly common in the early 1970s. Mysterious 'blooms' of previously rare micro-organisms began to appear in offshore waters. Red tides – killer outbreaks of a minute single-celled plant – returned to the Florida Gulf coast and were sometimes accompanied by tides of other exotic hues.

It was clear by 1975 that the entire ecology of the ocean was changing. A few types of phytoplankton were becoming resistant to chlorinated hydrocarbons and were gaining the upper hand. Changes in the phytoplankton community led inevitably to changes in the community of zooplankton, the tiny animals which eat the phytoplankton. These changes were passed on up the chains of life in the ocean to the herring, plaice, cod and tuna. As the diversity of life in the ocean diminished, its stability also decreased.

Other changes had taken place by 1975. Most ocean fishes that returned to fresh water to breed, like the salmon, had become extinct, their breeding streams so dammed up and polluted that their powerful homing instinct only resulted in suicide. Many fishes and shellfishes that bred in restricted areas along the coasts followed them as onshore pollution escalated.

By 1977 the annual yield of fish from the sea was down to 30 million metric tons, less than one-half the *per capita* catch of a decade earlier. This helped malnutrition to escalate sharply in a world where an estimated 50 million people per year were already dying of starvation. The United Nations attempted to get all chlorinated hydrocarbon insecticides banned on a worldwide basis, but the move was defeated by the United States. This opposition was generated primarily by the American petrochemical industry, operating hand in glove with its subsidiary, the United States Department of Agriculture. Together they persuaded the government to oppose the UN move – which was not difficult since most Americans believed that Russia and China were more in need of fish products than was the United States. The United Nations also attempted to get fishing nations to adopt strict and enforced catch limits to preserve dwindling stocks. This move was blocked by Russia, who, with the most modern electronic equipment, was in the best position to glean what was left in the sea. It was, curiously, on the very day in 1977 when the Soviet Union announced its refusal that another ominous article appeared in *Science*. It announced that incident solar radiation had been so reduced by worldwide air pollution that serious effects on the world's vegetation could be expected.

Apparently it was a combination of ecosystem destabilization, sunlight reduction, and a rapid escalation in chlorinated hydrocarbon pollution from massive Thanodrin applications which triggered the ultimate catastrophe. Seventeen huge Soviet-financed Thanodrin plants were operating in underdeveloped countries by 1978. They had been part of a massive Russian 'aid offensive' designed to fill the gap caused by the collapse of America's ballyhooed 'Green Revolution'.

It became apparent in the early 1970s that the 'Green Revolution' was more talk than substance. Distribution of high yield 'miracle' grain seeds had caused temporary local spurts in agricultural production. Simultaneously, excellent weather had produced record harvests. The combination permitted bureaucrats, especially in the United States

Department of Agriculture and the Agency for International Development (AID), to reverse their previous pessimism and indulge in an outburst of optimistic propaganda about staving off famine. They raved about the approaching transformation of agriculture in the underdeveloped countries (UDCs). The reason for the propaganda reversal was never made clear. Most historians agree that a combination of utter ignorance of ecology, a desire to justify past errors, and pressure from agro-industry (which was eager to sell pesticides, fertilizers, and farm machinery to the UDCs and agencies helping the UDCs) was behind the campaign. Whatever the motivation, the results were clear. Many concerned people, lacking the expertise to see through the Green Revolution drivel, relaxed. The population–food crisis was 'solved'.

But reality was not long in showing itself. Local famine persisted in northern India even after good weather brought an end to the ghastly Bihar famine of the mid 1960s. East Pakistan was next, followed by a resurgence of general famine in northern India. Other foci of famine rapidly developed in Indonesia, the Philippines, Malawi, the Congo, Egypt, Colombia, Ecuador, Honduras, the Dominican Republic, and Mexico.

Everywhere hard realities destroyed the illusion of the Green Revolution. Yields dropped as the progressive farmers who had first accepted the new seeds found that their higher yields brought lower prices – effective demand (hunger plus cash) was not sufficient in poor countries to keep prices up. Less progressive farmers, observing this, refused to make the extra effort required to cultivate the 'miracle' grains. Transport systems proved inadequate to bring the necessary fertilizer to the fields where the new and extremely fertilizer-sensitive grains were being grown. The same systems were also inadequate to move produce to markets. Fertilizer plants were not built fast enough, and most of the underdeveloped countries could not scrape together funds to purchase supplies, even on concessional terms. Finally, the inevitable happened, and pests began to reduce yields in even the most carefully cultivated fields. Among the first were the famous 'miracle rats' which invaded Philippine 'miracle rice' fields early in 1969. They were quickly followed by many insects and viruses, thriving on the relatively pest-susceptible new grains, encouraged by the vast and dense plantings, and rapidly acquiring resistance to the chemicals used against them. As chaos spread until even the most obtuse agriculturists and economists realized that the Green Revolution had turned brown, the Russians stepped in.

In retrospect it seems incredible that the Russians, with the American mistakes known to them, could launch an even more incompetent program of aid to the underdeveloped world. Indeed, in the early 1970s there were cynics in the United States who claimed that outdoing the stupidity of American foreign aid would be physically impossible. Those critics were, however, obviously unaware that the Russians had been busily destroying their own environment for many years. The virtual disappearance of sturgeon from Russian rivers caused a great shortage of caviar by 1970. A standard joke among Russian scientists at that time was that they had created an artificial caviar which was indistinguishable from the real thing – except by taste. At any rate the Soviet Union, observing with interest the progressive deterioration of relations between the UDCs and the United States, came up with a solution. It had recently developed what it claimed was the ideal insecticide, a highly lethal chlorinated hydrocarbon complexed with a special agent for penetrating the external skeletal armor of insects. Announcing that the new pesticide, called Thanodrin, would truly produce a Green Revolution, the Soviets entered into negotiations with various UDCs for the construction of massive Thanodrin factories. The USSR would bear all the costs; all it wanted in return were certain trade and military concessions.

It is interesting now, with the perspective of years, to examine in some detail the reasons why the UDCs welcomed the Thanodrin plan with such open arms. Government officials in these countries ignored the protests of their own scientists that Thanodrin would not solve the problems which plagued them. The governments now knew that the basic cause of their problems was overpopulation, and that these problems had been exacerbated by the dullness, daydreaming, and cupidity endemic to all governments. They knew that only population control and limited development aimed primarily at agriculture could have spared them the horrors they now faced. They knew it, but they were not about to admit it. How much easier it was simply to accuse the Americans of failing to give them proper aid; how much simpler to accept the Russian panacea.

And then there was the general worsening of relations between the United States and the UDCs. Many things had contibuted to this. The situation in America in the first half of the 1970s deserves our close scrutiny. Being more dependent on imports for raw materials than the Soviet Union, the United States had, in the early 1970s, adopted more and more heavy-handed policies in order to insure continuing supplies. Military adventures in Asia and Latin America had further lessened the international credibility of the United States as a great defender of freedom – an image which had begun to deteriorate rapidly during the pointless and fruitless Vietnam conflict. At home, acceptance of the carefully manufactured image lessened dramatically, as even the more romantic and chauvinistic citizens began to understand the role of the military and the industrial system in what John Kenneth Galbraith had aptly named 'The New Industrial State'.

At home in the USA the early 1970s were traumatic times. Racial violence grew and the habitability of the cities diminished, as nothing substantial was done to ameliorate either racial inequities or urban blight. Welfare rolls grew as automation and general technological progress forced more and more people into the category of 'unemployable'. Simultaneously a taxpayers' revolt occurred. Although there was not enough money to build the schools, roads, water systems, sewage systems, jails, hospitals, urban transit lines, and all the other amenities needed to support a burgeoning population, Americans refused to tax themselves more heavily. Starting in Youngstown, Ohio, in 1969 and followed closely by Richmond, California, community after community was forced to close its schools or curtail educational operations for lack of funds. Water supplies, already marginal in quality and quantity in many places by 1970, deteriorated quickly. Water rationing occurred in 1723 municipalities in the summer of 1974, and hepatitis and epidemic dysentery rates climbed about 500 per cent between 1970–1974.

Air pollution continued to be the most obvious manifestation of environmental deterioration. It was, by 1972, quite literally in the eyes of all Americans. The year 1973 saw not only the New York and Los Angeles smog disasters, but also the publication of the Surgeon General's massive report on air pollution and health. The public had been partially prepared for the worst by the publicity given to the UN pollution conference held in 1972. Deaths in the late 1960s caused by smog were well known to scientists, but the public had ignored them because they mostly involved the early demise of the old and sick rather than people dropping dead on the freeways. But suddenly our citizens were faced with nearly 200,000 corpses and massive documentation that they could be the next to die from respiratory disease. They were not ready for that scale of disaster. After all, the UN conference had not predicted that accumulated air pollution would make the planet uninhabitable until almost 1990. The population was terrorized as TV screens became filled with scenes of horror from the disaster areas. Especially vivid was NBC's coverage of hundreds of unattended people choking out their lives outside of New York's hospitals. Terms like nitrogen oxide, acute bronchitis and cardiac arrest began to have real meaning for most Americans.

The ultimate horror was the announcement that chlorinated hydrocarbons were now a major constituent of air pollution in all American cities. Autopsies of smog disaster victims revealed an average chlorinated hydrocarbon load in fatty tissue equivalent to 26 parts per million of DDT. In October, 1973, the Department of Health, Education and Welfare announced studies which showed unequivocally that increasing death rates from hypertension, cirrhosis of the liver, liver cancer and a series of other diseases had resulted from the chlorinated hydrocarbon load. They estimated that Americans born since 1946 (when DDT usage began) now had a life expectancy of only 49 years, and predicted that if current patterns continued, this expectancy would reach 42 years by 1980, when it might level out. Plunging insurance stocks triggered a stock market panic. The president of Velsicol Inc., a major pesticide producer, went on television to 'publicly eat a tablespoonful of DDT' (it was really powdered milk) and announce that HEW had been infiltrated by Communists. Other giants of the petro-chemical industry, attempting to dispute the indisputable evidence launched a massive pressure campaign on Congress to force HEW to 'get out of agriculture's business'. They were aided by the agro-chemical journals, which had decades of experience in misleading the public about the benefits and dangers of pesticides. But by now the public realized that it had been duped. The Nobel Prize for medicine and physiology was given to Drs J. L. Radomski and W. B. Deichmann, who in the late 1960s had pioneered in the documentation of the long-term lethal effects of chlorinated hydrocarbons. A presidential Commission with unimpeachable credentials directly accused the agro-chemical complex of 'condemning many millions of Americans to an early death'. The year 1973 was the year in which Americans finally came to understand the direct threat to their existence posed by environmental deterioration.

And 1973 was also the year in which most people finally comprehended the indirect threat. Even the president of Union Oil Company and several other industrialists publicly stated their concern over the reduction of bird populations which had resulted from pollution by DDT and other chlorinated hydrocarbons. Insect populations boomed because they were resistant to most pesticides and had been freed, by the incompetent use of those pesticides, from most of their natural enemies. Rodents swarmed over crops, multiplying rapidly in the absence of predatory birds. The effect of pests on the wheat crop was especially disastrous in the summer of 1973, since that was also the year of the great drought. Most of us can remember the shock which greeted the announcement by atmospheric physicists that the shift of the jet stream which had caused the drought was probably permanent. It signalled the birth of the Midwestern desert. Man's air-polluting activities had by then caused gross changes in climatic patterns. The news, of course, played hell with commodity and stock markets. Food prices sky-rocketed, as savings were poured into hoarded canned goods. Official assurances that food supplies would remain ample fell on deaf ears, and even the government showed signs of nervousness when Californian migrant field workers went out on strike again in protest against the continued use of pesticides by growers. The strike burgeoned into farm burning and riots. The workers, calling themselves 'The Walking Dead', demanded immediate compensation for their shortened lives, and crash research programs to attempt to lengthen them.

It was in the same speech in which President Edward Kennedy, after much delay, finally declared a national emergency and called out the National Guard to harvest California's crops, that the first mention of population control was made. Kennedy pointed out that the United States would no longer be able to offer any food aid to other nations and was likely to suffer food shortages herself. He suggested that, in view of the manifest failure of the Green Revolution, the only hope of the UDCs lay in population control. His statement, you will recall, created an uproar in the underdeveloped countries. Newspaper editorials accused the United States of wishing to prevent small countries from becoming large nations and thus threatening American hegemony. Politicians asserted that President Kennedy was a 'creature of the giant drug combine' that wished to shove its pills down every woman's throat.

Among Americans, religious opposition to population control was very slight. Industry in general also backed the idea. Increasing poverty in the UDCs was both destroying markets and threatening supplies of raw materials. The seriousness of the raw material situation had been brought home during the Congressional Hard Resources hearings in 1971. The exposure of the ignorance of the cornucopian economists had been quite a spectacle – a spectacle brought into virtually every American's home in living color. Few would forget the distinguished geologists from the University of California who suggested that economists be legally required to learn at least the most elementary facts of geology. Fewer still would forget that an equally distinguished Harvard economist added that they might be required to learn some economics, too. The overall message was clear: America's resource situation was bad and bound to get worse. The hearings had led to a bill requiring the Departments of State, Interior, and Commerce to set up a joint resource procurement council with the express purpose of 'insuring that proper consideration of American resource needs be an integral part of American foreign policy'.

Suddenly the United States discovered that it had a national consensus: population control was the only possible salvation of the underdeveloped world. But that same consensus led to heated debate. How could the UDCs be persuaded to limit their populations, and should not the United States lead the way by limiting its own? Members of the intellectual community wanted America to set an example. They pointed out that the United States was in the midst of a new baby boom: her birth rate, well over 20 per thousand per year, and her growth rate of over one per cent per annum were among the very highest of the developed countries. They detailed the deterioration of the American physical and psychic environments, the growing health threats, the impending food shortages, and the insufficiency of funds for desperately needed public works. They contended that the nation was clearly unable or unwilling to properly care for the people it already had. What possible reason could there be, they queried, for adding any more? Besides, who would listen to requests by the United States for population control when that nation did not control her own profligate reproduction?

Those who opposed population controls for the US were equally vociferous. The military-industrial complex, with its all-too-human mixture of ignorance and avarice, still saw strength and prosperity in numbers. Baby food magnates, already worried by the growing nitrate pollution of their products, saw their market disappearing. Steel manufacturers saw a decrease in aggregate demand and slippage for that holy of holies, the Gross National Product. And military men saw, in the growing population–food–environment crisis, a serious threat to their carefully nurtured Cold War. In the end, of course, economic arguments held sway, and the 'inalienable right of every American couple to determine the size of its family', a freedom invented for the occasion in the early 1970s, was not compromised.

The population control bill, which was passed by Congress early in 1974, was quite a document, nevertheless. On the domestic front, it authorized an increase from 100 to 150 million dollars in funds for 'family planning' activities. This was made possible by a general feeling in the country that the growing army on welfare needed family planning. But the gist of the bill was a series of measures designed to impress the need for population control on the UDCs. All American aid to countries with overpopulation problems was required by law to consist in part of population control assistance. In order to receive any assistance each nation was required not only to accept the population control aid, but also to match it according to a complex formula. 'Overpopulation' itself was defined by a formula based on UN statistics, and the UDCs were required not only to accept aid, but also to show progress in reducing birth rates. Every five years the status of the aid program for each nation was to be re-evaluated.

The reaction to the announcement of this program dwarfed the response to President Kennedy's speech. A coalition of UDCs attempted to get the UN General Assembly to condemn the United States as a 'genetic aggressor'. Most damaging of all to the American cause was the famous 'Twenty-five Indians and a dog' speech by Mr Shankarnarayan, Indian Ambassador to the UN. Shankarnarayan pointed out that for several decades the United States, with less than 6 per cent of the people of the world, had consumed roughly 50 per cent of the raw materials used every year. He described vividly America's contribution to worldwide environmental deterioration, and he scathingly denounced the miserly record of United States foreign aid as 'unworthy of a fourth-rate power, let alone the most powerful nation on earth'.

It was the climax of his speech, however, which most historians claim once and for all destroyed the image of the United States. Shankarnarayan informed the assembly that the average American family dog was fed more animal protein per week than the average Indian got in a month. 'How do you justify taking fish from protein-starved Peruvians and feeding them to your animals?' he asked. 'I contend', he concluded, 'that the birth of an American baby is a greater disaster for the world than that of twenty-five Indian babies.' When the applause had died away, Mr Sorensen, the American representative, made a speech which said essentially that 'other countries look after their own self-interest, too'. When the vote came, the United States was condemned.

This condemnation set the tone of US–UDC relations at the time the Russian Thanodrin proposal was made. The proposal seemed to offer the masses in the UDCs an opportunity to save themselves and humiliate the United States at the same time; and in human affairs, as we all know biological realities could never interfere with such an opportunity. The scientists were silenced, the politicians said yes, the Thanodrin plants were built, and the results were what any beginning ecology student could have predicted. At first Thanodrin seemed to offer excellent control of many pests. True, there was a rash of human fatalities from improper use of the lethal chemical, but, as Russian technical advisors were prone to note, these were more than compensated for by increased yields. Thanodrin use sky-rocketed throughout the underdeveloped world. The Mikoyan design group developed a dependable, cheap agricultural aircraft which the Soviets donated to the effort in large numbers. MIG sprayers became even more common in UDCs than MIG interceptors.

Then the troubles began. Insect strains with cuticles resistant to Thanodrin penetration began to appear. And as streams, rivers, fish culture ponds and onshore waters became rich in Thanodrin, more fisheries began to disappear. Bird populations were decimated. The sequence of events was standard for broadcast use of a synthetic pesticide: great success at first, followed by removal of natural enemies and development of resistance by the pest. Populations of crop-eating insects in areas treated with Thanodrin made steady comebacks and soon became more abundant than ever. Yields plunged, while farmers in their desperation increased the Thanodrin dose and shortened the time between treatments. Death from Thanodrin poisoning became common. The first violent incident occurred in the Canete Valley of Peru, where farmers had suffered a similar chlorinated hydrocarbon disaster in the mid-50s. A Russian advisor serving as an agricultural pilot was assaulted and killed by a mob of enraged farmers in January 1978. Trouble spread rapidly during 1978, especially after the word got out that two years earlier Russia herself had banned the use of Thanodrin at home because of its serious effects on ecological systems. Suddenly Russia, and not the United States, was the *bête noir* in the UDCs. 'Thanodrin parties' became epidemic, with farmers, in their ignorance, dumping carloads of Thanodrin concentrate into the sea. Russian advisors fled, and four of the Thanodrin plants were leveled to the ground. Destruction of the plants in Rio and Calcutta led to hundreds of thousands of gallons of Thanodrin concentrate being dumped directly into the sea.

Mr Shankarnarayan again rose to address the UN, but this time it was Mr Potemkin, representative of the Soviet Union, who was on the hot seat. Mr Potemkin heard his nation described as the greatest mass killer of all time as Shankarnarayan predicted at least thirty million deaths from crop failures due to overdependence on Thanodrin. Russia was accused of 'chemical aggression', and the General Assembly, after a weak reply by Potemkin, passed a vote of censure.

It was in January 1979, that huge blooms of a previously unknown variety of diatom were reported off the coast of Peru. The blooms were accompanied by a massive die-off of sea life and of the pathetic remainder of the birds which had once feasted on the anchovies of the area. Almost immediately another huge bloom was reported in the Indian ocean, centering around the Seychelles, and then a third in the South Atlantic off the African coast. Both of these were accompanied by spectacular die-offs of marine animals. Even more ominous were growing reports of fish and bird kills at oceanic points where there were no spectacular blooms. Biologists were soon able to explain the phenomena: the diatom had evolved an enzyme which broke down Thanodrin; that enzyme also produced a breakdown product which interfered with the transmission of nerve impulses, and was therefore lethal to animals. Unfortunately, the biologists could suggest no way of repressing the poisonous diatom bloom in time. By September, 1979, all important animal life in the sea was extinct. Large areas of coastline had to be evacuated, as windrows of dead fish created a monumental stench.

But stench was the least of man's problems. Japan and China were faced with almost instant starvation from a total loss of the seafood on which they were so dependent. Both blamed Russia for their situation and demanded immediate mass shipments of food. Russia had none to send. On 13th October, Chinese armies attacked Russia on a broad front ...

71 Noam Chomsky

The Role of the Intellectual

Excerpt from Noam Chomsky, *American Power and the New Mandarins*,
Pantheon Books, 1969, Penguin, 1969, pp. 251–4.

Traditionally the role of the intellectual, or at least his self-image, has
been that of a dispassionate critic. In so far as that role has been lost, the
relation of the schools to intellectuals should, in fact, be one of self-
defence. This is a matter that should be seriously considered. It is, to be
sure, ridiculous to propose that the schools, in any country, deal objectively with contemporary history – they cannot sufficiently free themselves from the pressures of ideology for that. But it is not necessarily
absurd to suppose that in Western democracies, at least, it should be
possible to study in a fairly objective way the national scandals of the
past. It might be possible in the United States to study, let us say, the
American occupation of the Philippines, leaving implicit its message for
the present. Suppose that high-school students were exposed to the best of
current American scholarship, for example, G. Taylor's recent study for
the Council on Foreign Relations, *The Philippines and the United States*.
Here they would learn how, half a century after the bloody suppression
of the native independence movement at a cost of well over 100,000 lives
in the years 1898 to 1900, the country achieved nominal independence
and the surface forms of democracy. They would also learn that the
United States is guaranteed long-term military bases and unparalleled
economic privileges; that for three fourths of the population, living standards have not risen since the Spanish occupation; that 70 per cent of the
population is estimated to have tuberculosis; that profits flowing to the
United States have exceeded new investment in each post-war year; that
the democratic forms give a new legitimacy to an old élite, allied now to
American interests. They would read that 'Colonial policy had tended to
consolidate the power of an oligarchy that profited ... from the free
trade relationship and would be likely to respect, after independence, the
rights and privileges of Americans'; that economically, 'the contrast between the small upper class and the rest of the population ... [is] ... one
of the most extreme in Asia'; that the consequences of American colonial policy were 'that little was done to improve the lot of the average
Filipino and that the Philippine economy was tied to the American to the

advantage of the few'; and so on. They would then read the book's final recommendation, that we go on with our good work: 'In spite of our many shortcomings, the record shows that we are more than equal to the task.' It is at least possible that to a young mind, still uncontaminated by cant and sophistry, such a study can teach a revealing lesson, not only about what American dominance is likely to mean concretely, in the Third World, but also about the way in which American intellectuals are likely to interpret this impact.

In general, the history of imperialism and of imperialist apologia, particularly as seen from the point of view of those at the wrong end of the guns, should be a central part of any civilized curriculum. But there are other aspects to a programme of intellectual self-defence that should not be overlooked. In an age of science and technology it is inevitable that their prestige will be employed as an ideological instrument – specifically, that the social and behavioural sciences will in various ways be made to serve in defence of national policy or as a mask for special interest. It is not merely that intellectuals are strongly tempted, in a society that offers them prestige and affluence, to take what is now called a 'pragmatic attitude', that is, an attitude that one must 'accept', not critically analyse or struggle to change, the existing distribution of power, domestic or international, and the political realities that flow from it, and must work only for 'slow measures of improvement' in a technological, piecemeal manner. It is not merely that having taken this position (conceivably with some justification, at a particular historical moment), one is strongly tempted to provide it with an ideological justification of a very general sort. Rather, what we must also expect is that political élites will use the terminology of the social and behavioural sciences to protect their actions from critical analysis – the non-specialist does not, after all, presume to tell physicists and engineers how to build an atomic reactor. And for any particular action experts can certainly be found in the universities who will solemnly testify as to its appropriateness and realism. This is not a matter of speculation; thus we already find, in congressional testimony, the proposal by a leading political scientist that we try to impose mass starvation on a quarter of the human race, if their government does not accept our dictates. And it is commonly argued that the free-floating intellectual, who is now outdated, has no business questioning the conclusions of the professional expert, equipped with the tools of modern science.

This situation again carries a lesson for the schools, one to which teachers in particular should be quite sensitive, bombarded as they have been in recent years by authoritative conclusions about what has been 'demonstrated' with regard to human learning, language, and so on. The social and behavioural sciences should be seriously studied not only for their intrinsic interest, but so that the student can be made quite aware of exactly how little they have to say about the problems of man and society that really matter. They should, furthermore, be studied in the context of the physical sciences, so that the student can be brought to appreciate clearly the limits of their intellectual content. This can be an important way to protect a student from the propaganda of the future, and to put him in a position to comprehend the true nature of the means that are sure to be used to conceal the real significance of domestic or international policy.

Suppose, however, that contrary to all present indications, the United States will stop short of using its awesome resources of violence and devastation to impose its passionately held ideology and its approved form of social organization on large areas of the world. Suppose, that is, that American policy ceases to be dominated by the principles that were crudely outlined by President Truman almost twenty years ago, when he suggested in a famous and important speech that the basic freedom is freedom of enterprise, and that the whole world should adopt the American system which could survive in America only if it became a world system. It would nevertheless remain true that the level of culture that can be achieved in the United States is a matter of overwhelming importance for the rest of the world. If we want to be truly utopian we may consider the possibility that American resources might be used to alleviate the terrorism that seems to be an inevitable correlate of modernization, if we can judge from past and present history. We can conceive of the possibility that the schools, or the intellectuals, might pay serious attention to questions that have been posed for centuries, that they might ask whether society must, indeed, be a Hobbesian *bellum omnium contra omnes*, and might inquire into the contemporary meaning of Rousseau's protest that it is contrary to natural right that 'a handful of men be glutted with superfluities while the starving multitude lacks necessities'. They might raise the moral issue faced, or avoided, by one who enjoys his wealth and privilege undisturbed by the knowledge that half of the children born in Nicaragua will not reach five years of age, or that only a few miles away there is unspeakable poverty, brutal suppression of human rights, and almost no hope for the future; and they might raise the intellectual issue of how this can be changed. They might ask, with Keynes, how long we must continue to 'exalt some of the most distasteful of human qualities into the position of the highest virtues', setting up 'avarice and usury and precaution ... [as] ... our gods', and pretending to ourselves that 'fair is foul and foul is fair, for foul is useful and fair is not'. If American intellectuals will be preoccupied with such questions as these, they can have an invaluable civilizing influence on society and on the schools. If, as is more likely, they regard them with disdain as mere sentimental nonsense, then our children will have to look elsewhere for enlightenment and guidance.

Acknowledgements

Permission to reproduce the Readings in this volume is acknowledged
to the following sources:

1 Population Reference Bureau Inc.
2 Population Reference Bureau Inc.
3 Population Reference Bureau Inc.
4 Macmillan Co. and William Petersen
5 Victor Gollancz Ltd, Pantheon Books and E. P. Thompson
6 American Sociological Association and Fred Cottrell
7 Collins, Sons & Co. Ltd, Tony Lane and Kenneth Roberts
8 Merlin Press and V. L. Allen
9 American Sociological Association and Herbert Blumer
10 John Wiley & Sons Inc. and Robert Blauner
11 Canadian Political Science Association and Everett C. Hughes
12 UNESCO - Mouton and Philip M. Hauser
13 University of Chicago Press and C. A. Valentine
14 Jonathan Cape Ltd and Random House Inc.
15 Routledge & Kegan Paul Ltd, Humanities Press Inc. and Hilda Jennings
16 H M S O, Ingrid Reynolds and Charles Nicolson
17 Free Press
18 American Political Science Association and Alvin W. Gouldner
19 *Berkeley Journal of Sociology* and Nigel Young
20 Free Press and R. T. McKenzie
21 Penguin Books Ltd and J. P. F. Blondel
22 Pioneer Publishers
23 *Sociological Review Monographs* and John H. Goldthorpe
24 University of Washington Press, East Asian Research Centre (Harvard
    University) and Roy Holfheinz Jr
25 Deborah Rogers Ltd
26 Free Press
27 Random House Inc.
28 M I T Press and Herbert J. Gans
29 Political and Economic Planning
30 *British Journal of Sociology*
31 Routledge & Kegan Paul Ltd, Humanities Press Inc. and David Hargreaves
32 Horizon Press and Paul Goodman
33 Methuen & Co. Ltd.
34 *New Left Review* and David Adelstein
35 *American Journal of Sociology* and Howard S. Becker
36 Prentice-Hall Inc.
37 *American Journal of Sociology* and William Foote Whyte
38 American Sociological Association

39 Holt, Rinehart & Winston Inc. and Gilbert Geis
40 University of Chicago Press
41 Prentice-Hall Inc. and Erving Goffman
42 *Social Problems*
43 Free Press and Edwin M. Lemert
44 *Southwestern Journal of Anthropology* and Edwin M. Lemert
45 Prentice-Hall Inc. and Edwin M. Schur
46 American Sociological Association and Irving K. Zola
47 *Journal of Social Issues*
48 Harvard University Press and Emily Mumford
49 *American Journal of Sociology* and Fred Davies
50 William Alanson White Psychiatric Foundation and Erving Goffman
51 William Alanson White Psychiatric Foundation and Erving Goffman
52 Houghton Mifflin Co. and Rosica Colin Ltd
53 Yale University Press and Leo Kuper
54 Weidenfeld & Nicolson Ltd, Schocken Books Inc. and John Rex
55 Pathfinder Press Inc. and Betty Schabazz
56 Oxford University Press for the Institute of Race Relations and Ulf Hannerz
57 Oxford University Press for the Institute of Race Relations and Roger Bastide
58 Jonathan Cape Ltd, Viking Press and Ronald Segal
59 Prentice-Hall Inc., and Robin M. Williams Jr
60 Basic Books and S. N. Eisenstadt
61 Routledge & Kegan Paul Ltd, Schocken Books and David Martin
62 Liverpool University Press
63 Faber and Faber Ltd, Doubleday & Co. Inc., and Peter Berger
64 Weidenfeld & Nicolson Ltd.
65 *American Journal of Sociology* and Bryan R. Roberts
66 Princeton University Press
67 Frank Cass, and Humanities Press Inc.
68 Merlin Press
69 Weidenfeld & Nicolson Ltd, W. W. Norton & Co. Inc. and Peter Worsley
70 *Ramparts* and Paul Ehrlich
71 Chatto & Windus Ltd, Pantheon Books and Noam Chomsky

Author Index

Subject Index

Peer-groups, 289–94
Planners, 133, 136–7, 159
Planning, 139, 144, 146, 604–5
Police, 133, 156
Political parties, 185–211
  see also Communism, Conservative
    Party, Labour Party, Liberal Party
Pollution
  air, 36
  radioactive, 40
  thermal, 33, 39
Population, active, 75–6
Population increase, 25
  in big cities, 63
  by regions, 479
  and standards of living, 56
  of world's twenty largest metropolitic
    areas, 66
Population problems, 46, 143
  demographic solutions, 56
Poverty, 132, 144, 149–53, 155
  culture of, 132, 149–51
  in the underdeveloped world, 54
Power
  hydro-electric, 34
  nuclear, 37–8
Prepatient, 433, 459
Priesthood, decline in recruitment to,
    544–5
Protestant ethic
  and spirit of capitalism, 525–6
  in underdeveloped societies, 526, 575
Protestantism, 532–8
Psychology, educational, 286–8

Race relations, 469
  and African independence, 502
  and cultural nationalism, 472
  and distribution of power, 471, 474
  and economic interests, 492–4
  and ethnic relations, 470
  and ideological factors, 473
  and industrialization, 509–14, 519,
    522
  and militancy, 472–3, 500–504, 515–18

paternalist, 509–12
  and physical differences, 469, 479
  and slavery, 474, 509, 512
  and status, 522–3
Race riots, 515–6
Racial discrimination
  and education, 519–20
  and ethnic discrimination, 470
  and racial prejudice, 491, 495
Racialism, 470–72
  and constructive use of conflict, 476,
    523
  and counter-racialism, 494–6
  and education, 475, 519–20
  factors reducing, 475–7, 519–23
  and industrialization, 475
  and legislation, 475–6, 522
  and recognition of common interests
    476, 523
  and religion, 472, 492, 493–4, 500–504
Racialization (Apartheid)
  moral justification of, 487, 488, 491–2
  and nationalism, 487
  and race consciousness, 489, 490–91
  sanctions upholding, 489–90
Racial prejudice
  and class prejudice, 512–14
  and education, 475, 519–20
  and racial discrimination, 491, 495
  respectability of, 521
  role of, 471–2
Racism
  definition of, 470
  and imperialism, 474
Reactors, nuclear, 41
Reading, 295
Reference group, 132
Relations personal, structural and
    categorical, 470–71, 476
Relationships
  inter-organizational, 130, 141, 164
  multiplex, 130
  strong, diffuse, 134
  weak, segmental, 134–5, 165
Relative deprivation, 132, 136

Religion
and bureaucracy, 556–7, 559
decline of, 526 *see also* Secularization
effects of convention on, 526,
549–54
institutional framework of, 549–54
and integration of Society, 528–9
knowledge about, 545–6
and the market, 558
and moral values, 528
and pluralism, 555, 559
and political systems, 528
and social change, 528
and social problems, 525
transformative capacities of, 531
Religious sects
consequences of membership in,
574–7
and coping with urban problems,
571–8
and economic benefits, 574–6
functions of, 571–2
maintenance of boundaries by, 572
network of relationships in, 571–3,
575, 578
Pentecostal, 571–8
and political behaviour, 576–7
popularity of, 529
relation to society, 578
Residential mobility, 156, 161, 166
Revolution, 104, 607–9
Industrial, 85–90
social, 180
trade unions and, 103–4
Robbins Report, 314–17
Roles
changing role of men and women, 236,
270–75
of trade union leader, 107–9

Safety on streets, 133–4
Science, 446, 452, 457
Scientism, 547
Secondary deviation, 16, 403
in mental illness, 434
and stuttering, 411

Sects, religious, *see* Religious Sects
Secularization, 526–7, 543–8
and democracy, 569
responses to, 527–8
Sex
norms and regularity in sexual
relationships, 351, 356
role-differentiation, 236, 257, 270–75
Sex-ratios, 28
Sexuality, 297
Shanty towns, 131, 142
Social change, relation to economic
change, 91–8
Social class
and education, 279
meaning of, 287
Social control
informal, 133, 156, 158–60
Social mobility, 277
Social movements, 180–232
Social problems and sociological
problems, 11–19
Socialist, 182, 187–9, 216
Soul, meaning of, 505–8
Space, geographical, 129–30, 137
private and public, 157–8
social, 129–30, 137, 164
Standards of living, 29
and population, 56
and technology, 53
State, 181, 182, 184, 185, 194, 196
Stigma, 382
Streaming in schools, 290–94
Street safety, 133–4
and public order, 154–61
Strikes, 99–102, 109
Student
drop-outs, 299–300
radicalism, 281, 317–23
unions, 322–3
Stuttering
and relation to cultural factors, 410
and secondary deviation, 411
Sub-cultures, 18
of drug-addicts, 422

636 Subject Index

Other sociology books of related interest from Penguin Education

Introducing Sociology
Peter Worsley

Roy Fitzhenry, J. Clyde Mitchell, D. H. J. Morgan, Valdo Pons, Bryan Roberts, W. W. Sharrock, Robin Ward

Introducing Sociology is an exciting and wholly original text which is, first and foremost, an *introduction* to sociological ideas and practice, not an exhaustive summary. It is written in a style which, at no sacrifice or scientific rigour, is refreshingly free from jargon. Its subject matter is drawn from the common life-experiences of most people born into the mid-twentieth century. Indeed, the examples used in the book have been deliberately chosen from a wide range of cultures and societies to underline the international roots and relevance of modern sociology.

The first part of the text begins by examining the relationship between sociology, as a profession and a discipline, and contemporary society. It stresses the way moral choices are implicit in all inquiries into human affairs and discusses the implications of this for the other two themes of the first section: the logic and methods of sociological inquiry. Part Two looks at the four major areas of social experience through which an individual passes: family, education, work and community. Each chapter in this section has the dual purpose of introducing the reader to a substantive area of social life, and familiarizing him with a range of fundamental concepts and theoretical ideas. In doing so it demonstrates firmly that 'description' and 'theorizing' are inextricably linked.

The final section of the text picks up certain themes introduced in Part One. It examines the way in which societies hold together in spite of the divisions discussed in Part Two, and in spite of the existence of groups who reject the norms of orthodox social behaviour.

In addition to the three main sections there is an extensive list of books for further reading, and author and subject indexes.

Introducing Sociology was specially commissioned by Penguin Education from a team in the Department of Social Anthropology and Sociology at Manchester University. A first draft was tested with a wide range of students. Their comments have been taken into account in the revised draft, and the book is therefore very much a collective product, reflecting – as much as arousing – the excitement of those coming to sociology for the first time, whether in school, college or university.

Modern Sociology Introductory Readings

edited by Peter Worsley

Roy Fitzhenry, J. Clyde Mitchell, D. H. J. Morgan, Valdo Pons,
Bryan Roberts, W. W. Sharrock, Robin Ward

Sociology is now a major area of intellectual inquiry in most of the countries of
the world. It is also seen by an increasing number of its students as one of the
most relevant of contemporary disciplines. This collection of Readings
acknowledges both these points. It is, first and foremost, an *introductory*
collection, designed not just to give a background to the main strands of
sociological thought, but to acquaint the reader with a wide range of styles of
sociological writing in their original form. The bulk of the pieces are taken from
works published since the Second World War, and underline the relevance of
sociology to anyone living in the second half of the twentieth century.

The book begins by examining the relationship between sociology, as a profession
and a discipline, and contemporary society. It stresses the way moral choices are
implicit in all inquiries into human affairs, and discusses the implications of this
for the other themes of this first part: the logic and methods of sociological
inquiry. The next sections look at the four major areas of social experience
through which an individual passes: family; education; work and organizations;
and community. Each of these sections has the dual purpose of introducing the
reader to a substantive area of social life, and familiarizing him with a range of
fundamental concepts and theoretical ideas. In doing so it demonstrates firmly
that 'description' and 'theorizing' are inextricably linked.

The final sections pick up certain themes introduced in the first part of the book.
They examine power and order, and the way in which societies hold together in
spite of the existence of groups which reject the norms of orthodox social
behaviour.

Modern Sociology: Introductory Readings was specially commissioned by Penguin
Education from the same team in the Department of Sociology at Manchester
University that produced *Introducing Sociology*. It has evolved very much from
their experience of teaching newcomers to sociology, and will prove invaluable
to anyone – in school, college or university – wishing to encounter, first hand,
the writings of the leading figures in modern sociology.

Sociological Perspectives
edited by Kenneth Thompson and Jeremy Tunstall

The primary intention of this book is to show that the sociological perspective provides a distinctive approach to the study of the relation between man and society. The continuities in the classic sociological tradition are illustrated by selections from the works of the chief figures in that tradition, and by focusing on some of the major debates that have excited sociologists.

In the first Part the emergence of sociology is related to the problems posed by the transition to a modern industrial society. The second Part examines efforts that have been made to analyse the basic processes and forms of social interaction. The focus then shifts to two important substantive areas – stratification and belief. Some of the great debates over developments in both these areas serve to illustrate continuities in the sociological tradition. The final Part deals with fundamental issues regarding the logic and methods of sociology. In keeping with the title of the book, it faces up to the possibility that the sociological perspective can at times become fragmented into radically opposed perspectives on the relation between man and society.

Sociological Perspectives is unusual in its blend of both the theoretical and empirical pieces, and in the manner in which it arranges its selections so as to present important debates that have enlivened sociological theory and research. By concentrating on a few major issues, this book provides a strikingly cohesive collection of Readings.

Sociological Perspectives emerged in the preparation of a course at The Open University, where both the editors teach sociology. Kenneth Thompson is the author of *Bureaucracy and Church Reform*, and has published articles on the sociology of religion and sociological theory. Jeremy Tunstall is the author of *The Fishermen, Old and Alone, The Westminster Lobby Correspondents* and *Journalists at Work*.